# Painting Dixie Red

*New Perspectives on the History of the South*

UNIVERSITY PRESS OF FLORIDA

Florida A&M University, Tallahassee
Florida Atlantic University, Boca Raton
Florida Gulf Coast University, Ft. Myers
Florida International University, Miami
Florida State University, Tallahassee
New College of Florida, Sarasota
University of Central Florida, Orlando
University of Florida, Gainesville
University of North Florida, Jacksonville
University of South Florida, Tampa
University of West Florida, Pensacola

# Painting Dixie
# **RED**

When, Where, Why, and How
the South Became Republican

———————

Edited by Glenn Feldman

*John David Smith, Series Editor*

University Press of Florida
Gainesville · Tallahassee · Tampa · Boca Raton
Pensacola · Orlando · Miami · Jacksonville · Ft. Myers · Sarasota

16  15  14  13  12  11   6  5  4  3  2  1

*Library of Congress Cataloging-in-Publication Data*
Painting Dixie red : when, where, why, and how the South became
Republican / edited by Glenn Feldman.
p. cm.—(New perspectives on the history of the South)
Includes bibliographical references and index.
ISBN 978-0-8130-3684-7 (alk. paper)
1. Southern States—Politics and government—1951– 2. Republican Party
(U.S. : 1854– )—History—20th century. I. Feldman, Glenn.
F216.2.P35   2011
324.27340977—dc22   2011011178

The University Press of Florida is the scholarly publishing agency for the
State University System of Florida, comprising Florida A&M University,
Florida Atlantic University, Florida Gulf Coast University, Florida In-
ternational University, Florida State University, New College of Florida,
University of Central Florida, University of Florida, University of North
Florida, University of South Florida, and University of West Florida.

University Press of Florida
15 Northwest 15th Street
Gainesville, FL 32611-2079
http://www.upf.com

For James M. "Jimmy" Wooten and Danny Feldman, two generous spirits,
and
For Jeannie, as always, my treasure

Plus ça change, plus c'est la même chose.

*Jean Baptiste Alphonse Karr*

# Contents

Acknowledgments  xi

Introduction: Has the South Become Republican?  1
*Glenn Feldman*

**Part I. Religion and Partisan Realignment**

1. Voting for God and the GOP: The Role of Evangelical Religion in the
   Emergence of the Republican South  21
   *Daniel K. Williams*

2. "Out-Democratin' the Democrats": Religious Colleges and the Rise of
   the Republican Party in the South—A Case Study  38
   *Barclay Key*

3. With God on Our Side: Moral and Religious Issues, Southern Culture,
   and Republican Realignment in the South  55
   *Frederick V. Slocum*

**Part II. State, Section, Suburb, and Race**

4. A Suburban Story: The Rise of Republicanism in Postwar Georgia,
   1948–1980  79
   *Tim Boyd*

5. Virginia's Northern Strategy: Southern Segregationists and the Route to
   National Conservatism  98
   *George Lewis*

6. Kennedyphobia and the Rise of Republicans in Northwest Louisiana,
   1960–1962  122
   *J. Eric Pardue*

7. Race, Grassroots Activism, and the Evolution of the Republican Right in
   South Carolina, 1952–1974  138
   *John W. White*

8. A Southern Road Less Traveled: The 1966 Gubernatorial Election and (Winthrop) Rockefeller Republicanism in Arkansas   172
*John A. Kirk*

**Part III. Economics, Faction, and the Neo-Confederacy**

9. "Gun Cotton": Southern Industrialists, International Trade, and the Republican Party in the 1950s   201
*Katherine Rye Jewell*

10. The First Southern Strategy: The Taft and the Dewey/Eisenhower Factions in the GOP   220
*Michael Bowen*

11. The Black Cabinet: Economic Civil Rights in the Nixon Administration   240
*Leah M. Wright*

12. M. E. Bradford, the Reagan Right, and the Resurgence of Confederate Nationalism   291
*Fred Arthur Bailey*

Conclusion: America's Appointment with Destiny—A Cautionary Tale   314
*Glenn Feldman*

List of Contributors   361
Index   363

# Acknowledgments

I am grateful to many people who made this book possible. John David Smith showed faith and interest in the project from its inception. For that, and his wise counsel, I am very appreciative. Meredith Morris-Babb, director of the University Press of Florida, demonstrated faith, support, wisdom, and encouragement throughout. I am deeply grateful to her. Project editor Marthe Walters and managing editor Michele Fiyak-Burkley guided the manuscript professionally through its various stages. Copy editor Susan A. Murray did an excellent job. The whole staff at the University Press of Florida was a pleasure to work with. Marjorie Julian Spruill served as an external reader. Professor Spruill and an unknown reader provided intelligent, insightful, and constructive remarks that clearly made this a stronger work. My sincere thanks go to them.

Hallie and Rebecca, my daughters, are a constant source of love, joy, encouragement, and pride. My brother Danny and Glenda Curry showed generosity when it was needed. My other brother, Richard, is always one of the people closest to me, as are my parents, Brian Feldman and Julia Garate Burgos San Sebastian Feldman. Friends too numerous to mention furnished fellowship and support, among them: Johnny Sherman, Jak and Judy Karn, Vicky Menke, Gloria Feldman, Frank LaRussa, Marc Dierikx, Matt Farrar, Amy Flanagan, Vickie Cox-Edmondson, Lois McFadyen Christensen, Flowers Braswell, Natalie Davis, Lori Jack, Tilla Durr, Roger Shuler, Wendy Price-Murch, Bill Trimble, Larry Gerber, Jody Coombs, Kaki O'Flynn, Owen Stayner, Tracy Wooten, and Bob and Shannon Saunders were particularly supportive. I am a blessed and wealthy man to have all of these people, and so many others, in my life. This book is dedicated to James M. "Jimmy" Wooten, a true friend in good times and bad, and my brother Danny Feldman. It is also dedicated to my wonderful wife of almost a quarter century, Jeannie, for whom there are no words.

*Glenn Feldman*

# Introduction

## Has the South Become Republican?

GLENN FELDMAN

Yes. Yes, it has.

That is the short answer to this question, a profoundly important one for the trajectory of American politics and the fortunes of our two major political parties. It is accurate; it is succinct. It has all the benefits of brevity and none of the liabilities of length. Yet, in all honesty, we cannot conclude that it is a complete, total, or even wholly satisfying answer.

The South *has* become Republican when it was once Democratic. But is this all we can say? Is this all we must say? The answers to those two questions are more complicated, less black-and-white, and thus more extended. But, in the final analysis, the answers to these two subquestions are "no." Hence this book.

Still, in a place like Alabama—the heart of Dixie, the cradle of the Confederacy, the deepest of the Deep South states—the answer to our first and overarching question must be a resounding "yes." Alabama has become Republican when it was once Democratic. In the last *thirteen* presidential election cycles, since 1956 (one-half of a century), Alabama has been carried by the national Democratic nominee exactly one time. And that was the aberration of 1976, when Alabamians got the chance to vote for a neighboring Georgia boy, whose liberalism they did not accurately gauge. Since 1986, a heavy majority of Alabama's governors, senators, and congressmen have been Republicans. More important, perhaps, the state has clearly been transformed into something "Republican" in a more esoteric and cultural sense.

Still, in a place as Deep South and Republican as Alabama, people can (and have) made the argument that the state has not really turned into a Republican stronghold.[1] Even now; even in the face of all that has happened. They argue that although there have unquestionably been what we may politely term "Republican gains," the state now constitutes something more along the lines of two-party contested terrain. Clearly this conclusion cannot be called correct in even the most charitable sense of the word. Yet, just as clearly, the argument (with evidence that is impossible to ignore) may still be made—and be made in a plausible (if somewhat tortured) fashion. How, then, are we to reconcile this state of affairs?

In large part, the answer is a matter of degree. No, the South has not become completely Republican in every sense of the word. Yes, there are many "Souths." There is a Deep South and an Outer South. There is the rich, fertile swath of soil called the Black Belt, sweeping majestically across the region. There is the less hospitable Pine Belt, as well as wiregrass, hill country, red clay, and sandy plain. There is upland and lowland; gulf coast and tidewater; cotton field and skyscraper; city, country, and suburb; rolling piedmont and dripping wet marsh and swamp. There are the mountains of western North Carolina and east Tennessee, the rice plantations of South Carolina, and the strip malls of most any southern state. Even within individual states there is shocking and meaningful variation—much of it geographic. Take Florida: can it not be argued that we are, in fact, dealing with two separate and distinct "states" north and south of the I-4 corridor stretching from Tampa to Orlando? Can it be said that the Florida Panhandle is actually—culturally and geographically—merely the southernmost part of Georgia and Alabama? What about Oklahoma? Is it a southern state or a western one? How about *parts* of the various states: Southern Missouri? The Eastern Shore of Maryland? Everything in Virginia besides the northernmost regions? East Texas versus West Texas? Florida's southern Atlantic coast? Downtown Atlanta? When, exactly, did Washington, D.C., cease to be a "southern" town? Such questions do not lend themselves to absolute black-and-white answers. Nevertheless, they are important.

No, not all of the South has become Republican, even in 2011. There are still more than mere pockets of Democratic strength depending on where in the South one cares to look. There are even a few bastions of liberalism. There is Austin, Texas; Chapel Hill, North Carolina; and the Black Belt of Alabama. Even a place as enduringly conservative as Birmingham, Alabama, has its eclectic Southside. And, of course, there is the all-important color line still at work here: politics in the white South and politics in the black South are two completely, unutterably different things. There are still Democratic governors in the South; Democratic senators (though not many); Democratic congressmen (a few more); and Democratic legislators, judges, sheriffs, tax collectors, postmasters, highway commissioners, mayors, attorneys general, and Speakers of statehouses. Indeed (and this is where the argument is most solid), there is still Democratic power at the state, local, and courthouse levels in the South—even in the Deep South states. And, while much of the region's Republican strength is dependent on a white majority that is evaporating before our very eyes, race and racism has not led to a seamless, perfectly linear transition from a conservative Democratic to a Dixiecrat to a Republican South (although there is considerable power and validity in tracing such a route).

Yet even with all of these disclaimers on the table, there *is* a "South." There is still something we can point to—definitely, assuredly, and with precision—as "the South." And, at least for our present purposes, it is this South that we must recognize as having become Republican.

Sometimes it is necessary—even vitally important—to take a moment to stipulate the most obvious. This is one of those times. Despite C. Vann Woodward and the majesty of his work in discontinuity, despite the transition from cotton belt to skyscraper and the massive influx of Yankees into burgeoning Sunbelt cities like Houston, Charlotte, Tampa, and Atlanta, and despite the fact that the South is now Republican, the South has still *never really changed*.[2] At its deepest root, this is a tale of continuity. This is perhaps the central message I wish to communicate. Despite the myriad disclaimers and the admitted crudity of the generalization put forward here, the essential accuracy of the tenet remains. As the world has flown by, the South has remained largely still. While the two major political parties have swapped places, the region has not undergone a paradigm shift. This recognition of continuity is particularly accurate when applied to the southern white voter. And that—that *has* had a great deal to do with the issue of race.

It is about race—there can be no question or minimization of that basic premise. The South's partisan realignment from Democratic to Republican is about race. But it is also about more than just race. It is about the fundamental continuity of the region itself. To a great extent, the South has consistently gravitated toward the political party that best reflects and represents its—if not indigenous, then at least deep-seated, ingrained, and stubbornly inculcated—conservative personality and culture. While this is certainly true, especially in the context of race relations and the white-supremacist movement, race isn't the only issue to engage the region's reactionary spirit. The southern outlook is more than just "white backlash" to civil rights; it is an ethos, a milieu, a *mentalité*, a worldview.

A "politics of emotion" better captures the essence of the South's enduring distinctiveness. This term refers to the power of emotional (some would call them moral or social) issues to eclipse economic and material issues. Race—or white supremacy—was long the king of such issues south of the Mason-Dixon Line. It could make a poor man forget just how poor he was for as long as it took to vote a conservative Democratic ticket that stood for low taxes, fiscal retrenchment, hostility toward government, more than just run-of-the-mill American individualism, and freedom defined as governmental aid and succor to business and profits at the expense of labor, and nearly every other competing entity in society. But, in the politics of emotion that has so long dominated the South, racial tension can be supplemented and even eclipsed by other electorally useful hot-button issues: abortion, gay rights, prayer in school, war, terrorism, tax fury, uber-patriotism, and a notion of "Americanism" that brooks little or no dissent. As such, the politics of emotion is broader and more flexible than what is sometimes defined by historians as the "white backlash" thesis—which relies primarily, if not solely, on the preservation of traditional racial attitudes and practices.[3]

Finally, what about this book's title, *Painting Dixie Red*? Red is surely a grotesque misnomer here, a screamingly inappropriate descriptor. Red has always meant communism. Yet, only very recently, our modern media has changed all of this. In the last several national election cycles, the mainstream media chose to reduce the whole galaxy and complexity of political choice in national affairs down to two kindergarten colors (easily recognizable by the masses): red and blue.

Still, red has always been associated with Marxism and communism—as rare in the South as the kudzu that grows there is common. But, upon reflection, the paradox is only chimerical. To be more precise, red has always stood for "radicalism" (leftist radicalism, to be sure, but still radicalism). A good argument can be made that it still does—even in the context of the present book. This is so because the Republican South is a thing of relatively recent vintage—but it is a Republicanism that has been, at its core, radical in the extreme: uber-patriotism to the point of talking about the use of nuclear weapons and defending torture; laissez-faire and pro-business to the point of neoliberalism, Austrian economics, the Chicago school, and the implied nihilism of F. A. Hayek, Ayn Rand, and Milton Friedman; and fundamentalism—not only religious but economic.

Various themes run throughout this book. Not least is a consideration of how the conservative tendency to cherish things exclusive, special, superior, has flourished in the modern age while the physical and partisan embodiment of conservatism in America—the modern Republican Party—has of late managed to convey a populist concern for the masses and the regular fellow. This is a contradiction that, while not readily apparent to many Americans, has been one of the most powerful secrets of modern GOP ascendance, especially in the South. In his intriguing essay in this book, Fred Arthur Bailey tells us that the pioneering conservative thinker Melvin Bradford flatly condemned faith in human equality as worse than naive, as something actually malevolent and weak. This is a theme that also appears in the life and work of conservative icons such as William F. Buckley Jr.[4] Despite Bradford's venerated place near the top of modern-day conservative philosophers, his affection for what may be called a "superiority gene" cannot be said to typify all modern conservatives. It can, though, be described as being present among a disturbingly large portion of them.

How exactly did the South become Republican? There is much in the unsettling answer to suggest that, in fact, the South did not become Republican so much as the Republican Party became *southern*. For Melvin Bradford (and other leading conservative ideologues), opposition to civil rights flowed freely and logically from the conviction that, indeed, all men were not created equal—nor should an overreaching national government seek to make them so. Of course this argument was not put in terms as crass as the purely racial or ethnic. More often than not it was couched in terms of "natural rights" and the natural order of things (à la Social Darwinism and a concern for the harmonious relations of different creations). Eventually it would devolve to the transparently racial and sectional, and find its fruition in Bradford's stunning attack on Abraham Lincoln as the most dangerous and diabolical of all American presidents, and his comparison of Lincoln to Hitler. This sentiment is with us even now in the shocking pronouncements against civil rights by Tea Party favorite Rand Paul of Kentucky.[5]

Yet Bradford's ascension—despite having savaged the memory and legacy of a national treasure with the status of Lincoln—provides an interesting lesson. Like so many disenchanted white conservatives in the South, Bradford did not chart a linear route from conservative Democracy straight to Republicanism. First he hitched his wagon to the presidential ambitions of George C. Wallace (he served as the Alabama governor's point man in Texas). By 1975, with the Wallace-Independent alternative gone, Bradford moved formally into the GOP, tying himself to rising Republican star and California governor Ronald Reagan. The Great Communicator rewarded the English professor by tapping him to chair the National Endowment for the Humanities (NEH). Despite enthusiastic backing by the most reactionary of southern Republicans (Jesse Helms and Bob East of North Carolina among them), Bradford's extremism was about a decade too early. More temperate (not to mention northern Jewish) voices, like neoconservative godfather Irving Kristol, torpedoed Bradford's nomination as too extreme. The Texan had to settle for a less-celebrated post in the Reagan administration, overseeing the awarding of Fulbright scholarships to international students. Despite this temporary setback, the future of domestic Republican politics belonged more to the Bradfords than to the Kristols.

But it was not simply white supremacy acting alone that fueled the drive toward "superiority" and, in the South, partisan conversion to the GOP. In his essay on Christian colleges, Barclay Key provides a poignant example of how the acids of racism, sectionalism, and religious conservatism all combined in the late 1940s and 1950s to eat away the foundations of southern white support for the Democratic Party. Chris Elliott, a student journalist at religious Harding College and a "proud white southerner by any standard," recounted how his family's traditional Democratic allegiance ("what his 'dear old mother' ... told about the great depression and Roosevelt's 'bread on the table' reconstruction program") had given way to the more enduring cultural norms of conservative Dixie. Claiming a "rebel temper" that flared whenever he read *Gone With the Wind*, and a southern heart that "does something romantic" whenever he saw the Confederate flag flutter by, Elliott explained his conversion to Republicanism as the result of Harry Truman's attempt to "cram Civil Rights and camouflaged socialism" down the throats of white southerners. A fellow journalist at the Arkansas college concurred. "I looked around one day to find the Democratic party, but it wasn't there," she said. "[T]his is no time to vote like your father, grandfather, and great-grandfather voted, but to vote like they would have voted if faced with . . . choosing between Socialism and Democracy." Striking are the echoes of this equation of civil rights with "socialism," especially in Barack Obama's America. From a church pulpit, Harding's president, George Benson, instructed his students that segregation was providential: "the nigra race . . . is under the curse of Ham. . . . [T]here is no reason to think the Lord wants a mixing of the races and the creating of just one mongrel race." Furthermore, liberal preachers and educators who "stir up strife and confusion" in the South were "not following Christian examples."

Daniel K. Williams's essay in this book goes even further, in some respects. Williams postulates that religion was even more important than race in pushing the South toward the GOP. In an essay that spans the early Cold War through the 1990s, Williams recounts the roles of evangelicals and fundamentalists like W. A. Criswell, Bob Jones Jr., Billy James Hargis, Jerry Falwell, Anita Bryant, Pat Robertson, and Ralph Reed in making the South Republican. Catholic conservatives such as Fr. Richard John Neuhaus, George Weigel, and Robert P. George are not mentioned, but they might as well be—especially in closing the gap between Protestant and Catholic conservatives in service to the GOP. On this note, it is nothing less than shocking when Williams reminds us that the Southern Baptist Convention (SBC) actually *supported* the *Engel v. Vitale* public school–prayer decision in 1962 and argued *in favor* of the separation of church and state—so great was the fear of John Kennedy and the influence of Catholic schools upon proper Christian America.[6]

After reading an essay like Williams's it is not difficult to connect the dots between religious and racial conservatism in making the South Republican.

In the Cold War period, and even before, so frenzied was American think-ing about communism that an actual "transitive law of politics" can be dis-cerned in vitro—much to the later detriment of Democratic liberalism in the country, and especially the South. New Deal–style liberalism (then as now) was castigated by conservatives as "socialism." Yet in the McCarthy years this epithet was emotional dynamite. Socialism, for all intents and purposes, was equated with communism. Therefore, it followed logically for many Ameri-cans that liberalism must then be communism: Liberalism is socialism; social-ism is communism; therefore, liberalism must be communism and thus active subversion and revolt against Americanism. Such was the Transitive Law of Politics.

Faith and patriotism became increasingly inseparable in this climate—as the evangelical icon Billy Graham openly joined Republican Richard Nixon over Vietnam and "law and order" issues. "God and Country" issues became the private domain of the Republican Party and a national civil religion. And in 1979–80, the marriage was formally consummated as conservatives "purged" the SBC of any moderate taint, and Ronald Reagan rambled to vic-tory. The circle became complete, Williams tells us, in the 1990s when conser-vative evangelicals took over the GOP and made it into "an instrument of the Religious Right."

Enter economics. The mirror side of millions of white southerners leaving the Democratic Party for the GOP in national elections was the eventual exo-dus of northern whites from the Republican Party. More important, perhaps, was the erasure of any viable tie between the old democracy and southern economic populism. In the South, populism became the purview of evangeli-calism—and thus Republicanism, as Williams correctly notes.

Yet, while racial exclusivity has been a central (perhaps *the* central) under-pinning in the Republican takeover of southern politics, the form it takes is not constant across all the subregions of Dixie. A recent perceptive essay on post-Katrina New Orleans hints at the interesting and shifting ways race may play into future GOP politics in the region, as well as providing further docu-mentation of the power that coded words and symbols have in the racial(ly muted) politics of the modern South.[7] Again, the Bradford example is instruc-tive. For the Texas literature professor, antipathy to civil rights and suspicion of democracy and universal suffrage followed easily from his certainty that some men (white, Anglo-Saxon, Protestant, conservative men) were the "natural" superiors of others—and therefore should enjoy disproportionate influence in matters of governance. Such convictions resulted in his insistence (and that of the many other conservatives he influenced) that America was a *republic* and not a democracy, less representative rather than more, more exclusive rather than less—a position they would eventually learn they held in common with libertarian exile cum celebrities of the stripe of Milton Friedman and F. A. Hayek of the Austrian school.

Nor has all of this been constrained to the hallways of neoliberal academia or radio talk shows, or even a few modern Machiavellian Republicans like Tom DeLay. There is an important and undeniable spiritual tie between the South's post-Reconstruction Redeemers—with their willingness to "count in" or "count out" black and progressive white ballots—and modern GOP efforts at the state level to engage in racial and partisan redistricting, and other electoral hanky-panky. As the political scientist David Lublin makes plain in his examination of southern state legislatures, the incidence of racial gerrymandering rose sharply during the Second Reconstruction when blacks gained real access to the polls in the wake of the Voting Rights Act.[8] The Reconstruction tie is made even clearer in J. Eric Pardue's essay on Kennedyphobia in northwest Louisiana and Frederick V. Slocum's work on religion and culture in this volume. In present-day southern politics, Slocum concludes, the Republican Party, not the Democratic Party, is clearly the "closer philosophical and ideological descendant of the old southern Democrats." Katherine Rye Jewell's essay adds an economic twist to the Reconstruction element—one involving free trade, textiles, and tariffs—and perhaps identifies one reason why southern industrialists clung to the Democratic Party for a while even after 1948.

The New Deal—not the modern civil rights era of the 1950s and 1960s—stands out as the critical watershed in southern partisan realignment to Republicanism. While the New Deal was in no way a perfect exercise in progressive politics and policy, it did mark a powerful and steady, if incremental, move toward reform, democratization, and racial liberalism in this nation's history. Conservative backlash in the form of the Nashville Agrarians, so influential to conservative thinkers, found New Deal echoes in the dark years of Reconstruction—a redux of a federal leviathan run amok in the interest of seeking, among other things, a wrongheaded egalitarianism. Not incidentally, Melvin Bradford found incubation for his thought in the warm confines of Nashville Agrarianism, and George Benson's ascendancy at Arkansas's Harding College traced its origins to 1936—in the midst of New Deal liberalism, Barclay Key reminds us. Other forbears of modern Republicanism analyzed within these pages also trace formative moments to their opposition to the New Deal. In Texas, later Dixiecrat Pappy O'Daniel spearheaded conservative hostility to liberal 1930s policies. In a sneak-preview of what would become commonplace character assassination in the modern conservative South, he claimed Franklin Roosevelt was a greater threat than Hitler and—apparently without a pause to consider the logical problem of the Fuehrer's fascism—charged the New Deal with dragging America into communism.

Yet, without question, the flashpoint of recent Republican success in the South has been religion. Of course, this too is traceable to the phenomenon of extreme right-wing thought long before it ever actually came into vogue. Melvin Bradford's enthusiastic defense of southern sectionalism—replete with all the trappings of slavery and aristocracy—found cosmological moorings in the curious theology of the late-nineteenth-century Southern Presbyterian theologian Robert L. Dabney, and endorsement by the Chicago historian Richard M. Weaver. Specifically, this was a belief that the decline of biblical morality in America was directly traceable to New England Unitarianism and Yankee intellectual affection for rationality, Enlightenment values, and (as Fred Bailey puts it in his essay) "secularism's soul-killing self-righteousness."

Frederick Slocum agrees that fundamentalist religious traditions have galvanized the rise of the Republican Party in the South, as does Barclay Key in his piece on religious colleges. Slocum's gripping essay makes clear that the involvement of the Religious Right in politics since the late 1970s has resulted in ever-more-extreme positions for its allied political party. As far-fetched as it may have once seemed, today there are even echoes of Dominionism and Christian Reconstructionism in the contemporary GOP—evident when elected Republican officials such as Alabama chief justice Roy Moore and Oklahoma senator Tom Coburn weigh and recommend, respectively, the death penalty for homosexuals and abortion providers.

Nor is support for war, as counterintuitive as it may first seem, unrelated to this kind of fundamentalist fervor. Slocum's essay takes us through various scholars' interpretations of George W. Bush's foreign policy on the Middle East; from the Iraq War as an exciting opportunity for evangelicals to convert Muslims; to pro-Israeli policies as the fulfillment of apocalyptic biblical prophecies; and war in Iraq and saber-rattling with Iran as welcome and necessary military precursors to Armageddon, the second coming of Christ, and the forcible conversion of all remaining Jews.

In all of this, the American South has shown itself the purest expression of a "status quo society" that Western civilization has yet to conjure.[9] In such a society, cultural norms have taken a whole step—or more—to the right. Right-wing reaction passes for conservatism, conservatism is moderation, centrism is liberalism, liberalism is radicalism, and a genuine radical alternative is impossible. The upshot is that, over time, right-wing extremes become mainstream conservatism—in other words, the general history of modern Republicanism in the United States. We have now reached a point where Kevin

Phillips, the GOP's leading wunderkind of the 1960s and 1970s, has renounced the party and become an outspoken anti-Bush independent; where the Eisenhower family is now voting for Democrats; and where Richard Nixon's relative "liberalism" might make it difficult for him to be nominated as a *Democratic* candidate today. "At this point," a Nobel laureate recently concluded, "whatever dividing line there was between mainstream conservatism and the black-helicopter crowd seems to have been virtually erased."[10]

The hijacking of the modern GOP by the radical Right has not come naturally or without a great deal of time, money, planning, effort, expertise, and vision. Yet things were not always so. John A. Kirk, in his essay on Arkansas, relates that Winthrop Rockefeller assured voters early on that "it is both a moral obligation and in society's best interest to help those unable to help themselves." Imagine for a moment a prominent southern Republican saying that today. Bob Riley tried it in Alabama a few years ago on a bold and biblically based initiative to overhaul the state's tax system, and got demolished—most badly by his former gubernatorial supporters. As George Lewis reports in his essay on the southern segregationist roots of modern Republicanism, in 1950s Virginia even the most fervent firebrands of resistance to racial integration referred to the John Birch Society as "a bunch of nuts." Could the same claim be made today? To ask the question is to answer it.

Other essays in this book speak to opportunities perhaps missed. Leah M. Wright describes in fascinating detail the potential—partially realized during the Nixon years—for black progress to move beyond the street and federal court and into the realm of entrepreneurship in partnership with the federal government. She writes of what amounts to a hybrid of Booker T. Washington's ideas of self-help and economic uplift with W.E.B. DuBois's concept of a "Talented Tenth" of black Americans leading the way. Michael Bowen's examination of 1950s Republicanism tantalizingly dangles the possibility of Dewey/Eisenhower moderation winning the day over Taft conservatism. But it was not to last. And John A. Kirk's examination of Republicanism, Winthrop Rockefeller–style in Arkansas, turns the traditional narrative of white backlash and reactionary politics almost on its head—if only for a spell, with a large amount of cash, in one southern state. Katherine Rye Jewell complicates matters even further by describing how national Democratic and Republican policies on trade protections and tariffs evolved over time to add a powerful economic incentive for discontented southern states'-righters (especially business interests) to push their region toward the GOP.

Here the role of fundamentalist religion must not be underestimated. Fundamentalism—Christian or Muslim, religious or economic—shares the common tendency toward justifying the unjustifiable; understanding no means as off-limits as long as the ultimate end of victory or conversion is achieved. In their essays, Daniel K. Williams and Fred Slocum document the critically important conservative rout of moderates within the Southern Baptist Convention, the largest Protestant denomination in the country, and that group's subsequent increasing stress on literalism and biblical inerrancy. The SBC, like many other Protestant denominations, became openly and actively involved in politics in the late 1970s, with abortion, feminism, homosexuality, and other social hot-button issues dominating its agenda. In this journey, as both contributors show, the SBC has moved so close to the Republican Party that some scholars have described the party and the denomination as virtually one and the same thing.

In his essay, Slocum takes note of the fundamentalist predilection toward winning at all costs, and proposes the intriguing concept of "cultural defense" to describe this phenomenon. He defines it as a propensity for conservative white southerners to go to extremes in defending cherished values or attacking those understood as threatening them—and ties the concept to well-known southern traditions of honor and militarism. Cultural defense is "the tendency to 'stop at nothing' . . . to 'defend' a cherished local practice or institution against attack from perceived 'outsiders.'" Extremism is thus part and parcel of the southern conservative experience, and, as the Republican Party has become increasingly dominated by the South, the results have been predictable. Many of its adherents find it difficult—if not impossible—to ever back down, accept losses, admit mistakes, change direction, reassess, or take responsibility—almost a character study of that most southern of presidents, George W. Bush.

On the other side, modern Democrats have repeatedly made it clear that they have trouble processing such ruthlessness, and no stomach to engage in it even if they did understand it. As the GOP has become more southern, the Democratic Party has become less so. The modern GOP of Lee Atwater, Tucker Eskew, and Karl Rove has distinguished itself with brass-knuckle politics and scorched-earth policies. With the partial exception of the Clinton/Daschle years, Democrats have too often countered with weakness, division, confusion, and ineptitude. For five years after Democrats achieved control of both houses of Congress in 2006, there has been little sign of letup in the paralyzing timidity that has crippled Democratic fortunes and, it must be admitted, done much to enable Republican ascendance—including that party's extremism—in recent years. So far, unfortunately, Barack Obama seems as culpable here as any of his Democratic peers. Can anyone imagine a Democrat the stripe of Lyndon Johnson or Harry Truman or even John Kennedy behaving this way?

Part of the recent GOP formula for success has been a talent for ignoring the obvious: that the party and its policies have become radicalized. In some ways this is a curious stance; one with which prime architects such as Barry Goldwater and Melvin Bradford certainly would not have bothered. For his part, Bradford claimed proudly his conservative moniker and even, in his more candid moments, radicalism—for him a distinction of virtue higher than mere conservatism. As Bradford himself put it: "'Reaction' is a necessary term. . . . Merely to conserve is sometimes to perpetuate what is outrageous." And we all remember what Barry Goldwater had to say about extremism.[11]

It is not surprising that the "status quo society" and its skewing of what constitutes "mainstream" several places to the right has been aided and ameliorated by those who occupy the Far Right. Consigned to the wilderness for decades, fringe figures have of course been anxious to gain more widespread acceptance for ideas that were previously and correctly considered radical. Yet it is not just those on the fringe that have abetted the growth and power of a status quo society. Almost as effective, ironically, have been the efforts of moderate and even progressive historians so desperate to detect some sign of reformist life in the South that they have been willing to label any centrist or even law-abiding action as "liberal." This practice has led to a debasement of that term itself, and consequently perpetuated (perhaps unwittingly) the status quo concept.

Yet the modern conservative movement has been nothing if not patient. Mentorship by succeeding generations of conservative intellectual icons and the creation of an accepted canon has engendered an artificial and constructed respectability, as well as additional mainstreaming. Russell Kirk and the journal he famously edited, *Modern Age*, heavily influenced Melvin Bradford, especially in matters pertaining to the superiority of Western civilization and white, European culture. Bradford's racial, sectional, and antidemocratic inclinations found strong reinforcement in the Nashville Agrarian nirvana of Vanderbilt University, and especially in the orbit of southern poet Donald Davidson. More recently William F. Buckley, Milton Friedman, F. A. Hayek, and Margaret Thatcher have done little to hide their disdain for democratic institutions and processes. There is evidence the Tea Party movement has followed suit.[12]

Massive investment in the infrastructure of ideas since the Goldwater debacle of 1964—think tanks, policy institutes, magazines, newspapers, radio and television outlets—has moved mountains to mainstream formerly radical rightist ideas. Harding College's National Education Program (NEP) and the sponsorship of right-wing thinkers and talkers in "Freedom Forums" and a national lecture circuit nurtured and gave sustenance to conservative icons such as Orval Faubus, Ken Starr, Ann Coulter, Sean Hannity, and Judge Janice Rogers Brown. In this lineage, the ugly anti–civil rights roots of conservative outreach are apparent and important. George Lewis catalogues in his essay that one Virginia segregationist and sovereignty group distributed over 2 million pamphlets and sixteen thousand books alone during the 1960s. The propaganda arm of powerful groups such as the National Association of Manufacturers did the same. This conservative strategy has constituted nothing less than the intellectual carpet-bombing of the American cultural landscape.

The status quo society that is, especially, the Deep South is characterized by two main points. One is its ability to reorder the political spectrum and conventional political understandings at least one full place to the right. The other is the intricate interweaving and interdependence of cultural elements that impede meaningful change: class, race, gender, ethnicity, hyperpatriotism, and their central adhesive, a rope of religion.

Christian institutions of higher education have played an integral role in bolstering and cementing ties between these cultural elements. Schools such as Harding College, the subject of Barclay Key's essay, served as important nurseries of what may be called "The Great Melding"—a seamless combination of racial and religious rightism with economic fundamentalism.[13] Harding and other colleges like it across the South represent a right-wing backlash that countered the New Deal and (at least in the minds of conservatives) its socialism, communism, godlessness, and tyranny with the wholesome antidotes of liberty, Americanism, free enterprise, Christianity, and constitutionalism. Daniel K. Williams and J. Eric Pardue reinforce similar messages in their essays. In the way the rightist dichotomy was constructed, any choice other than their version of conservatism represented an ineluctable march toward collectivism and personal slavery. James Bales, a young Harding professor and church leader, pointed to this "melding" of religious and economic rightism: "If we lose the battle for economic freedom, we lose the battle for religious freedom," he explained. "How much money have you got for evangelism if the government takes it all?"

At religious universities, disgust with the Democratic Party dovetailed with rejection of the New Deal and Fair Deal roads to "complete socialism," a hearty dislike of civil rights, an insidious brand of conformity, and profound—indeed, mythic—obsequiousness toward the business heroes who "provide jobs, a higher standard of living, and through production and their capital a better America." When a lone Harding student body president circulated a petition in support of racial desegregation, he was chastised by a college administrator who warned him in material terms about the consequences of nonconformity: "no employer would ever hire him" because "when one works for an institution he should accept all [of] its thinking and keep silent about contrary beliefs." Grist for life?

In the 1970s, this phenomenon took physical form in the marriage of rural East Texas working-class social conservatives to the middle-class urban and suburban economic conservatives of Houston and Dallas. In his 1968 bid for the presidency, small-town and rural blue-collar Texans formed the core of George Wallace's support in the Lone Star State and represented the long-term target of the Republican Party. A study of more recent New Orleans politics explores how Democratic mayor Ray Nagin, an African American considered "safe" by the white business community, and even a Republican by some, was able to win reelection by forging a curious coalition of black Democrats and white conservatives in the Crescent City.[14]

Of course Melvin Bradford's brand of conservatism managed to tie together religious fundamentalism (specifically literalism and scriptural inerrancy) with a sectional and racial rejection of modernism, liberalism, intellectualism, science, and Enlightenment rationality. Once formed, he linked these to a tainted Yankee appetite for egalitarian heresies—chief among them abolitionism, and later civil rights, multiculturalism, pluralism, and "tolerance" of all kinds. In the struggle to preserve white, Anglo, Christian cultural norms and values—what would eventually become known as the "culture wars"—the South was central to Bradford's triumphalist understanding of an ascendant American conservatism. As Fred Bailey writes in his essay of Bradford: "If the infidel Yankee stood as the enemy in 1861, his spiritual descendants remained a threat more than a century later. 'For all of the great issues fought out in the 1860s are still with us,' Bradford wrote, 'sometimes disguised, but in their fundamental character never changing.'" For Bradford and his conservative intellectual compatriots—men like Thomas Fleming, Clyde Wilson, Grady McWhiney, Forrest MacDonald, and those at the *Southern Partisan* and the League of the South—the late Confederacy, Bailey tells us, "represented far more than a nostalgic might-have-been; to them it stood as a political and social model, an ordered alternative to the anarchy they associated with the late twentieth century." Viewed in this proper context, Mississippi senator Trent Lott's infamous remarks at Strom Thurmond's hundredth birthday party are perfectly consonant with the ascendant South-based modern Republicanism that he and others like him represent.[15]

There is still the question, though, of when and where the South became Republican. George Lewis's essay challenges the received wisdom that party loyalties changed at the presidential level prior to affecting state patterns and down-ticket races—and, in any event, these changes did not begin in Virginia before 1964. Michael Bowen offers a similar argument South-wide. Andrew S.

Farmer confirms this observation in his essay on the 1970 elections in Texas. But, in their South-wide studies of more recent state legislatures, David I. Lublin and Thomas F. Schaller provide abundant quantitative evidence to bolster the more traditional view. The Farmer, Lublin, and Schaller works emphasize the essential test local Democrats must pass—distinguishing themselves from the national party—if they are to have any chance of winning in the South. J. Eric Pardue's in-depth examination in this volume of "Kennedyphobia" in northwest Louisiana during the early 1960s does the same. Farmer, Lublin, and Schaller also stress the significance of racial and partisan gerrymandering in rising Republican fortunes in the South.[16] Texas, Florida, and Virginia stand out in this regard, and, as Slocum's essay intimates, right-wing religion and the modern GOP have worked on each other, very often with the result that "changing the rules in order to win becomes no [ethical or practical] problem at all."

It is an undeniable mark of modernity that mass marketing, public relations, and imaging techniques have taken on added importance in the information age. The use of the word "freedom" is a prime example. Co-opted by the Right early on, this most American of terms has proven itself a convenient, all-purpose label for practically any conservative and even reactionary program—from Harding College's "Freedom Forums," to neoliberalism's fetish with libertarianism and "economic freedom," to southern resistance to school desegregation euphemistically termed "freedom of choice," to recent absurdist screeds like Sean Hannity's *Let Freedom Ring*. No matter how radical, extreme, or outrageous the use of the term might be, "freedom" is a label against which it has proven remarkably difficult—if not impossible—to argue.

"Constitutionalism" has enjoyed a similar career. Groups such as the Virginia Commission on Constitutional Government (CCG) were little more than fronts for states'-rights propaganda. But, given time, in the hands of groups such as the CCG, "constitutionalism" became especially useful in broadening and mainstreaming southern "massive resistance" into a movement that could appeal to nonsouthern conservatives in terms they could accept. As George Lewis illustrates, with concern for legal and "constitutional government" at its core, the modern conservative appeal could be made to northerners on the more euphemistic basis of law and order, fiscal responsibility, limited government, local control, and states' rights—in other words, on a respectable and even, ostensibly, a *nonracial* basis. To be sure, an onion-skin-thin facade and plenty of self-deception was involved. Yet, as a leading Virginia segregationist put it: "We can never win this thing on votes from Southern representatives alone. If we are to win, and I am confident that in the end we will . . . it must be with help from other areas of the country."

All of this leads us, finally, to the dissenting—yet rapidly growing—narrative on the topic of southern partisan realignment as represented in this book most clearly in the Tim Boyd, George Lewis, Michael Bowen, and John W. White essays. All—to greater and lesser extents—follow the lead of the historian Matthew D. Lassiter in *The Silent Majority* (2006) as well as that of the political scientists Byron Shafer and Richard Johnston in *The End of Southern Exceptionalism* (2006). Lassiter, and others since, have argued strongly against what they term the "white backlash" narrative of the South becoming Republican in reaction to national Democratic identification with civil rights and racial liberalism. The "suburban school," as it may now be called, stresses a "suburban strategy" versus what it deems a "southern strategy"—and insists that post–World War II white southern suburbanites were relatively "color-blind" in their approach to politics. The argument goes on to reject the notion of a distinctive South as well as to downplay—and even at times dismiss—the role of race in motivating white southerners to leave the Democratic Party for the GOP. Race was just not something they cared a whole lot about—this better-educated, upwardly mobile, suburban elite.[17] In this volume, the suburban school approach is probably most clearly exemplified in the essays authored by Tim Boyd on Georgia and John W. White on South Carolina, though it pops up in Dan Williams's and Leah Wright's essays, as well as elsewhere.

The brewing debate between the "backlash" theorists and the "suburban school" is so important that I have chosen to include as many sides as possible in this volume. The reader is perfectly capable of plunging in and weighing for themselves the rich, textured, and provocative essays within. In doing so, special attention should be paid to how different contributors conceptualize "the suburb," calibrate what constitutes "color-blind" issues and analyses, determine what qualifies as adequate evidence of partisan change, and decide where economics and politics, taxes and race, begin and end.

This collection is, of course, not exhaustive or definitive. No claim is made that it is. But, in the editor's humble opinion, this is an asset rather than a liability. My hope is that this book will serve as a jumping-off point to stimulate further research and exploration of this fascinating and all-important subject.

## Notes

1. Al LaPierre Oral Interview by Melody Izard, 21 January 2002; Mac Parsons Oral Interview by Melody Izard, 30 January 2002; Oral Interview #18 by Melody Izard, 11 March 2002; Lenora Pate Oral Interview by Melody Izard, 9 May 2002; and Marc Givhan Oral Interview by Melody Izard, 16 November 2007. All of the above interviews took place in Birmingham, Alabama, and are in the possession of the author. The interviewees above consisted of Democratic state strategists and consultants,

judges, candidates, contributors, and attorneys, one of whom (Marc Givhan) did not declare a party. The interviewees vary widely in their stridency, sophistication, and/or level of reasoning and logic in their denial that Alabama is a Republican stronghold. Recent books that deemphasize the importance of race in southern politics are not uncommon (see, for example, Glen Browder, *The South's New Racial Politics: Inside the Race Game of Southern History* [Montgomery: NewSouth Books, 2009]).

2. C. Vann Woodward, *Origins of the New South, 1877–1913* (Baton Rouge: Louisiana State University Press, 1951).

3. Tim Boyd, in his otherwise excellent article in the *Journal of Southern History*, grouped my concept of a "politics of emotion" with other "white backlash" theories. However, this requires some elucidation and expansion as noted here (see "The 1966 Election in Georgia and the Ambiguity of the White Backlash," *Journal of Southern History* 75 [May 2009]: 305–40, esp. 305 n. 2 and 306). Boyd listed other standard works that he properly described as examples of the "white backlash" school. Some of them are: Kevin P. Phillips, *The Emerging Republican Majority* (New Rochelle, N.Y.: Arlington House, 1969); Kirkpatrick Sale, *Power Shift: The Rise of the Southern Rim and Its Challenge to the Eastern Establishment* (New York: Vintage Books, 1975); Alexander P. Lamis, *The Two-Party South* (New York: Oxford University Press, 1984); Thomas Byrne Edsall with Mary D. Edsall, *Chain Reaction: The Impact of Race, Rights, and Taxes on American Politics* (New York: Norton, 1991); Dan T. Carter, *From George Wallace to Newt Gingrich: Race and the Conservative Counterrevolution, 1963–1994* (Baton Rouge: Louisiana State University Press, 1996); Ronald Radosh, *Divided They Fell: The Demise of the Democratic Party, 1964–1996* (New York: Free Press, 1996); and Earl Black and Merle Black, *The Rise of Southern Republicans* (Cambridge: Belknap Press of Harvard University Press, 2002). The *Journal of Southern History* article also referenced Glenn Feldman, ed., *Before Brown: Civil Rights and White Backlash in the Modern South* (Tuscaloosa: University of Alabama Press, 2004)—especially the prologue and epilogue—but those two essays actually go beyond analysis of a white backlash to probe the more expansive meaning of a "politics of emotion." For an excellent essay, somewhat related to this question on race, see Bethany Moreton, "Why Is There So Much Sex in Christian Conservatism and Why Do So Few Historians Care Anything about It?" *Journal of Southern History* 75 (August 2009): 717–38, esp. 720–21.

4. Michael Lind, "Can Obama Give 'em Hell before It's Too Late?: Why Can't Democrats Mobilize the Public for Healthcare Reform? Blame the Demagogy Gap," www.salon.com, 1 September 2009.

5. For the Hitler comparison, see Nancy MacLean, "Neo-Confederacy Versus the New Deal: The Regional Utopia of the Modern American Right," in *The Myth of Southern Exceptionalism*, ed. Matthew D. Lassiter and Joseph Crespino, 309 (New York: Oxford University Press, 2010). Linda Feldmann, "Rand Paul: Civil Rights Brouhaha Clouds Senate Campaign," *Christian Science Monitor*, 20 May 2010.

6. Williams's essay also reminds readers that the SBC endorsed the 1964 Civil Rights Act and did not oppose abortion until 1980. These "surprises," along with the 1962 stance on *Engel*, point to the chasm between the social attitudes of southern

Protestant leaders and those of their lay followers, something that bolsters Paul Harvey's side in his celebrated yet friendly debate with David Chappell. The surprises also point to the absolutely critical nature of the conservative "takeover" of the SBC in 1979, a topic discussed as well in Frederick V. Slocum's essay (see David L. Chappell, *A Stone of Hope: Prophetic Religion and the Death of Jim Crow* [Chapel Hill: University of North Carolina Press, 2003]; and Paul Harvey, *Freedom's Coming: Religious Culture and the Shaping of the South from the Civil War through the Civil Rights Era* [Chapel Hill: University of North Carolina Press, 2005]).

7. I thank Professor Alecia P. Long for sharing with me, in draft form, an unfinished essay that she ultimately decided was not ready to be included in this volume.

8. David Lublin, *The Republican South: Democratization and Partisan Change* (Princeton: Princeton University Press, 2004).

9. This term was first introduced and explained in Glenn Feldman, ed., *Politics and Religion in the White South* (Lexington: University Press of Kentucky, 2005), 292–99.

10. Paul Krugman, "The Big Hate," *New York Times*, 11 June 2009 (quoted).

11. "Extremism in defense of liberty is no vice" is the famous line from Goldwater's concession speech at the 1964 National Republican Convention in Miami.

12. On Buckley and philosopher Albert Jay Nock, see Lind, "Can Obama Give 'em Hell Before It's Too Late?" On Friedman, Hayek, and Thatcher, see Glenn Feldman, "Unholy Alliance: Suppressing Catholic Teachings in Subservience to Republican Ascendance in America," *Political Theology* 7 (April 2006): 137–79. See also Estelle Rogers, "Tea Party, GOP Groups, Target Minorities for Voter Suppression Schemes," *Forbes*, www.forbes.com, 28 October 2010; Michael Stone, "Tea Party Targets Minorities for Voter Intimidation, Suppression," *Portland Progressive Examiner*, 29 October 2010.

13. See Glenn Feldman, "Southern Disillusionment with the Democratic Party: Cultural Conformity and 'the Great Melding' of Racial and Economic Conservatism in Alabama during World War II," *Journal of American Studies* 43 (August 2009): 199–230.

14. Again, I thank Professor Alecia P. Long of Louisiana State University for making a draft of her unpublished essay available to me, as did Andrew S. Farmer.

15. Senate majority leader Trent Lott famously came under a firestorm of criticism for his racially charged remarks at Senator Thurmond's hundredth birthday party, an incident that eventually cost Lott dearly. Thomas B. Edsall, "Lott Decried for Part of Salute to Thurmond," *Washington Post*, 7 December 2002.

16. Lublin, *The Republican South*. See also Thomas F. Schaller, *Whistling Past Dixie: How Democrats Can Win without the South* (New York: Simon and Schuster, 2006). I thank Andrew S. Farmer for making available his unfinished essay on 1970 Texas.

17. Matthew D. Lassiter, *The Silent Majority: Suburban Politics in the Sunbelt South* (Princeton: Princeton University Press, 2006); Byron Shafer and Richard Johnston, *The End of Southern Exceptionalism: Class, Race and Partisan Change in the Postwar South* (Cambridge: Harvard University Press, 2006). See also Boyd, "The 1966 Election in Georgia and the Ambiguity of the White Backlash"; and, more recently, Lassiter and Crespino, eds., *The Myth of Southern Exceptionalism*.

# I

# Religion and Partisan Realignment

# 1

## Voting for God and the GOP

### The Role of Evangelical Religion in the Emergence of the Republican South

DANIEL K. WILLIAMS

When Barack Obama won the presidential election of 2008, he received strong support from nearly every demographic group in the United States. But one group remained staunchly opposed to his candidacy: white evangelicals—a group that pollsters usually define as Bible-believing, "born-again" Protestants who believe in personal salvation through Jesus Christ. Three-quarters of them cast their ballots for Republican presidential candidate John McCain. In the South, where approximately half of the nation's evangelicals live, the impact of the evangelical Republican vote was huge. In 2008, 94 percent of white evangelical voters in Mississippi, and an overwhelming majority of those in other southern states, supported the McCain-Palin ticket, allowing the GOP to maintain its hold on the Deep South in spite of Obama's landslide victory.[1]

At first glance, white evangelicals voting against Obama might appear to have merely been one more manifestation of the effect of race on voting patterns. But, along with race, religion played a key role in determining partisan preferences. In every state, white evangelicals were more likely than non-evangelical whites to vote Republican. The southern states that Obama lost were strong evangelical enclaves, such as Mississippi, where 74 percent of white voters were born-again Christians, and Alabama, where 72 percent were. On the other hand, the southern states that Obama carried, like North Carolina and Virginia, had a lower percentage of evangelical voters.[2] White opposition to Obama in the South was primarily an evangelical phenomenon. As had been the case for more than two decades, one of the best ways to determine whether a white voter was a Republican was to ask her where she went to church.

Studies of the rise of the GOP in the South have traditionally focused on race. But especially important in the emergence of a Republican South has been the role of evangelical ministers. For many southerners, the virulent anticommunism that bolstered the right wing of the GOP during the Cold War was a religious ideology, which southern evangelicals absorbed from fundamentalist radio evangelists and Christian periodicals. The "law and order" issue that brought so many southern whites into the GOP during the late 1960s and 1970s came not only from Richard Nixon but also from Billy Graham. In 1980, the Reagan campaign relied on Christian Right leaders such as Jerry Falwell to mobilize southern white voters with a message of social conservatism and Cold War ideology. In the 1990s, the political strategists who succeeded in creating a Republican South and a southernized national GOP included not only Newt Gingrich, but also Christian Coalition head Ralph Reed. Throughout the postwar era, evangelical religion has served as a principal transmitter of the Republican message in the South.[3] Southern evangelicals also infused the GOP with their religiously inspired concerns, pushing the party to the right on cultural issues: the perceived moral disorder caused by race riots, the sexual revolution, the feminist movement, and "secular humanism."

Christian Right activists who sought to establish a moral order through politics were not the first southern evangelicals to try. Southern Baptists and Methodists had pushed Prohibition, and, in the 1920s, southern fundamentalists succeeded in outlawing the teaching of evolution in public schools in a few states. But unlike the later Christian Right movement, these campaigns were not identified with a particular political party, and did not produce political realignment. In contrast, late-twentieth-century southern evangelical activism helped transform millions of traditionally Democratic voters into staunch champions of the GOP, a change that helped to make the once-solidly Democratic South a strongly Republican region.

Before World War II, southern white evangelicals, like other voters in the region, were overwhelmingly Democratic. In 1928, southern evangelical pastors made a rare break to campaign against Democratic presidential candidate Al Smith, a Catholic opposed to Prohibition.[4] During the 1930s, most pastors in the economically depressed South valued the benefits the New Deal provided for their impoverished parishioners; some became outspoken fans of FDR. In Alabama, 79 percent of the pastors who responded to a survey supported Roosevelt's New Deal: even the few critics generally complained that it was not radical enough. Hardly any wanted to see the federal government become less involved in their parishioners' lives. As one rural preacher in Apex, North Carolina, told his congregation, Roosevelt was "following more nearly the program of Jesus than any president we have ever had."[5] But after the war, as southern evangelicals began moving into the middle class, their commitment to the Democratic Party lessened, and they became more receptive to the message of moral order that the Republican Party promised. Anticommunism was the first issue on which southern evangelicals and northern Republicans found common ground. Fundamentalists—that is, independent Baptists and other Protestants who were more theologically conservative and separatist than the Southern Baptist Convention—were the first southern Protestants to link religion with anticommunism. Tulsa fundamentalist radio preacher Billy James Hargis spoke out strongly against communist influence in the United States, and in the mid-1950s, began working closely with J. B. Matthews, a former staffer for Republican Senator Joseph McCarthy.[6] Other fundamentalists in the South likewise began echoing McCarthy's charges that the State Department was filled with "fellow travelers" and subversives. In 1951, Bob Jones Jr. held an anticommunist World Outlook Conference at his South Carolina fundamentalist college.

Before the 1950s, southern Christian anticommunism was not explicitly partisan. At a time when both Democrats and Republicans endorsed the anticommunist investigations of the House Committee on Un-American Activities (HUAC), southern fundamentalists saw no need to abandon their region's traditional party. In 1944, a national survey of Baptists revealed that they were more likely than other Americans to view the USSR as a threat and yet also more likely to vote Democratic. In the early years of the Cold War, southern fundamentalists, Baptists, and other evangelicals viewed Harry Truman as a strong anticommunist.[7]

But by the 1950s, some fundamentalists began to view the GOP as their most reliable ally in the struggle against communism. Southern fundamentalists such as Jones and Hargis lauded Republican Senator Joseph McCarthy's attacks on Democrats in the State Department and began to associate New Deal and Fair Deal liberalism with "socialism," which they considered only one step removed from communism. In 1951, Bob Jones University's World Outlook Conference broadened its anticommunist message to encompass "Americanism," a term that was synonymous with what would eventually be called political conservatism. The conference offered a critical examination not only of Truman's foreign policies, but also of his health-care plan. The South's leading fundamentalist periodical, the *Sword of the Lord*, also published several editorials criticizing Truman and the Democratic Party, which it claimed was "now committed to socialism." The "class hatred so carefully cultivated by New Dealers and Communists is wicked, un-Christian and un-American," editor John R. Rice declared in 1952.[8] These moves demonstrated the power of right-wing anticommunism to turn southern Christians away from an economic populism that they had enthusiastically championed earlier.

Seeking an alternative to Truman, many conservative Protestants in the South supported Dwight Eisenhower in 1952. As a wartime general with southern family ties, Eisenhower had widespread appeal in the region. Among evangelicals he was even more popular because his candidacy symbolized strong military leadership and moral order. Although Ike was not a regular churchgoer before he became president, he began invoking religion on the campaign trail as a spiritual force to unite Americans in the Cold War, a struggle that he called a "war of light against darkness, freedom against slavery, Godliness against Atheism." When the Democratic Party nominated a divorced Unitarian—Illinois governor Adlai Stevenson—millions of fundamentalists and evangelicals in the South crossed party lines to vote for Eisenhower. At Bob Jones University, 80 percent of students favored him. When Billy Graham polled Protestant ministers on their election preferences, he found that 77 percent of them did as well.[9]

Graham was one of Eisenhower's staunchest supporters, primarily because he believed that the general would offer the country a strong defense against communism. Communism, Graham said, was "against God, against Christ, against the Bible, and against all religion," and therefore must be opposed with strong military action. Although he was a registered Democrat—like most North Carolinians in the late 1940s—Graham had lost faith in Truman. When the ecumenically minded Southern Baptist became closely associated with Eisenhower, many moderate southern evangelicals embraced the general as an ally in their quest for an anticommunist moral order.[10]

During his time in office, Eisenhower solidified his standing with evangelicals by promoting the role of religion in American society and infusing the cause of anticommunism with religious rhetoric. He frequently referenced God in his speeches, and signed into law bills that put the words "under God" in the pledge of allegiance and "In God We Trust" on the nation's currency. He began cabinet meetings with prayer and adopted a habit of weekly church attendance. At a time when church attendance rates were reaching record levels, Graham viewed Ike as an officiator of a "national spiritual awakening," a role that made him "God's man of the hour."[11]

Evangelicals' association of the Republican Party with a national civil religion became more pronounced in 1960, when the Democratic Party nominated a Catholic candidate, Senator John F. Kennedy, for the presidency. Because they believed that the nation's tradition of individual liberty was rooted in its Protestant heritage, evangelicals viewed a Catholic presidential candidate as a threat not only to Protestantism, but to the nation's identity. In contrast, they viewed the Republican presidential candidate, Richard Nixon, as a representative of the Protestant-dominated, anticommunist, civil religion of the Eisenhower administration. The Southern Baptist Convention passed a resolution in May 1960 warning of the dangers of a Catholic president, and several leading Southern Baptist pastors campaigned against Kennedy—as did Graham and Billy James Hargis. W. A. Criswell, a Dallas pastor whose congregation was the largest in the SBC, distributed 100,000 copies of a sermon predicting that JFK's election would "spell the death of a free church in a free state and . . . full religious liberty in America."[12]

When southern evangelicals lost their campaign against Kennedy, they reacted with despair. No longer could they take the nation's Protestant identity and moral and religious order for granted. "You, Dick, stood for the things which have made America great, while Mr. Kennedy appealed to the most venal elements in individuals and society as a whole," North Carolina Presbyterian pastor L. Nelson Bell, Billy Graham's father-in-law, told Nixon a few days after the election. "The judgment of God hangs over a people to whom He has given so much and who have rejected spiritual values for those which are material."[13] Some southern Protestants—especially fundamentalists—enlisted in a larger conservative movement developing in opposition to Kennedy's civil rights policies and social programs. Southern fundamentalists recognized the common goals they shared with the conservative movement. Bob Jones Jr., who continued his attacks on Kennedy throughout his presidency, invited Senator Strom Thurmond and Rep. Mendel Rivers (D-SC) to give speeches on campus denouncing the Kennedy administration.[14]

Billy James Hargis, who made criticisms of the administration a staple of his radio sermons, launched a new effort to elect self-proclaimed "conservatives" to Congress. By the early 1960s, Hargis, Jones, and other fundamentalists feared the country was moving away from the vigilant anticommunism of the late 1940s and early 1950s. They blamed the Kennedy administration and its associated "liberals" for this alleged appeasement of the enemy. "Liberalism," Hargis said, was a "broad, slick runway straight into Communism," and "conservatism," therefore, was the only political stance that a Christian could legitimately take. "Christ is the heart of the Conservative cause," Hargis proclaimed. "We conservatives are fighting for God and Country." Linking aggressive anticommunism with an equally adamant opposition to civil rights, Hargis campaigned for congressional candidates who were declared opponents of the president. At the local level, this movement was bipartisan, because most of the southern conservatives that Hargis aided, such as Arkansas governor Orval Faubus, were Democrats. But at the national level, Hargis, Jones, and other fundamentalists supported conservative Republicans such as Barry Goldwater, a move that drew them closer to the GOP. In 1964, Hargis declared that if Goldwater were elected with a conservative Congress, it "would be the millennium."[15]

Outside of fundamentalist circles, many southern Protestants, including most of those in the SBC, refused to join the fundamentalists' conservative coalition, primarily because of the issue of race. In 1960, southern conservative Protestants across the theological spectrum, including fundamentalists, Southern Baptists, and other evangelicals, had united in opposing JFK. But in 1964, the coalition fragmented. Fundamentalists who endorsed segregation supported Goldwater, an opponent of the Civil Rights Act of 1964, but many evangelicals who took a moderately progressive stand on civil rights, such as Billy Graham, favored Lyndon Johnson. The SBC officially endorsed Johnson's Civil Rights Act. Although the majority of Southern Baptist churches remained entirely white, and although many of the Convention's pastors supported Jim Crow and denigrated Martin Luther King Jr., the Convention's leadership generally tried to avoid being tarred with the overt racism of the region's fundamentalists.[16]

Only after the accomplishment of legal desegregation defused the contentious issue of civil rights were the region's evangelicals and fundamentalists able to unite in a lasting political coalition. The race riots of the late 1960s caused evangelicals such as Graham, who had once supported civil rights legislation, to break with the civil rights movement and begin calling for "law and order, no matter how much power and force it takes." At the same time, the desegregation of public facilities throughout the South caused fundamentalists such as Lynchburg, Virginia, Baptist pastor Jerry Falwell, who had campaigned for school segregation, to recognize the futility of that policy and accept the reality of legal integration. Falwell welcomed the first blacks to his church in 1968, and accepted the first African American students at his Christian school in 1969. By the end of the decade, fundamentalists and evangelicals who had been at odds over civil rights were able to unite in a coalition of nominally color-blind "law and order" politics. When Nixon ran for president in 1968, he received strong support, not only from Graham, but also from southern fundamentalists and Southern Baptists who had been politically divided four years earlier. Although third-party candidate George Wallace attracted widespread support from rural whites, few southern church leaders were interested in his presidential campaign. *Christianity Today*, the nation's leading evangelical magazine, denounced him. On election day, 69 percent of the nation's white evangelical voters cast their ballots for Nixon.[17]

Nixon appealed to conservative Protestants because his rhetoric opposed the secular trends that evangelicals believed were undermining America. Secularization, which included court-ordered discontinuation of traditional civil religious observations in the nation's public institutions, as well as the perception that religion was losing its influence in public life, was a new concern for southern evangelicals in the early 1970s. In 1962, when the Supreme

Court ruled against school prayer in *Engel v. Vitale*, the SBC did not denounce the ruling as an attack on religion—as it would a generation later—but instead lauded the decision as necessary to maintain the separation of church and state and prevent Catholics from obtaining federal funding for parochial schools. But the sexual revolution, the feminist movement, and a rising crime rate convinced many evangelicals and fundamentalists that Christians—both Catholic and Protestant—were losing control of the nation's culture, and they longed for a politician who would challenge what they viewed as a liberal secular establishment and a culture of permissiveness. Nixon's call for "law and order," *Eternity* magazine declared in January 1973, was a clarion call against cultural liberalism and would "guide the nation out of its ethical morass."[18]

Evangelicals who wanted a return to moral order appreciated Nixon's use of civil religion. They commended him for inviting Billy Graham to deliver sermons at White House church services and for appearing at a few evangelical gatherings. Viewing Nixon as an exemplar of public morality and Christian faith, the SBC invited him to speak at its annual meeting in 1972, the first time that the Convention had ever issued such an invitation to a U.S. president. Nixon was a "born-again" Christian, the president of the SBC declared, a view Graham shared. During the president's reelection campaign, Graham broke precedent by openly endorsing him, and he met regularly with H. R. Haldeman to give campaign advice on how to reach evangelical voters. On election day in 1972, Nixon received more than 80 percent of the white evangelical vote.[19]

One poll showed that more than 80 percent of Southern Baptist pastors supported Nixon's strategy in Vietnam in the summer of 1970, a time when the president was facing sharp criticism from many other Americans for his bombing of Cambodia.[20] For many southern evangelicals of the early 1970s, faith and patriotism were becoming increasingly inseparable, a situation that benefited Nixon, who was eager to endorse both.

Southern evangelicals' longing for moral order in the nation was so strong that Nixon's fall from grace and Graham's subsequent retreat from politics did not quell their fledgling political movement or their commitment to the Republican Party. Evangelical women who were concerned about the future of their families and the maintenance of traditional gender roles organized their own grassroots political campaigns to keep "secular humanism" out of schools, save their children, and protect the "traditional" family against profanity and "anti-Christian" stories in school curricula. In 1975, evangelical women in Texas, Oklahoma, and North Carolina lobbied their state legislatures against the Equal Rights Amendment. In 1977, fifteen thousand socially conservative women gathered at the Houston Astro Arena to protest against the International Women's Year conference, which they claimed was dominated by liberal, pro-choice, pro-ERA feminists. The Christian singer Anita Bryant led a successful campaign to repeal a gay rights ordinance in order to prevent homosexuals from teaching children in Florida public schools.[21]

Most of the women who launched these campaigns did not view themselves as conservative activists. Many were registered Democrats, and few had connections to the national conservative movement or had any aspirations for political office. But their campaigns for the preservation of an evangelical Christian version of "family values" brought them into alliance with conservative Republican politicians who were eager to blame government bureaucrats for the threats to the "traditional" family that evangelical activists perceived. Alice Moore received help from Heritage Foundation founder Paul Weyrich in her campaign against "humanist" textbooks in West Virginia, because the New Right activist viewed the campaign as a fight for local parental control of school curriculum against the opposition of liberal educational bureaucrats. The evangelical women who campaigned against the ERA in the South worked closely with Phyllis Schlafly, a veteran conservative Republican activist who had written a campaign book for Barry Goldwater in 1964. Anita Bryant received funding from Senator Jesse Helms in her campaign against gay rights.[22] Across the South, socially conservative Democratic women began to view the federal government as a threat to the family, and conservative Republicans as their allies.

At the end of the 1970s, the "pro-family" movement directed much of its ire against the nation's most politically prominent Democrat, President Jimmy Carter. As a Southern Baptist Sunday school teacher and Georgia governor, Carter had won a majority of the white Baptist vote in 1976. Once in office, Carter confirmed these evangelical skeptics' worst fears about his candidacy and also alienated many of his erstwhile supporters by strongly supporting the ERA, filling his administration with pro-choice advocates, and reaching out to gay rights activists. Tarring Carter with the charge of having "secular humanist" sympathies, San Diego Baptist pastor and best-selling Christian author Tim LaHaye suggested that the president was either "naïve about humanism" or, worse yet, was "a humanist who masqueraded as a Christian to get elected and then showed his contempt for the 60 million 'born agains' by excluding them from his government."[23]

In 1978, the Carter administration further angered fundamentalist and conservative evangelical Protestants by threatening to revoke the tax exemption of private Christian schools that did not comply with federal civil rights policy by enrolling a sufficient number of African Americans and other minorities. By the late 1970s, most Christian schools, including Falwell's, enrolled at least a token number of African Americans, but few of them made efforts to expand their minority enrollment, and many of them would have been affected by the IRS's proposed policy. Rather than comply with the ruling, Falwell and other Christian school administrators chose to fight the policy, calling it an unwarranted federal intervention in their religious establishments.[24]

Fundamentalists' successful fight against the IRS in 1978 ensured that the national movement that they launched the following year would be an explicitly conservative political effort, because it was founded on opposition to federal control of religious institutions and private enterprise, a cause that many conservative Republicans championed. By arguing that the federal government—and especially the Carter administration—had unjustifiably intervened in private family matters to prosecute Christian schools and promote feminism, abortion, and homosexuality in opposition to the values of conservative Christian parents, Falwell succeeded in making the emerging Christian political movement a campaign against the intrusion of the federal government in church and family life.

But that changed in the 1970s. A new generation of evangelicals moved into the suburban middle class and found church homes in the thriving Sunbelt, a region that fostered some of the nation's fastest-growing congregations. Evangelicals also improved their socioeconomic standing. By the mid-1970s, 23 percent of evangelicals had a college education. With their newfound education came increased wealth, which could easily be channeled into political causes. By the end of the 1970s, Falwell was collecting more money per year than either the Democratic or Republican parties, and he had to employ a staff of one thousand to oversee his vast ministerial operations.[25]

Evangelicals discovered in the mid-1970s that they were the nation's largest religious group. In 1976, the Gallup poll revealed that one-third of Americans were "born-again" Christians, prompting *Newsweek* magazine to declare it the "year of the evangelical." Some evangelicals realized that if they united with conservative Catholics outside of their movement, they could easily take power in Washington. "We have together, with the Protestants and the Catholics, enough votes to run the country," Pat Robertson said in 1979. "We are going to take over."[26]

As conservative evangelicals prepared to exercise their political power, savvy Republican politicians decided to ally with the movement and solicit its votes. One of those politicians was Ronald Reagan, who correctly sensed that southern conservative evangelicals' staunch anticommunism and opposition to federal intrusion in their Christian schools would lead them to support his presidential candidacy in 1980. Although the former California governor had not been known for his support of the Christian Right's religiously inspired moral causes—and, in fact, had spoken out in 1978 against a California anti-gay rights referendum that Falwell had endorsed—his antigovernment rhetoric accorded well with Falwell's goals. During his 1980 presidential campaign, Reagan spoke at the evangelical National Religious Affairs Briefing in Dallas, where he affirmed his support for private Christian schools, and at Falwell's Liberty Baptist College in Lynchburg, Virginia, where he declared his approval of classroom prayer in public schools. "I know you can't endorse me," he told a group of fifteen thousand evangelical ministers in Dallas, in a nod to their professed tradition of nonpartisanship, "but I want you to know that I endorse you and what you are doing." Christian Right leaders were ecstatic. In the election of 1980, Reagan carried 67 percent of the white evangelical vote, and in 1984, he did even better, winning nearly 80 percent of white evangelicals. Reagan's campaigns marked the beginning of evangelicals' lasting commitment to the Republican Party; after 1980, Republican presidential candidates would consistently win a majority of the white evangelical vote, regardless of whether or not they won a majority among the general voting population.[27]

Falwell's Moral Majority, which registered at least 2 million new conservative voters in 1980, may have helped Reagan win the South, but the 13 million–member Southern Baptist Convention provided a much more influential source of support. Many prominent pastors in the SBC had been leaning Republican for at least a decade before Reagan took office, but as late as 1979, several of the denomination's leaders were still supportive of Carter and were reluctant to enlist the denomination in the Christian Right's causes. The denomination's politics changed rapidly in June 1979, when a group of self-styled "conservatives" took control of the SBC and moved it sharply to the right on cultural issues, especially on abortion. For most of the 1970s, abortion had not been a major issue of concern for the SBC. In 1971, the SBC, which had had a long-standing suspicion of Catholic causes, had officially endorsed the liberalization of state abortion laws in a direct repudiation of the predominantly Catholic pro-life movement. But the conservatives who took control of the denomination in 1979 objected to the SBC's moderately pro-choice position, because they viewed the nation's rising abortion rate as a sign of sexual promiscuity, feminism, and moral decline. The fact that the Supreme Court had ruled in favor of abortion rights confirmed their suspicion that the federal government was anti-Christian. In an effort to challenge the political status quo on the issue and enlist the denomination in a broader culture war to reclaim the nation for Christian values, the SBC's new leaders reversed the denomination's official stance on abortion in 1980, and replaced its moderately pro-choice position with a strong show of support for fetal life.[28]

Under conservative leadership, the denomination also passed a resolution in 1980 criticizing Carter's White House Conference on the Family for its support of abortion, and issued other resolutions condemning pornography, homosexuality, and even the "marriage tax." In 1982, the SBC moved closer to the Republican fold by rescinding its long-standing opposition to prayer in public schools, and passing a resolution supporting the school-prayer constitutional amendment that the Reagan administration had proposed. Five years later, the denomination supported one of Reagan's judicial appointments by lobbying for Judge Robert Bork's confirmation to the Supreme Court.[29] Using opposition to abortion as their justification, the SBC's conservatives enlisted the denomination in support of the Christian Right and the Republican Party.

The SBC's support of the Reagan administration led to an increase in the number of Southern Baptist pastors and other white southern evangelicals who identified themselves as Republican. Even though southern evangelicals had been voting for Republican presidential candidates since Eisenhower's first presidential campaign, they were more likely than their region's non-evangelicals to remain registered Democrats, even as late as 1980. Republican partisan identity among Southern Baptist pastors was only slightly higher. But during Reagan's first term in office, southern evangelical voters abandoned the Democratic Party, and by 1984, the rate of Republican registration among Southern Baptist pastors increased to 66 percent. Non-evangelical white southerners experienced an increase in Republican identity during this period, but not to the same extent that evangelicals did. After 1984, white evangelicals would remain more Republican than Democratic in their party identification, and they would consistently support Republican presidential candidates at a higher rate than their non-evangelical peers. For Christian Right activists, the Democratic Party was on the wrong side of the culture war in its support of abortion rights and on the wrong side of the Cold War in its opposition to Reagan's defense policies. As Jerry Falwell told his supporters in 1984, "The Democratic party is basically controlled by the radical ideas of a dangerous minority—homosexuals, militant feminists, socialists, freezeniks [advocates of a nuclear freeze], and others of the ilk."[30]

If the 1980s was the decade in which southern evangelicals became committed Republicans, the 1990s was the time when they, with the help of the Christian Coalition, took over the party and reshaped it into an instrument of the Religious Right. The Christian Coalition was the brainchild of the religious broadcaster Pat Robertson, who used the mailing list from his unsuccessful campaign for the 1988 Republican presidential nomination to launch the organization in 1989. But the political strategist behind the operation was Ralph Reed, a young Emory Ph.D. who had been active in Republican Party politics since his undergraduate years at the University of Georgia in the early

1980s. Previous Religious Right organizations had gained national attention, but Reed sought something greater: genuine political power, which he knew could be won only with control of party organizations. Employing a "stealth strategy" that largely avoided the scrutiny of the media, Reed's candidates won a string of local election victories, and then parlayed local political power for more substantial influence in the Republican Party. By 1994, the Christian Coalition controlled eighteen state Republican parties and exercised a strong influence in eighteen others, including the state GOP organizations of Alabama, Georgia, Texas, Louisiana, North and South Carolina, and Virginia. Party control gave the Christian Coalition the ability to replace moderate Republican congressional candidates with staunch social conservatives.[31]

When the Christian Coalition succeeded in making the national Republican Party more southern and evangelical, some of the party's long-standing northeastern members decided to leave. By the end of the twentieth century, only a minority of white mainline Protestants, including the Episcopalians and Presbyterians who had once been the mainstay of the GOP, voted Republican in presidential elections. In contrast, approximately three-quarters of white evangelicals were reliable Republican voters. As a result of this turnabout, the party became increasingly dependent on its evangelical members. Republican politicians realized that they could not win a national race without the support of the Christian Right.[32]

In 2000, Senator John McCain learned the perils of alienating the Christian Right when he angered evangelicals by denouncing Jerry Falwell and Pat Robertson as "agents of intolerance." McCain went on to win a majority of non-evangelical votes in southern primaries, but he failed to win any of these contests. McCain learned his lesson. In preparation for his campaign of 2008, he spoke at Falwell's Liberty University, solicited endorsements from evangelical pastors, and highlighted his opposition to abortion. During the general election campaign, he chose as his running mate the overtly evangelical, strongly pro-life Alaska governor Sarah Palin in order to solidify his support in the South. If McCain's goal was to win white evangelical support, the tactic worked. Nearly 40 percent of his votes came from evangelicals, and in the South, he received nearly monolithic support from white, born-again Christians. McCain won the votes of 85 percent of white evangelicals in South Carolina, 89 percent of those in Georgia, and 92 percent of those in Alabama.[33]

Voting patterns in the 2008 election, and in 2010, provided further confirmation that southern white evangelicals, who had once been solidly Democratic partisans and economic populists, were the nation's most loyal Republicans in the early-twenty-first century. By moving into the GOP en masse, they had succeeded in transforming the party into an agent in the culture wars.

This move alienated many of the party's traditional supporters in the North, which in turn made the GOP increasingly dependent on southern evangelical votes. Christian Right activism thus not only made the South more Republican, but also made the Republican Party more southern.

## Notes

1. E. J. Dionne Jr., *Souled Out: Reclaiming Faith and Politics after the Religious Right* (Princeton: Princeton University Press, 2008), 54; CNN Election Center 2008, www.cnn.com/ELECTION/2008/results/polls.

2. CNN Election Center 2008.

3. Analyses of the late-twentieth-century southern political realignment that emphasize race include Earl Black and Merle Black, *Politics and Society in the South* (Cambridge: Harvard University Press, 1987); Earl Black and Merle Black, *The Rise of Southern Republicans* (Cambridge: Belknap Press of Harvard University Press, 2002); Thomas Byrne Edsall and Mary D. Edsall, *Chain Reaction: The Impact of Race, Rights, and Taxes on American Politics* (New York: Norton, 1991); Dan T. Carter, *From George Wallace to Newt Gingrich: Race in the Conservative Counterrevolution, 1963–1994* (Baton Rouge: Louisiana State University Press, 1996); and Glenn Feldman, "Epilogue: Ugly Roots: Race, Emotion and the Rise of the Modern Republican Party in Alabama and the South," in *Before Brown: Civil Rights and White Backlash in the Modern South*, ed. Feldman, 268–309 (Tuscaloosa: University of Alabama Press, 2004). For studies of the role of religion in the growth of the Republican Party in the South, see Clyde Wilcox, *Onward Christian Soldiers: The Christian Right in American Politics*, 3rd ed. (Boulder, Colo.: Westview Press, 2006); Steven P. Miller, *Billy Graham and the Rise of the Republican South* (Philadelphia: University of Pennsylvania Press, 2009); and Glenn Feldman, "The Status Quo Society, the Rope of Religion, and the New Racism," in *Politics and Religion in the White South*, ed. Feldman, 287–352 (Lexington: University Press of Kentucky, 2005).

4. Paul Harvey, *Freedom's Coming: Religious Culture and the Shaping of the South from the Civil War through the Civil Rights Era* (Chapel Hill: University of North Carolina Press, 2005).

5. Kenneth K. Bailey, *Southern White Protestantism in the Twentieth Century* (New York: Harper and Row, 1964), 114–15; Southern Baptist Convention, Untitled Resolution, June 1933, www.sbc.net/resolutions/amResolution.asp?ID=60; Wayne Flynt, "Religion for the Blues: Evangelicalism, Poor Whites, and the Great Depression," *Journal of Southern History* 71 (2005): 28, 33–34, 38.

6. George M. Marsden, *Fundamentalism and American Culture: The Shaping of Twentieth-Century Evangelicalism, 1870–1925* (New York: Oxford University Press, 1980), 209; Peter T. Beckman, "The Right Wing and the Christian Faith" (Ph.D. diss., University of Chicago Divinity School, 1968), 149–66; Louis Gasper, *The Fundamentalist Movement* (The Hague: Mouton, 1963), 66–67; Erling Jorstad, *The Politics of Doomsday: Fundamentalists of the Far Right* (Nashville: Abingdon, 1970),

48, 51; Billy James Hargis to Jim Ryerson, 14 January 1958, "Fundamentalism" File, J. S. Mack Library, Bob Jones University, Greenville, S.C.

7. Wesley and Beverly Allinsmith, "Religious Affiliation and Politico-Economic Attitude: A Study of Eight Major US Religious Groups," *Public Opinion Quarterly* 12 (1948): 385; Lyman Kellstedt et al., "Faith Transformed: Religion and American Politics from FDR to George W. Bush," in *Religion and American Politics: From the Colonial Period to the Present*, ed. Mark A. Noll and Luke E. Harlow, 2nd ed. (New York: Oxford University Press, 2007), 272.

8. Bob Jones Jr., "No Harm Investigating," *Trade Union Courier*, 9 September 1953; *Christian Echoes*, September 1950, 6–7; "BJU Session Opens Dec. 14," *Greenville Piedmont*, 23 November 1951; *Sword of the Lord*, 15 August 1952, and 19 September 1952.

9. William R. Conklin, "Eisenhower Says Farewell to Columbia University," *New York Times*, 17 January 1953; Kellstedt et al., "Faith Transformed," 272; "BJU Students Favor Ike in 'Convention,'" *Greenville News*, 20 October 1952; William Martin, *A Prophet with Honor: The Billy Graham Story* (New York: Morrow, 1991), 148–49.

10. Billy Graham, "We Need Revival!" and "Prepare to Meet Thy God!" in *Revival in Our Time: The Story of the Billy Graham Evangelistic Campaigns* (Wheaton, Ill.: Van Kampen Press, 1950), 72–73, 122–23; William G. McLoughlin Jr., *Billy Graham: Revivalist in a Secular Age* (New York: Ronald Press, 1960, 108–14, 151; Billy Graham to Dwight Eisenhower, 3 December 1951, Folder 1–12, Collection 74, Billy Graham Center Archives (BGCA), Wheaton, Ill. (original in Dwight D. Eisenhower Presidential Library [hereafter EPL]); Gary Scott Smith, *Faith and the Presidency: From George Washington to George W. Bush* (New York: Oxford University Press, 2006), 222.

11. Sydney Ahlstrom, *A Religious History of the American People* (New Haven: Yale University Press, 1972), 954; Stephen J. Whitfield, *The Culture of the Cold War*, 89; James DeForest Murch, *Cooperation without Compromise: A History of the National Association of Evangelicals* (Grand Rapids: Eerdmans, 1956), 150–51; Billy Graham to Dwight Eisenhower, 19 August 1955 and 18 November 1959, Folder 1–12, Collection 74, BGCA (original in EPL).

12. John Wicklein, "Baptists Question Vote for Catholic," *New York Times*, 21 May 1960; AP, "Kennedy Is Attacked," *New York Times*, 4 July 1960; Billy Graham to Richard Nixon: 17 November 1959, 27 May 1960, 29 August 1960, 17 October 1960, and 23 August 1960, Microfilm reel 1, Collection 74, BGCA (originals in Nixon Presidential Library); W. H. Lawrence, "Nixon Forecasts Reuther Control If Kennedy Wins," *New York Times*, 4 November 1960; Bob Jones Sr., "Shall President Take Orders from the Pope?" Chapel Talk, Bob Jones University, Greenville, S.C., 14 March 1960, reprinted in *Sword of the Lord*, 20 May 1960; Shaun A. Casey, *The Making of a Catholic President: Kennedy vs. Nixon, 1960* (New York: Oxford University Press, 2009).

13. L. N. Bell to Richard Nixon, 11 November 1960, Folder 39–15, Collection 318, BGCA.

14. "Senator Strom Thurmond Speaks," *Bob Jones University Bulletin: Voice of the Alumni*, November 1961; "BJU to Present Political Issues," *Greenville Piedmont*, 29

January 1962; Public Relations Scheduling Form #4, "Americanism Conference—BJU Conservative Position, Etc.," 27–28 January 1962, "Americanism Releases, Feb. 5–10, 1962" Folder, Bob Jones University Archives, Greenville, S.C. For a history of conservatism in the early 1960s, see Jonathan M. Schoenwald, *A Time for Choosing: The Rise of Modern American Conservatism* (New York: Oxford University Press, 2001).

15. John Harold Redekop, *The American Far Right: A Case Study of Billy James Hargis and Christian Crusade* (Grand Rapids: Eerdmans, 1968), 38, 43; Donald Janson, "Vote Push Urged for U.S. Rightists," *New York Times*, 31 January 1962; Donald Janson, "Rightists Called to Unity Meeting," *New York Times*, 2 February 1962; Richard V. Pierard, *The Unequal Yoke: Evangelical Christianity and Political Conservatism* (Philadelphia: Lippincott, 1970), 17.

16. Martin, *Prophet with Honor*, 302; *Christianity Today*, 6 November 1964, 47; Mark B. Newman, *Getting Right with God: Southern Baptists and Desegregation, 1945–1995* (Tuscaloosa: University of Alabama Press, 2001), 30; "A Question of Values," *Christianity Today*, 20 November 1964, 44; Wayne Flynt, *Alabama Baptists: Southern Baptists in the Heart of Dixie* (Tuscaloosa: University of Alabama Press, 1998), 455–516.

17. Religious News Service, "Graham to Candidates: Americans Wants Change in U.S. Moral Direction," *Western Voice*, 7 November 1968, 3; Steven P. Miller, "The Politics of Decency: Billy Graham, Evangelicalism, and the End of the Solid South, 1950–1980" (Ph.D. diss., Vanderbilt University, 2006), 121–24, 162–67; William Martin, *With God on Our Side: The Rise of the Religious Right in America* (New York: Broadway Books, 1996), 58; Wallace Henley, "The Clergy on George Wallace," *Christianity Today*, 25 October 1968, 36–37; Kellstedt et al., "Faith Transformed," 272.

18. "School Prayer Declared Unconstitutional," *Alabama Baptist*, 5 July 1962, 3; *Eternity*, January 1973, 7.

19. C. E. Bates to William Covington Jr., 10 March 1972, Folder 1, Carl E. Bates Papers, Southern Baptist Historical Library and Archives (SBHLA), Nashville; George Strachan to H. R. Haldeman, 10 February 1972; George Strachan, Talking Papers for Billy Graham, 11 April 1972, 16 May 1972, 27 June 1972, 20 September 1972, 25 October 1972, Folder 3–7, Collection 74, BGCA (originals in Nixon Library); Martin, *Prophet with Honor*, 395–98; Kellstedt et al., "Faith Transformed," 273.

20. "Nixon's Support among Baptists Increases," *Baptist Courier*, September 1970; Billy Graham, press release, "Statement to Define Dr. Billy Graham's Position Regarding the Recent Conduct of the Vietnam War," 5 January 1973, Folder 3–7, Collection 74, BGCA (original in Nixon Presidential Library); Martin, *Prophet with Honor*, 370–71.

21. Martin, *With God on Our Side*, 122–27, 135–36; David W. Brady and Kent L. Tedin, "Ladies in Pink: Religion and Political Ideology in the Anti-ERA Movement," *Social Science Quarterly* 56 (1976): 564–75; Ruth Murray Brown, *For a "Christian America": A History of the Religious Right* (Amherst, N.Y.: Prometheus Books, 2002), 111–14, 117–20; Judy Klemesrud, "Equal Rights Plan and Abortion Are Opposed by 15,000 at Rally," *New York Times*, 20 November 1977.

22. Melissa M. Deckman, *School Board Battles: The Christian Right in Local Politics* (Washington, D.C.: Georgetown University Press, 2004), 15; Brown, *For a "Christian*

*America,"* 63–76; Anita Bryant, *The Anita Bryant Story* (Grand Rapids, Mich.: Fleming H. Revell, 1977), 43, 122.

23. Sara Diamond, *Roads to Dominion: Right-Wing Movements and Political Power in the United States* (New York: Guilford Press, 1995), 173; Myra MacPherson, "Evangelicals Seen Cooling on Carter," *Washington Post*, 27 September 1976; Smith, *Faith and the Presidency*, 307–11, 317–19; Tim LaHaye, "The Questions?" *Moral Majority Report*, 6 June 1980, 10.

24. Joseph Crespino, "Civil Rights and the Religious Right," in *Rightward Bound: Making America Conservative in the 1970s*, ed. Bruce J. Schulman and Julian E. Zelizer (Cambridge: Harvard University Press, 2008), 90–105; A. O. Sulzberger Jr., "Private Academies Protest Tax Plan," *New York Times*, 11 December 1978; "Politicizing the Word," *Time*, 1 October 1979, 68.

25. Jeffrey K. Hadden and Anson Shupe, *Televangelism: Power and Politics on God's Frontier* (New York: Holt, 1988), 83; *Christian Life*, September 1971, 28; "Pastor Keeps Up Attack on Carter," *Lynchburg Daily Advance*, 14 November 1979; Ruth McClellan, *An Incredible Journey: Thomas Road Baptist Church and 50 Years of Miracles* (Lynchburg, Va.: Liberty University, 2006), 98, 134, 218; Jerry Falwell, Chapel Talk, 30 January 1980, "Falwell Sermons—1980" Folder, FAL 5–3, LUA; Robert Wuthnow, *The Restructuring of American Religion: Society and Faith since World War II* (Princeton: Princeton University Press, 1988), 197; Anthony Gierzynski, *Money Rules: Financing Elections in America* (Boulder, Colo.: Westview Press, 2000), 72.

26. Kenneth L. Woodward, "Born Again! The Year of the Evangelicals," *Newsweek*, 25 October 1976; "Mobilizing the Moral Majority," *Conservative Digest*, August 1979, 14.

27. Lisa McGirr, *Suburban Warriors: The Origins of the New American Right* (Princeton: Princeton University Press, 2001), 258; George J. Church, "Politics from the Pulpit," *Time*, 13 October 1980, 34; Bruce Nesmith, *The New Republican Coalition: The Reagan Campaigns and White Evangelicals* (New York: Peter Lang, 1994), 74–77; Howell Raines, "Reagan Is Balancing 2 Different Stances," *New York Times*, 4 October 1980; Howell Raines, "Reagan Backs Evangelicals in Their Political Activities," *New York Times*, 23 August 1980; James Mann, "Preachers in Politics: Decisive Force in '80?" *U.S. News and World Report*, 15 September 1980, 24; Kellstedt et al., "Faith Transformed," 273.

28. Seymour M. Lipset and Earl Raab, "The Election and the Evangelicals," *Commentary*, March 1981; Bob Maddox to Rosalynn Carter, White House memo, n.d. [early 1980], "Memos" Folder, Box 107, Robert Maddox Papers, Public Outreach Papers, Jimmy Carter Presidential Library, Atlanta, Ga.; Paul L. Sadler, "The Abortion Issue within the Southern Baptist Convention, 1969–1988" (Ph.D. diss., Baylor University, 1991), 11–128; Barry Hankins, *Uneasy in Babylon: Southern Baptist Conservatives and American Culture* (Tuscaloosa: University of Alabama Press, 2002), 42–48; Religious Coalition for Abortion Rights, "A Call to Concern," 1977, AR 658, Southern Baptists for Life Collection, SBHLA; Southern Baptist Convention, Resolutions on Abortion, June 1971 and June 1980, www.sbc.net/resolutions.

29. Southern Baptist Convention, Resolutions, 1980, www.sbc.net/resolutions; SBC, Resolution on Prayer in Schools, June 1982, www.sbc.net/resolutions/am Resolution.asp?ID=862; Charles Austin, "Baptist Meeting Backs School Prayer Amendment," *New York Times*, 18 June 1982; Nancy T. Ammerman, "SBC and New Christian Right," *SBC Today*, February 1988, 1, 4; Ray Waddle, "Baptist Support of Bork Hit," *[Nashville] Tennessean*, 1 September 1987.

30. Corwin E. Schmidt, "Born-Again Politics: The Political Behavior of Evangelical Christians in the South and Non-South," in *Religion and Politics in the South: Mass and Elite Perspectives*, ed. Tod A. Baker, Robert P. Steed, and Laurence W. Moreland (New York: Praeger, 1983), 36; Ellen M. Rosenberg, *The Southern Baptists: A Subculture in Transition* (Knoxville: University of Tennessee Press, 1989), 183; Bruce Nesmith, *The New Republican Coalition: The Reagan Campaigns and White Evangelicals* (New York: Peter Lang, 1994), 120; Stratos Patrikios, "American Republican Religion? Disentangling the Causal Link between Religion and Politics in the US," *Political Behavior* 30 (2008): 368; Jerry Falwell, *Moral Majority Report*, July 1984, 1.

31. Justin Watson, *The Christian Coalition: Dreams of Restoration, Demands for Recognition*, 2nd ed. (New York: St. Martin's, 1999), 51–80; Barry M. Horstman, "Christian Activists Using 'Stealth' Tactics," *Los Angeles Times*, 8 April 1992; John F. Persinos, "Has the Christian Right Taken Over the Republican Party?" *Campaigns and Elections*, September 1994, 22; Schneider, "Impact of the Christian Right Social Movement," 117.

32. Lyman A. Kellstedt et al., "Religious Voting Blocs in the 1992 Election: The Year of the Evangelical?" *Sociology of Religion* 55 (1994): 311, 317; Charles Reagan Wilson, "Mobilized for the New Millennium," in *Religion and Public Life in the South*, ed. Wilson and Silk, 197; Corwin E. Schmidt, "Evangelicals and the American Presidency," in *Religion, Race, and the American Presidency*, ed. Gastón Espinosa (Lanham, Md.: Rowman and Littlefield, 2008), 22–24.

33. "Excerpt from McCain's Speech on Religious Conservatives," *New York Times*, 29 February 2000; Dan Balz, "McCain Reconnects with Liberty University," *Washington Post*, 14 May 2006; CNN 2008 exit polls.

# 2

## "Out-Democratin' the Democrats"

### Religious Colleges and the Rise of the Republican Party in the South—A Case Study

BARCLAY KEY

Less than two years before then First Lady Hillary Rodham Clinton complained to a national television audience of a "vast right-wing conspiracy," the conservative icon William F. Buckley detailed his own conspiracy in an essay for the *New Yorker*. Buckley described an annual gathering of nine men, some of the "most conspicuous right-wing figures in the United States." The cadre included four U.S. senators—Barry Goldwater, Strom Thurmond, John Tower, and Frank Lausche—along with Edgar Eisenhower and Buckley himself. Clarence Manion, former dean of the University of Notre Dame Law School and a John Birch Society board member, and George Benson, president of Harding College in Searcy, Arkansas, were also involved. Indeed, the political activities of Buckley, Manion, and Benson were conspicuous enough to warrant their own chapters in a 1964 volume authored by the directors of the Anti-Defamation League titled *Danger on the Right*.[1]

These annual meetings were occasioned by the final wishes of John Gaty of Wichita, Kansas. Facing dire medical circumstances, Gaty composed a will that instructed trustees to dispose of his estate by giving special consideration to purposes that would "promote individual liberty and incentive as opposed to socialism and communism." From 1963 to 1973, Gaty's trustees distributed $1.3 million to more than fifty conservative enterprises, and, while the amount is negligible by current standards, Buckley contended that it partially explained Ronald Reagan's 1980 victory: "Millions of words were printed, spoken, and preached by recipients of Gaty money. Sweaty work, over a period of ten years, but then revolutions take time."[2]

As the former president of Harding College, a private institution in Arkansas affiliated with Churches of Christ, George Benson channeled his trustee funds toward the school and what he dubbed his National Education Program

(NEP), a veritable factory of conservative political propaganda. Benson and Harding were not alone. In the wake of perceived threats to public education (such as desegregation, secularization, alleged communist infiltration, etc.) and increased enrollment due to the GI Bill, private education became an increasingly popular option for evangelicals—particularly white southerners—who were lured to colleges that offered professional degrees in an environment that suited their religious predilections. Enrollment in private grade schools and colleges exploded during the 1960s, and Christian colleges like Harding enjoyed a huge influx. Within the confines of such private academies across the South, conservative political values were instilled in generations of students who departed college with both a degree and a resolve to support the Republican Party.[3] The confluence of private education, evangelical Christianity, conservative politics, and the GOP in the South is exemplified by Harding College and its maturation from the end of World War II to 1970. During these twenty-five years, students, faculty, administrators, and campus guests pressed issues that would galvanize the GOP and contribute to the South becoming Republican.

When George Benson first accepted the presidency of Harding College in 1936, he inherited an almost unknown college with sizable debt. As a counterpoint to the New Deal, Benson began promoting both Christian education and a version of Americanism that emphasized free enterprise and constitutional government. By 1939, Benson retired the school's whole debt by securing $25,000 from DuPont Chemical, a frequent contributor to right-wing causes. Two years later he created the NEP, multiplying Harding's assets.[4]

Benson's version of Americanism was forged in part by his experience as a missionary working to wean the Chinese away from communism through "education, particularly Christian education." He gained national prominence before several congressional committees during the early 1940s when he recommended that Congress curb expenditures unrelated to defense and dissolve New Deal programs. These appearances were important in establishing his reputation as a fiercely patriotic, fiscal conservative, and Benson's influence grew. Churches of Christ had a rich, if uneven, pacifist tradition that finally succumbed to the militarism and patriotism aroused by the fight against communism and fascism during and after World War II. A preacher in his own right, Benson fashioned himself as a prophet whose objective in life was to warn people of the communist danger and direct them toward salvific action. His influence aided the demise of pacifism within the denomination, and many Harding students soon followed Benson's lead.[5]

James Bales was an early convert. One of several church leaders who preached pacifism in the years preceding World War II, as a young professor at Harding, he came under Benson's influence and began to perceive communism as a threat that demanded a military response. Many equated communism with atheism, and southerners were urgent in their opposition to any organization or person who did not believe in God. Harding's student newspaper, the *Bison*, would later warn that communists desired "complete control over the human mind. . . . The Communists will destroy religion here in America if they have the opportunity." Religious overtones could also be discerned from the most avid champions of free-market capitalism.[6]

The names Benson and Bales soon became synonymous with political conservatism and anticommunism, perspectives they worked to instill in the students who matriculated at Harding. The NEP was an important component of their strategy. The program's sole purpose was to disseminate conservative political literature and provide a platform for speakers whose perspectives on economics and government aligned with Benson's. The "Freedom Forum," created in 1949 as a method of educating both students and the public, became one of the NEP's most popular programs. Seminars stressed "the American way of life" and included sessions on Christian morality, constitutional government, history, comparative economics, and the latest techniques in promoting Americanism. This missiological focus meshed well with the "other" Great Commission—that church members should make every effort to share the gospel with the lost—and students attended the seminars in droves, soaking up the "wealth of experience and knowledge [from] men who hold top business positions." By 1965, more than 3,500 executives from more than one thousand organizations had visited Harding College for the Freedom Forums.[7]

In January 1952, students requested a mock presidential election. A proud white southerner by any standard, student journalist Chris Elliott recalled what his "dear old [Democratic] mother told . . . about the great depression and Roosevelt's 'bread on the table' reconstruction program." He confessed that his "rebel temper" flared whenever he read *Gone with the Wind*, and his "heart does something romantic when I see the confederate flag flutter by." "On the other hand," Elliott continued, "I remember . . . Harry Truman and his attempts to cram Civil Rights and camouflaged socialism down gullible throats. . . . It looks to me as if the Republicans are out-Democratin' the Democrats." Elliott supported the Republicans.[8] Another student explained that she was a Democrat voting for Republican Robert Taft, while a young man proclaimed, "I'm supporting the Republicans because I'm an American and anybody who supports the Democrats [just] couldn't be an American." The student Democratic committee chief complained that he had called two meetings and "no one has shown up."[9] "Fair Deal and New Deal politicians are determined to put us further along the road to complete Socialism," a typical

Republican supporter charged. Elliott later complained of Truman's pressure on Congress to establish a permanent Fair Employment Practices Committee. This "proposal means more Negro, Japanese and other 'group' votes . . . without regard to the success of men who provide jobs, a higher standard of living, and through production and their capital[,] a better America."[10]

Mary Ann Whitaker, in her weekly column, penned a piece titled, "Southerner Explains Political Position—No Democrat Now." She recalled her roots in Tennessee along the Mississippi River, "where Colonel Memphis is pictured as looking down over his white Van Dyke mustache and beard into a mint julep, his Confederate hat askew . . . and his string tie trembling slightly as he murmurs, 'Ah, sur, hate them Yankees.'" Whitaker noted that she "was no longer of a tender age when I saw my first white Republican." Asserting that she was "typical of every other young Southerner—or old Southerner for that matter," Whitaker declared: "we had been given a pretty raw deal by the Republicans after the Civil War. . . . We were for the good old . . . Democratic candidate no matter who he was or what he stood for. And that was fine as long as he stood for things American and things Southern (above all things Southern). . . . I looked around one day to find the Democratic party, but it wasn't there. In its place, taking its name, and corrupting its ideals and traditions was the Fair Deal."[11] "Socialism" and civil rights legislation were too much for many white southerners to bear. "How could I, a true-blue (oh, what a heresy, I mean grey) daughter of the Confederacy ally myself with the 'carpet-bagging' Yankees?" Whitaker asked, as she gave herself and her peers permission to vote Republican. Everyone who is interested in keeping "free enterprise and their personal freedoms" must realize that "this is no time to vote like your father, grandfather, and great-grandfather, but like they would have . . . if faced with choosing between Socialism and Democracy."[12]

In 1952, Benson capitalized on the success of the Freedom Forums by creating a School of American Studies. A four-year degree program incorporated economics, government, history, and political science to provide "solid grounding in American and Christian principles" and the "American Way of Life." "My aim is to move public opinion at the grass roots in the direction of godliness and patriotism," Benson later told the *New York Times*.[13] When officials questioned Harding's accreditation for the NEP, he incorporated it as a private educational institution with a separate board, although Benson remained president of both the college and the NEP.[14]

Blacks were not part of Benson's vision of Americanism and were not even admitted until 1963. Benson was open about his belief that segregation was providential. Shortly after the 1957 Little Rock school desegregation crisis, more than 90 percent of Harding students and faculty signed a petition in favor of admitting African Americans. Benson was not persuaded, arguing during a chapel assembly that "the redbirds, the bluebirds, the blackbirds, they don't mix and mingle together, young people!" A student recalled a class in 1959 at which Benson articulated his belief that "the nigra race . . . is under the curse of Ham." As late as 1966, Benson continued to espouse racial segregation in a sermon, insisting that "there is no reason to think the Lord wants a mixing of the races and the creating of just one mongrel race." The "race problem" was created and perpetuated by "communist agitators;" the protests were "largely illegal and therefore contrary to Christian principles. Preachers and others who go S[outh] to stir up strife and confusion are not following Christian examples."[15]

Benson's guest speakers at Harding had comparable opinions. Leon Burns, minister for Churches of Christ in Columbia, Tennessee, spoke at Harding, and other Christian colleges, on several occasions after his sermon "Why Desegregation Will Fail" was disseminated widely in 1957. Notre Dame conservative Clarence Manion spoke at Harding, as did Fred Schwarz of the Christian Anti-Communism Crusade, who featured Ronald Reagan on his California radio program. Conservative politicians with national acclaim also appeared at Harding. Senator John McClellan, who signed the 1956 Southern Manifesto in opposition to the Supreme Court's desegregation orders, was an occasional guest of Benson's and received an honorary doctorate from Harding in 1963. Governor Orval Faubus, best known for his opposition to desegregation during the Little Rock crisis of 1957, enjoyed a warm reception in 1964. In 1973, Vice President Spiro Agnew was welcomed to campus. The guests represented unabashed efforts to instill and buttress the same conservatism that soon came to characterize the GOP.[16]

Although Harding students were mostly supportive, some grew disillusioned with the bombardment of right-wing guests. For example, students certainly did not summarily endorse their president's racial attitudes. While they harbored misgivings about the level of interaction that was acceptable between blacks and whites, some students had always favored desegregating the college. When a University of Mississippi student penned an editorial in 1950 that advocated desegregation, demonstrations and a cross burning soon followed in Oxford. The *Bison*, however, endorsed the essay and congratulated the author for "his stand for freedom, toleration, and anti-discrimination." Throughout the 1950s, other articles and editorials supportive of desegregation appeared in the *Bison*, and in 1957, more than 90 percent of the student body and most faculty favored desegregation according to the aforementioned petition. Benson's cold dismissal of the statement troubled a number of students. Student body president Bill Floyd was privately chastised for his role in circulating the petition and told by administrators that "no employer would ever hire me, when one works for an institution he should accept all its thinking and keep silent about contrary beliefs, and that if I wanted to crusade for integration I should go where everyone believes in it." Another school official told Floyd that student government should be "an agency to indoctrinate the students with the ideas of the administration."[17] The night after Benson's chapel speech about redbirds, bluebirds, and blackbirds not mixing, a daring student waded into the lily pond in front of the administration building and hung a sign on the birdbath at center that read, "WHITE ONLY." Thus, indoctrination—explicitly stated by one administrator—met with varying degrees of success. Most Harding students favored some form of desegregation, but even the students' position on desegregation did not preclude other racialized activities or inspire wholehearted support for integrating African Americans into all aspects of college life. During the following spring, for example, a chapel program included a minstrel show where white students and at least one professor donned blackface for an Amos 'n' Andy routine. (Other Christian colleges in the South held minstrel shows into the mid-1960s.)[18]

During the fall of 1959, a sociology professor at Harding administered a student poll that included questions about racial attitudes. When asked if they favored "allowing Negro students to attend Harding," 56 percent answered affirmatively. Another 15 percent indicated that desegregation would be acceptable with some qualifications, while 29 percent simply answered "no." When this line of questioning extended to the inclusion of African Americans in Harding's social clubs, the responses were more evenly split. The acceptance of desegregation, along with the persistence of racial stereotypes and the supposed discomfort of socially mingling with blacks, illustrate the variations of racial attitudes among southern whites in this era.[19]

Harding finally accepted its first African American student in the fall of 1963, and the *Bison*'s praise for the decision was so over-the-top as to be almost disingenuous. "Those who know us will testify that we are not prone to fawn," an associate editor wrote, "but Dr. Benson's leadership in the movement for equal opportunity makes us proud, even boastful; it makes us happy, even ecstatic." This student clearly missed the events of 1957 at Harding, and he apparently failed to appreciate that the primary reason for admitting black students was economic. Federal monies required compliance with court desegregation orders. It seems that when the resources potentially available from the federal government exceeded the funds that would be lost due to contributors disgruntled over desegregation or students who would no longer attend, private colleges like Harding admitted a few token African American students. But the stipulation that applicants be admitted regardless of race troubled whites, who offered dire warnings. If the federal government can require one to admit African Americans, the thinking went, what might come next? "Hire this teacher, fire that one. Use this textbook, scrap the other one. No Bible reading, no prayer."[20] Once formal steps had been taken to admit black students to Harding, many whites concluded that they had done their part to bring about racial justice. Some whites simply assumed that racial equality and harmony would inexorably follow the desegregation of public institutions, that access could be equated with opportunity.[21]

A month later, another editorial foreshadowed white attitudes for the remainder of the decade. Editor Phil Sturm, in an essay titled "Racial Demonstrations Causing Shift in Pro-Integration Opinion," described his experiences as an observer of a civil rights demonstration in Chicago. Sturm opened the piece by expressing his belief in racial equality and in the justice of past demonstrations. "I approved of this 'passive resistance' as a legitimate method in their fight for equal rights," he wrote. However, his opinion changed, and the essay that he wrote illuminates the concerns that Republicans would soon use as political capital. "The crowd was peaceful and nondestructive but it was nevertheless a mob which required close supervision by policemen." The sight of thousands of African Americans in a demonstration—one that he even described as "peaceful and nondestructive"—made Sturm extremely uncomfortable. The "mob" required white supervision, in part because it "was highly emotional and fear-inspired. . . . They marched on the streets and sidewalks chanting in a primitive manner, 'What do you want? Freedom! When? Now!' and other similar phrases," Sturm recalled. The verbiage of this assessment underscores white fears. Demonstrators, "urged on by a few leaders," were dangerously malleable, and their actions were not inspired so much by injustice as by uncontrolled emotion and rampant fear. Perhaps unconsciously, Sturm even used the term "primitive," an allusion to old colonial stereotypes of Africa. The sight of these demonstrations led him to conclude, "Unless integration leaders realize their mistakes and change their tactics, they will continue to lose support and sympathy in the traditionally pro-integration North."[22]

Throughout the remainder of the decade, the few voices for social justice at Harding faced opposition from students, faculty, and administrators. Gone were the days when more than 90 percent of the student body would speak as one voice on an issue raised by the African American freedom struggle. In February 1965, as civil rights demonstrators drew attention to voting in Selma, Alabama, the *Bison* printed a story that described how voter literacy tests were administered differently for blacks and whites. The report decried the fact that "voter registration procedures have limited suffrage to a minute fraction of Negro applicants"—an assessment that bothered a number of

Harding students. One insisted, "The majority of the people in Alabama do not deny the Negro the right to vote," before launching a tirade against Martin Luther King and those African Americans who had recently sought the franchise. Another complained about the *Bison* itself. "Southerners are labeled as prejudiced against the Negro," but this "labeling itself is prejudiced for it places the accusation on all Southerners." He further asked readers to consider whether or not decisions made by civil rights leaders and, by implication, African American voters, would be "best for the Negro masses as compared to the 'decisions of the Southern whites.'" Although these white students could accept token integration at their college, the possibility of black political participation and influence seemed frightening.[23]

Within this Arkansas context, a young Ken Starr—now infamous for making the public aware of President Bill Clinton's marital indiscretions—began cutting his political teeth. Starr served as editor of the *Bison* in 1965. In "Starr Dust," he voiced new concerns that would help precipitate Republican ascendancy in the South. He denounced the "modern city" and its myriad problems, singling out New York for special criticism. The city "has been plagued through the years with everything from Tammany Hall to Malcolm X, Adam Clayton Powell," Starr complained. "Race rioters, junkies, perverts and yes, even striking subway workers, call the city 'home.'" Conscious or not, Starr's list communicates the easy association that future Republican stalwarts employed for their "undesirables" [my word, not Starr's]. Here, junkies and perverts are placed alongside workers on strike, as if these people all belonged to one amorphous problem that Republicans could blame on communist influence, the federal government, welfare dependency, or immorality. Many white southerners would simply ascribe urban problems to racial integration, and they heard Republicans expressing solidarity with their discomforts.[24]

Harding students were not the only ones reevaluating their racial perspectives and political allegiances. James Bales, the professor who had previously expressed ambivalence about desegregating the college, focused his energies on castigating Martin Luther King. Bales was active in the anticommunist crusade throughout the 1960s, authoring several books, writing numerous letters to newspaper editors, and engaging in public debates. In February 1966, Bales debated members of the Student Nonviolent Coordinating Committee (SNCC) and Students for a Democratic Society (SDS) about Vietnam. His publication of *The Martin Luther King Story* in 1967 was a classic attempt to disparage the civil rights leader and the causes he supported.[25]

Bales spent years collecting information that could be used to damn King, poring through magazine and newspaper articles, press releases, and books. Bales's book attempted to expose King as both an anarchist and a communist—two distinct ideologies that Bales conflated. In each chapter title, Bales employed a vocabulary intended to malign King, his faith, and his political activism: anarchist, apostate, pacifist, leftist, and "collaborator with the Reds." He did admit that King's relationships with communist sympathizers might not have been conscious, "but it has certainly ended with conscious collaboration with Communists in an effort to defeat investigation of internal communism and to defeat our resistance to external Communist aggression." Guilt by association served as Bales's weapon of choice in arguing that King was heavily influenced (if not controlled) by communists. Other influential figures at Harding gave at least tacit approval to this assessment. Benson, who retired in 1965, later claimed to have encouraged Bales to write the book, and his successor generally stood by Bales's work.[26]

As the 1960s wore on, Harding students continued to express regret and dismay over incidents of gross racial injustice, but they failed to comprehend the ubiquitous impact of systemic racism. Persistent "prejudicial attitudes" were conceived as "barriers to heaven's gates and to the presence of God," rather than the root causes of African American poverty, inequitable educational opportunities, and urban rioting. No one spoke of social reform because the solution presumably lay in personal relationships, in making "an effort to judge others on an individual basis." Thus, the tragic death of MLK—whose messages about wealth redistribution and pacifism had long departed from the goal of integrating public facilities—was met with mixed reactions at Harding. A *Bison* editorial indicated that some students laughed at the assassination, saying "he got what was coming," or expressed a desire "to pin a medal on the guy who did it." It is impossible to determine if these harsh opinions were widespread, although they were certainly shared by many white southerners. And while the *Bison* itself expressed grief over the assassination, its articles about King's death focused not so much on the man as on the riots that soon erupted. One emphasized: "The color of a man's skin, regardless of his background, does not give him the right to live off the efforts of others, to demand something for nothing, to deface the property of others, to kill at will. Mass reactions of violence to Dr. King's death only emphasize the white racist's claim that the Negro is only one step removed from the black jungles of Africa, barely better than his cannibal ancestors." Another that started to criticize Harding students' "regrettable" response to King's death actually gave more space to condemning the violence that ensued, using King's own words. By the time of King's funeral, whites were already using his rhetoric to frame discussions of race relations around control and order rather than social justice and equality of opportunity.[27]

Just one month later, a nationwide poll of college students illustrated how the perspectives of Harding students were antithetical to King. The *Bison* recognized that the voting of Harding students differed radically from the national norm by being much more conservative. Nearly 60 percent of Harding students favored increasing the war effort in Vietnam, with 40 percent advocating an "all-out war." The percentage of Harding students insisting on increased riot control more than doubled the national numbers, and more than half of Harding students favored Nixon or George Wallace in the upcoming presidential election in double the percentages nationwide.[28]

If, as an administrator once suggested, indoctrinating students was Harding's goal, these numbers indicate a level of success. One frustrated student asked, "How often are liberal religious and political views expounded from our chapel? . . . How often are we objectively presented with moral and social issues without an overhanging mood of prohibition and restriction? . . . Either let us reconsider the purposes of this school or rename it Harding Institute for the Propagation of Conservative Philosophy." On one occasion, a few students won several meetings with President Clifton Ganus and two other administrators. One of the students later recalled that "the one question which we tried to ask in all three meetings was this, 'If a student, or group of students, does not agree with an administration action or policy and does not feel that his voice will be heard through the 'normal channels' of this institution, does he have the right to publicly express his views?' The answer was NO." Despite these sentiments, most students imbibed or were apathetic about the college's political philosophies. Even those who might have otherwise been critical of Harding's previous exclusion of blacks continued to attend a college that practiced other forms of discrimination. Although Harding admitted a few blacks in 1963, several years passed before the races were permitted to live together, as at other Christian institutions. Neither was Harding alone in monitoring its students' dating habits, particularly in regard to race. Administrators personally contacted the parents of students involved with members of another race, while some colleges arranged counseling sessions or simply prohibited interracial dating.[29]

If colleges such as Harding began admitting African Americans into their classes, they failed to fully integrate them into the life of the college. The behavior of black students was closely monitored and tightly controlled, and since the primary goal of desegregation was to secure federal money, little effort was made to recruit minority students. By the end of the decade, African Americans accounted for less than 2 percent of Harding, and the few who chose to attend grew increasingly frustrated with the college. In the fall of 1968, they formed a new organization, Groove Phi, and during the spring mounted a series of protests. Although they found a few supporters among white students, the overwhelming majority of the student body gave full support to the administration's suppression of these protests. In doing so, the white students illustrated whites' perpetual discomfort with integration and with politically organized blacks.

The *Bison* included pieces from both sides of issues raised by Groove Phi, but editor Kay Gowen was a staunch supporter of the administration. Her interpretation of Groove Phi suggests that integration came much too fast for some whites. Furthermore, once educational access and voting rights had been nominally extended to blacks, many whites believed that any additional efforts to correct past injustices were superfluous. Meanwhile, the failure to fully incorporate its black students into the life of the college was clear. In 1969, the annual leadership conference sponsored by the Student Association organized a forum for discussing race relations on campus; blacks readily voiced their displeasure. One described the indignity of hearing references like "boy," "Nigra," and "colored" and complained that intramural teams curtailed the participation of blacks. Another noted the absurdity of claiming that race riots were inspired by communists, and several students wished to ban Bales's book on King from the library. Some complained about Harding's band playing "Dixie" at athletic events and excluding blacks from social clubs. A white student even complained that Harding students showed much more enthusiasm for "Dixie" than for the national anthem.[30]

A few white students cast their lots with the dissenters from Groove Phi. One student urged *Bison* readers to "look how often in our own Christian school the Black Man is made aware of his 'inferiority,'" but for the most part, white students expressed the ideas that had already transformed the South into a Republican stronghold. When asked about the cause of racial unrest at Harding, one student remarked, "We are so afraid that we might help the Negroes that don't deserve help that we won't go an extra mile with them in order to deal fairly with those that have not been treated fairly." Others complained about blacks who "are not satisfied with equal rights but want superior rights" and the "hypersensitivity of the Negro students." One person concluded: "Black people know they have the right to rebel against whatever they want to, so they take advantage of that right. As Christians, it seems that Black people should be able to take a little bit of abuse from unthoughtful White people to be able to get along in a peaceful society." While a few students acknowledged the culpability of whites, these answers are illustrative of the dissatisfaction that whites felt about the militancy of black demands.[31]

On March 20, 1969, President Ganus gave a chapel speech intending to show that Harding's racial unrest was primarily the work of a few students. The speech exemplifies the white backlash that led to the Democratic Party's demise in the South. Ganus opened by claiming he had only "been prejudiced toward helping people regardless of color." He then recited a list of examples that proved his point. The list included helping to integrate Harding, giving financial aid to blacks, and permitting the family maid to eat with him. Ganus said he appreciated a committee report on race at Harding but then attacked black students themselves. "I guess most are better fed and housed and better treated than at home," Ganus told his audience before reciting his own list of grievances against black students. He alleged that some were guilty of falsifying time sheets, stealing, making lewd comments to or inappropriately touching girls, acting "ungentlemanly in cafeteria," exhibiting disrespect and bad attitudes, and being overly sensitive. "I thought that if we tried to help you, all of you would grow up and mature," Ganus lectured the blacks. "Irresponsibility is a terrible curse to any man and too long it has been winked at in the Black man because his great grandfather was a slave." The speech closed with an admonition to stop wasting time and "be about their reason for being here—to give and receive a good education, to grow in wisdom and stature and in favor with both God and man."[32]

Ganus received a standing ovation during both chapel services that day and support later from faculty and whites at the college and in the community. Leading members of Groove Phi did not surrender immediately, but their poses for the media after a walkout show their slumped shoulders. Later in the semester a small group staged a brief protest in which they burned pamphlets titled *The Communist Blueprint for the American Negro*. The demonstration included a few speeches and drew about 150 students and complaints that courses in black history were not taught. Groove Phi's leader and several other black students chose not to return to Harding in the fall.[33]

Statistics show that private educational institutions continued to favor whites after the 1960s. Christian colleges across the nation lagged behind public institutions in minority enrollment and in the amount of financial aid offered to minority students. By the mid-1980s, institutions in the Christian College Coalition (composed of evangelical colleges) were experiencing declines in minority student enrollment. Numerous reasons might explain the decline, but financial aid statistics are especially revealing. From 1978 to 1983, for example, one study found that "the average financial aid sum awarded per black student at private colleges and universities dropped by 1.9 percent and aid per Hispanic student dropped 4.5 percent. Yet during the same period, aid per white student in private colleges and universities actually increased 15.6 percent." Through the mid-1980s, Christian colleges trailed their public counterparts in almost every statistical category that examined minority enrollment, recruitment of minority students and faculty, the presence of minorities as presidents or board members, and budgetary expenditures relating to minority students.[34]

In writing about the French Revolution, the French historian Jules Michelet once remarked: "Religious or political, the two questions are deeply, inextricably intermingled at their roots. Confounded in the past, they will appear tomorrow as they really are, one and identical." In another context, "tomorrow" arrived in the South during the middle of the twentieth century. Private Christian colleges like Harding united religion and politics in an unprecedented fashion, giving the Republican Party a powerful device for claiming the South as a stronghold. These colleges served as bastions of political conservatism and havens for whites who wished to avoid blacks. During the last decades of the twentieth century, Christian colleges effectively became mouthpieces for the Republican Party in the South, as whites increasingly sought educational options that would insulate them from secular influences and from blacks. Thus, it is especially ironic that Harding University would publish a school history titled *Against the Grain*, and proudly boast of its place as "the first private college in Arkansas to integrate." President Benson, the reader learns, "received a standing ovation in chapel when he announced it," though he must have shared the news with great reservation.[35]

Although today's Harding is more integrated than the Harding of the 1960s, its political conservatism has not waned. Freedom Forums that once featured anticommunist crusaders and staunch segregationists have been replaced by the American Studies Institute's Distinguished Lecture Series. Recent invitations have been extended to Ann Coulter, Sean Hannity, and Judge Janice Rogers Brown, and the annual lecture series helps secure Harding's place in the "Top 10 Conservative Colleges," as determined by Young America's Foundation. Five of the "Top 10" are Christian colleges in the South or Border South, suggesting once more the significance of these institutions in explaining how the South became Republican.[36]

## Notes

Editor's note: Some of the material in this chapter previously appeared in Barclay Key, "On the Periphery of the Civil Rights Movement: Race and Religion at Harding College," *Arkansas Historical Quarterly* 68 (Autumn 2009): 283–311. The editor is grateful for the permission granted by the *Arkansas Historical Quarterly* to reprint the article here.

1. William F. Buckley Jr., "My Secret Right-Wing Conspiracy," *New Yorker* (21 and 28 October 1996): 120, 122–24, 126, 128–29; Arnold Foster and Benjamin R. Epstein, *Danger on the Right* (New York: Random House, 1964), 87–99, 115–31, 240–61.

2. Buckley, "My Secret Right-Wing Conspiracy," 122–23, 129. FBI Director J. Edgar Hoover was also named as a trustee, but he declined; L. Edward Hicks, *"Sometimes in the Wrong, but Never in Doubt": George S. Benson and the Education of the New Religious Right* (Knoxville: University of Tennessee Press, 1994), 112–30.

3. Buckley, "My Secret Right-Wing Conspiracy," 124; William C. Ringenberg, *The Christian College* (Grand Rapids: Eerdmans, 1984), 186; Hicks, *"Sometimes in the Wrong, but Never in Doubt,"* xxii; Clyde Wilcox, "Popular Backing for the Old Christian Right: Explaining Support for the Christian Anti-Communism Crusade," *Journal of Social History* 21 (Autumn 1987): 129; Thomas A. Askew, "The Shaping of Evangelical Higher Education since World War II," in *Making Higher Education Christian: The History and Mission of Evangelical Colleges in America,* ed. Joel A. Carpenter and Kenneth W. Shipps (Grand Rapids: Eerdmans, 1987), 137–38, 142; Marvin Wayne Lishman, "An Historical and Status Survey of the Member Schools of the Mississippi Private School Association from 1974–1989" (Ph.D. diss., University of Mississippi, 1989), 1–4, 25; Melinda Bollar Wagner, *God's Schools: Choice and Compromise in American Society* (New Brunswick, N.J.: Rutgers University Press, 1990), 18–19.

4. Richard T. Hughes, *Reviving the Ancient Faith: The Story of Churches of Christ in America* (Grand Rapids: Eerdmans, 1996), 154–60; Hicks, *"Sometimes in the Wrong, but Never in Doubt,"* 19–22, 141.

5. Hicks, *"Sometimes in the Wrong, but Never in Doubt,"* 11, 41; Henry N. Dorris, "Doughton Denies Tax 'Shenanigans,'" *New York Times,* 16 May 1941; Henry N. Dorris, "Direct Tax Urged on All Incomes," *New York Times,* 22 August 1941; "College Head Urges Ending of CCC, NYA," *New York Times,* 15 April 1942; Michael W. Casey, "From Religious Outsiders to Insiders: The Rise and Fall of Pacifism in the Churches of Christ," *Journal of Church and State* 44 (Summer 2002): 470–72.

6. David Edwin Harrell, *The Churches of Christ in the 20th Century: Homer Hailey's Personal Journey of Faith* (Tuscaloosa: University of Alabama Press, 2000), 51–57, 164–67; Hughes, *Reviving the Ancient Faith,* 214; Hicks, *"Sometimes in the Wrong, but Never in Doubt,"* 85–86; "Thunder on the Far Right: Fear and Frustration . . . Rouse Extremists to Action across the Land," *Newsweek* (4 December 1961), 22; "Communism Seeks to Destroy Religion," *Bison,* 12 October 1955, 4.

7. "To Study 'American Way,'" *New York Times,* 21 January 1949; Hicks, "Sometimes in the Wrong, but Never in Doubt," 52–54; "Freedom Forums Have Meant a Lot to Us," *Bison,* 24 March 1951, 2.

8. Lin Wright, "Faculty Approves Sham Presidential Election," *Bison,* 1 December 1951, 1; Chris Elliott, "The Light That Failed; Backing Republican Party," *Bison,* 1 December 1951, 1, 3.

9. "Republicans Nominate Taft. . . . ," *Bison,* 12 January 1952, 1; "What Do You Think of the Idea. . . . ," *Bison,* 1 December 1951, 3; Irma Coons, "Students Favor Senator Taft. . . . ," *Bison,* 19 January 1952, 1; "The Student's Voice," *Bison,* 12 January 1952, 2.

10. Bill Bell, "Childs to Show GOP Ideals Are Those of People," *Bison,* 19 January 1952, 1; Chris Elliott, "80th Congress 'Unsympathetic'?: Fortunately, Yes," *Bison,* 26 January 1952, 1, 3.

11. Mary Ann Whitaker, "Southerner Explains Political Position—No Democrat Now," *Bison*, 26 January 1952, 1, 3.

12. Ibid.

13. "American Studies: Integration of Courses Planned in New Four-Year Program," *New York Times*, 12 October 1952; Giles M. Fowler, "A Label Ultra-Rightist Puts the Spotlight on a Small College Town in Arkansas," *Kansas City Star*, 4 February 1962; Cabell Phillips, "Wide Anti-Red Drive Directed from Small Town in Arkansas," *New York Times*, 18 May 1961.

14. Hicks, *Sometimes in the Wrong, but Never in Doubt*," 84–85; Phillips, "Wide Anti-Red Drive," 26; Linda Charlton, "Agnew Relaxes Attack on Media," *New York Times*, 13 April 1973.

15. Norman Adamson, telephone conversation with author; Don Haymes, interview by author, tape recording; "Christ & Current World Problems, 10–13–66," George S. Benson files, Folder "Sermons, 1960–1969," Special Collections, Harding University, Searcy, Arkansas. See also Haymes, Race & the Church of Christ, www.mun.ca/rels/restmov/texts/race/haymes12.html.

16. Leon C. Burns, "Why Desegregation Will Fail," copy in possession of author; "Chapel Schedule," *Bison*, 19 November 1959, 1; Leon C. Burns, "Some Dangers Which Faced the First Century Church," in *Harding College Bible Lectures, 1961* (Austin: Firm Foundation Publishing House, 1962), 15–19; David L. Chappell, *A Stone of Hope: Prophetic Religion and the Death of Jim Crow* (Chapel Hill: University of North Carolina Press, 2004), 109; Carl Holladay, "Leon C. Burns Lectures on Communism," *Skyrocket* [school newspaper, Freed-Hardeman College, Henderson, Tenn.] (10 December 1962): 1; Charlton, "Agnew Relaxes Attack on Media,"18; Hicks, *Sometimes in the Wrong, but Never in Doubt*," 60–61; George S. Benson to John L. McClellan, 3 July 1959, John L. McClellan Papers, Box 25-A, Folder "Speech–Pepperdine College," Special Collections, Ouachita Baptist University, Arkadelphia, Ark.; Clifton Ganus Jr., address at the Annual Freedom Forum, Little Rock, February 1961, Orval Faubus Papers (MC MS/F27/301/Faubus), Series 17, Box 588, Folder 5, Special Collections, University of Arkansas Libraries, Fayetteville.

17. "What Would You Have Done?" *Bison*, 11 November 1950, 2; "Results of Recent Poll on Racial Integration Show Student Attitudes," *Bison*, 14 November 1957, 1; William K. Floyd, "Why I Could Not Be a Career Preacher," in *Voices of Concern: Critical Studies in Church of Christism*, ed. Robert Meyers (St. Louis: Mission Messenger, 1966), 166–69.

18. Haymes, Race & the Church of Christ, www.mun.ca/rels/restmov/texts/race; "Chapel Program," *Bison*, 17 April 1958, 1; "Minstrel Planned," *Skyrocket*, 11 February 1963, 3.

19. Grace Davis, "Opinion Poll Reflects Student Attitudes," *Bison*, 19 November 1959, 1.

20. Jimmy Arnold, "Now Is the Time to Stand," *Bison*, 26 September 1963, 2; Floyd, "Why I Could Not Be a Career Preacher," 168; "A Doubt Dispelled," *Skyrocket*, 16 April 1962, 2; Ringenberg, *The Christian College*, 209–14.

21. Arnold, "Now Is the Time to Stand," 2.

22. Phil Sturm, "Racial Demonstrations Causing Shift in Pro-Integration Opinion," *Bison*, 31 October 1963, 2.

23. Don Johnson, "Voter Literacy Test Used in Alabama Often Varies According to Applicant," *Bison*, 18 February 1965, 2; "Letters—Alabama Voting," *Bison*, 4 March 1965, 2.

24. Ken Starr, "Crowded Cities, Plentiful Problems," *Bison*, 12 January 1966, 2.

25. James Bales to Carl Spain, 6 March 1960, James Bales Papers, Unprocessed, Special Collections, University of Arkansas Libraries, Fayetteville; "Bales Debates at 'Teach-in,'" *Bison*, 16 February 1966, 1; James D. Bales, *The Martin Luther King Story* (Tulsa: Christian Crusade Publications, 1967).

26. James D. Bales to Erle Johnston Jr., 31 January 1965, Mississippi State Sovereignty Commission Records, SCR ID #99–38–0–236–1–1–1, Mississippi Department of Archives and History, www.mdah.state.ms.us; James D. Bales to Martin Luther King Jr., 21 June 1967, James Bales Papers, Unprocessed, Special Collections, University of Arkansas Libraries, Fayetteville; Bales, 114; Robert Christy Douglas, "Power, Its Locus and Function in Defining Social Commentary in the Church of Christ, Illustrated by a Case Study of Black Civil Rights" (Ph.D. diss., University of Southern California, 1980), 273; Clifton L. Ganus Jr. to Cled Wimbish, 10 July 1968, C. L. Ganus Jr. Papers, Administration Building, Harding University, Searcy, Ark.

27. D. Johnson, "Comments of Students in Chapel Should Shame White Society," *Bison*, 8 March 1967, 2; Lynn McCauley, "Last Friday's Chapel Program Proved Harding Not Afraid of Hurting Image," *Bison*, 15 March 1968, 2; D. McBride, "Laughter at Assassination of King Exemplifies Indifferent Attitude—An Attitude Harmful to America," *Bison*, 12 April 1968, 2; J. Flippin, "This Matter of Equality," *Bison*, 12 April 1968, 2; L. McCauley, "A Christian Reaction," *Bison*, 12 April 1968, 2.

28. Don Wilson, "McCarthy Tops National Choice '68 Poll: Nixon Gets Nod at Harding," *Bison*, 10 May 1968, 5.

29. "Letters," *Bison*, 7 March 1969, 2; "Letters," *Bison*, 14 March 1969, 2; "Letters," *Bison*, 15 April 1965, 2; John E. Acuff to Brothers, 11 January 1971, John Allen Chalk Papers, Box 1971 Correspondence, Folder A, Special Collections, Harding University Graduate School of Religion, Memphis; Ginger Shiras, "Blacks Get Up, Leave as Harding Head Explains. . . . ," *Arkansas Gazette*, 21 March 1969; John C. Stevens to Mrs. Billy Carlile, 21 September 1972, John C. Stevens Papers, Box 21, Folder General Correspondence, Special Collections, Abilene Christian University, Abilene, Tex.; Harry Ward to Jack Evans, 13 October 1975; Jack Evans, *The Curing of Ham* (DeQueen, Ark.: Harrywell, 1976), 115.

30. Kay Gowen, untitled, *Bison*, 17 January 1969, 2; Kay Gowen, untitled, *Bison*, 21 February 1969, 2; "SA Holds Non-Typical Conference; Campus Leaders Hear Negro Panel," *Bison*, 18 March 1969, 1, 3; Jean Flippin, "'Dixie' Incites More Participation Than Playing of National Anthem," *Bison*, 15 February 1968, 2.

31. "Letters," *Bison*, 21 March 1969, 2; Donna Holmquist and Jerry Flowers, "Bison Poll Draws Variety of Comments," *Bison*, 18 March 1969, 4.

32. "Race Relations at Harding," Race Relations file, Special Collections, Harding University, Searcy, Ark.

33. Edwin Hendrix to Dr. Ganus, 20 March 1969, Clifton L. Ganus Jr. Papers, Unprocessed, Administration Building, Harding University, Searcy, Ark.; Wayne Jordan, "NEP Pamphlets Are Burned in Harding Negroes' Protest," *Arkansas Gazette*, 17 April 1969; Wayne Jordan, "Students Using Techniques of Communists, Forum Told," *Arkansas Gazette*, 18 April 1969.

34. Alvaro L. Nieves, "Minorities in Evangelical Higher Education," in *Making Higher Education Christian: The History and Mission of Evangelical Colleges in America*, ed. J. A. Carpenter and K. W. Shipps (Grand Rapids: Eerdmans, 1987), 281–93.

35. Michelet quoted in Suzanne Desan, *Reclaiming the Sacred: Lay Religion and Popular Politics in Revolutionary France* (Ithaca: Cornell University Press, 1990), xviii; David B. Burks, ed., *Against the Grain: The Mission of Harding University* (Searcy, Ark.: Harding University, 1998), 58.

36. Doug Lederman, "Calling Off Ann Coulter," *Inside Higher Ed*, 1 September 2005, http://insidehighered.com/news/2005/09/01/harding; "Harding University Announces 2006-06 Distinguished Lecture Series," www.harding.edu/news_2006/news_ASI%20lineup.html; "Top 10 Conservative Colleges," http://media.yaf.org/latest/2005_2006_top_ten.cfm.

# 3

## With God on Our Side

### Moral and Religious Issues, Southern Culture, and Republican Realignment in the South

FREDERICK V. SLOCUM

In the popular imagination, the American South is an especially religious and conservative region. V. O. Key documented southern whites' thoroughgoing resistance to racial change, and political scientists Earl Black and Merle Black demonstrate change and continuity in southern politics, with increasing racial equality in the region, coupled with continuing conservative domination of the region's politics.[1] Recent elections reinforce the South's conservative reputation. The region was a stronghold for George W. Bush in 2000 and 2004, and Barack Obama's weakest region in 2008. While racial conflict no longer dominates southern politics today as it did forty years ago, conflicts over social and moral issues in the South are often expressed with striking intensity, as evidenced by conflicts over evolution, gay and lesbian issues, Ten Commandments displays, school prayer, and other social issues.

In the South,[2] Christian fundamentalist (especially Southern Baptist) religious traditions and political conservatism are closely related, and their confluence fueled the rise of the Republican Party to dominance in southern politics, primarily between 1980 and 2006. However, the agenda shift toward economic issues in 2008–9 may have blunted the continuing Republican advance in the South, creating conditions favorable for Democrats. The blending of southern religion and politics is nothing new: the 1845 founding of the Southern Baptist Convention is traceable to conflicts over slavery. The rise of the Ku Klux Klan was catalyzed by racism and hostility toward Catholics and Jews. The nexus between religion and politics in the South evidences both continuity and change. The continuity is that religion has frequently been invoked to justify and maintain social, economic, and political dominance by existing elites. The change is that the political party that best expressed the values of this "traditionalistic" political subculture was, for decades, the

Democratic Party—but today is the GOP. Thus, in contemporary southern politics, the Republican Party, not the Democratic Party, is the closer philosophical and ideological descendant of the old southern Democrats.[3]

## Social and Religious Conservatism in the South

The South is "home base" to the moral and social conservatism of Religious Right groups such as Focus on the Family and the Christian Coalition. Such groups derive power from the pronounced southern geographical concentration and flavor in incidents and social conflicts into which Religious Right groups commonly wade. In each case, Republicans nationwide—and even more so in the South—have positioned themselves on the conservative pole, an advantageous position in southern politics.[4]

### Disputes over Prayer and Religion in the Public Schools

Since the Supreme Court's early 1960s rulings banning organized prayer and Bible reading in the public schools, disputes over public-school prayer and religious practices have usually surfaced in rural and/or Deep South communities. In 1981, in Little Axe, Oklahoma, Lucille McCord and Joann Bell challenged religious meetings encouraged by the local school district and faced bloodcurdling hostility and abuse, including a physical assault on Bell by a school employee, death threats, an arson attack that destroyed Bell's home, and the slashing of Bell's pet goats.[5] Eventually, McCord and Bell won their case in a federal appeals court.[6] In *Wallace v. Jaffree* (1985), the Supreme Court overturned, on Establishment Clause grounds, an Alabama statute authorizing a "moment of silence" in public schools "for prayer or meditation." Another case, *Chandler v. James* (1997), heard in federal district and appeals courts, overturned Alabama's law authorizing "student-initiated" nonsectarian prayer at school events and barred captive-audience prayers and devotional Bible readings in DeKalb County. In Douglasville, Georgia, in 1986, student Doug Jager successfully challenged pre–football game prayers, but his family was bombarded with threats. In a Mississippi case, *Herdahl v. Pontotoc County School District* (1996), a federal district judge ordered a halt to Bible study classes and captive-audience intercom prayers. In Pike County, Alabama, a Jewish family whose children were coerced into Christian prayers and observances and who endured religious persecution by fellow students settled a lawsuit with the school district, which agreed to protect students against religious harassment and cease overtly Christian prayers and observances in the public schools.[7] In *Doe et al. v. Rhea County Board of Education*

(2002), a federal judge ordered an end to proselytizing Bible classes in the Rhea County, Tennessee, public schools—a ruling upheld on appeal in 2004.[8] The most recent major Supreme Court case on school prayer, *Doe v. Santa Fe Independent School District* (2000), overturned a Texas school district's policy of allowing a student-spoken prayer over the public address system at athletic events.

All of these controversies arose in southern states, and Religious Right groups invariably supported disputed religious practices. The GOP is more supportive of Religious Right causes, including school prayer, than the Democratic Party, and nowhere is the prevalence of religious conservatives among Republican activists greater than in the South, especially in states with large Southern Baptist populations such as Alabama, Mississippi, and Texas.[9] "The Republican Party and the Southern Baptist Convention are not only in firm alliance, they are sometimes indistinguishable," according to Oran P. Smith. Other leading political scientists concluded that "the white Protestant alliance is being recreated in the Republican Party," where it once was dominant in the Democratic Party.[10]

Democratic candidates face a difficult choice: echo Republican conservatism on religious issues and eschew support from the national party, thereby risking cutting themselves off from money and political expertise—or adopt positions distinct from the Republicans at a high risk of being branded as hostile to religion, beholden to unpopular liberal interest groups and a liberal national Democratic Party, or both. Generally, "national Democrats" attract little white southern support, owing to the Democratic Party's more secular and liberal philosophy.

Ten Commandments Controversies and the Roy Moore Case

As with school-prayer issues, Ten Commandments controversies, when they arise, tend to arise in southern states. In *Stone v. Graham* (1980), the Supreme Court overturned Kentucky's state law mandating the posting of the Ten Commandments in the state's public-school classrooms. In *Van Orden v. Perry* (2005), the Court upheld a Ten Commandments display on the grounds of the Texas state capitol in Austin. In *McCreary County v. ACLU of Kentucky* (2005), the Court struck down displays of the Commandments on courthouse walls in two Kentucky counties. The most enduring controversy over displaying the Ten Commandments was sparked by Roy Moore, the former chief justice of the Alabama Supreme Court. A Southern Baptist, Moore first attracted controversy as a lower state court judge by having courtroom prayers delivered by a local minister and displaying a Ten Commandments plaque on the wall of his Etowah County courtroom. Sued in 1995 over both practices, Moore was ordered by another judge to stop the prayers, but won a technical ruling on the plaque,[11] rode his notoriety to election as the chief justice of the Alabama Supreme Court in 2000 by declaring himself "the Ten Commandments judge" and promising to restore God and Christianity to American law.

Late at night and without the knowledge of any of his fellow justices, Chief Justice Moore oversaw the installation of a one-ton, granite Ten Command-ments monument in the rotunda of the Alabama Supreme Court building. The Rev. D. James Kennedy of Coral Ridge Ministries in Florida taped the event to sell videos. The monument sparked another lawsuit, and in 2002, black federal district judge Myron Thompson ruled that the monument violated the First Amendment's Establishment Clause and ordered it removed—a ruling that was upheld in 2003 by the Eleventh Circuit Court of Appeals in Atlanta. Defiant to the end, Moore again refused to remove the monument. Moore's eight associate justices overruled him, and he was then prosecuted by a special Alabama judicial ethics court for deliberately violating a federal court order. In November 2003, the ethics court convicted Moore on all counts, automati-cally removing him from office, but Moore remains a hero in Religious Right circles.[12]

As with school prayer, Republicans have declared ringing support for Ten Commandments displays. Democrats face pressure to support them as well, to avoid being branded as "liberal" or cozy with unpopular groups such as the American Civil Liberties Union or People for the American Way, and many southern Democrats join Republicans at least rhetorically, muting partisan difference on this subject.[13]

Conflicts over Gay and Lesbian Rights

Given the entrenched social conservatism that dominates southern opinion with a strong religious basis, increased hostility toward policies "friendly" to gays and lesbians in the South is common. Indeed, a startling array of antigay statements and actions has emerged, chiefly in the South, but not exclusively so.[14] One such controversy involves Roy Moore of Ten Commandments fame. As Alabama's chief justice, in a child custody case involving a lesbian mother, Moore wrote a long optional concurring opinion focusing on the mother's sexual orientation, proclaiming homosexuals "presumptively unfit" to raise children, and describing homosexuality as "abhorrent, immoral, detestable, [and] a crime against nature." Moore stipulated that "the State carries the power of the sword, that is . . . execution" in this regard.

Alabama GOP chair Marty Connors (a Catholic) told the press that "some people are going to condemn his outspokenness, but I'm certainly not. I think he's right." Similarly, a Mississippi judge published a letter expressing regret over a California law granting same-sex partners the same rights to sue as spouses or family members, opining that "gays and lesbians should be put in some type of a mental institute instead of having a law like this passed for them." In 2004, Republican Jim Deming, running for Democrat Fritz Hollings's open U.S. Senate seat, favored a state GOP plank supporting a ban on homosexual teachers.[15] He easily won a race in a state where, outside majority-black areas, Democrats are nearly certain to lose. U.S. Senator Tom Coburn (R-OK) claimed that in one Oklahoma town, lesbianism was "so rampant in the schools, that they'll let only one girl go to the bathroom" (at a time). Coburn has also been quoted as saying that a gay agenda is "the greatest threat to our freedom today" and provides "rationalization for abortion and multiple sexual partners."[16]

Southern hostility to gays and lesbians is also reflected in custody cases involving lesbian mothers. In 1995, a Florida judge awarded custody of Mary Ward's then eleven-year-old son to his father, John Ward, even though he had murdered his first wife and spent eight years in prison for it; the judge said the child should have a chance to grow up in "a non-lesbian world." The Virginia Supreme Court awarded custody of Sharon Bottoms's son Tyler to her mother, Pamela Kay Bottoms, in 1995, citing Bottoms's sexual orientation and stating "Conduct inherent in lesbianism is punishable as a Class 6 felony in the Commonwealth."

Opposition to gay marriage was an often-cited contributor to George W. Bush's 2004 reelection. Of the thirteen states enacting constitutional bans on gay marriage in 2004, six were southern: Arkansas, Georgia, Kentucky, Louisiana, Mississippi, and Oklahoma. More telling, southern states passed gay-marriage bans by wider margins than elsewhere: in Kentucky, Louisiana, Georgia, and Arkansas, the bans passed with 75 percent or greater support; in Mississippi, the margin was 86 percent in favor. Tennessee voters passed a gay-marriage ban in 2006 with 81 percent for the ban.

Before the Supreme Court's *Lawrence v. Texas* (2003) ruling overturning state anti-sodomy laws, distinct regional patterns were evident. Nine of the thirteen southern states (69 percent) still had sodomy laws on the books in 2003; only four, or 11 percent of the thirty-seven non-southern states, still had them. More tellingly, of the four southern states *without* an anti-sodomy law on the books in 2003 (Georgia, Arkansas, Tennessee, and Kentucky), *all four* reached that outcome via a state supreme court ruling overturning such laws as violations of the state constitution. No southern state has repealed such a law through legislative action, indicating the radioactive nature of the issue, with southern lawmakers fearing offending religious conservatives.[17]

Other Government Actions Promoting Traditional Values

On other miscellaneous "values" issues, similar calculations are likely to pose conflicts for southern Democrats, while leading to a headlong, unvarnished rush to the right for southern Republicans. A case study is North Carolina's anticohabitation law, on the books from 1805 until 2006, when it was overturned in court. Debra Hobbs, then a Pender County sheriff's dispatcher, filed suit to block enforcement of the law after her boss learned of her live-in relationship with her boyfriend and, citing the law, gave her three choices: move out, quit her job, or marry her boyfriend.[18] Hobbs left her job, but she also sued. In July 2006, a North Carolina judge ruled that the anticohabitation law was unconstitutional. Religious Right groups, such as the North Carolina Family Policy Council, vigorously defended the law. Carl Horn III, a Republican federal judge in Charlotte (and hero to religious conservatives in North Carolina), frequently questioned defendants about their living arrangements and refused to release those unmarried and living with an opposite-sex partner unless they agreed to end such living arrangements.[19]

Southern states often lead the nation in passing restrictive abortion laws. Mississippi and Louisiana have passed "trigger laws" that would ban nearly all abortions should the Supreme Court overturn *Roe v. Wade* (1973); the Republican-controlled Texas legislature considered, but defeated, a similar trigger law in 2007. A federal appeals court overturned a case upholding South Carolina's right to market a "Choose Life" license plate in 2004 because the plates provided a public forum for pro-life supporters but none for pro-choice supporters. In 2007, South Carolina, where Republicans hold the governorship and legislative majorities, enacted a law—the first of its kind in the nation—requiring a pregnant woman considering abortion to view an ultrasound and wait at least an hour thereafter before making a final decision. Both political calculations and personal views, then, should motivate southern Republican officeholders and candidates to pursue hard-line conservative positions on gay and lesbian issues, and on other "values" issues. For southern Democrats, we can expect more diverse positions, and for some, conflict between sincere convictions and political motivations to avoid being branded as liberal.

## Cultural Conservatism: A Case of Southern Exceptionalism?

One might question just how uniquely southern these phenomena really are. While these conservative reactions to cultural issues could conceivably occur in another part of the country, they would not have this frequency or vehemence. As the 2006 and 2008 elections illustrated, the Northeast and West Coast states and parts of the Mountain West and upper Midwest are trending increasingly Democratic, and the increasingly conservative and geographically southern tilt[20] of the Republican Party is alienating many nonsouthern voters, especially in the Northeast. No Republicans remain in New England's twenty-two-member U.S. House delegation, and former senators Jim Jeffords (VT) and Lincoln Chafee (RI), and Senator Arlen Specter (D-PA) all left the Republican Party, disenchanted with the its dominant conservatism. The Terri Schiavo end-of-life case (2005), where congressional Republicans (with lopsided southern support) and then-president Bush intervened to force Schiavo to remain connected to a feeding tube against her and her husband's wishes, is often cited as evidence that the Republican Party has moved too far right for most northeastern voters, and other socially conservative issues have a similar effect.[21] After the Schiavo case, former representative Chris Shays (R-CT), who in 2008 lost his seat to a Democrat, said, "This Republican Party of Lincoln has become the party of theocracy." Specter also cited the party's rightward drift in his 2009 decision to switch to the Democratic Party.

Outside the Northeast, there is no region that can equal the repeated, wideranging cultural conservatism that surfaces in the South on many issues, including abortion, religion, and gay and lesbian rights, among others. To be sure, another conservative area is Utah, Idaho, and Wyoming—states with strong Mormon influence that supported John McCain over Barack Obama. But tellingly, the outbursts of social conservatism frequent in the South are rare in the Mountain West, possibly because western conservative ideology is more informed by strong suspicion of government action that can conflict with the Religious Right's moral-values agenda. The kind of strident cultural conflicts evident in the South are generally far scarcer in other regions. Some nonsouthern episodes occasionally arise: for example, the 2004 conflict over intelligent design in Dover, Pennsylvania, and the 2006 and 2008 efforts in South Dakota to pass near-total abortion bans. However, in the Dover case, the school-board members who had supported intelligent design lost their seats in the November 2004 election, and both abortion-ban measures in South Dakota were defeated. Overall, the cultural conservatism evident in the foregoing cases is hardly seen in other regions, either in frequency or in the wide range of social and cultural conflicts that arise. Social conservatism is by no means uniquely southern, but its expression attains an intensity in the rural and Deep South that is unmatched elsewhere.

## The Conservative Takeover of the Southern Baptist Convention

The Southern Baptist Convention (SBC), the largest Protestant denomination in the United States, numbers about 16.5 million members and arose out of disputes over slavery. Early Southern Baptists were ardent defenders of slavery and, later, segregation and the subordination of blacks.

Before 1979, the SBC was controlled by a theologically and politically more moderate faction. However, the SBC soon faced rising disputes over social issues by a growing cadre of conservatives who emphasized biblical inerrancy and socially conservative views like opposition to abortion and feminism.[22] In 1979, the conservatives elected one of their own, Adrian Rogers, as SBC president. Conservatives used their control of the SBC presidency to cement dominance through a cumulative process, appointing like minds to key committees and boards at Southern Baptist seminaries year after year. Today, most moderates have left the SBC altogether to form the Cooperative Baptist Fellowship.

Theologically, moderates are more flexible in interpreting the Bible and more open to forming ecumenical partnerships. Politically, moderates tend to deemphasize divisive social issues like abortion, school prayer, and gay rights, leaving individual members to decide their positions on these issues. Conservatives generally hew to a fundamentalist or "literalist" interpretation of the Bible, and use that to justify strongly conservative positions on a wide range of issues from opposition to abortion, gay rights, and feminism to support for religious displays and school prayer, the war in Iraq, and the GOP. In 1998, SBC messengers adopted a resolution prohibiting women from serving as pastors and stating that wives should be "graciously submissive" to their husbands, prompting former president Jimmy Carter to sever his lifelong ties to the SBC. The close alliance between southern Republicans and Southern Baptists and other fundamentalist denominations like the Assemblies of God is particularly striking. More than one scholar has stated that the GOP and the SBC are "not only in firm alliance, they are sometimes indistinguishable from each other . . . interchangeable."[23]

Other analyses generally confirm the pattern: Peter Applebome's study of the connection between republicanism and conservative Christianity in Cobb County, Georgia; David Goldfield's work on the Christian Coalition; and the work of John Green and his colleagues. The latter concluded that the traditional "white Protestant alliance" that once was foundational to Democratic Party supremacy in the South "is being recreated in the Republican Party." As a result, "by the 1990s the Southern electoral order had two new religious centers of gravity: high-commitment [white Protestant] evangelicals for the GOP and black Protestants for the Democrats."[24]

Current events, too, evidence the connection between the SBC and south-ern Republicanism. At the East Waynesville Baptist Church in the North Carolina mountains, Pastor Chan Chandler spearheaded the expulsion of nine members because they refused to support President George W. Bush's 2004 reelection. Chandler endorsed Bush from the pulpit and advised Kerry supporters to "repent or resign."[25] The North Carolina GOP asked churches to send their membership directories for mobilizing.[26] Nationwide, the 2004 Bush-Cheney campaign asked Republican activists to provide church direc-tories for use in making their churches into political organizing bases.

The swing toward fundamentalist dominance in the SBC dates primarily to the 1968–88 period, with the pivotal year being 1979, when the first conserva-tive president was elected. During the late 1970s, the Religious Right became a prominent political force in the GOP, arising originally as a reaction against feminism and the counterculture of the late 1960s and a perceived breakdown in sexual morality and traditional moral values. The *Roe v. Wade* decision (1973), overturning state abortion bans, lent further impetus, as did beliefs that President Jimmy Carter (1977–81), despite his Southern Baptist past, was abandoning traditional moral values. The Religious Right soon broadened its emphasis to other issues, such as school prayer and pornography, with the Moral Majority founded by the Rev. Jerry Falwell in 1979, the same year as the fundamentalist takeover in the SBC. After his unsuccessful 1988 bid for the Republican presidential nomination, the Rev. Pat Robertson founded the Christian Coalition. Both groups—and others like the Traditional Values Co-alition, Coral Ridge, and Focus on the Family—maintain a strong (in some states dominant) influence in the GOP, particularly in the South. Moderate or liberal positions on social issues flatly disqualify any candidate from winning contested party endorsements, caucuses and primaries.[27]

## Politically Significant Elements of Southern Cultures

A culture of honor, southern militarism, and cultural defense also define the South. In previous works, I have defined "cultural defense" as a tendency for some tradition-minded white southerners to go to extremes in "defending" cherished values or attacking those deemed to challenge those values.[28]

### Southern Militarism

Many historians have long noted a military tradition in the American South. Even some book titles reveal the theme. Rates of military enlistment have always been higher in the South than in much of the rest of the country. Most modern observers confirm the tradition's existence. Michael Lind writes of the

Bush administration's eager militarism overseas since 9/11 and connects it to southern military traditions, reinforced by religious fundamentalism. As Lind notes elsewhere, southerners are overrepresented in today's volunteer military—especially in the officer corps—more tolerant of wartime casualties, and more supportive of military action overseas, including Vietnam and Iraq.[29] Politically, the pro-military bent in the South likely propels Republican support, especially among white southerners, as the GOP has traditionally been more hawkish on national defense and was more stridently anticommunist before the decline of communism in most of the world. For example, Ronald Reagan won 70 percent of southern white male votes in 1984.

The Southern Culture of Honor

The cultural psychologists Richard Nisbett and Dov Cohen (1996) argue that a "culture of honor" is prominent in certain societies with a history of raising animals. Such is the case for many native-born white southerners, whose ancestors often raised animals on the fringes of Great Britain. In outlying areas of England and Scotland, two factors—a herding tradition and a lack of effective law enforcement—combined to foster a culture of honor that was transplanted via migration to the American South and instilled primarily in white males.[30] In a "culture of honor" society, a male who perceives a challenge, insult, or material threat is widely expected to confront the other party, possibly with threatened or actual violence; extreme cases include killing the perceived offender. To not respond to a challenge or insult is seen as "unmanly," indicative of someone who can be "pushed around" or taken advantage of easily.[31]

Thus, men must always be vigilant and act to preserve their reputation (or that of their family) against slights; no challenge can go unanswered; no insult can be shrugged off. Other situations might also call for violent action: defense of property, or ensuring social control. The political ramifications of the culture of honor among white southerners include, among other things, a pro-defense, pro-military ethic, greater support for and more frequent use of capital punishment, and the greater propensity in the South to favor violence for maintaining social control (for example, corporal punishment), and harsh policies in the criminal-justice system, such as the "hitching post" used briefly in 1995–96 by Alabama authorities to restrain inmates.[32]

Southern "Cultural Defense" and Southern Religious Disputes

Cultural defense is the tendency to "stop at nothing"—even including threatened or actual violence—to defend a cherished local practice or institution against attack from perceived "outsiders," or retaliate against them. In earlier work, I cited examples of cultural defense in the areas of civil rights and antiunion activity by southern employers.[33]

School-prayer disputes in southern communities provide a striking additional example of cultural defense in practice. Time and again, when a family (typically a religious minority) sues to stop (overwhelmingly popular) organized prayer or religious practices in a southern school district, the family faces vicious reprisals. In the 1997–98 Pike County, Alabama, case cited earlier, the Jewish children involved endured taunts and harassment; other children took their yarmulkes, yelled slurs, and drew swastikas on their lockers and personal belongings. The school superintendent said the harassment would stop when the Jewish children converted to Christianity. In a 1996 Mississippi case, the Herdahl children were called "atheists" and "devil worshippers" and ostracized for not joining other children in classroom or intercom prayers. Their mother received death threats and threats to firebomb the family home,[34] was declared "unemployable in the state of Mississippi," and could not find work anywhere in Pontotoc County. In Little Axe, Oklahoma, Joann Bell sued in 1981 to stop religious meetings in public schools, and received bloodcurdling threats, was physically assaulted by a school employee, and had her house set on fire.

The cases cited here all furnish striking evidence of southern cultural defense over a religious issue. In each case, those challenging a cherished religious status quo in the South found themselves branded outsiders or "outside agitators" and became potential targets for severe reprisals. Some status-quo defenders resort to extreme measures or flatly refuse to accept losing. Local authorities, in cultural defense of public-school prayer, usually "litigate to the hilt" and appeal adverse court rulings with little regard to their prospects for success. Such recalcitrant behavior, strikingly similar to the "still fighting the Civil War" mentality identified by David Goldfield, can be costly.[35] In the Herdahl case, Pontotoc County authorities were ordered to pay plaintiffs' attorneys $144,000 in legal fees. Lacking these funds, the school district resorted to bake sales, concerts, and other public fund-raising events. Contributors faced the galling reality that their money was going to hated "outside, liberal" groups like People for the American Way and the ACLU, both of which joined the Herdahl suit.

Cultural defense is also evident in other kinds of religious issues. When federal judges strike down school prayer and religious practices in southern districts, Religious Right activists and some community members not uncommonly brand them "rogue, activist" judges and alleged sympathizers with outside liberal groups. Cultural defense is also apparent in Alabama's repeated legislative actions to circumvent 1960s-era Supreme Court rulings banning organized prayer in the public schools; in Alabama governor Fob James's 1997 promise to "call out the state police and mobilize the National Guard if necessary" to defend Roy Moore's defiance of federal court orders to remove his Ten Commandments monument; in Moore's own defiance;[36] and in southern local governments' efforts to provide for student-initiated oral prayer to circumvent the requirement that teachers and school officials not sponsor or endorse prayer themselves (as in the *Ingebretsen* and *Santa Fe ISD* cases). When southern officials repeatedly persist in reinstating religious practices ruled unconstitutional by federal judges, or in creatively circumventing those rulings, cultural defense is evident again. Cultural defense on religion issues may be a manifestation of the white southern pattern identified in Goldfield's *Still Fighting the Civil War*. Goldfield noted the common white southern tendency to vehemently resist liberal policies and/or impose reactionary policies in a crusade to continually "redeem" the Lost Cause and strike out at outsiders seeking to undermine what they view as traditional southern values. By imposing conservative views on their communities and the nation, southerners can "win" the larger battle, sometimes with God's perceived endorsement.[37] On religious issues, then, cultural defense is a prominent and recurring pattern in many rural southern communities. Democrats occasionally follow suit (as in the 2006 Eaves gubernatorial campaign in Mississippi), but southern Democrats usually prefer to emphasize economic issues over social issues,[38] and fare better in elections to the extent that holds true.

## Militarism, the Culture of Honor, Cultural Defense, and Religion in the South

Military traditions, the culture of honor, and cultural defense are strongly interconnected. Nisbett and Cohen note that the culture of honor leads southern lawmakers toward more "hawkish" positions on defense, wars, and military intervention overseas. As Michael Lind noted, southerners were more supportive of the war in Iraq than were nonsoutherners.[39] But why? As discussed earlier, the culture of honor requires that a perceived challenge or insult *must* be answered somehow, or the insulted person will lose esteem in the eyes of peers. If male, this may mean being seen as "not much of a man," a costly proposition. The culture of honor and southern militarism are connected when one considers that perceived insults can be societal, or even international, as well as individual. The 9/11 attacks can be seen as a colossal national insult—a seemingly unprovoked attack that killed nearly three thousand Americans. Not surprisingly, white evangelicals registered unusually high support for invading Iraq (77 percent in March 2003), a figure that would probably be even higher if it surveyed only white southern evangelicals. Viewed as a colos-sal *national* insult, 9/11 would merit a decidedly aggressive response—which George W. Bush, a southern president, delivered in spades.[40] Perhaps other foreign-policy events—the expansion of communism into Cuba and Viet-nam, or socialism in Nicaragua, or the 1979 seizure of American hostages in Iran—were also interpreted by conservative (and not coincidentally, famously anticommunist) southern whites as national insults demanding all-out war, or at least a strong military response. Southern lawmakers have a long history of especially strong support for military action overseas.

If national insults can trigger a "culture of honor" response, the southern propensity for favoring harsh, "eye for an eye" Old Testament justice in the criminal justice system is a product of the "insult" to a community that violent crime is perceived to represent. The enthusiastic use of the death penalty—no-where more evident than in Texas—can represent a form of state militarism as well as a legitimate "culture of honor" response to the social insult of violent crime.

In the South, religion, specifically evangelical Protestantism, seems to re-inforce these propensities. The biblical injunction to "spare the rod, spoil the child," cited by evangelicals is also commonly invoked. Conservative religious traditions (within and outside the South) usually staunchly support the death penalty, to "punish the evildoers." Religion also appears to underlie support for invading Iraq. The Southern Baptist leader Charles Stanley has urged support for the Iraq War, for "God battles people who oppose Him, who fight against Him and His followers." Other evangelical leaders have spoken of occupied Iraq as an exciting opportunity to convert Muslims to Christianity. In the Feb-ruary 2006 issue of *Christianity Today*, 77 percent of white evangelicals sup-ported invading Iraq in March 2003, while in October 2005, approval of Bush's job performance was only 37 percent overall, but still 64 percent among white evangelicals. As Lind argued, many southern evangelicals viewed George W. Bush's pro-Israel foreign policy as a fulfillment of biblically based mandates.[41] Similarly, some evangelicals view the Iraq War (and possibly, today's rising tensions between the United States and Iran) as a fulfillment of biblical proph-ecy and a welcome sign of impending Armageddon and the second coming of Christ.

The enthusiastic white southern support for Bush's aggressive Middle East policies, including warrant-less domestic spying, torture and harsh treatment of detainees, and rendition for terror suspects, might also represent an exten-sion of "cultural defense" ideology into U.S. foreign policy—a justifiable lash-ing out against the "outside threat" of Islamic extremism. Several controversial statements by southern lawmakers (all white, conservative Republicans) and some southern evangelical leaders seem revealing in this regard, indicating a pattern of approval of profiling of Middle Easterners and/or a stereotype or all Arabs or Muslims as security threats.

In 2001, Congressman John Cooksey (R-LA) said that someone "wearing a diaper on his head" should expect to be questioned in the investigation of 9/11. Republican U.S. representative (now senator) Saxby Chambliss of Georgia told a November 2001 gathering of Georgia law-enforcement officers that an appropriate response to terrorism would be to "turn the sheriff loose and have him arrest every Muslim that crosses the state line."[42] Two Republican U.S. representatives from North Carolina, Howard Coble and Sue Myrick, also made comments widely viewed as racially insensitive toward Middle Easterners. In a 2003 radio talk show, Coble defended FDR's decision to intern Japanese Americans in camps during World War II. In 1988, Coble had voted against a congressional bill providing monetary reparations to survivors of the internment. In a speech to the conservative Heritage Foundation on domestic terrorism, Myrick said, in reference to Arab Americans, "Look who runs all the convenience stores across the country" as she linked her remarks to the danger of "illegal trafficking of food stamps . . . for the purpose of laundering money to countries known to harbor terrorists."

One of these remarks could be shrugged off as an isolated incident. Four of them, all coming out of the mouths of conservative white southern Republican elected lawmakers, seem more like a pattern. The comment by the North Carolina evangelist Franklin Graham (son of Billy Graham) that Islam is "a very evil and wicked religion" fits the pattern as well. Other southern evangelical leaders have offered similar comments. In an October 2002 interview on CBS, Jerry Falwell called the prophet Mohammed a "terrorist . . . a violent man, a man of war," and in November 2002 Pat Robertson denounced Muslims as "worse than the Nazis" and bent on exterminating Jews. This pattern of comments seems to suggest a version of southern "cultural defense"—a closing of ranks in righteous defense against the perceived outside threat. Republican U.S. congressman Virgil Goode warned Virginia constituents to "wake up," adding that if stricter immigration laws are not passed, "there will likely be many more Muslims elected to office and demanding use of the Koran." He was referring to the 2006 election of Keith Ellison, a Democrat and Muslim, to Minnesota's Fifth Congressional District.[43] Political conflicts are rife with religious overtones for many white southerners. Their more conservative religious leaders, and the officials they elect today (heavily Republican, especially in federal elections), seem to act in ways that support them. Southern religious traditions (particularly fundamentalist), militaristic traditions, the culture of honor, and cultural defense often combine to provide justifications for the often stridently conservative views advocated by southern elected officials today.

## Southern Culture, Religious Values, and Party Politics

The culture of honor, cultural defense, southern militarism, and southern evangelical religion have combined in a potent stew in contemporary southern politics—a combination evident in national politics today. The combination of these factors has fostered a potent strain of take-no-prisoners ruthlessness, which was most evident when Republicans held all levers of power in Washington during most of the 2001–7 period. This argument is developed more thoroughly elsewhere,[44] but a brief mention of some illustrative cases might include the following. George W. Bush zealously pursued the Iraq War despite escalating violence and falling approval ratings, having announced that he would never consider troop reductions there. In 2005, Republican congressional leaders persisted in forcing the Terri Schiavo case into federal court despite opposition from a majority of the public, but with die-hard support from religious conservatives, an important Republican base group.[45] Also in 2005, Republicans pushed congressional ethics rule changes clearly designed to hinder ethics investigations of Tom DeLay, who has since resigned from Congress and been charged with illegally laundering corporate contributions to the Texas GOP. Republican leaders, notably Tennessee's Bill Frist, pushed the "nuclear option" to kill Democratic filibusters of Bush's judicial nominees, paving the way for Republicans to crush Democratic opposition with fifty-one votes. The 2003 Texas redistricting, a mid-decade redistricting engineered by Tom DeLay to gain more Republican congressional seats, and the 2005 mid-decade redistricting in Georgia, were both steamrolled through by newly dominant Republicans in their respective states. Republicans scuttled the once-understood rule of "one redistricting per decade" except when a court ruling required a second redistricting. In each of these cases, the crusade to change the rules for political benefit is consistent with the ruthlessness inherent in southern cultural defense ideology—and reinforced by the religious and political arch-conservatism of the "high commitment evangelicals" that Green et al. identify as the center of Republican support in southern politics today. As David Goldfield wrote, today's evangelicals evidence

> a lack of respect for other faiths, because evangelicals believe there is only one Truth, only one way to attain heaven: through their faith. As Southern Baptist leader Bailey Smith noted in 1980 and again in 1987, "God doesn't hear the prayer of the Jew." This comment implies a certitude over a range of issues, from free trade to feminism. In response to

a 1992 survey of churchgoers in Charlotte, North Carolina, a member of Northside Baptist Church admitted that "people who don't have a Christian background think we're fanatical." She added not an apology but a confirmation: "Well, I guess we are. We have all the answers." . . . [S]uch statements . . . are understandable in light of the fact that evangelical Southerners believe they are uniquely chosen by God. Historian Charles Reagan Wilson explained, "the self-image of a chosen people leaves little room for self-criticism." Since the end of the Civil War, and because of the result of that war, white Southern evangelicals have believed this with all their hearts and souls.[46]

The take-no-prisoners ruthlessness of southern Republicans evident in state and national politics, then, has easily discernable roots in, and derives outright encouragement from, the region's Southern Baptist and other fundamentalist religious traditions. Tom DeLay's entire political career, with its signature brass-knuckled ruthlessness that earned him the moniker "The Hammer," is a textbook example. With God on their side in political matters, the ends can, all too often, justify the means, and changing the rules in order to win becomes no problem. This pattern has historical parallels in white southern elites' often vicious efforts to oppress blacks and destroy the civil rights movement, and in the ruthless, often illegal, and sometimes violent tactics used by southern textile mill management to crush workers' efforts to establish and join labor unions.

Republican advantages in southern politics today are built on the combination of Earl Black and Merle Black's "conservative advantage" in white public opinion, the convergence of ideological and partisan divisions, making Republicans the uniformly more conservative party, and the willingness of southern Republicans to stake out unrestrained hard-line conservative positions, especially on social and moral issues with religious overtones, and pursue them with extreme zeal.[47] Before the 2006 elections installed Democratic majorities in both houses of Congress, George W. Bush and Republican congressional majorities pursued conservative goals with a zeal and unity unmatched by any party in decades. As the political scientists Jacob Hacker and Paul Pierson document, the ideological center in the Republican Party continues to shift rightward, both among the party's activist base and in Congress.[48] After Republican defeats in the 2006 midterm elections, GOP senators chose Trent Lott of Mississippi as their minority whip. This action elevated Lott back into the Republican leadership just four years after he lost his position as Senate majority leader, embarrassing President Bush by making racially insensitive remarks at Strom Thurmond's hundredth birthday party (implying the country would have been better off if Thurmond's racist Dixiecrat Party had won the presidency in 1948). In the Democratic-controlled 110th Congress, southern influence in Republican leadership waned in the House but not the Senate, where Mitch McConnell (KY) is Senate minority leader and Lott is minority whip. Nor is southern domination in Republican-controlled congresses anything new: from 1995 to 1999, the House's majority party (Republican) included Newt Gingrich (GA), Richard Armey (TX), and Tom DeLay (TX); their Senate counterparts included Trent Lott (MS) and Don Nickles (OK) as majority whip. That said, the 2006 and 2008 elections have sharply eroded southern influence in national politics, as Barack Obama's winning electoral coalition was built largely outside the South.[49]

The lockstep unity and zeal on conservative causes exhibited by southern Republicans in Congress cannot be surprising, given the confluence of various southern cultural elements and southern fundamentalist religion. In 2004, with Bush running as a southern conservative against a northeastern liberal Democratic opponent,[50] in a "war on terror" environment, with cultural issues like gay marriage and "culture of honor" issues like Iraq, it was virtually inevitable that Bush would crush Kerry among white southerners, thereby guaranteeing a regional sweep. Only in Florida was the contest close. Furthermore, the successful election and reelection of archconservative southern lawmakers like Jesse Helms, Kirk Fordice, Bob Barr, Tom DeLay, Tom Coburn, Jim Bunning, and Jim DeMint indicate that southern Republicans have nearly unlimited latitude to tack to the extreme right and still win elections. Meanwhile, southern Democrats walk an endless and increasingly harrowing tightrope between echoing Republican conservatism (minimizing intercandidate differences, but pushing away the national Democratic Party and alienating more liberal donors and constituencies like organized labor) and tacking more to the left (risking making the dangerous "liberal" label stick, and abandoning more whites to the Republican candidate). These realities probably have more potency when social issues are prominent (2004), and less potency when economic issues are prominent (2008).

Republican dominance in southern politics has been attenuated in the 2006 and 2008 elections. But it was back in full force in the 2010 midterm elections. Nonetheless, even in 2006 and 2008, Democratic gains nationwide were heavily concentrated in the Northeast and Midwest. Despite the pro-Democratic political climate nationwide and dominance of economic issues in 2008, Republicans continued their dominance in state elections in Texas, Mississippi, Alabama, South Carolina, and Georgia—all states in which the Republican realignment among whites is virtually complete. In Tennessee and Oklahoma, Republicans continued their advance at the state level, despite their poor performance nationwide. In south-central, interior southern, and Appalachian districts, Barack Obama fared worse electorally than John Kerry had in 2004. On the other hand, Democrats gained ground in North Carolina and Arkansas. In addition, Barack Obama broke the Republican presidential lock on the South by carrying the South Atlantic states Virginia, North Carolina, and Florida. These realities emphasize that Republican realignment in the region is not uniform from state to state, and that other factors remotely related to religion (like population shifts and Latino immigration) may be eroding Republican dominance in some states. In congressional elections, Democratic gains in the South were modest: Democrats brought their share of southern U.S. House seats from 36 percent in 2005 to 44 percent in 2009, and of southern U.S. Senate seats from 15 percent in 2005 to 27 percent in 2009.

Still, Republican dominance in the region among white southerners owes much to religion—particularly the political shift of Southern Baptists and other fundamentalist Christians into the GOP—a striking confluence of religious conservatism with Republican partisan identification. In politics today, Republican opponents of the Christian Right's agenda are most prevalent in the Northeast, and largely nonexistent in the South. In contemporary southern politics, "evangelical Christian" in theology and "Republican" in politics are increasingly interchangeable terms. As the Mississippi State University political scientist Marty Wiseman told the *Jackson Clarion-Ledger*, "I've heard people say, 'If you're a Christian, you vote for Bush, and if you voted for Kerry, it's obvious you haven't been saved.'"[51] With little doubt the same sentiments motivated Southern Baptist pastor Chan Chandler's efforts to expel John Kerry supporters from his Waynesville, North Carolina church.

## Notes

1. V. O. Key Jr., *Southern Politics in State and Nation* (New York: Knopf, 1949); Earl Black and Merle Black, *Politics and Society in the South* (Cambridge: Harvard University Press, 1987).

2. This essay considers thirteen states as "southern": Alabama, Arkansas, Georgia, Florida, Kentucky, Louisiana, Mississippi, North Carolina, Oklahoma, South Carolina, Tennessee, Texas, and Virginia.

3. Daniel J. Elazar, *American Federalism: A View from the States* (New York: Harper and Row, 1984).

4. Black and Black, *Politics and Society in the South*.

5. http://blog.au.org/2008/11/25/hell-in-little-axe-an-oklahoma-moms-chilling-battle-with-religious-bigotry/.

6. *Bell v. Little Axe Independent School District #70*, 1985.

7. The case, *Paul Michael Herring v. Dr. John Key, Superintendent of Pike County*

*(Alabama) Schools*, was filed in 1997 and settled in 1998. The plaintiffs alleged a teacher had said, "If parents won't save souls, we have to."

8. Rhea County, Tennessee, was the site of the 1925 Scopes "Monkey Trial"; the county seat, Dayton, is the home of Bryan College, an evangelical Christian school named after William Jennings Bryan. In March 2004, the county again made international headlines when county supervisors asked state legislature to allow the county to prosecute homosexuals for "crimes against nature" (Rhea County Seeks Change in Law to Ban Gays," www.wkrn.com/Global/story.asp?S=1718183&nav=1ugFLb9D).

9. At its 2004 convention, the Texas Republican Party adopted platform language calling the United States "a Christian nation . . . founded on fundamental Judeo-Christian principles based on the Holy Bible" and decrying "the myth of the separation of church and state." This resolution was eerily reminiscent of the claim by Mississippi's governor, Kirk Fordice, at the 1992 Republican Governors' Association that "the United States is a Christian nation."

10. Oran P. Smith, The *Rise of Baptist Republicanism* (New York: New York University Press, 1997), 2 (first quotation); John C. Green, James L. Guth, Lyman Kellstadt, and Corwin Schmidt, "The Soul of the South: Religion and Southern Politics at the Millennium," 283–98, 296 (second quotation), in *The New Politics of the Old South*, ed. Charles Bullock III and Mark J. Rozell, 2nd ed. (Lanham, Md.: Rowman and Littlefield, 2003).

11. Bill Pryor, a Republican and Alabama attorney general, was a strong Moore supporter, but was legally required to prosecute Moore at the ethics court trial that removed him from office. In 2004, Robert Aderholt, a Republican U.S. representative from Alabama, sponsored a bill to strip the Supreme Court of jurisdiction in cases concerning government officials' "acknowledgment of God as the sovereign source of law, liberty or government."

12. Governor Bob Riley's repeated and public penance was absolutely essential in Alabama. It worked well as, suitably reassured on taxes, fiscal conservatives and all but the most fervent social conservatives abandoned Moore. Riley and conservative Catholic attorney general Bill Pryor had rhetorically defended Moore's wisdom before his defiance of a federal district court and his calling on the Alabama National Guard turned him into a Frankenstein to the state's GOP leadership. Previously Moore's rhetoric had served the Alabama GOP well in rallying social and religious conservatives to their standard. Riley, Pryor, and the whole GOP-controlled state supreme court turned on Moore. One of Moore's lasting supporters was the conservative Catholic state GOP chairman, Marty Connors.

13. *New York Times*, 10 October 2007.

14. Black and Black, *Politics and Society in the South*; Smith, *The Rise of Baptist Republicanism*; and Green et al., "The Soul of the South."

15. MSNBC, "Meet the Press: Transcript for October 17 [2004]," www.msnbc.msn.com/id/6267835/.

16. Coburn also recommended the death penalty for abortion providers (http://

en.wikipedia.org/wiki/Tom_Coburn). Charles Babbington, "Two Opponents of Abortion Are Tapped," *Washington Post*, 21 December 2004.

17. Graphic in the *New York Times*, 19 March 2003.

18. AP, "N.C. Anti-Cohabitation Law Comes under Legal Attack," MSNBC online, 9 May 2005, http://msnbc.msn.com/id/7794211/.

19. Anti-Cohabitation Laws Still Being Enforced," Unmarried America, 28 March 2004, www.unmarriedamerica.org/News-About-Us/Anti-cohabitation.htm.

20. Republicans hold 47 percent of Senate seats nationwide, but 76.9 percent (20 of 26) of the Senate seats from the thirteen-state South. Put differently, of the Republicans' 47 Senate seats, close to half (20, or 42.6 percent) are southern. In the 2010 midterm elections, Republicans captured a net of 21 previously Democratic-held House seats in the South, including at least one seat in *every* former Confederate state. Republicans gained three House seats in Texas, three in Virginia, four in Florida, three in Tennessee, two in Mississippi, two in Arkansas, and one each in North Carolina, South Carolina, Georgia, Alabama, and Louisiana. That adds up to 22 seats, but Democrats gained one previously Republican-held seat in Louisiana by defeating Rep. Joseph Cao in the heavily Democratic New Orleans district. That yields a net Republican gain of 21 seats across the region. Even more striking is that in the five core Deep South states of Louisiana, Mississippi, Alabama, Georgia, and South Carolina, there is exactly *one* white Democrat remaining in those states' U.S. House delegations combined: John Barrow of Georgia. In the Texas House of Representatives, Republicans gained 24 seats to go to a 100–50 majority (previously 76–74), and the ranks of white Democrats plummeted from 28 to 9. Republicans held 79 southern U.S. House seats before the election (after Parker Griffith's party switch from Democratic to Republican in Alabama), and their numbers increased by 21, to 100 after the election. Republicans will hold 100 out of 142 House seats in the thirteen-state South, or 70.4 percent. Republicans will hold 243 seats in the House. Thus, 100 of the Republicans' 243 seats, or 41.2 percent, are southern.

21. Keith B. Richburg, "In Northeast, Lost in a Blue Wave." *Washington Post*, November 11, 2008, www.washingtonpost.com/wp-dyn/content/article/2008/11/10/AR2008111003026.html.

22. Ellen M. Rosenberg, *The Southern Baptists: A Subculture in Transition* (Knoxville: University of Tennessee Press, 1989).

23. Smith, *Rise of Baptist Republicanism*, 2 (first quotation), 56, 207 (second quotation).

24. Peter Applebome, *Dixie Rising: How the South Is Shaping American Values, Politics, and Culture* (San Diego: Harcourt Brace, 1997), esp. chap. 2; David R. Goldfield, *Still Fighting the Civil War: The American South and Southern History* (Baton Rouge: Louisiana State University Press, 2002), 80 (first quotation); Green et al., "The Soul of the South," 294 (third quotation), 296 (second quotation).

25. "Church Split in Dispute over Bush," *New York Times*, 11 May 2005.

26. Alan Cooperman, "In N.C., GOP Requests Church Directories," *Washington Post*, 18 February 2006.

27. Green et al., "The Soul of the South."

28. John Hope Franklin, *The Militant South, 1800–1861* (Boston: Beacon Press, 1956); John Temple Graves II, *The Fighting South* (New York: Putnam's, 1943), Jonathan F. Phillips, "Superbase: Fort Bragg and the Origins of Militarization in the American South" (Ph.D diss., University of North Carolina at Chapel Hill, 2003); Richard Nisbett and Dov Cohen, *Culture of Honor: The Psychology of Violence in the South* (Boulder: Westview Press, 1996); Fred Slocum, "Connecting the Past and the Present: Historical Realities and Current Political Trends in the South," paper presented at the Southern Political Science Association Annual Meeting, Atlanta, January 2006.

29. Ibid. See also Rod Andrew Jr., *Long Gray Lines: The Southern Military School Tradition, 1839–1915* (Chapel Hill: University of North Carolina Press, 2001); Tim Kane, "The Demographics of Military Enlistment After 9/11," The Heritage Foundation, www.heritage.org, 3 November 2005; Michael Lind, *Made in Texas: George W. Bush and the Southern Takeover of American Politics* (New York: Basic Books, 2003), esp. chap. 5; and, also by Lind, "Bush's Martyrs," *New Statesman*, 1 March 2004.

30. Nisbett and Cohen, *Culture of Honor.*

31. For other examples of the culture of honor (and other white male themes) in southern rock music, see Ted Ownby, *Subduing Satan: Religion, Recreation, and Manhood in the Rural South, 1865–1920* (Chapel Hill: University of North Carolina Press, 1993).

32. On dueling, see Bertram Wyatt-Brown, *Southern Honor: Ethics and Behavior in the Old South* (New York: Oxford University Press, 1982).

33. Slocum, "Connecting the Past and the Present."

34. The Herdahl case is portrayed by the 1999 video *School Prayer: A Community at War* by Slawomir Grunberg and Ben Crane (LOGTV, Ltd.); see also www.school-prayer.com.

35. Goldfield, *Still Fighting the Civil War.*

36. Moore has proclaimed that he honors God's laws over human laws, and that the First Amendment's Establishment Clause does not apply to the states, despite unambiguous federal court rulings (e.g., *Everson v. Board of Education*, 1947).

37. Goldfield, *Still Fighting the Civil War*, 76–88. As Goldfield notes (83), Alabama requires the display of a sticker in textbooks disclaiming evolution as "theory, not fact." Cobb County, Georgia, required the posting of a similar sticker in biology textbooks, which a federal district judge overturned. In *Edwards v. Aguillard* (1987), the Supreme Court overturned Louisiana's law requiring that if evolution was taught in the public schools, creationism must also be taught. IMAX wide-screen theaters in Texas, Georgia, North Carolina, and South Carolina have refused to show a film on volcanoes because it mentions evolution ("IMAX Movie about Volcanoes Banned in South Because It Mentions Evolution," *Associated Press*, 23 March 2005).

38. James Glaser, *The Hand of the Past in Contemporary Southern Politics* (New Haven: Yale University Press, 2005).

39. Nisbett and Cohen, *Culture of Honor;* and Lind, "Bush's Martyrs."

40. Slocum, "Connecting the Past and the Present."

41. Charles Marsh, "Wayward Christian Soldiers," *New York Times*, 20 January 2006, Tony Carnes, "Disappointed But Holding: While Overall Support for George W. Bush Has Plummeted, Evangelicals Remain Surprisingly Loyal," *Christianity Today*, 26 January 2006; Lind, *Made in Texas*, chap. 5.

42. CNN, *Crossfire*, 2002.

43. Zachary Goldfarb, "Virginia Lawmaker's Remarks on Muslims Criticized," *Washington Post*, 21 December 2006 (quotations).

44. Slocum, "Connecting the Past and the Present."

45. An aide to Sen. Mel Martinez (R-FL), Brian Darling, resigned after admitting authoring a memo citing the political advantage to Republicans of intervening in the Schiavo case (Mike Allen, "Counsel to GOP Senator Wrote Memo on Schiavo," *Washington Post*, 7 April 2005).

46. Goldfield, *Still Fighting the Civil War*, 81.

47. Black and Black, *Politics and Society in the South*.

48. Jacob Hacker and Paul Pierson, *Off Center: The Republican Revolution and the Erosion of American Democracy* (New Haven: Yale University Press, 2005).

49. See www.nytimes.com/2008/11/11/us/politics/11outh.ntml.

50. Sen. Trent Lott (R-MS), addressing a conservative audience in Neshoba County, described John Kerry as a "French-speaking socialist from Massachusetts" (Curtis Wilkie, "Mississippi Leads Red State Wave," in "The South: Awash in Red in 2004," *SouthNow*, January 2005, 6 [quotation], www.southnow.org). In Mississippi, this is potent code for "a scary liberal 'outsider' from a state that allows gay marriages."

51. Wilkie, "Mississippi Leads Red State Wave."

# I I

## State, Section, Suburb, and Race

# 4

# A Suburban Story

## The Rise of Republicanism in Postwar Georgia, 1948–1980

TIM BOYD

Toward the end of 1963, the Republican leadership in Fulton County, Georgia—home to Atlanta and the most populous county in the state—published an upbeat assessment of their party's prospects for electoral success in the form of a booklet. The main message of *Operation Breakthrough* was that Republican strength in Georgia had been steadily growing since the end of World War II and that the end of the Democratic Party's stranglehold on political office in the state was tantalizingly close. In fact, the booklet boasted, thanks to the efforts of Republicans in Fulton County, even such unsuccessful campaigns as the 1956 attempt to unseat the Democratic congressman from the Fifth District, James C. Davis, in which the Republican candidate lost by nearly twenty percentage points, had made it "apparent that Fulton County, and Georgia, was on its way to an effective two-party system." Further grounds for optimism could be found in the election of two Republican aldermen to the Atlanta City Council in 1961 and the relatively narrow twelve-point defeat suffered by Republican James O'Callaghan in the Fifth District in 1962. All of this meant that those voters in Georgia who had "always believed in Republican principles" but whose voices had been stifled by the one-party system were poised to deliver lasting political success to a resurgent GOP in the near future.[1]

Depending on which metric one wishes to use, it is possible to conclude that the analysis and predictions in *Operation Breakthrough* were either hopelessly optimistic or remarkably prescient. In fact, they were both. From the perspective of 2011, the fact that since 1960 Georgia has gone from being the second-most Democratic state in the nation to voting Republican in eight of twelve presidential elections suggests that the hopes of the Fulton County Republicans were broadly realized.[2] Similarly, that Georgians voted for John McCain in 2008 by a 5.2-point margin, that both of Georgia's current U.S.

senators are Republicans, that the U.S. House delegation contains a Republican majority, that the governor is a Republican, and that there are Republican majorities of 36–20 and 103–77 in the state senate and House respectively, all suggest that a Republican "breakthrough" has occurred.[3] On the other hand, this breakthrough did not occur in full until thirty to forty years later, which suggests that the transition to a majority in the state was not as straightforward as many Republicans had hoped. From 1963 to 2000, Republicans won only three of twelve contests for U.S. Senate, they did not manage to capture more than two U.S. House seats from Georgia until 1992, and not until the twenty-first century did Republicans win a majority in either a gubernatorial contest or a chamber of the General Assembly.

The discrepancy between the widespread predictions of an imminent Republican majority and the delay in the actual appearance of that majority is one of the most intriguing aspects of postwar politics in Georgia and most other southern states. This discrepancy does not fit well with the prevailing "white backlash" narrative of the rise of southern Republicanism. This narrative suggests that the key to GOP growth in the South was the party's ability to capture disaffected white voters who had once been staunch Democrats but who—after 1964 in particular—felt betrayed by the party's support for civil rights and cultural liberalism.[4] If the central dynamic in this process was indeed a white backlash, then it is reasonable to ask why it took so long to work.

One way to answer is to downgrade white backlash from its leading role to that of a supporting actor. Although anger at both civil rights and cultural liberalism were often present, in the end neither was as significant as the less dramatic growth of the state's suburban population. Ultimately, it was the ability of the GOP to position itself as advocating the political interests of the suburbs that was critical. While suburban voters were by no means always immune to the appeals of racial or cultural traditionalism, as a whole they were not as interested in focusing on these issues as the rural and small-town voters who had given overwhelming support to the preservation of Jim Crow in the 1950s and 1960s. Rather, suburban residents were generally more interested in a political agenda that prioritized economic growth, low taxes, and what they deemed to be their "property rights" (and property values). Winning support from these voters meant adopting what the historian Matthew Lassiter has called "suburban strategies" that stressed economic prosperity and racial moderation, rather than the "southern strategy" of appealing to the white backlash.[5] Indeed, a too-zealous pursuit of the white backlash was one of the main reasons that building a majority took such a long time. While embracing the southern strategy could, in certain cases, be effective, it also carried with it the risk of systemic electoral failure, such as the regionwide disappointment suffered by Republican candidates who tried it in 1970.[6]

Choosing whether to campaign on a suburban or a southern strategy turned out to be the central dilemma that the Georgia Republican Party faced in the postwar years. How to respond to civil rights, how much to focus on anticommunism, on evangelical voters, on elections at the state, congressional, or presidential level—all tactical issues were framed by this overarching choice. Changes in terms of the nature of party competition in the South and the salience of particular political issues in a given campaign also played a large part in determining the possibilities for either of these two strategies at any given moment.

The Fulton County Republicans unquestionably intended *Operation Breakthrough* to be a "battle plan" for continuing the suburban strategy developed in the 1950s. This strategy involved promoting a "progressive conservatism" that stressed "free enterprise," individual rights, smaller government, reaching out to women, and not indulging in the "backwards" politics of massive resistance. In fact, appeals to a racial backlash were generally to be eschewed. The Fulton Republican Planning Committee warned that Georgia must not allow its public schools to be closed as in Arkansas and parts of Louisiana, and pushed for the state party to condemn "most strongly the injection of the struggle for [civil rights] into the area of political expediency." Instead, the GOP should commend those who had sought "with brotherly love for their fellow man" to pursue equal rights through "constitutional means" and welcome "all citizens" into its ranks.[7] This stance on civil rights reflected a combination of principle and calculation central to the suburban strategy. The principle was the belief that a "color-blind" position on race was the most just and in the best interests of the state. The calculation was that high-income suburban voters would have little sympathy for either civil rights activists or militant segregationists. The sincere (if myopic) belief in the meritocratic, racially "innocent" nature of suburban life also informed the worldview of suburban voters and suggested the value of a color-blind approach: a belief in individual merit regardless of race while avoiding any commitment to using government to adopt race-conscious policies to address structural racism.[8]

In 1963, the suburban strategists of Fulton County also had a particular incentive: the 1964 Republican presidential nomination of Arizona senator Barry Goldwater. Goldwater's boosters in Georgia hoped to shape a platform for the state GOP more in line with the southern strategy and, in the mid-1960s, it appeared the southern strategists had the upper hand. They recruited to their ranks several former Democratic Party leaders who had opposed accommodating racial change. In 1966, one of these former Democrats came within a whisker of becoming the first Republican governor of Georgia since Reconstruction. When a wave of senior Democrats, all racial and cultural conservatives, defected to the GOP in 1968, it also suggested momentum toward a southern strategy. In 1970, however, that momentum was decisively checked by the success of Hal Suit, a candidate who ran on a suburban strategy. Even after 1980, it was not until 2000 that the GOP enjoyed consistent success at all levels of Georgia politics.

This unsettled and uneven ascendancy was both a symptom and a cause of the party's gradual progress to majority status in Georgia. On the one hand, it reflected instability caused by the transition from one- to two-party politics as well as the Georgia Democratic Party's ability to successfully adapt to the post–Jim Crow landscape: challenges the Republicans simply could not have avoided. On the other, the inability to present a coherent message at the state level and the political infighting this caused also damaged party prospects. In particular, it contributed to a near electoral collapse in the ten years after 1964 that slowed overall Republican growth. Amidst all this, the only constant was suburban support. From the 1950s to the 1990s, GOP success was first and foremost reliant on majorities in the suburbs. On several occasions, suburban support was sufficient for Republicans to win even while losing the rest of the state. As a result, the best way to understand GOP growth in postwar Georgia is to see it as primarily the result of suburban expansion. The best way to understand the slow pace is to see it as the inability of the party after 1964 to realize that its best prospects lay in resisting the temptations of the southern strategy.

### Early Inroads: The Suburban Strategy in the 1950s

No Republican candidate came close to winning a statewide or congressional election in Georgia from World War II until 1964. By 1960, there were still only three Republicans in the entire General Assembly, all from a cluster of Appalachian counties that contained legacies of "mountain Republicanism."[9] Thomas E. Dewey had received only 30 percent of the vote in Fulton County in 1948.[10] Republicans had received even lower scores before World War II with the lack of any kind of agenda and a sense of amateurism.

Nonetheless, 1948 was still the base on which the party would build. Dewey's strength was centered on the north Georgia mountains and Atlanta,[11] and he had done best in counties with high median incomes, above-average levels of education (for the state), and the largest rates of absolute growth in population since 1940.[12] It is also worth noting that there was little to no connection between Dewey's support and that for J. Strom Thurmond, only a statistically insignificant 0.15.[13] These features all suggested that the best prospects for Republican growth lay among the more prosperous and educated voters in the growing urban and suburban parts of the state as well as the heavily white mountain areas north of Atlanta. The 1952 presidential election confirmed this impression. Overall, Dwight Eisenhower raised the Republican share of the vote to 30.3 percent, with fully three-quarters of the votes coming from urban, suburban, and northern counties—not winning over Thurmond supporters.[14]

Although Eisenhower had improved on Dewey's performance by 158 percent, the range of structural and tactical problems remained daunting. Urban and suburban voters seemed willing to vote GOP in presidential contests in significant numbers (Eisenhower won 39.9 percent of their support in 1952), but Georgia's heavily malapportioned election mechanism, the county unit system, allocated electoral power on a per-county rather than a per-capita basis, vastly inflating the political influence of small, sparsely populated rural counties where Republicans were all but nonexistent.[15] Additionally, Republicans had to deal with a state political machine that was operated entirely by and in the interests of the Georgia Democratic Party—a machine that was quite willing to bend and break rules to maintain one-party hegemony.[16]

State Republican leaders in the 1950s—almost to a man young, white professionals from Atlanta and its suburbs—objected to both the liberalism of the national Democratic leadership and what they saw as the reactionary rural politics of the state Democrats. As such, they had to carve out a political position that looked two ways: more conservative than Democratic presidential candidate Adlai Stevenson, and more progressive than Georgia governor Herman Talmadge. The simultaneous desire of Republican leaders not to take part in a Dutch auction on preserving segregation with master race-baiters such as Talmadge, yet also not wanting to be tagged as "black Republicans" supporting civil rights, presented the party with a further challenge.

These various considerations manifested themselves in the first significant postwar effort to challenge the Democrats' monopoly of the Georgia congressional delegation. In 1954, the Republicans decided to take on James Davis, the four-term U.S. representative from the Fifth District, which was made up of Fulton, DeKalb, and Rockdale counties, encompassing all of metropolitan Atlanta and many of its suburbs. It had given Eisenhower over 40 percent support in 1952 and had provided him with more than a quarter of his state-wide votes. Davis presented an ideal target, as he was a reactionary Democrat in a district that was widely believed to contain the most progressive voters in the state. The Republicans nominated Charlie Moye as their candidate, an Atlanta-based attorney who was chair of the party in DeKalb County.[17] In

1954, Moye pursued a suburban strategy to try to unseat Davis, stressing his support for Ike's economic policies and positioning himself as the candidate of business-friendly prosperity.[18] Reflecting the delicate ideological balancing act that the situation in 1950s Georgia required, Moye's campaign both praised Eisenhower for having halted the slide toward "socialism" favored by the national Democratic Party, while also criticizing Davis as being too reactionary, pointing to Davis's opposition to Social Security and the United Nations.[19] Moye also framed his stance as forward-looking on a two-party system in Georgia and the need to end county unit voting, carving out a position that hewed closely to the principles of color-blindness—simultaneously distancing himself from massive resistance while not openly supporting civil rights.

Moye spoke out against a proposed constitutional amendment that would allow Georgia to close its public schools rather than desegregate them due to be voted on in a statewide referendum and clearly intended to thwart the *Brown* decision. His opposition was not because the amendment maintained segregation but rather because relying on a private-school system was class-based. It would prevent the son of "a janitor" from attending school with the "son of a corporation president"—an example of the color-blind rhetoric of the suburban strategy: based on individual merit, not race.[20] The Fifth District voted against the amendment by 58.2 to 41.4 percent even as the measure carried the state by 53.7 to 46.3 percent.[21]

On election day, Moye lost out to Davis 64 to 36 percent, some four points below what Eisenhower had managed in 1952. But state Republican leaders stepped up the emphasis on rejecting massive resistance to civil rights in Randolph Thrower's 1956 challenge to Davis. Like Moye, Thrower linked himself closely to Eisenhower, attacked the county unit system, called for two-party politics, and cast Davis as an extremist.[22] He also resisted Davis's characterization of his Democratic supporters as renegades.[23] Like Moye, Thrower wanted to be seen as the rational moderate between liberal national Democrats and reactionary local Democrats.

Thrower also pursued a more direct attack on Davis as someone who stirred up racial resentments, declaring that "not for one hundred thousand votes will I become a peddler of hatred and rancor and bitterness."[24] Although Davis prevailed for a second time against Republican opposition, Thrower polled nearly 59,000 votes—1,700 more votes than President Eisenhower received in the Fifth District that same day.[25]

The campaigns by Moye and Thrower were the most high-profile efforts launched by the Georgia Republican Party in the 1950s and the best available measure of the "public message" the party wanted to present. As with the congressional campaigns, the statewide leadership sought to tie itself ideologically to the Eisenhower administration on economic matters. On civil rights, the state party echoed Moye and Thrower's approach: denounce massive-resistance rhetoric, but avoid any commitment to desegregation. Accordingly, Bill Shartzer, the Republican state chairman for much of the 1950s, welcomed the very mild endorsement of *Brown* in the 1956 Republican platform as "thoughtful" and acceptable to all but the most die-hard "extremists" on either side, a desire to position the party between local and national Demcrats.[26]

By 1960, the suburban strategy was well established as the preferred strategy of the state party organization. Although no breakthrough victory had yet occurred, Georgia's Republicans could nonetheless look back on a decade that had witnessed sustained gains in presidential elections: from 18.9 percent in 1948 the Republican ticket improved to 30.3 percent in 1952, 33.7 percent in 1956, and 37.9 percent in 1960. Nearly two hundred thousand more Georgians were willing to vote for Nixon in 1960 than had voted for Dewey in 1948. Of those two hundred thousand new Republicans, more than 60 percent were from the fifteen counties that contained the state's most populous urban and suburban areas where Nixon polled 47.6 percent overall, and had carried Savannah, Augusta, and Columbus, three of the six largest cities in the state.[27] By contrast, south Georgia and the Black Belt—the heart of resistance to ending Jim Crow—contributed just over 20 percent of the new GOP voters and had given Nixon only 26.8 percent support in 1960. In short, even with massive resistance to desegregation at its zenith, a business-friendly, color-blind Republicanism was gaining strength in Georgia during the 1950s, and was doing so most rapidly among urban and suburban voters.

## The Lure of the Backlash

During the 1950s, Georgia Republicans had little choice but to position the party as a moderate intermediary between New Deal liberalism and massive resistance, constrained by meager resources to focusing on their footholds in the cities, suburbs, and the Appalachian Mountains. In the 1960s, they faced the opposite problem—too many choices. Growing disaffection with the national Democratic Party among rural white voters and the possibility of Barry Goldwater winning the 1964 Republican nomination as an opponent of federal civil rights laws both suggested that there was a substantial number of racially and culturally conservative voters who could be won over to the GOP through a southern strategy. Conversely, the continued growth of the suburbs, the ending of massive resistance and the county unit system, the rise of more moderate "New South" Democrats within the state party who could compete for suburban white support, and the expected need for Republicans to continue winning some significant portion of the black vote all suggested that a "suburban strategy" might continue to be effective.

In the 1960 presidential election, black Republican leaders John H. Calhoun and John Wesley Dobbs had been influential enough to help Richard Nixon secure a majority of the black vote in Atlanta, despite the personal intervention of John Kennedy in the effort to get Martin Luther King Jr. released from jail.[28] In 1962, however, James Davis was defeated in the Democratic primary by Charles L. Weltner, a New South Democrat who would be the only congressman from the Deep South to vote for the 1964 Civil Rights Act. With Weltner likely to appeal to black voters also, Republican candidate James O'Callaghan faced a difficult decision. In the end, both candidates focused on a more classically liberal-conservative axis, with deep cuts in New Deal and New Frontier programs, and big government and higher taxes.

Weltner eventually prevailed by nearly 2 to 1—a margin that was depressingly comfortable. That the loss had come about without the GOP making civil rights a major issue provided ammunition to those favoring a southern strategy, particularly as the black vote had ultimately gone heavily for Weltner. The disappointment of state chairman Jack Dorsey, a suburban-strategy advocate, over this loss of black support was palpable. He predicted that black voters would return to the GOP in due course. After all, Dorsey claimed, the Republican Party has always "done more to promote [black] rights than the Georgia Democratic Party."[29] Whether or not this actually reflected a sincere desire to work for racial justice, both Dorsey's statements and the rhetoric of *Operation Breakthrough* about not exploiting racial divisions showed what would happen if the Republicans became seen as actively hostile to black interests.

By contrast, appearing hostile to black interests was a risk supporters of a southern strategy were quite willing—even eager—to take. By 1964, the momentum had also clearly shifted in their favor. Dorsey was replaced as state chairman by Joe Tribble, a Goldwater supporter, one of the clearest signs of the transition away from the priorities of the 1950s leadership. Another was the party switch of prominent businessman Howard "Bo" Callaway. An enthusiastic supporter of Goldwater, Callaway became a Republican in 1964 and that November became the first Georgia Republican elected to Congress since the nineteenth century. Further evidence of the shifting balance of power in the state party came in the way Goldwater supporters sought to marginalize the "Old Guard," particularly Atlanta alderman Rodney Mims Cook, a leader of the Fulton County Republicans.[30]

Despite Cook's concerns, 1964 turned out to be a banner year for the southern strategy in Georgia. Goldwater became the first post-Reconstruction

Republican to win the state, improving seventeen percentage points on Nixon's 1960 vote, and carrying south Georgia and the Black Belt—the two regions of the state with the fewest Republican roots—by more than 60 percent each. In what was seen as a further vindication of the value of the southern strategy, Goldwater won in traditional Democratic strongholds while also expanding Republican support in urban and suburban Georgia from 47.6 percent to 54.1 percent. Only in north Georgia did LBJ prevail, and even there, the Republican vote had jumped by thirteen percentage points.[31] In addition, Callaway's victory in the Third District along with an increase in representation in both houses of the General Assembly only seemed like further proof of the southern strategy's potential.[32]

In 1966, Georgia Republicans hoped to parlay their breakthrough in the coalition that had supported Goldwater two years earlier.[33] For a while, things went according to plan for gubernatorial aspirant Callaway. With neither former-governors Ernest Vandiver nor Herman Talmadge in the race, it seemed the likely Democratic nominee would be another former governor, Ellis G. Arnall, perhaps the most high-profile white liberal in Georgia and a vocal supporter of the national Democratic Party. It would have been hard to find someone southern strategists in the Georgia Republican Party would rather have run against than Arnall. Accordingly, Callaway's campaign planned to emphasize their candidate's conservative credentials: a record of near total opposition to the Great Society and civil rights laws. During the summer of 1966, Callaway stressed his support for "states' rights," his hostility to federal welfare programs, and the need for two-party politics in Georgia, thereby laying the groundwork for running against Arnall on a southern strategy.[34] Unfortunately for Callaway, events then took an unexpected turn. Arnall was defeated in the Democratic runoff by arch-segregationist Lester Maddox. Suddenly, almost by default, Callaway found himself as the less racially conservative candidate and it was no longer clear that sticking to the southern strategy made sense.[35]

Despite this, Callaway showed little interest in moving back to a suburban strategy. He gave a speech scathingly critical of outgoing governor Carl E. Sanders, angering many of his white moderate supporters without producing any political gain.[36] Aside from no longer calling himself a segregationist, Callaway also made no real effort to appeal to black voters.[37] In the end, Callaway was able to eke out a narrow plurality over Maddox, but the election was ultimately decided by the overwhelmingly Democratic General Assembly, which duly elected Maddox. The election results contained ambiguous lessons for the GOP. Having set out to capture the support of rural and small-town white conservatives through a southern strategy, Callaway saw Republican support in those areas plummet while it rose sharply in the more tradition-ally pro-Republican cities and suburbs.[38] This might have been interpreted as evidence that it was a mistake for Callaway not to utilize a suburban strategy. On the other hand, Callaway had become the first Republican to outpoll his Democratic opponent in a gubernatorial contest and his conservative, anti–civil rights image had still won a record level of urban and suburban support for the GOP. This way the Maddox candidacy could be interpreted as simply a *force majeure* that would not be repeated: against any other Democrat, Cal-laway's approach would have prevailed.

Over the next few years, there were signs that Callaway's defeat had not lessened the appeal of the southern strategy for Georgia Republicans. Fletcher Thompson and Ben Blackburn both won their congressional races in 1966 and were successfully reelected two years later. Also in 1968, following a bitter dispute over the seating of the Georgia delegation at the Democratic National Convention, five conservative Georgia Democrats switched to the GOP. All five had held significant statewide office and were recognized as powerful political figures, none more so than Comptroller General James L. "Jimmy" Bentley, who would seek the Republican nomination for governor by deploy-ing the southern strategy. And yet, there were also clear signs that the core of the party's strength was still in the suburbs and that rural and small-town white voters were a volatile political group who remained ambivalent toward the GOP. In the 1968 presidential election, arch-segregationist George Wal-lace carried the state and reduced the Republican vote to 30.4 percent (what it had been in 1952). Overall, the regional and demographic breakdown of the 1952 and 1968 Republican vote was also close to identical (see figures 1 and 2). In fact, Nixon actually did *worse* in south Georgia and the Black Belt in 1968 than Eisenhower had sixteen years earlier. The 1968 General Assem-bly elections provided further evidence of the suburban nature of the party's base. Seven Republicans were elected to the state senate and twenty-eight to the state House. All but one of them came from just six counties—all with substantial suburban populations. The most Republican county in 1968 was DeKalb, which consisted of parts of metro Atlanta and its eastern suburbs. Only one of four counties in which Nixon polled over half the votes, it had a 3–2 GOP edge in its state senate representation and a 7–7 tie in its delegation to the Georgia House. In sum, the 1960s had seen the GOP make several ef-forts to secure the support of backlash voters with varying degrees of success. And yet, despite the apparent momentum, underneath the surface the party's suburban base that had been established in the 1950s remained its electoral stronghold.

Figure 1:

Support for Republican Presidential Ticket in Georgia by county demographic, 1952 and 1968

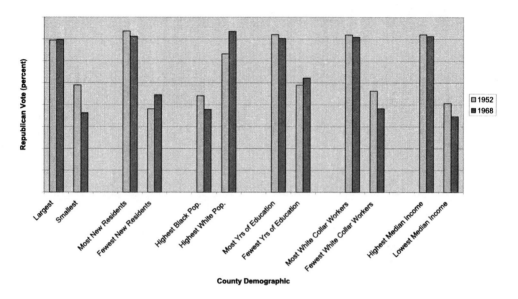

Figure 2:

Support for Republican presidential tickete in Georgia by region, 1952 and 1968

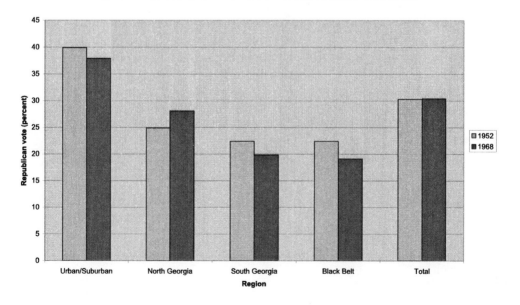

**Figure 3:**

**Republican Vote in Georgia by Region, 1980-1996**

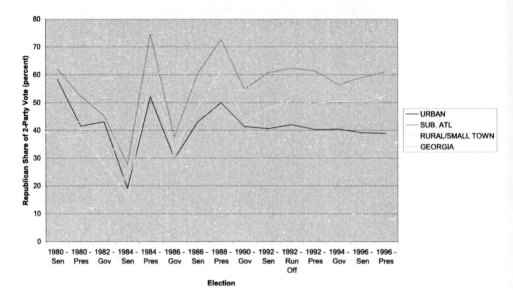

**Figure 4:**

**Net Republican Vote in Georgia, 1980-1996**

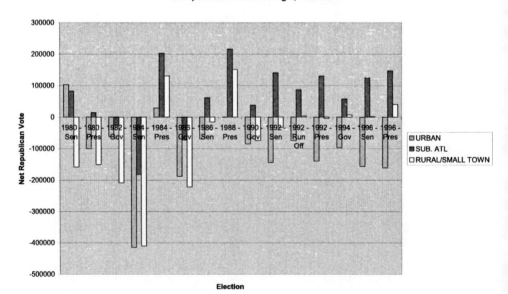

## Adjusting to Sunbelt Politics

For the first time in its history, in 1970 the Georgia Republican Party held a statewide primary to nominate a gubernatorial candidate. Many Republican leaders and the media assumed that the party rank-and-file were of the same mind as the southern strategists who had gained the upper hand during the 1960s. Jimmy Bentley intended to follow in Bo Callaway's footsteps as a former Democrat seeking the state House as a Republican. A seasoned veteran with strongly conservative credentials, Bentley was considered likely to prevail over his opponent, Hal Suit, a TV journalist from Atlanta making his first run for public office.[39]

Bentley's campaign for the nomination was southern strategy, emphasizing opposition to any government-sponsored policies to bring about school desegregation—busing in particular. Bentley's TV ads on busing were so obvious that the *Atlanta Constitution* sarcastically reassured the candidate "don't worry, Jimmy"—even though the word "race" was never used in the ad, "all good white folks know exactly what you mean[t]."[40] Bentley also expressed his support for the "freedom of choice" plans that were designed as thinly veiled attempts to sidestep integrated schools.[41] Finally, Bentley was not shy of stressing cultural traditionalism.[42] He publicly wondered whether the choice of April 22 as "Earth Day" was evidence that the environmental movement was pro-communist, as that date was also Lenin's birthday.[43]

Suit responded to Bentley's ruminations on Earth Day by asking, "oh my gosh, how far out can you get?"[44] Just as Bentley embodied the southern strategy, so Suit embodied the suburban strategy. Throughout the campaign, Suit sought to minimize the impact of racial and cultural issues, and suggested that those using them were appealing to extremists. Early in the year, Suit described himself as "conservative—but liberal on the race issue."[45] While he never championed school integration as morally desirable, he refused to endorse any attempts to subvert it through school boycotts or closures.[46] In addition, while Suit took generally conservative positions on most economic questions, he did not have traditionalist views on the "red button" cultural issues that were a corollary of the southern strategy. Suit favored legalized gambling and gun control, and opposed the death penalty. He even had to deny that his lack of church membership made him an atheist.[47] The Bentley-Suit race also revolved around tension within the Georgia Republican Party: the extent of the national party's influence. While Bentley picked up the endorsement of Bo Callaway, many in the state party, including southern strategists, chafed at what they perceived as an attempt by the national party to impose a candidate on them. U.S. representative Fletcher Thompson and G. Paul Jones, who had chaired the state party from 1965 to 1969, were both partial to the southern strategy, but both backed Suit in 1970 over what they saw as excessive meddling in state affairs by the national GOP.[48]

Suit scored a resounding triumph, outpolling Bentley by 61 to 39 percent and highlighting the continuing centrality of Atlanta and its suburbs to Georgia Republicanism. Suit received more votes in Fulton, DeKalb, and Cobb counties than Bentley did in the state as a whole. In fact, Suit would have trailed Bentley had the contest been held without these three counties. As it was, Fulton, DeKalb, and Cobb enabled Suit to win a landslide victory.[49] It was above all a sign of the skepticism much of the Republican electorate in the suburbs felt toward the southern strategy.

In the general election against Jimmy Carter, Suit was able to poll just 41 percent despite winning 58 percent support from suburban Atlanta, and 51.2 percent support from urban and suburban counties statewide.[50] The suburbs were still clearly the most reliably Republican parts of the state, and had shown in the GOP primary that they were hesitant to embrace too overt a southern strategy. Nonetheless, pursuing the suburban strategy had resulted in another dispiriting defeat. The new concern was personified by Carter: the rise of the "New South Democrat." All across the South, Democrats who stressed racial moderation and economic progress had shown in 1970 that they were a formidable electoral force. Within Georgia, Carter and other New South Democrats consolidated their hold on the state party with remarkable rapidity during the 1970s and nominated a succession of candidates who campaigned on this message.

For the remainder of the decade, Georgia's Republicans seemed unable to decide which strategy to pursue against them. Following Suit's defeat, the party nominated southern strategists in the next two major statewide contests. In 1972, Fletcher Thompson ran for the U.S. Senate on massive resistance and a car blaring out "Dixie."[51] Thompson repeatedly attacked attempts to integrate housing and called for a statewide boycott of the public schools[52] Despite this message, greater name recognition, and more money, Thompson still lost to Democrat Sam Nunn, who portrayed the Republican as exploiting racial fears.[53] While Thompson improved on Suit's statewide showing and boosted the Republican vote in small towns and rural counties, he actually underperformed Suit by 3 percent in Atlanta's suburbs.

In 1974, Republicans nominated Ronnie Thompson, the mayor of Macon, to run for governor. Thompson deployed an even more overt southern strategy to tag Democratic candidate George Busbee as the "black candidate" by repeatedly invoking Busbee's connections to high-profile black legislator

Julian Bond.[54] Busbee won in a landslide—trouncing Thompson by 69 to 31 percent. Even in suburban Atlanta, the Republican vote was down to 37 percent: in urban and suburban areas across the state, it was down to 30.4 percent, nearly ten points below what Ike had in 1952.[55] In 1978, the Republicans reverted to a suburban strategist, Rodney Mims Cook, as their gubernatorial candidate, but Cook fared even worse than either Thompson, losing to Busbee 80.6 to 19.4 percent. Overall, the Republican Party seemed in danger of becoming irrelevant in state politics. In 1972 and 1974, the GOP had lost control of the Fourth and Fifth Districts, leaving it with zero congressional delegates (in 1978, Newt Gingrich put the Republicans back on the board by winning an open congressional seat). Neither suburban nor southern strategies seemed capable of providing consistent success.

## 1980 and Beyond

Just as the Republican optimism of the 1960s had eventually been tempered, so the Republican despondency of the 1970s did not last. Beginning in 1980 with the defeat of four-term U.S. senator Herman Talmadge, the GOP restored itself to competitiveness. For the next decade, there still remained a good deal of volatility in the Republican performance at various electoral levels, but by the mid-1990s a more stable pattern of support was established. Throughout, the one constant was the dependence of the party on suburban voters. The backlash vote that had gone to Thurmond, Goldwater, and Wallace remained a secondary factor.

The 1980 election set the tone for the next twenty years. The results from the contest between Mack Mattingly and Herman Talmadge for the U.S. Senate and the presidential race in Georgia between Jimmy Carter and Ronald Reagan showcased the key partisan divisions in the state. Mattingly was able to defeat Talmadge in 1980 only because of the overwhelming support he received from urban and suburban Georgians. Talmadge's lead in rural and small-town Georgia was close to 160,000 votes.[56] Reagan was not able to carry the state against Carter, but he also ran strongest in Atlanta's suburbs, outpolling Carter there by 52.3 to 47.7 percent. Over the next several elections, Republican candidates consistently won suburban Atlanta while Democrats consolidated their strength among urban voters.[57] Rural and small-town voters swung. Republicans generally did better in rural and small-town counties with small black populations, but never as well as they did in the suburbs. Democrats ran strongly in rural and small-town counties with higher black populations, but generally not as well as in urban areas. In each case, the implication is clear. The Republican Party in Georgia was a suburban party. While Republican candidates could win majorities in other parts of the state, they could not win without majorities in Atlanta's suburbs. In fact, on several occasions, Republicans won *only* because of majorities in Atlanta's suburbs. Fulton County's Republicans of 1963 had been vindicated: the same suburban parts of the state that had been the base of the party in the 1950s had, by the 1990s, provided the GOP with the necessary platform to dominate the state's politics in the early twenty-first century. As tempting an opportunity as the southern strategy had appeared to be in the 1960s and 1970s, in the end, the voters it was intended to attract remained consistently more reluctant to commit to the GOP than did those in the high-income, highly educated suburban communities that built postwar Republicanism in Georgia.

## Notes

1. Fulton County Republicans, "Operation Breakthrough" (1963), "Fulton County Republicans—Operation Breakthrough," Box 14, Rodney M. Cook Papers, Richard Russell Library, University of Georgia, Athens (hereafter RRL).

2. In 1960, Georgia gave Kennedy 62.5 percent of the vote, exceeded only by Rhode Island (Alice M. McGillivray, Richard M. Scammon, and Rhodes L. Cook, *America at the Polls, 1960–2004: A Handbook of Presidential Election Statistics* [Washington, D.C.: Congressional Quarterly Press, 2005], 25). Since 1960, Georgia has failed to vote Republican in presidential elections in 1968, when it voted for George Wallace; in 1976 and 1980, when it voted for Jimmy Carter; and in 1992, when it voted for Bill Clinton.

3. Election returns for 2008 listed on the Web site of the Georgia secretary of state, http://sos.georgia.gov/elections/election_results/2008_1104/Default.htm.

4. The "white backlash" narrative has existed for at least forty years and has dominated the scholarly discussion of southern politics in that time and produced much excellent scholarship. Among the most significant works that emphasize the "white backlash" are Kevin Phillips, *The Emerging Republican Majority* (New Rochelle, N.Y.: Arlington House, 1969); Thomas D. and Mary Edsall, *Chain Reaction: The Impact of Race, Rights, and Taxes on American Politics* (New York: Norton, 1991); Earl and Merle Black, *The Rise of Southern Republicans* (Cambridge: Belknap Press of Harvard University Press, 2002); Glenn Feldman, ed., *Before Brown: Civil Rights and the White Backlash in the Modern South* (Tuscaloosa: University of Alabama Press, 2004); Kevin Kruse, *White Flight: Atlanta and the Making of Modern Conservatism* (Princeton: Princeton University Press, 2005); and Thomas D. Schaller, *Whistling Past Dixie: How the Democrats Can Win without the South* (New York: Simon and Schuster, 2006). Two significant recent challenges to this narrative are Byron Shafer and Richard Johnston, *The End of Southern Exceptionalism: Class, Race and Partisan Change in the Postwar South* (Cambridge: Harvard University Press, 2006); and Matthew D. Lassiter, *The Silent Majority: Suburban Politics in the Sunbelt South* (Princeton: Princeton University Press, 2006).

5. Lassiter, *Silent Majority*, 225–26; Lassiter "The Suburban Origins of Colorblind Conservatism: Middle-Class Consciousness in the Charlotte Busing Crisis," *Journal of Urban History* 30, no. 4 (2004): 549–82.

6. Lassiter, *Silent Majority*, 251–75.

7. Memo from the Fulton County Republican Planning Committee, January 1961, and Recommendations of the Planning Committee on the Public Schools, 1961–62, "Planning Committee, 1961–63"; "Operation Breakthrough"; Proposed Resolution for the Georgia Republican Party, 12 July 1963, "Planning Committee, 1963," Box 14, *Cook Papers*.

8. Lassiter, *Silent Majority*, 1.

9. The roots of Appalachian Republicanism are discussed in Gordon B. McKinney, *Southern Mountain Republicanism, 1865–1900: Politics and the Appalachian Community* (Knoxville: University of Tennessee Press, 1998). See also V. O. Key Jr., *Southern Politics in State and Nation* (Knoxville: Knopf, 1949), 33–34, 75–81, 218–23.

10. Fulton County Republicans, "Operation Breakthrough." For the official figures, see Richard M. Scammon, *America at the Polls, 1920–1956: A Handbook of Presidential Election Statistics* (Washington D.C.: Congressional Quarterly Press, 2005), 158–60.

11. The ten Georgia counties in which Dewey did best formed a contiguous bloc from the northern mountains to Atlanta (see Scammon, *America at the Polls, 1920–1956*, 158–60).

12. Calculations for the 1948 election are based on the returns listed in Scammon, *America at the Polls, 1920–1956*, 158–60 and cross-referenced with census data taken from the *Sixteenth Census of the United States: 1940*, vol. 2, *Characteristics of the Population*, pt. 2, Florida to Iowa (Washington D.C., 1943), Georgia table 21, pp. 216–25; and the *U.S. Census of Population: 1950*, vol. 2, *Characteristics of the Population*, pt. 2, Georgia (Washington, D.C., 1952), table 5, pp. 9–11 and table 12, pp. 37–38.

13. Ibid.

14. The correlation between Eisenhower's support in 1952 and Thurmond's in 1948 remained a weak 0.15, while the correlation between the two Republicans at the county level was a strongly significant 0.62. See note 12 for the calculations for the 1952 presidential election. Descriptions "urban and suburban" and "northern" are taken from Numan Bartley's *From Thurmond to Wallace: Political Tendencies in Georgia, 1948–1968* (Baltimore: Johns Hopkins University Press, 1970), 13–19.

15. The county unit system was based on allocating a certain number of "units" to each county depending on its size. Of Georgia's 159 counties, the 8 largest were given six unit votes each; the next 30 in terms of population were given four unit votes, and the remaining 121 counties had two unit votes each. To win any statewide contest required 206 unit votes—which could be achieved without any support from the 8 counties that included nearly one-third of the population by 1940 (see Key, *Southern Politics*, 117–24).

16. "GOP's King Is Ruled off District 7 House Ballot," *Atlanta Constitution*, 21 September 1956; "GOPs Ruled off DeKalb," *Atlanta Constitution*, 28 September 1956; "School Post Okay Denied Towns GOP," *Atlanta Constitution*, 5 December 1956.

17. "Moye, LeCraw Petitions Are Circulated," *Atlanta Constitution*, 26 August 1954.

18. "GOPs Say 5th District to Elect Moye," *Atlanta Constitution*, 9 October 1954.

19. Charlie Yates to Judge Gunby, 12 October 1954, Box 12, "1954 Campaign: Strategy (General Election)," Davis Papers; Copy of letter from Moye campaign organizer Randolph Thrower and unsigned memo to James C. Davis, 28 October 1954, Box 12, "1954 Campaign: Strategy (General Election)," Davis Papers.

20. "GOP's Moye Opposes Amendment," *Atlanta Constitution*, 16 October 1954.

21. Results for the 1954 amendment are based on the returns listed in the *Georgia Official Register, 1953–54* (Atlanta: Georgia Department of Archives and History, 1954), 688–92.

22. "5th & 7th District GOPs Qualify for House Races," *Atlanta Constitution*, 20 September 1956; "Thrower Gains Support from 9 More Democrats," *Atlanta Constitution*, 19 October 1956.

23. "Thrower Hits Left-Wing Jab," *Atlanta Constitution*, 23 October 1956.

24. Handwritten Notes of Speech by Thrower Given in Avondale, Georgia, 29 October 1956, Box 13, "1956 Campaign: Strategy (Primary)," Davis Papers.

25. Scammon, *America at the Polls, 1920–1956*, 152–54.

26. Ralph McGill, "Rights Plank Pleasing," *Atlanta Constitution*, 21 August 1956; "GOPs Woo Georgia's Democrats," *Atlanta Constitution*, 23 October 1958.

27. Figures for 1960 taken from Scammon et al., *America at the Polls, 1960–2004*, 247–49.

28. Numan V. Bartley, *The New South, 1945–1980* (Baton Rouge: Louisiana State University Press, 1995), 238–39.

29. "The Militant Mood of the Georgia Republicans," clipping from *Atlanta Magazine*, February 1963, Box 14, "Militant Mood of the Georgia Republicans," Cook Papers.

30. Rodney M. Cook to John Stokes, June 26, 1964, "Planning Committee, Fulton County, 1961–63," Box 14, Cook Papers.

31. Figures for the 1964 election are taken from the *Georgia Official Register, 1963–1964* (Atlanta: Department of History & Archives, 1964), 1500–1505.

32. Robert Sherrill, "Nixon's Man in Dixie," *New York Times Magazine: Campaign 1968*, clipping, "Politics, Georgia, Callaway, Bo," Box 3, *New York Times Research Collection*, RRL.

33. Harold P. Henderson, "The 1966 Gubernatorial Election in Georgia" (Ph.D. diss., University of Southern Mississippi, 1982), 7. The structure and strategy of the Callaway campaign is also discussed on 220–21.

34. Henderson, "The 1966 Election," 192–96.

35. Ibid., 196–98, 211.

36. Ibid., 223–25.

37. Ibid., 223.

38. All calculations for the 1966 general election, and comparisons with the 1964 presidential election in Georgia are taken from voting returns listed in, respectively, the *Georgia Official and Statistical Register, 1965–66*, 1786–88; and Scammon et al.,

*America at the Polls, 1960–2004,* 244–46. The demographics come from the *Census of Population: 1970,* vol. 1: *Characteristics of the Population,* pt. 12, Georgia (Washington D.C., 1973), table 16, pp. 53–54, table 43, pp. 232–33, and table 44, pp. 234–35.

39. Steve Ball Jr., "Survey Shows Bentley Holds Lead over Suit," *Atlanta Constitution,* 26 April 1970.

40. Bill Shipp, "Bentley v. Bus," *Atlanta Constitution,* 18 August 1970.

41. Gene Stephens, "GOP Hopefuls State Positions on Schools," *Atlanta Constitution,* 28 August 1970; Gene Stephens and Terry Adamson, "Bentley Launches Stop-Busing Drive," *Atlanta Constitution,* 2 September 1970.

42. "Bentley Unveils T.V. Film Telling Why He Switched," *Atlanta Constitution,* 3 March 1970.

43. "Earth Day on Lenin's Birthday," *Atlanta Constitution,* 10 April 1970.

44. Ibid.

45. "Hal Suit May Enter Gubernatorial Race," *Atlanta Constitution,* 6 January 1970.

46. "GOP Hopefuls State Positions on Schools," *Atlanta Constitution,* 28 August 1970.

47. Duane Riner, "Suit Backs 3-Day Wait on Purchase of Guns," *Atlanta Constitution,* 12 August 1970; Duane Riner and Diane Stepp, "Hal Suit Lays Religion Smear to 2 GOPs," *Atlanta Constitution,* 14 August 1970; "Nine Questions for Carter, Suit," *Atlanta Constitution,* 1 November 1970.

48. Bill Shipp, "Bentley Troubled by Own Party," *Atlanta Constitution,* 18 February 1970; Mike Bowler, "Pressure in GOP Charged," *Atlanta Constitution,* 21 March 1970; "G. Paul Jones to Campaign for Hal Suit," *Atlanta Constitution,* 9 August 1970.

49. All calculations for the 1970 Republican primary are taken from the official voting returns by county listed in the Georgia Official and Statistical Register, 1969–70, 1669–71. The demographic information comes from the tables listed in note 38 above.

50. Georgia Official and Statistical Register, 1969–70, 1752–53.

51. Bob Hurt: "Thompson Stresses Busing and Job Quotas," *Atlanta Constitution,* 2 September 1971.

52. Beau Cuff, "Thompson Urges Statewide Boycott," *Atlanta Constitution,* 16 February 1972.

53. Bob Fort, "Nunn-Wallace Visit Fake, Says Thompson in Debate," *Atlanta Constitution,* 30 September 1972.

54. "Ronnie Ups Security," *Atlanta Constitution,* 12 October 1974.

55. All calculations for the 1974 elections are taken from the official voting returns by county listed in the Georgia Official and Statistical Register, 1973–74, 1898–1900.

56. Figures for the 1980 election are taken from the *Georgia Official Register* (Atlanta: Georgia Department of Archives & History), 1832–34.

57. Prior to the 1970s, urban and suburban counties had been treated as a single unit. From then onward, it makes sense to distinguish between the two groups, as with the process of white flight, the former swung heavily Democratic, while the latter remained heavily Republican. Fulton and DeKalb Counties became solidly "blue," while Cobb, Gwinnett, and others around Atlanta became solidly "red."

# 5

# Virginia's Northern Strategy

## Southern Segregationists and the Route to National Conservatism

GEORGE LEWIS

In late July 1962, thirty Republican legislators from Pennsylvania arrived in Williamsburg, Virginia.[1] Among the party were some of the Keystone State's most powerful and influential politicians, including Albert W. Johnson, Republican minority leader in the state House; W. Stuart Helm, chair of the state Republican Party; and state senator Alvin C. Bush. They were met by a number of Virginia's leading political figures, including Governor Albertis S. Harrison Jr., former governor J. Lindsay Almond Jr., and James Jackson Kilpatrick, editor of the *Richmond News Leader*. The presence of so many high-ranking northern Republicans in a city not fifty miles from Richmond, the former Confederate capital, contrasts sharply with the political landscape of the region in 1962. As Earl Black and Merle Black have noted, midway through the twentieth century, the U.S. Congress included no Republican senators and only two Republican representatives from the South.[2] A decade later, of the 106 congressmen the South sent to Washington, only seven were Republicans, and there were still no Republican governors or senators from the region.[3] At the state level, Virginia was still in thrall to the political machine of Harry Flood Byrd Sr., the state's senior senator and a thoroughgoing southern Democrat who had molded his organization into a crystalline image of his own political, fiscal, and racial conservatism. Granted, pockets of watery Republicanism existed in the mountainous southwestern corner of the state, but in 1962 Virginia was still so staunchly Democratic that the greatest challenges to Byrd's political hegemony had come from within his own party.[4]

While grassroots, state-level politics remained steadfastly Democratic, signs of a delicate change in southern voting patterns had begun to surface in presidential politics. Even Byrd had been shaken by Harry S. Truman's decision to run on a strong civil rights plank in 1948, and, starting in 1952, Virginia voted for three successive Republican presidential candidates. In 1952, Byrd settled instead for what became known as his "golden silence" when asked to endorse Democratic front-runners. Political choices between presidential candidates became yet more problematic in 1954 when Chief Justice Earl Warren, an appointee of Dwight D. Eisenhower's Republican administration, oversaw the *Brown v. Board of Education* decision, and in 1957 when Ike used federal troops at Little Rock. Many of the state's white segregationists returned to their previous view that the GOP was the party of Lincoln, abolition, and emancipation.

The Pennsylvania and Virginia delegates who met at Williamsburg in 1962 were representative of state-level party politics, however, and commentators have long held that traditional party loyalties remained firmly entrenched at the state level for far longer than at the presidential level—at least until 1964.[5] Nonetheless, the Pennsylvania Republicans were received warmly by Governor Harrison, who, along with Lieutenant Governor Mills E. Godwin Jr., had run successfully as Byrd's anointed Democratic candidate in the 1961 state elections. The bipartisan nature of the gathering was also clear in the only detailed newspaper report of the Williamsburg meeting of Pennsylvania Republicans and Virginia Democrats.[6]

The links between two such apparently disparate political groups can be explained most clearly by examining their "common problems." A deeper analysis of those issues—and of the political processes that brought the two groups together—reveals much that has remained hidden about southern segregationists and resistance to *Brown*. The Pennsylvania Republicans had not been invited to Williamsburg on a spur-of-the-moment whim; rather, their presence represented a careful process four years in development. Disentangling the motives and machinations behind that process reveals the need for a more nuanced understanding of southern segregationist ideology in the post-*Brown* era, of the very different strategies that existed within the apparently homogeneous segregationist response to the Supreme Court's decision, and, finally, of the ways in which certain elements of that response merged effortlessly into what has been termed the "new conservatism" of the late 1960s and 1970s.

The roots of the alliance that brought the Pennsylvanians to Williamsburg in 1962 were buried in the Byzantine terrain of Virginia's attempts to formulate a response to *Brown*. While a number of states—especially those of the Deep South—chose to follow a path of unyielding, open defiance of federally mandated desegregation, some in the Upper South clung to the possibility of fashioning a legislative rejoinder that would engage, rather than ignore, the Supreme Court's decision. Proponents of such an approach hoped that it would provide a legally tenable answer to *Brown* that would stave off desegregation indefinitely. In Virginia, therefore, Byrd and his close lieutenants searched for solutions that would not brazenly ignore the *Brown* decision but that would nonetheless render it unworkable at a local level. The so-called Gray Commission, chaired by state senator Garland "Peck" Gray, revolved around a euphemistic "freedom of choice" plan that gave local school boards wide discretion regarding the assignment of public-school pupils in an attempt to circumvent meaningful desegregation. By August 1956, Byrd and his governor, Thomas "Bahnse" Stanley, became more confident, and their resistance more strident. Stanley managed to force through the legislature a series of bills and amendments that left pupil placement not in the hands of local school boards but directly in the hands of the governor, who also gained the power to close any school that was threatened with immediate desegregation and subsequently to deny state funding to any school that reopened on an integrated basis. This was neither the carefully choreographed segregationist bluster that would later see George C. Wallace and Ross R. Barnett standing menacingly in schoolhouse doors nor the open violence that characterized Bull Connor's Birmingham and Jim Clark's Selma. Instead, these measures against desegregation resulted from the passage of bills through Virginia's state legislature and the legitimate adoption of changes to the Old Dominion's constitution.[7]

In three separate localities, Front Royal, Charlottesville, and Norfolk, Stanley invoked his newfound powers and closed public schools, the ultimate circumvention of *Brown*. For whites in those communities, the establishment of private academies and state-funded scholarships for students ameliorated the school closures. On January 19, 1959, however, both the Virginia Supreme Court and a three-judge federal court in Norfolk overturned the legal basis of the school-closure measures and brought an end to Stanley's hard-line resistance plans. Although a new committee returned Virginia to the original anti-*Brown* strategy of "freedom of choice" plans, the striking down of Stanley's hard-line resistance has often been taken by historians to signal an end to Virginia's resistance effort.[8] It did not. Instead Byrd and his supporters underwrote a second, parallel strategy. On March 7, 1958, the General Assembly established the Virginia Commission on Constitutional Government (CCG), whose mandate differed expressly and significantly from that of any other resistance organization in the South.

In theory, the CCG was a states'-rights propaganda agency.[9] In reality, its purpose quickly evolved. The commission's chairman, David J. Mays, had long been adamant that southern resistance would fail if the region's segregationists continued to fight the federal government in purely sectional terms. Too many of his segregationist peers, he believed, were focusing exclusively on the need to appeal to fellow southerners for support and thus were achieving little other than preaching to the converted. Mays had long believed that an isolated South would be defeated if the national will supported an end to segregation—a belief that Little Rock only strengthened. As a result, Mays and his lieutenants created two strategic priorities for the CCG: to broaden the base of support for the southern status quo, and to entice northerners to form alliances with southern segregationists. It was the CCG that had established links between Virginia Democrats and the Pennsylvania Republicans and issued the invitation to Williamsburg.

For a number of reasons, historians have largely overlooked the work of the CCG.[10] In recent decades, the African American side of the civil rights struggle has received unprecedented historical attention, adding nuance to the original view of the civil rights movement as a top-down phenomenon that relied on charismatic leaders and national organizations.[11] In stark contrast, with one or two notable exceptions, historians have failed to modify or complicate the original view of the freedom struggle's white segregationist opponents: Orval Faubus at Little Rock in 1957, plumes of smoke pouring from a Freedom Riders' coach in 1961, and, in Virginia, the closure of the state's public schools. Historians have, therefore, yet to bring out the full complexity of the segregationist response to the civil rights movement. Massive resistance has been seen either in simplistic terms as a movement that petered out in the face of civil rights gains or in expressly deterministic terms as a movement that was always bound to fail.[12]

A close analysis of the CCG is therefore essential. Its activities begin to bring out the true resourcefulness of the segregationist response to the civil rights movement and to federal pressure for racial change. More specifically, the commission's activities show that there were concomitant, multilayered approaches in the campaign to resist *Brown*, each with different strategies, agendas, and modi operandi. Beyond the bluster of totemic segregationists such as Wallace and Barnett lay a second strategy, pioneered by those segregationists who were quick to see the limitations and ultimate futility of the first. The second approach was a product of greater realism and objectivity. As a result, it had greater appeal beyond the confines of the South, which in turn imbued it with a far healthier long-term outlook. Under David Mays's guidance, the CCG proved remarkably adept at pinpointing and then publicizing issues that would enable southern segregationists to garner northern support. Indeed, so skillful was the CCG's work that many of its issues reemerged well over a decade later as central tenets of Richard Nixon's "southern strategy." The most notable of these were the primacy of states' rights and limited government, fiscal conservatism, a strong emphasis on law and order, and a play upon white constituents' racial fears that was sufficiently subtle, in most cases, to avoid reference to race altogether.

In many ways, Mays was the ideal candidate to lead the CCG. He was a well-respected member of the Virginia Bar, had close ties to the Byrd machine, and cultivated them as an active member of Richmond's patrician Forum Club, where many of Byrd's closest confidants and protégés met informally. Nevertheless, neither Mays nor his contemporaries viewed him as a member of the machine. That independence allowed him a degree of crucial objective detachment from the excesses of Byrd's regime.[13] Mays was a voice of moderation on successive attempts to formulate Virginia's legislative response to *Brown*. That was not, however, because he was halfhearted in his defense of segregation. Mays was constantly moderated by pragmatism and realism. While Byrd demanded legislative plans that offered total—if technically constitutional—resistance regardless of the consequences, Mays would not support anything that he knew to be legally untenable.[14] Mays tried to modify Stanley's hard-line response to *Brown* but ultimately was unable to change the governor's strategy. As Mays expected, the courts overturned Stanley's plan in January 1959.[15]

That careful, moderated approach infused the work and direction of the CCG from its inception, and Mays steered what he consistently referred to in his diaries as "*my* CCG" away from the more hard-line, extremist polemics of many of his peers and toward a solution to the segregation question that would, he believed, endure.[16] After years of vituperative intemperance, J. J. Kilpatrick of the *Richmond News Leader* came to share Mays's view, and he agreed to serve as head of the CCG's publications department. "We can never win this thing on votes from Southern representatives alone," Kilpatrick realized by 1957. "I am confident that in the end we will win [but] it must be with help from other areas of the country."[17] Reaching out to nonsoutherners became the commission's main aim. Mays and his circle devised a simple strategy: concentrate on matters of sound legal and constitutional principle rather than on details peculiar to the South; remove race from the equation as often as possible, since the issue would only serve to polarize; and disseminate the CCG's ideas and educate potential supporters.[18]

At every conceivable juncture of its campaign to maintain segregation, the CCG remained supremely disciplined in its attempts to transform the peculiarly sectional concerns of southern resistance into matters of broader national principle. In 1960, for example, Mays orchestrated the CCG's official response to the sit-ins that were sweeping across the South. While a succession of the region's coarser segregationist leaders spluttered angrily at the impudence of the sit-in protestors, labeling many of them "outside agitators," communists, and insurrectionists, the CCG chose instead to emphasize the illegality of their protests, that the Fourteenth Amendment had no hold over discrimination on what it described as "private" premises.[19] From Mays's point of view, there was no need to linger on discussions of the moral issues of segregated restaurant facilities; he had the words of a federal district court judge in *Williams v. Howard Johnson's Restaurant* to disseminate and the backing of the U.S. Constitution upon which to rely. The situation would give northern conservatives as much to think about as southern segregationists. Indeed, he was so certain that the CCG pamphlet *Race and the Restaurant* would succeed that he postponed a planned reprint of John C. Calhoun's Fort Hill address of 1831, which famously made the case for states' rights: "This effort of the Negroes is self-defeating since they have now turned from the federal courts to extra—and illegal—actions."[20]

This line of attack could be tailored to many of the white South's most pressing concerns. The CCG did not deride the *Brown* decision in broad-brush strokes as the harbinger of racial cataclysm and societal chaos but held it up as clear, specific evidence that the Supreme Court had exceeded its constitutional authority. During its lifetime, for example, the commission distributed some thirty-seven thousand copies of a booklet tellingly entitled *Democracy and Despotism* and nearly forty thousand of *Did the Court Interpret or Amend?* These were no repeats of Senator James O. Eastland's claims that *Brown* was evidence of a communist-laden Supreme Court; these were entreaties to respect the Tenth Amendment and appeals to the will of the delegates to the Constitutional Convention of 1787, who had insisted upon the separation of federal powers.[21] A later pamphlet, *"State Action" and the 14th Amendment*, even managed to avoid specific mention of *Brown* altogether. Instead, it examined the origins of the Fourteenth Amendment in the discussions surrounding Senator Lyman Trumbull's proposed Civil Rights Act of 1866 and traced the history of the amendment's implementation. In a final section, the pamphlet claimed that the "first breach" occurred with *Smith v. Allwright* in 1944, but that "it was not until 1948 that the original understanding of the Fourteenth Amendment was completely forgotten" in *Shelley v. Kraemer*. "After this," the document concluded, "came the deluge."[22] The commission had fallen upon a formula that depicted the problems facing southern segregation as but one outgrowth of an assault on national constitutional principles.

The commission's other members aided Mays in the production of that material. The CCG's original charter stipulated that it would have fifteen members, plus the governor ex officio. Four were to be appointed by the state senate, three by the state house of delegates, and eight by the governor, who also appointed the chairman and vice chairman. The vast majority of those selected to serve on the commission had legal training, a reflection of the style that Mays wished to impose upon the CCG and of the implicit need to exclude the brash excesses of many of the South's other resistance bodies.[23] Their expertise helped Mays in his attempts to keep the content of the commission's output in sharp focus, and the sheer scale of its publications—and the manner in which they were disseminated—were central to its attempts to win new allies from beyond the segregationists' traditional heartland in the white South. By 1969, the total number of publications printed and distributed by the CCG stood at over 2 million booklets and pamphlets and more than sixteen thousand books. Nor were these mailed randomly. Mays compiled a distribution list that included the state legislators, governors, and chief justices of every state; U.S. congressmen; federal judges, including Supreme Court justices; college, junior college, and city public libraries "throughout the nation"; state libraries, law school libraries, and state law libraries; chambers of commerce in every U.S. city with a population over one hundred thousand; selected daily newspapers throughout the United States; and "Magazines of national circulation." "Where I could get them to do [so]," he wrote, "I have used senators and congressmen as my 'newsboys' to distribute my pamphlets on Civil Rights, because people in Washington are far [more] likely to read them when asked by a legislator."[24] In stark contrast, the focus of Birmingham's Bull Connor and Selma's Jim Clark was never far beyond their own local bailiwicks.

Mays and his fellow commission members were so determined to promote a distinct brand of resistance and to elevate the CCG from the open racism and demagoguery that dogged so much of the white South that they were wary of the slightest association that might tarnish the CCG's standing above the Mason-Dixon Line. In 1961, for example, commission supporters took umbrage at the linking of a CCG pamphlet on communism with the name of the John Birch Society.[25] Even Kilpatrick, perhaps the greatest firebrand of the CCG, referred to the John Birch Society as "a bunch of nuts."[26] He was slightly more restrained when, in July 1962, the chairman of the Lynchburg American Legion's "Americanism Committee" asked for access to the CCG's mailing list to aid in the distribution of Carleton Putnam's racist tract *Race and Reason: A Yankee View*, but Kilpatrick nonetheless remained adamant that the venture should not be allowed to taint the commission's reputation as the CCG had "fought hard to stay absolutely free of the race issue as such. Our concern is constitutional government, especially the relationship of the Federal and State governments. We want to keep it that way."[27]

Mays showed similar signs of caution. In August 1962, for example, he declined to attend a meeting of the League of Conservative Voters "at which such wild people as Judge Billy Old will be on the program."[28] Judge William "Wild Billy" Old, in August 1955, had urged Virginia's leaders to resuscitate the theory of "interposition" as a way to resist desegregation edicts. Mays refused to have anything to do with Virginia's foremost Citizens' Council group, the Defenders of State Sovereignty and Individual Liberties: "a rabid crowd who . . . have given me as wide a birth [sic] as I am glad to give them."[29]

With Virginia's front-line legislative measures in disarray, the state's segregationists found the CCG's success to be increasingly important. In essence, the commission developed a two-pronged strategy: encourage other southern states to follow more rational, defensible positions, and look simultaneously for national support, as Virginia governor J. Lindsay Almond Jr. explained to the South Carolina Bar Association in 1958.[30]

Mays realized that, in attempting to convert a greater number of southern segregationists to his style of resistance, he and his commission would have to deal with proponents of rabid demagoguery. On August 12, 1959, with some reluctance, Mays wrote to resisters in Arkansas, Mississippi, Louisiana, and Florida to outline the approach that the CCG was taking. As he confided in his diaries, that reluctance was born of the desire not to become entangled with those segregationists who continued to believe that staunch, all-out resistance might yet be victorious. He was a little apprehensive.[31] Kilpatrick was equally wary.[32] In September 1960, Almond chaired the Southern Governors' Conference in Hot Springs, and he gave Mays the chance to address the governors in person. "I was careful to begin by pointing out," reported Mays, "that my Commission was not set up to deal with school litigation, but was to put on an educational program concerning basic constitutional concepts." The talk was applauded and, according to Mays, "received vocal approval by Faubus, [Ernest] Hollings [of South Carolina], [Mississippi's Ross] Barnett, [North Carolina's Luther] Hodges, and [Alabama's John] Patterson."[33] The extent to which Mays's work impressed the governors was revealed at the end of the conference, when they unanimously adopted a resolution not just to praise Mays's and the CCG's work but also to "urge other states of the union to follow their example."[34]

The CCG's stock kept rising throughout the South and beyond. Kilpatrick went to Arizona in February 1962 to "spread a bit of Gospel" and then went on to "try his hand" with the "hapless 'liberals' of Antioch College in Ohio" in May. The commission was asked to send speakers all over the country, from Mobile in the summer of 1962 to the Student Congress of Young Americans for Freedom Convention at the University of Indiana in the summer of 1963. The University of Georgia asked Mays to make a television recording espousing the commission's views, and, in his home state, the Central Virginia

Educational Television Corporation asked him to make a "canned film" for use "where desired in different parts of the country." In spring 1961, Mays had welcomed a delegation of Louisiana segregationists to Richmond. By March 1964, the governor-elect of Louisiana was planning to realign the state sovereignty commission along the lines of Virginia's CCG, a move that Alabamians looked set to follow in April when it placed a large order for materials from Mays's commission.[35]

The links that the CCG forged with the Pennsylvanians most excited Mays. On May 29, 1961, they contacted him with a proposal to send a delegation south to establish links with the CCG. After three years of painstaking work, Mays could barely contain his excitement. "This is the first real break we have had in the North," he wrote. A preliminary meeting with a vanguard of the Pennsylvanians was held in Richmond on November 10—again including an evening at the Forum Club—in preparation for a more formal affair to be held in Pennsylvania the following month. That meeting, thought Mays, would provide the "finest opportunity to place our views where they could have national repercussions."[36] However, inclement weather grounded the delegates' airplane, and the entire trip appeared to be in jeopardy. Indicating the importance that the CCG's members placed on this nascent northern alliance, Mays et al. drove the whole way in hastily arranged limousines. They were met by approximately thirty legislators and some specially invited guests, and laid plans for the weekend-long seminar in Williamsburg the next summer.[37]

The CCG had clearly stated its interest in garnering support outside the South. The motives underpinning the Pennsylvania Republicans' decision are, however, not so readily apparent. Their interest confirms the existence of a core of ideological precepts shared by both southern and northern conservatives by the mid- to late 1950s, for it was those beliefs that Mays was able to exploit and to which the Pennsylvanians were attracted. By the time that the CCG established tangible links with the Pennsylvanians, the party affiliations of northern and southern conservatives were becoming more fluid, even at the state level. Having proclaimed at the time of the Williamsburg meeting that he believed both groups shared common problems, Alvin C. Bush, a leader of the Pennsylvania delegation, conceded some forty years later that "the people we met [there] were about as Democrat as we were Republican."[38]

There were also state-specific reasons for the Pennsylvania Republicans' interest. When the CCG reached out to it, the Pennsylvania Republican Party was emerging from an exhausting intraparty struggle and attempting to bring eight years of Democratic rule in the state to an end. Many in the state felt that the party was in steep decline after losses in the gubernatorial elections of 1954 and 1958 and John F. Kennedy's success in Pennsylvania in 1960. Trying to arrest that decline, the GOP's power brokers in Pennsylvania electioneered savagely during the 1962 gubernatorial race, and the state's Democratic leadership matched their tactics resulting in "one of the bitterest in Pennsylvania history."[39] A progressive Republican, William W. Scranton, won the election in November 1962 but not until a vicious political battle had been fought. Eisenhower had been drafted to speak on Scranton's behalf, and Kennedy—whose sister Kathleen had dated Scranton while they were college students—had spoken in support of his Democratic opponent, Richardson "Dick" Dilworth.[40] The battle that led up to Scranton's nomination, though, had caused much of the turmoil within Republican ranks. Scranton had, initially, withdrawn himself from the race, but the acrimonious chaos that existed within the party prompted him to change his mind, especially after he had received the encouragement of the grand old man of Pennsylvania Republican politics, George I. Bloom. Bloom's comment that he did not want "a funeral in November" was widely reported, and he devised a compromise ticket of Scranton for governor and Raymond P. Schafer for lieutenant governor. Both men were a comparatively youthful forty-five years old and represented a more progressive Republicanism than many of their peers.[41] On polling day, Scranton defeated Dilworth by almost half a million votes, and the Republicans carried both houses of the state legislature.[42]

The divisions of the campaign left a number of visible scars on Republican state politics, and within Republican ranks its caustic nature laid bare factional differences that had previously been papered over. As a result, some uneasy alliances followed. Standing clearly on the right of the party's ideological spectrum was W. Stuart "Stu" Helm, a native of Cowansville in Armstrong County, who served continuously for twenty-four years as a member of the state House. A very conservative Republican, Helm cultivated a vigorous relationship with big business and had close links to the Sun Oil Company, based in Philadelphia.[43] Scranton, by contrast, was an out-and-out progressive, but it was a reflection of the party's attempts to restore unity and of Helm's political acumen that, despite never knowing quite what to make of each other, the two put ideological differences aside and forged a meaningful working relationship once the party returned to power.[44] The Republicans' resounding victory in 1962 not only confirmed the status of entrenched political veterans such as Helm, but also ushered new members into the legislature, many of whom lacked direct political experience.[45]

The majority of those new Republican legislators were progressives in the mold of Scranton, including the two driving forces in the creation of the forum, Alvin C. Bush, from Lycoming County, and Guy A. Kistler, from Cumberland County. The inclusion of Bush, Kistler, and Helm is, therefore, another apparent anomaly of the Pennsylvania delegation to Williamsburg: Bush and Kistler were young, inexperienced, and progressive, while Helm was a veteran and a conservative. Different motives were apparently at work within Pennsylvania's delegation for the establishment of the alliance with the southern segregationists of the CCG. Kistler in particular was an enthusiastic amateur historian and was as keen to visit the home state of Patrick Henry and Thomas Jefferson as he was to develop his belief in the need for stronger states' rights.[46] Kistler's avocation did not, however, dilute the vigor of the belief that was unanimously held by those who were present at Williamsburg: that the federal government had begun to overstep its bounds. Bush, for example, declared to the press on the first morning of the Williamsburg meeting that "We, too, are concerned over the trend of federal encroachments."[47]

In articulating southern concerns over the erosion of states' rights, perceived federal encroachment, and the economic cost to states of the federal grants-in-aid program, Mays and the CCG had clearly pinpointed issues that were as central to Pennsylvania conservatives as they were to southern segregationists. Despite their apparent lack of dynamism, Bill Stauffer and Ed Lafferty had been dispatched in February 1962 to the National Taxpayers' Conference in Washington as the CCG's delegation, and they had presented material on the same subject to the Pennsylvanians during the initial Harrisburg meeting the same month.[48] Mays's interest in the two men's in-depth knowledge of the subject, rather than their oratorical ability, exemplifies his working methods. Stauffer was a former director of research and statistics for the Virginia State Department of Taxation, as well as former commissioner of public welfare and director of statistics for Virginia's Unemployment Compensation Commission. Unsurprisingly, therefore, Mays called upon Stauffer to draw up more than half of one of the CCG's most successful publications, simply titled *Federal Grants-in-Aid*.[49] The publication was cleansed of the brutally racist dialogue of much of massive resistance. In the months following the Williamsburg weekend, Pennsylvanians W. Stuart Helm and Albert W. Johnson used much that they had learned from Mays about emphasis, language, approach, and ideology as they attempted to forge their own national alliance constructed around their own particular conservative agenda. Mays had devised a program that essentially supported southern resistance, but he skillfully framed it in terms that appealed to a wider audience, including members of both the progressive Republican Legislative Forum and the conservative Helm-Johnson axis. Both factions had at least some interest in the ideas that the CCG was promoting, and, more important, Helm and Johnson were willing to use those ideas and the continued input of CCG members as part of a broad effort to influence national politics. As well as being a stalwart of the conservative wing of his state's Republican Party, Helm had, by the early 1960s, taken over the chairmanship of the National Legislative Conference (NLC), which was a bipartisan subsidiary of the Council of State Governments (CSG) and was composed of highly regarded representatives from all fifty states. Moreover, as chair he was able to establish, via covert discussions and maneuvers, an independent group from within the NLC's ranks. In 1962, that group, known widely as the Dual Sovereignty Committee (DSC), emerged fully formed, with Helm as its chair.[50]

The DSC's purpose was to alter the landscape of U.S. politics fundamentally and in a resolutely conservative manner. From the outset, the DSC's program had much in common with the ideology of southern resistance. The commission's name indicated, for example, that it was in essence a states'-rights organization, whose members, like proponents of massive resistance, believed that successive federal administrations had encroached so greatly on the power of individual states that drastic action was necessary. Unlike many of those resisters—but in line with the approach of the CCG—the Dual Sovereignty Committee did not see interposition or open, outright defiance as appropriate. Instead, in December 1962, the DSC began to coordinate a nationwide plan to alter the basic compact of the United States. The group aimed to pass resolutions in favor of three constitutional amendments through a sufficient number of state legislatures to trigger a constitutional convention, which would then consider adoption into the U.S. Constitution. The first amendment would have given state legislatures the ability to directly approve amendments to the Constitution on the basis of support from two-thirds of the states; the second would have removed apportionment cases from the jurisdiction of federal courts; and the third would have established a "super court," made up of the fifty state chief justices, with the power to overrule the Supreme Court on constitutional questions. The DSC's network of political operatives may have been wildly optimistic in hoping to secure the support of a sufficient number of state legislatures, but their guile and political shrewdness allowed them to make significant progress toward their goal. By the time the press first broadly latched onto the campaign, ten state legislatures had already approved the apportionment measure, and eleven had passed the declaration aiming to streamline constitutional change. Finally President Kennedy, Chief Justice Warren, the American Bar Association, and the American Civil Liberties Union all released statements warning against the amendments' adoption.[51]

The way in which the three "silent amendments" were introduced in Pennsylvania gives one example of the Machiavellian political maneuvering and considerable planning that lay behind their development. Soon after Scranton's election, Helm was elected once again to be Speaker of the state House.

From that post, he was able to guarantee the introduction of the amendments as House Bills 9, 10, and 11 of the 1963 legislative session. No sooner had they been introduced than they were referred to the rules committee—chaired at the time by none other than Helm's fellow Williamsburg weekender Albert W. Johnson.[52] The early success of the "silent amendments" was not solely the result of a well-developed practical approach or of the prime positioning of the Helm-Johnson axis, however, for the DSC's campaign also tapped into increasingly popular ideological concerns. Crucially—and starkly reminiscent of the importance of the CCG's work to Helm—those concerns appealed to southern segregationists as strongly as to northern conservatives. As Helm well knew, many white-supremacist legislatures and governorships in the South, including those run by Byrd's organization in Virginia, depended on their control of a limited franchise to maintain their political dominance.[53] In March 1962, however, the Supreme Court signaled the end of such schemes in *Baker v. Carr*. The Court dramatically changed constitutional interpretation, maintaining that remedial action for malapportioned state legislatures was a matter of federal concern.[54]

Only the second of the three "silent amendments" directly attacked *Baker v. Carr* with a bid to return all decisions on apportionment to state legislatures. The other two amendments encompassed broader aims, although both were tangentially associated with apportionment. Many nonsouthern states had voting wards that were as unrepresentative as those that served to underpin segregationist dominance in the South. In Pennsylvania, those inequalities contributed directly to the continued power of rural conservatives in the state, just as the overrepresentation of Southside voters in Virginia shored up the Byrd regime. As the 1960 census made plain, the population of urban centers such as Philadelphia and Pittsburgh and the number of African Americans registered to vote had grown to such an extent that existing voting districts were no longer representative of the population's geographical distribution. As a result, Pennsylvania had to redraw its electoral boundaries. Two of the districts most at risk of being combined into others were rural Kittaning and McKean Counties, the seats of Helm and Johnson respectively.[55]

In one sense, therefore, the early success of the campaign for the "silent amendments" rested on its coordinators' ability to pinpoint ideological links that bound northern conservative interests with southern segregationist ones. At the same time, however, those links also proved to be the amendments' Achilles heel, for Pennsylvania's mainstream press was quick to seize upon them. Walter S. Farquhar, editor of the *Pottsville Republican*, wrote to the governor's office to warn of a "degrading" movement at least partly organized by "Dixiecrats." The dean of Harrisburg's Episcopal cathedral thought it "obvious that these amendments are aimed at civil rights proponents and are actually the babies of southern minds." A Philadelphia lawyer said they were "fraught with real danger to individual rights and liberties, particularly to Negroes."[56]

Where support for the DSC's nascent conservative movement did exist, it was both practical and ideological in character: a practical wish to cling to power was bolstered, in many cases, by a fervent belief in the primacy of states' rights. Only when the "silent amendments" campaign is analyzed in more specific detail does the full extent of Mays's and the CCG's influence on it become clear. A close analysis reveals that the amendments' instigators and coordinators were profoundly affected by the ways in which Mays chose to set out the parameters, strategies, and content of his campaign for continued southern segregation and shows the extent to which Helm and Johnson were intently soaking up information on the three separate occasions when they met CCG members. Indeed, Mays's metaphorical fingerprints were all over the Dual Sovereignty Committee's work. First and foremost, the "silent amendments" were expunged of any potentially divisive reference to conservatism, race, or even states' rights, while still retaining their appeal to committed conservatives, segregationists, and states'-rights advocates. Any possible link to the segregationist South had been bleached out, which was all the more important given that the DSC's only full-time, paid staff member was George R. Prentice, who, although a native Kansan, had worked as a newspaperman in Birmingham, Alabama. Just as Mays sought to distance the CCG from the demagoguery of some of Virginia's wilder resisters, so the DSC was careful to ensure that the vast majority of its members were nonsouthern. In a clear echo of CCG member William T. Muse's words on the Birchers and Mays's own views on the Virginia Defenders, journalist Robert L. Riggs reported that one of Prentice's tasks was to ensure "that the committee avoids undesirable companions. . . . Anyone who wants to do so can join the cheering section, [but] he tries to keep the working ranks cleared of members of the John Birch Society, the racist White Citizens Council, or any other groups on the radical right."[57] In a more tangible link, both J. J. Kilpatrick and CCG executive director Hugh V. White Jr. were present at the CSG's annual convention in Chicago in December 1962 when the amendments were first proposed. In a confidential memo to the CCG, Kilpatrick reported that he and White "found ourselves strongly in favor of the principles involved" in all three of the amendments, even if the language used in their drafting left something to be desired.[58]

Helm's strategy of trying to secure the introduction of the three amendments in all of the fifty state legislatures on a single day was an astute political move. As the press began to report the events of the DSC's thrust on January 16—and the public was alerted to the genuine threat that the amendments posed—constituents began to urge their legislators to block their adoption. In Pennsylvania, that development put Helm once more at odds with his governor. Although Scranton was a strong supporter of states' rights, there was no need to make changes to the Constitution, he believed, as the states themselves should be reenergized into assuming their proper role. "Too often," he concluded, the states had "screamed about state rights, but ignored state responsibilities."[59] Nonetheless, Scranton was slow to come out against the amendments publicly and slower still to offer any sort of legislative leadership on the matter. In no small part, that hesitation was because there were already strong indications that he might run for the Republican Party's nomination for the 1964 presidential election—a process that would pit him directly against the archconservative Barry Goldwater.[60] Even as Scranton was seriously considering running, conservative interests in his own state were openly supportive of Goldwater. John G. Pew Jr., of the Philadelphia-based Sun Oil Corporation that backed Helm, was a national leader in the Goldwater movement.[61]

Part of Scranton's appeal for other, less dogmatically conservative Republicans, though, was his integrity and his respect for political principle. That stance led him to pronounce repeatedly that his role as governor did not include telling Pennsylvania's elected legislators how to vote on any issue. The amendments had already been introduced and were under consideration by the legislature when Scranton publicly denounced them at a press conference on May 23. The legislature did act in Pennsylvania, as others did elsewhere, and the quiet momentum that had begun to build behind the amendments ebbed away. By August 1963, when Helm traveled to Honolulu for the annual meeting of the National Legislative Conference, which he still served as president, even he was publicly stating that he wished no further action to be taken.[62]

Helm's volte-face marked the demise of the close alliance between his conservative cadre and the CCG, although some of the other Williamsburg weekenders continued to press for the establishment of a sister commission to the CCG in Pennsylvania.[63] By 1964, though, there were open channels through which northern and southern conservative forces could pursue their agenda—channels that had not been developed when the CCG was concocted in 1958. The mooted presidential candidacy of George C. Wallace as a conservative Democrat and the very real challenge of Barry Goldwater as a conservative Republican gave southern Democrats two options that were, for the segregationists among them, far more palatable than the "socialization and centralization" that LBJ offered. The defection of South Carolina's Strom Thurmond to the GOP later in 1964 blurred partisan lines in the South yet further.[64] Nevertheless, Mays was wary of tarnishing the CCG's carefully crafted image

with open support of Wallace, a man who was still too close to the rabid demagoguery from which Mays was keen to distance his work.[65]

Although supporting Wallace was not part of Mays's resistance plan, he
did think there were some positives to his campaign. "The enormous vote
that he got is as gratifying as it is amazing and probably indicates a real awakening in the Northwest as to what the Civil Rights bill really is."[66] Mays was
evidently committed to the alliance with the Pennsylvanians and valued the
acquisition of northern support, but he had always industriously ensured that
the CCG independently busied itself with several lines of attack. All were designed to appeal to a broad, conservative audience, but the principles underlying that allure were always easily tailored to the specifics of the southern racial
situation.[67]

Once the association with the Pennsylvanians had clearly run its course,
Mays and the CCG members turned their attention to the pending civil rights
bill. The commission published vast amounts of information in an attempt to
turn both public and legislative opinion against its passage. Once again, Mays
turned his wrath on what he believed to be the act's violation of constitutional
principles.[68] Indeed, the preface to the CCG's twenty-four-page publication
on the proposed civil rights act—titled *Civil Rights and Federal Powers* and
with the word "Constitution" squeezed by a vise on the front cover—eruditely
restated the commission's ideological standpoint and strategy. "This Commission is not concerned with race relations as such; this is not our function." Instead, the stated purpose of the booklet was to ask, "Is the bill constitutional?"[69] The pamphlet proved hugely popular, with requests for copies
flooding in from across the South and the nation. Tacitly recognizing that
Mays had conceived the most intelligent and sustainable means of resistance
for Virginia, Harry Byrd read the pamphlet into the *Congressional Record* in
its entirety as part of his filibuster against the civil rights bills.[70]

The failure of that filibuster and the passing of first the Civil Rights Act
in 1964 and then the Voting Rights Act a year later effectively neutered the
most openly abrasive and violent aspects of southern resistance. Certainly,
the form of resistance that pricked the national conscience in reports from
Birmingham and Selma was no longer a viable option for southern segregationists. The type of resistance pioneered by the CCG, however, had a longer
shelf life. Indeed, that the members of the Dual Sovereignty Committee, in
promoting a national states'-rights campaign, relied on the work of a southern segregationist agency—created by Virginia's white-supremacist oligarch,
Harry Flood Byrd Sr., in an era of massive resistance to federally mandated
desegregation—underscores the long-term vision, political pragmatism, and
tactical acumen of that agency's chairman, David Mays. The DSC was, after

all, an offshoot of the National Legislative Conference, an organization that was truly national in scope. Mays and his fellow CCG members proved the feasibility of elevating arguments made in defense of the southern status quo above the base, racist demagoguery so common to the majority of massive resistance's proponents. The program that the CCG put forward was sufficiently devoid of sectional concerns to continue to draw allies from both sides of the Mason-Dixon Line; after building the relationship with the Pennsylvanians, Mays received interest from Texas and even had "a nibble from Idaho."[71] Not only the program itself but also its style and delivery contributed to the CCG's success, and both aspects were also visible in the DSC's attempts to convince state legislatures across the nation to alter the Constitution in ways that would appeal to a broad coalition of conservatives.

Mays remained wedded to the belief that the CCG alone was making the best case for the South, but even he could never be quite sure of the extent of the inroads the commission was achieving. In no small part, that was because the CCG had no way of knowing how many reprints of its material were being made. In the spring of 1964 alone, for example, there were rumors that an Alabama newspaper, a group in Texas, and the Illinois Manufacturers' Association were all distributing reprinted CCG materials—and there is no concrete record of how wide an audience read reprints.[72] Although Mays was never shy about promoting the work that "his" CCG was performing, the commission clearly had a more widespread effect than was credited either at the time or later in the historical record.[73]

The amount of support that Mays received from other segregationist politicians and agencies across the South at the end of the 1950s and the early 1960s indicates the growing reputation that he was building among his peers in the region. The segregationist cause, though, was demonstrably weaker because neither Mays nor the CCG was in a position to shape the resistance movement at its outset. Byrd did not deign to nurture the CCG and its more thoughtful resistance strategies until his favored strategy—that of outright circumvention of *Brown*—clearly began to fail. As massive resistance laws were being dismantled and the force of white northern public opinion was swinging inexorably toward support for southern civil rights protesters, segregationists increasingly realized the efficacy of the tactics promulgated by the CCG: its efforts to distance itself from the more rabid displays of racist segregationists; its espousal of legal arguments; and its educational approach. Ultimately, perhaps because Mays's style of resistance was deployed so late in the struggle and because his careful, thoughtful response to the challenges of court-ordered desegregation remained, in his phrase, in the periphery, determined southern resistance was no match for the forces arrayed against it. The civil rights movement proved to be tactically astute in its attempts to place and keep racial segregation at the top of the domestic political agenda, a task far easier when facing the vituperative racism of Bull Connor and Jim Clark than when encountering the carefully crafted white supremacy of David Mays.

In the wider field of national conservative politics, the CCG certainly made its mark. From both tactical and ideological points of view, the commission's continued emphasis on the primacy of states' rights, economic conservatism, and race-free appeals to racist constituencies presaged Barry Goldwater's rough-hewn Republican campaign of 1964 and much of the more polished "southern strategy" that Richard Nixon crafted later in the decade. As such, the work of Mays and the CCG necessitates fresh analysis of the South's role in the development of the new conservatism of the late 1960s and 1970s. Their ventures indicate that southern segregationists were capable of more subtle forays into the national political arena than George Wallace's, however effective Wallace proved to be. Where Wallace played upon his folksy roots and reveled in bringing southern-style stump politics to a national audience, Mays perfected the unemotional—even clinical—dissemination of legal arguments and historical precedents. The CCG's ability to woo nonsouthern, non-Democratic supporters in terms that simultaneously appealed to traditional southern Democrats was an early indicator of changing political sympathies. More fundamentally, perhaps, it reveals that such political changes were not solely the consequence of top-down initiatives from the national Republican Party but were in full flow well below the presidential level. Mays may not have been courting Republicans specifically, but he was sufficiently astute to realize that, if the CCG were going to be successful in its quest for northern allies, those allies were less likely to be Democrats. Finally, the zeal with which the CCG went about its focused activities alters the view of the South as the passive, objectified prize of imaginative northern political strategists. To borrow from Goldwater's oft-quoted remarks, the CCG's theoreticians were not mere political ducks waiting to be shot.[74] Instead, the work of the CCG shows incontrovertibly that a number of southern segregationists were active, energetic, and perceptive players in the formulation of conservative ideology that constituted the cornerstone of the new political alliances that emerged in the mid- to late 1960s and that they were fundamental to those ideas' dissemination and popularization. Indeed, beginning in 1958, a full decade before Nixon won the presidency, David Mays and the CCG were using many of the same ideological touchstones to broaden the base of support for massive resistance that Nixon used as part of his strategy to win the 1968 election. The CCG even produced a booklet on the decline of law and order a year before Nixon launched his own assault on lawlessness.[75] As a result, the brand of thoughtful segregationist that Mays typified had no need for a Damascene conversion away from the sectional politics and excesses of southern resistance before entering the arena of national politics. The ideological focus that they had maintained throughout the massive resistance years allowed them to segue seamlessly into the currents of the new national conservatism.[76]

## Notes

1. Editor's note: This essay originally appeared as George Lewis, "Virginia's Northern Strategy and the Route to National Conservatism," *Journal of Southern History* 72 (February 2006): 111–46. I am grateful to the author, George Lewis, and Professor John B. Boles, editor of the *Journal of Southern History*, for their permission to reprint the essay here.

2. Earl Black and Merle Black, *The Rise of Southern Republicans* (Cambridge: Harvard University Press, 2002), 2. Lewis would like to acknowledge the assistance of a Small Research Grant that he received from the British Academy.

3. Numan V. Bartley and Hugh D. Graham, *Southern Politics and the Second Reconstruction* (Baltimore: Johns Hopkins University Press, 1975), 92.

4. Figures from Ralph Eisenberg, "Virginia: The Emergence of Two-Party Politics," in *The Changing Politics of the South,* ed. William C. Havard (Baton Rouge: Louisiana State University Press, 1972), 48. Miller quoted in J. Harvie Wilkinson III, *Harry Byrd and the Changing Face of Virginia Politics, 1945–1966* (Charlottesville: University Press of Virginia, 1968), 210.

5. Thomas Byrne Edsall and Mary D. Edsall, *Chain Reaction: The Impact of Race, Rights, and Taxes on American Politics* (New York: Norton, 1991), 6, 10, 35–36. Joseph A. Aistrup's analysis rests upon what he refers to as "Republican top-down advancement" (see Aistrup, *The Southern Strategy Revisited: Republican Top-Down Advancement in the South* [Lexington: University Press of Kentucky, 1996], 3 and passim).

6. Bush quoted in "Harrison Asks Pennsylvanians for Support," *Richmond Times-Dispatch,* 24 July 1962.

7. In January 1956, Virginians voted 304,154 to 146,164 for a constitutional convention to draft changes that would legitimate the use of public funds for tuition grants to allow "some educational opportunities" for those school-age children "whose parents conscientiously object to integration" (State Referendum Information Center, "Questions and Answers on Constitutional Convention," quoted in Robbins L. Gates, *The Making of Massive Resistance: Virginia's Politics of Public School Desegregation, 1954–1956* [Chapel Hill: University of North Carolina Press, 1964], 73 [quotations]; W. D. Workman Jr., "The Deep South: Segregation Holds Firm," in *With All Deliberate Speed: Segregation-Desegregation in Southern Schools,* ed. Don Shoemaker [Westport, Conn.: Negro Universities Press, 1957], 98–99).

8. J. Douglas Smith, "'When Reason Collides with Prejudice': Armistead Lloyd Boothe and the Politics of Moderation," in *The Moderates' Dilemma: Massive Resistance to School Desegregation in Virginia,* ed. Mathew D. Lassiter and Andrew B. Lewis

(Charlottesville: University Press of Virginia, 1998), 46. This essay adopts Numan Bartley's broader, more metaphorical—and, to the historian, more instructive—definition of massive resistance as a movement encompassing the broad arsenal of resistance measures created by white southerners in defense of segregation (Numan V. Bartley, *The Rise of Massive Resistance: Race and Politics in the South During the 1950's* [Baton Rouge: Louisiana State University Press, 1969]).

9. "Report to Governor, December, Yearly," in Box 1, Virginia Commission on Constitutional Government Papers (Record Group 70, State Government Records Collection, Library of Virginia, Richmond) (hereafter CCG Papers).

10. The CCG does not appear at all in specific studies of Virginian resistance such as Lassiter and Lewis, eds., *Moderates' Dilemma*; and Wilkinson, *Harry Byrd and the Changing Face of Virginia Politics*; and neither the CCG nor Mays appears in Ronald L. Heinemann, *Harry Byrd of Virginia* (Charlottesville: University Press of Virginia, 1996). Bartley, *Rise of Massive Resistance*, 183; James W. Ely Jr., *The Crisis of Conservative Virginia: The Byrd Organization and the Politics of Massive Resistance* (Knoxville: University of Tennessee Press, 1976), 93–95.

11. For overviews of historiography that are far too lengthy to be listed here, see Charles W. Eagles, "Toward New Histories of the Civil Rights Era," *Journal of Southern History*, 66 (November 2000): 815–48; Adam Fairclough, "Historians and the Civil Rights Movement," *Journal of American Studies* 24 (December 1990): 387–98; and George Rehin, "Of Marshalls, Myrdals and Kings: Some Recent Books about the Second Reconstruction," *Journal of American Studies* 22 (April 1988): 87–103.

12. In his seminal work, Bartley described massive resistance as the product of a "neobourbon elite" (Bartley, *Rise of Massive Resistance,* 116). Those notable exceptions include Jane Dailey, "Sex, Segregation, and the Sacred after *Brown*," *Journal of American History* 91 (June 2004): 119–44; and David L. Chappell, "Religious Ideas of the Segregationists," *Journal of American Studies* 32 (August 1998): 237–62.

13. "Scrapbooks, Dec 1953–May 1954," Box 2, David John Mays Papers, Virginia Historical Society, Richmond; entries dated 19 November 1954, 6 January 1955, and 30 November 1956, David John Mays Diary, Virginia Historical Society (hereafter Mays Diary).

14. Entry for 7 September 1956, Mays Diary.

15. Entry for 5 July 1957, Mays Diary. On 19 January 1959—Robert E. Lee's birthday—Virginia's Supreme Court struck down the Old Dominion's resistance laws in *Harrison v. Day* (see Benjamin Muse, *Virginia's Massive Resistance* [Bloomington: Indiana University Press, 1961], 122–26).

16. James Latimer, "The Rise and Fall of Massive Resistance," *Richmond Times-Dispatch*, 22 September 1996; entries for 17 July 1961, and 31 May 1962.

17. Kilpatrick quoted in Joseph J. Thorndike, "'The Sometimes Sordid Level of Race and Segregation': James. J. Kilpatrick and the Virginia Campaign against *Brown*," in *Moderates' Dilemma*, ed. Lassiter and Lewis, 64; Kilpatrick to Mills E. Godwin Jr., copied to Gravatt, Gray, Moore, Smith, Boatwright, and Mays, July 23, 1958, Folder "CCG Minutes, Meetings, 1958–1960," Box 39, Papers of James J. Kilpatrick 6626-b (Albert

and Shirley Small Special Collections Library, University of Virginia, Charlottesville) (hereafter Kilpatrick Papers).

18. Kilpatrick to Verbon E. Kemp, Virginia State Chamber of Commerce, undated, "Correspondence K 1961," Box 34, Kilpatrick Papers, 6626-b.

19. *Race and the Restaurant: Two Opinion Pieces* (Richmond, [1960]); *Williams v. Lewis; Williams v. Howard Johnson's,* 342 F.2d 727 (4th Cir. 1965).

20. Entry for 8 April 1960, Mays Diary.

21. *Democracy and Despotism: An Excerpt from Part II of Democracy in America, by Alexis de Tocqueville* (Richmond: Virginia Commission on Constitutional Government, 1963); *Did the Court Interpret or Amend? The Meaning of the Fourteenth Amendment* . . . (Richmond: Virginia Commission on Constitutional Government, [1960]). Circulation figures are in "Final Report, Virginia Commission on Constitutional Government, January 25, 1969," Box 1, CCG Papers. For a populist reprint of Eastland's remarks, see, for example, *On Whose Side Is the Supreme Court?* a pamphlet produced by the Independent American organization of New Orleans, in Folder 109, Box 14, Wesley Critz George Papers #3822 (Southern Historical Collection, Wilson Library, University of North Carolina at Chapel Hill).

22. *"State Action" and the 14th Amendment: A Study of Judicial Misinterpretation* (Richmond, [1966]), 15–17.

23. Various documents regarding the creation and structure of the CCG may be found in Boxes 1 and 2 of the CCG Papers. Entry for January 18, 1964, Mays Diary; Albertis S. Harrison Jr. letter of appointment to John Dos Passos, January 26, 1965; Mills E. Godwin letter of appointment to John Dos Passos, September 8, 1966, both in Folder "P-14 Oversize," Box 125, John Dos Passos Papers #5950 (Small Special Collections Library).

24. *Report of the Virginia Commission on Constitutional Government* (Richmond, 4 January 1962), p. 6, Box 1, CCG Papers (first and second quotations); entry for 19 February 1964, Mays Diary (third and fourth quotations). "Final Report, Virginia Commission on Constitutional Government, January 25, 1969," p. 2. *Report of the Virginia Commission on Constitutional Government* (4 January 1962), 6.

25. William T. Muse to Members of the Executive Committee, Virginia Bar Association, 24 March 1961, Box 1, CCG Papers.

26. James Kilpatrick quoted in Hugh V. White Jr. to Mills E. Godwin Jr., 13 March 1961, Box 1, Mills E. Godwin Jr. Papers, Manuscripts and Rare Books Department, Earl Gregg Swem Library, College of William and Mary, Williamsburg, Va.

27. Kilpatrick's undated reply to 16 July 1962 letter from Fred M. Davis, Folder "Correspondence D—1962," Box 38, Kilpatrick Papers 6626-b.

28. Entry for 17 August 1962, Mays Diary.

29. Entry for 26 June 1964, Mays Diary.

30. *"The Achilles Heel of America*: Address by Governor J. Lindsay Almond, Jr, Governor of Virginia, South Carolina Bar Association, Columbia SC, May 2 1958," Box 13, J. Lindsay Almond Jr. Papers, Virginia Historical Society.

31. Entry for 12 August 1960, Mays Diaries.

32. Kilpatrick to Godwin, copied to Gravatt, Gray, Moore, Smith, Boatwright, and Mays, 23 July 1958, Folder "CCG Minutes, Meetings, 1958–1960," Box 39, Kilpatrick Papers, 6626-b.

33. Entry for 28 September 1960, Mays Diary.

34. 28 September 1960, Resolution appended to CCG Minutes, 8 December 1960, Folder "CCG Minutes, Meetings, 1958–1960," Box 39, Kilpatrick Papers 6626-b.

35. See the following entries in Mays Diary: Arizona quotation from 28 February 1962; Ohio quotations from 7 May 1962; Mobile request mentioned 27 August 1962; Indiana request mentioned 9 August 1963; Mays agreeing to request from University of Georgia noted 7 August 1963; request by Central Virginia Educational Television Corporation mentioned 29 April 1965; Louisiana delegation mentioned 4 May 1961; Louisiana governor-elect's interest noted 25 March 1964; Alabama interest and Mays's final quote both from entry for 6 April 1964.

36. Entries for 29 May and 17 November 1961, Mays Diary.

37. Entries for 23 and 26 February 1962, Mays Diary; CCG Minutes, March 15, 1962, Folder "CCG Minutes, Meetings, 1960–1963," Box 39, Kilpatrick Papers 6626-b.

38. Alvin C. Bush, telephone interview by author, 12 April 2004 (hereafter Bush interview).

39. Philip S. Klein and Ari Hoogenboom, *A History of Pennsylvania* (New York: McGraw-Hill, 1973), 464; George D. Wolf, *William Warren Scranton: Pennsylvania Statesman* (University Park: Pennsylvania State University Press, 1981), 61.

40. Wolf, *William Warren Scranton*, 53–64.

41. See ibid., esp. 58–61; and Paul B. Beers, *Pennsylvania Politics Today and Yesterday: The Tolerable Accommodation* (University Park: Pennsylvania State University Press, 1980), chap. 9 (quotation on 275). Beers, *The Republican Years* (Harrisburg, Pa., n.p., 1971), 1–6. For Bloom quotation, see also ibid., 2.

42. Harold F. Alderfer, *William Warren Scranton: Pennsylvania Governor, 1963–1967* (Mechanicsburg, Pa.: Local Government Service, 1976), 5.

43. William Kiesling, telephone interview by author, 12 April 2004; James Reichley, telephone interview by author, 13 April 2004.

44. Indeed, by 1965, Helm had been appointed by Scranton to the position of secretary of the commonwealth. See press releases regarding Helm's duties as secretary of the commonwealth in Folder 3, Box 56, William W. Scranton Papers #208, Pennsylvania State Archives, Harrisburg.

45. Bush interview.

46. Bush interview; CCG Minutes, 15 March 1962, Folder "CCG Minutes, Meetings, 1960–1963," Box 39, Kilpatrick Papers 6626-b.

47. Bush quoted in "Harrison Asks Pennsylvanians for Support," *Richmond Times-Dispatch*, 24 July 1962.

48. Entries for 7 and 26 February 1962, Mays Diary.

49. *Federal Grants-In-Aid* (Richmond, 1961). Stauffer alone was responsible for part 1 of the publication, which ran to more than seventy pages, and part 2, a similar

length, was compiled by T. Jack Gary Jr. under Stauffer's supervision. For details on authorship, see David J. Mays, "Introduction," *Federal Grants-In-Aid*, iii–iv.

50. "States Rights Sparks Dispute," *Harrisburg Patriot*, 24 August 1963. See also clippings of Anthony Lewis, "10 States Ask Amendment to Gain Districting Rights," New York *Times*, 14 April 1963; Robert L. Riggs, "States' Votes Quietly Push Court Curbs," *Louisville Courier-Journal*, 28 April 1963; Associated Press releases, 24 and 25 May 1963, in Jack L. Conmy Press Secretary Category Files, Box 10, Scranton Papers; "U.S. Power Curbs Sought in Six States," *Washington Post*, 31 January 1963; Richard L. Strout, "How U.S. Constitutional Change," *Christian Science Monitor*, 14 May 1963; and Dave Hess, "Rightists Aim to Change Constitution," *Christian Science Monitor*, 21 May 1964.

51. *Pittsburgh Post-Gazette*, 27 May 1963; *Chambersburg Public Opinion*, 25 May 1963, Jack L. Conmy Press Secretary Category Files, Box 10, Scranton Papers.

52. Press release, 6 January 1965, Folder 3, Box 56, Scranton Papers. The three proposals were first introduced by Johnson ("Retreat from Reality," *Pittsburgh Progress*, 29 May 1963). See also Associated Press press release, 25 May 1963, and transcript of Governor Scranton Press Conference, 23 May 1963. All three are in Jack L. Conmy Press Secretary Category Files, Box 10, Scranton Papers.

53. "Reapportionment Cases," *State Government News*, 7 (July 1964): 2. More damningly, as Peter Wallenstein has recently noted, the 1960 census showed that, while the average Virginia delegate served a population of 40,000, the variation was such that one delegate from a rural area represented only 20,000 people, and each of the two delegates from Fairfax County represented 143,000 (Wallenstein, *Blue Laws and Black Codes: Conflict, Courts, and Change in Twentieth-Century Virginia* [Charlottesville: University Press of Virginia, 2004], 192).

54. *Baker v. Carr*, 369 U.S. 186 (1962), at 267. Frankfurter and Harlan's dissent is quoted in *Reapportionment: A Transmittal of Certain Resolutions Approved by the General Assembly of Virginia on December 3, 1964* (Richmond, [1965]), 1.

55. "The Virginia Commission on Constitutional Government and the Pennsylvania Republican Legislative Forum: Minutes of Meeting Held at the Williamsburg Inn, Williamsburg, Virginia, July 23 and 24, 1962," Folder "CCG Minutes, Meetings, 1960–1963," Box 39, Kilpatrick Papers, 6626-b. For the specific risk to the rural seats of Helm and Johnson, see *Harrisburg Evening News*, 10 November 1961; and "Retreat from Reality," *Pittsburgh Progress*, 29May 1963, clippings in Jack L. Conmy Press Secretary Category Files, Box 10, Scranton Papers.

56. Walter S. Farquhar to James Reichley, 7 June 1963; the Very Reverend Arnold E. Mintz to Scranton, 14 June 1963; Austin Morris, of the Law Offices of Norris, Green, Harris & Brown, to Scranton, 26 June 1963, all in Folder 13, Box 1, Scranton Legislative Files, 1963–66, Scranton Papers.

57. Riggs, "States' Votes Quietly Push Court Curbs," 24.

58. "Report of General Assembly of the States, 17 December, 1962," Folder "CCG Minutes, Meetings, 1960–1963," Box 39, Kilpatrick Papers, 6626-b.

59. Tom Seppy, "First Lead Dentists," press release, 14 October 1963, Jack L. Conmy Press Secretary Category Files, Box 10, Scranton Papers.

60. Beers, *Pennsylvania Politics Today and Yesterday*, 296.

61. Wolf, *William Warren Scranton*, 104.

62. "States Rights Sparks Dispute," *Harrisburg Patriot*, 24 August 1963.

63. Entry for 17 January 1963, Mays Diary; CCG Minutes, 13 December 1962, 14 March 1963, 12 September 1963 (quotations), Folder "CCG Minutes, Meetings, 1960–1963," Box 39, Kilpatrick Papers, 6626-b.

64. Mays himself voted for Goldwater. "I supported him as the only way of protesting against the socialization and centralization of Johnson," he recorded, "both of which I shall continue to fight" (entry for 3 November 1964, Mays Diary).

65. Entry for 5 May 1964, Mays Diary.

66. Entry for 8 April 1964, Mays Diary.

67. Conference of Chief Justices, *Report of the Committee on Federal-State Relationships as Affected by Judicial Decisions, Adopted . . . August 1958* (1958; repr., Richmond, [1959]); *A Question of Intent: The States, Their Schools, and the Fourteenth Amendment* (Richmond, [1959]); *On the Fixing of Boundary Lines* (Richmond, [1958]); *The Rational Approach* (Richmond, [1961]). Descriptions of and commentaries on these publications are in *Report of the Virginia Commission on Constitutional Government* (4 January 1962), 5.

68. The civil rights bill, he wrote, "would violate the most basic concepts of the Constitution, although drafted in its name" (entry for 12 June 1963, Mays Diary).

69. *Civil Rights and Federal Powers* (Richmond, [1964]).

70. Harry Flood Byrd to Kilpatrick, 23 March 1964, with *Congressional Record* clipping enclosed, Folder "1963–1966 JJ Kilpatrick Correspondence with Harry Flood Byrd," Box 1, Kilpatrick Papers, 6626-e.

71. Entry for 27 November 1963, Mays Diary.

72. Entry for 14 March 1964, Mays Diary.

73. Entry for 19 March 1964, Mays Diary.

74. In Atlanta in 1961, Goldwater remarked that he was going "hunting where the ducks are" (Jack Bass and Walter DeVries, *The Transformation of Southern Politics: Social Change and Political Consequence Since 1945* [New York: Basic Books, 1976], 27).

75. *Every Man His Own Law* (Richmond, 1967), 2.

76. Even George Wallace strove to distance himself from what Dan T. Carter has referred to as the "tawdry trappings" of his massive resistance–era attempts to rouse the primal fears of suburban white Americans (Dan T. Carter, *The Politics of Rage: George Wallace, the Origins of the New Conservatism, and the Transformation of American Politics*, 2nd ed. [Baton Rouge: Louisiana State University Press, 2000], 347 [quotation], 455–74).

# 6

# Kennedyphobia and the Rise of Republicans in Northwest Louisiana, 1960–1962

J. ERIC PARDUE

The death of Congressman Overton Brooks of Louisiana's Fourth District created the need for a special election in 1961 to choose a replacement. This election became the first test for Republicans in Louisiana to use Kennedyphobia as an issue to increase GOP vote totals. John Kennedy's 1960 presidential victory had unalterably changed party politics and partisanship in the South, continuing a trend of voter realignment away from the Democratic Party as Republican support in the region increased.[1] Prior to Kennedy's election, no Republican since Reconstruction had come close to winning a congressional seat in Louisiana. But in 1961, Charlton Lyons, a Republican from Shreveport, came within a hair of defeating a young, conservative Democrat for the Fourth District seat. He ran on a platform tying him to a national Democratic Party perceived as excessively liberal, soft on communism, and out-of-touch with white north Louisianans on race. In this GOP effort, JFK became the shorthand unifier against whom the Republican campaign concentrated its accusations. The Shreveport oil man melodramatically declared that "today, the United States is in the throes of choosing between two irreconcilable philosophies of government—a Republic . . . [and] a Socialist-Totalitarian State."[2]

While the 1961 special election is not new to historians, the role of Kennedyphobia in the election has yet to be examined. In his study of Lyons, Dino Alberti notes that the 1961 election showed that normal partisan voting lines were "beginning to diminish."[3] Alberti, though, overlooked the role of Kennedyphobia in the campaign, only mentioning in passing the vicious anti-Kennedy rhetoric expressed by the candidates. But Kennedyphobia was a huge aspect of the race, and it provided Lyons *the* issue upon which not only to draw a partisan distinction between him and his opponent, but also to drum up support from an apprehensive electorate.

As an older, successful businessman who was well respected in the Shreveport community, Charlton Lyons was an ideal Republican candidate to capitalize on Kennedyphobia. His Lyons Petroleum company became immensely successful, and he served as president of the Independent Petroleum Association of America as well as a director for the American Petroleum Institute, National Petroleum Council, and National Association of Manufacturers.[4] Formerly a Democrat, Lyons publicly renounced his party membership in September 1960 by red-baiting the party as supporting programs akin to socialism. In a full-page article in the *Shreveport Times,* Lyons laid bare for north Louisianans his reasons for leaving the Democrats, taking offense at the 1960 Democratic platform, which he called "a veritable blueprint for a complete Socialist State, if not, indeed, a Totalitarian State."[5] He joined the Republican Party, he said, because it offered the "greatest hope of perpetuating Constitutional Government in America," coded language for states' rights, which represented for southerners the best vehicle to maintain segregation.[6] The GOP, Lyons contended, "has a long record of advocating and supporting 'conservative' as opposed to 'socialist' government."[7]

While Lyons drew no Republican opposition, five Democrats entered the Democratic primary. The front-runner and eventual nominee was Joe Waggonner, who dispatched his opponents in the September primary with ease, capturing 79 percent of the vote.[8] Like Lyons, Waggonner was involved in the oil industry, owning a marketing business for petroleum products in Plain Dealing, a small town in northern Bossier Parish. Also a veteran, he had served as a navy midshipman in the Pacific theater of World War II.[9]

Waggonner was also politically experienced and a strong segregationist, which made him a difficult opponent for Republicans to challenge. Elected to the Bossier Parish School Board in 1954, Waggonner became a leader of the White Citizens' Council. In 1959, he ran unsuccessfully for state comptroller on the segregation-driven gubernatorial ticket of William Rainach, and in 1960 he served as Fourth District campaign chairman for the States' Rights Party's slate of unpledged presidential electors. Also in 1960, Waggonner was elected to the State Board of Education, a position he held during his 1961 candidacy for Congress.[10]

The press noted that there were few ideological differences between Lyons and Waggonner as both were avowed southern conservatives.[11] Each pressed his conservative credentials as well. "I will speak for . . . vote for . . . work for . . . a return to the conservative principles that made this country the Free World's last great bulwark of freedom," an early Waggonner advertisement proclaimed. "Turn to the Right," it continued, "Vote Conservative!"[12] Defining himself as a conservative Republican out of the mold of Barry Goldwater, Lyons similarly wanted "to fight to preserve our free society."[13] His principles were simple and straightforward—opposition to "federal controls" (another veiled reference to states' rights and the role of the federal government in the South), "communism and socialism in every form," and "force[d] integration."[14] On many of the key political issues in the campaign—states' rights, segregation, communism, and the role of the federal government—the two were nearly identical.

Even before Waggonner won the Democratic primary, the ideological similarities between Waggonner and Lyons were obvious. At an October "Meet the Candidate" function hosted by the Farm Bureau that included the other Democratic contenders, Lyons and Waggonner answered questions in near unanimity. Both rejected federal aid to education as unconstitutional. Both agreed that the federal government lacked the constitutional authority to standardize voter-registration requirements, which would infringe upon states' rights and the ability of states to disenfranchise black voters. Both felt federal spending should be cut "in every area." To a question on the role of the federal government in establishing wage and hour minimums and maximums, Lyons answered, "they have no function." Waggonner responded to the same query by saying that "fundamentally, I don't believe they [the federal government] have any function there."[15] Later in the campaign, both candidates spoke out against wasteful spending and federal deficits. They both called the federal agricultural policy of subsidies and price controls "socialistic" and advocated getting "the government out of agriculture."[16]

Neither differed significantly from the other on issues related to foreign policy either, since both Lyons and Waggonner were aggressive Cold Warriors. Both advocated ending foreign aid to communist nations. Waggonner called this aid program "degenerate," while Lyons noted that the United States was "giving away money like a drunken sailor" and should not provide aid "unless it could be proved that it was in our self-interest."[17] Both also supported American withdrawal from the United Nations if the body admitted Red China. Waggonner said he would introduce legislation to withdraw America from the world body if "representatives of Godless Communism are seated."[18] Additionally, both candidates encouraged overthrowing the communist government in Cuba as well as a potential blockade of trade to that nation.[19] Because there was virtually no separation between the two candidates on these major domestic and foreign-policy issues, Lyons would have to rely on Kennedyphobia to distinguish himself from his Democratic opponent and gain support from northwest Louisianans.

An important part of Kennedyphobia was segregation. Although there was no major Louisiana segregation issue dominating headlines (like the New Orleans integration crisis during the 1960 election), several regional incidents like the Freedom Rides of early 1961 reminded white voters of the importance of preserving Jim Crow.[20] The integration of athletics at the University of Texas at Austin in the spring of 1960 drew the ire of the vocal citizenry.[21] A letter to the editor in the *Shreveport Times* called anyone favoring the action "subversive, criminal, and a traitor."[22] A Louisiana reminder finally occurred on Halloween 1961, when Shreveport officials defied an order by the Interstate Commerce Commission to integrate bus terminals, a refusal that eventually led Justice Department officials to file a lawsuit against the city.[23] Leaders from the Joint Legislative Committee on Segregation, a governmental group led by segregationist state senator Willie Rainach, called for a change in election laws. They wanted to tighten voter requirements and eliminate "minority bloc" voting, which segregationists believed would give black voters a pivotal role in deciding elections.[24]

But both Lyons and Waggonner firmly supported segregation and states' rights.[25] As such, both readily played to voters' racial fears and pro-segregation views. "I believe segregation to be imperative and mandatory," proclaimed a Waggonner advertisement.[26] Another Democratic spot bragged that 95 percent of black voters in Shreveport had voted against Waggonner in the Democratic primary. The *Shreveport Journal* reiterated this appeal to white voters, declaring in an editorial that the "Negro Bloc Opposes Waggonner," thus "his hopes for victory . . . lie in his ability to claim the votes of a substantial majority of white citizens."[27] Similarly, Lyons's platform forthrightly declared his support of segregation and opposition to "any and all" efforts to integrate southern institutions.[28] Lyons also distanced himself from the Eisenhower-style "moderate" Republicanism and the infamous use of troops to integrate Little Rock. One Lyons advertisement exclaimed that Lyons understood southerners and would "wage an aggressive fight against outsiders meddling in the South's affairs," while another Lyons newspaper spot observed that the Republican would vote for "preserving the Southern way of life and right to live that way" while voting against "integration in any form."[29]

The only major segregation challenge Lyons and Waggonner faced emerged from an incident concerning the Louisiana State University football team, but even in this situation both candidates reiterated similar views against integration. On November 18, 1961, the LSU Board of Supervisors approved a policy that allowed the university's sports teams to participate in interracial athletic contests.[30] Attorney W. M. Shaw, in a public letter to the candidates, used the incident to probe Lyons and Waggonner on segregation, asking them to give their opinions on the issue. The LSU decision "represents one of the first voluntary steps by a state institution toward the abandonment of our historic policy on segregation," railed Shaw. "Before I vote," he continued, "I would certainly like to know just how strong each of you are on this matter in particular and on the question of the separation of the races in general."[31] "I strongly oppose integration on principle," Lyons answered, "and would not change the principle even for the sake of football"—an institution closely akin to religion in the South.[32] Waggonner responded by citing his record on the State Board of Education: "my record . . . clearly shows that I have voted against interracial athletic contests in college under the Board's jurisdiction. Nothing could cause me to change that stand."[33] Because both Lyons and Waggonner advocated segregation, the issue—like socialism, communism, and "big" government— did little to separate the candidates.

Waggonner and Lyons were not completely without differences though. Since Lyons was sixty-seven and Waggonner forty-three, the disparity in their ages became one of the most obvious differences between the two candidates and an issue on which Lyons could easily tie his opponent to the youthfulness of JFK and many of his advisors. But Waggonner tried to make age a positive. Early in the campaign, he drew attention to the age difference by calling himself a "vigorous, dedicated, young conservative."[34] While this simple description did not directly attack Lyons, it subtly portrayed him as old and tired while depicting Waggonner as young and energetic. To bolster this claim, the Waggonner campaign released an advertisement saying it would take a young, active man to succeed in such a stressful job as that of a congressman. This advertisement called the job "one of the most demanding, grueling tasks in existence," thus someone with "vigor and stamina to see the job through" was needed to seriously accomplish something for the Fourth District.[35] "It stands to reason," he asserted, "that a younger man can give more service and longer hours to the backbreaking task of representing almost a quarter of a million people in the Fourth District."[36] Waggonner also used the issue of age to argue that Lyons could not receive good committee assignments in Congress. He speculated that because of Lyons's age, Republicans would not "waste" an important committee assignment on him because he would not be around long enough to gain seniority or a chairmanship.[37]

Lyons responded to Waggonner's charges about his age by stressing his health and strength, replying that he "never felt better physically" and intended to "be around for a long time to come."[38] He ridiculed Waggonner for "trying to do something that I can't do—predict the date of my death."[39] "If he is saying that a 67 year old man can't serve his country, then I say to you that we may as well ship all people my age to Siberia. Churchill, Adenauer, DeGaulle."[40]

Aware of the vital import of Kennedyphobia in trying to create a divide between the candidates, the Lyons campaign worked relentlessly to tie Waggonner to the president. After Waggonner brought up the age issue, Lyons and his supporters turned it on him, subtly connecting Waggonner to the president. Many Lyons advertisements described his age as a sign of "maturity," contrary to the perceived youthfulness of the Democratic administration in Washington that included many high-level officials in their thirties and forties.[41] The *Shreveport Times,* in particular, stressed this aspect of the age issue. Its editors urged voters to "take a good look at Washington" so they would "realize the need for a bit of maturity there."[42] Tying the notion of age to the youthfulness of the Kennedy administration, the *Times* averred, "take a look at Jack and Bobbie [*sic*] and see if you don't agree [that Washington needs maturity]."[43]

But perhaps the greatest boon for Lyons was the poor perception of the national Democratic Party and the Kennedy administration by northwest Louisianans. Criticism so strongly expressed during the 1960 presidential election continued into 1961, with some citizens voicing concern over Kennedy's integration creating what the writer believed amounted to a police state in the South.[44] An area woman, voicing concerns over federal policies toward segregation, communism, and federal spending, asked, "Mr. Kennedy, how can a person live his life and halfway heed the mess of government you are putting or trying to put into effect?"[45] Other residents more broadly admonished the president for a general mishandling of government.[46] The *Caddo Republican,* a newsletter published by the Caddo Parish Republican Party, noted, "It appears obvious that the voters of this district have no wish to send to Washington, as their congressional representative, a man who would be a partisan of the Kennedy clan."[47] Waggonner himself even agreed that people "around here don't like the President," although he argued that they then "shouldn't care what he thinks about the election."[48]

Lyons cultivated popular opposition to Kennedy's programs as justification for rejecting Waggonner by linking the Democrat to New Frontier policies through the association of his party label. The primary issue of the campaign, according to Lyons, was "the present sins" of what he derisively termed the "Democratic-Socialist Party."[49] Lyons told one radio audience that a Waggonner victory would be "a stamp of approval of the socialistic program of the New Frontier."[50] In reference to the Kennedy administration's role in the election, a Lyons advertisement claimed in bold letters, "Washington wants to be able to say 'THE SOUTH APPROVES OF WHAT WE ARE DOING IN WASHINGTON.'"[51] On one occasion, the Republican charged, "Every time a Democrat is elected . . . [it] indicates approval of [Kennedy's] program."[52] By tirelessly referencing the image of the national Democratic Party and its standard-bearer—John Kennedy—Lyons attempted to make the special election less about issues and policies concerning the Fourth District and more a referendum on the national Democratic Party and the Kennedy presidency.

Southerners increasingly viewed both as too liberal and hostile to states' rights, therefore giving Republicans an avenue to make gains in the region by attracting these disillusioned voters.

Faced with being tied to the Kennedy administration by the Lyons campaign, Waggonner tried to distance himself from national Democrats and assert his independence. "I am independent in the race," he avowed, "although I am running as a Democratic nominee."[53] In a newspaper advertisement with the headline "Men and Party Labels," Waggonner divorced himself from the Kennedy administration and downplayed the notion that a vote in support of him was also a vote for Kennedy: "I have opposed much of the Kennedy program and will continue to oppose much of it when elected. . . . My election will not be an endorsement of Democratic errors."[54] In its endorsement of the Democrat, the *Shreveport Journal* called Waggonner "politically independent," noting that "citizens who understand the principles of states' rights are not likely to be fooled by the claim that the election of Waggonner could be viewed as a victory for the Kennedy regime."[55] Another *Journal* editorial called Waggonner's political independence "unassailable."[56] Waggonner's efforts to evade Lyons's contention that he was tied to the Kennedy administration demonstrate that Kennedyphobia was a serious issue with the potential to create Republican gains in a traditionally non-Republican region like northwest Louisiana.

Despite Waggonner's efforts to counteract its charges, the Lyons campaign continued its strategy, promoting the Republican's candidacy as an opportunity for voters to register a protest against the president and, by extension, the Democratic Party as a way of swaying voters to the GOP. Lyons called for voters to reject the policies of the New Frontier and "send an unmistakable message to the Kennedy Bros." that "the South is no longer 'in the bag.'"[57] Similarly, the Lyons campaign asked voters to look toward the GOP for a change. One advertisement called Lyons "your voice of protest to Washington."[58] Another proclaimed Lyons "a leader in the SOUTHERN VOICE OF PROTEST to Washington," while yet another called Lyons's candidacy "A REBELLION AS VITAL AS THAT WHICH FOUNDED OUR COUNTRY!"[59] Lyons told voters that their vote could send a message to the White House that northwest Louisiana did not support the policies and programs of the Kennedys. He informed one group that national Democrats would feel the effects of their votes for him, saying that electing a Republican "would jar the Kennedy administration to the marrow of its bones."[60] Declaring that "Washington and the rest of the nation are watching for your decision," another Lyons spot alleged that voting for the Republican was a way for northwest Louisiana to send a message to the rest of the nation.[61]

Many Caddo citizens concurred with the notion that a vote for Lyons was a protest against Kennedy and the national Democrats. Election of Waggonner, the *Shreveport Times* proclaimed, will mean "new prestige and new power for the present Democratic Party and its Kennedy domestic socialism and Kennedy foreign policy blunders."[62] A self-identified Shreveport Democrat, stepping out to support the Republican, offered a red-baiting theme similar to that used in the *Times* when he wrote that Lyons afforded northwest Louisianans "an opportunity to register their protest to the trend of our republic toward socialism and the moral decay of the welfare state and away from the constitutional government and the rights and responsibilities of the states and individuals, in terms that cannot be misunderstood by Washington or the rest of the country."[63] Others wrote that by voting for Lyons, "Mr. Kennedy will have no doubts as to how we really feel."[64] As one Shreveporter put it, "If [a voter] endorses the aims of the Kennedy administration and wishes to expand them, a vote for Mr. Waggonner would be in order."[65]

By casting the election as a referendum on Kennedy, Republicans positioned themselves to be the saviors of the South, capable of defeating the creeping socialism and radical racialism of national Democrats. Several voters built upon the theme of a revolt against national Democrats by declaring that the Republican Party was the only institution capable of rescuing the South from the throes of Democratic liberalism. They aggrandized the GOP with Redeemer language similar, ironically, to that used to describe post-Reconstruction southern Democrats in the 1870s. Val Irion, chair of Democrats for Lyons, took out an advertisement in the Shreveport newspapers that stated, "We must look to the Republican Party to save not only the South but the nation."[66] Similar Redeemer language permeated an advertisement from several registered Democrats supporting Lyons. "OUR BALANCE OF POWER . . . CAN FREE THE SOUTH," the spot proclaimed, but only if voters elect a Republican to strike "an effective blow" against the National Democratic Party.[67] In a Lyons advertisement addressed "To Democrats Who Love the South," more than four hundred Democrats declared their support for the Republican Lyons, stating that he was just "the kind of man the SOUTH needs in this trying hour."[68]

With Republican efforts to tie his candidacy to Kennedyphobia in north Louisiana gaining traction, Waggonner responded by attacking the GOP's charges. He rebutted the calls for voting against the Democrat as a protest by urging voters to vote for a man and not against a party.[69] On a similar note, he pointed out: "This is a contest between *men* . . . not parties. No matter which candidate you vote for, vote for HIM, not just his PARTY."[70] The Democratic *Shreveport Journal* also espoused the idea of a race between men,[71] and

Waggoner dismissed the notion that voting for him was an endorsement of Kennedy and liberalism a "hobgoblin."[72] During a radio broadcast, Waggonner again tried to stress his independence from JFK by informing voters that Kennedy's name would not be on the ballot, only his own "because I am the candidate."[73] In a speech before the Shreveport Lions Club, he appeared worried that "some people think they are going to vote for John Kennedy again."[74] In a December debate in Caddo Parish, Waggonner argued, "You can't spite the President[;] you can only spite yourself."[75] Waggonner's responses to charges that he was tied to Kennedy suggest that Kennedyphobia was strong enough in northwest Louisiana to become the primary campaign issue—not only for Lyons but also for Waggonner, who worked tirelessly to refute Lyon's allegations.

Yet, while Waggonner strongly denounced the Republican efforts to attack his partisan ties to the Kennedy administration by stressing his political independence on the national level, he was just as quick to appeal to state Democratic Party loyalty as a reason for Louisianans to support him.[76] "I am the same sort of Democrat today that most of you out there are, and most of you are Democrats," he explained.[77] In one advertisement, Waggonner asked voters what kind of Democrats they were because the GOP was attacking them also with its insinuations that all Democrats were tied to the national party. "There has been an all out effort in this campaign," he noted, "to label every member of the Democratic Party as a liberal or radical and solely responsible for the socialistic policies of the national party . . . regardless of how you as individual Democrats have felt about this trend."[78] Pandering to voters' old partisan pride, Waggonner attested that Republican attacks on the Democratic Party are "not just an indictment of me, [they are] an indictment of you as well."[79] Democratic Congressional Executive Committee chairman N. B. Carstarphen placed a similar spot in the *Shreveport Times*, noting that never before had electing a Democrat in local and congressional elections been described as "a tragedy or a disaster"—an obvious reference to the Solid Democratic South's decades-long protection of white supremacy.[80] At the end of the campaign, Waggonner charged that his district had always been Democratic, and should remain so "[d]espite the disagreements we may have with the liberal wing of the Democratic Party."[81]

Waggonner also tried to play down Kennedyphobia by evoking a language similar to the States' Rights slate of electors in 1960, which he had openly supported. He drew negative attention to the Republican record on states' rights and foreign policy during the Eisenhower administration to show that neither party was suitably conservative at the national level. The *Shreveport Journal* called the notion that Waggonner's election would be a tragedy "spurious" and turned the issue of partisanship on the Republicans by proclaiming that identification with one party might "easily be considered as much of a liability as identification with the other."[82] Waggonner himself called out the "black marks of the Republican party," including the Republican administration appointment of Chief Justice Earl Warren, "their bayonet troops at Little Rock," and the "Republican stamp of approval on the Castro seizure of Cuba."[83] One Waggonner advertisement claimed that Republicans had done more to "strip the states of their constitutionally guaranteed rights than any administration in history."[84] During a debate between the two candidates, Waggonner maintained that both national Democrats and national Republicans were controlled by liberals, drawing attention to the fact that "our states' rights have been lost in the last eight years of Republican administration."[85] Eisenhower's use of troops during the integration of Central High School in Little Rock, Arkansas, represented, according to Waggonner, "the greatest set-back to States' Rights in the history of this Republic."[86] It was difficult for the Democrat to have been more direct: "When some people say they're going to vote Republican because they're tired of the Democrats they have a short memory. They forget about the Republican Judge Earl Warren who is trying to ram school integration down our throat . . . that it was Republican incompetence or indifference that lost Cuba to the Communists."[87]

Waggonner continued to counter GOP charges linking him to Kennedy and Kennedyphobia in the region by attacking the usefulness of a Republican congressman. Because Democrats were the majority party, Waggonner argued he would be able to accomplish things for the district whereas a Republican in the minority party could only block efforts by Democrats. A conservative Democrat could "lead," "initiate action," and "promote and take *positive* steps in association with his fellow conservatives."[88] Similarly, he urged voters not to "trade a record for a promise," but instead to help southern Democrats in Congress "with another Conservative."[89] Waggonner also recalled Reconstruction to challenge the idea of Redeemer Republicans.[90]

But toward the end of the campaign, Lyons, replying to Waggonner's charges, questioned his opponent's usefulness by continuing to link him to the national Democratic Party. "I don't believe it is possible for a man to go to Congress running under the national Democratic emblem and return constitutional government to the people," Lyons told a crowd from the back of a flatbed truck.[91] Democrats for Lyons chairman Val Irion, in his newspaper advertisements, offered a similar contention, urging voters to elect Lyons because "in Washington, Mr. Waggonner will be like a fish out of water, shunted aside, ignored, cold-shouldered by the socialists who have seized control of our Democratic Party."[92]

Waggonner also attempted to sidestep the role of national party politics in the election by praising the southern one-party system's success at limiting the political power of blacks. He appealed to racial disgust among voters by equating a two-party system with empowering African Americans because it would allow "bloc voting"—the idea that with two parties competing for the vote of the white majority, a small minority of black "bloc" voters would be capable of swinging elections whichever way they desired.[93] Waggonner even asserted that the black voters were supporting Lyons.[94] "If you have any doubt about how the Negroes are going to vote," he proclaimed, "then drive across the river and look at the bumper stickers on the Negroes' cars."[95] The Democratic *Shreveport Journal* echoed this claim.[96]

Lyons responded to Waggonner's implications that a two-party South would lead to black voting power by attacking the idea of a one-party South. He pointed out that communist nations such as Russia, China, and Cuba had one-party systems and declared that a one-party system was what "Washington liberals" wanted, continuing his Kennedyphobia theme.[97] The Democratic Party that dominated the South, Lyons argued, had allowed the Freedom Riders, ordered in federal marshals, "crawfished in Cuba," and adopted an "80% Socialistic program . . . sa[ying] the South is 'in the bag.'"[98] Urging white voters to look to the GOP for a new direction, Lyons perhaps unconsciously, echoed Karl Marx: "Southerners, throw off your chains!"[99]

While southerners in northwest Louisiana did not throw off their chains, Lyons nevertheless made a very impressive showing in a traditional Democratic stronghold. As election day passed, the Republican came just five thousand votes shy of victory, receiving 28,275 votes to Waggonner's 33,486. Most of Lyons's support came from Shreveport and the surrounding Caddo Parish, both of which he won by a substantial margin of more than six thousand votes. He also carried the two predominantly black precincts in Shreveport by almost a three-to-one margin.[100] But Lyons's 46 percent of the ballots (and 28,275 votes) represented the strongest showing ever by a Republican in the Fourth District. It is quite conceivable that, had his Democratic opponent not been so unflinchingly conservative and pro-segregationist, Lyons might well have won the seat. Lyons's victory in Caddo was the first time a Democrat lost the parish in a congressional race. The Waggonner-Lyons matchup drew a spectacular 61 percent turnout rate for an election where the congressional seat was the only item on the ballot.[101] The issue of Kennedyphobia and the competitiveness of the GOP excited the electorate enough to bring almost as many people to the polls in 1961 as the hotly contested Kennedy-Nixon states'-rights presidential race had brought for the down-ticket congressional election a year before.

The highest hurdle for the Lyons campaign to surmount turned out, ironically, to be the strength of partisanship in favor of a conservative Democrat. Political scientists Earl and Merle Black cite the 1961 special election as a classic example of "Democratic Smother"—a campaign strategy in which Democrats "smother[ed] the conservative Republican threat by emphasizing their own conservatism and acute unhappiness with the national Democratic party [sic]."[102] Therefore, Joe Waggonner was the perfect Democratic candidate for a district as conservative as the Louisiana Fourth District—a conservative segregationist stressing his independence from national Democrats and the Kennedy administration. Against an ideologically similar right-wing opponent, Lyons could not differentiate the GOP brand sufficiently or consolidate conservative support for his candidacy as a Republican. As Earl Black and Merle Black claim, at this point, "white majorities still preferred an ultraconservative Democrat to a conservative Republican."[103] Therefore, a Republican, anti-Kennedy campaign was limited in its capabilities when running head-on into a similar anti-Kennedy Democrat.

But what did Lyons's showing in the 1961 special election accomplish in the scope of Republican progress in north Louisiana and more broadly the South? For one, it solidified the notion that the GOP was becoming a viable, vote-getting option in southern elections *prior to the Goldwater presidential candidacy in 1964*. After the election, the *Caddo Republican* proclaimed that "Fourth District Republicans lost a battle, but won a war"[104] While Republican registration numbers were not rising significantly, Republican vote totals were. Compared to the 1960 congressional election in the Fourth District between incumbent Overton Brooks and Republican Fred McClanahan, the GOP vote grew significantly while the Democratic vote decreased, highlighting the importance of Kennedyphobia. Lyons received over eleven thousand more votes than McClanahan, whereas Waggonner received almost fourteen thousand fewer than Brooks.

Electoral support for Republicans in northwest Louisiana grew substantially after Kennedy's victory in 1960. Although Lyons lost in 1961, his impressive showing in northwest Louisiana illustrated that Kennedyphobia was a key factor in the support given to Republican candidates. Lyons declared, "The vote of 28,275 people, most of them lifelong Democrats, shows that there is a well-defined trend for a change to a type of leadership that will aggressively and effectively work for the re-establishment of Constitutional Government in America."[105]

Although Louisianans had proved more than willing to vote for Republican presidential candidates in the 1950s and 1960, the 1961 Lyons campaign was the first instance of a Republican running strongly in a congressional race in the northern part of the state. It demonstrated clearly that John Kennedy and racial liberalism had become a liability and campaign issue for Democrats facing strong challenges from conservative Republicans. His success confirmed that the roots of conservative congressional Republicanism in Louisiana, as well as the South, were evident well before Goldwater in 1964.

## Notes

1. These voters, though, were not realigning completely into the Republican column because the GOP was still losing most nonpresidential elections in the South and continued to lag behind Democrats in voter-registration totals (see Earl Black and Merle Black, *The Rise of Southern Republicans* [Cambridge: Belknap Press of Harvard University Press, 2002]).

2. C. H. Lyons Sr., "The Responsibility of the Republican Party of the Fourth Congressional District of Louisiana," address to the Convention of the Republican Party of the Fourth District of Louisiana, Shreveport, La., 5 August 1961, Manuscript vol. 3, Charlton Havard Lyons, Sr. Papers, Mss. 3075, Louisiana and Lower Mississippi Valley Collections, LSU Libraries, Baton Rouge.

3. Dino Alberti, "Republican Resurgence in North Louisiana: The Impact of Charlton H. Lyons, Sr., 1960–1965" (master's thesis, Louisiana Tech University, 1967), 47.

4. Alberti, "Republican Resurgence in North Louisiana," 15–21; Julia Morrow Gilmore, "A Statesman in Business and Politics," *Shreveport* Magazine, August 1962, 21; *Shreveport Journal*, 1 October 1961; *Shreveport Times*, 10 December 1961.

5. *Shreveport Times*, 25 September 1960.

6. Ibid.

7. Ibid.

8. Ibid., 29 October 1961.

9. Ibid., 10 December, 10, 1961.

10. Ibid.; *Shreveport Journal*, November 2, 1961; "Small Comfort," *Time*, 29 December 1961; Neil R. McMillan, *The Citizens' Council* (Urbana: University of Illinois Press, 1971); Michael J. Klarman, "How Brown Changed Race Relations: The Backlash Thesis," *Journal of American History* 81 (June 1994): 81–118.

11. *Shreveport Times*, 10 December 1961.

12. Ibid., 15 October 1961.

13. Ibid., 1 October 1961.

14. Ibid.

15. Ibid., 15 October 1961; *Shreveport Journal*, 11 November 1961; Alberti, "Republican Resurgence in North Louisiana," 27.

16. *Shreveport Times*, 5 and 19 November 1961, 1 and 2 December 1961.

17. Ibid., 5 and 19 November 1961, 1 December 1961.

18. Ibid., 5 and 19 November 1961, 3 December 1961.

19. Ibid., 5 and 19 November 1961.

20. Raymond Arsenault, *Freedom Riders: 1961 and the Struggle for Racial Justice* (New York: Oxford University Press, 2007); and Arsenault, "'You Don't Have to Ride Jim Crow': CORE and the 1947 Journey of Reconciliation," in *Before* Brown: *Civil Rights and White Backlash in the Modern South*, ed. Glenn Feldman, 1–20 (Tuscaloosa: University of Alabama Press, 2004).

21. "Texans for Integration," *Time*, November 10, 1961.

22. Hartley Brown, letter to the editor, *Shreveport Times*, 31 October 1961.

23. *Shreveport Times*, 1 November 1961.

24. Ibid., 3 and 12 November 1961.

25. Ibid., 17 December 1961.

26. Ibid., 5 November 1961.

27. Ibid., 14 and 17 November 1961; *Shreveport Journal*, 15 November 1961.

28. *Shreveport Times*, 19 November 1961.

29. Ibid., 4 and 14 December 1961.

30. W. M. Shaw to John Doles, 27 November 1961, Box 1, Folder 1, Joe Waggonner Papers, Special Collection, Louisiana Tech; *Shreveport Times*, 5 December 1961.

31. W. M. Shaw to Joe Waggonner and Charlton Lyons, 27 November 1961, Box 1, Folder 1, Joe Waggonner Papers, Special Collection, Louisiana Tech University.

32. *Shreveport Journal*, 4 December 1961; *Shreveport Times*, 4 December 1961; *Caddo Republican*, 15 December 1961, Maggie Bell Hodges Republican Party Materials, 1952–1964, Box 1, Folder 29, Noel Memorial Library, Louisiana State University, Shreveport.

33. *Shreveport Journal*, 4 December 1961; *Shreveport Times*, 4 December 1961; *Caddo Republican*, 15 December 1961, Maggie Bell Hodges Republican Party Materials, 1952–1964, Box 1, Folder 29, Noel Memorial Library, Louisiana State University, Shreveport; *Shreveport Times*, 5 December 1961; J. D. Waggonner, Jr., undated note, Box 1, Folder 1, Joe Waggonner Papers, Special Collection, Louisiana Tech University.

34. *Shreveport Times*, 5 November 1961.

35. Ibid., 19 November 1961.

36. Ibid., 19 December 1961, *Shreveport Journal*, 18 December 1961.

37. *Shreveport Times*, 7 and 15 December 1961; *Shreveport Journal*, 7 and 8 December 1961.

38. *Shreveport Journal*, 8 December 1961.

39. *Shreveport Times*, 15 December 1961.

40. Charlton Lyons, notes on "Age," Box 2, Folder 48, Charlton Havard Lyons, Sr. Papers, Mss. 3075, Louisiana and Lower Mississippi Valley Collections, LSU Libraries, Baton Rouge.

41. *Shreveport Times*, 16 November 1961, 12 December 1961; *Shreveport Journal*, 12 December 1961

42. *Shreveport Times*, 11 December 1961.

43. Ibid.

44. J. Leon Williams, letter to the editor, *Shreveport Journal*, 9 October 1961.

45. Mrs. McCullen, letter to the editor, *Shreveport Journal*, 25 October 1961.

46. M. C. Durr, letter to the editor, *Shreveport Times*, 10 October 1961; Kirk Railsback, letter to the editor, *Shreveport Times*, 24 October 1961.

47. *Caddo Republican*, 20 October 1961, Box 1, Folder 29, Maggie Bell Hodges Republican Party Materials, 1952–1964, Noel Memorial Library, Louisiana State University, Shreveport.

48. *Shreveport Journal*, 15 December 1961.

49. *Shreveport Times*, 13 December 1961; Benjamin L. Alpers, *Dictators, Democracy, and American Public Culture: Envisioning the Totalitarian Enemy, 1920s-1950s* (Chapel Hill: University of North Carolina Press, 2002).

50. *Shreveport Times,* 5 December 1961.

51. Ibid., 8 December 1961; *Shreveport Journal*, 7 December 1961.

52. Ibid., 15 December 1961.

53. Ibid., 1 December 1961.

54. Ibid., 11 November 1961.

55. *Shreveport Journal*, 8 December 1962.

56. Ibid., 13 December 1961.

57. *Shreveport Times*, 11 November 1961, 8 December 1961.

58. *Shreveport Journal*, 7 December 1961.

59. *Shreveport Times,* 17 December 1961, 15 December 1961.

60. Ibid., 8 December 1961; *Shreveport Journal*, 8 December 1961.

61. Ibid., 17 December 1961.

62. Ibid., 3 December 1961.

63. R. Lee Rogers, letter to the editor, *Shreveport Journal*, 13 November 1963; and in *Shreveport Times,* 10 December 1963.

64. Robert Marlowe, letter to the editor, *Shreveport Times,* 17 December 1961.

65. R. M. Nevin, letter to the editor, *Shreveport Times,* 17 December 1961.

66. *Shreveport Times*, 10 December 1961; *Shreveport Journal*, 11 December 1961.

67. *Shreveport Times*, 12 December 1961; a variation of this ad appeared in the *Shreveport Journal* on 11 December 1961.

68. *Shreveport Times*, 17 December 1961.

69. Ibid., 28 November 1961.

70. Ibid., 19 November 1961.

71. *Shreveport Journal*, 11 November 1961.

72. *Shreveport Times*, 17 December 1961.

73. Ibid., 6 December 1961.

74. Ibid., 7 December 1961.

75. Ibid., 15 December 1961.

76. This was a tremendous advantage for Waggonner because registered Democrats vastly outnumbered registered Republicans. In 1961, only nine-tenths of 1 percent of Louisiana voters was registered Republican while over 98 percent was registered Democrat (see Wayne Parent and Huey Perry, "Louisiana: African Americans, Republicans, and Party Competition" in *The New Politics of the Old South: An Introduction to*

*Southern Politics,* ed. Charles S. Bullock III and Mark J. Rozell [Lanham, Md.: Rowman and Littlefield, 1998], 118).

77. *Shreveport Times,* 8 December 1961.

78. Ibid.; *Shreveport Journal,* 8 December 1961.

79. *Shreveport Times,* 15 December 1961; *Shreveport Journal,* 15 December 1961.

80. *Shreveport Times,* 10 December 1961.

81. Ibid., 19 December 1961.

82. *Shreveport Journal,* 19 December 1961, 18 December 1961.

83. *Shreveport Times,* 19 November 1961.

84. Ibid., 15 November 1961.

85. Ibid., 17 November 1961.

86. Ibid., 3 December 1961.

87. *Shreveport Journal,* 14 December 1961.

88. *Shreveport Times,* 19 November 1961.

89. *Shreveport Times,* 18 December 1961; *Shreveport Journal,* 18 December 1961.

90. *Shreveport Times,* 15 November 1961.

91. Ibid., 10 December 1961.

92. Ibid.; *Shreveport Journal,* 11 December 1961.

93. "Bloc voting" had been used by conservative southern Democrats in Congress, which Waggonner and other Democrats making this charge do not mention.

94. Waggonner was correct. Blacks did support Lyons more than the Democrat. In the two predominantly black Shreveport precincts, Lyons received 687 votes to 281 for Waggonner (*Shreveport Times,* 20 December 1961).

95. *Shreveport Journal,* 14 December 1961.

96. Ibid., 15 December 1961.

97. *Shreveport Times,* 10 December 1961.

98. Ibid.

99. Ibid.

100. Ibid., 20 December 1961.

101. Ibid., 21 December 1961, 20 December 1961; *Caddo Republican,* 12 January 1962, Box 1: Folder 29, Maggie Bell Hodges Republican Party Materials, 1952–1964, Noel Memorial Library, Louisiana State University, Shreveport.

102. Earl Black and Merle Black, *The Rise of Southern Republicans* (Cambridge: Belknap Press of Harvard University Press, 2002), 171.

103. Ibid., 166.

104. *Caddo Republican,* 12 January 1962, Box 1: Folder 29, Maggie Bell Hodges Republican Party Materials, 1952–1964, Noel Memorial Library, Louisiana State University, Shreveport.

105. *Shreveport Times,* 24 December 1961.

# 7

# Race, Grassroots Activism, and the Evolution of the Republican Right in South Carolina, 1952–1974

JOHN W. WHITE

At the onset of the Great Depression, South Carolina was a single-party state with a political system dominated by rural elites. Democratic primaries were the only competitive elections and restrictive voting laws limited political participation. This one-party system was maintained by a combination of Jim Crow laws, poll taxes, and corrupt voter-registration practices that severely limited the voting rights of African Americans and poor whites. In the three decades after World War II, however, the state experienced unprecedented industrial expansion, striking modifications in racial customs, and the emergence of the Cold War economy—all of which led to the birth of a competitive two-party political system for the first time in nearly a century. Although the Democratic Party retained its control of the state legislature and remained a potent force in local politics well into the 1990s, the emergence of a competitive and well-organized opposition party in the 1950s and 1960s laid the groundwork for the modern Republican ascendancy in the Palmetto State.[1]

Between 1952 and 1974, the Republican Party of South Carolina constructed a viable political coalition that was centered around consistent and complex appeals to mainstream white voters who were concerned about heavy-handed federal policies, but were unwilling to jeopardize their own interests by siding with the South's most intransigent segregationists in an unwinnable battle to preserve Jim Crow. Moreover, Richard Nixon's so-called "southern strategy" was not the beginning of the state's move toward Republican dominance, but the culmination of nearly two decades of grassroots political change. Contrary to many accounts, the presidential elections of 1952 and 1960—along with a host of local and statewide races in 1961, 1962, 1966, and 1970—provided important benchmarks in the emergence of the modern GOP in South

Carolina—even more so than the extensively studied contests in 1948, 1964, and 1968.

The presidential election of 1948 may have exposed some initial stirrings of the factional schisms and popular discontent that would later develop within the Democratic Party, but it also demonstrated that those cracks had not widened enough to create room for two-party competition. As a number of scholars have pointed out, Strom Thurmond's Dixiecrat campaign was only victorious in states where Thurmond's name appeared on the ballot as a regular Democrat. Additionally, the lack of even token support for Republican Thomas Dewey revealed that, although the Democratic Party suffered from some internal divisions, white southern voters had not yet softened on their antipathy to the GOP. Combined with Thurmond's inability to unseat popular Democratic Senator Olin Johnston in 1950, the results from 1948 revealed the continued, if somewhat diminished, potency of the New Deal coalition in South Carolina.[2]

It was not until 1952 that white South Carolina voters gave the first unambiguous indication that the Democratic Party's stranglehold on the region was legitimately threatened. The candidacy of Dwight D. Eisenhower posed an interesting dilemma for southern Democrats. The popular former general and war hero appealed to southern whites' sense of honor and patriotism, but it was his reputation as the more conservative of the two major candidates that intrigued grassroots activists in South Carolina. In the wake of a number of court cases that had challenged the legality of the white primary (*Rice v. Elmore* and *Brown v. Baskin*), the constitutionality of segregated education (*Briggs v. Elliott*), and the fairness of unequal pay (*Thompson v. Gibbes*) in South Carolina, white voters faced a deep uncertainty over the Democratic Party's nascent interests in civil rights and the future of Jim Crow. And yet, most South Carolinians recognized that the state had experienced a significant increase in the average standard of living during the New Deal and World War II. Especially in the Black Belt, many rank-and-file whites attributed to Democrats these improvements to federal investments in the defense industry and thus improvements in their own economic well-being.

World War II had saved the Charleston Naval Base and Naval Shipyard, the Korean War rescued Fort Jackson, and the Cold War helped pump money into the state's other defense facilities. The Charleston Naval Shipyard alone employed between ten thousand and fifteen thousand workers during the late 1940s and early 1950s, and the atomic-weapons plant under construction near Aiken was rapidly becoming South Carolina's largest employer. Federal jobs, like those at the navy yard, paid employees on average nearly twice as much as other workers and helped fuel statewide population changes. The construction of the Savannah River Site nuclear-weapons facility alone brought almost forty thousand new people to the Aiken area, and once the facility was operational it employed four thousand full-time workers. Almost overnight the sleepy southern backwater known for its fertile soil and red clay mud became a federal town. According to historian James Farmer, the impact on Aiken was greater than that of the Civil War: "Sherman's army was larger, but it did not have families in its train and it only passed through."[3]

This atmosphere of racial uncertainty and rapid demographic transformation had a dramatic impact on South Carolina's electorate. The combination of the changing population and the elimination of voting restrictions as a result of *Brown v. Baskin* fostered an increase of nearly 140 percent in the number of registered voters in South Carolina between 1948 and 1952: "new, relatively independent party members" less inclined to trust Democratic Party elders, and more unpredictable. This trend was exemplified by a new "grass roots citizens' club" in Charleston that urged its members to capture control of local Democratic Party machinery so they could more effectively pressure the national party to reverse its drift toward the political left. By the spring of 1952 similar grassroots organizations had formed throughout the South Carolina Black Belt and began to function as loosely organized interest groups within the Democratic Party.[4] Nonetheless, the South Carolina Democratic Party still hoped to avoid another schism like that of 1948. Democratic loyalists, such as state senator Edgar Brown, House Speaker Sol Blatt, and Senator Olin Johnston called for unity, and more fiscally conservative leaders, such as Governor James F. Byrnes, initially rejected appeals for a revival of Dixiecrat separatism.

The new grassroots groups, which were dominated by middle-class businessmen, tended to support racial and fiscal conservatism but were not necessarily the intellectual descendants of South Carolina conservatives such as Senator "Cotton" Ed Smith. They were opposed to many of President Truman's Fair Deal reforms (such as proposed national health care) and disinclined to promote Roosevelt-style economic liberalism. Although they supported traditional racial controls, these new grassroots clubs were suspicious of the economic effects of unrestrained race-baiting. They were also frustrated by their inability to unseat the state's Old Guard. After finding it difficult to undermine the more entrenched loyalist members of the party, the citizens' clubs refocused their efforts on organizing a movement to place Ike on the state's ballot and pressured the state's political elite to endorse the general, forming an organization, South Carolinians for Eisenhower (SCE), to run the campaign autonomous from the state GOP.[5]

Despite this growing pressure from hard-core segregationists and professional whites to bolt the Democratic Party for the second presidential election in a row, most of South Carolina's political elite endorsed Stevenson. That did not, however, stop the grassroots activists from applying pressure to even the most devout defenders of states' rights. For example, one faction of South Carolinians for Eisenhower, the Grass Roots Crusade, targeted First District congressman L. Mendel Rivers with subtle reminders of his white constituents' allegiance to "states' rights." Rivers was an unlikely target for any conservative political organization. He was a die-hard segregationist and a strict anticommunist. Nonetheless, his uncertain efforts to navigate the intersections of local and national politics regarding racial and sectional concerns encapsulated the dilemmas facing white segregationists on the eve of the *Brown* decision. Despite his record, Alice Beckett, of the Colleton County Grass Roots Crusade, wrote to Rivers in April 1952 and urged the congressman to use his "best efforts to protect States' Rights . . . and to see that the Constitution is preserved." Rivers heartily agreed and bragged that he had spoken out on "States Rights' in 1948," and wished the Grass Roots Crusade had been around then.[6]

Other political leaders, especially those who considered themselves staunch New Dealers, were less confident than Rivers in the party's ability to navigate another Dixiecrat-like schism. The "political situation in South Carolina," warned Senator Burnet R. Maybank, was "very bad. . . . The people are very bitter" about civil rights and the Supreme Court decisions. By midsummer, politicians throughout the state were under enormous pressure from SCE. For example, H. Sanford Howie Jr. of Greenville wrote to Byrnes to encourage the governor to lend his support to Eisenhower unless, of course, a pro-segregation southerner was named as the Democratic nominee: "Too long we have allowed the Northern wing of the party to completely ignore our interests and candidates; to vote Republican . . . would not mean a divorce from the Democratic Party."[7] Edgar Brown, who directed the Stevenson-Sparkman campaign in South Carolina, predicted that "many good people" would vote for Eisenhower, and that the Republican supporters would "organize a definite Eisenhower campaign and try to make a strong showing in the State." To counter this challenge, Brown insisted that "rallies," "speakers," "radio programs," and a significant fund-raising effort would be necessary.[8]

Brown had good reason to be alarmed. In early fall, a number of Black Belt political leaders succumbed to pressure from white activists and endorsed the independent Eisenhower campaign: Governor Jimmy Byrnes, Mount Pleasant mayor Francis Coleman, and former Charleston mayor Thomas P. Stoney. In addition, SCE received the support of prominent newspapermen Thomas

R. Waring and William D. Workman and hired the public-relations firm of Bradley, Graham, and Hamby to manage the campaign. Even Rivers, who had nearly lost his congressional seniority for supporting Thurmond in 1948, tempered his support for the national ticket and signed a petition calling on the state party not to punish individuals who voted "independent."[9]

Rivers was in a particularly precarious situation as he attempted to strike a balance between his outraged constituents and losing seniority within the national party. His district had a substantial number of hard-core segregationists and a growing number of white professionals who were less committed to New Deal economic liberalism than were middle-class whites in the textile belt upstate. Therefore it was no surprise that Rivers's attempt to have his cake and eat it too was unpopular with the Grass Roots Crusade. Crusade member and former state senator Paul Quattlebaum felt Rivers's decision to sign the resolution allowing Democrats to vote for Eisenhower without repercussions while formally endorsing Stevenson was hypocritical and told the congressman so.[10] Though he was unlikely to face a serious challenge from the political right, Rivers did worry that a divided conservative vote would create an opportunity for a biracial moderate alliance to emerge in the Low Country.[11] Nonetheless, Rivers understood that Eisenhower had received a groundswell of popular support in South Carolina. Ever the pragmatist, Rivers left the door open for a political change of heart and insisted, "I have not made up my mind the part I propose to take in this campaign other than vote." He arranged to be out of the country on a congressional trip for most of September; like many southern Democrats, he was hoping to protect his congressional seniority without taking part in the campaign.[12]

As Rivers began to waffle on his support of Stevenson, the ability of SCE to mobilize community resources was bolstered by a highly effective public-relations campaign. Dolly Hamby, a relative political novice, drafted a series of ads that resonated with South Carolina whites, underscoring the fact that voting for Eisenhower wouldn't "in any way affect their party loyalty on a state basis." Hamby insisted the campaign remain an independent group with no political aspirations of its own and no affiliation with any party."[13] Furthermore, she began to refine some of the organization's amorphous and undisciplined criticisms of the national Democratic Party into a sophisticated campaign of well-placed catchwords that presaged later mainstays of the GOP in the South. Under her direction, SCE emphasized Truman-era "graft, corruption, socialism, inefficiency, big government [and] . . . bureaucracy."[14]

Under Hamby's direction, South Carolinians for Eisenhower adeptly navigated the difficult intersections of race and politics in the South. For the most part, the group was able to appeal to whites alienated by national

Democratic support for African American voting rights without appearing to be reactionaries or extremists. SCE consistently assailed corrupt government bureaucracies and rights-based liberalism knowing that, despite specific references to blacks, most white South Carolinians would draw a connection with federal entitlement programs and civil rights legislation. For example, SCE proclaimed that "extravagant Federal spending, high taxes, inflation, and the many Federal 'handouts' hiding under the name of welfare are leading us down the dead end road of socialism and ruin." "WE BELIEVE that all sovereign states should be free to handle local problems locally and to govern themselves according to the expressed wishes of the people in each state." Overall, SCE managed to garner support from Black Belt segregationists with varying degrees of support for preserving Jim Crow, and it did so while running a mainstream campaign absent of palpable racial demagoguery. By joining together the fragmented coterie of white conservatives, the organization helped fuel a groundswell of support for the Republican candidate that united what historian Bruce H. Kalk has christened as a coalition of cosmopolitan whites with their ultra-segregationist neighbors.[15]

The success of South Carolinians for Eisenhower did not go unnoticed by national GOP leaders. When Eisenhower stopped in Columbia, his visit was not sponsored by the Republican Party, but by SCE and Governor Byrnes. During his speech, Ike promised to uphold the constitutional principle of states' rights; southern white grassroots activists intensified their pressure on local political leaders to jump on the Eisenhower bandwagon. Rivers told Representative E. E. Cox of Georgia's Second Congressional District: "In my locality people are frenzied . . . everybody is supporting Eisenhower. . . . I have never seen such bitter opposition to Truman and Stevenson as exists in the whole South Carolina Low country. . . . [Eisenhower] is going to get a whale of a vote . . . Jim Byrnes is really going to bat for [him]."[16]

Three days later, on October 25, Rivers caved to constituent pressure and endorsed Eisenhower. Eager to rationalize his abandonment of Stevenson, Rivers professed loyalty to the Democratic Party of Jefferson, Calhoun, and Wade Hampton, but claimed that the national party had "been captured" and was "controlled by elements with ideologies foreign to democracy." He insisted the party's turn to the left was a result of dangerous outsiders with communistic ideas. In a nod to Cold War xenophobia, Rivers declared: "America has been a mecca for many people from across the seas. They have come to this country and grown rich . . . and many of them now seek to change the very type and form of Government under which they have waxed so rich. [These people] are now charting the course of the National Democratic Party."[17]

Rivers worked throughout the fall to convince voters he had not changed his basic ideology. "When Governor Stevenson was nominated at Chicago, I had hopes that he would lead the party of our fathers back to the road of States Rights and local government," said Rivers, but "upon my return, I find that the president proclaimed a strong Civil Rights program." Rivers warned his constituents that his decision to support the independent movement could cost him his "political job," but he claimed any other action would cost him his "self-respect." "It is often the practice of some Democrats, when they don't like their candidate, to 'go fishing' come Election Day," said Rivers, "I call these men cowards."[18] "I followed this course in 1948." [On election day I will] "cast my vote for the Democratic electors for Eisenhower."[19]

Rivers, it seems, was dragged onto the Eisenhower bandwagon by the potent grassroots effort within his district. In a very short time, South Carolinians for Eisenhower had built a powerful campaign and altered the state election ballots. By election day, SCE had raised nearly $100,000 and the GOP attempted to remove itself from the ballot so as not to confuse voters, prevented from doing so only because the ballots had already been printed.[20] Although Rivers agonized over his decision and was a latecomer to the cause, the choice to support Eisenhower was, ultimately, not a difficult one for many South Carolina whites. The former general seemed to transcend party. He was popular with widespread name recognition, and most South Carolinians considered him the racially conservative candidate. Of course, many southerners also liked Ike's military credentials, lending credence to the notion that he would also maintain high levels of federal spending at defense installations. His perceived racial conservatism attracted hard-core segregationists and more moderate whites who feared that increased federal management of local race relations would push more and more whites into the hard-core camp.

It was no coincidence then that the Stevenson-Sparkman campaign's most concerted attempt to diminish Eisenhower's appeal in the Black Belt was targeted at defense workers. The Democrats implied that a Republican victory would cause the loss of jobs in the state's Low Country defense industries. No South Carolinian was in a better position to refute such claims than Rivers. The congressman's position on the Armed Services Committee and his reputation for steering defense dollars to the region made him an authority. "It is an insult to the intelligence of these fine, patriotic Americans for . . . Stevenson to try to pressure these employees into believing that a vote for Eisenhower would affect these installations," Rivers insisted. The congressman promised workers they would get "every protection" if they voted for Eisenhower.[21]

Despite such fierce opposition from Rivers, Byrnes, and SCE, Stevenson won the state in 1952 by five thousand votes. Loyal Democrats upstate voted two to one in favor of Stevenson. White textile workers and the strong support of African American voters helped the Stevenson-Sparkman ticket achieve one of its few victories. Republicans did, however, learn an important lesson. Eisenhower's strong showing verified that the "Solid South" was cracking. Eisenhower overwhelmingly carried the Black Belt areas where fears of widespread racial change were most acute. Rivers's First Congressional District provided the most support for the independent ballot, giving over 65 percent of its vote to Eisenhower.[22]

In an election postmortem, Jimmy Byrnes estimated that about fifty-nine thousand blacks had voted for the national Democrat and nearly all of Eisenhower's votes came from white voters. Thus Ike carried the state's white vote by a significant margin. Correspondent Ray Moley concluded that Stevenson's total vote among South Carolina whites was a scant 114,000. After Eisenhower's election, most of SCE's members refused to abandon the Democratic Party because the GOP had little to no official structure, almost no ability to raise funds, and was incapable of electing anyone to a statewide office. In other words, the road to political success in South Carolina was through the state Democratic Party, and few whites were willing to abandon those advantages.[23]

Despite winning the majority of the white vote in 1952, Eisenhower's support in South Carolina quickly fizzled. In the year following the general's inauguration, his administration desegregated the navy base in Charleston and the civilian workforce at the naval yard. Then, in May 1954, the United States Supreme Court ruled against South Carolina in *Briggs v. Elliott*—a decision handed down as part of the *Brown* decision. White South Carolinians were outraged and blamed Eisenhower for nominating Supreme Court Chief Justice Earl Warren.[24] In the firestorm of southern protests that followed *Brown*, white South Carolinians voiced opposition to both national parties and there was talk of another Dixiecrat movement from South Carolina governor George Bell Timmerman. That same month, state attorney general T. C. Callison declared the only option was to "abandon the public schools." Timmerman's rhetoric encouraged South Carolina's radical fringe to push for a unified and resolute response against any efforts to desegregate southern society.[25]

Perpetually concerned that they might lose the political advantage to white backsliders on race or that apathy would erode white commitment to resisting the Supreme Court's order, hard-core segregationists took every opportunity to discredit the possibility of a moderate solution. For example, after a number of white ministers encouraged congregations to refrain from harmful actions toward their black neighbors, they were quickly silenced. The governor's father, George Bell Timmerman Sr., for instance, orchestrated the resignation of the pastor of the First Baptist Church in Batesburg by convincing the conservative congregation that he was too liberal to continue. Orangeburg conservative worshipers forced the Methodist Church to relocate Reverend John V. Murray for speaking out against segregation.[26]

Intractable white South Carolinians, many of whom had supported Eisenhower in 1952, flocked to join White Citizens' Councils (WCC) and encouraged the state to engage in dilatory legal tactics to forestall desegregation. Determined to combat thoroughgoing racial change, hard-core segregationists were encouraged in early 1956 when the University of Alabama expelled the school's first African American student, Arthurine Lucy. South Carolinians passed a series of laws to crack down on civil rights activists, promised to close public schools, made it illegal for black educators to claim membership in the NAACP, and launched an intimidation campaign against student and faculty activists at South Carolina State College.[27] Unlike in 1948 and 1952, a viable third option was not immediately available to disgruntled southern whites. Despite the best efforts of Timmerman to convince southern governors to support a Dixiecrat-like third party, there was little interest in abandoning the Democrats among other well-known politicians.[28]

Many whites felt that the state had no option but to return to the Democratic Party and hope for the best. After the national convention in Chicago, even Timmerman attempted to put a positive spin on the party's position on civil rights, dismissing the idea of supporting the Republican candidate. He declared that Eisenhower's efforts to desegregate the school system in the District of Columbia were "100 percent more damaging than the decision of the court itself." Neville Bennett, the South Carolina Democratic Party chairman, claimed that he had received assurances from Adlai Stevenson that the party would not forcibly implement federal desegregation rulings, and Stevenson himself wrote to the *Camden News* and promised to use the "prestige" of the presidency to work out a compromise on the desegregation issue.[29] Most of South Carolina's leading Democrats eventually endorsed Stevenson, convinced that protecting southern seniority in Congress was cause enough to remain loyal. Like most elected officers, the state Democratic Convention also endorsed Stevenson. Even though the vote was close, it offered a sharp contrast to the previous two elections. The party had endorsed Stevenson in 1952, but it did so with a special caveat that allowed party members to support and vote for Eisenhower. There was no such stipulation in the first post-*Brown* presidential contest. Moreover, after the state Democratic Convention, even hard-core segregationists like Timmerman and Rivers issued calls for party unity and endorsed Stevenson. Their approval of the national Democrat is evidence that South Carolina's elected officials recognized the futility of supporting a third-party candidate. Timmerman said Stevenson was "the best of a bad lot."[30]

Nonetheless, many rank-and-file white South Carolinians still felt alienated by the national party. By the end of September, South Carolinians for Independent Electors demanded that the state place their organization on the presidential ballot of 1956. The group, which had promised to award all "un-pledged" ballots to Virginia senator and massive-resistance proponent Harry F. Byrd, issued a statement declaring its belief in "the restoration of constitutional government," respect for "states' rights," and against "federal interference in school matters." In order to assure itself a place on the ballot, the organization recorded more than thirty-six thousand signatures on its petition, even though state laws required only ten thousand. It also received the endorsement of Senator Strom Thurmond and former governor Jimmy Byrnes.[31] South Carolinians for Independent Electors was a hodgepodge of WCC leaders, former Dixiecrats, and veterans of the SCE. Nearly all of the organization's leaders had voted Dixiecrat in 1948, for Eisenhower in 1952, and had supported the Citizens' Councils after *Brown*. For example, Farley Smith, Micah Jenkins, S. E. Rogers, Stanley Morse, and Thomas Stoney all played leadership roles.[32]

After a strong start, the "un-pledged electors" movement sputtered. In doing so, it revealed some deep-seated schisms among white voters and gave the first indication that many white professionals in the state's cities would not join their more intractable neighbors in support of third-party protest. Three separate studies of the presidential election of 1956 later found that white voters were divided across regional and socioeconomic lines. Overall, Stevenson collected just over 45 percent of the vote, compared to less than 30 percent for Byrd and 25 percent for Eisenhower. In contrast to the previous two elections, a majority white vote failed to emerge. The "un-pledged electors" movement, unlike the Dixiecrats and the independent Eisenhower campaign, was a complete failure. Once again, white professionals near Charleston and Columbia tended to vote for Ike, and working-class whites upstate continued to vote for the national Democrats. Voters in only eleven of South Carolina's forty-six counties cast a majority for Byrd. Even Black Belt counties like Berkeley, Orangeburg, and Dorchester demonstrated limited support for the WCC-backed campaign and awarded the independent ticket a mere plurality. Moreover, according to political scientist Gregory Sampson, the socioeconomic and regional divisions among whites combined with a decrease in voter turnout to demonstrate ambiguity "as to which party or candidate held the least objectionable position" on black civil rights.[33]

The presidential election of 1956 was the only contest between 1948 and 1972 in which fewer South Carolinians voted than in the prior election. More than forty thousand voters in South Carolina chose to stay home. Sampson concluded that "when given the choice of a racially moderate Republican presidential candidate and the symbolic representation of a movement organized around racially reactionary politics, white voters in the Black Belt counties overwhelmingly preferred the latter," but, in more urban and suburban areas, many white (and even some black) voters were conflicted. Sampson and political scientists Bruce Kalk and Donald Fowler agree that persistent New Deal loyalties combined with a divided white vote to hand victory to Stevenson in the election, thereby revealing the thin veneer of white unity.[34]

Between the reelection of Eisenhower and 1960, whites rarely questioned the state's commitment to Jim Crow and only a tiny handful of white liberals, such as Jack O'Dowd and Alice Spearman, even dared to suggest that the state comply with the 1955 *Brown* implementation order. Despite this superficial unity, the widespread white endorsement of South Carolina's system of racial apartheid remained a complex and often contradictory phenomenon. Many whites privately sensed that token compliance and bureaucratic obstacles were more effective long-term strategies for preserving both public order and white privilege without doing irreparable harm to state and local economies, but such concerns were undercut by the continued reluctance of most moderate whites to endorse even minimal compliance. Whether from apprehension that doing so would open the way to greater desegregation, or from fear of being branded "race traitors" by the most extreme proponents of massive resistance, moderate whites rarely questioned the effectiveness of uncompromising resistance—at least not publicly.

These cracks in the façade of white unity were exacerbated by the increased toll of federal pressure and the excessive tactics of South Carolina's most committed white segregationists. The confidence among hard-core white supremacists following the expulsion of Lucy from Alabama was shattered in 1957 when Eisenhower ordered the forced desegregation of Central High School in Little Rock, Arkansas. A wave of protests followed, but most educated whites could see that Jim Crow's days were numbered. After the home of a prominent white moderate, Claudia Sanders, was bombed by Klansmen in Gaffney, South Carolina, the private concerns of white political and economic leaders in the state began to percolate to the surface. The state's newspapers offered a "lukewarm" condemnation of the violent episode, but as usual blamed the incident on the heightened racial tensions and insisted that it was civil rights activists who had "incited" the Klan in the first place. Although public officials condemned Klan activity in general, no one of note declared their support for

Sanders's right to opine on the matter. One white moderate noted that state leaders responded to Klan violence with far less fervor than they had shown in their condemnations of the president's use of force in Little Rock.[35]

Still, according to contemporary observers, "respectable South Carolinians were appropriately shocked." Sanders was a member of at least four "old Charleston" families. She had graduated from the prestigious Ashley Hall girls' school, and her husband was a physician. For middle-class whites, the idea of working-class white men blowing up the home of a prominent white woman was an affront to southern notions about gender and class.[36]

Finding those responsible was not difficult, Howard Quint observed. It required neither Sherlock Holmes nor Dick Tracy to track down the culprits; the trail led directly to the Klan. Luther Boyette, Robert Martin, James Roy McCullough, Cletus Sparks, and John E. Painter were soon arrested. Investigators found the minutes from Klan meetings in Boyette's car, and the FBI determined that dirt in the nail-keg bomb was from the yard of the Klan's meeting house. Martin gave a full confession and implicated the other men in the attack.[37]

The next day, the five men were released on bond. They did not in any way attempt to conceal their involvement in the crime, and all five spoke about the attack at a KKK rally in Gaffney. Shortly after that Klan meeting, a car under which Martin was working mysteriously fell, killing him, but his death was ruled an accident. After his death, magistrate I. B. Kendrick reasoned that, even though Martin's testimony was witnessed by law-enforcement officers and notarized, it was "hearsay" and therefore inadmissible in a court of law. Kendrick also threw out the KKK minute book found in Boyette's car. The case disintegrated, and only Painter and McCullough were brought to trial, both of whom won an acquittal.[38]

Following the Sanders bombing—the capstone of increasingly violent and desperate attempts to hold the line of complete segregation—white South Carolinians were left to ask themselves whether they were willing to tolerate overt violence in order to silence dissension in their own ranks. They were also left to wonder if their efforts would be better served by supporting a carefully managed desegregation than by combating each and every attempt to alter traditional racial arrangements. With the specter of federal enforcement of the *Brown* decision hanging over the entire region, many whites came to realize that the preservation of Jim Crow would no longer ensure public order. In fact, some whites finally began to appreciate that it could have precisely the opposite effect. The attack on Claudia Sanders was a reminder that when state leaders implicitly encouraged whites to resist any alteration in the racial status quo, more militant segregationists would light the fuse of racial violence.

South Carolina's state courts, civic leaders, and elected officials had helped to create a climate where some white extremists felt comfortable taking drastic measures to defend the state's rigid system of Jim Crow. In the process, however, they also convinced many whites that unchecked white resistance was not necessarily in the state's best interests.[39]

With that in mind, mainstream white voters revisited the idea of supporting a Republican in 1960. Despite Texan Lyndon Johnson's appearance on the ticket as the Democratic Party's nominee for the vice presidency, white segregationists had largely given up any hope that the national party would soften its stance on race. They also had no faith in the GOP to defend any vestige of racial segregation, but given the growing sense that national Republicans were more amenable to token desegregation, there was hope for the creation of a potent conservative political alliance. Nationally, the Republican Party was more homogeneous than the Democrats. Thus GOP candidates outside the South faced less pressure from African Americans and New Deal liberals to push for immediate and far-reaching integration. By 1960, Republican strategists began to recognize that they could pursue the votes of southern whites without jeopardizing important blocs within their own party. Richard Nixon, the candidate in 1960, proclaimed, "It's time for the Democratic candidates to quit taking the South for granted and it's time for the Republican Party to quit conceding the South to the Democrats." Although Nixon was a former member of the NAACP and had courted black voters for Eisenhower in 1956, he presented himself as a more racially conservative candidate than his opponent, John F. Kennedy.[40]

Nixon and his campaign staff knew that Kennedy was vulnerable in the South, with the Democratic platform reading "all men are created equal" and recommending "equal access for all Americans." Leading up to the Democratic National Convention, Kennedy and his future running mate, Lyndon Johnson, campaigned for an active federal role in desegregating schools and ending racial discrimination in federal housing. Though Kennedy downplayed that role in the general election, his nominal interest in civil rights was disturbing to southern whites, who were uneasy after the Democratic candidate telephoned Martin Luther King's wife, Coretta, on the eve of the election after King was jailed in Georgia during a civil rights protest.[41]

Kennedy enjoyed a reputation as a political moderate throughout much of the nation, but southern whites tended to view the northern Democrat with skepticism. South Carolina's delegates to the national convention protested the civil rights plank. Although this was futile, conservative South Carolina Democrats were once again able to convince the state party to adopt a resolution allowing party members to vote for the presidential electors of their choice without jeopardizing their standing within the state Democratic Party. That, however, was not enough to convince many hard-core segregationists to remain loyal. In the weeks following the national convention, several leaders from the 1956 independent elector movement, such as former Association of Citizens' Councils of South Carolina (ACCSC) chairman Micah Jenkins, announced their defection to the GOP. In the metropolitan areas around Columbia and Charleston, the Republican Party seemed to win scores of converts almost overnight. One study of these "new Republicans" found that most of them had followed a similar path: they were political novices or they were former Democrats alienated by the party's new "liberal" image. According to Sampson, they supported Thurmond in 1948 and Eisenhower in 1952 and 1956.[42]

Given the Democratic Party's strong state organization and lingering distrust of the GOP among working-class whites, some political hopefuls chose to endorse national Republicans without formally leaving the party of their grandfathers. For the fourth consecutive presidential election, dissident Democrats formed an "independent" organization that endorsed a candidate other than the party's nominee for the presidency. Under the direction of Albert Watson, a Columbia attorney, South Carolinians for Nixon and Lodge campaigned for the Republican candidates. In a portent of things to come, the organization revisited the rhetoric of South Carolinians for Eisenhower and avoided crass race-baiting and steered clear of calls to preserve de jure segregation. Instead the campaign returned to making more subtle overtures to whites.[43]

In the national campaign, the ideological differences between Nixon and Kennedy were hardly perceivable. Both argued in favor of civil rights, but downplayed the issue; both were staunch anticommunists; and they both called for increases in the defense budget. On the state level, however, Republican Party officials and dissident Democrats drew a stark contrast between the two. Once again, the Republican campaign was managed by Bradley, Graham, and Hamby, and, once again, the campaign focused on a few central themes that would portray Nixon favorably to white voters without presenting him as an extremist. Hamby's campaign ads were especially adept at portraying Nixon as the only true "conservative" in the race. It worked with Watson to spread rumors that communists were hopeful of a Kennedy victory, and arranged for ex-Dixiecrat and former governor of Texas Allan Shivers to campaign for Nixon in South Carolina.[44] Much like her campaign in 1952, Hamby's advertisements tended to combine different, yet complementary, issues that appealed to conservative white South Carolinians. A film quoted Watson's and Thurmond's opinions that the national Democratic platform was antisouthern, would promote "racial amalgamation," and was a "road map for economic collapse."[45] The film's focus on the real or imagined "abuses" of federal power was a conscious effort to attract white professionals and merchants who were concerned about heavy-handed federal policies but were unwilling to jeopardize their own interests to fight an unwinnable conflict over Jim Crow. Hamby realized (much earlier than most political strategists) that, by criticizing the bureaucratic impediments and federal power in general, rather than focusing solely on race, her clients could attract more voters.[46] In another spot, the women's chairman of South Carolina Democrats for Nixon, a former member of the Citizens' Councils, insisted: "South Carolina women are deeply concerned about Kennedy, strange people, foreign influence and morals."[47]

Nixon's claim that he was the most conservative choice did not go unnoticed by the state's political elite. ACCSC executive director Farley Smith refused to endorse any candidate, but declared that the Republican civil rights plan was less offensive. Thurmond did not campaign for, or endorse, Kennedy. Jimmy Byrnes, who had endorsed Ike in 1952, publicly declared his support for Nixon. Other former Dixiecrats such as Mendel Rivers preached party loyalty, but took little or no part in the campaign. The end result was that "opponents of black civil rights" implied that Kennedy would "inflict the most damage on southern racial convictions."[48]

Conversely, Senator Olin Johnston, Edgar Brown, and other Democratic stalwarts reminded voters of Nixon's membership in the NAACP, his courtship of black voters in 1956, and his support of civil rights legislation. However, their efforts did not persuade many white segregationists that Nixon and the Republicans would be more aggressive on civil rights than a Democratic Kennedy White House. A typical Nixon voter was either a middle- or upper-class white professional living in or around one of South Carolina's major cities or a less-educated white living in a county with a significant black population. Population growth, economic changes, and national political realignments all contributed to this change, but racial politics united poor Black Belt whites and urban educated whites under the Republican banner as both factions seemed convinced that rapid desegregation would lead to widespread social unrest, economic instability, and a palpable loss of white status and advantage.[49]

Despite the stirrings of a significant Republican presence, Kennedy narrowly defeated Nixon with 51.2 percent of the vote in South Carolina. His victory was due to a combination of votes from white workers in the piedmont region, white farmers in the Pee Dee area who were suspicious of Republican efforts to restructure farm subsidies, and black voters. The fact that Nixon did win the majority of the white vote was evidence of underlying changes in South Carolina's political atmosphere; Nixon's white majority was almost identical to Eisenhower's from 1952. Once again, the combination of segregationists and white professionals nearly carried the state for a Republican, only this time Nixon was only on the ballot as a member of the GOP. Furthermore, Nixon was able to preserve his reputation on the national stage as a racial moderate while simultaneously giving the perception to South Carolina whites that he would be less apt to force rapid and sweeping racial change on the South. Though his "southern strategy" had not yet matured, Nixon's campaign tactics both foreshadowed his later political agenda and reflected the evolution of a modern conservative movement in South Carolina.[50]

In South Carolina, two distinct trends emerged from the Republican's strong showing. First, the election was the first time that many white Democrats in South Carolina openly endorsed a Republican candidate on the Republican ticket. Second, it was the first election in which a large number of Democrats changed their official party affiliation on a permanent basis. Even Albert Watson, who had been reluctant to switch parties, later announced that he would change his affiliation. The strong support for Nixon among white middle-class segregationists like Micah Jenkins demonstrated a sharp contrast between South Carolina's hard-core segregationists and recalcitrant resisters in other Deep South states. In Alabama and Mississippi, for example, whites handed their votes to unpledged electors rather than endorse Nixon, while white South Carolinians, it seems, had abandoned last-ditch political protest.[51]

Despite Nixon's success with white voters in 1960, the nascent conservative coalition in South Carolina faced numerous obstacles. Rural southerners were not yet comfortable with the suburban "Sunbelt Republicanism" that was emerging in southern and western cities. South Carolina Democrats such as Olin Johnston, Edgar Brown, and even Mendel Rivers had campaigned in rural counties by perennially supporting popular farm subsidies, rural electrification, and other New Deal programs. As popular as the conservative wing of the GOP was with South Carolina's rank-and-file Republicans, its opposition to programs like the Santee-Cooper hydroelectric plant was a significant impediment to building a dominant Republican Party in South Carolina. So long as rural whites believed that there was a significant difference between the Democratic Party of South Carolina and the Democratic National Convention, winning state and local elections was nearly impossible for the South Carolina GOP.

Nevertheless, there were some indications that the kinds of economic concerns that still animated urban working-class whites and rural Democratic voters had begun to wane in South Carolina's suburban areas. As the state moved further away from the poverty of the Great Depression, many of South

Carolina's leading businessmen, such as Charles Daniel and textile executive John Cauthen, had stepped up their support for laws that were anti-union, anti–minimum wage, and pro–corporate tax cuts. More important, however, was their increasing tendency to call for an alternative to die-hard massive resistance that took economic considerations into account. To some extent, among the state's business elites race relations had been in the process of a slow, uneven thaw for some time. Between 1958 and 1962, industrial construction in South Carolina surpassed $850 million and created nearly sixty thousand new jobs, and the *New York Times* had acknowledged that South Carolina did "not want to create an atmosphere of rebellion that would discourage the economic development of the state." By 1961, it was clear that, as the influence of conservative Republican ideas gained strength among business elites, fiscal concerns would have a dramatic impact on the tenor of white resistance. Daniel and others continued to argue that the state had to solve its "race problem" or face the same kind of fiscal setbacks that plagued Mississippi and Arkansas during massive-resistance campaigns. Public disorder, he argued, would limit the state's economic potential. Likewise, Cauthen preached that "law and order" was absolutely necessary to ensure economic success.[52]

The kind of law-and-order conservatism preached by Daniel, Cauthen, and other business leaders sharply contrasted with the working-class campaigns directed by Olin Johnston, Edgar Brown, and other racially conservative South Carolina Democrats. It was also quite different from the conservative populism espoused by other southern leaders, such as George Wallace and Herman Talmadge, and less acerbic and demagogic than the rhetoric emanating from rural social conservatives in South Carolina like John D. Long. The appeal of law-and-order conservatism in South Carolina was undeniable; therefore, Republican strategists tailored their efforts to appeal to business-minded whites suspicious of rapid social change.[53]

For conservative whites, the need for a new political option seemed to become even more urgent after Kennedy was elected. Soon after his inauguration, Kennedy named several African Americans to his cabinet. He also named Thurgood Marshall to the Second Court of Appeals. The combination of Kennedy's support for the Peace Corps, the bungled Bay of Pigs Invasion, and his endorsement of African American appointees convinced many conservative white South Carolinians that Kennedy was a liberal. Moreover, the increase in black direct-action campaigns—notably the student sit-ins and freedom rides—was further evidence to many segregationists that the president was encouraging civil rights. By the time Kennedy federalized the Mississippi National Guard and ordered troops into Oxford, Mississippi, in 1962, southern whites had grown increasingly hostile to the Democratic president.

The perception that South Carolina had no choice but to desegregate Clemson College peacefully in 1963 provided even further evidence to conservative whites that the federal government was acting beyond its constitutional authority.[54]

Republicans in South Carolina hoped to capitalize on this growing dissatisfaction and hostility and launched a concerted effort to win state and local elections with a monolithic campaign strategy. They simply reminded white voters that the Democratic Party was the "liberal" party. The GOP's first opportunity to score an electoral victory in a state election occurred in Richland County in 1961 during a special race to fill a vacant seat in the South Carolina House of Representatives. The Republican was Columbia attorney Charles E. Boineau Jr. Like most of the state's GOP members, Boineau formally joined the GOP in 1960, but actually had not supported the Democratic nominee in a presidential election since 1944.[55]

Boineau and his opponent, Joe Berry, held similar political views. Both men were avowed conservatives who believed in segregation. The biggest difference between them was their party affiliation. Even though the election was for a state office, Boineau was able to win by a landslide simply by campaigning against the national Democratic Party. He condemned the Kennedy administration for "telling us whom we should hire" and attacked federal "control" of education. Unlike many conservative whites who had cut their political teeth in the massive-resistance campaigns of late 1950s, Boineau made subtle commitments to defend white privilege without promoting the most virulent strains of white extremism. In a half-hour television commercial produced by Dolly Hamby, one woman declared that she was voting for Boineau because the GOP was the more conservative party and the "defender of states' rights." Another interviewee praised Boineau for speaking out against "socialism in Washington."

The combination of economic conservatism and white supremacy made Boineau an attractive candidate to both white professionals and die-hard segregationists. His economic conservatism, more subtle criticisms of desegregation, and carefully constructed defense of white rights spoke to his belief in white privilege without the kind of "ugliness" that was typical in racial campaigns. His victory in a solid Democratic state was evidence of the groundswell of support for an alternative political option in the South Carolina midlands.[56]

White conservatives in South Carolina took Boineau's victory as a sign that the GOP had emerged as a serious political contender. Republican leaders confirmed that the fastest road to victory in South Carolina was a combination of racial politics and economic conservatism. They were determined to build on their victory in Richland County by using Boineau's strategy to win a

statewide office in 1962 and nominated newspaperman and outspoken conservative William D. Workman to challenge Olin Johnston. Workman had good
name recognition, and his book *The Case for the South* was an indictment of
federal intrusion and a defense of Jim Crow.[57]

The 1962 election was also notable in that it featured a strong Republican
challenge in the Second Congressional District, which included Columbia and
several mostly rural counties and was dominated by hard-core segregationists.
Its Democratic representative, Albert Watson, was a well-known segregationist, but that did not stop ultra-segregationist Floyd Spence from challenging
the maverick Democrat. Though there was a large African American community in Columbia and Richland County, it was dwarfed by the size of the
white population. Furthermore, most of the blacks in the surrounding rural
counties were not registered voters.[58]

Like Boineau, both Workman and Spence reminded voters that a vote for
Johnston or Watson was an endorsement of the national Democratic Party,
its platform, and "liberal" politics, and urged southern voters to find a new
political home in the conservative wing of the GOP. Unlike Boineau, however,
Workman rarely strayed from connecting his criticisms of national Democrats directly to the race issue. He seemed especially intent on blaming the
judiciary.[59]

For many whites, the GOP strategy made for a compelling argument. Olin
Johnston had to rely on class politics and a strong black turnout to defeat the
GOP challenge. He labeled Workman the candidate of big business and declared that the Republican platform was at odds with the well-being of working people. He also defended his support for popular New Deal programs
such as the minimum wage and Social Security; Workman would be loyal to
corporations and Republican fat cats. He also noted that his own record as
an "independent" Democrat in the Senate was impeccable and demonstrated
that he rarely voted along the "liberal" party line.[60] Workman was unable to
overcome Johnston's strong support from white textile workers and African
Americans. Nevertheless, he captured over 44 percent of the popular vote,
nearly the entire Black Belt, and the majority of the white vote. Moreover, the
election was an important step in the GOP's long-term plan for South Carolina. Workman's defense of white supremacy helped secure a white majority.
Nonetheless, Hamby worried that Workman had been too focused on race
and, as a result, had alienated some voters who might have otherwise supported his candidacy. To Hamby's dismay, he seemed incapable of reproduc-
ing Boineau's subtle commitment to racial conservatism and instead related
every issue to segregation.[61]

Though it achieved similar results, Spence's campaign was more difficult. Watson had been a frequent critic of the national Democratic Party and supported Nixon in 1960. Nevertheless, Spence's relentless attacks on northern "liberals" won him 47.2 percent of the popular vote. Like Workman, however, he was unable to unseat his Democratic opponent, who, ironically, most likely owed his narrow victory to the small number of black voters in Richland County. Still, the small margin of victory worried the conservative Democrat. With the exceptions of Mendel Rivers and Strom Thurmond, no representative from South Carolina had a more credible reputation than Watson for defending white privilege and endorsing conservative candidates, and yet, Spence was still able to win over white conservatives—a core of his base.[62]

The strong showing by Workman and Spence was a defining moment. It became clear to many state Democrats that without black ballots they risked losing future elections to conservative Republicans. As Democrats became more reliant on black voters, however, they also became, reluctantly, more open to negotiation with African American leaders. Though decisive change was still years away, Workman's ability to take the white vote away from one of South Carolina's most entrenched Democrats and Spence's ability to challenge one of the state's most uncompromising segregationists served as important lessons to later Democrats. For example, in the election for the deceased Johnston's senate seat in 1966, Fritz Hollings, who had been elected governor in 1958 on a promise to preserve segregation, worked with black leaders to ensure a high African American turnout to offset the widespread defection of whites to the GOP. As more segregationist whites sought refuge in the conservative wing of the Republican Party, they also helped usher in a new, fragile, biracial Democratic Party in South Carolina.[63]

Republicans were slow to adjust to the change in Democratic tactics. For two decades after the federal judiciary initially ruled against the lily-white primary, white conservatives had worried about the potential of a black/white coalition in South Carolina. Nonetheless, only a few political strategists recognized that blatant race-baiting would not lead to success in the polling booths. Dolly Hamby, for example, was very critical of Spence and Workman—both of whom had been her clients—for not adopting a more nuanced critique of "liberalism." She warned that although racial demagoguery would energize 35 to 45 percent of voters, the lingering strength of loyal New Deal Democrats (including the roughly seventy thousand to ninety thousand registered black voters) would undermine GOP campaigns.[64] But most Republican leaders were overjoyed to win a white majority in the 1960 and 1962 contests. Their confidence boomed after Barry Goldwater carried the state with nearly 60 percent of the popular vote in the 1964 presidential election. Combined with Thurmond's official conversion to the GOP, the election gave Republican activists confidence that the state was on the verge of a major electoral shift in favor of the GOP.

The first major sign that the Republican Party would build on Thurmond's defection to the GOP came from longtime Democratic malcontent Albert Watson. Watson, who represented South Carolina's Second Congressional District, was stripped of two years of his seniority after campaigning on behalf of Goldwater. He resigned from office, changed his party affiliation, and ran for reelection in a special contest as a Republican. His opponent, Preston Harvey Callison, was a moderate Democrat who advocated compliance with the Civil Rights Act. Both Spence and former governor Byrnes endorsed Watson. Throughout the short campaign, Watson race-baited his opponent, and his campaign circulated a pamphlet entitled *The South is Under Attack* as both a repudiation of Democratic civil rights initiatives and as an appeal to alienated whites. This strategy was successful, and Watson won with almost 70 percent of the popular vote.[65]

Race was clearly the most important issue in these campaigns, but the argument that Goldwater (or Watson) supporters had exercised little more than a "protest vote" is superficial. For South Carolina's emerging conservative GOP, the Goldwater campaign was more than a "last gasp" or a "final fling of stand-pat racists." Granted, many were drawn to the GOP because of Goldwater's denunciation of the Civil Rights Act of 1964, but he offered more than just a way to voice voter displeasure with the national Democratic Party. Goldwater and the conservative wing of the GOP offered another way of protecting white privilege without forcing a showdown with the executive branch. A February 1963 *National Review* article claimed "the Republican Party in the South is, in general, far less committed to all-out segregation than the Democrats."[66]

Though many white voters were undoubtedly drawn to Goldwater through a combination of rage and racism, it is important to note that the Republican Party platform actually called for an end to racial segregation. The more sophisticated members of the emerging GOP of South Carolina understood that, no matter what Goldwater desired, the national party would not endorse segregation and that, even under a Republican administration, at least a minimum amount of desegregation would occur, even in recalcitrant South Carolina. It was the GOP's less forceful language and willingness to settle for slow change that helped encourage Thurmond, Watson, Jenkins, Spence, and other segregationist Democrats to join. Goldwater may have been a protest candidate for some alienated southern whites, but grassroots Republicanism in

South Carolina signified the desire of white professionals to find an alternative to massive resistance.

In spite of the GOP successes of 1964 and the emergence of a dependable Republican base, the party had yet to form a well-rounded political philosophy. Although it had become a legitimate threat to Democratic dominance in the Palmetto State, it suffered mixed results during the 1966 midterm elections. In 1952, there were fewer than ninety thousand registered black voters in South Carolina. By 1966, that number had increased to roughly two hundred thousand, which represented just over 20 percent of the total electorate.[67] Largely due to the Voting Rights Act of 1965 and the persistent efforts of black activists like Modjeska Simkins to register African Americans, the number of black ballots increased to more than 220,000 (or 35 percent of all voters) by 1970.[68]

Democratic leaders, such as gubernatorial candidate Robert McNair, were quick to adjust to these changes. McNair, whose campaign public relations were managed by Bradley, Graham, and Hamby, ran as a moderate candidate dedicated to maintaining public order, calling for minimal compliance with federal laws and court decisions regarding desegregation. His opponent, J. O. Rogers, a former Democrat who had supported the Citizens' Councils, mimicked Goldwater and Watson. Like many of his Republican predecessors, he won the majority of the white vote, but was unable to overcome the combination of white moderates and African American voters in the general election. McNair won with over 58 percent.[69] Likewise, Republican Inez Clark Eddings failed to overcome a coalition of moderate whites and African Americans in her run for state superintendent. Her open appeals to hard-core white supremacists offered a stark contrast to her opponent, who insisted that "quality" education for all South Carolinians should be the state's primary concern.[70] Like McNair and Busbee, Democrat John West also defeated his Republican opponent, Marshall Mays, in the race for lieutenant governor by openly campaigning as a "moderate." When combined with Democrat Grady Patterson's landslide victory over another former leader in the Citizens' Council movement, the Democrats managed to secure every statewide elected office. The Democrats also retained one of the state's seats in the United States Senate when Hollings defeated GOP nominee Marshall Parker.[71]

In spite of failing to capture a single victory in any of the statewide races, Republicans were, nonetheless, able to secure several important victories. Thurmond successfully defended his Senate seat for the first time running as a Republican, Watson was reelected to represent the Second District in the House of Representatives, and local GOP candidates won 17 of 124 seats in the state House and six in the state senate. Although these gains paled in comparison with Goldwater, the GOP's limited success did serve as a harbinger of future Republican strategies.[72]

The GOP was especially successful when its candidates endorsed policies to control the process of desegregation. For example, one of the few successful Republicans in the 1966 elections, Carolyn E. Frederick, avoided the more virulent strains of extremism that had motivated large numbers of white supremacists to vote for J. O. Rogers in the gubernatorial contest. By mimicking the more moderate Boineau campaign, Frederick became the first Republican woman elected to the South Carolina House of Representatives. Frederick endorsed dilatory legal tactics, but refused to support the far-right Jacobinism of the most committed white supremacists. Frederick's defense of discriminatory "freedom of choice" plans and her opposition to court-ordered busing won over conservative white voters in Greenville without alienating more moderate whites.[73] The inability of former Citizens' Council leaders, hard-core segregationists, and intransigent white supremacists to overcome the Democratic advantages in 1966 was an early warning sign that Goldwater's landslide victory in 1964 would not be easily replicated. Thurmond and Watson were closely identified with their commitment to segregation and their opposition to the Civil Rights Act. However, they were both established candidates with well-organized political operations. It was much more difficult for their GOP allies to overcome lingering Democratic loyalties. The increase in black voters meant that the margin of victory was increasingly decided by white moderates who were put off by hard-core race-baiting.

By 1968, it was obvious to all but the most committed segregationists that rigid dedication to de jure Jim Crow was an electoral dead end. Moreover, it was apparent that black ballots had reenergized the New Deal Coalition in South Carolina. Democratic governor Robert McNair went so far as to enroll his daughter in a desegregated public school in Columbia, a gesture that symbolized his party's new reliance on biracial moderate politics. By the time the Republican National Convention nominated Richard Nixon as its candidate for the presidency in 1968 and George Wallace announced his candidacy as an independent, it seemed as if the white vote might be divided enough to ensure a Democratic victory in South Carolina that would usher in a new era of racial moderation. In any event, it seemed to most South Carolinians that the election would determine the extent to which the state would be required to move beyond token desegregation. Of course, it would also give white Democrats a clear indication of the lingering strength of recalcitrant segregationists and of the true depths of the white defection to the GOP.

By the time of the election, most white South Carolinians had acquiesced to minimal segregation. Therefore, the key issue for them was how and to what extent desegregation would be enforced. Like the nation, this issue typically revolved around busing. During the campaign, Nixon assured Strom Thurmond's key strategist Harry Dent that he did not favor forced busing as a means of enforcing desegregation. In doing so, Nixon left open an opportunity for whites to continue the use of district gerrymandering and pupil-placement restrictions to limit school desegregation. The GOP candidate also met with Thurmond and promised to appoint "strict constructionists" for Supreme Court vacancies as a way to allow freedom of choice to continue. These pledges promised to limit the federal government's regulatory control over school desegregation and the threat of continued federal court demands for meaningful desegregation.[74]

In return for Nixon's commitment to scaling back federal interference with school desegregation, Thurmond pledged to campaign for the GOP nominee in the primary and general elections, an endorsement that gave Nixon instant credibility with white southerners. However, the independent candidacy of Alabama governor and ultra-segregationist George Wallace provided an alternative for hard-core whites that threatened to divide the white vote and ensure a Democratic victory in the general election. Thurmond and Dent tried to limit Wallace's appeal in South Carolina with a series of ads saying that a vote for the independent would put Hubert Humphrey in the White House, but they were unable to convince many working-class whites that the former member of the NAACP was a true conservative who would defend white rights.[75]

Thanks mostly to the vigorous campaigning of Dent and Thurmond, Nixon won South Carolina, but, as GOP strategists had feared, his victory exposed an acutely divided white electorate and demonstrated the significant power of black ballots. The three presidential candidates nearly divided the state's votes evenly—only 38 percent for Nixon, 32 percent for Wallace, and nearly 30 percent for Humphrey. Though he won a plurality, Nixon's inability to secure a majority or near-majority vote confirmed that, when given a choice, hard-core segregationists would continue to support the most racially conservative candidate in any election, irrespective of party affiliation. Nixon's endorsement of gradualism and conservative judicial appointments was popular with middle-class whites in South Carolina's major cities—a group that prized "law and order" and limits on federal activism—but it also alienated working-class whites across the state who had chosen to endorse Wallace's particular brand of racism and economic populism. Other Republicans took notice of these results and concluded that without a unified white vote they had no hope of defeating the cautiously, but increasingly biracial Democratic Party that had emerged in the South in the wake of the Voting Rights Act of 1965.[76]

National elections aside, in state contests the Democratic Party still held significant advantages in South Carolina. With nearly uniform black support and a solid foundation of white loyalists, state Democrats had a more stable political base. Though conservative Republicans had managed to lure the support of a white plurality in statewide elections, they had not consistently been able to overcome these Democratic advantages. In spite of Nixon's victory, the GOP lost seventeen of its twenty-five seats in the state legislature. Within this context, the Republican nominee for governor in 1970, Albert Watson, hoped that a combination of Nixon and Wallace voters would end the Democratic control of the governor's office that had been unbroken since Reconstruction. In order to accomplish that goal, Watson vigorously denounced federal desegregation policy and engaged in a blatant race-baiting campaign against his Democratic opponent, Lieutenant Governor John West.[77] Watson's strategy criticized the Supreme Court for ruling against freedom-of-choice plans, accused West of sacrificing states' rights for black bloc voting, and promised to fight to the bitter end against federal desegregation. Furthermore, he frequently utilized Wallace-like rhetoric that reminded voters of his militant segregationist past.[78]

West and his Democratic allies worried that the relatively new biracial political alliance was not strong enough to ward off Watson's relentless attacks and were concerned that Thurmond's endorsement of the GOP nominee would be impossible to overcome. West, who did not share Watson's flair or charisma, called for voters to support the same kind of steady leadership that had navigated the state during the desegregation crises with minimal bloodshed—and also minimal desegregation. West hoped that voters would recognize that the Democratic Party had managed the problem of desegregation without resorting to the kind of unproductive demagoguery associated with Georgia under Lester Maddox and Alabama's George Wallace.[79]

Democratic leaders understood that most white South Carolinians (and their black neighbors) took pride in the state's peaceful reputation, but they also worried that white outrage over the end of freedom of choice would give Watson the edge. West and his supporters hoped that white voters would recognize that the state's Democratic leadership had made the inevitable more palatable and would refuse to allow Watson's race-baiting to alter the state's commitment to conservative measured change. Moreover, he urged voters to ignore outrageous GOP promises, such as a pledge to save freedom of choice, that Watson was simply incapable of keeping.[80]

The political differences between Watson and West were encapsulated in their attitudes toward busing. Shortly after declaring his candidacy, Watson spoke at an antibusing rally in Lamar. On February 22, 1970, he and 2,500 white protesters called on Darlington County to resist any further federal pressure to integrate its public-school system through busing, appealing to the county's white population to resist forced busing to the bitter end. Shortly after the rally, another protest turned violent when a mob of angry whites overturned two school buses that had carried black children to a newly de-segregated school. The incident brought national attention. Yet, despite wide-spread criticism for stirring up white emotions, Watson's campaign did not desist from further controversy, leading to a racial fight at a Columbia high school. The two eruptions were enough to convince some white moderates that Watson's inflammatory style would bring unwanted attention to South Carolina and generate poor publicity.[81]

No one was more aware of Watson's tendencies toward far-right hyperbole than Hamby, who at the behest of Thurmond had reluctantly agreed to man-age public relations for the campaign. Throughout the contest, she had clashed with Watson, who refused to moderate his message on racial issues. Hamby was furious with Watson for ignoring her advice to avoid language and actions that might cast him as an extremist. Watson, however, continued to ignore her advice and authorized advertisements that featured television footage of Na-tional Guardsmen firing into a crowd of African Americans during the Watts riots. The ads, which were done without her approval, infuriated Hamby. She later called them "the worst example of raw racism I have ever seen" and con-cluded that they were "offensive to almost any decent person."[82]

Outrage over these episodes combined with near-uniform black support to help West win the election with 52 percent of the popular vote. However, Wat-son won an overwhelming majority of the white vote. Less than half of West's votes came from white voters. The outcome further confirmed the newfound power of black ballots in the wake of the Voting Rights Act and proved defini-tively that overtly racist campaigning was a losing strategy in South Carolina. The results also confirmed what Hamby had argued for nearly two decades—that extremism would alienate just enough moderate whites to ensure defeat at the polls.[83]

Some Republicans, such as Arthur Ravenel of Charleston, had argued even before the election that the state's GOP could not overcome its Democratic op-ponents on a consistent basis unless it abandoned its blatant racism. Ravenel called on the Republican Party to reach out to blacks. The GOP, he claimed, could not win while campaigning to just 65 percent of the registered vot-ers. Reaching out to blacks would also soften the party's image among white moderates who shared the GOP's economic and moral agenda.[84] Hamby warned Thurmond that Ravenel was right, encouraging him to alter his own political strategy. She insisted that West's ability to label Watson as a "racist" "REALLY hurt!" Moreover, Hamby implored Thurmond to adopt a more moderate position and abandon any last-ditch efforts to restore Jim Crow. Thurmond, apparently, took the advice seriously, hired black staffers, and began actively campaigning to black voters.[85]

In sum, the Watson-West election taught the same lesson to white racial conservatives that the 1968 presidential contests taught George Wallace: race-baiting and overt white supremacy could still capture a white plurality in the Deep South, but it might also alienate enough white voters to ensure electoral defeat. Watson, like Wallace, learned that in South Carolina, a racist campaign would lure scores of loyal voters, but it would also create a sizable biracial voting bloc for the opposition. His election defeat, therefore, represented an end to the politics of massive resistance in South Carolina. Racially conservative but less overt forms of white politicking would continue in South Carolina, but the context within which it existed and operated was significantly changed after 1970. A near-uniform white vote propelled Nixon to a stunning victory in South Carolina in 1972. Opposition to rights-based liberalism (especially to busing), criticisms of "activist judges," and a strict adherence to the "law-and-order" conservatism that had nearly won the state for Nixon in 1960 helped the president win over 70 percent of the popular vote.[86] These new messages were evident in 1974 when South Carolinians elected the first Republican governor since Reconstruction, James B. Edwards.[87]

Though he was considered a long shot in both the primary and general elections, Edwards embodied the brand of law-and-order conservatism that had helped Nixon build a successful electoral majority in the elections of 1968 and 1972. Edwards was an outspoken opponent of busing, a fiscal conservative, and a proponent of dramatic increases in defense spending. He was able to win the support of Nixon voters and just over 50 percent of the vote.[88] In many ways, Edwards epitomized the modern conservative movement in South Carolina. He volunteered to campaign for Goldwater in 1964. Raised in a middle-class family, he appealed to middle-class voters who valued his work ethic and commitment to personal responsibility.

Unlike Watson, Edwards was circumspect in his use of rhetoric regarding race. Like other "new" Republicans, he challenged rights-based liberalism and rapid social change in broad strokes. He told the *State* newspaper in 1975 that the "true enemy" was "the irresponsible people in America who are trying to undermine us." At a Lions Club event in Charleston, he complained that far too many people were rewarded with life's necessities without having to work for them—a thinly veiled criticism of the Great Society welfare programs. Edwards later went so far as to say that the double-digit inflation that was crippling economic growth in 1974 was the result of government handouts. He insisted that he became politically active because he was "fed up with . . . irresponsible government . . . where there is no regard for the taxpayers' money and the experiment with all the great schemes that came out of Washington in the sixties." In an indirect reference to the 1969 Charleston Hospital workers' strike, Edwards declared that he, unlike the Democrats, opposed engaging public employees in collective bargaining. According to Edwards, doing so would reward "rioting" and social unrest with pay increases at taxpayer expense.[89]

Although Edwards made no explicit mention of African Americans, Republican activists recognized that the vast majority of white South Carolinians would draw a connection between his critique of riots and "irresponsible government experiments" and their resentment over federal entitlement programs and civil rights initiatives. Edwards also realized that his calls for "responsible" monetary policy combined with an endorsement of increased defense spending would ensure that voters understood that his brand of fiscal conservatism would limit social welfare spending but would not jeopardize defense-industry jobs in the Palmetto State. The distinction was an important one for the state's middle-class voters. In many of South Carolina's cities, military installations were the largest employers. Nearly half of the federal funds spent in South Carolina originated from the military budget or the Atomic Energy Commission in 1971. In the First Congressional District, where Edwards first campaigned, 35 percent of the total payroll—or more than $460 million—came from defense-related employment or associated industries that were entirely dependent on military spending. In Charleston, the district's largest city, the Department of Defense spent $800 for every person (compared to a national average of less than $300). Overall, the federal government spent nearly $1 billion in the First District in 1971, and even conservative white leaders were unwilling to jeopardize that arrangement by challenging federal authority directly.[90]

Whether it was his opposition to busing, his endorsement of military spending, his support of right-to-work laws, his opposition to the Equal Rights Amendment, or his vague criticisms of social welfare spending, Edwards's campaign both echoed the strategy developed by Hamby for Eisenhower in 1952 and served as a precursor to later efforts to build a GOP majority in South Carolina. Regardless, his election as the first Republican governor since Reconstruction marked the emergence of a mature and competitive GOP in South Carolina. The party, which had gained a strong grassroots following during the 1960s, offered what segregationist Democrats had not—a manner to oppose federal intervention when possible while simultaneously preserving public order and economic development. The success of candidates such as Frederick, Boineau, and Edwards, who were elected without resorting to Watson/Spence-style racial demagoguery, indicated that conservative whites in South Carolina remained suspicious of rapid social change but were disinterested in fighting a losing battle over Jim Crow.[91] The Republican candidates who first recognized this established the foundations of the modern party in South Carolina.

## Notes

1. James O. Farmer, "Memories and Forebodings: The Fight to Preserve the White Democratic Primary in South Carolina, 1944–1950," in *Toward the Meeting of the Waters: Currents in the Civil Rights Movement of South Carolina during the Twentieth Century,* ed. Winfred B. Moore and Orville Vernon Burton, 243–51 (Columbia: University of South Carolina Press, 2008); Jack Bass and Walter DeVries, *The Transformation of Southern Politics: Social Change and Political Consequence since 1945* (Athens: University of Georgia Press, 1995), 248–83; Patricia Sullivan, *Days of Hope: Race and Democracy in the New Deal Era* (Chapel Hill: University of North Carolina Press, 1996), esp. 170–220; Kari Frederickson, "'Dual Actions, One for Each Race': The Campaign Against the Dixiecrats in South Carolina, 1948–50," *International Social Science Review* (1997): 14–25; Kari Frederickson, "'The Slowest State' and the 'Most Backward Community': Racial Violence in South Carolina and Federal Civil Rights Legislation, 1946–48," *South Carolina Historical Magazine* (April 1997): 177–202; Kari Frederickson, *The Dixiecrat Revolt and the End of the Solid South, 1932–1968* (Chapel Hill: University of North Carolina Press, 2001), 118–216.

2. Matthew D. Lassiter, *The Silent Majority: Suburban Politics in the Sunbelt South* (Princeton: Princeton University Press, 2006), 1–42; Frederickson, "Dual Actions," 14–25; Frederickson, *Dixiecrat Revolt*, 118–216.

3. Fritz Hamer, "A Southern City Enters the Twentieth Century: Charleston, Its Navy Yard, and World War II, 1940–1948" (Ph.D. diss., University of South Carolina, 1998); Albert Herbert Myers, "Black, White, and Olive Drab: Military-Social Relations during the Civil Rights Movement at Fort Jackson and in Columbia, South Carolina" (Ph.D. diss., University of Virginia, 1998); I. D. Carson to B. R. Maybank, 3 March 1952, E. J. McGrath to B. R. Maybank, 28 February, 27 May, and 10 March 1952, and H. J. Sears to B. R. Maybank, 6 October 1952, Maybank Senatorial Papers, Special Collections; James O. Farmer Jr., "A Collision of Cultures: Aiken, South Carolina Meets the Nuclear Age," *Proceedings of the South Carolina Historical Association* (1995): 40–49. On Aiken, see also Kari Frederickson, "The Cold War at the Grassroots: Militarization and Modernization in South Carolina," in *The Myth of Southern Exceptionalism,*

ed. Matthew D. Lassiter and Joseph Crespino, 190–209 (New York: Oxford University Press, 2010).

4. Gregory Sampson, "The Rise of the 'New' Republican Party in South Carolina, 1948–1974" (Ph.D. diss., University of North Carolina, 1984), 217–19, 230; *Charleston News and Courier*, 30 January 1952.

5. Frederickson, *Dixiecrat Revolt*; Howard Quint, *Profile in Black and White: A Frank Portrait of South Carolina* (Washington: Public Affairs Press, 1958); Frank E. Jordan, *The Primary State: A History of the Democratic Party in South Carolina, 1876–1962* (ca. 1965, n.p.); P. Quattlebaum to J. L. Platt, *Myrtle Beach News*, 15 March 1952, Quattlebaum Papers, Thurmond Institute; Jack Bass and Marilyn Thompson, *Ol' Strom: An Unauthorized Biography of Strom Thurmond* (Atlanta: Longstreet, 1998), 135–38; and Bass and Thompson, *Strom: The Complicated Personal and Political Life of Strom Thurmond* (New York: Public Affairs, 2005), 136–52. For Byrnes, see Frederickson, *Dixiecrat Revolt*, 180–229.

6. Alice T. Beckett, Secretary, Colleton County Citizens Grass Roots Crusade to L. Mendel Rivers, 21 April 1952, L. M. Rivers to A. T. Beckett, 23 April 1952, Rivers Papers, SCHS.

7. Maybank to Wright Morrow, 11 January 1952, H. S. Howie Jr. to J. F. Byrnes, 11 July 1952, both in the Maybank Senatorial Papers, Special Collections.

8. J. K. Case to B. R. Maybank, and Edgar Brown to B. R. Maybank, both 8 August 1952, Maybank Senatorial Papers, Special Collections.

9. *State*, 19 September 1952, *News and Courier*, 20 August 1952, in John W. White, "Dolly Hamby and the Rise of Two-Party Politics in South Carolina, 1951–1970," in *South Carolina Women: Their Lives and Times,* ed. Marjorie Spruill, Joan Johnson, and Valinda Littlefield (Athens: University of Georgia Press, 2009).

10. P. Quattlebaum to L. M. Rivers, 16 August 1952, Rivers Papers, SCHS.

11. L. M. Rivers to P. Quattlebaum, 20 August 1952, Rivers Papers, SCHS.

12. Ibid.

13. "Recommendations to Publicity Committee, South Carolinians for Eisenhower," 1952, Hamby Papers.

14. Ibid.

15. Donald Fowler, *Presidential Voting in South Carolina, 1948–1964* (Columbia: Bureau of Governmental Research and Service Publications, 1966), 35–62; Sampson, "Rise of the New Republican Party," 255–61; Bruce H. Kalk, *The Origins of the Southern Strategy* (New York: Lexington Books, 2001); Quint, *Profile in Black and White*, 137–38.

16. L. M. Rivers to E. E. Cox, 22 October 1952, Rivers Papers, SCHS.

17. Statement by Congressman L. Mendel Rivers, 25 October 1952, Rivers Papers, SCHS.

18. Ibid.

19. *Greenville News*, 26 October 1952; *News and Courier*, 26 October 1952; L. M. Rivers to R. L. Scott, 4 November 1952; *Hampton Guardian* (n.d.). *Jasper Record*, 29 October 1952; and L. M. Rivers to E. E. Cox, 22 October 1952, both in the Rivers Papers,

SCHS. Jeff Broadwater, *Adlai Stevenson and American Politics* (New York: Twayne, 1994), 117–20; Frederickson, *Dixiecrat Revolt*, 200–300.

20. "Slim Suttle's Viewing the South," 31 October 1952, Rivers Papers, SCHS.

21. *News and Courier*, 30 October 1952, Rivers Papers, SCHS.

22. Ibid., 11 November 1952; Sampson, "Rise of the New Republican Party," 230–32.

23. Raymond Moley, "A Political Perspective," *Newsweek*, 15 December 1952, 108.

24. Ibid.

25. *State*, 14 August 1955; *Southern School News* (August 1955): 6, *News and Courier*, 18 October 1955.

26. Southeastern Office of the American Friends Service Committee, Dept. of Racial and Cultural Relations, National Council of Churches of Christ, Southern Regional Council, "Intimidation, Reprisals, and Violence in the South's Racial Crisis," n.d., South Carolina Council on Human Relations Papers, South Caroliniana Library, University of South Carolina, Columbia (hereafter SCCHR Papers in SCL); Lowe, "The Magnificent Fight," 213–14.

27. John W. White, "Managed Compliance: White Resistance and Desegregation in South Carolina, 1950–1970 (Ph.D. diss., University of Florida, 2006).

28. Hallie Henry, "Governor George Bell Timmerman and the 1956 Southern Solidarity" (master's thesis, University of South Carolina, 1972).

29. *Southern School News* (September 1956): 4.

30. *News and Courier*, 17 August 1956; Sampson, "Rise of the New Republican Party," 254–57.

31. *Southern School News* (October 1956): 4.

32. Fowler, *Presidential Voting in South Carolina*, 35–52; Sampson, "Rise of the New Republican Party," 255–61; Kalk, *Origins of the Southern Strategy*, 26–36; Quint, *Profile in Black and White*, 137–38.

33. Ibid.

34. Ibid.

35. Ibid.

36. Quint, *Profile in Black and White*, 172–73.

37. Timothy Tyson, "Dynamite and 'The Silent South': A Story from the Second Reconstruction in South Carolina," in *Jumpin' Jim Crow: Southern Politics from Civil War to Civil Rights*, ed. Jane Dailey, Glenda Elizabeth Gilmore, and Bryant Simon, 275–97 (Princeton: Princeton University Press, 2000).

38. Ibid.

39. White, "Managed Compliance," Paul Lofton, "Calm and Exemplary: Desegregation in Columbia, South Carolina," in *Southern Businessmen and Desegregation*, ed. David Colburn and Elizabeth Jacoway, 70–81 (Baton Rouge: Louisiana State University Press, 1982); John Sproat, "Firm Flexibility: Perspectives on Desegregation in South Carolina," in *Race and Slavery in America*, ed. Robert H. Abzug and Stephen E. Maizlish, 165–81 (Lexington: University Press of Kentucky, 1986); Richard Phillip Stone II, "Making a Modern State: The Politics of Economic Development in South Carolina, 1938–1962" (Ph.D. diss., University of South Carolina, 2004), 387–518; Marcia Synnott,

"Desegregation in South Carolina, 1950–1963: Sometime "Between 'Now' and 'Never,'" in *Looking South: Chapters in the Story of an American Region*, ed. Winfred B. Moore Jr. and Joseph F. Tripp, 51–64 (New York: Greenwood Press, 1989). Business leaders also expressed concern that recalcitrant resistance would do irreparable harm to the state's economy and impede progress (see E. R. McIver Jr. to William Workman, 21 August 1961, Workman Papers, MPC; George Grice to Charles W. Coker, 24 March 1965, College of Charleston Archives, Special Collections.

40. *News and Courier*, 7 November 1960, clipping in the Rivers Papers, ADHS; Mark Stern, *Calculating Visions: Kennedy, Johnson, and Civil Rights* (New Brunswick, N.J.: Rutgers University Press, 1992).

41. "Democratic Party Platform of 1960," reprinted in Arthur M. Schlesinger Jr., ed., *History of American Presidential Elections*, 1940–1948 (New York: Chelsea House, 1971), 3508. The Kennedy call to King is discussed in Jonathan Rosenberg, *Kennedy, Johnson, and the Quest for Justice* (New York: Norton, 2003), 27–29.

42. Sampson, "Rise of the New Republican Party," 313–16.

43. Ibid., 317–19.

44. Ibid., 318–23; Billy B. Hathorn, "The Changing Politics of Race: Congressman Albert William Watson and the S.C. Republican Party, 1965–1970," *South Carolina Historical Magazine* (October 1988): 227–41.

45. Script from an untitled film produced by Bradley, Graham, and Hamby for South Carolina Democrats for Nixon and Lodge" (1960), Hamby Papers; Taylor Branch, *Pillar of Fire: America in King Years, 1963–65* (New York: Simon and Schuster, 1998), 242.

46. Script from an untitled film produced by Bradley, Graham, and Hamby for South Carolina Democrats for Nixon and Lodge" (1960), Hamby Papers.

47. Ibid.

48. Sampson, "Rise of the New Republican Party in South Carolina," 323.

49. Fowler, *Presidential Voting in South Carolina*, 99–127; Kalk, *Origins of the Southern Strategy*, 25–54; Sampson, "Rise of the New Republican Party," 274–343.

50. Ibid.

51. Bass and DeVries, *Transformation of Southern Politics*, 58–59, 470–71; Jack E. Davis, *Race Against Time: Culture and Separation in Natchez since 1930* (Baton Rouge: Louisiana State University Press, 2001), 161.

52. Cox, "1963: The Year of Decision," 10–17; *New York Times*, 17 October 1962; Sproat, "Firm Flexibility"; Stone, "Making a Modern State," 387–518.

53. Dan T. Carter, *The Politics of Rage: George Wallace, the Origins of the New Conservatism, and the Transformation of American Politics* (Baton Rouge: Louisiana State University Press, 1995); Mark Royden Winchell, *Talmadge: A Political Legacy, A Politician's Life* (Atlanta: Peachtree, 1987). On conservative populism, see Michael Kazin, *The Populist Persuasion* (New York: Basic Books, 1995).

54. Sampson, "Rise of the New Republican Party," 337; Carl Brauer, *John F. Kennedy and the Second Reconstruction* (New York: Columbia University Press, 1977).

55. Sampson, "Rise of the New Republican Party," 332–35.

56. Ibid., 333–35; *News and Courier*, 18 July 1961.

57. William Workman, *The Case for the South* (New York: Devin-Adair, 1960).

58. Russell Merritt, "The Senatorial Election of 1962 and the Rise of Two-Party Politics in South Carolina," *South Carolina Historical Magazine* (July 1997): 281–301; Hathorn, "The Changing Politics of Race, 227–41.

59. Ibid.

60. Ibid.

61. Ibid.

62. Hathorn, "The Changing Politics of Race," 228.

63. Sproat, "Firm Flexibility"; Synott, "Desegregation in South Carolina"; Tony Badger, "From Defiance to Moderation: South Carolina Governors and Racial Change," in *Toward the Meeting of the Waters*, ed. Moore and Burton, 3–21.

64. Untitled speech to the Republican Women of Augusta, Ga. 1965, Hamby Collection.

65. Ibid.

66. Hathorn, "Changing Politics of Race," 230.

67. Sam Ragain, "Dixie Looked Away," *American Scholar* (Spring 1965): 202–12.

68. Richard Barnard, "Strom Thurmond, Republican Senator from South Carolina"; John Hancock, "Ernest F. Hollings, Democratic Senator from South Carolina"; Edie Reno and Elaine Strassborg, "Tom S. Gettys: Democratic Representative from South Carolina"; Miles Hawthorne, "W. J. Bryan Dorn: Democratic Representative from South Carolina"; Ellen A. Kaplan and Arthur Magida, "James R. Mann: Democratic Representative from South Carolina"; Bonnie Miller, "John L. McMillan: Democratic Representative from South Carolina"; Sally Keeble, "Mendel Davis: Democratic Representative from South Carolina"; and Steven Reddicliffe, "Floyd Spence: Republican Representative from South Carolina," all in Ralph Nader Congress Project, *Citizens Look at Congress* (Washington, D.C.: Grossman, 1972), vol. 8; Robert Coles, "The Way It Is in South Carolina," *New Republic*, November 30, 1968, 17–21.

69. Robert Coles, "The Way It Is in South Carolina," *New Republic*, November 30, 1968, 17–21. See also Barbara Woods Aba-Mecha, "Black Woman Activist in Twentieth Century South Carolina: Modjeska Monteith Simkins" (Ph.D. diss., Emory University, 1978); and Brian Ward, *Radio and the Struggle for Civil Rights in the South* (Gainesville: University Press of Florida, 2004), 326–29.

70. Philip G. Grose, *South Carolina at the Brink* (Columbia: University of South Carolina Press, 2006), 82–158.

71. *Southern Education Report* (March 1966), South Carolina, 17–18; Grose, *South Carolina at the Brink*, 132–41.

72. Grose, *South Carolina at the Brink*, 132–45.

73. Bass and DeVries, *Transformation*, 254–56. See also Harriet Keyserling, *Against the Tide: One Woman's Struggle* (Columbia: University of South Carolina Press, 1998), 271–77; Archie Vernon Huff Jr., *Greenville* (Columbia: University of South Carolina Press for the Greenville Historical Society, Inc., 1995), 409; and *Southern Education Report* (March 1966), South Carolina, 17–18.

74. Ibid.

75. Sampson, "Rise of the New Republican Party," 499–502; Bass and Thompson, *Strom*, 199–209.

76. Kalk, *Origins of the Southern Strategy*, 79–88.

77. Ibid., 86–89; Sampson, "Rise of the New Republican Party," 511–23; Badger, "From Defiance to Moderation," 3–21.

78. Bass and DeVries, Transformation, 254–55; Randy Sanders, *Mighty Peculiar Elections: The New South Gubernatorial Campaigns of 1970 and the Changing Politics of Race* (Gainesville: University Press of Florida, 2002), 113–45.

79. Ibid.

80. Ibid.

81. Ibid.

82. Hamby quoted in Kalk, *Origins of the Southern Strategy*, 124.

83. Kalk, *Origins of the Southern Strategy*, 123–26.

84. Ibid.

85. Ibid.

86. "Race Memo Prodded Thurmond," *State*, 3 October 2004.

87. Bass and DeVries, *Transformation*, 256–57.

88. Ibid.

89. Ibid., 269–71.

90. Ibid., 264–65 (Edwards quoted); Shirley, *Uncommon Victory*, 105–42.

91. Shirley, *Uncommon Victory*, 105–42. See also note 68 above.

# 8

# A Southern Road Less Traveled

## The 1966 Gubernatorial Election and (Winthrop) Rockefeller Republicanism in Arkansas

JOHN A. KIRK

When Winthrop Rockefeller met the seven-year residency requirement to run for governor of Arkansas in 1960, that fact did not go unnoticed. The Louisiana newspaper the *Monroe World* ran an article that began: "The noisiest, struttingest and presumably richest northern 'Yankee' liberal in Arkansas—Winthrop Rockefeller—is being talked of as a possible candidate for governor of that state." The article concluded: "If a northern-born 'liberal' integrationist were to be elected governor of a deep-south, conservative, segregationist state it would be the biggest overnight about-face in the history of the United States, if not the entire world."[1] Less than seven years later, on January 10, 1967, Winthrop Rockefeller was sworn in as governor of Arkansas. He became the first Republican governor of the state in almost a century and only the sixth Republican governor of any former confederate state since Reconstruction, closely following the fifth, Florida's Claude R. Kirk Jr., a former Democrat, by just one week. Rockefeller and Kirk became the first southern Republican governors in forty-four years.[2]

How did such a seemingly earth-shattering turnaround occur? Answering that question complicates the established narratives of how, when, and why the South became Republican. For many years the received wisdom about the Republican ascendency in the region involved the "southern strategy" whereby Republicans wooed traditionally conservative southern voters by promoting conservative policies, particularly in the area of civil rights, where they exploited the white backlash to the civil rights movement and won over southern Democrats who were increasingly alienated from the more liberal policies of the national Democratic Party.[3] More recently, historians have begun to challenge the centrality of race in the Republican ascendency in the South by pointing instead toward what historian Matthew Lassiter terms a "suburban strategy." According to this interpretation, the Republican Party's success in the South was based on an appeal to the shared values of an emerging nationwide suburban white middle class that included a preference for color-blind policies over affirmative action, individual freedom over federal control, and free-market consumerism over federal regulation. Whereas the "southern strategy" suggested that the Republican Party was successful in appealing to the distinctive regional politics of the South, the "suburban strategy" makes the case for a regional convergence of shared white middle-class suburban values across the United States.[4]

Neither the "southern strategy" nor the "suburban strategy" helps explain Rockefeller's election in 1966. So much about that election turns established wisdom on its head. Rather than appealing to southern racial conservatism, Rockefeller, standing against a strong segregationist Democrat, actively courted the African American voters on whom his opponent turned his back, and they turned out to be the pivotal constituency in his victory. By contrast to other Republican victories in the South, Rockefeller was strongest in urban areas and among liberal and progressive members of the electorate, among affluent whites, and among African Americans.[5]

What Rockefeller's 1966 election does do is provide an intriguing glimpse at southern politics in flux before any discernable Republican strategy had begun to emerge in the region. Without any established template for success, Rockefeller took a Republican road less traveled that held its own unswerving logic. In a cripplingly poor state dominated by southern conservative Democratic politics, Rockefeller dared to offer a genuine alternative of liberal, socially progressive reform that included ambitious spending plans as a vital and necessary way to propel it into the twentieth century. In doing so, Rockefeller set the political agenda in Arkansas for at least the next thirty years, forced far-reaching reform in both the state's Republican and Democratic parties, and promulgated nothing short of a revolution in the state's political culture.

The *Monroe World* depiction of Arkansas as a "deep-south, conservative, segregationist state" was not entirely accurate. Undoubtedly that perception was colored by the recent events of September 1957 in the state capital of Little Rock, when Arkansas governor Orval Faubus called out National Guard troops to surround the city's Central High School, thereby preventing the court-ordered entry of nine African American students in the wake of the U.S. Supreme Court's 1954 *Brown v. Board of Education* school-desegregation decision. The situation was only resolved when President Dwight D. Eisenhower sent in federal troops to escort the African American students into the school.[6]

Yet the Little Rock school crisis was uncharacteristic of what was a relatively racially moderate state. Bordered on its northern and western boundaries by Missouri and Oklahoma, northwest Arkansas had more in common with the Midwest and West than the South. Rolling hills and a small-farm economy dominated the area in the mid-1950s. Since cotton had never reached that part of the state, the African American population was small, and in some counties nonexistent.[7] The University of Arkansas Law School in Fayetteville, northwest Arkansas, was the first in the former Confederate states to voluntarily admit an African American graduate student in 1948.[8] Fayetteville and the nearby town of Charleston were the only two school districts in the South to voluntarily desegregate between the 1954 *Brown* decision and the Supreme Court's 1955 implementation order (known as *"Brown* II").[9] However, on its eastern and southern boundaries, Arkansas bordered Mississippi, Louisiana, and Texas, and the southeastern half of the state did more closely resemble the Lower South. The traditionally cotton plantation areas of the Arkansas Delta contained over 90 percent of the state's African American population.[10]

Little Rock was perched precariously at the center of the state between the two very different regions. As the most urban area of the state in the 1950s, with a population of around one hundred thousand, it had developed a reputation for progressive race relations—a fact that even the most critical members of the African American community were willing to acknowledge was true.[11] African American police officers had patrolled African American neighborhoods since World War II, the University of Arkansas Medical School at Little Rock began admitting African American graduate students in 1948, and buses desegregated without trouble in 1956.[12]

Nevertheless, rural Arkansas Delta interests still exercised considerable power in state politics. The Democratic Party was its voice and it was all-powerful. V. O. Key in his landmark 1949 political survey of the South characterized Arkansas as "pure one-party politics," and more than twenty-five years later political scientists Jack Bass and Walter DeVries agreed that "No state has been more traditionally Democratic than Arkansas."[13] National elections underscored the state's Democratic loyalty. In 1948, despite Arkansas governor Ben Laney being the first choice to head the National States' Rights Party (South Carolinian Strom Thurmond got the job after Laney turned it down) in a so-called Dixiecrat protest against the national Democratic Party and their candidate Harry S. Truman's pro–civil rights platform, Arkansas still voted for Truman in the presidential election. As other southern states voted for Republican presidential candidate Dwight D. Eisenhower in the 1950s, Arkansas remained Democrat. Even after President Lyndon B. Johnson signed the Civil Rights Act in 1964, leading to the wholesale decamping of the Lower South to Republican presidential candidate Barry Goldwater, Arkansas remained Democrat. However, in 1968, Arkansas went for American Independence Party candidate George Wallace, and finally, in 1972, decamped to Republican candidate Richard Nixon, along with the rest of the South and most of the nation. In 1972, Arkansas became the penultimate state in the nation to vote for a Republican presidential candidate since Reconstruction. (A few hours later Hawaii, a state only since 1959, became the last U.S. state since Reconstruction to vote for a GOP presidential candidate).[14]

For the *Monroe World* to describe Winthrop Rockefeller as noisy and strutting was likewise wide of the mark. True, since his move to Arkansas in 1953, Rockefeller often dressed in flamboyant western wear and he had made a big impression on the state, but despite his handsome features and striking build—six foot, four inches and 200-plus pounds—Rockefeller was relatively quiet, shy, and often awkward and ill-at-ease in public. As for being a rich northern-born Yankee liberal integrationist, Rockefeller was guilty as charged. Born May 1, 1912, Winthrop Rockefeller was the grandson of John D. Rockefeller, one of the founders of Standard Oil Company in 1870 and reputedly one of the richest men ever to have lived. He was the son of John D. Rockefeller Jr., the sole male heir to the Standard Oil fortune, and Abby Aldrich, the daughter of Rhode Island Republican senator Nelson W. Aldrich. Winthrop grew up in the Rockefeller family home in New York with his older sister and as the second-youngest of five brothers.

Winthrop attended Lincoln High School at Columbia University's Teachers College in New York City and Loomis School in Windsor, Connecticut, before enrolling at Yale as an undergraduate. Deciding that he was not cut out to be a scholar, he left Yale in his junior year to work in the Texas oil fields with Humble Oil and Refining Company—part of what had been Standard Oil before the Supreme Court ordered it to be broken up in 1911 because it breached antimonopoly legislation. Rockefeller then spent a brief time at the family-controlled Chase National Bank before becoming a junior executive at another Standard Oil subsidiary, Socony-Vacuum Oil Company. In the summer of 1940, he volunteered for military training at the Businessmen's Camp at Plattsburg, New York, and on January 22, 1941, he enlisted as a private in the U.S. Army. Rockefeller saw active service in the Pacific at Guam, Leyte, and Okinawa. On April 2, 1945, Rockefeller's ship, the *Henrico*, was attacked by a kamikaze pilot; 75 men were killed, 150 wounded. Rockefeller suffered flash burns and was hospitalized for six weeks, after which he returned to Okinawa. By the end of the war, Rockefeller had risen from the rank of private to lieutenant colonel.[15]

After the war, Rockefeller worked for a short time making a nationwide survey of veterans' readjustment problems before again becoming involved in various family business interests. As the only unmarried Rockefeller brother, Winthrop was one of America's most eligible bachelors, and he soon established himself as a fixture on the New York social scene, gaining a reputation as something of a playboy. It was during these years that Rockefeller met Barbara Sears, whom most people knew as "Bobo." At the time she was estranged from her husband, the Boston socialite Richard Sears Jr., who was in the diplomatic service and stationed in Paris. Eighteen months after they met, two months after Bobo's divorce, and with Bobo already two months pregnant, Winthrop and Bobo married on February 14, 1948. Winthrop's only son, Winthrop Paul, was born seven months later. After just over a year together, the couple split, leading to an acrimonious and much-publicized divorce which ended in a $6 million settlement in 1954. The pain and publicity of the divorce, the desire to leave the public glare of New York's high life, and the need to chart his own course within the Rockefeller family were all factors in Winthrop's move to Arkansas in 1953.[16]

Rockefeller chose to move to Arkansas at the recommendation of an old army friend, Frank Newell. Once there, Rockefeller bought a 927-acre tract on top of Petit Jean Mountain just outside the small town of Morrilton, sixty miles northwest of Little Rock. He immediately began building Winrock Farms and stocked its fields with prime Santa Gertrudis cattle. Rockefeller's interests stretched well beyond Petit Jean as he continued the Rockefeller family tradition of philanthropy by giving money to various causes around the state.[17]

Rockefeller's extravagance was not the only thing that set him apart in Arkansas. One of the things he did in setting up Winrock Farms was to put his old friend from Harlem, African American private detective Jimmy Hudson, in charge of running day-to-day matters there.[18] This raised more than a few eyebrows in a state that, despite the limited progress that had been made in certain areas, was still saturated with southern racial mores. For Rockefeller, it was a continuation of a racially moderate, color-blind attitude. As a youngster, he had spent holidays with his family on campus at Virginia's African American Hampton Institute where he mixed freely with African American students. Rockefeller also took an interest in African American medical care while living in Houston, and in the late 1940s he became a trustee of the National Urban League, continuing the Rockefeller family interest in this organization dedicated to addressing the urban problems and needs of the African American population. While not a racial liberal—he later opposed the 1964 Civil Rights Act on the grounds that it handed the federal government too

much power, and he preferred voluntary change—he was certainly more progressive in his racial views than most Arkansans. This continued throughout
his life. In 1968, after the assassination of civil rights leader Martin Luther
King Jr., Rockefeller was the only southern governor to arrange a memorial
service on the grounds of the state capitol to dissipate racial tensions. The following year he appointed William "Sonny" Walker as the South's only African
American state head of the Office of Economic Opportunity (an agency of the
War on Poverty); this was one of many minority hirings during Rockefeller's
two terms in office.[19]

Arkansas was in dire straits when Rockefeller arrived. In almost every index of poverty and social backwardness, the state came second only to Mississippi. The state's population was plummeting rapidly as residents moved
elsewhere to look for jobs.[20] In 1955, newly elected governor Orval Faubus
sought to address the problem by getting the Arkansas General Assembly to
declare a state of emergency and urging it to pass legislation to address the
state's predicament. One of these measures created the Arkansas Industrial
Development Commission (AIDC), which was charged with the task of lur-
ing new industries to the state to halt the population drain. Faubus appointed
Rockefeller as AIDC chair in March 1955, hoping that he could use his influential name to bring business to the state. Rockefeller was a huge success at
the AIDC. In the next nine years, six hundred new industrial plants opened
in Arkansas, creating ninety thousand new jobs and adding $270 million to
the annual payroll. Around $100 million was spent in capital construction,
the state's per-capita income rose from $960 to $1,500, and Arkansas led the
southern states in new factory jobs per capita. The success made Rockefeller a
popular and highly visible figure in the state.[21]

Just as Rockefeller and the AIDC were was kick-starting Arkansas's recovery, the 1957 Little Rock school crisis broke. The state made news both
nationally and internationally as the epitome of southern massive resistance
to school desegregation and a symbol of racial prejudice. Many business leaders and potential investors shied away from such negative publicity, and new
industries went into a temporary lull until the schools peacefully reopened
on a token integrated basis in August 1959.[22] Rockefeller had spent two-and-
a-half hours with Faubus before the governor called out the National Guard
in September 1957, trying to persuade him not to intervene for the sake of the
Arkansas economy. "I reasoned with him, argued with him, almost pled with
him," Rockefeller later recalled. Faubus would not listen. "I'm sorry," he told
Rockefeller, "but I'm already committed. I'm going to run for a third term [for
governor in 1958], and if I don't do this, [segregationist politicians] Jim Johnson [head of the Citizens' Councils in Arkansas, an organization dedicated to

opposing school desegregation] and Bruce Bennett [the pro-segregation state attorney general] will tear me to shreds." Faubus had taken a moderate stance on school desegregation when first elected in 1954, but challenged by Jim Johnson in the Democratic primary in 1956, he had been pushed into taking a stronger segregationist line. In September 1957, Faubus's actions cemented his segregationist credentials and proved to be politically expedient. He was elected to an unprecedented six terms as governor.[23]

The Little Rock crisis soured the relationship between Rockefeller and Faubus. Though they remained on cordial, even good-humored terms on a personal level, the two men recognized that they were on opposite sides of the political fence. Rockefeller had been reticent to speak out against Faubus in September 1957 since he did not want to stir up even more controversy. By October, however, he was criticizing Faubus's actions in the national media, while still steering clear of direct engagement with the racial controversy. He instead labelled Faubus's actions as "bad for business."[24]

The rivalry between Rockefeller and Faubus intensified in 1960 when Rockefeller met the seven-year residency requirement for governor. That year, Rockefeller organized a Committee for the Two-Party System (CTPS) and hosted a "Party for Two Parties" evening at Winrock Farms. Aware of the overwhelmingly pro-Democrat feeling in the state, a call for two competing parties, rather than an outright appeal for the Republican Party, seemed the most prudent first step forward. Some friends urged Rockefeller to run as a Democrat if he was truly serious about political success. However, coming from a Republican family background, he would not commit himself to the Democratic Party simply for political convenience.[25]

In May 1961, Rockefeller was elected Arkansas's Republican national committeeman. One reason why Rockefeller had initially steered clear of Arkansas's Republican politics was the factionalism that existed in the state party despite its small size and almost total ineffectiveness. As historian Cathy Urwin writes, the party had not "elected even one governor, senator, representative or state senator in the whole of the twentieth century." The dominant figures in the organization were state chair Osro Cobb and national committeeman Wallace Townsend. Both men were conservative, old guard, states' rights'–supporting, "post office" Republicans whose primary purpose for existence was to dispense federal patronage in the state during Republican presidential administrations. When Townsend retired in 1961 after thirty-three years, it provided Rockefeller with the opportunity to gain control. Despite some murmurings, Rockefeller met with little resistance in winning the appointment. The party had little to lose and much to gain by having such a wealthy and influential figure in charge. Rockefeller quickly set about overhauling the party. The appointment of John Paul Hammerschmidt as state chairman—a young and emerging new Republican figure in the state—went a long way in establishing a new Arkansas Republican regime.[26] In March 1964, Rockefeller resigned as chair of the AIDC, and three days later he announced his candidacy for governor in November's general election.[27]

On June 20, 1964, Rockefeller released a sixteen-point "Statement of Beliefs." He dedicated himself to serving only two terms if elected; eliminating election fraud and abuse; improving the education system; cracking down on illegal gambling; pursuing racial change through voluntary action; running government in a financially accountable way; opposing exertion of political pressure on state employees; striving to establish a two-party system; supporting health and welfare programs; reforming the state's prison system; developing the state's cultural and intellectual activities; conserving and managing the state's natural resources; promoting the conduct of fair and equitable relationships between state government, state citizens, and private business; supporting local and state control of governmental matters; striving for full employment; and providing positive and forward-looking leadership for "economic and cultural growth."[28]

The same day, Faubus addressed a statewide audience on television. Contrasting starkly with Rockefeller's policy statement, Faubus set the tone for a bitterly personal campaign in which he painted Rockefeller as an outsider, interloper, and misfit. Faubus continually returned to Rockefeller's wealthy and privileged background, his custom of serving drinks at Winrock Farms in a predominantly dry state, and his habit of holding conferences at Winrock Farms that brought in outsiders for fresh perspectives on Arkansas's problems. "Faubus could make 'Rockefeller' sound almost like an obscenity," Rockefeller later recalled.[29]

Ever the politician, Faubus often conveyed these messages surreptitiously. "By hint and innuendo," reported one newsman, "Faubus constantly conveys the impression that he considers Rockefeller morally unfit for high office."[30] At other times, Faubus was more straightforward. In his televised speech, Faubus promised to guard against "a state policy of immorality, atheism, and forced integration" and to protect the rights of citizens to "live a moral, upright, Christian life." Faubus warned voters not to be swayed by his opponent's "unlimited campaign funds," and he declared that under his guidance the executive mansion "will not become the scene of drinking parties, and guest houses will not become the headquarters of beatniks from other states." Neither would state authority be "used in the interests of a band of Communist-trained invaders, bent on creating discord in our various communities." Faubus pledged that he would not "give preferential treatment to the rich and powerful" but that he would instead "promote programs for the care of the helpless and unfortunate" and "further the economic and educational betterment of all of our citizens." "If you agree these are worthy objectives," he concluded, "I need your help and your vote."[31]

Rockefeller ignored personal mudslinging and focused instead on campaigning hard on the issues. As one aide observed, Rockefeller, "travelled 12,000 miles, [shook] more than 300,000 hands and visited on the courthouse lawns and main streets of towns in all of Arkansas' 75 counties."[32] It was not enough. Faubus defeated Rockefeller by 337,489 to 254,561 votes (57 percent to 43 percent) in the general election.[33]

National trends certainly helped Faubus. Even though Lyndon Johnson was out of favor in much of the South because of his support for the 1964 Civil Rights Act, Faubus, after initial hesitancy, remained loyal and supported the national Democratic ticket. So too did the majority of the Arkansas electorate, who cast their votes for Johnson even as all five Lower South states went for conservative Republican Barry Goldwater in protest.[34] Meanwhile, the Goldwater campaign did not help Rockefeller at all. Winthrop's older brother Nelson, who had served as governor of New York since 1958, was Goldwater's main opponent for the Republican presidential nomination in 1964. Nelson Rockefeller represented the liberal Republican wing of the national party to the extent that its members were dubbed "Rockefeller Republicans." His increased national profile flagged the more liberal side of Rockefeller politics, something that did not play particularly well with voters in Arkansas. Once Goldwater had won the nomination, Winthrop Rockefeller was in the awkward position of standing at the same election for the same party as a man who was in many ways his ideological opposite. When asked where he stood between his brother Nelson and Goldwater, Rockefeller cryptically replied: "That's just what I do. I stand between Nelson and Goldwater." The Winthrop Rockefeller camp was divided over what to do. If they supported Goldwater, they potentially stood to gain from a rise in Republican votes. At the same time, it would alienate liberal Democrat supporters who were disaffected with Faubus. If they supported Johnson, they would look like they were turning their back on the Republican Party even as they were asking Arkansas voters to embrace it. It also risked confirming the electorate's fears that Rockefeller was too liberal. Rockefeller ultimately decided to distance himself from Goldwater, just as the Goldwater campaign held Rockefeller distinctly at arm's length.[35]

There were a number of things to be salvaged form the 1964 defeat. Rockefeller's 43 percent share of the vote was twice that of any previous Republican candidate for governor in Arkansas since Reconstruction. Rockefeller performed best in urban areas, precisely where the state's population was expanding.[36] Political corruption and the control over the electoral process exercised by an entrenched Democratic political machine had aided Faubus, but significant electoral changes were afoot. In 1964, the passage of Amendment Twenty-four to the U.S. Constitution outlawed the use of the poll tax in federal elections. The following year, Arkansas abolished the poll tax as a requirement for voting and introduced a permanent personal voter-registration system. The new system required only a free, one-off registration that in most cases lasted a lifetime. Qualifying to vote therefore became much easier, and exerting control over the electoral process became more difficult. The number of qualified electors began to rise rapidly.[37]

African American voters in particular saw the benefits of these changes. The civil rights organization the Student Nonviolent Coordinating Committee had been active in the state since 1962, and it worked hard to register and mobilize African American voters.[38] Faubus received 84 percent of the African American vote in 1964, partly because he cultivated established leaders in the African American community and partly because of corruption in the Arkansas Delta, where influential white planters still controlled large blocks of African American voters.[39] The prospect of a larger and more politically aware African American electorate in 1966 cast a large element of uncertainty over the outcome of the election.

After defeat in 1964, Rockefeller immediately began campaigning for governor in 1966. "We lost," Rockefeller recalled, "but we never stopped running. . . . On election night, when Governor Faubus had his sixth term in the bag, someone pasted a '66 over the '64 camping button and we were off that very night toward victory in 1966."[40] As one Rockefeller aide noted, the 1966 campaign "was professionally directed by an experienced core of loyal specialists who had teethed on the miscalculations of the 1964 campaign and spent the next two years learning to work together as a well-disciplined team."[41] Arkansas political scientists Diane D. Blair and Jay Barth called it "one of the most sophisticated partisan apparatuses in America, complete with professional pollsters, elaborate headquarters, well-paid field workers, and a public relations campaign."[42] Coordinating the campaign was a small cluster of advisors known as "The Group," whom Rockefeller selected as the best and brightest of young political talent in the state. With Rockefeller's campaign chest to hand, a huge effort was made to mobilize grassroots support.[43]

The Rockefeller campaign team could not control or predict every move. The first shock came when Orval Faubus announced that he did not intend to run for reelection in 1966. With an eye on the polls, which were telling him that voters were turning against his long tenure and control over the state

Democratic machine, Faubus decided to retire rather than chance an igno-minious defeat. Much of the Rockefeller campaign since the 1964 election had been run with Faubus in mind as the opponent. Many in the campaign team refused to take Faubus's withdrawal seriously. He had pulled similar stunts in the past only to throw his hat in the ring at the last moment. Not until the deadline for filing had passed did the Rockefeller people begin to consider the alternatives.[44]

The man to emerge from a highly competitive Democratic Party primary in Faubus's absence was Faubus's old nemesis James D. Johnson. Born in the small lumber town of Crossett, Arkansas, on August 20, 1924, Johnson was the son of an independent grocer. Educated in local schools, he then went to Cumberland University Law School in Birmingham, Alabama, where he entered politics at the age of twenty-three, working for Strom Thurmond in his 1948 bid for the presidency as head of the independent National States' Rights Party. In 1950, Johnson was elected as the youngest state senator in Arkansas history. After two terms in office, in 1954 he made a failed bid to win statewide office as attorney general. The following year, Johnson emerged at the forefront of Arkansas's massive-resistance movement against school de-segregation. In 1956, he unsuccessfully challenged incumbent governor Orval Faubus in the Democratic Party primary.[45]

After Faubus's 1957 stand at Central High, it became unrealistic for Johnson to paint the governor as soft on integration—he later ruefully recalled that Faubus "took my nickel and hit the jackpot."[46] Johnson instead settled for election to a seat on the Arkansas Supreme Court in 1958. In 1964, while still a member of the court and going against its tradition of impartiality, Johnson openly campaigned for conservative Republican presidential candidate Barry Goldwater, and he appeared alongside Goldwater and South Carolina segre-gationist politician Jimmy Byrnes on a South-wide campaign telecast.[47]

In 1966, with Faubus finally out of the way, Johnson made a second bid for governor. Billing himself as "Justice" Jim Johnson, he campaigned in the same folksy, revivalist, conservative, pro-segregation mold as he had done ten years earlier. Johnson's main selling point in the Democratic primary was that he could distance himself from the Faubus Democratic machine; he cast him-self instead as "the only choice for change."[48] To almost everyone's surprise, Johnson won the first round of primary voting in a field of candidates, with his nearest rival fellow Supreme Court justice Frank Holt.[49] The defeat al-lowed the Democratic Party establishment to get fully behind Holt. However, in another shock victory in the runoff election ("a fluke," Rockefeller called it), Johnson won, albeit by a much closer margin.[50]

The Arkansas Republican Party gubernatorial primary that year was the first to be held in almost a decade. A 1957 state law required political parties to hold primary elections for contested posts which the Republicans duly began to comply with in 1958.[51] However, the winner of the primary for governor that year went on to poll so few votes that the Republicans decided to save money and nominate just one candidate for each office, thus removing the need for party primaries. In 1966, to force a primary election, Gus McMillan, an old Faubus supporter, filed against Rockefeller. It was a futile gesture: Rockefeller handily won the primary by 19,956 to 310 votes. Moreover, it proved a political miscalculation: "Our Democratic opponents . . . hoped we would have to hold a statewide primary, with the idea that the expense and trouble would weaken us," said state chair John Paul Hammerschmidt. "On the contrary, it will make us stronger." The primary provided a useful electoral dry-run ahead of the general election and a chance to mobilize grassroots support.[52]

Once the Democrat and Republican candidates for governor had been decided, the campaign for the general election began in earnest. For Jim Johnson, how to position himself against Rockefeller proved something of a dilemma. He had run as the candidate for change in the Democratic primary, but as he was standing against a Republican in the general election, the claim of being the freshest face was more difficult to sell. Initially, Johnson chose to distance himself from Faubus to emphasize the difference between his candidacy and the old Democratic regime, telling the press that he did not need the former governor's support to win the election. Looking to put his own stamp on the party, and in a break with the past when individual candidates had run their own campaigns for various offices, plans were made to run a Johnson Democratic ticket with James J. Pilkinton and Joe Purcell running alongside him for lieutenant governor and attorney general. Joe Basore, a defeated primary candidate for lieutenant governor, took charge of managing the ticket.[53]

The joint opening of the campaigns at Democratic Party headquarters in Little Rock's Albert Pike Hotel on August 28 did not bode well. None of Arkansas's congressional delegation turned up. Pilkinton and Purcell both subsequently distanced themselves from Johnson and set up their own campaign offices.[54] Things did not improve at the Democratic State Convention held September 15 and 16 at Little Rock's Robinson Auditorium. Faubus stole the show on the first day with a triumphalist speech recalling his achievements as governor. Johnson, who had to be persuaded to invite Faubus to the convention at all, refused to appear alongside him. Johnson showed up the following day to deliver his televised speech. He was introduced by Arkansas congressman Wilbur Mills, the only member of Arkansas's congressional delegation willing to openly endorse Johnson's candidacy. In his speech, Johnson railed against the "Madison Avenue Cowboy" and "prissy sissy" Rockefeller as well as the liberal *Arkansas Gazette* newspaper. Johnson declared that he stood for "the preservation of our Christian faith and heritage, the preservation of constitutional government, and the preservation of our right to own and control private property."[55]

Discontent over Johnson's candidacy within Democratic ranks led to the formation of a "Democrats for Rockefeller" organization made up of "anti-Faubus stalwarts left over from 1964" and liberal Democrats who did not like Johnson's conservative politics. "Democrats for Rockefeller" was chaired by Robert E. Lee Wilson III, a northeast Arkansas plantation millionaire, and Dansby A. Council, a businessman from the northwest Arkansas city of Fort Smith. Johnson attempted to counter the move with a "Republicans for Jim Johnson" organization but, as one Rockefeller man noted, it "could have met in a telephone booth." Operating from a two-room office at the Marion Hotel in Little Rock, "Democrats for Rockefeller" ran stinging campaign ads with slogans such as, "Do the Democratic Party a favour . . . Vote for Rockefeller!" It also lent experienced assistance in mobilizing disgruntled and disaffected Democrats across the state.[56]

Developments in the national Democratic Party also went against Jim Johnson in 1966. The growing unpopularity of Lyndon Johnson in Arkansas threatened to weaken support for all Democratic candidates in the state. "There can be no doubt about it," noted one Democrat pollster, "President Johnson is in a poor shape in Arkansas today." This was put down to "frustration over the Vietnam War, unhappiness at the high cost of living and the feeling that he has gone too far on racial problems."[57] Republican pollsters had Lyndon Johnson's approval rating down as low as 27 percent of the vote in the state. Jim Johnson sought to distance himself from his presidential namesake, reassuring voters that, "I'm . . . not kin to Lyndon Johnson, either by blood or philosophically." As proof of this, Jim Johnson could point to the fact that he had strongly endorsed Barry Goldwater for president in 1964. Yet neither Jim Johnson's rejection of Lyndon Johnson nor his support for Barry Goldwater played well. His attacks on the incumbent president only succeeded in pushing more liberal Democrats to Rockefeller. Meanwhile, Rockefeller exploited Johnson's support for Goldwater in 1964 by asking in campaign ads: "If Jimmy Johnson can support a Republican, why can't everybody else?"[58]

As it had in 1964, much of the 1966 campaign focused more on personalities than policies. Johnson, as Faubus had successfully done in 1964, portrayed himself as the heir to southern Democrat, rural, working-class, conservative values, and campaigned on the slogan "For the Love of Arkansas."[59] Clearly differentiating his candidacy from Johnson's, Rockefeller painted himself as the new, forward-looking, break-with-the-past candidate. On the campaign trail, Johnson sounded much like Faubus had in 1964, honing in on personal attacks: "It's the hard knocks of life that tempers the steel that makes the man," he told voters. "His [Rockefeller's] jet-set status has shielded him from the realities that confront the people of the state." Johnson's political ads reinforced this with statements like: "Justice Jim has something in common with all of us. He is a man who understands our problems in paying the grocery bill, rent, car payments, doctor bills and for the rest of the necessities of life. . . . If you have three hundred million dollars ($300,000,000), the Rockefeller Party may understand your problems. If you have less, the Democratic Party does understand YOUR problems and YOUR way of living."[60]

Rockefeller, ready for what was coming this time around, hit back more effectively. After Johnson's "prissy sissy" comments about Rockefeller at the state convention, which Republican polls showed the voters disapproved of by an over 80 percent margin, an endorsement ad was run featuring two former University of Arkansas Razorback footballers who had later turned professional, John David Crow of the Chicago Bears and Washington Redskins, and Fred Williams of the St. Louis Cardinals and San Francisco 49ers, that declared, "Us Sissies Gotta' Stick Together!" In answer to charges about his wealth and privilege, Rockefeller responded: "I thank God that the people of Arkansas are not for sale to anyone. To imply that they are is a slap at their integrity and at their right to vote for the candidate of their choice." When a cartoon depicting "King Winnie I" sitting on overflowing bags of money atop Petit Jean Mountain was published by Johnson's campaign, Rockefeller turned the tables and pointed to his extensive philanthropy in the state since his arrival: "I'm mighty proud of that picture with all the money spilling over," he said. "I haven't built a wall around the mountain to keep my money in. I've invested it in young people."[61]

For those who were interested in the issues, the slogan, "Which candidate can do most for Arkansas?" proved a distinct asset for Rockefeller. The polls told the Rockefeller camp that the three main issues of interest to the voters were education, jobs, and roads. On education, Johnson's opposition to *Brown* and his involvement with the school crisis in Little Rock contrasted with Rockefeller's investment of money in a model-school program in his hometown of Morrilton. On jobs, Rockefeller's record with the AIDC to bring industry into the state was unsurpassed. On roads, Rockefeller was committed to developing the state's infrastructure. Collectively, what many voters appeared to want in 1966 was change: a new politics, a new direction, and new ideas for advancing Arkansas's politics, economy, society, and culture. Johnson benefited from this in the Democratic primary as the anti-Faubus establishment candidate, but up against Rockefeller, Johnson's conservative brand of Democrat politics only accentuated the distinction between the old and the new in the voters' minds. As a member of Rockefeller's campaign team summed it up, "the segregationist, evangelical appeal of Jim Johnson just did not fit the 20th century image Arkansans were so anxious to achieve."[62] Or, as political scientist Earl Black put it, "a majority of Arkansas voters in 1966 preferred a nonsegregationist Republican who promised to create jobs through economic development to a local version of George Wallace."[63]

Fortunately for Rockefeller, many of the hot-button issues that would later prove so beneficial to conservative Republicans—and which would have benefited Jim Johnson in 1966—did not yet appear relevant. Voters were of two minds over Johnson's fusion of religion with politics. While 65 percent thought that a candidate's churchgoing would make a difference in their vote, 75 percent thought that religion should not play a major role in the campaign. Likewise, almost three-quarters of voters did not see Rockefeller's status as a divorcee as a big issue. In the pre-*Roe* world, abortion did not figure at all as a campaign issue. Neither did the question of teaching evolution in schools, which was already outlawed in Arkansas. This meant that two-thirds of Arkansas voters did not even know what evolution theory was. The third that did were evenly split over whether it should be taught in schools. Johnson's scepticism of federal government hurt him when Rockefeller raised the question of how safe federal aid to the state would be in his opponent's hands—a crucial factor in Arkansas which saw three dollars of federal money enter the state for every one dollar of taxpayers' money that left. Many in Arkansas relied on some sort of federal welfare check, and supporting increases in such payments was a political necessity. Johnson promised an extra ten dollars per head in welfare payments within a year of election. Rockefeller assured voters that "it is both a moral obligation and in society's best interest to help those unable to help themselves."[64]

If there was one substantive issue that proved a tiebreaker in the 1966 election campaign, it was civil rights. Yet neither candidate explicitly made race central to their campaign, largely because both took it as read that the voters already understood their position. Rockefeller was known to be the more racially liberal candidate though he was reluctant to trumpet this for fear of alienating conservative white voters. Johnson, the state's former Citizens' Council head, made it perfectly plain from the outset where he stood. Early in the campaign, Johnson refused to shake hands with African Americans, saying that he "did not campaign in their community." His segregationist past kept coming back to haunt him. Former Mississippi governor Ross Barnett declared at a Citizens' Council rally in Marvell, Arkansas, that the country needed "men the calibre of Justice Jim Johnson and George Wallace to return it to normalcy." At a Klan rally in Star City, Arkansas, shortly before election day, amid robed participants and a fifteen-foot burning cross, Louisianan Grand Dragon Jack Helms declared that, "The Klan has come out for Lurleen Wallace [the wife of George Wallace, who successfully ran for Alabama governor that year in place of her husband who was term-limited], Lester Maddox [a segregationist who was appointed governor of Georgia in 1966 by the Georgia General Assembly, despite gaining slightly fewer votes than his opponent in the general election, Republican Howard "Bo" Calloway] and Jim Johnson, and we're electing them one by one." Such endorsements did not help Johnson. With increasing racial violence in the nation in the mid- to late 1960s, Arkansas voters were concerned about what would happen in their state. They were unsure about Johnson's ability to handle such disturbances without further fanning the flames of racial discord. In 1964, Faubus outscored Rockefeller among voters when asked who could best keep the racial peace. In 1966, they went for Rockefeller over Johnson by a three-to-one margin.[65] As Rockefeller noted, "The reckless course of white supremacy at any cost was running out of appeal; it was losing its credibility with the people."[66]

The African American vote turned out to be the decisive factor in the outcome of the election.[67] Irene Samuel, a veteran of Little Rock's Women's Emergency Committee to Open our Schools (WEC), which had mobilized community support for opening schools with token integration in the city in 1959, played a key role in mobilizing the African American vote for Rockefeller in 1966. Samuel noted that the campaign for African American votes was conducted in a low-key manner to avoid a backlash from white voters. Not until the final four weeks of the campaign was an all-out attempt made to court African Americans. Samuel believed that the permanent voter-registration system had "a real impact on the results of this election." Rockefeller won the election by 306,324 to 257,203 votes (54.4 percent to 45.6 percent), a margin of just 49,121 votes. Overall, Samuel estimated that Rockefeller had actually narrowly lost to Johnson on white votes alone by about 18,000 votes. But Rockefeller claimed at least 67,000 more African American votes than Johnson, enough to make up the winning margin.[68]

Rockefeller won reelection in 1968, serving two terms as governor. In a largely hostile, Democrat-dominated state legislature, he battled with mixed success to push through his reform agenda. Nevertheless, among his achievements in office, in addition to a more progressive racial agenda of tolerance and affirmative action in hiring practices, was the adoption of the state's first minimum-wage law, a freedom of information law, a tightening of tax legislation, and a crackdown on illegal gambling. The most wide-ranging reforms came in the state's notoriously archaic penal system. Rockefeller brought better medical care, better food, and an educational program to Arkansas's prisons. During his tenure as governor, Rockefeller also replaced a trustee system of inmate supervision with hired guards to weed out day-to-day corruption. Rockefeller was an ardent opponent of the death penalty, and his final act in office was to commute the death sentences of all fifteen men on death row. Defeated in the 1970 election, Rockefeller gradually withdrew from the political scene. In 1971 he divorced his second wife, Jeanette Edris, a New Yorker whom he had married shortly after his arrival in Arkansas in 1956. On February 22, 1973, Rockefeller died at age sixty of pancreatic cancer in Palm Springs, California. He was buried in Arkansas on top of Petit Jean Mountain.[69]

The longest-lasting legacy of the 1966 election was its impact on the Democratic Party. Bill Clinton recalls, "Ironically . . . it was the Democratic Party which benefitted most from Rockefeller's Republican administration."[70] As the Democratic governor of Arkansas from 1979 to 1981, and then again from 1983 to 1992, and a two-term Democratic president from 1993 to 2001, Clinton was well-positioned to make such a judgement. In 1970, Dale Bumpers, a political unknown, won the Democratic Party's nomination for governor and soundly defeated Rockefeller in the general election by a near two-to-one margin, 375,648 to 197,418 votes (61.7 percent to 32.4 percent).[71] Bumpers had previously held only one elected office in his life as city attorney in a one-attorney town.[72] Yet he offered what Arkansans had perhaps wanted all along: a Rockefeller program for reform run and implemented by a Democrat. Bumpers was one of a number of so-called "New Democrats" to emerge in the 1970s, alongside politicians such as Jimmy Carter, who was elected governor of Georgia the same year and who, even before Clinton, went on to become president of the United States (1977–81). Rockefeller was not too perturbed by this transformation in Arkansas's Democrats, once reflecting: "One of the most encouraging things . . . is the frequency with which I hear it said that the Democratic Party will never be the same again. . . . It's amazing what a little competition can do to make anybody—individual, company, political party— turn out a better product. That, I hope, will be one of the great legacies that the effort to establish a second party will leave Arkansas."[73]

The New Democrats were progressive-minded and eschewed the segregationist past of the old southern Democrats. Bumpers went on to serve as a U.S. senator for Arkansas (1975–99), replacing Arkansas's more liberal

Democratic senator, William Fulbright. Bumpers was succeeded by Democrat Blanche Lincoln in 1999, but she was ousted by Republican John Boozman in the 2010 midterm elections. Bumpers's elected successor as governor was Democrat David Pryor (1975–79), who was in turn elected as Arkansas's other U.S. senator (1979–97). Pryor replaced John McClellan, "the last of the old Arkansas conservatives."[74] Bill Clinton followed Pryor as the next elected Democratic governor, eventually going on to win two terms in the White House as the national Democratic Party presidential candidate (1993–2001). The procession of highly successful liberal Democrats in the governor's mansion was a direct consequence of Rockefeller's 1966 election victory. By beating Jim Johnson, Rockefeller put the sword to the old-guard Arkansas Democratic Party, just as he had done to the old-guard Arkansas Republican Party in the early 1960s, thereby allowing a very different set of politicians with many similar reform-minded programs and ideas to emerge.[75]

A number of political scientists prematurely wrote off Rockefeller's impact on the fortunes of the Republican Party in Arkansas, noting that once he and his wealth disappeared, so too did the party in the state. But that proved only partially true. Republicans have become ever more competitive in Arkansas since Rockefeller's term in office, and the state is today by no means the Democratic stronghold it once was.[76]

While without question a number of different national, regional, state, and local factors have determined the more recent Republican rise in Arkansas, Rockefeller's election broke the partisan taboo that smoothed the way for other Republicans to run for office. When Rockefeller was elected in 1966, so too was the first Arkansas Republican lieutenant governor since Reconstruction, Maurice "Footsie" Britt, and the first Arkansas Republican congressman since Reconstruction, the party's state chair John Paul Hammerschmidt. At a local and county level, Republican's fared less well. Though they gained their first three seats in the state legislature that year, they were still up against 132 Democrats. Republicans won only a handful of county offices.[77] Nevertheless, John Paul Hammerschmidt's Third District congressional seat has remained in Republican hands ever since. Bill Clinton tried but failed to unseat Hammerschmidt in the 1974 congressional election. Hammerschmidt held the seat for twenty-six years in total (1967–93) and has since been succeeded by Tim Hutchinson (1993–97), Tim's brother, Asa Hutchinson (1997–2001), and John Boozman (2001–11). Boozman was succeeded by Republican Steve Womak in 2010. Boozman had moved up to oust Democrat Blanche Lincoln from her U.S. Senate seat. Hammerschmidt's immediate successor, Tim Hutchinson, gave up the congressional seat in 1997 to become the first Republican U.S.

senator from Arkansas since Reconstruction (1997–2003). He was unseated by David Pryor's son, Mark Pryor, who has retained the seat in the family name ever since (2003–present).

At various points, Republicans have also picked up two other of Arkansas's four congressional seats: Ed Bethune (1979–85) and Tommy F. Robinson (1989–91) in the First District, and Jay W. Dickey (1993–2001) in the Fourth District. From 1997 to 2001, half of Arkansas's congressional delegation was Republican, with Tim Hutchinson serving as U.S. senator, his brother Asa Hutchinson serving in the Third Congressional District, and Jay Dickey serving in the Fourth Congressional District.

Republican governors have also succeeded Winthrop Rockefeller. Frank D. White defeated Bill Clinton in 1980 to serve one term (1981–83), and Mike Huckabee served for more than a decade (1996–2007). Democrat Mike Beebe currently holds the office (2007–present). Huckabee ran a surprisingly strong race in the 2008 Republican primaries for president as a dark-horse candidate, and he has since established himself as a national political personality as a commentator on the Fox News Channel, with his own Fox weekend show, *Huckabee*, with a daily commentary show on ABC Radio Network's *The Huckabee Report*, and as the author of several books. Speculation about a run for the Republican presidential nomination in 2012 has continued, with Huckabee remaining noncommittal about the prospect, saying that, "I'm not ruling anything out for the future, but I'm not making any specific plans."[78]

Huckabee's emergence as a darling of the national Republican Right, as well as the elections of the Hutchinson brothers, indicate that national politics has increasingly caught up with Arkansas, which now embraces conservative Republicans as eagerly as any other southern state. While the state voted for New Democrat southern presidential candidates Jimmy Carter and Bill Clinton in 1976, 1992, and 1996, it also voted for Republican presidential candidates Ronald Reagan in 1980 and 1984, George H. W. Bush in 1988, and George W. Bush in 2000 and 2004. In 2008, when Arkansas voted for John McCain, it was on the losing side for the first time since voting for George Wallace fifty years earlier. Indeed, McCain won Arkansas in 2008 by an even bigger percentage than George W. Bush did in 2004, the only state in the nation in which the Republican presidential candidate did this—though this may well have been linked to a Democrat backlash at the failure of former First Lady Hillary Clinton to secure the Democratic Party's nomination over Barack Obama.

There was no better illustration, however, that Rockefeller Republicanism retained a presence in the state than the fact that Mike Huckabee's elected lieutenant governor between 1996 and 2006 was Winthrop Paul Rockefeller, Winthrop Rockefeller's only son. Knowing that Huckabee would retire in 2006, Winthrop Paul announced his intention to run for governor to replace him. However, on July 20, 2005, he withdrew his candidacy from the Republican Party primary after being diagnosed with the blood disorder myeloproliferative disease. He underwent unsuccessful bone marrow transplants in October 2005 and March 2006. Winthrop Paul Rockefeller died in Little Rock's University of Arkansas for Medical Sciences on July 16, 2008, at the age of fifty-seven, in a tragic echo of his father's early death.[79] The Rockefeller name lives on in southern politics only through Winthrop Rockefeller's nephew, Jay Rockefeller (John D. Rockefeller IV), who was a regular visitor to Winrock Farms in his youth. Jay Rockefeller was secretary of state for West Virginia (1968–72), then governor (1977–85), before becoming a U.S. senator (1985–present). All of these offices he filled—breaking with family tradition—as a Democrat.[80]

As for Jim Johnson, he saw little immediate gain from his 1966 bid for governor other than a large amount of debt for his trouble. That did not stop him from running in 1968 against incumbent William Fulbright for a seat in the U.S. Senate (Johnson's wife, Virginia, meanwhile contested and lost the Democratic primary for governor). Johnson was persuaded to run for the senate seat by Henry Salvatore, a political advisor and confidant of California governor Ronald Reagan, who offered up conservative donations to bankroll the campaign. As one historian tells it, Johnson "allowed himself to be run as a front man for a group of Reagan Republicans." He lost again. The same year, Johnson campaigned for American Independence Party presidential candidate George Wallace. Though Wallace carried Arkansas, Johnson had none-too-fond memories of the experience, remembering how "that little bastard" Wallace left Johnson to borrow money to fund Wallace's appearances in the state only to take the money and run afterward. In the 1980s, Johnson was an enthusiastic Reagan supporter, and he became head of Arkansas's conservative Moral Majority organization. In the 1990s, Johnson described himself as an anti-Clinton southern Democrat. "The old breed of Southern Democrats were a law unto themselves," he wistfully recalled. "Maybe they're all dead now and I just don't know it." Through it all, Johnson remained an old-guard southern Democrat, being so "ultra-critical of the conservatives who fail to live up to my expectations that I feel a personal disgust for the Republicans."[81] On February 13, 2010, at the age of eighty-five, Johnson, who had been suffering from a terminal illness, was found dead at his rural home in Conway, Arkansas, killed by a self-inflicted gunshot wound.[82]

No doubt conservative Republicans would point to Rockefeller's experience in Arkansas as an anomaly, and an instructive one at that. Rockefeller's attempts to introduce progressive reform were not as politically profitable to Republicans in Arkansas as conservative policies were to them elsewhere in the South. While this is by and large true, Rockefeller's case was not totally unique. In 1969, for example, A. Linwood Holton Jr. became the first Republican governor of Virginia in circumstances similar to Rockefeller's in 1967. To dismiss these developments as anomalies is to miss a crucial part of the overall story of the Republican ascendency in Dixie.[83] What happened in Arkansas suggests that although the Republican Party certainly needed the South to advance its conservative agenda, the South did not necessarily need the Republican Party's conservative agenda to advance. True, Arkansas has been one of the quieter success stories of the New South to emerge since the 1970s, but its growth has been no less spectacular for it. Few could have believed when Rockefeller took over as head of the AIDC in 1955 that just fifty years later a homegrown Arkansas company like Walmart would become the largest retailer in the world. Tyson Foods and transportation company JCB Hunt are other northwest Arkansas success stories. Arkansas today is mid-table among states containing Fortune 500 companies, a remarkable feat for a state of its size. While economic development in the state has been uneven, and problems of poverty still persist in the Arkansas Delta, the state today is generally in much better shape than it was at midcentury.[84]

Moreover, Rockefeller was not in Arkansas just to promote the Republican Party, but first and foremost to improve his adopted state. His central goal was to transform Arkansas from a one-party state into a two-party state that would be more responsive to the demands of the electorate.[85] He certainly did not want to see a new Republican one-party state replace the old Democratic one-party state. "If I had found Arkansas under almost a hundred years of Republican domination with the political stagnation just as bad," Rockefeller once wrote, "I very probably would have set out to reorganize a Democratic Party in Arkansas."[86] Some still mutter that Rockefeller simply bought the election in 1966, and the state with it, with his tremendous wealth. But there were cheaper ways to buy into state politics at a time when votes were quite literally for sale to the highest bidder. Right on Rockefeller's doorstep in Morrilton was Conway County sheriff Marlin Hawkins, the rural equivalent of the city machine boss, whose candidly titled 1991 autobiography *How I Stole Elections* tells its own story.[87] Rockefeller did not buy Arkansas or its voters. Rather, he invested heavily in the state in the hope that the people there were willing to share in his vision for betterment. "Who can do most for Arkansas?" Rockefeller asked in 1966. The voters gave their answer. Few candidates in

Arkansas, or elsewhere, can claim to have delivered in a more wide-ranging and impactful way. As one of Rockefeller's Democrat heirs, David Pryor, said of Rockefeller, he "extended a greater—and more beneficial—influence on a single state than any figure of his generation."[88]

## Notes

1. The author wishes to gratefully acknowledge the receipt of a grant-in-aid in April 2009 and a month as a scholar-in-residence in August 2009 funded by the Rockefeller Archive Center, Sleepy Hollow, New York, which facilitated the research and writing of this essay. My thanks go to the staff at the archive for their help and support during my time there.

"Rockefeller in Arkansas," *Monroe (La.) World*, 1 March 1960, newspaper clipping, Record Group I, Box 59, Folder "Newspaper Clippings—Photostats, 1954–1957," Papers of Winthrop Rockefeller, 1911–1973 (microfilm), Rockefeller Archive Center, Sleepy Hollow, N.Y. (hereafter WR Papers, RAC Microfilm). The other four Republican governors from former Confederate states since the end of Reconstruction (I exclude West Virginia, which seceded to the Union early in the Civil War, as an exceptional case) up to 1967 are Florida's David Lindsay Russell (1897–1901), and Tennessee's Alvin Hawkins (1881–83), Ben W. Hooper (1911–15), and Alfred A. Taylor (1921–23).

2. Edmund F. Kallina, *Claude Kirk and the Politics of Confrontation* (Gainesville: University Press of Florida, 1993).

3. The idea of the "southern strategy" was coined in Kevin P. Phillips, *The Emerging Republican Majority* (New Rochelle, N.Y.: 1969).

4. On the "suburban strategy," see Matthew D. Lassiter, *The Silent Majority: Suburban Politics in the Sunbelt South* (Princeton: Princeton University Press, 2006); and Byron E. Shafer and Richard Johnston, *The End of Southern Exceptionalism: Class, Race and Partisan Change in the Postwar South* (Cambridge: Harvard University Press, 2006).

5. Richard E. Yates, "Arkansas: Independent and Unpredictable," in *The Changing Politics of the South*, ed. William C. Havard (Baton Rouge: Louisiana State University Press, 1972), 233–93.

6. John A. Kirk, *Beyond Little Rock: The Origins and Legacies of the Central High Crisis* (Fayetteville: University of Arkansas Press, 2007), 1–14; John A. Kirk, "Bigger Than Little Rock?: New Histories of the 1957 Central High Crisis," *Reviews in American History* 36, no. 4 (December 2008): 624–38.

7. John B. Mitchell, "An Analysis of Arkansas' Population by Race and Nativity, and Residence," *Arkansas Historical Quarterly* 8 (Summer 1949): 115–32.

8. Guerdon D. Nichols, "Breaking the Color Barrier at the University of Arkansas," *Arkansas Historical Quarterly* 27 (Spring 1968): 3–21.

9. For Arkansas's response to *Brown*, see John A. Kirk, *Redefining the Color Line: Black Activism in Little Rock, Arkansas, 1940–1970* (Gainesville: University Press of Florida, 2002), 86–105.

10. Mitchell, "An Analysis of Arkansas' Population," 115–32.

11. Daisy Bates, *The Long Shadow of Little Rock* (New York: McKay, 1962), 2.

12. Kirk, *Redefining the Color Line*, 34–74.

13. V. O. Key Jr., *Southern Politics in State and Nation* (New York: Knopf, 1950), 183–204; Jack Bass and Walter DeVries, *The Transformation of Southern Politics: Social Change and Political Consequence since 1945* (repr., Athens: University of Georgia Press, 1995), 87–106.

14. In addition to Key, *Southern Politics;* and Bass and DeVries, *Transformation of Southern Politics,* useful overviews of Arkansas politics include Earl Black, *Southern Governors and Civil Rights: Racial Segregation as a Campaign Issue in the Second Reconstruction* (Cambridge: Harvard University Press, 1976), 98–106; Andrew Dowdle and Gary D. Wekkin, "Arkansas: The Post-2000 Elections—Continued GOP Growth or a Party That Has Peaked?," in *The New Politics of the Old South,* 3rd ed., ed. Charles S. Bullock III and Mark J. Rozell (Lanham, Md., Rowman and Littlefield, 2007); Alexander Lamis, *The Two-Party South: Expanded Edition* (New York: Oxford University Press, 1988), 120–30; Neal Pierce, *The Deep South States of America* (New York: Norton, 1974), 123–61; and Yates, "Arkansas," 233–93. The definitive contemporary guide to Arkansas politics and government is Diane D. Blair and Jay Barth, *Arkansas Politics and Government,* 2nd ed. (Lincoln: University of Nebraska Press, 2005).

15. "WR Biography, May 18, 1964," 1–5, Record Group 1, Box 99, Folder, "Biographical Material (WR and JDR Jr.) 1957–1960," Reel 26, WR Papers, RAC Microfilm.

16. Alvin Moscow, *The Rockefeller Inheritance* (New York: Doubleday, 1977), 206–12.

17. For a thorough and comprehensive account of Rockefeller's philanthropy in Arkansas, see John L. Ward, *Winthrop Rockefeller, Philanthropist: A Life of Change* (Fayetteville: University of Arkansas Press, 2004).

18. "Rockefeller's Right-Hand Man," *Ebony,* August 1955, 17–24, copy in Record Group I, Box 57, Folder "Winrock Farms, 1953–1959," Reel 21, WR Papers, RAC Microfilm.

19. On Rockefeller and race, see John L. Ward, *The Arkansas Rockefeller* (Baton Rouge: Louisiana State University Press, 1978), 159–78; and Ward, *Winthrop Rockefeller, Philanthropist,* 23–34.

20. The state population dropped 6.5 percent in the 1950s, from 1,909,511 people in 1950 to 1,786,272 people in 1960, a figure just above the 1920 census count (Yates, "Arkansas," 239).

21. Cathy Kunzinger Urwin, *Agenda for Reform: Winthrop Rockefeller as Governor of Arkansas, 1967–71* (Fayetteville: University of Arkansas Press, 1991), 20–21, 26–29.

22. On the economic impact of the school crisis, see James C. Cobb, "The Lesson of Little Rock: Stability, Growth and Change in the American South," in *Understanding the Little Rock Crisis: An Exercise in Remembrance and Reconciliation,* ed. Elizabeth Jacoway and C. Fred Williams (Fayetteville: University of Arkansas Press, 1999), 107–22; and Gary Fullerton, "New Factories a Thing of Past in Little Rock," *Nashville Tennessean,* 31 May 1959.

23. On Faubus, see Roy Reed, *Faubus: The Life and Times of an American Prodigal*

(Fayetteville: University of Arkansas Press, 1997). Rockefeller quoted from an interview with Neal Pierce in Pierce, *The Deep South States of America*, 132.

24. Rockefeller's comments during the school crisis are documented in numerous newspaper clippings in Record Group I, Box 56, Folder "Little Rock Situation 1957," Reel 21, WR Papers, RAC Microfilm.

25. Winthrop Rockefeller, "Rebel with a Cause," 1970, 73–75, unpublished manuscript, Record Group IV, Box 54, Folder "Book (Doubleday) 1969," Reel 415, WR Papers, RAC Microfilm; "WR in Arkansas: The Story of Win Rockefeller's Campaign for Governor 1966," 4, Record Group IV, Box 115, Folder "WR in Arkansas—The Story of Win Rockefeller's Campaign for Governor," Reel 428, WR Papers, RAC Microfilm; Ward, *Arkansas Rockefeller*, 14–20.

26. Urwin, *Agenda for Reform*, 31–57; Winthrop Rockefeller, interview by John L. Ward, 1972, 27, series 1: adm. files, subseries 2: Winthrop Rockefeller Foundation, 1964–2005, Folder "Interviewed by John Ward, 1972," Winthrop Rockefeller Foundation Archives 1956—(1978–1999)—2005, Rockefeller Archive Center, Sleepy Hollow, N.Y.

27. Rockefeller, "Rebel with a Cause," 76.

28. "Statement of Beliefs," Record Group IV, Box 84, Folder "Rockefeller, Winthrop—Statement of Belief 1964 and Undated," Reel 422, WR Papers, RAC Microfilm.

29. Rockefeller, "Rebel with a Cause," 1.

30. Quoted in Ward, *Arkansas Rockefeller*, 36.

31. "Television address of Governor Orval E. Faubus, July 20, 1964," Record Group II, Box 192, Folder "Faubus, Orval E. (Governor), 1961, 1962, 1964," Reel 139, WR Papers, RAC Microfilm.

32. "WR in Arkansas," 6.

33. Yates, "Arkansas," 275.

34. The vote in Arkansas went 56.1 percent Johnson; 43.4 percent Goldwater; 0.5 percent John Kasper, National States' Rights Party (Jim Ranchino, *Faubus to Bumpers: Arkansas Votes* [Arkadelphia, Ark.: Action Research, Inc., 1972], 35).

35. Ward, *Arkansas Rockefeller*, 23–27 (Rockefeller quote, 34).

36. Ranchino, *Faubus to Bumpers*, 37–38.

37. Yates, "Arkansas," 242–46; Ward, *Arkansas Rockefeller*, 29–32; Calvin Ledbetter Jr., "Arkansas Amendment for Voter Registration without Poll Tax Payment," *Arkansas Historical Quarterly* 54 (Summer 1995): 134–62.

38. On SNCC in Arkansas, see Jennifer Jensen Wallach and John A. Kirk, eds., *Arsnick: The Student Nonviolent Coordinating Committee in Arkansas, 1962–1967* (Fayetteville: University of Arkansas Press, 2011).

39. Ranchino, *Faubus to Bumpers*, 73; Edwin E. Dunaway, interview by John A. Kirk, 26 September 1992, Little Rock, Pryor Center for Arkansas Oral and Visual History, University of Arkansas Special Collections, Fayetteville.

40. Rockefeller, "Rebel with a Cause," 77.

41. "WR in Arkansas," 193.

42. Blair and Barth, *Arkansas Politics and Government*, 67.

43. "WR in Arkansas," 220–24.

44. Ibid., 13–14.

45. Elizabeth Jacoway, "Jim Johnson of Arkansas: Segregationist Prototype," in *The Role of Ideas in the Civil Rights South*, ed. Ted Ownby (Jackson: University Press of Mississippi, 2002), 139–41.

46. Bass and DeVries, *Transformation of Southern Politics*, 92.

47. Jacoway, "Jim Johnson of Arkansas," 149.

48. "WR in Arkansas," 20.

49. Ranchino, *Faubus to Bumpers*, 42.

50. Rockefeller, "Rebel with a Cause," draft chapter "II," 8.

51. Yates, "Arkansas," 269–70.

52. "WR Story in Arkansas," 27–29; Ward, *Arkansas Rockefeller*, 55–56.

53. "WR Story in Arkansas," 34–37.

54. Ibid.

55. "WR in Arkansas, 79; Ward, *Arkansas Rockefeller*, 63.

56. "WR in Arkansas," 49–52.

57. Ibid., 45.

58. Ibid., 45–46, 52.

59. Ranchino, *Faubus to Bumpers*, 43.

60. "WR in Arkansas," 58.

61. Ibid., 59–60, 63.

62. Ibid., 257.

63. Black, *Southern Governors and Civil Rights*, 104.

64. "WR in Arkansas," 95–96.

65. Ibid., 105.

66. Rockefeller, "Rebel with a Cause," 3.

67. Bass and DeVries, *Transformation of Southern Politics*, 93.

68. "An Analysis of Negro Voting in the General Election 1966—Governor's Race," confidential memorandum from Irene G. Samuel to Edwin Dunaway, 17 November 1966, Record Group 3, Box 83, Folder "Campaign Information—Misc.," WR Papers, RAC Microfilm. Ranchino, *Faubus to Bumpers*, gives roughly the same analysis but with slightly different figures: "Rockefeller received 71 per cent of the black vote; Jim Johnson received 29 per cent . . . Johnson lost by some 63,000 votes, the approximate number of black voters who chose Rockefeller," 74–75.

69. On Rockefeller's terms in office, see Urwin, *Agenda for Reform*; and Tom W. Dillard, "Winthrop Rockefeller (1912–1973)," The Encyclopedia of Arkansas History and Culture, www.encyclopediaofarkansas.net/encyclopedia/entry-detail.aspx?search=1&entryID=122

70. Urwin, *Agenda for Reform*, quoted from cover.

71. Walter Carruth, American Independent Party candidate, won 36,132 votes (5.9 percent). Bass and DeVries, *Transformation of Southern Politics*, 95; Ranchino, *Faubus to Bumpers*, 70; Yates, "Arkansas," 293.

72. Dale Bumpers, *The Best Lawyer in a One-Lawyer Town: A Memoir* (New York: Random House, 2003).

73. Rockefeller, "Rebel with a Cause," draft chapter "II," 9–10.

74. Bass and DeVries, *Transformation of Southern Politics*, 98.

75. Earl Black and Merle Black, *The Rise of Southern Republicans* (Cambridge: Belknap Press of Harvard University Press, 2002), 111–12.

76. Lamis, *Two-Party South*, 124–26, 129.

77. Yates, "Arkansas," 280.

78. "Huckabee Won't Rule out 2012 Run," Associated Press, 18 November 2008, www.msnbc.msn.com/id/27805664/wid/21370087/.

79. "Arkansas Lt. Gov. Winthrop Rockefeller Dies at 57," *New York Times*, 17 July 2006, www.nytimes.com/2006/07/17/us/17rockefeller.html?ex=1310788800&en=d7ea 97306cfad739&ei=5090&partner=rssuserland&emc=rss.

80. Richard Grimes, *Jay Rockefeller: Old Money, New Politics* (Parsons, W.V.: McClain Printing, 1984).

81. Jacoway, "Jim Johnson of Arkansas," 149–51.

82. *Arkansas Leader*, 16 February 2010, www.arkansasleader.com/2010/02/top-story-justice-jim-was-man-of-his.html

83. David Lublin, *The Republican South: Democratization and Partisan Change* (Princeton: Princeton University Press, 2004), 43.

84. A very useful overview of modern Arkansas history is Ben F. Johnson III, *Arkansas in Modern America: 1930–1999* (Fayetteville: University of Arkansas Press, 2002). The Fortune 500 table (Arkansas is placed twenty-fourth out of fifty states) is cited in J. David Woodard, *The New Southern Politics* (Boulder: Rienner, 2006), 419.

85. Winthrop Rockefeller, interview by John L. Ward, 1972, 1, Series 1: Administrative Files, Subseries 2: Winthrop Rockefeller Foundation, 1964–2005, Folder "Interviewed by John Ward, 1972," Winthrop Rockefeller Foundation Archives 1956—(1978–1999)—2005, Rockefeller Archive Center, Sleepy Hollow, N.Y.

86. Rockefeller, "Rebel with a Cause," 75.

87. Marlin Hawkins and C. Fred Williams, *How I Stole Elections: The Autobiography of Sheriff Marlin Hawkins* (Morrilton, Ark.: New Leaf Press, 1991).

88. Blair and Barth, *Arkansas Politics and Government*, 46.

# III

## Economics, Faction, and
## the Neo-Confederacy

# 9

## "Gun Cotton"

### Southern Industrialists, International Trade, and the Republican Party in the 1950s

KATHERINE RYE JEWELL

In 1959, Donald Comer—son of former Alabama governor Braxton Bragg Comer, president of Avondale Mills and a prominent advocate for the textile industry—reflected, "In [19]36 I wrote an article . . . in which I asked, 'When Japan buys our cotton, whether she turns it into gun cotton and shoots shells at us or whether she ships it back as cloth, there would be casualties in either case.' At the time I never dreamed that she was going to do both." In the 1930s, Japanese dumping of surplus cotton textiles in the United States prompted Comer, along with other representatives of the domestic industry, to travel to Japan and arrange a voluntary quota agreement. War decimated Japan's industry, and in 1948 Comer benevolently returned to Japan at the request of General Douglas MacArthur to provide consultation for industrial recovery. Comer believed demand in war-torn Asian countries would provide markets for the recovering textile industry, but his hopes proved to be erroneous. By 1951, only three years after Comer's second trip to Japan, U.S. textile manufacturers looked with alarm toward rising Japanese imports and the reemergence of Japanese "gun cotton." As far as Comer was concerned, Japanese attempts to gain access to the U.S. market constituted a second Pearl Harbor—but this time cotton towels, not bombs, were the ammunition.[1]

Protectionism was certainly not new in the 1950s, but the profile of its prominent political advocates in the 1950s was, and their arguments included imperatives and rationales divergent from those of their predecessors. Comer's trenchant criticism of Japanese imports reflected the growing arguments of an emerging political movement in states formerly dedicated to free trade. While in the 1930s the textile industry achieved protections via voluntary agreement, in the 1950s domestic producers found it necessary to wage a political battle in an atmosphere dominated by the Cold War and complicated by regional tensions over civil rights. As the United States strove to keep Japan as an ally, even if it meant granting access to domestic markets, Comer and his industrial allies believed the government was needlessly sacrificing domestic industry for international peace. Furthermore, while southern politicians across the ideological spectrum emphasized southern unity in the face of social unrest (desegregation), southern industrialists found themselves at distressing odds with their representatives over protection of the region's economic base. The political insurgency among cotton textile producers in the 1950s, as well as among other industries that felt threatened by mounting imports of Asian-produced products, suggests that the traditional Democratic-Republican split over foreign trade policy—where Smoot-Hawley (1930) represented the triumph of protectionist Republicans against freer-trade Democrats usually hailing from rural, agricultural areas like the South—was becoming anachronistic.

Foreign trade debates led southern industrial representatives to consciously break with regional tradition and develop critiques of reciprocal trade within a politically conservative framework. The Reciprocal Trade Agreements Act of 1934 (RTAA) granted greater latitude to the executive branch in negotiations of trade agreements, and had been endorsed by Secretary of State Cordell Hull, himself a Tennessean. This negotiating power, previously reserved for Congress, confirmed the suspicions of many industrialists of the danger inherent in centralized bureaucratic government relatively free from legislative or judicial oversight—though internationalists justified the power as key in the nation's fight to contain communism in developing countries. Moreover, foreign trade issues in the 1950s exacerbated deep divisions between this constituency and its national Democratic leaders—some of whom had already broken faith in their support of a liberal legislative agenda—and allowed for stronger congruence with Republicans than was offered by solidarity on racial segregation. As Kari Frederickson argues, national Democratic Party support for the Fair Employment Practices Commission (FEPC) and civil rights broke this constituency from the party, and the Dixiecrat revolt, led by men such as Donald Comer, "precipitated the weakening of the Democratic Party's grip on presidential elections in the Deep South" and "laid the foundation, if only in presidential voting, for the creation of a two-party region."[2] Foreign trade issues in the mid-1950s built on this centrifugal pressure and helped push this constituency into greater cooperation with congressional Republicans. Thus, while the breaks with the Democratic Party formed over the issue of states' rights, economic issues like trade protectionism helped exacerbate those cracks while also building bridges to the GOP. Although Eisenhower, an internationalist, endorsed and expanded presidential preferences in trade negotiations, southern industrialists increasingly trusted Republican presidential candidates to wield the greater executive authority granted—as they argued—under the dangerous presidencies of Roosevelt and Truman. Emergence of new economic threats, however, in the form of Japanese imports, galvanized a broader, more practical, and economically based southern revolt in the mid-1950s that forged a strong southern conservative business interest that intersected with emerging business conservatism nationally. The 1950s issues of international trade, which played out in the tumultuous context of Cold War spending and politics, helped coalesce southern business interests and political movements with the kind of institutional and ideological developments described by Kim Phillips-Fein.[3]

David Carlton and Peter Coclanis have demonstrated the economic impact of globalization on the southern textile industry, but international economic developments during the height of the Cold War came with political consequences as well. Southern industrialists' protectionist arguments, while often xenophobic and defensive, demonstrate the emergence of a new version of the "southern viewpoint." Diversification of economic interests in the South led to a diversity of political imperatives where economic interest played a more divisive role among southerners than did civil rights. Southern industrialists largely supported efforts to stop desegregation, and resented federal "meddling" in regional affairs. On this point, they found an easy alliance with southern Democrats who defied the national party on civil rights. However, those same Democrats in the 1950s continuously irked southern industrialists with their allegiance to agricultural interests and failure to pursue legislation adequate to the developing industrial sector of the region. Southern industrial political arguments, consequently, began to diverge from the traditional southern defensive position against federal intervention. As the activism of the Southern States Industrial Council (SSIC) and its supporter, Donald Comer, reveals, the nationalization and internationalization of the southern economy weakened the political salience of an underdeveloped, misunderstood, and homogeneous South in the 1950s.[4]

New South industrialists formed a key constituency in the South's break from the old Democratic Party dominance, and in the 1950s trade policy debates revealed the impact of economic changes on southern industrial political activity. While white backlash to civil rights and the resurgence of states'-rights arguments helped break southern conservatives from the Democratic Party, international trade contributed to this shift by giving practical economic significance to what was largely an ideological conservative resurgence. Like businessmen elsewhere, southern industrialists had grown wary during the New Deal and World War II of the growing power of centralized federal bureaucracies, exemplified by their criticisms of the National Labor Relations

Board, their rejection of the FEPC, and their embrace of Taft-Hartley and state right-to-work laws. While internationalist sentiment had increased among Republicans, the party still "remained closely tied to the small and medium sized manufacturer who continued to look abroad with suspicion." President Truman's failure to enact Tariff Commission recommendations in nineteen of twenty-one cases between 1947 and 1951 led congressional Republicans to mandate escape clause inclusion in all agreements, as well as introduce the "peril point." The escape clause guaranteed industries the ability to petition for protection if a bilateral agreement allowing increased imports would cause "serious injury" to a domestic producer. The peril-point provision, opposed by Truman, required the Tariff Commission to calculate a rate prior to negotiations that would ensure the safety of domestic industry. In 1949, Congress repealed the provision, but in 1951, it restored the peril point and added the escape clause. By 1955, when Democrats had regained control and instituted a leadership favoring lower tariffs, southern industrialists emerged as a galvanized force for protection, exerting significant influence on southern representatives.[5] In particular, the 1955 House debate on the RTAA's renewal, H.R. 1, and the Senate Finance Committee hearings chaired by Virginia's Harry Byrd revealed the consequences of internationalization among this constituency. The compromise bill was a product of the resistance of industries like textiles, wallpaper, zinc, and oil, but there were larger points of convergence emerging between southern industrialists and their GOP allies.[6]

As southern industrialists organized around business issues rather than a defense of southern identity or a "southern way of life," they articulated concurrent and seemingly paradoxical arguments for free enterprise and protectionism. However, proponents based their arguments on consistent reasoning and were partisans in a "fundamental battle over the nation's governing ideology in the age of economic globalization."[7] Protectionism brought them into conflict with Democrats on economic issues but halted effective alliances with Republicans on international politics. Southern industrialists interpreted trade negotiations that aimed to contain communism as a violation of American constitutional government. Though the SSIC maintained a strong anticommunist stance, its leaders established limits to policies and sacrifices the United States could make in fighting communist expansion abroad. SSIC industrialists managed to stake out a conservative position that would provide ideological consistency when conservatives united under the GOP. Free enterprise was a cornerstone of the American "way of life," they argued, but executive or bureaucratic excess—especially if domestic industry was sacrificed—undermined the American system. Thus they were able to marry their protectionism with their conservative ideology, and thereby create new possibilities for partisan realignment in ensuing decades.

## Breaking with Tradition

The rising significance of trade politics to American foreign policy after the passage of the RTAA and the industrialization of the South placed southern industrialists in a position in which they turned toward policies divergent from their region's traditional stance. Accelerating industrialization and modernization magnified the role of manufacturing in the region's economy, and its leaders developed political imperatives different from those of a predominantly agricultural society. Men like Donald Comer reversed the southern Democratic tradition of openness to unfettered international trade based in the region's agricultural past. The region of Calhoun, which abhorred the "tariff of abominations" harbored within it a century later a constituency inclined toward the protectionist stance traditionally embraced by the GOP.[8]

New South industrial leaders became energized politically during the New Deal, having organized the Southern States Industrial Council. Representing more than 3,500 industrial establishments in the South, including some of the region's most prominent textile, chemical, coal, and forest-product companies, the SSIC framed its role as to "protect and defend" the South from ill-informed, misguided, and sometimes hostile policymakers and bureaucrats. Free enterprise, fiscal restraint, anticommunism, and a return to federalism proved particularly potent arguments in resisting civil rights and labor policy—especially after the postwar onset of the CIO's Operation Dixie. Although their commitment to "protect and defend" had not disappeared by the 1950s, SSIC leaders largely abandoned arguments defending a unique "southern way of life" or socially homogeneous character in favor of more universal, economic rationalizations.[9]

Industrial manufacturers in the South felt particularly threatened by Asian-produced low value–added products. Like the South, Asian manufacturers employed their competitive advantage in low wages as the basis for modernization. Lower-wage American industries, now well established in the South, protested allowing cut-rate competitors to access their markets. In 1954, SSIC general counsel Tyre Taylor took pleasure in reporting increasing opposition to the RTAA's extension. The four major industries he named—textile, coal, chemical, and lumber—comprised the core of the SSIC in money and leadership. In 1954, ten of the SSIC's sixteen vice presidents represented these four categories, and included the presidents of companies like South Carolina's

Alice Manufacturing, Fortune 500 company and fertilizer manufacturer Monsanto Chemical, and the Tomlinson Company of High Point, North Carolina, a furniture business.[10]

The knee-jerk response of industrialists to Japanese competition was to invoke the South's past. One textile manufacturer wrote Senator Harry Byrd to argue the Japanese threat to American employment. "The South . . . has made great progress in industrialization, but even today, 90 years after the Civil War, we have not fully recovered from the devastation of that holocaust." This defensive response embodied the "parochial and sometimes xenophobic" protectionist attitude among textile manufacturers, particularly in their unwillingness to confront their own faulty management practices, outdated equipment and factory procedures, or their "commitment to bulk staple production."[11]

By the 1950s, northern and southern textile interests had converged considerably, although northern mills often concentrated production in different, more specialized lines than the southern staples. Many northern mills had relocated to the South, drawn by low wages, cheap land, and a supportive business climate. Southern manufacturers, however, soon found themselves articulating arguments against Japanese competition similar to those northern competitors had made about the South. Southern industrialists had long argued for greater access to American markets in order to remain competitive, pointing to their disadvantage in interterritorial freight rates, distance from purchasing centers, and the rural location of industry, particularly when it came to availability of skilled labor. Competition from foreign-made goods, produced at even cheaper wages than in the South, served to further weaken their competitive advantage. Comer's nephew J. Craig Smith, president of Comer's Avondale Mills and vice president of the SSIC, told the Alabama Cotton Manufacturers Association, "To bridge [the wage gap between countries like India] we would have to be three times as efficient as the Japanese and 12 times as efficient as India." The textile industry was a global industry, and the postwar South in global context paid high wages, second only to the higher-wage North and West.[12]

In the debate over RTAA extensions in the 1950s, manufacturers largely replaced policy arguments for the old emotional appeals based on the South's position as an underdeveloped region. Rather, industrial representatives argued that expanding presidential authority and the undermining of American business were counterproductive in the fight against communism. Even Byrd's petitioner presented an alternative strategy to the senator that affirmed the goals of anticommunism, suggesting, "that 'selective' or 'commodity by commodity' treatment is the practical course in protection of our . . . American economy. The tariff should at least equalize wage differences. [I]t is important that we maintain a high level of economic activity. . . . That is really the way to outbid Communism." Greater executive authority under Eisenhower led to alarming policies that complicated planning and coordination of production and marketing.[13]

In particular, the SSIC and its brethren moved away from describing injured industries as southern to highlighting the injury to small firms caused by executive action. Furthermore, SSIC leaders began to grapple with the consequences of advocating a more national position, not just in the area of trade policy. In defending Taft-Hartley, a balanced budget, and in protesting the FEPC and antilynching legislation, the SSIC cast itself as halting the nation's slide toward socialism. SSIC leaders increasingly saw the South not as a *special* interest, but as a region whose needs and values best represented those of the entire nation. As contributions from other regions continued to increase in the early 1950s, some suggested the SSIC change its name to the United States Industrial Council. Vice President Thurman Sensing convinced the board to remain a regional organization but stressed that it was no longer a parochial organization whose only goal was to defend southern exceptionalism. "The voice of free enterprise from the Southern view point" is rendering a "service to the nation as a whole." Sensing and the SSIC itself emphasized their southern heritage to portray the region as a bastion of anticommunism and free enterprise, allowing greater room for common ground with Republicans outside the region.[14]

## Critiquing Reciprocal Trade

As the SSIC began to drop its defensive southern position, textile producers fell in line with representatives of other textile-producing states in advocating a strong escape clause and peril point in all reciprocal trade agreements. Former domestic textile adversaries found themselves allied against internationalists in Congress and an administration that advocated for Japan's increased access to American markets. Proponents of these protective measures increasingly believed Eisenhower would not follow through on his promise that no domestic industry would be harmed by trade agreements. Comer's concerns, shared by other industrialists in chemicals, oil, raw materials, and producers of low value–added goods in the South, helped develop an increasingly cohesive business movement through the series of RTAA renewals in the 1950s. These renewals and the United States' participation in the General Agreement on Trade and Tariffs (GATT) increased the country's multilateral trading and considerably reduced tariffs. Freer trade was coming, and at higher volumes.

The activism of groups like the SSIC represented accommodation with new circumstances—albeit grudgingly. After 90 percent of textile products appeared on a 1955 concession list, producers stepped up their efforts to achieve binding protective amendments to the RTAA. Donald Comer once again took center stage.[15]

Southern industrial arguments, which aligned with arguments from other protectionist concerns, struck recurrent themes that criticized internationalists' agenda, especially after Eisenhower appealed for Japan's special treatment given its position near the conflict in French Indochina. Japan's clear intention to pave its path to redevelopment on cheap textile production caused industrialists to question the entire premise of the U.S. trade program. Comer's main problem, reiterated by the SSIC, was that reciprocal trade had deviated from the spirit of Secretary Cordell Hull. SSIC vice president John U. Barr, an oil manufacturer, concurred with Comer but also rejected Hull's use of foreign trade in international relations. "One of the most damnable things under the Reciprocal treaty," he complained, "is the fact that it is not truly reciprocal." Barr, a WCC leader, reflected the second argument of threatened industries like textiles: the unfair encroachment of foreign goods into American markets after the United States had aided in the redevelopment of foreign economies. Others remarked that the United States could not "buy friends" to keep them from turning to communism.[16]

Reciprocity, from Comer and the SSIC's vantage, meant a fair exchange of goods. Since the United States had an ample supply of domestically produced textiles, reciprocal trade would limit imports of duplicate goods. The situation, Comer argued, was manifestly unfair. Instead of accepting needed raw materials from Japan, under the "miscalled" RTAA, "Japan takes from us only what she needs and wants, while we take from her only what we do not need and do not want." Criticized as greedy by Ralph McGill, editor of the *Atlanta Constitution*, Comer argued fairness of trade. He cited unfair practices in the implementation of trade policy, particularly compared with the protections afforded farmers.[17] "The price of what he grows is directly protected . . . the same cotton I buy is sold to the Japanese spinner for less money. The world market is open to him and closed to me. American industry is not asking for any new deal, just simple justice."[18]

Moreover, agricultural policies directly disadvantaged domestic textile producers to Japanese competitors. While Section 22 of the Agricultural Adjustment Act protected cotton prices in domestic markets, the U.S. government, he argued, sold discounted cotton to foreign competitors who, unlike American producers, could pay cut-rate wages that corresponded to lower living standards abroad.[19]

Not only a lack of reciprocity in trade agreements offended textile industry representatives. Comer declared he was not averse to Japanese development, and he had credibility on this point. In 1948, General Douglas MacArthur had invited textile manufacturers, including Comer, to Japan to give advice on the rebuilding of the industry. However, the markets Comer envisioned were American. Comer indicted the unwillingness of administrations past and present to weigh the protection of domestic industry over international concerns. Japanese manufacturers, alarmed by American response to the 1955 RTAA extension, contacted Comer directly. Kojire Abe infuriated Comer when he asked if the two countries could coexist in a spirit of "live and let live." For years Comer looked back on the letter with contempt, explaining that the American cotton industry had approached the Japanese in a spirit of "live and *help* live," referring to his mission to help rebuild the country's shattered industry.[20] Incensed, Comer wrote a public response to Abe in the *Cotton Trade Journal*. While damage to American industry was Comer's paramount protest against the opening of America's consumer market, he also opposed access to competitive Japanese textiles. "Mr. Eisenhower cannot build a bridge of good will between America and Japan over a wrecked American textile industry." From Comer's vantage point, not only had the American textile industry aided in Japan's resurgence as an industrial producer, but through trade liberalization the United States was attempting to promote good feelings between the two countries in order to prevent Japan from trading with Communist China. These goals, though worthwhile in the eyes of many manufacturers, did not weaken Comer's imperative, repeated often, "We must have the American market."[21]

Southern industrial representatives, like their northern counterparts, pressed for protections rather than outright rejection of H.R. 1. Though many were sympathetic, they, especially in the cotton-producing states, still owed electoral success to rural areas rather than the growing urban and suburban areas. Though southern industry developed in the countryside, its political power remained in urban districts. As the bill moved from the House to the Senate, Tennessee senator Albert Gore ridiculed the "tariff lobby." James Eastland (D-MS), Estes Kefauver (D-TN), and Alben Barkley (D-KY) all joined Gore. Even Senator Walter George (D-GA), who Tyre Taylor reported was a key leader for protections, spearheaded this fight due to an impending challenge from Governor Herman Talmadge at home, who promised greater protections for industry. Representative Joe Martin (R-MA) had secured a written promise from Eisenhower in February 1955 that no domestic industry would be harmed by any trade agreement he signed, but many protectionist senators remained unconvinced. Harry Byrd represented a moderated position, though he was not an avowed protectionist himself. Others such as Leverett Saltonstall (R-MA) and Eugene Milliken (R-CO) tepidly supported the bill as long as it provided adequate safeguards for domestic industries. Senator Styles Bridges of New Hampshire, however, declared he could not support a policy "that can create boomtowns in Japan and ghost towns in New England." J. Bryan Dorn, however, a representative from South Carolina, reflected the more conservative-oriented position toward which the SSIC and Comer were moving when he declared, "This House should surrender no more of its power to the President, the Supreme Court, or any agency of the evermore central- ized federal government." Adding restrictive power to the escape clause and exemptions on tariff reductions in the case of national defense helped bring many senators and representatives around to the bill. In the final vote, only thirteen voted against the amended H.R. 1. Olin Johnston (D-SC) was the sole southerner to vote "nay."[22]

During the Senate Finance Committee hearings, Tyre Taylor admitted to Milliken, one of the more critical voices of H.R. 1, that his personal feelings were more in line with the senator's: "I think the whole thing is wrong," Taylor admitted. "To me it just doesn't make sense, under the guise of a reciprocal trade agreement, to have certain industries assume a large part of the bur- den of foreign relief." The SSIC's official position resembled the moderated position, which endorsed the continuation of the RTAA and advocated for Committee protections. In its *Declaration of Policy*, the Council affirmed: "The South has a special interest in foreign trade and commerce. Its exports account for a large part of the region's two main money crops—cotton and tobacco." However, the SSIC—despite its strident anticommunism and dedi- cation to what it called the nation's natural system of free enterprise—predi- cated its position on limit to anticommunist action, bringing it more in line with the protectionist position that rejected the rationale behind the RTAA itself. Council leaders argued that fighting communism abroad required stable and ideologically based institutions and policies at home. The United States could support anticommunist action abroad only when it had eradicated all "socialistic" practices at home, which included the promotion of a balanced budget, the rollback of bureaucratic programs, and a pay-as-you-go plan for defense spending. Their divergence from the Cold War anticommunism of the Eisenhower administration included placing limits on executive authority. "Foreign trade policy based upon subsidy is unsound," the *Declaration* read. "There is a limit to which this country can go . . . without inflicting serious injury upon the American economy. The [RTTA] should provide adequate safeguards against unreasonable and unethical competition which would seri- ously injure American producers and American labor." The SSIC, representing mostly small and medium-sized manufacturers, contradicted the traditionally free trade southern position while also placing limits on U.S. commitments to stem the spread of communism. Their emphasis on conservative practices forged alliances with other conservative advocates in both parties, but also complicated their relationship with cold warriors in the GOP.[23]

In making these arguments, self-declared representatives of southern industry made a conscious break with another long-standing political tradition. Donald Comer broke with the Democratic Party in 1952, and, even though Eisenhower clearly took an internationalist approach, Comer told *Life* magazine, "My family broke a tradition of many years when we voted for President Eisenhower." But southern industrialists broke traditions beyond the sphere of presidential politics in the 1950s. Thurman Sensing directly attributed this political break to changing economic conditions: "The time was—and not so long ago—when Southerners were almost unanimous in their support of Free Trade. . . . Now industry has moved in and the Representatives of [rural] areas are anxious to protect their industries from low-wage foreign competition." Despite Sensing's interpretation, industrialists observed promising splits within the Republican Party while finding reasons to doubt their representatives in Congress.[24]

## Foreign Trade and Southern Political Change

The issue of trade protectionism strengthened the SSIC's hopes for a conservative realignment in Congress. In 1952, the Council's president, Paul Redmond of Alabama Mills, had celebrated that the region was no longer solidly "in the bag" for the Democratic Party. In that year's election, the SSIC hailed the return of a two-party South, citing Republican wins in Tennessee, Florida, and Virginia, as well as relatively close votes in three other states. Redmond, interpreting the election as a sign of "the importance of the power that can be wielded by Southern Delegations in the coming Congress," hoped that congressional conservatives would "prevent the scuttling of sound legislation and the imposition of more and more socialism." He considered it ironic that the South, which he felt had been "ignored and rejected," was now the "cornerstone upon which to restore a government dedicated to upholding the Constitution." Tyre Taylor added hope, stating, "for the first time in a generation, the President of the United States will be free to act in the best interests of the people—even including the employers."[25]

Following Eisenhower's election, however, the SSIC became disappointed in the "New Deal–Fair Deal" orientation of the administration. Though states' rights proved to be the greatest unifying principle between southern conservatives and Republicans—at least in the eyes of SSIC leaders—international considerations played a key role, particularly as Eisenhower lauded the removal of barriers to trade. The problem for these southern industrialists lay in the split within the GOP between "representatives of the Eastern Internationalists or the Taft wing of the party." Thurman Sensing observed a similar split among their own representatives. While the national debt and lack of fiscal restraint continued to irk conservatives, and civil rights—particularly the *Brown* ruling in 1954—inflamed southern massive resistance, Thurman Sensing declared the Eighty-third Congress a failure and lamented, "it would seem, therefore, that the true conservative in this country has nowhere to turn, no party to which to give his allegiance."[26]

During the 1955 RTAA renewal, the SSIC sensed promising political congruence among economic interests across regions that would bring about changes in the political status quo. While the war between the northeastern urban, union faction and the southern contingent of the Democratic Party continued to worry conservative and segregationist southern Democrats, international trade worsened a similar Republican division. Taylor reported from Washington, "Republicans are split right down the middle on the President's recommendation for extension of the [RTAA], while the Democrats are similarly divided over the issue of so-called Civil Rights." RTAA negotiations in 1955 occurred in a context of events that helped drive home to SSIC's leaders that their old standby arguments about a homogeneous South—ethnically, politically, and ideologically—no longer applied. Economic issues, SSIC leaders observed, increasingly divided southerners. In 1949, Council president Kirby Longino considered greater participation from other regions and argued: "There is no reason why people of other regions who are actuated by a desire to maintain our individual liberties and a free competitive economy, should not participate. However, we must not overlook the fact that the growth and strength of the Council has resulted because the people of the South are like minded. There are no essential differences of opinion in our ranks." By 1955, no such certainty existed among the ranks of the SSIC's leadership.[27]

One-party politics in the South created a fractious unity between politicians of very different types within the Democratic Party, but the chaotic political climate of the 1950s exacerbated divisions. For southern protectionists, the "obligatory stands" for segregation taken by some representatives were no longer enough to satisfy them.[28] Alabama's liberal senator and 1952 vice-presidential candidate John Sparkman, in particular, felt the wrath of indignant industrialists in 1955. A Birmingham businessman, PG Shook, wrote J. Craig Smith: "I despise him! Give me some ammunition to fire at him." Sparkman had told Shook that the Senate Finance Committee amendments to the re-newal bill would not protect many industries. The greater issue that Sparkman ignored, Shook wrote, was the Senate's failure to explicitly protect domestic industry and curb presidential authority by rejecting the amendment outright. If "he and other Southern Senators had voted *against* the Bill the threat to the textile industry would have been removed . . . by depriving the President of the power to further cripple the industry by further reduction in the tariff." Sparkman could not be counted as a friend to Alabama industry: "He is ut-terly hopeless. He should be a 'Senator at large' . . . instead of the State of Alabama."[29]

The amended H.R. 1 proved unacceptable to textile producers, who felt that even a stiff tariff was not equal to the task of reducing imports given Japanese advantage in wages. The final 1955 bill still granted the president authority to reduce tariffs by 5 percent every year for three years, plus it only modified the base date for the president's prerogative to cut rates up to 50 percent on goods imported in "negligible quantities." Smith stated that these two categories "took in practically everything the textile industry makes." Although Comer admitted that Japanese imports accounted for barely 1 percent of American production, he stated, "We would like to keep the house from being set on fire rather than to put it out after it has burned down." Furthermore, the Tariff Commission had proved unreliable in the past. "Asking the Tariff Commis-sion for relief one fabric at a time is just like picking seed out of cotton by hand," Comer told his employees. "We need the equivalent of a cotton gin, . . . an all-over textile quota. . . . escape clauses one production line at a time seemed wasteful and unproductive."[30]

Northern textile producers similarly lamented the political situation. Lawton Brayton, the president of the Northern Textile Association, thanked Comer for his activism. Brayton had met with Ellison McKissick, a SSIC vice president and president of South Carolina's Alice Manufacturing. Both agreed that, while Brayton and his associates had been able to secure strong support from northern representatives, particularly Joe Martin, "There really is no-body [who] has battled for us . . . particularly some of your influential South-ern Congressmen."[31]

By 1956, Donald Comer despaired of Congress's support, and the textile industry pushed for voluntary agreements with the Japanese. Neither political party, in his estimation, stood for the needs of his industry. "We have had the opposition of the leaders of the Republican Party, the Democratic Party, pow-erful business organizations which are interested in building their exports, Walter Reuther and the CIO, and free traders and world-wide 'do-gooders' too numerous to count." Comer's greatest annoyances were representatives'

assurances that the textile industry was not being hurt, or that injured production lines should petition the Tariff Commission, a practice he had already
summarily dismissed. Comer and the SSIC alike preferred honest competition
and personal agreements in a free-enterprise system to "subsidy" and the use
of trade policy ends beyond economic prosperity. In their eyes, the RTAA
acted as an unnatural, bureaucratic system that distorted the national free-
enterprise system.[32] The textile industry received scant reason to hope from
national business organizations like the National Association of Manufacturers or the Chamber of Commerce, both of which endorsed freer trade.[33]

In 1956, state-based resistance sprang up in Alabama and South Carolina
in the form of laws requiring signs that would identify stores selling Japanese-
made cotton goods. Georgia, Louisiana, and Mississippi narrowly defeated
sign-requirement initiatives. Comer, in reaching out to the Alabama Republican Executive Committee, thanked the chairman for his help in the matter
because "Washington has thrown our textile industry to the wolves." Increased
and varied tactics from textile states to pressure consumers to "buy American"
revealed the growing depth of political sentiment in the region led by textile
manufacturers.[34]

During the summer GATT negotiations in 1955, some southern senators
pleased industrialists by calling for government action regarding the pricing
of cotton exports and import quotas for textiles. Strom Thurmond, Harry
Byrd, and James O. Eastland defended their states' industries vigorously, and
southern representatives "let the White House know that the sacrificing of this
regional interest at the altar of GATT would never be forgiven or forgotten."
Though their arguments reflected the older SSIC reliance on regional solidarity, the underlying protectionist rationale was economic rather than based in a
sense of homogeneous, shared identity. Maine senator Margaret Chase Smith,
a moderate Republican who represented textile concerns, called Japan's use of
the communist threat to gain greater access for textiles in the United States
"economic blackmail." Japanese exporters, alarmed by the vehemence of textile states' protests, agreed to enter voluntary quota talks out of concerns for
"self-preservation." Though voluntary agreements stemmed the growing tide
of Japanese imports, industrialists again moved to secure protections during
the RTAA's renewal in 1958, with some success, as Congress established its
own veto power to force the president to allow industries to claim protection
from foreign competition on the basis of national security.[35]

Despite expanded trade in the 1950s and after, textiles continued to be one
of the nation's most protected industries, even when John Kennedy attempted
to somewhat placate the politically powerful textile industry. Only in the 1980s
did the Uruguay round of GATT negotiations manage to secure an agreement

to eliminate textile quotas and tariffs by 2005. Other manufacturers stepped into Donald Comer's shoes, particularly Roger Milliken, the South Carolina billionaire who funded strong "Buy American" campaigns in the 1980s and 1990s. Another of Milliken's funding recipients was the SSIC—renamed in the 1970s the United States Industrial Council. By the 1990s, trade protectionism was the USIC's sole focus. Presently, on its Web site the organization boasts a trade deficit tally similar to the national debt clock.[36]

On the political end of the trade question, internationalists in the Republican Party had not scared away Donald Comer. Civil rights, social welfare, deficit spending, and unionism continued to split the Democrats, though trade issues had formed important alliances between southern manufacturers and protectionist Republicans. James Stahlman wrote to Comer as the 1956 presidential election neared: "I am glad that . . . regardless of what has happened in the textile situation, you are sticking with Ike and Dick. I am sure they will be elected, but it is going to take the interest and support of real Americans like yourself to see that the left-wingers, the Reuthers, and the crackpots don't take over." Even though the SSIC resented excessive Cold War deficit spending and Eisenhower's support of New Deal–type policies, the critiques they offered found greater purchase in Republican circles than in Democratic ones. Southern industrialists had galvanized under new issues that brought them closer to the national GOP than the old southern Democrats, many of whom, the industrialists felt, could not be counted on to protect American industry. In 1958, the SSIC's president declared that the "average businessman" was "milk fed" by the representatives of business in Washington, and needed to increase their activism. He invoked a statement by a promising senator from Arizona, Barry Goldwater, who told the U.S. Chamber of Commerce, "I have seen the weakness and even cowardice in businessmen across the country." The SSIC represented the emergence of conservative arguments and organized constituencies that would build behind candidates like Goldwater in the years to come. These arguments and constituencies, moreover, represented a break with traditional southern political defenses and allowed for the diversification of the "southern viewpoint." Concurrent with regional development, southern industrialists emerged as a politically powerful voice in a region traditionally dominated by rural and agricultural interests. Their arguments, though conservative—as had been those of the traditional southern Democrats—broke with the region's traditional variety by emphasizing economic and industrial development concerns and solutions over racial unity and traditional social structures—thus opening up sympathetic constituencies for a reinvigorated Republican Party in the 1960s.[37]

Since the 1980s, popular "Buy American" campaigns and resistance to increased foreign trade and globalization have been union-led or humanitarian in nature, and associated politically with Democrats or Independents, particularly in the case of Ross Perot. The 1950s RTAA renewals and GATT negotiations, however, demonstrate how conservative resistance to foreign imports broke down regional political barriers and helped move southern political arguments in new directions that would open up opportunities for Republicans to build upon in the 1960s and 1970s. In the 1950s, these industrialists had yet to impact the region's partisan alignment, but they were playing a transitional role in the emergence of Sunbelt conservatism. Furthermore, their position in a political no-man's-land regarding Cold War policies created space where they could articulate conservative positions that emphasized smaller government, fiscal responsibility, and limited commitments abroad. These arguments provided continuity with the traditional southern brand of conservatism and the emergent national business conservatism of the 1960s and 1970s, and contributed to the complex process of partisan realignment in the South yet to come.[38]

## Notes

1. Donald Comer, "Our Misnamed Foreign Policies," *Southern Textile News,* 3 October 1959, 20, James McDonald Comer Avondale Office Files, 1920–1958, Archives, Birmingham Public Library, Birmingham, Ala. [hereafter DC]; "Spinner's Treaty," *Time,* 8 March 1937; "Memo between the Representatives of the Japanese Cotton Textile Industry and the American Cotton Textile Mission," Osaka, Japan, 22 January 1937, DC. See Louis Galambos, *Competiton and Cooperation: The Emergence of a National Trade Association* (Baltimore: Johns Hopkins University Press, 1966).

2. Kari Frederickson, *The Dixiecrat Revolt and the End of the Solid South, 1932–1968* (Chapel Hill: University of North Carolina Press, 2001), 238; William Barnard, *Dixiecrats and Democrats: Alabama Politics 1942–1950* (Tuscaloosa: University of Alabama Press, 1985), 118.

3. Kim Phillips-Fein, *Invisible Hands: The Making of the Conservative Movement from the New Deal to Reagan* (New York: Norton, 2009).

4. David Carlton and Peter Coclanis, "Southern Textiles in Global Context," in *Global Perspectives on Industrial Transformation in the American South,* ed. Susan Delfino and Michelle Gillespie (Columbia: University of Missouri Press, 2005), 151–74.

5. *Congressional Quarterly Almanac* (Washington, D.C.: Congressional Quarterly News Features, 1955), 11:290.

6. Alexander Heard, *A Two-Party South* (Chapel Hill: University of North Carolina Press, 1952); George B. Tindall, *The Emergence of the New South, 1913–1945* (Baton Rouge: Louisiana State University Press, 1967); Bruce J. Schulman, *From Cotton Belt to Sunbelt: Federal Policy, Economic Development, and the Transformation of the South, 1938–1980* (New York: Oxford University Press, 1991); Sayuri Shimizu, *Creating People*

*of Plenty: The United States and Japan's Economic Alternatives, 1950–1960* (Kent: Kent State University Press, 2001) 20, 22; Thomas Edsall and Mary Edsall, *Chain Reaction: The Impact of Race, Rights, and Taxes on American Politics* (New York: Norton, 1991); Dewey Grantham, *Life and Death of Solid South: A Political History* (Lexington: University Press of Kentucky, 1988), 178. See Phillips-Fein, *Invisible Hands*, chaps. 1–3; Barbara Griffith, *The Crisis of American Labor: Operation Dixie and the Defeat of the CIO* (Philadelphia: Temple University Press, 1988); Robert A. Pastor, *Congress and the Politics of U.S. Foreign Economic Policy: 1929–1976* (Berkeley and Los Angeles: University of California Press, 1980), 96–100.

7. Shimizu, *Creating People of Plenty*, 19.

8. See James C. Cobb and William W. Steuck, *Globalization and the American South* (Athens: University of Georgia Press, 2005), xi; Gavin Wright, *Old South, New South: Revolutions in the Southern Economy since the Civil War* (New York: Basic Books, 1986); and James Cobb, *Industrialization and Southern Society, 1877–1984* (Lexington: University Press of Kentucky, 1984).

9. See Griffith, *The Crisis of American Labor*.

10. Tyre Taylor, "Exhibit H," in Minutes, Meeting of the Board of Directors, 13 May 1954, Box 2, Folder 1, Southern States Industrial Council Records, 1933–1973, Tennessee State Library and Archives, Nashville (hereafter SSIC). Account Books, 1934–1964, Oversize Material, SSIC.

11. Carlton and Coclanis, "Southern Textiles in Global Context," 172; John Reeves, Chairman of Board to Byrd, 15 March 1955. DC.

12. Carlton and Coclanis, "Southern Textiles in Global Context," 174; Peter Coclanis and Louis Kyriakoudes, "Selling Which South?: Economic Change in Rural and Small-Town North Carolina in an Era of Globalization, 1940–2007," *Southern Cultures* (Winter 2007): 95, 96.

13. Shimizu, *Creating People of Plenty*, 41; J. Reeves, Chairman of Board to Harry F. Byrd, 15 March 1955, DC; T. Taylor, "Report from Washington," *Bulletin*, 15 February 1955, Box 8, Folder 3, SSIC.

14. Thurman Sensing, "Exhibit B," Annual Report before the Board of Directors, 22–23 May 1952, SSIC; Sensing, Report to the Board, 1 May 1953, Box 2, Folder 2, SSIC.

15. "Global Responsibilities," Report of the Board of Directors, 11–12 May 1956, Box 2, Folder 2, SSIC. For more figures on tariff reduction in the 1950s, see Pastor, *Congress and the Politics of U.S. Foreign Economic Policy*; Senator Milliken, Testimony of the National Association of Wool Manufacturers, Senate Finance Committee Hearings on Trade Agreements Extension, 84th Cong., 9 March 1955, p. 859.

16. Stahlman to Clement, 15 November 1955, Stahlman Papers; John U. Barr to Donald Comer, 15 August 1958, DC.

17. Donald Comer, "Fifty Years of Progress and Developments in the Textile Industry as I Have Seen Them Unfold," unpublished speech, March 1958, DC.

18. Comer, letter to the editor, *New York Times*, 15 April 1956, DC.

19. Comer to Ralph McGill, editor of *Atlanta Constitution*, 27 January 1958; response to "Grapples with Greed," *Atlanta Constitution*, 16 January 1958, DC.

20. "Cotton Experts Off to Tokyo," *New York Times* (1857-Current file), 11 January 1948; ProQuest Historical Newspapers, *New York Times* (1851–2005); Burton Crane, "Mission Would Aid Textiles of Japan," *New York Times*, 1 February 1948; Donald Comer, Avondale Annual Report 1951, DC; Kojire Abe to Seton Ross, editor of *Cotton Trade Journal*, 6 June 1955, DC.

21. Donald Comer, letter to the editor, *Cotton Trade Journal*, 9 September 1955, DC; Donald Comer, "Our Misnamed Foreign Policies," *Southern Textile News*, 3 October 1959, 20. DC.

22. Albert Gore, in *Congressional Quarterly Almanac*, 11:297; Shimizu, *Creating People of Plenty*, 41; *Congressional Quarterly Almanac*, 11:294.

23. Southern States Industrial Council, *Declaration of Policy*, pamphlet, May 12–13, 1954, SSIC; Tyre Taylor in "Hearings before the Committee on Finance," U.S. Senate, 84th Cong., 1st. sess., on H.R. 1, *Trade Agreements Extension* (Washington D.C.: U.S. Government Printing Office, 1955), 985.

24. Comer to *Life* magazine, 28 April 1955, DC; Thurman Sensing, "The Changing South," *Bulletin*, 1 March 1955, Box 7, Folder 3, SSIC; see also Donald Comer, letter to the editor, *New York Times*, 15 April 1956, DC.

25. Tyre Taylor, "Report from Washington," *Bulletin*, 16 February 1948, SSIC; Paul Redmond, "The Voice of the South," *Bulletin*, 15 November 1952, Box 7, Folder 2, SSIC.

26. Tyre Taylor, "Report from Washington," *Bulletin*, 1 December 1952, Box 7, Folder 2, SSIC; Thurman Sensing, "Come Back, Coalition!" *Bulletin*, 15 October 1952, Box 7, Folder 2, SSIC.

27. Tyre Taylor, "Report from Washington," *Bulletin*, 15 January 1955, Box 8, Folder 3, SSIC; R. Kirby Longino, "Annual Report," Minutes, Meeting of the Board of Directors, 29 January 1949, Box 2, Folder 1, SSIC.

28. Jack Bass and Walter DeVries, *The Transformation of Southern Politics: Social Change and Political Consequence since 1958* (Athens: University of Georgia Press, 1995), 58.

29. PG Shook to J. Craig Smith, 5 June 1955, DC; Shook to Comer 21 June 1955, DC; Bass and Devries, *The Transformation of Southern Politics*, 58. Sparkman's election in 1954, 1960, and 1966 revealed the growing strength of Republican challenges. In 1954, J. Foy Guin received only 17.5 percent of the vote, but in 1960, Republican challenger Julian Elgin received 29 percent. By 1966, the Republican challenger received 39 percent.

30. J. Craig Smith to PG Shook, June 8, 1955, DC; Donald Comer, "Additional Facts Concerning Japanese Imports," draft for *Avondale Sun*, 5 March 1956, DC.

31. Northern Textile Association; Lawton Brayton to Comer, 10 April 1956, DC.

32. Donald Comer, "Additional Facts Concerning Japanese Imports," draft of article for *Avondale Sun*, 5 March 1956, DC.

33. Charles A. Cannon to Comer, 14 December 1956, DC.

34. Shimizu, *Creating People of Plenty*, 150; Donald Comer to Claude O. Vardaman, 23 April 1956, DC.

35. Shimizu, *Creating People of Plenty*, 113; Robert Pastore, *Congress and the Politics of U.S. Foreign Economic Policy, 1929–1976* (Berkeley and Los Angeles: University of California Press, 1980), 103–4.

36. United States Business and Industrial Council, "About Us," www.american economicalert.org.

37. James Stahlman to Donald Comer, 5 October 1956, James G. Stahlman Papers, Vanderbilt University Special Collections, Nashville, Tenn. [hereafter Stahlman] VIII–1, F15; Hon. Ralph W. Gwinn, (NY) "The State of the Unions," Pittsburgh, on 27 February 1958 in Condon, "Reports of President, Vice President, and the Secretary-Treasurer," presented at Annual Meeting of the Board of Directors at Hot Springs, Va., May 29, 1958, Box 2, Folder 2, SSIC.

38. See Dana Frank, *Buy American: The Untold Story of Economic Nationalism* (Boston: Beacon Press, 1999); and Susan A. Aaronson, *Taking Trade to the Streets* (Ann Arbor: University of Michigan Press, 2001).

# 10

## The First Southern Strategy

### The Taft and the Dewey/Eisenhower Factions in the GOP

MICHAEL BOWEN

Henry Zweifel was livid. As the Republican national committeeman from Texas, he had served his party loyally through the 1920s and the hard times of the Great Depression, when being a Republican in the Lone Star State was somewhat akin to hailing from the planet Gallifrey, but he had never witnessed anything like he saw during the first weekend of May 1952. He had opened his home in Granbury for the quadrennial party precinct convention, an event usually attended by a handful of his friends and neighbors. From the moment his wife unlatched the front door, however, a sizable group of strangers had taken over his living room. As the newcomers helped themselves to tea and snacks and made small talk, it became clear to the experienced attendees that these interlopers had not undergone some sort of miraculous conversion experience to Republicanism, but rather came for the sole purpose of selecting state convention delegates pledged to General Dwight D. Eisenhower. Zweifel, a fervent backer of Eisenhower's chief rival, Ohio senator Robert A. Taft, did what any self-respecting Texas politico would when faced with such an overwhelming display of populism: he quietly led those he knew to the front lawn and called the precinct meeting to order while the larger group of Ike supporters held a simultaneous convention in air-conditioned comfort around his coffee table.[1] In thirty other precincts across Texas, similar scenes played out as Democrats crossed party lines to participate in their first Republican meetings and gave Eisenhower a contested victory in the most enthusiastic showing of GOP support in Texas since the late 1800s.

These results are a testament to Eisenhower's staggering popularity but, more important, are indicative of a comprehensive, long-term strategy to assume control of the southern GOP. The architect of this plan, former Republican national chairman and future attorney general Herbert Brownell, designed Eisenhower's national pre-convention campaign to directly challenge the more conservative Taft in his areas of strength, most notably the South.[2] As Brownell's program came to fruition, the infusion of manpower, resources, and electoral competition in the region gave the party a solid foundation on which to build in subsequent decades, shaking the southern GOP out of its apathy and "post office politician" mentality. Though he set out solely to recruit delegates to secure the Eisenhower nomination, Brownell laid the foundation for a viable two-party system throughout the Democratic Solid South: one that conservatives would successfully capture more than a decade later.

Over the years, historians and political scientists have attributed the South's embrace of the Republican Party to racial issues. Scholars such as Dan T. Carter and Thomas Edsall and Mary Byrne Edsall have explored various aspects of the 1960s-era "white backlash," the white working-class abandonment of the Democratic Party over civil rights, taxation, and welfare policies. The discussion has become more nuanced during the past decade, but race still remains the driving force in the South's transformation narrative. Kevin Kruse, in his study of suburban conservatism in Atlanta, notes that "the connections between the Old South and the New Right run much deeper than mere rhetorical appeals to racism."[3] Along the same lines, Joseph Crespino, William Link, and Matthew Lassiter contend that southern politicians capitalized on resentment over various civil rights policies, from fair-housing legislation to affirmative action, to solidify their conservative base from the late 1960s forward. Though their analyses are not mono-causal by any means, these accounts, when taken as a whole, imply that southerners' move from the Democrats to the Republicans was largely reactionary. It was as if, as Lyndon Johnson famously proclaimed upon signing the Civil Rights Act of 1964, the South had been lost for a generation, but only when the civil rights policies of the national Democratic Party became too much to bear.[4] By itself, however, the white backlash remains an insufficient explanation for this transformation.

Animosity over civil rights legislation, on its own, did not guarantee a Republican realignment. Southern Democrats had lodged protests over their national party's limited agenda of equality since the 1930s, and, in 1948, disgruntled partisans broke off and ran their own presidential and vice-presidential candidates in response to a strong endorsement of civil rights at the national convention. Though Democratic leaders had continually made strides for unity in the decade since the Dixiecrat revolt, tensions would remain into the mid-1960s. Even then, though, disaffection did not translate to defection. Southern Democrats, quite simply, had nowhere else to go. Between Reconstruction and the mid-1940s, the GOP had maintained little more than a token presence in the region. As V. O. Key famously noted, aside from a handful of mountain Republicans, southern state parties were generally small, ineffective, and usually served the sole purpose of dispensing patronage from Washington. Setting aside the fact that the GOP was hated due to the Civil War, the party did not have the resources, field workers, communications infrastructure, or competent leaders to mount successful campaigns. Southern Democrats understood that they had to stay with their party or lose their political viability. The Democratic Party was a powder keg over issues of race, to be sure, but the Republican organization had to be built and strengthened in order to accommodate converts from across the aisle.[5]

National Republican leaders understood this as well and, beginning in 1944, New York governor Thomas Dewey's organization cultivated a new generation of southern leadership. Unlike the infamous presidential campaign of 1968, in which Richard Nixon amassed a "silent majority" around the concept of law and order, the Republicans' first southern strategy was not based on racial considerations.[6] Indeed, it was only when the region factored in the national party's internal politics that the GOP made inroads into the South. In 1944, the Republicans suffered their fourth consecutive presidential defeat and, despite some gains in Congress that election cycle, appeared destined to lose again in 1948. In early 1945, Dewey and Ohio senator Robert A. Taft began amassing support in preparation for the 1948 nomination. Though over time these two factions would solidify into ideologically driven groups, in 1945 they were largely candidate-centered and focused on short-term goals. Most of Taft's support came from two areas: the Midwest and the South. Brownell, at the time the RNC chairman, was Dewey's chief political strategist and believed the South was the key to a Dewey victory. Though the actual GOP presence in Dixie was miniscule, it controlled roughly one-sixth of the national convention delegates. Brownell devised a plan to challenge the post-office Republicans, who to a man backed Taft, and groom new leaders committed to Dewey. In response, Taft defended the existing Old Guard leadership. Though these maneuvers did not result in electoral victories, the national party lavished unprecedented resources and manpower on the South, breaking state parties out of their "palace politician" mentality, solidifying their organizations and structures, and ultimately preparing them to receive the surge of ex-Democrats in the mid-1960s.

Brownell, arguably the most gifted political operative of his day, devised a strategy to exploit the unique circumstances of the South. He understood that the weakness of the existing Republican organizations and the South's changing demographics made the area ripe for change. To capitalize, he reached out to ambitious junior members of each state party, offering to steward their political advancement if they would organize and lead a fight against the pro-Taft, Old Guard leadership. If Dewey won the nomination, the national headquarters would push for their elevation to state party chairmanship or a seat on the RNC and give them control over patronage appointments. If he could not find an upstart official, Brownell went outside the party and built a rival organization, often composed of Republicans who had recently relocated from the North. Brownell approached a number of these individuals and offered financial support and patronage jobs in exchange for fighting the pro-Taft state leaders. Once these new factions became operational, Brownell used the resources of his well-financed campaign war chest to insulate the new leaders from rival factions and ensure that they gained control of their state parties. After Eisenhower's victory in 1952, he backed them with the full weight of the White House. Though a full account of Brownell's program is beyond the scope of this paper, events in a number of states, including Alabama, Texas, Louisiana, Florida, and Mississippi, illustrate its success. Building a bloc of committed partisans with a vested interest in the GOP's future, and the subsequent infusion of resources and attention from the national headquarters, energized the southern GOP and ended the rule of the post-office Republicans of the pre–World War II period.

In late 1947, Brownell began organizing the South. Alabama was one of his highest priorities because, as the first state alphabetically, it opened the nomination process at the national convention—usually a good bit of political theater. Candidates vied to control the Alabama delegation solely for this reason, as the state remained heavily Democratic. The local Republican organization was virtually invisible in Montgomery and existed solely for patronage distribution when the GOP occupied the White House. In early 1947, the state's national committeeman, real-estate developer and banker Lonnie Noonjin; and the state party chairman, utility executive Claude Vardaman, remained noncommittal on their candidate preferences. Noonjin expressed interest in Dewey but, according to one insider, agreed with Taft on "national defense." Brownell and other Dewey partisans reached out to Vardaman, offering him control of patronage in exchange for assembling a pro-Dewey slate. By the fall, it was clear that he had taken the deal, as Brownell regularly consulted Vardaman on strategy for the region.[7]

Vardaman's support for Dewey was out of step with grassroots Republican sentiment and shows the unpredictable role of race and racism in the southern GOP. Taft's legislative record in Congress, heavily based on federalism and limited government, clearly resonated with a segment of white upper- and middle-class Alabamians. One correspondent wrote to Taft claiming that he and his congressional cohort were the only people who could save the nation from the "evil forces" and "New Deal foul ideas." Another declared, "We conservatives of the South are depending on you conservative Republicans to rescue the country from the radical New Dealers."[8] Numerous voters also thought a Taft presidency would safeguard segregation. A dentist and avowed lifelong Democrat from Evergreen, Alabama, wrote to Taft protesting the "pernicious Anti–States' Rights Legislation." In cases like this, Taft responded with a form letter extolling the virtues of federalism while downplaying the correspondent's racist overtones. When one supporter from Birmingham signed Taft's Capitol Hill office up for a "States' Righter" newspaper, Taft responded with a noncommittal defense of his education bill and pledged to uphold the Constitution.[9] He was clearly cognizant of the role of race in southern politics, though, confiding in Noonjin that "I shouldn't think Mr. Dewey's stand on the FEPC [Fair Employment Practices Commission] would do him any good in Alabama."[10] Yet Taft characterized the FEPC, the major civil rights issue of the 1948 cycle, essentially as a race-blind extension of the federal bureaucracy and opposed it on constitutional, rather than racial, grounds. Alabama voters seemed receptive to his policy positions, much more so than Dewey's.[11]

Early reports from Old Guard operatives indicated that this approach was a safe political strategy and that Taft had an above-average chance of picking up the votes of thousands of disaffected Democrats and, more importantly, the state's Republican national convention delegates. These predictions clearly underestimated Vardaman's role. A report from John Gordon Bennett, Taft's key field worker in the South, noted that Brownell had made progress in Alabama but concluded that Noonjin still controlled the delegation.[12] Ultimately, Bennett's predictions fell wide of the mark. Brownell and Vardaman outflanked the Taft team and recruited a slate of Dewey delegates that were popular and well known to Republican precinct members. In early 1948, the Alabama Republican Executive Committee took a straw poll that resulted in forty votes for Dewey, twelve for Taft, two for Stassen, and eight for others. At the 1948 Alabama state convention, the GOP selected a delegation of mostly Dewey delegates, but retained Noonjin as state party chair, likely as part of a compromise with the Old Guard. Alabama placed a committed Dewey delegate on the Credentials Committee and, during the nomination process, yielded to New York, which placed the governor's name in nomination first. Dewey, the most progressive of all the GOP candidates on civil rights, received overwhelming support from this Deep South state, a sign that racial conservatism did not yet guarantee an endorsement from southern Republicans.[13]

Alabama was a best-case scenario for Brownell's strategy, but states where the leadership stuck together proved more difficult and labor intensive. A good example is Texas, a state that had actually gone Republican in 1928 over the Catholicism of Democratic candidate Al Smith. Texas, like Alabama, voted solidly Democratic, but important players in the cattle and oil industries including oilmen Marrs McLean, H. R. Cullen, and H. L. Hunt sent reliable and steady financial contributions to the national GOP.[14] Colonel Rentfro B. Creager, the Texas national committeeman, dominated the state party. Creager, the archetype of a southern Republican boss, joined the RNC in 1923 and had maintained his grip on power by faithfully rewarding party workers with patronage positions ever since. One Texas reporter referred to him as "the Japanese Gardner," because the Texas GOP, like a bonsai tree, was cultivated to be small and controllable, traits that strengthened Creager's hold on the organization.[15] Creager's conservative worldview made him a strong proponent of Taft, who in turn counted on Creager to swing the Texas delegation in his favor at the national convention and fill his war chest with oil money.

By 1948, however, Creager's self-interested leadership had angered many Texas Republicans, causing an open revolt that forced Taft and Dewey to become involved in matters well beyond their control. During the 1944 presidential election, Brownell had worked closely with Hobart McDowell, a former judge from San Angelo, and W. C. "Colley" Briggs, a lawyer from Paducah. Both men were leaders of the emerging anti-Creager movement and favored moderately liberal policies. Briggs regarded the Creager faction as "reactionary and isolationist," claiming that "the whole of his crowd think a union member should be shot at sun rise. They are against the FEPC and the Civil Rights program." To further complicate matters, H. Jack Porter, an oilman closely allied with H. R. Cullen, offered to make extremely large campaign contributions in exchange for more power within the state GOP, primarily to further the ambitions of the petroleum industry. Porter was a wild card in the organizational structure and gave Brownell the opportunity to disrupt the Texas party and steer its delegation to Dewey.[16]

As in Alabama, race was a tangential factor in the 1948 Texas situation. Brownell and some associates visited Texas in January and February 1948 to build a base of support. Many party chairmen pledged to oppose Creager, but a few refused to sign on due to Dewey's advocacy of the FEPC. For example, Philip Eubank, a San Antonio Republican who published an anti-Creager newsletter, flatly told Brownell that, while he despised the regular Republican organization, he could not support any politician who advocated racial equality.[17] Eubank was clearly in the minority, however, as many county leaders joined with Brownell, giving McDowell and Briggs enough cover to overpower Creager from within the state organization.

The anti-Creager group planned to build their challenge from the ground up and dominate the state's precinct meetings. Since the Democrats controlled the state, Republican precinct and county conventions had always been rather limited affairs, usually with single-digit attendance. The Creager forces normally had total control of these meetings, giving them free reign to appoint loyal delegates to the state convention and, in turn, the national convention. When the anti-Creager people made their challenge in 1948, the Old Guard leadership took proactive—and in many cases illegal—measures to ensure their victory. The most prominent example of this occurred in San Antonio, where Mike Nolte, the 1946 gubernatorial candidate and the local supplier of fine ales and lagers, chaired the Bexar County GOP.[18] In April 1948, Nolte approved thirty-nine precinct conventions, thirty fewer than in 1947. Instead of publicizing the list of meeting sites and their precinct captains, however, he speedily dictated them to a subordinate and promptly adjourned the meeting. The events happened so fast that the Dewey/anti-Creager backers could not record the information and, if they did not know when or where the meetings were, Nolte would handpick the county delegation for Taft. This was certain to happen since most of the Bexar party officials were allegedly Nolte's truck drivers, employees, customers, and friends.

The anti-Creager faction filed a lawsuit in district court, and, three days before the date of the precinct meetings, a judge ordered Bexar party officials to produce a written location list at a party meeting. That night, Nolte arrived at the specially called gathering with a handwritten list on the back of a beer napkin. He laid the note on the table, thus meeting the requirements of the court, and in less than two minutes calmly placed the napkin in his pocket and left. Dewey supporters sued again the next day, and this time the judge ruled that the list must be posted publicly on the courthouse door. Nolte evaded deputy sheriffs dispatched to enforce the order for two days until May 1, the day of the precinct meetings, when he reluctantly posted the document. The anti-Creager forces packed the meetings and defeated Nolte's faction. This mattered little though, as Nolte contested the results at the next county party meeting. The Nolte-appointed executive committee ruled in favor of the Nolte-backed Taft delegates and invalidated the elections in favor of the regular Republicans. Later that month, the Creager-controlled state committee endorsed this decision and sent a delegation of thirty for Taft and three for Dewey to the national convention.[19] One supporter wrote to Creager lamenting the fact that Taft had an estimated 10 percent of the popular support but 90 percent of the delegates. Creager responded with a terse letter, saying: "You speak of an unfortunate political system in Texas so that 10% of the Republican voters can control Conventions. Did you ever know of a State anywhere, where at anytime a very small percentage of the leaders do not control the large majority?"[20] Clearly democracy was a concept with which the leadership of the Texas GOP was not very familiar.

Taft's strength in the South made little difference, however, as Dewey easily won the 1948 Republican nomination, due to an excellent national pre-con-vention campaign. In one of the most unusual presidential election cycles of the modern era, Dewey found himself in a four-way contest with the Demo-crats split into three groups: the left-leaning Progressive Party under former vice president Henry Wallace; the regular organization led by incumbent pres-ident Harry Truman; and the conservative States' Rights Democratic Party, or Dixiecrats, running South Carolina governor Strom Thurmond. Though poll numbers showed Dewey with an overwhelming lead early on, Truman campaigned hard against the Taft-led Eightieth Congress, blaming most of the nation's economic woes on Republican obstructionism. Dewey, purposefully trying to stay above the fray, left these charges unanswered and ran as if he had already won. As the results were tallied and the Republicans suffered their fifth straight defeat, the Taft and Dewey factions each blamed the other for the loss. Dewey reasoned that the people had rejected the conservative legislative pro-gram, while Taft believed that Dewey's stump speeches had been too weak. As a result, the national GOP remained divided between the Taft and Dewey fac-tions, keeping Brownell's southern strategy in play for the foreseeable future.

On the heels of the shocking 1948 defeat, Taft backers on the RNC took over the party machinery, ousting its pro-Dewey chairman, Pennsylvania congress-man Hugh Scott. In preparation for the 1950 congressional elections, newly appointed chairman Guy Gabrielson, a Taftite from New Jersey, launched a number of initiatives to further entrench the Old Guard leadership in the South through generous campaign funding and publicity programs. While in truth it would take much more than Gabrielson's proposal to make southern Republicanism viable in a general election, his actions showed that the region was still central to Taft's strategy. The remnants of the Dewey faction, believ-ing that the conservatism of Gabrielson and Taft meant certain defeat, soon countered. In late May 1950, Scott accused six southern RNC members of colluding with the Democrats to maintain the one-party system in the region. Scott's statement, made during a national radio interview, specifically named the Taft-backing committeemen of Alabama, Louisiana, Mississippi, South Carolina, Tennessee, and Texas. He accused them of "selling their party down the river for . . . personal advantage." Scott praised the RNC members from Florida, Georgia, and Virginia, all of whom had, conveniently, backed Dewey in 1948, for building a two-party system in the South.[21] Two days later, Taft is-sued a statement defending those Scott had targeted and arguing that they had actually expanded the GOP. While the merits varied from state to state, Taft's remarks sent the clear message that he had a special interest in the South.[22]

Extraordinary events at the start of the 1952 election cycle raised the stakes for the southern GOP even higher. Dewey and his associates recruited Dwight Eisenhower, war hero and commander of the D-Day invasion, as their candidate for the nomination. Though "Ike" had near-universal popularity and a bipartisan following nationally, a majority of Republican insiders believed Taft had a legitimate claim to lead the ticket. Eisenhower had no political experience. Yet, just as in 1948, the GOP delegates would ultimately decide the nominee regardless of popular sentiment. So while Ike supporters were criticizing Taft, Brownell was resurrecting his southern strategy. The RNC planned the convention for 1,206 delegates and allotted the South a sixth of the nominating votes. Brownell later noted that the southern delegates "represented almost no one at home . . . but they constituted a sizable bloc in the 1952 convention's balloting, and by and large they were Old Guard conservatives strongly in favor of Taft."[23] The South once again looked to be fertile ground for planting the seeds of discontent in the Taft camp.

Political columnists forecast that Dixie would be a pivotal battleground. In early 1952, Marquis Childs reported that Taft had built the bulk of his base from roughly 100 pledged delegates in the South and 150 in the Midwest. Unlike 1948, however, the presence of Eisenhower had changed the political equation. In March, Joseph Alsop and Stewart Alsop detailed a survey of the editors of fourteen major newspapers in the South. Only one, the editor of the *Tampa Morning News*, predicted that Taft would win their state over Truman. All of the editors agreed that Ike had the popularity to win, but the southern Republican leadership was solidly behind Taft. In commenting on the gulf between party leaders and their voters, which they termed "The Great Republican Mystery," the Alsops concluded that Taft's inability to break the Democratic hold on the South would bring another Republican defeat. Eisenhower, in their opinion, was the only hope for the GOP in 1952, thanks to his bipartisan appeal in the region.[24]

Once again, Texas factored heavily in Brownell's plan. Since 1950, the situation had become more favorable to his top lieutenants, Colley Briggs and Hobart McDowell, as Creager's death had left a power vacuum. Harry Zweifel, Creager's state party chair, had taken the vacant RNC seat and frozen out the Dewey supporters. Brownell, however, found a new ally in the form of Texas oil tycoon Jack Porter, who had unsuccessfully challenged Zweifel for the national committee seat.[25] Porter saw Eisenhower as the most viable candidate and the most likely to prevent the federal takeover of the mineral rights to offshore oil deposits, the so-called "tidelands" question.[26] Porter's presence and fortune changed the dynamics of the Texas GOP and bolstered Brownell in the state. Porter lobbied successfully for a bill, written by Brownell, to outlaw the shenanigans surrounding precinct conventions, and Brownell convinced Porter to join Briggs and McDowell and become the public face of "Draft Eisenhower" in Texas.[27]

Brownell's team had a common mission: to expand the state party and create a viable two-party system. They did not, however, have similar ideological or long-term goals. Brownell told Briggs that he hoped that "it will be possible to induce a group of progressive young fellows to run for office on the Republican ticket," but Porter, the energetic newcomer, disagreed.[28] Porter made numerous attempts to link Ike to causes that he and many disgruntled Democrats believed in regarding taxes, foreign policy, tidelands oil, and race relations. In May 1952, he claimed that "If we passed an F.E.P.C., which tells you whom you can hire, the next step will be to tell the worker for whom he can work, which will complete the cycle of physical and economic slavery." Eisenhower, to his credit, refused to acknowledge these claims and made general statements in favor of employer rights and reduced taxation. Eisenhower, much like Taft, would not support the southern racial view and deflected Porter's racist comments with silence. Porter's ideas did not mesh with the moderate line Eisenhower took during the campaign, but he was too valuable a player in the local situation to be removed from Brownell's setup.[29]

Eisenhower's popularity and the successful precinct organization of the Deweyites created a wave of support that overwhelmed the Old Guard Republicans. As indicated earlier, the heavy-handed tactics of a number of Creager supporters led to contested results in thirty-one precincts. At the county conventions three days later, Taft forces were defeated and, once again, bolted from proceedings to elect their own delegates to the state convention. Three weeks later, on May 26, the state party met and, with Zweifel firmly in control of the machinery, rejected the Eisenhower delegates, appointing a slate of thirty for Taft, four for Eisenhower, and four for General Douglas MacArthur. The Eisenhower suppers then walked out and nominated their own set of delegates with thirty-three for Eisenhower and five for Taft.[30]

The fallout from the state convention became central to the national Republican narrative. Both Eisenhower and Taft had regional campaign managers present to guide the Texas factions, making the candidates themselves look somewhat culpable in the disarray. The press claimed that the Old Guard had driven the "Taft steamroller" through the convention and invalidated the legitimate delegates, despite the legal and binding votes of the county meetings. The Taftites claimed that the Eisenhower supporters were only "one-day Republicans" and that Zweifel had protected the integrity of the party by removing the outsiders. The press, especially Joseph Alsop and the editors of the *Houston Post,* claimed that Taft had stolen the delegates from Eisenhower.

The description of the "Texas Steal" was picked up by reporters around the nation, and the Eisenhower campaign quickly adopted the "Texas Steal" rhetoric. Eisenhower surrogates made the controversy into a moral question and claimed that justice would be vindicated at the national convention in Chicago once its delegation had been seated.[31]

Events in Texas turned on Brownell's efforts to expand the GOP beyond the control of the local post-office Republicans, a goal that was replicated in one form or another in the ten other states of the Old Confederacy. It is important to note, though, that Brownell only cultivated local factions that were on the outs with the Old Guard when it benefited Eisenhower's nomination prospects. There was no motivation to challenge Democratic one-party systems when it could harm, or have no impact on, the national convention. Florida was the most prominent example of this, as the Eisenhower group snubbed the leader of a prominent Republican reform movement in favor of a local pro-Eisenhower organization that refused to even label itself as Republican. The Florida Citizens for Eisenhower-Nixon was largely a group of northern transplants who portrayed themselves as nonpartisan in order to secure independent and Democratic votes. In Mississippi, Brownell ostracized black RNC member Perry Howard, longtime leader of the state's "Black and Tan" faction and a committed Taftite, in favor of an openly racist all-white Republican group. This occurred despite Eisenhower's public stance as a racial moderate. Brownell was clearly willing to work with segregationists if they could contribute to his cause.[32]

Brownell's cultivation of rival factions in the South created five delegate contests at the 1952 Republican National Convention: Texas, Mississippi, Louisiana, Georgia, and Florida. The Taft and Eisenhower forces agreed not to get involved in the Florida contest,[33] but the contests in the remaining states hinged on the question of whether the Old Guard–dominated parties had used their institutional control to reject Eisenhower majorities illegally. The Taftite state leaders each argued that Eisenhower voters were "one-day Republicans" who had temporarily switched party affiliation. The state Eisenhower forces and national campaign managers argued that the Taftite Republican organizations had disenfranchised thousands of voters. In Louisiana, as in Texas, the state convention had ruled against the Eisenhower group and selected delegates for Chicago who favored Taft but clearly did not have the backing of their constituents in their parishes and wards. While the specific details and names were different, the four remaining contests all raised questions regarding the closed nature of the southern GOP.[34]

Because Taft had control of the Credentials Committee at the national convention, it seemed likely that the pro-Taft delegations would be seated. In light of this, Brownell devised a surprise maneuver that, in the end, gave the nomination to Eisenhower. Ike's campaign team announced their intention to pass a rule change, dubbed the "Fair Play" amendment, to prevent delegates from the four contested states from voting on the seating of any contested delegations; contested delegates from Georgia would not be able to vote to seat Louisiana's delegation, and vice versa. Taft's campaign manager, Clarence Brown, mishandled the situation and gave Eisenhower an early victory on the Fair Play question. To the assembled faithful, this was an indication of Taft's weakness, and Taft support withered, handing the nomination to Eisenhower.[35]

Eisenhower ran well in the South during the November election, carrying Texas, Tennessee, Florida, and Virginia on his way to the first Republican victory since 1928. During the first years of the new administration, the RNC and the White House hoped to build on their success in the region, but met resistance from the remaining Old Guard leaders. Patronage still remained the political lifeblood of Dixie. Ike's lieutenants established a Southern Advisory Group, chaired by legendary golfer and Eisenhower confidant Bobby Jones and composed primarily of individuals Brownell had recruited during the 1948 and 1952 campaigns, to challenge the post office Republicans. Its membership included Elbert Tuttle of Georgia and John Minor Wisdom of Louisiana, both of whom Ike would elevate to the federal bench, and who would become instrumental to school desegregation in the post-*Brown* era.[36]

Charles Willis spearheaded the anti–Old Guard campaign from his office in the White House, and achieved varied levels of success. In Florida, he gave financial and publicity support to Tampa businessman William Cramer, who went on to win a congressional seat in 1954 and turn the Bay Area into a Republican stronghold.[37] In Tennessee, the leadership of the 1952 Citizens for Eisenhower, a nonpartisan organization created to woo independent and Democratic voters, publicly recruited House candidates in middle and west Tennessee against the wishes of state party leader B. Carroll Reece. Willis targeted Reece for replacement, but the congressman shrewdly traded his vote on the House Rules Committee to discharge pro-Eisenhower tax legislation in exchange for unrestricted control over patronage in Tennessee, exasperating Willis and staying in power.[38] Reece was one of a handful of pro-Taft Republicans to do so after 1952.

As in the pre-convention campaign, the Eisenhower administration allied with segregationists and white supremacists when the need arose. In Mississippi, Perry Howard, one of only two African Americans on the RNC, retained his seat and expected to continue as patronage distributor. The Mississippi Citizens for Eisenhower teamed up with the racist "Lily-White" Republican faction to challenge Howard, and RNC chair Leonard Hall developed a solution in which E. O. Spencer, head of both the Mississippi CFE and the Lily-Whites, would chair a state advisory committee to determine patronage appointments.[39] The leader of the Lily-Whites sued in federal court to remove Howard and assume full control of the Mississippi GOP,[40] and a letter to Eisenhower from a concerned citizen of Meridian, Mississippi, is indicative of the true motivations for this lawsuit: "Mr. President, don't you think that it is extremely embarrassing to the 112,000 very fine men and women of this state who gave so freely of their time and influence to help elect a man worthy of the name of President to be held at bay by one negro man. It is an unwarranted indignity heaped upon us."[41] The Eisenhower administration, nominally moderate on civil rights, worked with southern segregationists to oust the most prominent African American on the RNC. Eventually the Supreme Court ruled in favor of the Lily-Whites. Spencer's organization became the officially recognized Mississippi GOP. Howard kept his seat on the RNC through 1956, but had less say in local matters.[42]

Eisenhower initially proved to be a boon for southern Republicans, as events in Louisiana indicate. From 1952 through 1957, when he took his place on the Fifth Circuit Court of Appeals, John Minor Wisdom continued to expand the GOP using Eisenhower's image to recruit new members. Once the GOP took over the White House in 1952 after a twenty-year absence, some party leaders believed that Eisenhower was a transformative figure who could rally the public and possibly realign the political parties behind his policies. An internal campaign memo from the White House during the 1954 congressional elections claimed that "Every people in every age has required its Moses" and argued that Eisenhower would revitalize the Republican Party much like FDR did for the Democrats in 1932.[43] Wisdom subscribed to this belief wholeheartedly and hoped to use Eisenhower's name as a way to convince disaffected Democrats that it was acceptable to become a Republican. In campaign letters from 1956, the central qualification of the individuals he backed for the state Republican committee was their devotion to Eisenhower. One letter noted that their opponents "opposed the President's nomination. They sat on their hands after 1952. They have consistently opposed the President and his policies. Long before the President's illness, they loudly stated their opposition to the President's re-election."[44] The sample ballot sent to voters in the Tenth Ward included a logo of an elephant draped in an "Ike" banner, as well as multiple assurances that Democrats could legally vote for Eisenhower.[45] Wisdom did work to build the party infrastructure through established methods, such as setting up women's clubs and district committees throughout the state, but he also understood that convincing voters to abandon their Democratic roots would not be easy. The Eisenhower-centered appeals generated short-term results and ultimately accounted for the surge of Republicanism during the 1956 election cycle.

Wisdom's determination to use Eisenhower as a sort of halfway house for Democrats wary of becoming Republican fit in well with his larger political strategy. The postwar South experienced rapid economic growth, with most development concentrated in metropolitan areas. Wisdom concentrated the lion's share of his efforts on New Orleans, and to a lesser extent in Shreveport, and promoted Eisenhower's economic policies to wealthy and powerful business leaders as an incentive to leave the Democratic Party. In a letter to New Orleans businessman Samuel Israel, Wisdom noted, "It just seems to me, however, that there is no cause so vital to business men, especially in the South, as the continued support of the present administration."[46] The success of using Eisenhower's image as a recruiting tool and promoting the GOP as the party of business was readily apparent in Wisdom's fund-raising efforts during the 1956 election cycle. He created a nonpartisan "Americans for Eisenhower" committee fronted by a prominent and wealthy Democrat and solicited the most prominent members of Louisiana society for donations. A donor list from September shows 310 names responsible for 301 donations totaling $314,950 to Americans for Eisenhower. Only sixteen of the individuals listed were from outside New Orleans, showing the importance of the city to Wisdom's vision. A breakdown of the list by occupation shows large contributions from a cross-section of the city's most important economic interests. For example, twenty-two individuals affiliated with the shipping industry gave $25,400; twenty-two bankers and financiers contributed $21,000; eight auto dealers gave $7,500; and twenty-seven associated with agriculture, including officials of the United Fruit Company and a number of sugar companies, sent in $30,250. These numbers were quite extraordinary for Louisiana, whose entire quota to the Republican National Committee for the years 1950 through 1955 was just under $111,000, and has to be read as a positive endorsement of Wisdom's strategy. A letter from the state treasurer to an associate noted that it was easy to raise money for Eisenhower during a presidential year, but difficult to bankroll the GOP in its own right. Promoting Eisenhower's economic policies and raising capital did, however, provide a financial foundation for his broader party-building efforts and contributed to the state going Republican in the 1956 presidential election.[47]

Following Eisenhower's landslide reelection in 1956, the RNC and the White House continued party-building activities along the same lines. With fewer and fewer Old Guard Republicans, their efforts were highly targeted. In Mississippi, where Perry Howard remained by virtue of his election to the RNC, the relationship between the two factions remained tumultuous.

Howard had been seated as a delegate at the 1956 national convention but, in the subsequent months, had been further ostracized in patronage matters and general party business. In complaints to the White House, Howard claimed outright racial discrimination and argued that the Lily-Whites had been publicly protesting against civil rights legislation.[48] In September 1957, after Eisenhower dispatched federal troops to oversee the integration of Little Rock High School, the head of the Lily-White Republicans formally renounced his party affiliation in protest. Howard immediately asked for a restoration of his patronage powers and his standing within the RNC as the official representative of the Mississippi GOP, but his pleas fell on deaf ears. Wirt Yerger, who in September had criticized Eisenhower's civil rights record and Little Rock, was made the sole arbiter of patronage in the state. This marked the end of Howard's importance in Mississippi Republican circles. The Lily-Whites, despite their unwillingness to back the administration on civil rights, remained the dominant force in the state party. Yerger, a much more active leader then Howard, set out to build the Mississippi GOP into a vehicle for conservatives who felt estranged from the national Democratic Party.[49]

From the mid-1940s through the Eisenhower administration, the southern and the national Republican campaigns pursued two different goals. Regionally, the aim was to revitalize the party in order to nominate Dewey and Eisenhower. Nationally, Brownell and his associates recast the GOP as a moderately progressive institution. In 1956, it appeared that both of Brownell's plans would succeed. Thirty-nine new state chairs were elected during the Eisenhower years, including a number in the South.[50] Yet, by 1964, it was clear that the conservative wing of the party was ascendant and that Brownell's work in the region transformed the state parties into viable institutions for his ideological opponents. Political scientist Bernard Cosman reported that, in April 1964, three-fourths of the counties in Alabama, Georgia, Mississippi, and South Carolina had active GOP chairmen and vice chairmen, with Louisiana projected to reach this threshold by the end of the year. Most backed the candidacy of Arizona senator Barry Goldwater. In 1964, the year of Goldwater's nomination, Mississippi fielded its first Republican gubernatorial candidate in the twentieth century. He polled a respectable 38 percent of the vote.[51] The Alabama Republican Party mounted an effective campaign against incumbent Senator Lister Hill that tallied 49 percent of the vote. Walter Dean Burnham attributed this success to a conservative message that contrasted the GOP candidate with Hill's support for the civil rights and liberal economic policies of the Kennedy administration.[52] The racially charged politics of the South clearly attracted voters to the GOP well before the Civil Rights Act became law, and the Republican Party was now poised to crack the Democrat's hold on the South for good.

Separating the politics of the twentieth-century South from race is impossible. Segregation was an undeniable foundation for the Democratic Solid South and was a strong impetus for the shift to the Republican Party in the civil rights era. Isolating the cause of this transformation to a reaction to social change, however, ignores other political factors. The initial postwar Republican foray into the region had virtually nothing to do with race. In fact, in a number of situations segregationists worked side by side with moderate liberals to both nominate a popular candidate and build an effective Republican organization in their states. The concerted effort to clear out the post-office Republicans and replace them with a committed and active leadership paid dividends well before the mass exodus of the southern Democrats. In fact, the first southern strategy elevated racial moderates like Elbert Tuttle and John Minor Wisdom alongside segregationists like Jack Porter and Wirt Yerger. Rather than being wholly reactionary, the southern embrace of the Republicans was an extended process that had its impetus in party politics. Nearly two decades after Brownell's first southern strategy, conservative Republicans associated with Barry Goldwater capitalized on the benefits of Brownell's plan and used them to tilt the two-party system well to the right. Nevertheless, the impetus of the southern GOP was more color-blind than historians have thus far claimed.

## Notes

1. Interview by Alvin Lane, 22 December 1968, copy in Eisenhower Library Oral History Collection, Dwight D. Eisenhower Library, Abilene, Kans. (hereafter Eisenhower Library Oral History Collection).

2. *Washington Post*, 5 February 1952.

3. Kevin Kruse, *White Flight: Atlanta and the Making of Modern Conservatism* (Princeton: Princeton University Press, 2005), 10.

4. Dan T. Carter, *Politics of Rage: George Wallace, the Origins of the New Conservatism, and the Transformation of American Politics* (New York: Simon and Schuster, 1995); Thomas Byrne Edsall and Mary Edsall, *Chain Reaction: The Importance of Race, Rights, and Taxes on American Politics* (New York: Norton, 1991); Matthew D. Lassiter, *The Silent Majority: Suburban Politics in the Sunbelt South* (Princeton: Princeton University Press, 2006); Joseph Crespino, *In Search of Another Country: Mississippi and the Conservative Counterrevolution* (Princeton: Princeton University Press, 2007); William A. Link, *Righteous Warrior: Jesse Helms and the Making of Modern Conservatism* (New York: St. Martin's Press, 2008).

5. V. O. Key, *Southern Politics in State and Nation* (New York: Knopf, 1949), 277–97; Earl Black and Merle Black, *The Rise of Southern Republicans* (Cambridge: Belknap Press of Harvard University Press, 2002).

6. Lewis L. Gould, *1968: The Election That Changed America* (New York: Dee, 1993); Rick Perlstein, *Nixonland: The Rise of a President and the Fracturing of America* (New York: Scribner, 2008); Robert Mason, *Richard Nixon and the Quest for a New American Majority* (Chapel Hill: University of North Carolina Press, 2004).

7. Paul Lockwood to Thomas E. Dewey, memo, 19 February 1947, copy in Folder 2 ("Alabama"), Box 21, Series II, Dewey Papers; Herbert Brownell, Letter to Claude Vardaman, 13 September 1947, copy in Folder 2 ("Alabama"), Box 21, Series II, Thomas Dewey Papers, Department of Rare Books and Special Collections, University of Rochester (hereafter Dewey Papers).

8. Claude Vardaman to Thomas E. Dewey, 8 February 1948, copy in Folder 2 ("Alabama"), Box 21, Series II, Dewey Papers; Andrew Hurst to Robert A. Taft, 12 December 1947, copy in Folder "1948 Campaign—Alabama—A–H," Box 164, Robert A. Taft Papers, Manuscript Division, Library of Congress, Washington, D.C. (hereafter Taft Papers); John Hill to Robert A. Taft, 30 December 1947, copy in Folder "1948 Campaign—Alabama—A–H," Box 164, Taft Papers.

9. H. C. Fountain to Robert A. Taft, 8 March 1948, copy in Folder "1948 Campaign—Alabama—A–H," Box 164, Taft Papers; Robert A. Taft to William Logan Martin, 14 May 1948, copy in Folder "1948 Campaign—Alabama—J–M," Box 164, Taft Papers.

10. During Dewey's tenure, New York had passed the first state level FEPC in the nation.

11. Robert A. Taft to Loonie Noonjin, 20 February 1948, copy in Folder "1948 Campaign—Alabama—N–W," Box 164, Taft Papers; *Human Events* 5, no. 14 (7 April 1948).

12. John Gordon Bennett, memo, 25 October 1947, copy in Folder 31 ("Alabama"), Box 16, Clarence Brown Papers, Ohio Historical Society, Columbus, Ohio (hereafter Clarence Brown Papers); Mildred Reeves to B. L. Noonjin, 23 December 1947, copy in Folder "1948 Campaign—Alabama—N–W," Box 164, Taft Papers; Colley Briggs to Herbert Brownell, 30 October 1947, copy in Folder 4 ("Texas"), Box 30, Series II, Dewey Papers; Herbert Brownell to Claude Vardaman, 13 November 1947, copy in Folder 2 ("Alabama"), Box 21, Series II, Dewey Papers.

13. The results were eight for Dewey, six for Taft, and one for Stassen. Thomas E. Stephens to Herbert Brownell, memo, 13 May 1947, copy in Folder 2 ("Alabama"), Box 21, Series II, Dewey Papers; Herbert Brownell to Claude Vardaman, 13 September 1947, copy in Folder 2 ("Alabama"), Box 21, Series II, Dewey Papers; Claude Vardaman to Thomas E. Dewey 8 February 1948, copy in Folder 2 ("Alabama"), Box 21, Series II, Dewey Papers; Memo "Result of Investigation—Alabama," unsigned, 18 December 1947, copy in Folder 2 ("Alabama"), Box 21, Series II, Dewey Papers; Herbert Brownell to Claude Vardaman, 1 June 1948, copy in Folder 2 ("Alabama"), Box 21, Series II, Dewey Papers; C. D. Moore to Herbert Brownell, 13 June 1948, copy in Folder 2

("Alabama"), Box 21, Series II, Dewey Papers; Claude Vardaman to Herbert Brownell, 15 June 1948, copy in Folder 2 ("Alabama"), Box 21, Series II, Dewey Papers.

14. James Anthony Clark, *Marrs McLean: A Biography* (Houston: Clark, 1969).

15. Roger M. Olien, *From Token to Triumph: The Texas Republicans since 1920* (Dallas: Southern Methodist University Press, 1982); interview by Joe Ingraham and H. Jack Porter, transcript in Eisenhower Library Oral History Collection; Colley Briggs to Herbert Brownell, 2 June 1948, copy in Folder 4 ("Texas"), Box 30, Series II, Dewey Papers.

16. Colley Briggs to Herbert Brownell, 16 July 1948, copy in Folder "Br–Bz (1)," Box 134, Herbert Brownell Papers, Dwight D. Eisenhower Library, Abilene, Kans. (hereafter Brownell Papers).

17. Herbert Brownell to Colley Briggs, 26 February 1948, copy in Folder 4 ("Texas"), Box 30, Series II, Dewey Papers; Herbert Brownell to Hobart McDowell, 26 February 1948, copy in Folder 4 ("Texas"), Box 30, Series II, Dewey Papers; Philip Eubank to Herbert Brownell, 8 March 1948, copy in Folder 4 ("Texas"), Box 30, Series II, Dewey Papers.

18. Interview by Joe Ingraham and H. J. Porter, Eisenhower Library Oral History Collection.

19. *Texas Republican*, March–June 1948.

20. Rentfro B. Creager to Enoch Fletcher, 3 June 1948, copy in Folder 4 ("Texas"), Box 30, Series II, Dewey Papers.

21. *Washington Post*, 28 May 1950.

22. Robert A. Taft in *New York Times*, 3 May 1950; *Birmingham News*, 9 June 1950.

23. Paul T. David et al. *Presidential Nominating Politics in 1952*, vol. 3, *The South* (Baltimore: Johns Hopkins Press, 1954). The introductory chapter is especially important; Herbert Brownell with John P. Burke, *Advising Ike: The Memoirs of Attorney General Herbert Brownell* (Lawrence: University Press of Kansas, 1993), 105–6.

24. *Washington Post*, 5 February 1952, 5 March 1952; *New York Times*, 28 February 1952.

25. W. C. Briggs to Herbert Brownell, 28 October 1950, copy in Folder "Br (1)," Box 24, Brownell Papers; W. C. Briggs to Herbert Brownell, 20 November 1950, copy in Folder "Br (1)," Box 24, Brownell Papers; W. C. Briggs to Herbert Brownell, 20 April 1951, copy in Folder "Br (1)," Box 24, Brownell Papers; David Ingalls to Walter Rogers, 13 November 1951, copy in Folder "1952 Campaign—Texas—L–Mc," Box 409, Taft Papers.

26. David Ingalls to Marrs McLean, 17 May 1951, copy in Folder "1952 Campaign—Texas—L–Mc," Box 409, Taft Papers; David Ingalls to H. Jack Porter, 18 September 1951, copy in Folder "1952 Campaign—Texas—L–Mc," Box 409, Taft Papers.

27. C. Briggs to William Pheiffer, 8 April 1951, copy in Folder "Br (1)," Box 24, Brownell Papers; interview by Joe Ingraham and H. Jack Porter, Eisenhower Library Oral History Collection; interview by Edward Dicker with John Luter, Eisenhower Library Oral History Collection; Edward Bermingham to Dwight D. Eisenhower, 7

February 1952, copy in Folder "Edward J. Bermingham (Jan. 1952–Feb. 1952)," Box 11, Eisenhower Pre-Presidential Papers, Dwight D. Eisenhower Library, Abilene, Kans. (hereafter Eisenhower Pre-Presidential Papers); W. C. Briggs to Herbert Brownell, 20 April 1952, copy in Folder "Br (1)," Box 24, Brownell Papers.

28. Herbert Brownell to W. C. Briggs, 20 November 1950, copy in Folder "Br (1)," Box 24, Brownell Papers; H. Jack Porter, speech to the Young Republican Federation of Nueces County, 21 June 1951, copy in Folder "Mc (2)," Box 26, Brownell Papers.

29. Dwight D. Eisenhower to H. Jack Porter, 28 March 1952, copy in Folder "Politics—1951–1952—Correspondence (5)," Box 127, Eisenhower Pre-Presidential Papers. Eisenhower did ask Clay to read the letters, lest Ike "cross-up" Clay (see Dwight D. Eisenhower to Lucius Clay, memo, 28 March 1952, copy in Folder "Lucius D. Clay [Jan. 1952–Feb. 1952]," Box 24, Eisenhower Pre-Presidential Papers; H. Jack Porter to Dwight D. Eisenhower, 14 May 1952, copy in Folder "H. J. Porter," Box 92, Eisenhower Pre-Presidential Papers). Porter explicitly asked Eisenhower to endorse a states'-rights position on civil rights (see Jack Porter to Dwight D. Eisenhower, 9 May 1952, copy in Folder "H. J. Porter," Box 92, Eisenhower Pre-Presidential Papers).

30. Henry Zweifel, press release, 27 May 1952, copy in Folder "1952 Campaign—Press Releases," Box 460, Taft Papers; Precinct Committee Meeting Report, Dallas County, Texas, undated, copy in Box 70, Katherine Kennedy Brown Papers, Department of Special Collections and Archives, Paul Laurence Dunbar Library, Wright State University, Dayton, Ohio (hereafter KKB Papers); David et al., *Presidential Nominating Politics in 1952,* 3:321; H. Jack Porter to Jesse Jones, 9 May 1952, copy in Folder "Citizens for, Advisory Council," Box 1, Oveta Culp Hobby Papers, Dwight D. Eisenhower Library, Abilene, Kans. (hereafter Hobby Papers); Henry Zweifel, "Statement of Henry Zweifel," 20 May 1952, copy in Folder "Citizens for, Advisory Council," Box 1, Hobby Papers.

31. *Houston Post*, 27 May 1952; *Houston Post,* 30 May 1952.

32. Michael D. Bowen, "'The Strange Tale of Wesley and Florence Garrison: Racial Crosscurrents of the Postwar Florida Republican Party," *Florida Historical Quarterly* 88, no. 2 (Fall 2009).

33. C. C. Spades to Hugh Scott, 24 March 1952, copy in Folder "1952 Convention Delegate Contests—Florida," Box 129, Brownell Papers.

34. *The Louisiana Story,* undated pamphlet, copy in Folder "1952 Campaign—Louisiana—The Louisiana Story," Box 356, Taft Papers.

35. Patterson, *Mr. Republican*, 555–58.

36. Jim McKillips, "Report on the Southern Committee Meeting," undated, copy in Folder "Southern Situation 1953 (1)," Box 166, Papers of the Republican National Chairman (Leonard Hall), Dwight D. Eisenhower Library, Abilene, Kans. (hereafter Hall Papers); David A. Nichols, *A Matter of Justice: Eisenhower and the Beginning of the Civil Rights Revolution* (New York: Simon and Schuster, 2007).

37. Jim McKillips to Charles Willis, memo, 27 November 1953, copy in Folder "OF-138-Florida," Box 691, Official File, Presidential Papers of Dwight D. Eisenhower,

Dwight D. Eisenhower Library, Abilene, Kans. (hereafter Official File); Henry Havens to Eisenhower, 30 October 1956, copy in Folder "Of-138-Florida," Box 691, Official File.

38. Val Washington to Sherman Adams, 24 November 1953, Folder 109-A-1 ("Oct–Nov–Dec 1953"), Box 466, General File, Presidential Papers of Dwight D. Eisenhower, Dwight D. Eisenhower Library, Abilene, Kans. (hereafter General File).

39. Leonard Hall, press release, 29 May 1953, copy in Folder "Mississippi Situation," Box 173, Hall Papers.

40. Jim McKillips to Leonard Hall, undated memo, copy in Folder "Southern Situation 1953 (1)," Box 166, Hall Papers.

41. Louise McCorkle to Dwight D. Eisenhower, 10 August 1953, copy in Folder "OF 109-A-2 Mississippi," Official File.

42. Newspaper clipping, 9 February 1954, copy in Folder "Mississippi Situation 1954," Box 180, Confidential File, Presidential Papers of Dwight D. Eisenhower, Dwight D. Eisenhower Library, Abilene, Kans.

43. Memorandum, "An Analysis of the 1934 Congressional Elections," undated, copy in Folder "Campaign 1954 (2)," Box 6, Papers of the Chairman of the RNC, Dwight D. Eisenhower Library, Abilene, Kans. (hereafter cited as Hall Papers).

44. Unsigned letter to "Fellow Republicans of the Twelfth Ward," undated, copy in Folder "Primary 1956," Box 3307, Wisdom Papers.

45. Campaign flyer, "Eisenhower Sample Ballot," undated, copy in Folder "Publicity 1956 Campaign," Box 3308, Wisdom Papers.

46. John Minor Wisdom to Samuel Israel, 13 September 1955, copy in Folder "Publicity 1956 Campaign," Box 3308, Wisdom Papers.

47. ASE Bennett to Thomas Stagg, 30 July 1956, copy in Folder "Republican National Finance Committee General Correspondence File," Box 3341, Wisdom Papers.

48. Perry Howard to Howard Pyle, 12 March 1957, copy in Folder "GF-109-A-2 Mississippi," Box 511, General File.

49. For more on the Mississippi GOP, see Crespino, *In Search of Another Country*.

50. Milton Eisenhower to Dwight D. Eisenhower, 16 January 1956, copy in Folder "Jan. '56 Miscellaneous (4)," Box 12, Ann Whitman DDE Diary Series, Dwight D. Eisenhower Library, Abilene, Kans.

51. Bernard Cosman, "Deep South Republicans: Profiles and Positions," in *Republican Politics: The 1964 Campaign and Its Aftermath for the Party*, ed. Bernard Cosman and Robert J. Huckshorn, 76–112 (New York: Praeger, 1968).

52. Walter Dean Burnham, "The Alabama Senatorial Election of 1962: Return of Inter-Party Competition," *Journal of Politics* 26, no. 4 (November 1964): 798–829.

# 11

## The Black Cabinet

### Economic Civil Rights in the Nixon Administration

LEAH M. WRIGHT

When readers opened the November 1968 special election issue of *Jet* magazine, they were inundated with slick political advertisements from the presidential candidates. The black weekly offered no-nonsense messages from Freedom and Peace Party representative Dick Gregory and Democratic contender Hubert Humphrey.[1] Not to be outdone, the Republican Party also tried its hand at wooing the magazine's African American audience. Nixon's two-page glossy insert opened with a close-up of a young, well-dressed black man clutching a thick stack of books. "This Time," the headline solemnly advised, "Vote Like Homer Pitts' Whole World Depended On It." On the next page, the party directly linked the fate of "Homer Pitts" with that of the black electorate:

> He'll get his degree. Then what? . . . laborer, factory job . . . or his own business? A vote for Richard Nixon for President is a vote for a man who wants Homer to have the chance to own his own business. Richard Nixon believes strongly in black capitalism. Because black capitalism is black power in the best sense of the word. It's the road that leads to black economic influence and black pride. It's the key to the black man's fight for equality—for a piece of the action. And that's what the free enterprise system is all about. This time . . . Nixon.[2]

The Republican Party implied that Nixon had viable solutions to address the ailments and aspirations of African Americans; that is, Nixon suggested that the GOP would succeed where the Democratic Party had failed. Implicit in Nixon's message was that this solution was not for all of the electorate, but rather was designed for middle-class, college-educated African Americans. In essence, as *Time* commented, the Republican Party was looking to develop a new "Negro managerial class to lead, hire, and inspire."[3] Further expounding on these ideas in a lengthy *Jet* questionnaire, Richard Nixon wrote, "I am the only candidate who truly believes that black people, on their own steam and with 'remedial' help from the government are going to make it." Increasingly irritated by the magazine's provocative questions, the presidential candidate abruptly asserted, "Men like Ed Brooke and Art Fletcher are symptomatic of what I hope will be an increasingly political phenomenon in this country; the realization by black people and their leaders that their best hope lies not in the Democratic plantation politics of the past, but in the kinds of programs as I have put forward."[4]

Richard Nixon's appeals for minority enterprise and alternative politics echoed a theme central to black Republican ideology and action. African American party members consistently proposed a unique agenda that wedded liberal appeals for racial equality with a belief in traditional Republican principles. In particular, they had long called for the creation and implementation of an aggressive movement for economic civil rights as an alternative means of reaching full equality and independence. A June 1968 article in *Time* highlighted this significant development, noting that the three Republican presidential primary candidates had incorporated this concept into their campaign rhetoric.[5] New York governor Nelson Rockefeller proposed "multibillion-dollar schemes for urban redevelopment," while his conservative counterpart in California, Ronald Reagan, promoted solutions aimed at the "economic salvation of the ghettoes."[6] Most notably, Richard Nixon outlined his sweeping program of black capitalism, emphasizing black pride and self-help. *Cleveland Call and Post* publisher W. O. Walker was so impressed by the initiative that he confidently declared: "Nixon will do more for [African Americans] than has been accomplished in the last hundred years. Sound economic gains and restoration of pride and dignity are in store for minority groups."[7]

And yet, black Republicans were divided in their support of Nixon's candidacy, with many initially rejecting the party's national ticket. The politician—heartily endorsed by black Republicans during the 1960 campaign—had fallen out of favor by 1968. African Americans recoiled at Nixon's attacks on the 1967 Kerner Report, berated him for using the racially charged language of "law and order," bemoaned the nominee's attempts to placate white southerners, and denounced his vice-presidential running mate, Spiro T. Agnew.[8] Simply put, as one black party member complained, "Nixon has a bad reputation among Negroes and so does Agnew."[9] To many, Nixon's actions belied his endorsement of black capitalism, universal human dignity, and party unity, and instead implied a willingness to spurn the black electorate.[10] Arguably, Jackie Robinson best expressed black liberal Republican frustrations with the Nixon-Agnew team in a September 5, 1968 letter to Arizona's Barry

Goldwater. "Picture yourself a black man, standing before your television set hearing Strom Thurmond. . . . Nixon . . . made a kingmaker out of the former Democrat.[11]

Despite such sentiments, the majority of black party members viewed Nixon's November 1968 presidential win as a cautious victory of their own. A Republican administration had the potential to be an extremely powerful venue for advancing, developing, and implementing black party members' solutions and policies. Floyd McKissick, former executive director of the Congress of Racial Equality (CORE), underscored this thinking when he announced that Nixon would do "one Hell of a job" in the White House. Echoing these sentiments, black Republican James Rhone of New York insisted that the president would "put forth more progressive programs than LBJ." John Silvera, deputy aide to Nelson Rockefeller, perhaps best conveyed black party members' opinions on Nixon, stating: "there needed to be a change."[12] The goal was clear: directly influence and inform the policies, programs, and direction of the Nixon administration with regard to issues of African American concern. As GOP Minorities Division director C. L. Townes surmised in 1969, the black community was "ripe for a Republican resurgence" so long as the party made good on its promise of economic uplift.[13]

Richard Nixon's "Black Cabinet" was central to this effort. Its members, a loosely assembled group of black Republican appointees, embraced this vision and used it to push an agenda directly aimed at the needs and aspirations of African Americans. They developed and promoted a specialized black outreach campaign; they specifically used the Nixon administration as a means of advancing an alternative social, economic, and political civil rights agenda. Ultimately, the Black Cabinet viewed economic uplift coupled with political shrewdness as the final, critical step in the struggle for racial equality and black independence. "Earning Power," Arthur Fletcher explained, "is the name of the Game. The black man's future, his rights to equality, his freedom of choice. . . . What matters for us blacks is economic liberation."[14]

This essay documents the role, strategy, and influence of this African American coalition in the development and promotion of an alternative civil rights agenda.[15] The first part of this essay investigates the roots and symbolism of the Black Cabinet, and explores their complicated motives, ideologies, and strategies. Part 2 examines policy initiatives promoted and implemented by members of the Black Cabinet, concentrating on minority enterprise, affirmative action, and federal funding initiatives. The conclusion suggests that black Republicans managed to launch an economic and political agenda through the Nixon administration, despite the hostility and failings of the greater Republican Party. Indeed, by the mid-1970s, black Republicans had, to some extent, influenced both the Republican Party and the larger black community by providing an alternative civil rights agenda, setting the stage for a larger debate on black alternative politics in the postwar era.

## Making the Black Cabinet

Within days of the Republican Party's November presidential victory, black party members publicly called for the president to appoint qualified African American Republicans to the new administration. According to the National Council of Concerned Afro American Republicans (NCCAR), black loyalists had "worn the battle cry in the heat of the day" and demonstrated their steadfast allegiance to the Republican Party. This unwavering commitment, the organization argued, compelled recognition for "those who have worked for and supported the party in season and out of season since the great exodus of 1932."[16] Echoing a similar, albeit less partisan refrain, *Ebony* magazine speculated on the prospects of a Nixon-appointed "black brain trust," consisting of prominent Republican figures such as Clarence Townes, Arthur Fletcher, former Equal Employment Opportunity (EEOC) commissioner Samuel C. Jackson, Michigan GOP vice chair Earl Kennedy, Black Power Conference secretary Nathan Wright, and, of course, the ubiquitous Edward Brooke.[17]

As an enigmatic advisor to Nixon throughout the fall 1968 campaign, Brooke and the president-elect had discussed, on a number of occasions, the possibility of a cabinet appointment. After the November election, Nixon offered the Massachusetts senator his choice of positions including secretary of Housing and Urban Development (HUD), secretary of Health, Education and Welfare (HEW), or ambassador to the United Nations (UN).[18] Brooke declined Nixon's offer; as he explained during a press conference, "I felt I could best serve the country and Mr. Nixon in the Senate."[19] Moreover, despite Brooke's assertion that he planned to work with the administration in "other capacities," many African Americans were disappointed as they had imagined the politician as the nation's first black attorney general. Giving voice to this anguish, the *Chicago Defender* issued a biting editorial criticizing the senator's decision: Brooke "made a misjudgment. . . . [As] Attorney General he [c]ould do more for civil rights in a manner that would inspire confidence" in the black masses. The diatribe concluded with a grim warning: placing the "wrong men" in the "wrong Cabinet posts" would bring "irreparable discredit" to the Nixon administration's fragile relationship with the black community.[20]

However, the White House did, in fact, manage to appoint a number of prominent African American Republicans to high-ranking positions in the new administration.[21] Among the first was Robert J. Brown, the designated

"White House ambassador to American Negroes." Dubbed a "true black capitalist" by the *Chicago Defender*, the thirty-three-year-old North Carolinian
was a wealthy self-made entrepreneur who "still carrie[d] a switchblade knife
in his White House attaché case as a reminder" of his impoverished upbringing. Brown was uniquely suited for his position in the Nixon administration.
As a former police officer and federal narcotics agent, he had a demonstrated
respect for law and order. But he also saw himself as a civil rights advocate,
active with both the National Association for the Advancement of Colored
People (NAACP) and the Southern Christian Leadership Conference (SCLC),
where he had formed close friendships with Martin Luther King Jr. and Jesse
Jackson during the early 1960s. As a member of the Democratic Party, he had
worked on the presidential campaign of Robert F. Kennedy; in the wake of
the candidate's June 1968 assassination, Brown quietly joined the GOP at the
urging of Clarence Townes. His work with the Minorities Division of the Republican National Committee (RNC) caught the attention of the Nixon team,
earning him a spot on the campaign trail as the authority figure on issues of
black concern. As the president's special assistant, Brown was charged with
developing a comprehensive black-capitalism campaign and advancing it as
a viable alternative to the Great Society programs of the Johnson administration. "There's a great challenge in this job," Brown shrewdly observed. "We're
not making any grandiose promises, but we want action." Moreover, Brown
equated this "action" with black economic enterprise, prompted through a
philosophy of black self-help and self-determination.[22] To those ends, he
sought inspiration from local models that had joined these principles successfully—like Reverend Leon Sullivan's Philadelphia Opportunities Industrialization Center (POIC), whose guiding principle was "Helping People Help
Themselves."[23] For Brown, the solution to racial equality lay not in violent
struggle, but rather in economic strength. "You've got to keep pressing," he
maintained. "I mean politically and economically, not with firebombs. . . . We
have to work with the framework of the system to change it and make it more
responsive to the people."[24] Still, Brown was fully aware of the onerous battle
facing him as a black Republican; this was never more apparent than on the
eve of December 20, 1968. During a televised broadcast from his New York
City office, President Nixon shocked the country and angered thousands of
black party members as he brought out Walter Washington and announced
the black Democrat's reappointment as mayor of Washington, D.C. What's
more, Nixon managed to frustrate African Americans from across the political spectrum in his closing address, when he introduced the new members of
his "lily-white" presidential cabinet. A lonely face in the crowded room, Bob

Brown somberly watched the events unfold, hidden by a television camera, but painfully conspicuous in his race and political loyalties.[25]

Civil rights groups and black media outlets reacted harshly to the political revelation, levying accusations of racism, neglect, and discrimination. Newspapers and magazines including the *Chicago Defender, Jet,* and the *Pittsburgh Courier* decried the president's cabinet and argued that it was symbolic of a significant civil rights setback. The charge was difficult to ignore, given that Lyndon Johnson had appointed the first black cabinet member, Robert C. Weaver, in 1966. "Johnson, a President from Texas, desegregated the Cabinet, while Nixon, a President from California, resegregated the Cabinet," NAACP official Clarence Mitchell sarcastically commented.

The countless accusations provoked an angry rejoinder from Robert Finch; in an embarrassingly candid interview, the HEW chief insisted that black leaders' fear of being labeled "Uncle Toms" was the sole reason for the lack of diversity in the presidential cabinet. "There will be Negroes in top jobs in the Nixon administration, that I guarantee you," he fumed.[26] Indeed, the administration had already created a task force on black federal appointees in early December 1968. Bob Brown and Len Garment, Nixon's former law partner and a liberal Democrat, headed the search committee, with a goal of integrating African Americans into the upper echelons of the federal government. Interestingly, Harry S. Dent—the architect of the "Southern Strategy"—also played a role in the task force, working with Garment and Brown to recruit black leaders into policy-making positions. The former aide to South Carolina senator Strom Thurmond explained this apparent paradox in his 1978 memoirs, writing: "Bob and I worked together closely. We were both southern boys, albeit black and white. But we understood our Southland and the practical problems associated with the race question. . . . While President Nixon was pursuing a southern strategy he was also putting more blacks in key government positions than ever before. Orders were issued to . . . concentrate on minority appointments."[27]

Brown's relationship with both Garment and Dent was significant in that it created a pipeline of access for members of the black community, establishing a system whereby African American federal appointees could make their "input" heard. Finally, Whitney Young, executive director of the National Urban League (NUL) assumed an important but discreet position in the selection process; for Young, adopting a flexible stance toward the administration was key in pushing a black empowerment agenda. In a December 1968 letter to Garment, the civil rights leader pledged to help "squelch" the rumors that surrounded the administration and festered in the black community. Responding to Young's missive, a frustrated Len Garment railed against "the aggressive black press" that had "placed their own construction on things" and soured the White House's progress. "We have been working very hard to find and suggest . . . the names of highly qualified Negroes," wrote Garment. "As we move along, these rumors will end—that has to be our common objective." Within one day of receiving Garment's letter, Young produced dozens of names, many of whom were appointed.[28] The NUL head also espoused cautious but optimistic statements in support of the administration. For instance, during an interview in early 1969, he casually suggested that African Americans accept federal appointments as a means of "faithfully" representing the views of the black community. "After all," he offered, "I don't think the President will respond to demands wrapped around a brick and thrown through the White House window."[29]

The behind-the-scenes machinations of the task force quickly helped the administration achieve its "first real breakthrough" with the appointment of James Farmer. Already a highly recognizable public figure for his leadership of the Congress of Racial Equality (CORE), and for his role in orchestrating the 1961 "Freedom Rides," Farmer had drawn further attention by running for a congressional seat in Brooklyn during the 1968 election.[30] In spite of his loss to Democratic dynamo Shirley Chisholm, he still managed to command the interest of the White House. Just weeks after his defeat, the liberal Republican found himself being wooed by Nixon officials, who offered him his choice of three subcabinet positions. While dining with HEW chief Robert Finch in New York City, Farmer admitted that he was hesitant to accept given that he had repudiated Nixon during the 1968 campaign. "I will not reject it out of hand," he stated, "But it will be a very difficult decision for me. . . . Nixon is very unpopular among blacks." In truth, Farmer was genuinely concerned that working in the administration would be political suicide. "I would be painting a bull's-eye on my chest, my back, and both of my sides," he explained to Finch. However, Farmer also acknowledged that the position was a valuable opportunity to play a significant role in federal policy-making; it was also a chance to demonstrate that African Americans could achieve "maximum political leverage" by "not being 'in the bag'" for the Democratic Party.

Seeking guidance, the activist spoke to former colleagues from CORE and civil rights leaders including Roy Wilkins of the NAACP and Whitney Young; he also spoke with countless college students during a two-week tour of black colleges. With few exceptions, black constituents urged Farmer to accept the position. As one black militant argued, "We have to have somebody who knows where the bodies are buried—somebody who knows where the pots of money are that the organizations can go to, to get funding for community projects. We have to have somebody we can trust there."[31] Farmer finally accepted the administration's offer, taking a job as the assistant secretary of HEW as it commanded "considerable power and influence." Aside from working on matters of "urban affairs," Farmer was also charged with establishing a line of communication between the administration and "strident young blacks interested in government . . . particularly a Republican government." The Nixon administration "got mileage" out of the presence of a high-profile civil rights figure, as Farmer himself astutely observed. "That fact gave me a good deal of leverage, which I was able to use for causes I was committed to."[32]

Moreover, the appointments carried multiple meanings for African Americans; for many, the embrace was both significant and symbolic in that it represented a genuine interest in the black community. For black Republicans, it was an illustration of their potential power and an opportunity to demonstrate their unique blueprint for America. The January inauguration of Richard Nixon gave black loyalists a national platform to broadcast their vision of racial equality, integration, and economic uplift. After years of existing on the margins, they now had an opportunity to be included in both party and community politics. In essence, the three-day celebration provided black party members with a brief glimpse of a nation that consisted of a responsible Republican institution and a receptive black population. Theirs was a tangible euphoria, undiminished by the chants of thousands of protestors storming the nation's capital. The contrast was notable; as black party members prepared to usher in the new administration, white "counter-inaugural" activists marched down Pennsylvania Avenue, gripping five-foot-tall posters of Martin Luther King Jr. and signs that read "Down with Racist Brass!" and "Non-Violence . . . Our Most Potent Weapon!" Adding to the irony, the dissenters were flanked by Nixon's massive security force—30 percent of which was black. The tension served to highlight the unusual social dynamic: white protestors on one side of the political uproar, and black Republicans and police officers on the other.[33]

Still, the "surprisingly integrated" inauguration crowd shocked many African Americans. As one reporter noted, "Democratic Negroes experienced difficulties in telling the story of the GOP inaugural that was supposed to be lily white." In truth, black members of the inauguration committee made an aggressive effort to incorporate minority presence into every aspect of the event, beginning with the arrival of 1,500 black VIPs. Edward Brooke hosted one of the largest GOP events, a glitzy affair that "thousands" attempted to crash. Watching white dignitaries "awed" at the sight of a powerful black politician was a "refreshing turnabout in roles," acknowledged one writer. In a sense, Brooke's reception was a showcase for black party members, as they asserted and displayed their sense of racial equality, progress, and independence. For

example, Cleveland councilman John Kellogg mingled effortlessly with Secretary of Transportation John Volpe, while Nathan Wright—secretary of the
Black Power Conference (BPC)—made a bold entrance, arriving in "flowing,
colorful African-style robes," and spent the entire night chatting about black
militancy. Newspaper editors reserved their highest praise for Ed Brooke,
writing that he had demonstrated "prestigious standing" and the color-blind
"pulling power of his name."[34] Black Republicans found other ways to highlight their vision as well; Berkeley Burrell, the party's first black chair of the
Concession Committee, arranged for African American businessmen to oversee most of the vital services of the inauguration, including souvenirs, tour-
ism, and photography. Maurice Moore, a soul-food entrepreneur, handled
meals for more than seven thousand guests, while Autoways executive Ernest
Matthews supplied them with chartered buses and limousines from his company. The spirit of black capitalism flourished during the festivities, netting
the proprietors more than $1 million in profits in just three days.[35] African
Americans also contributed a unique musical element to the presidential affair—Nixon supporters and jazz legends Lionel Hampton and Duke Ellington
dazzled guests, as did Dinah Shore, who belted out a heartfelt rendition of
"God Bless America." But the highlight of the celebration was the performance
of "Soul Brother No. 1"—James Brown; sliding out onto the stage in a tux-
edo, the singer shrieked, "Say It Loud, I'm Black and I'm Proud!" Black audience members shouted along, and soon "even a few whites . . . found themselves caught up . . . and they, too, were saying they were black and they were
proud."[36] Brown's closing number, "Maybe the Last Time," apparently stirred
deep emotions in quite a few black Republicans—after the concert, Earl Kennedy, president of Black Americans for Nixon Agnew (BANA), declared that
the GOP finally had a chance to help African Americans. "If it does not do
this job, this could be the last time," he warned. "There are people around who
have become very tired of waiting for this thing called equality—equality in
everything."[37]

Along similar lines, the presidential swearing-in ceremony motivated
the confidence of black Republicans for both symbolic and literal reasons.
Staunch Nixon supporter and longtime civil rights advocate Bishop Charles
Ewbank Tucker of the African Methodist Episcopal Zion Church opened the
ceremony, delivering the invocation in front of an audience of thousands.[38]
Surrounding him was a group of prominent religious figures, including South-
ern Baptist Billy Graham. As the president took the stage to deliver his speech,
African Americans watched him from "spots of honor" reserved for figures of
prominence; among them sat Supreme Court Justice Thurgood Marshall and
Republican Senator Edward Brooke.[39] The president delivered a purposefully

veiled moderate speech, urging Americans to "go forward together" and "give freedom new reach." His carefully crafted words resonated with black party members, as they deftly joined elements of conservatism with black aspirations and values. In a moment that simultaneously evoked and rebuked Goldwater conservatism, the president declared that the laws of the nation had "caught up with [its] conscience." All that remained, he asserted, was to abide by the law—ensuring that "as all are born equal in dignity before God, all are born equal in dignity before man." Nixon closed his inaugural statement thoughtfully, offering a vision that black party members eagerly embraced: "Our destiny offers not the cup of despair, but the chalice of opportunity. So let us seize it not in fear . . . let us go forward, firm in our faith, steadfast in our purpose . . . [with] sustained confidence in the will of God and the promise of man."[40]

The overt symbolism and promises of the inauguration spurred not only activity from African American Republicans, but also a cautious interest from the general black population.[41] Arguably, these factors contributed to the success of the administration's black-appointee task force and facilitated the development of a wide-ranging coalition committed to racial progress. By April 1969, ten African Americans were employed at the subcabinet level; in addition to Farmer, appointed officials included Arthur Fletcher, assistant secretary of labor; Samuel C. Jackson, assistant secretary of HUD; William H. Brown, chairman of the Equal Opportunity Employment Commission (EEOC); and Elizabeth Koontz, director of the Women's Bureau in the Labor Department.[42] With the guidance of Bob Brown, Clarence Townes, Whitney Young, and Ed Brooke, the cohort appeared ready to make a significant impact on the federal government and the nation. Impressed, *Ebony* mused that perhaps African Americans had been too hasty in their initial assessment of the Nixon administration and black Republicans. "The black man has been handicapped in the past because he did not have men 'on the inside' in government," reasoned the editors. "Now that he does have that opportunity, he should take every advantage of it. The very presence of a black man in an office . . . helps keep the white majority from forgetting us."[43] Reader Sandra Lee of Berea, Ohio, agreed, writing: "Negroes can accomplish a lot more by working within the system than by standing outside of it."[44]

In fact, Lee's mind-set did underscore the political motivations and thinking of those black GOP appointees; establishing a positive rapport and an influential relationship with the White House was crucial in the pursuit of their calculated agenda of equality and advancement. As several observed in a September 1969 interview with the *St. Petersburg Times*, theirs was a "quiet" approach to civil rights. This was understandable, sympathized reporter James

Naughton, since the "so-called southern strategy" was incompatible with an "open avowed civil rights crusade." However, the federal appointees—the Black Cabinet—were not necessarily concerned with pragmatic politics for the sake of southern white voters; instead they hoped to use the administration's resources to advance an economic and political campaign. They theorized that their strategy for racial equality would offer concrete results, rather than "idealistic" rhetoric. "This Administration is not going out promising more than it can deliver," Arthur Fletcher boasted. "[It] is not going to spread itself thin over the whole range of civil rights activities . . . it's going to concentrate on economic opportunities. We got so hung up on the idea that civil rights was a social problem that we failed to see the connecting links. We've got to talk economics." Indeed, black GOP appointees were firm in their belief that "now was the time to shift the civil rights focus" to an alternative movement. This philosophy, along with their linked racial heritage and experience, made their role in the administration vital—that is, African American party members maintained that they could offer both the Nixon administration and the black community a "viable alternative" to Democratic liberalism through solutions for racial advancement. "Civil rights is not on the back burner in this Administration," stressed one African American appointee. "We may be quiet, but we intend to get results."[45]

## The Black Cabinet, Federal Policies, and "Getting Results"

On March 5, 1969, surrounded by dozens of black business, community, and government leaders, Richard Nixon announced the first wave of the black-capitalism initiative.[46] In signing Executive Order 11458, the president established the Office of Minority Business Enterprise (OMBE), a federal coordinating agency designed to promote the "establishment, preservation and strengthening of minority business." The office was designed as a central clearinghouse where African American entrepreneurs could access information, specialized resources and training, and most importantly, project funding. In all, OMBE handled more than one hundred funding programs; it also had an outreach arm in the form of the Advisory Council for Minority Enterprise (ACME), comprised of community business-savvy leaders of color. "Encouraging increased minority-group business activity is one of the priorities of this Administration," Nixon declared during the press conference. Minorities deserved an equal chance to pursue success as managers and owners; and as such, the federal government was committed to providing "expanded opportunity to participate in the free enterprise system at all levels." The ultimate goal, Nixon confidently stated, was to share economic benefits and "encourage pride, dignity and a sense of independence" among communities of color. As the leaders and White House officials drifted into a celebratory reception honoring black entrepreneurs, they chatted excitedly about the future of OMBE and the potential for racial progress. Guests theorized that the agency would provide a hearty boost to black-owned businesses; Nixon special assistant Robert Brown agreed, telling the hopeful crowd that the administration intended to put "words into action—and within the next few weeks." And judging by the thousands of business proposals that soon swamped Brown's office, many African Americans did take his promise quite seriously.[47]

The launch of OMBE directly reflected the vision of African American party members. For years, black Republicans had pushed an aggressive sales effort that sought to capitalize on black dissatisfaction with the civil rights initiatives of the Democratic Party. Of particular concern was the burgeoning black middle class. African American Republican appointees theorized that this "increasingly sophisticated audience" would embrace an alternative civil rights movement grounded in economic uplift and traditional Republican principles.[48] Thus when Richard Nixon called for the "imaginative enlistment of private funds, private energies, and private talents" to solve the nation's racial crises through black private ownership and economic inclusion, he was appealing explicitly to a "segment of the black population that would be more apt to come aboard."[49] Or, as Edward Brooke later reflected, the Republican Party "wasn't reaching down to poor blacks. . . . [It] was reaching out to educated businessmen, the small businessman. People who could comprehend and be thankful for and benefit from this, if you know what I mean."[50] The senator bluntly advanced a parallel agenda as the keynote speaker for the National Insurance Association's annual conference in New Orleans in July 1967, telling the predominantly black audience that he wanted to see the same "energy and imagination that had developed the nation's system of free enterprise" injected into the development of African American economic opportunities. "We must act on this because it threatens the ultimate success of the civil rights movement," urged Brooke. Condemning most—if not all—of the economic programs of the Great Society, Brooke argued that Democratic liberalism perpetuated race-based economic inequality. He suggested that the programs were discriminatory as they assumed that African Americans were solely laborers, workers, and "potential employees," rather than managers, owners, and entrepreneurs.[51] Equal citizenship would arrive with the "development of a new Negro business class"—a task accomplished through the encouragement and training of talented African Americans whose "abilities and inclinations" qualified them for "more sophisticated position[s] on the economic ladder." Brooke closed his spirited address by offering his listeners a few words of warning. "These problems will not be solved solely by government," he cautioned. African Americans "must retain their sense of responsibility for their own . . . success. . . . [They] must be creative and develop their own solutions . . . and guard against mediocrity."[52]

Indeed, by structuring their outreach to the black middle class around economic uplift, African American party members blended liberal ideas and conservative principles to advance viable alternative solutions. In doing so, they appealed to a general philosophy of self-help, notions of which, such as economic and social uplift, self-reliance and determination, and personal accountability, cut across ideological and partisan lines. As a number of scholars have discussed, it was an ideology often embraced by affluent and middle-class segments of the population as a method of challenging a crippling system of American racism. Even as increasing significance was placed on the role of the federal government in securing equality, African Americans continued to employ philosophies of self-help in their day-to-day lives.[53] In truth, while black capitalism was the administration's general effort to tap into this history, it also signified something much deeper for many within the Black Cabinet. They viewed their work as an attempt to reconcile the enlarged role of the federal government with the "inherent conservatism" of African Americans and traditional Republican Party principles.[54] Of particular interest were those "ordinary" middle-class black citizens, disillusioned with the failures of Democratic liberalism but equally dissatisfied with the anarchy of urban disorder. Black appointees looked for communities where self-help ideology thrived, and where black rebellion had manifested as a surging dedication to self-reliance, self-preservation, and minority economic growth. Or, as *Time* crassly observed, "Instead of incinerating their neighborhoods, many [African Americans] have begun concentrating on building them up."[55] The Nixon administration reasoned that although the black middle class was not the largest segment of the population, the size of the group would increase with economic incentives and targeted assistance. For the president, this certainly had political advantages. "Middle-class Americans didn't riot. They had something to lose, homes and families to protect," he opined, "Valuing good schools and law and order, middle-class blacks . . . should rally to Republican virtues."[56]

While black appointees strongly agreed with this line of thinking from the president, their racial loyalty also demanded a more nuanced response. In many ways this approach paralleled the attitudes in political scientist Ellen Boneparth's 1971 study of black middle-class businessmen. According to the respondents, individual success was significant insofar as it ameliorated conditions for the entire black community. The achievements of the middle class facilitated uplift for the "less fortunate," they argued, thereby linking

"black business" to economic and political developments in African American communities. Their attitudes, Boneparth concluded, not only reflected
an acute awareness of their privilege and the strength of the individual, but
also revealed an overwhelming belief in the linked fate of all African Americans.[57] Like Boneparth's black businessmen, the members of the Black Cabinet
viewed individual success and the achievements of the middle class as vital
to the progress of the entire community. In this sense, "getting a piece of the
action" was more than a catchy campaign slogan—for the appointees, black
capitalism implied a complicated set of beliefs based on shared racial history,
commitment to racial progress, and an embrace of traditional conservatism.
Accordingly, as liaisons for the Nixon administration, they sought African
Americans who embraced community and minority enterprise initiatives,
like the collaborative efforts between Harlem's Freedom National Bank and
the NAACP. Highlighting, funding, or even replicating these types of local
self-help projects allowed black officials to display the "logical" connection
between African American values and traditional Republican principles. Assessing the Harlem project, the *Cleveland Call and Post* eloquently captured
black Republican attitudes, writing that the goals "are not to get something for
nothing . . . but to get their own without having to ask someone else."[58]

In this sense, OMBE was a starting point for a much broader outreach
agenda built on minority enterprise, equal employment, and economic uplift.
Black appointees were determined to attack what they considered the fundamental roots of racial inequality. Thus, ten days after the OMBE announcement, the president tapped Arthur Fletcher as the assistant secretary of labor,
making him, as *Ebony* proclaimed, "one of the highest ranking Negroes in
the Republican administration." While speaking with reporters, he spoke of
his eagerness to join George Schultz's team: "I am happy with the direction
of the Nixon administration," he cheerfully remarked. "I hope I can make an
added contribution."[59] Within weeks, Fletcher was asked to join the twelve-
member interagency OMBE committee, which hoped to marshal his ideas on
black economic uplift and funding resources.[60] The president had long viewed
Fletcher as the embodiment of black capitalism, but more importantly, the
lifelong black Republican had provided much of the early inspiration for the
actual program.[61] Between 1965 and 1967, Fletcher launched the East Pasco
Cooperative Association, a "model self-help program" in the state of Washington, designed as an alternative to urban renewal (or, as Fletcher liked to
call it, "black removal"). Locals were encouraged to invest in community redevelopment by purchasing shares of their own neighborhood. This promoted
feelings of pride, ownership, and independence among community members,
Fletcher asserted. It was a form of "sweat equity" whereby black residents

would be invested in the success of the entire community. By 1968, East Pasco was thriving, complete with a shopping center, police station, credit union, and supermarket. Fletcher—now a city councilman—observed that towns-people had created their own vision of the community instead of relying on a mandate from the "bureaucratic" government. "Self-help, not hand-outs is the answer," he argued. Fletcher's philosophy and his self-help success propelled him into the spotlight, but it was his bid for lieutenant governor that made him a major player in Republican circles. Running an aggressive campaign, he championed philosophies of self-help, rejected liberal government anti-pov-erty programs, and spoke of his desire to "build a bridge" between the GOP and the black community. Many even wondered if they were watching the "next Ed Brooke."[62] The would-be statesman did not disappoint when he ap-peared before the Republican Platform Committee in July 1968—his proposal for a new kind of "action politics" impressed the board so much that his ideas were incorporated into the national civil rights plank. Additionally, Richard Nixon invited Fletcher to serve as a campaign advisor, and used many of the black Republican's ideas to enrich and broaden the idea of black capitalism. The press soon dubbed the black statesman the "Godfather of the GOP black capitalism plank."[63]

Consequently, by the time Fletcher arrived at the White House in April 1969, he came with a very public and highly focused agenda: to create an eco-nomic civil rights movement and end discrimination in employment.[64] Eco-nomic inequality was the fundamental problem faced by African Americans, he argued. He both scandalized and intrigued audiences when he repeatedly proposed that "new civil rights legislation" was "not relevant to the needs" of African Americans. "I feel we have achieved all we are going to through legislation," he reasoned. According to the Nixon official, wealth and capital-ism were the most important components in the movement for racial equal-ity. "If you have money you can send your children to the best public and private schools. . . . We are now entering the most difficult period of the civil rights struggle, the struggle for economic freedom."[65] Fletcher's line of ap-proach also equated Democratic liberalism with ineffectual government poli-cies, "empty promises," and poor solutions that ignored the economic plight of black citizens. Much like Ed Brooke, Fletcher did not dismiss all principles of liberalism; rather, his criticism stemmed from his belief that the Johnson ad-ministration had created "demeaning" programs that encouraged government dependency and intensified economic disparities between races. The nation needed firm employment and action-oriented, results-driven goals that would aid African Americans in obtaining "their fair share" of the national wealth.[66]

Fletcher's solution to the black community's racial and economic dilemmas came through the framework of the Labor Department; the result was the Philadelphia Plan, a policy that firmly introduced the concept of compensatory preferential treatment into the nation's structure. At its most basic level, the Philadelphia Plan was simple: its aim was to end discrimination by increasing the number of highly paid minority construction workers employed on federally funded projects. The White House initially plucked the idea from the Johnson administration: Executive Order 11246, issued in 1965, required government contractors to take "affirmative action" toward underrepresented minority employees. What's more, employers were forced to document these measures, lest they risk contract termination—a threat enforceable through the Office of Federal Contract Compliance (OFCC).[67] During 1966 and 1967, the labor department instituted a series of "experimental solutions" designed to test the new policy on union-controlled construction industries in St. Louis, San Francisco, Cleveland, and Philadelphia, where discrimination was rampant. Clusters of unions thrived on nepotism, rewarding family members and friends with lucrative jobs and "incidentally" preventing equal access to nonwhites.[68] In the rare event that black workers did make it through the complicated system, they were forced to wait for the union to admit them; as the NAACP bitterly complained, that would be like "letting George Wallace decide who is qualified to vote in Alabama." The unions aggressively resisted the implementation of the policy, ironically accusing the government of violating the Civil Rights Act of 1964. The comptroller general agreed, prematurely killing the Johnson administration's efforts.[69]

Just two years later, the Nixon administration announced that it was reviving the employment policy under the direction of Secretary of Labor George Schultz and Arthur Fletcher. Schultz—arguably a moderate on issues of race and civil rights—concluded that the Philadelphia Plan was an opportunity to force the "hiring halls" of construction to include more minority workers.[70] Political pragmatists in the White House appreciated Schultz's approach but also recognized that the policy was a political gold mine. Aside from opening high-wage positions to minorities, the Philadelphia Plan had the potential to enlarge and diversify the nation's workforce, lower overall construction costs, alleviate racial tensions in urban centers, and destroy the Democratic Party's tenuous coalitions—namely, organized labor and the civil rights establishment.[71] And although Fletcher undoubtedly recognized the political advantages of the policy, his personal investment stemmed from a place of deep anguish and experience. "The Philadelphia Plan was my baby," Fletcher fondly recalled in an interview. "There was no specific standard for equal opportunity. It was viewed as social engineering and not as a labor standard enforceable at law. So, one of my conditions for accepting the [assistant secretary of labor] job was that I could make equal opportunity a labor standard."[72]

On June 27, 1969, the administration launched its reinvigorated Philadelphia Plan; Fletcher unveiled the labor policy to the "City of Brotherly Love" with a forceful, yet thoughtful, set of remarks designed to convey the significance of the moment. "A vital freedom guaranteed by our Constitution is the right to equal participation in the economic processes of our society. . . . Segregation didn't occur naturally—it was imposed." In many ways, Fletcher's speech paralleled Lyndon Johnson's Howard University address delivered four years before; both men drew connections among freedom, opportunity, equality, and results, and recognized the challenge of institutional racism. Much like its predecessor, the revised Philadelphia Plan provided a new interpretation of "fair play" in the construction industry. All federal contractors receiving funding in excess of $500,000 were required to submit affirmative action plans. These goals and timetables, Fletcher warned, were to be submitted *before* the contracts were rewarded and were non-negotiable. Failure to meet the "established standard" would result in a bid rejection.[73] "The Federal government has an obligation to see that every citizen has an equal chance at the most basic freedom of all—*the right to succeed*," Fletcher insisted. The Philadelphia Plan, then, was the "most fair, economical and effective way" to correct deep-rooted inequality.[74] In issuing the mandate, the Department of Labor bypassed any mention of color-blindness in racial equality, implying that compensatory preferential treatment was, in fact, constitutional as it concretely advanced racial freedom and equality. So, while the Philadelphia Plan was simple in concept, it was both complicated and controversial in its principles. In seeking to eradicate institutionalized racism—generations of discrimination ingrained in the fabric of the nation—Fletcher promoted a solution that prevented discrimination before it happened, by privileging underrepresented minority groups.[75] Predictably, the same angry foes that opposed the plan in 1967 quickly revived their "righteous" opposition in 1969. For Fletcher, this meant facing more than legal challenges—it also signaled a violent resistance, which he quickly encountered in September 1969. During a visit to Chicago for a series of OFCC hearings, Nixon labor officials found their courtroom invaded by five hundred hard hat–wearing construction workers who noisily disrupted the proceedings, forcing a trial postponement. The next morning, Fletcher was forced to spend the day hiding in his hotel room as two thousand rowdy unionists crowded the courthouse—blocking all entrances, swigging beer, singing "God Bless America," and occasionally yelling "no coalitions!" As witnesses and lawyers approached the doorways, they were "grabbed, punched and shoved" by the angry crowd. One man was badly beaten in a case of mistaken identity as his attackers had confused him for Fletcher. Finally, a full-blown riot erupted when a group of black men attempted to force their way into the building; not only did the bloodthirsty mob seize and beat these witnesses, they also attacked Chicago police officers, smashed cars, and defaced the surrounding public property.[76] Congress, in contrast, did not resort to such tactics; they did, however, launch an ugly "hypocrisy-laden" war over the Philadelphia Plan. In December 1969, Democratic Senator Robert Byrd of Virginia added a rider to an appropriations bill that would have invalidated the labor policy.[77] Ultimately, the Nixon administration "muscled" its opponents into acquiescence—the Byrd amendment was defeated 208 to 156 in the House, and the Senate later voted to accept the decision, 39 to 29.[78]

By February 1970, Fletcher and other labor officials had revised the Philadelphia Plan yet again, drastically expanding it to apply to all federal contractors across industries. Likewise, he also authored a "Washington Plan" aimed at making the District of Columbia's construction workforce 45 percent African American by 1975.[79] Fletcher's federal appointment was a large victory for black Republicans and African Americans alike; but more than that, it represented the impact potential of the black appointees—Fletcher had, after all, assumed a major policy-making role that deeply shifted how equality in the nation was understood. As Fletcher noted in April 1970, "I have access to life at the White House and to the decision makers there."[80] Such access, he argued, would facilitate the ultimate goal: complete economic equality for African Americans by 1980. Indeed, as he revealed in a speech to the St. Louis Urban League in May, he had already met with the president to discuss a ten-year plan for economic liberation, a proposal that had the strong backing of Schultz, as well. With the deafening roars and cheers from the enthusiastic crowd encouraging him, Fletcher closed with a booming proclamation: "If we can put a man on the moon, then both parties should be able to end economic discrimination in the next decade!"[81]

The Philadelphia Plan fell well within the boundaries of black capitalism, complementing the economic empowerment vision of OMBE, and providing another avenue for African Americans to achieve increased economic and social status.[82] "This is the chance to give the black worker [an opportunity] to put decent clothing instead of burdens on the backs of his family," argued Fletcher. "This gives him a chance to put food into their mouths and books into the hands of his kids. This is the golden opportunity for black workers to retrieve their manliness and family tradition."[83] Indeed, within the construct of black capitalism, the Philadelphia Plan, in theory, provided an economic base for working-class African Americans to advance to middle-class status, while OMBE, with a parallel agenda, strengthened and expanded the existing black middle class. As Commerce Secretary Maurice Stans proudly told *Jet* in April 1970, OMBE awarded more than $16 million to black businessmen in its first year of operation, and planned to hand out more than $100 million in contracts in 1971. Coordinating for all of the agencies and departments, OMBE delivered a total of $200 million in assistance to minority businessmen in 1969 and $315 million in 1970. "We are seeking to encourage minority manufacturers to participate in the annual federal procurement program," Stans eagerly remarked. "The government . . . provides a readily accessible market for newly organized businesses."[84] Likewise, black capitalism appeared to have somewhat of a tangible impact on the economic success of African Americans; as Boneparth's study on black businessmen illustrated, nearly 75 percent of participants declared an increase in economic opportunities, attributing the shift to various factors including greater availability of capital, educational and training advancements, protests from civil rights groups, government pressure, and assistance from white businessmen. More than 15 percent of respondents expressed overwhelming approval of both the "concept and the actual program of black capitalism," which they recognized as the "need and ability that exists in the black community to run businesses," and the "necessity for blacks to control economic resources in their own communities." Progress had been achieved in a number of areas, they argued, including an increased availability of credit, stronger enforcement of equal employment opportunity laws, and access to government contracts.[85]

Still, despite setting the groundwork for an economic and political uplift movement, African American Republican officials continued to struggle enormously with their party and their racial community. Black appointees were stunned by complaints over black capitalism. For instance, some African Americans argued that they could never trust the program since anything with Richard Nixon's name attached "must be a political trick." Others, like Federal Reserve board governor Andrew Brimmer, argued vehemently against the initiative, suggesting it was a form of racial separatism, which would only serve to marginalize the black community. As one disgruntled businessman complained, "No one ever stuck 'white' in front of the word 'capitalism.'" A surprising number of black men and women discounted public assistance in general; that is, they argued that federal aid implied government dependency, which they viewed as dangerous since "the government starts out helping people and ends up supporting them forever." Even among self-proclaimed conservative African Americans, black capitalism was viewed with some hesitation. Many called for a limited government role, stressing that the Nixon

administration should apply increased pressure to the private sector to facilitate the assimilation of black businesses. As one New York businessman
rationalized: "This is . . . a capitalistic country which means that most of the
wealth is owned by private sources. . . . Blacks should look to an alliance with
private industry. . . . If black business has a government-based foundation, it
will always be more socialistically oriented than traditional business, and . . .
wouldn't be business. . . . Private enterprise should do it—not Uncle Sam."[86]
Likewise, many expressed frustration with black capitalism's general rate of
success.[87] By April 1970, African Americans owned only 2.5 percent of the
nation's 5.4 million businesses, and although the size of the black middle class
had increased since the 1960s, many still found it nearly impossible to obtain
loans, contracts, and insurance as entrepreneurs. Black Congressman John
Conyers of Detroit railed against the administration, demanding significant
change in industrial and corporate racism and increases in employment and
manpower training programs. *Time* suggested that black capitalism was just
another "catchy and promising phase" as it had failed to produce substantive results. For members of the Black Cabinet and other black Republican
advocates of economic civil rights, such accusations were deeply unsettling;
as Floyd McKissick complained, "Black capitalism has not failed. It was never
given a chance."[88]

In truth, while black capitalism did have a significantly mixed record, it
was more expansive and influential than most realized. For instance, critics
of the program rarely linked the administration's involvement with higher
education with the notion of black capitalism; and yet, as Bob Brown observed
during an interview, "promoting colleges was a priority"—inextricably linked
to black progress and economic liberation. The Nixon aide devoted a significant amount of time fusing the notion of black economic independence with
higher education. Specifically, throughout the 1970s, he steadily lobbied for increased federal funding to historically black institutions. In doing so, he forced
the administration to examine a serious financial disparity between black and
white universities, and as *Jet* cheered, "generated new official interest in black
education."[89] In October 1969, after discovering that black colleges received
only 3 percent of the $4 billion allocated annually to higher education, Brown
convinced the president to take an active interest in the situation. In the spring
of 1970, Nixon held a gathering with nearly a dozen black college presidents.
Arranged by Brown, the session afforded the educators with a valuable private
forum to voice their concerns and resolve their grievances with the administration.[90] During the meeting, Nixon appeared greatly interested in the fate of
black colleges. Were "segregated" colleges necessary in a rapidly desegregating nation? Or should such schools be "phased out?" The college presidents

fiercely asserted that black institutions were a vital necessity, especially in racially polarizing times, as they provided African Americans with broad access to higher education and served as cultural and historical lodestones.[91] The administration appeared somewhat genuine in its commitment, appointing a White House special advisor on black colleges and issuing a forty-five-page report titled *Federal Agencies and Black Colleges*.[92] Significantly, during a July 1970 press conference on campus unrest and violence, Robert Finch and Bob Brown announced that black colleges would receive an additional $30 million in federal funding annually to address their unique needs.[93] In private, Brown also negotiated millions in future earmarks for scholarships, salaries, campus programs and resources, and overall building construction.[94] Between 1969 and 1973, the administration increased federal funding to black colleges by more than 230 percent ($129 million to $400 million).[95]

Indeed, Brown succeeded in creating an institutionalized pipeline that provided significant access to the administration, while merging black interests with those of the Republican Party. The White House also established a new kind of relationship with dozens of black colleges, using the schools in order to directly recruit talented African American students. Black appointees saw this as an opportunity to mix education with employment and economic opportunity. In this sense, many within the administration believed that they were facilitating the growth of the black middle class by providing black students with access to education, resources, and future high-level employment opportunities. James Farmer, for instance, instituted a policy at HEW that reserved an "equitable share" of management intern slots for minority students, many of whom hailed from black colleges. In essence, this allowed Farmer to place these students in federal policy-making positions, since management interns were eligible after graduation for midlevel appointments at HEW.[96] Along similar lines, African American administration officials established a Black Minority Recruitment program, traveling to schools like Clark College in Georgia and California State College and encouraging students to work for the federal government. As a result, by 1971 African Americans comprised 18 percent of the college-trainee pool at the General Services Administration (GSA) and 52 percent of the Training and Advancement Program (TAP), an initiative designed to facilitate "upward mobility" within the federal government.[97] In fact, by brokering a mutually beneficial working relationship with predominantly black schools, Brown had federally institutionalized minority advancement, paralleling the other black-capitalism initiatives including the Philadelphia Plan and OMBE.

Black Republican appointees found their agenda further reinvigorated by a black economic growth spurt of sorts. As the nation moved into the 1970s, more and more African Americans pursued higher education; and as they graduated, they found that they had greater access to economic and employment opportunities. Between 1960 and 1972, the number of black students enrolled in college increased from 10 percent to 18 percent, comprising 7 percent of the nation's total student body. Many of these students found careers with the federal government, while others became entrepreneurs or sought white-collar employment. Those without college degrees also found increased access to economic and employment opportunities through Philadelphia Plan policies, the Small Business Association, and OMBE specialized initiatives. In this way, black capitalism promoted entrance into a black middle class over the course of the 1970s.

Thus black capitalism, for all its failings, began to reap social and political rewards as early as 1970.[98] Although it experienced a difficult start, Arthur Fletcher's "baby"—the Philadelphia Plan—managed to boost minority manpower in the construction industry by more than 12 percent in a two-year period. *Ebony* was elated over the employment and economic developments of the policy. Singing his praises, the magazine anointed Fletcher the "Watchdog of Labor," triumphantly declaring him "one of the most powerful men in the Nixon industry, irrespective of color."[99] The OMBE umbrella widened considerably during the 1970s, and the administration anticipated that as the economic status of African Americans improved, many would "take advantage of new opportunities" made accessible by the civil rights legislation of the 1960s. Indeed, the Small Business Association (SBA) provided $217 million in minority enterprise loans in 1971, while 710 black firms received government contracts worth $58 million. Under OMBE, black citizens also received a number of training opportunities; the residents of Roosevelt City, Alabama, for example, received law enforcement materials, resources, and funding for skill development purposes.[100] African Americans also received greater access to credit and loans as the number of black-owned banks nearly doubled between 1969 and 1971, increasing total black lending power by 33 percent. Likewise, under the federal procurement program, the government purchased $200 million worth of minority services by 1973. For example, Garland Foods, Inc., a black-owned company from Dallas, Texas, earned a $5.2 million contract to supply the military with canned and smoked meat; likewise, that same year, SBA supplied Wood Oldsmobile Company of Washington, D.C., with a contract worth $200,000 to repair and maintain 1,700 government vehicles. In all, Brown and the Black Cabinet were responsible for pumping more than $1 billion into black colleges, businesses, and communities.[101]

Still, as many scholars have correctly suggested, the opportunities afforded by black capitalism were beyond the reach of many African Americans.[102] The economic outreach effort, did, however, work incredibly well for specific, targeted segments of the black community. For example, Reverend Leon Sullivan received $10.7 million through OMBE to expand his POIC program into forty cities over an eighteen-month period.[103] Former college and professional athletes were also among the prime beneficiaries of black economic outreach—in 1969 alone, more than one thousand new "black athlete-entrepreneurs" opened businesses with the help of the Nixon administration. Basketball star and Nixon pal Wilt Chamberlain received federal funds to support his franchise of Los Angeles diners, as did former Pittsburgh Steeler Brady Keys. In fact, the football player's "All-Pro Chicken" was popular enough to merit 150 franchises in eleven cities by 1970—many of which were opened by other black athletes with the help of federal financing. For black athlete-entrepreneurs, their degrees, reputation, and personal finances afforded them a certain kind of privilege that—combined with government support—created favorable conditions for entrepreneurial success. Jim Brown—the actor and former Cleveland Browns star—met regularly with White House officials to discuss OMBE funding for his Black Economic Union (BEU), an organization that provided financing for potential black entrepreneurs.[104] During a congenial meeting in August 1972 with Bob Brown, Stan Scott, John Wilks, John Ehrlichman (head of domestic policy), and Nixon, Jim Brown warmly expressed his appreciation for the administration, commenting, "I think you are moving in the areas in which blacks should be concerned . . . self-determination in the business world." After the meeting, Nixon instructed Scott and Bob Brown to set up a session between BEU and the Commerce Department in order to establish a permanent partnership.[105] On a community level, a number of black men and women took advantage of the employment, training, and funding available through federal outreach initiatives. Brown suggested the White House capitalize on this by inviting groups of successful black entrepreneurs to chat with the president. "These men exemplify action instead of mere rhetoric," Brown encouraged. "Just what the President wants to support." Approving the recommendation, Nixon hosted at least three events with "leaders in ghetto economic development" in 1971. Among those honored were DeForrest Brown of Cleveland (Hough Development Corporation), Lou Harris of Los Angeles (Operation BOOTSTRAP), and Bernie Gifford of Rochester (FIGHT). White businessmen who helped the black capitalists were also saluted: Richard Tullis of Harris Intertype, Ruth and Elliott Handler of the Mattel Corporation, and the senior executive team of XEROX.[106]

Moreover, the notion of an economic civil rights movement appeared to penetrate African American political consciousness throughout the 1970s. Although they often criticized the Nixon administration, many prominent black periodicals acknowledged that the Black Cabinet exerted significant influence in some areas of federal policy-making. Between 1971 and 1974, *Ebony* repeatedly listed Bob Brown, Arthur Fletcher, Sam C. Jackson, Ed Brooke, and Whitney Young among its annual "100 Most Influential Black Americans."[107] The editors had two criteria for making their decision: "Does the nominee affect, in a decisive way . . . the lives, thinking and actions of large segments of the nation's black population? Does the nominee command widespread national influence among blacks, and/or is the nominee unusually influential with those whites whose policies and practices significantly affect a large number of blacks?"[108] Stan S. Scott, a communications aide in the White House, highlighted the media's developing interest in the influence of the black appointees. While tracking periodical references in 1971, he celebrated the positive "maximum exposure" given to black outreach programs initiated by members of the Black Cabinet. The newspapers with wide circulations carried dozens of glowing headlines and stories that covered the Philadelphia Plan, recent black federal appointments, minority enterprise, federal aid to black colleges and black universities, and Nixon's meetings with black businessmen and civil rights leaders.[109] Arguably, the NAACP offered the most surprising about-face with regard to Nixon programs. In July 1971, in front of an audience of thousands, Bishop Steven Spottswood—who one year earlier denounced the White House as "anti-Negro"—declared that the administration had earned "cautious and limited approval" due in large part to the success of a number of federal economic and employment efforts.[110]

Like the NAACP, Whitney Young also offered coded criticism and support for the administration's economic civil rights movement. During a 1970 press conference, the NUL leader declared that the words and deeds of Richard Nixon left a "bitterness that must now be transcended." And yet, the NUL head qualified his remark just a few minutes later, commenting, "As critical as I have been of the Administration's actions, I do admit that there are some signs that elements of this Administration are moving forward to bring about this change."[111] Indeed, Young was a part of this "element," quietly advising the White House on issues of African American concern. His criticisms of the White House were tempered by his diplomatic faith in the administration and its black appointees. Specifically, Young recognized the inherent value in negotiating and working pragmatically with a Republican federal government. When the *New York Times* offered a spread exploring whether Young should be called an "Oreo Cookie," "Whitey Young," "Uncle Whitney," or a genuine civil rights leader, based on his work with the Nixon administrations and previous presidents, the NUL dismissed the chatter, arguing: "Nobody's who's working for black people is a moderate. . . . We're *all* militants in different ways. I can't afford the luxury of a completely dogmatic position that says, 'I won't make any compromises,' because I'm dealing with the real world.'"[112] In addition to working with the black-appointee task force, Young also worked directly with the administration, collaborating on a number of black-capitalism programs. On December 22, 1970, Young and several NUL officials met with President Nixon, Bob Brown, Arthur Fletcher, Sam Jackson, and Samuel Simmons to discuss the "unique capabilities of private, non-profit local organizations like the Urban League."[113] Pulling out a series of visual charts and reports, Young carefully outlined his theory, identifying $70 million in future collaborative efforts between NUL and various departments and agencies. The White House officials were impressed; within hours of the meeting, Nixon ordered all members of his cabinet to appoint a liaison to work directly with the organization as a means of exploring the "ways in which the League and its network of local affiliates can . . . help the Departments carry out their human resources programs." As the civil rights group envisioned it, the league's "special capabilities" would be used to monitor, evaluate, and operate a variety of social service programs with funds from federal agencies and departments. The relationship should not be a "rhetorical partnership," Nixon maintained, "but a real one" that would facilitate the development of new opportunities for African Americans and reflect the administration's "steady as you go" approach to policy and programs.[114]

In truth, the relationship was more than a partnership for racial progress. Indeed, the collaboration was a radical endeavor that allowed both the administration and NUL to broker influence. For the administration—particularly black Republicans and liberal and moderate staffers—this was an opportunity to appeal directly to a target group of African Americans and gain valuable publicity. For the Urban League, the relationship provided a means of obtaining valuable federal funds, influence in determining social policy, and an opportunity to further their civil rights agenda. As legal historian Dennis Dickerson rightly observes, the initial success of this relationship had less to do with savvy political skills than with the "enormous importance of the black freedom struggle."[115] For those African Americans—both in the White House and in the Urban League—such a partnership was, as Whitney Young declared, "a new start, a new day."[116]

Within weeks, the Nixon administration offered the civil rights organization over $21 million in federal contracts harnessed from eight government departments. "Judging by the tabs that the federal government picks up," *Ebony* slyly observed, "the marriage is mutually beneficial." Indeed, the Department of Commerce offered $140,000 for a project related to the U.S. Census, while the Department of Agriculture provided $430,000 to guarantee rural housing loans for NUL-approved applicants. Still, many of the programs served a dual purpose—they effectively introduced Republican ideas and initiatives into hard-to-reach black areas.[117] Proposals, like the one received in June 1971 from the league's southern office, were highly desirable, largely for this reason. The organization's suggestion for a yearlong series of economic education workshops in black localities in twelve southern states was well received; as Robert Brown commented in his evaluation, "The Administration has a strong interest in efforts of this nature." The seminars, approved with funding from the Departments of Labor and Education, outlined and promoted Nixon's revenue-sharing plan. Moreover, administration officials participated in the session, studying black opinions and offering insights on policy misconceptions.[118] The relationship suffered a devastating blow with the unexpected death of Whitney Young in March 1971. "I have lost a friend— black America has lost a gifted and commanding champion of its just cause," wrote Richard Nixon. "And this Nation has lost one of the most compassionate and principled leaders . . . since whites from Europe and blacks from Africa began building . . . toward the American dream."[119]

Despite the president's solemn avowal that the "effort launched so ably by Whitney Young will go forward," both sides began to chip away at the partnership almost immediately. As early as May, NUL officials accused the White House of discriminatory bureaucratic treatment; they demanded that the administration prove its loyalty in the wake of Young's death. For its part, the Nixon administration seemed genuinely bewildered by the accusations but promised to investigate.[120] Bob Brown attempted to repair the damage by arranging a meeting between Nixon and newly appointed NUL director Vernon Jordan: "We hope to explore," the White House aide stated, "the future of the Urban League and its relationship with this Administration." During the June 28 meeting, Republicans reassured Jordan that the "pertinent" departments and agencies were "responding positively" to the league's proposals. The group also discussed voting rights, the Family Assistance Plan (FAP) and NUL's future workshops on revenue sharing.[121] Likewise, at the urging of the black appointees, George Schultz gave the league's keynote address at its national conference in July 1971. In his speech, he reiterated the administration's commitment to the organization and to African American uplift. "Steadiness of policy leads to steadiness of growth," he told his audience. "This applies to race relations and black economic growth and progress as well." Schultz (now the director of the Office of Management and Budget—OMB) reminded the delegates that the Nixon administration viewed free-market enterprise as the key to racial equality. Black independence, then, would occur by returning "power and responsibilities to states, localities, and individuals." By suggesting that black liberation was "logically" in sync with conservative principles, Schultz diverted potential criticisms over the idea of "states rights"—a historically divisive topic.

The Republican official closed by calling on the memory of Arthur Fletcher's 1970 speech to the Urban League: "For the most part, we have the civil rights legislation that we require," Schultz reasoned. "The need is not for new programs or prohibitions but to make the ones we have work." By pitching the government's ideas in this manner, the OMB official could easily rationalize local hometown plans as black-controlled "hometown solutions," depict anti-busing approaches as federally funded "biracial state advisory committees," and propose welfare reform as a black self-empowerment initiative. The administration's effort appeared to mollify the NUL, as the league's officials showed renewed enthusiasm for future collaborations. "There is no question we are getting heard," Vernon Jordan later declared. "We have been able to disagree with them on basic issues and continue a creative partnership."[122]

In sum, as historian Robert Weems argues, the period between 1969 and 1973 witnessed an explosion of "unprecedented national interest in promoting substantive African American economic progress."[123] And to some extent, the Nixon administration contributed to this "unprecedented national interest" in black economic civil rights. Black appointees ushered in an agenda that penetrated the economic consciousness of the nation; writing in 1973, for example, both *Time* and *Jet* attributed the jump in black business revenue to an "infusion of federal funds" from the black capitalism programs.[124] *Black Enterprise* founder Earl Graves declared that the surge indicated that a number of "obstacles to black business ownerships" had been defeated. This, *Time* argued, provided the nation with "another confirmation of the growing economic strength of the black middle class."[125]

Members of the Black Cabinet hoped that through this new national interest in black economics, they could then appeal to a distinct set of amalgamated conservative and liberal principles, and thereby begin to reintegrate the Republican Party and attract substantial portions of the black electorate. Specifically, they attempted to appeal to the nation's black middle class—a group that had more than doubled its size in a fifteen-year period, surging from 12 percent of the African American population in 1960 to 30 percent by 1974.[126] African Americans could be found in corporations, banks, white-collar offices, government buildings, Congress, the classrooms of elite universities, and increasingly, even in the white suburbs.[127] Black homeowner Tom Allen of Seattle recalled: "15 years ago, you couldn't beg, borrow or steal a place outside the central area even if you had the money. . . . Today, if your money is green enough, you can live anywhere."[128] In this particular sense, the black middle class represented a "decisive break with tradition," drawing their inspiration from the civil rights movement, and imbued with a new sense of "pride, confidence, and political skill." This was the sentiment into which black Republicans attempted to tap. Echoing this feeling, Arthur Fletcher argued that resiliency, optimism, and strength had propelled the civil rights movement through the first half of the twentieth century; he proposed that African Americans' new economic path coupled with traditional resiliency would also drive the economic revolution of the second half of the twentieth century.[129]

And, as scholars like Cornel West have argued, as some individuals succeeded in their upward mobility, many did embrace the rhetoric and program of black Republicans. Indeed, some African Americans found appeals in black capitalism, while others found that their needs and aspirations exceeded the scope of Democratic liberalism; more specifically, while African Americans embraced racially liberal principles, some were eager for an alternative to the solutions offered by the Democratic Party. Arguably, not only did the civil rights movement transform the social fabric of the nation, it also created a new set of middle-class values and sensibilities.[130]

## Conclusion

Nixon's black appointees, wrote Milton Viorst of the *New York Times*, "are but mere window-dressing—with large titles but little influence—in an Administration bent on a 'Southern strategy.'" The reporter continued his brutal assessment, lamenting the apparent racial betrayals of, among others, Arthur Fletcher, James Farmer, and Bob Brown—who received perhaps the harshest critique: "Some would say that Brown . . . only serves a symbolic purpose," Viorst concluded. "In fact, he is not even President Nixon's 'house nigger.' That distinction belongs to Leonard Garment . . . who is white."[131] Significantly, criticisms like those of the *New York Times* were not unusual during this period, for in truth, the administration's forays into areas such as desegregation, voting rights, and urban disorder rankled innumerable African Americans, leading to a general distrust of the Republican government.[132] However, Viorst's portrayal of the members of the Black Cabinet failed to consider the heavy pressure of competing racial and political loyalties; neither did it acknowledge the power and influence of the appointees within the White House.

During the Nixon administration, the members of the Black Cabinet enacted a broad economic agenda for racial uplift. Under the umbrella of black capitalism, the officials advanced initiatives that joined ideas of racial liberalism with traditionally conservative principles. In doing so, they embraced the civil rights successes of the 1960s, but proposed an alternative economic civil rights agenda for the final step in the struggle for black liberation. While major public and private challenges marked their efforts, ultimately the Nixon appointees aided in the expansion of the modern black middle class. And, as Bob Brown detailed, the group institutionalized a "direct link" between African Americans and the GOP, providing the administration with access to the "ideas and problems of the black community and a vehicle for dealing with them."[133]

To be sure, Nixon's African American appointees also had an impact on party outreach, successfully convincing the administration to woo targeted segments of the black community.[134] In particular, members of the Black Cabinet launched a collaborative endeavor with Harry Dent to broaden the GOP's "New Republican Majority." Their political outreach message carried a theme of economic civil rights; by June 1970, spokesman Arthur Fletcher had reached more than 5.6 million constituents.[135] Their efforts, while varied, appeared to have had an impact. Despite the contradictory behaviors of the administration, the Minorities Division of the RNC could still boast of amassing important electoral victories on the state and local levels.[136] Likewise, a Harris Survey found that between 1968 and 1970, African Americans self-identifying as Republicans jumped from 7 percent to 17 percent. Gallup found equally significant results: though Nixon's nationwide black approval ratings were abysmal in 1970, his positive support among black southerners hovered at 42 percent—a figure that held well into the mid-1970s.[137] The group witnessed an astonishing increase in black Republican organizational activity with the establishment of the Black Elected Republican Officials (BERO), the National Black Silent Majority (NBSM), and the National Council of Concerned Afro American Republicans (NCCAR).[138] Likewise, during the 1972 Republican National Convention, the party passed a resolution granting the National Black Republican Council (NBRC) affiliation status with the national committee. As *Ebony* declared, "[B]lack Republicans around the country finally have a solid [affiliated] organization."[139]

Certainly, however, the turmoil of Republican politics would continue to reemerge, especially in the post-Watergate era. Still, the Black Cabinet had a lasting influence and, to a certain extent, a role in advancing their alternative economic, social, and political movement throughout the 1970s. As *Ebony* observed on the eve of Democratic president-elect Jimmy Carter's inauguration, "The Nixon-Ford years will be over—and so will the prime time for GOP black achievers in politics." Still, the black periodical called on its audience to acknowledge, "one last time," the African American Republicans who "struggled against the odds to bring some hope and relief to their people.[140]

# Notes

1. George Wallace proved to be the exception, as he showed no interest in wooing black voters through the magazine. Dick Gregory's advertisement included a personal statement and pictures from rallies. The subheader read: "On November 5th write in or vote for Dick Gregory." Citizens for Humphrey–Muskie produced an ad featuring a jovial Hubert Humphrey, surrounded by cheering members of the black community. "On November 5 you will have two choices," the announcement stated. "Vote for Hubert Humphrey and you'll help elect the right man President. Don't vote and you'll help elect the wrong one" ("Message from Dick Gregory," and "Citizens for Humphrey-Muskie," paid political advertisements, *Jet*, 7 November 1968).

2. "Nixon-Agnew Campaign Committee," paid political advertisement, *Jet*, 7 November 1968.

3. "The Birth Pangs of Black Capitalism," *Time*, 18 October 1968.

4. Nixon was offended by a question that probed whether he planned a "great sweep of Negroes . . . from government posts" after the election. "Not only do I not envision it," the politician angrily wrote, "but I find it somewhat disturbing that such a question could be seriously posed" ("Nixon Says No Clean Sweep of Blacks," *Jet*, 7 November 1968; Doris E. Saunders, "Confetti," *Chicago Daily Defender*, 18 November 1968).

5. Hubert Humphrey also advocated for expanded economic opportunities for African Americans. For more information, please see historian Timothy Thurber's work on Humphrey: *The Politics of Equality: Hubert H. Humphrey and the African American Freedom Struggle* (New York: Columbia University Press, 1999). See also Robert E. Weems Jr. with Lewis A. Randolph, *Business in Black and White: American Presidents & Black Entrepreneurs in the Twentieth Century* (New York: New York University Press, 2009), 89–109.

6. "In the 'New' Politics," *Time*, 7 June 1968.

7. William Walker, "Down the Big Road," *Call and Post*, 2 November 1968.

8. The phrase "law and order" carried an implicit message: racial peace would be maintained through repressive means devoid of justice. As Edward Brooke observed, the phrase implied "police-state attitudes toward urban problems" and had "racist undertones." Along similar lines, the *New York Times* suggested that law and order was geared toward the white-backlash crowd as it promised an end to rioting while serving as a reminder to "keep Negroes in their place" (John Henry Cutler, *Ed Brooke: Biography of a Senator* [New York: Bobbs-Merrill, 1972], 311; Thomas A. Johnson, "Alienating the Negro Vote," *New York Times*, 18 August 1968).

9. Black Republicans appeared angriest over Nixon's selection of his vice-presidential running mate, Spiro T. Agnew, a candidate they had vigorously supported just two years prior. But between 1967 and 1968, Agnew slowly alienated Maryland's black population. Initially, his early attacks on black militants (like H. Rap Brown) and rioters were applauded by some civil rights organizations, including the NAACP. But disagreements over fiscal budgets, insensitive racial statements, and clashes with black

college students eventually soured the relationship. Moreover, in the wake of Martin Luther's King Jr.'s death and the April 1968 riots, Agnew issued a vicious public state-ment denouncing black militants and skewing moderate black leaders as "cowards." Interestingly, Agnew thought he was "committing political suicide" by launching the attack; piles of fan mail from all over the nation quickly convinced him otherwise. As historian Gary Wills observes, Agnew's "tough statements" on the Kerner Report, "Cadillacs," and "shooting looters" quickly anointed him the new spokesman for "law and order" and white backlash. For more information, see "Spiro Agnew: The King's Taster," *Time*, 14 November 1969; Garry Wills, *Nixon Agonistes: The Crisis of the Self-Made Man* (Boston: Houghton Mifflin, 1970), 280–91; and Rhonda Y. Wil-liams, "Black Women, Urban Politics, and Engendering Black Power," in *The Black Power Movement: Rethinking the Civil Rights–Black Power Era*, ed. Joseph E. Peniel (New York: Routledge, 2006), 91–92, 307. For black Republican opinions on Nixon, see Nicholas Horrock, "Area GOP Negroes: 'Ouch,'" *Washington Daily*, 8 August 1968.

10. Many of Nixon's black critics argued that rejecting black voters was a foolish idea. Indeed, in the 1960 presidential election, black voters had provided the mar-gin of victory needed for John F. Kennedy to squeak by with a victory over Richard Nixon. The Republican politician received 52 percent of the white vote in the 1960 race, whereas John F. Kennedy collected only 48 percent. However, 68 percent of the black electorate pulled the lever for the Democratic nominee, providing just enough room to win the entire election. Interestingly, the 1960 loss inspired Barry Goldwater to "go hunting where the ducks are," *and* encouraged Ray Bliss's moderate "Big City, Big Tent" approach to politics. For more information, see Johnson, "Alienating the Ne-gro Vote," *New York Times*, 18 August 1968; Voter Strategy Reports of the Republican National Committee, 1961–1971, in Stanley S. Scott Papers, Gerald Ford Presidential Library, University of Michigan, Ann Arbor (hereafter SSS Papers); and Clarence L. Townes, Jr. Papers, Special Collections, Virginia Commonwealth University (hereafter CLT Papers).

11. Jackie Robinson to Barry Goldwater, 5 September 1968, in *First Class Citizenship: The Civil Rights Letters of Jackie Robinson*, ed. Michael G. Long (New York: Times Books, 2007), 282–84.

12. Black Republicans were not the only members of the African American commu-nity to express cautious support for Richard Nixon in the months following the elec-tion. Both Roy Wilkins of the National Association for the Advancement of Colored People (NAACP) and Whitney Young of the National Urban League (NUL) expressed their desire to work with the new administration and find an amicable solution to the problems of urban disorder and racial inequality ("Blacks Have Mixed Reaction to Nixon," *New York Amsterdam News*, 16 November 1968).

13. *Election Analysis: 1968 and the Black American Voter*, report by Minorities Divi-sion, Republican National Committee, 12 January 1969, Folder "Election Analysis 1968 and the Black American Vote," CLT Papers.

14. Irving A. Williamson, "Secretary Fletcher Goes to the White House," uniden-tified newspaper article [St. Louis, Mo.], 4 June 1970, all in Box 88, Folder "Arthur

Fletcher," WHCF (White House Central Files), SMOF (Staff Member and Office Files), Leonard Garment (hereafter Garment Files), Richard Nixon Presidential Library, National Archives and Records Administration, College Park, Maryland (hereafter Nixon Library).

15. This essay focuses on the stories of a core group of black Republican appointees as a representative sample. By no means is theirs the *entire* story; rather the individuals in this particular study highlight the major themes and battles faced by the larger black Republican coalition. To cover each and every narrative would be an undertaking worthy of its own large project since Richard Nixon appointed hundreds of African Americans during his tenure as president. By 1972, there were 156 senior-level black appointees in the Nixon administration. By the time the president resigned in August 1974, black employees comprised more than 16 percent of the federal workforce. For the sake of comparison, sixty-three African Americans were appointed to top-level positions during the Johnson administration, including Robert Weaver, the first black member of a presidential cabinet (see Stan Scott to Lerone Bennett, memo on black appointees, 18 December 1972, Box 3, Folder "Black Appointees 1971," SSS Papers).

16. "Black GOP Group Raps Nixon on Cabinet Picks," *Daily Defender*, 17 December 1968.

17. Also included: New York lawyer Samuel R. Pierce; Chicago Welfare director William Robinson; Cleveland businessman Charles Lucas; and Leadership Conference of Africa director Theodore R. Brown ("What Blacks Can Expect from Nixon," *Ebony*, January 1969).

18. Reportedly, Richard Nixon offered Ed Brooke the position of U.S. attorney general. Brooke refused to confirm or deny; nonetheless, the black press and many within the African American community *assumed* and *hoped* it to be true. The claim merits further archival inquiry, given that there is ample evidence that Nixon offered Brooke a number of high-ranking positions between 1969 and 1974. Moreover, as the senator mused, "I was even given some consideration for the [Supreme] Court . . . strangely." Taped conversations between Nixon and his advisors confirm Brooke's claim. Unaware that he was being scouted, the Massachusetts politician told a Nixon aide that he was "too young to sit and rock. . . . I wouldn't give up my Senate seat for the world" (please see "A New Administration Takes Shape," *Time*, 20 December 1968; Edward W. Brooke, *Bridging the Divide: My Life* [New Brunswick, N.J.: Rutgers University Press, 2007], 199; John Wesley Dean, *The Rehnquist Choice:* [New York: Simon and Schuster, 2002], 53–54; and White House Tapes Nos. 576–11, 577–3, 9–93, Nixon Library).

19. Brooke later revealed that he felt that a cabinet position would limit his political independence, his "free voice," and his ability to be his "own man." Brooke's own musings, speeches, and writings also indicate that he may have rejected the positions because he did not want to limit himself to "stereotypical" black issues ("Black Lawmakers in Congress," *Ebony*, February 1971, Box 137, Folder 3 ["Minorities Activities"], Garment Files).

20. "Nixon and Brooke," *Chicago Defender*, 4 December, 1968; "Cabinet Post Declined by Sen. Brooke," *New Journal and Guide*, 7 December 1968; "Senate Holds

Brooke, He Rejects Cabinet HUD Offer of Nixon," *New Pittsburgh Courier*, 7 December 1968; Robert B. Semple Jr., "Brooke Rejects Post on Housing in Nixon Cabinet; Other Options Also Studied as Two Confer—Senator Prefers His Present Job," *New York Times*, 28 November 1968; Stan Benjamin, "Nixon Is Giving More Top Jobs to Nonwhites," *New Observer*, 2 May 1970; "Black Lawmakers in Congress," unidentified article, n.d. [1968], Box 137, Folder 3 ("Minorities Activities") Garment Files.

21. Clarence Townes was reappointed head of the Minorities Division of the RNC in early December 1968. His selection marked the end of a tense battle between "warring factions" of black Republicans. Prior to the election, Earl Kennedy, chair of Black Americans for Nixon-Agnew (BANA), called for Townes to relinquish control of the Minorities Division. The Virginia Republican refused, well aware that the position could be "more meaningful and profitable [than] even membership in the Cabinet." Arguably, these ideological and methodological differences had been simmering for quite some time, and exploded after the 1968 election as a result of the party's newly acquired power and status (Simeon Booker, "Uneasiness in Nixon Camp," *Jet*, 5 December 1968; Diggs Datrooth, "National Hotline," *New Pittsburgh Courier*, 21 December 1968).

22. Gloria Wolford, "Black Businessman Is Nixon's Appointee," *Chicago Daily Defender*, 10 December 1968; "Meet First Black Nixon Staffer," *Chicago Daily Defender*, 11 December 1968; "New Man in White House," *New York Amsterdam News*, 14 December 1968; James K. Batten and Dwayne Walls, "Nixon Aide Has Murky Past," *St. Petersburg Times*, 5 April 1969.

23. Reverend Leon Sullivan, a "quiet" Nixon supporter, founded the Philadelphia Opportunities Industrialization Center (POIC) in 1964. The organization's mission was to help African Americans move from "welfare to work, from tax dependent to taxpayer, and from homelessness to homeownership."

24. Wolford, "Businessman" *CD*, December 1968; "Black Nixon *CD*, December 1968; "New Man," *NYAN*, December 1968; Batten and Walls, "Murky Past," *SPT*, April 1969.

25. Nixon's presidential cabinet initially included: William P. Rogers (secretary of state), David Kennedy (secretary of the treasury), Melvin Laird (secretary of defense), John N. Mitchell (United States attorney general), Walter J. Hickel (secretary of the interior), Clifford M. Hardin (secretary of agriculture), George P. Schultz (secretary of labor), Robert N. Finch (secretary of health, education and welfare), George Romney (secretary of housing and urban development), John Volpe (secretary of transportation), and Maurice Stans (secretary of commerce). Additionally, Alabama's Winton Blount was named postmaster general, making him the first southerner to hold a cabinet position in more than a century (Simeon Booker, "What Nixon Plans for Blacks," *Jet*, 26 December 1968; "Nixon Keeps Black D.C. Mayor, Names All-White Cabinet," *Chicago Daily Defender*, 12 December 1968; Batten and Walls, "Nixon Aide," *SPT*, April 1969).

26. "A New Administration Takes Shape," *Time*, 20 December 1968; "'Tom' Tag Fear Made Blacks Reject Nixon Posts," *Jet*, 6 February 1969.

27. Dent continued, proudly claiming, "By 1972 Nixon had set a new record in making key black appointments—more than Kennedy and Johnson together had appointed" (Dent, *Prodigal South*, 176–77).

28. Interestingly, Young urged Garment and Brown to appoint Grant Reynolds, of the National Negro Republican Assembly (NNRA), to a prominent federal position. "[He] is a highly qualified individual, knows as 'Mr. Republican' among Negroes . . . for many years," wrote Young. "It would be a smart move to find a spot for Mr. Reynolds' capabilities." Unfortunately for Reynolds, neither Garment nor Brown passed his name along for recruitment (Whitney Young to Leonard Garment, 21 December 1968; Garment to Young, 6 January 1969; Young to Garment, 7 January 1969; Garment to George Schultz, memo, 9 January 1969; Garment to Winton Blount, 9 January 1969; Garment to Clifford Hardin, 9 January 1969; Garment to Peter Flanigan, memo, 9 January 1969, all in Box 171, Folder "Whitney Young," Garment Files. See also "Nixon Set for Black Appointees," *New Pittsburgh Courier*, 28 December 1968.

29. Young had just turned down a cabinet position as secretary of HUD. Young stated that he declined for pragmatic reasons—his neutral public profile guaranteed him a certain amount of political leeway in both parties and with the black community. In short, he felt he could get more done without binding labels ("New Administration," *Time*, December 1968; "Tom Tag," *Jet*, February 1969).

30. As one of the founders of the Congress of Racial Equality (CORE) in 1942, Farmer played a transformative role in the battle for civil rights and racial equality. In 1961, he organized and led the Freedom Rides, a nonviolent effort to desegregate interstate transportation. He was anointed one of the "Big Four" civil rights leaders during the 1950s and 1960s; other members included Martin Luther King Jr. of the SCLC; Roy Wilkins of the NAACP, and Whitney Young of the NUL. He left CORE in 1966—Floyd McKissick was named his successor (see Farmer, *Lay Bare the Heart*, 104–6, 196–257, 301–9; "Pioneer Leader James Farmer, Last of Civil Rights Movement's 'Big Four,'" *Jet*, 26 July 1999; and Steven F. Lawson, *Civil Rights Crossroads: Nation, Community, and the Black Freedom Struggle* [Lexington: University Press of Kentucky, 2003], 73–77).

31. "Working from Within," *Time*, 21 February 1969; "Let's Give Him a Chance," *Ebony*, April 1969; "James Farmer Interview," in Strober, *The Nixon Presidency*, 59–60; Farmer, *Lay Bare the Heart*, 315–17.

32. "Working," *Time*, February 1969; Farmer, *Lay Bare the Heart*, 316, 330.

33. A small "handful" of African Americans participated in the protests. Explaining the lack of participation, a black-power advocate stated: "This ain't our bag. We don't need to get a lot of our people clubbed for nothing" ("Blacks Play Key Roles in Keeping Tight Inaugural Security," *Jet*, 2 February 1969; Garry Wills, *Nixon Agonistes: The Crisis of the Self-Made Man* (Boston: Houghton Mifflin, 2002), 403.

34. "Black Senator Tosses Big Bash for Nixon White Men," *Jet*, 6 February 1969; "Changing of the Guard: Nixon Inaugural," *Ebony*, March 1969.

35. "Changing of the Guard," *Ebony*, March 1969.

36. During the 1968 election, James Brown supported Hubert Humphrey. Nonetheless, the singer canceled a concert in Texas to accept the inauguration invitation,

declaring that he was "enough of a man to transcend political differences to heed the call of the President of the United States." By 1972, Brown (a strong proponent of minority enterprise) was supporting Richard Nixon, going so far as to endorse the politician publicly.

37. "James Brown, Lionel Hampton Headline Inaugural Gala," *Jet*, 23 January 1969; "Hamp's Harlem, Brown's Soul Score!" and "Words of the Week," *Jet*, 6 February 1969; "Changing," *Ebony*, March 1969.

38. Tucker's church, located in Louisville, Kentucky, was described as a "continuing stronghold of black Republicanism."

39. The D.C. mayor Walter Washington and approximately seven out of the nine black members of the House of Representatives were seated on the main dais as well.

40. Richard Nixon, "Inaugural Address," 20 January 1969, *American Presidency Project*, University of California, Santa Barbara; "What Nixon Said to Blacks at the Inauguration," *Jet*, 6 February 1969.

41. By the spring of 1969, Nixon's approval rating with African Americans reached 40 percent, outweighing the 17 percent who disapproved of his performance, while 43 percent did not hold an opinion. Among white communities, 64 percent approved of the president, 9 percent disapproved, and 27 percent were indifferent (Harry Dent to John Mitchell, Memo on Black Voters, 11 February 1971, in Dent, *Prodigal South*, 179; Republican National Committee, Research Division, "Report on the Polls: Blacks," undated [1971], Box 5, Folder "Black Vote," SSS Papers).

42. Other appointees included: Samuel Simmons (assistant secretary for equal housing opportunity at HUD), Barbara Watson (administrator of Bureau of Security and Consular Affairs, State Department), Ronald Lee (deputy postmaster general), James "Jim" Johnson (civil service commissioner), Ben Holman (Justice Department), and James Washington (general counsel in Department of Transportation). The majority of the appointees were Republicans; however, Watson, Lee, and Koontz, were Democrats ("Top People," *Chicago Daily Defender*, 24 May 1969).

43. "Chance," *Ebony*, April 1969.

44. Sandra Lee, letter to the editor, *Ebony*, July 1969.

45. James M. Naughton, "Civil Rights: 'The Quiet Way to Get Things Done,'" *St. Petersburg Times*, 30 September 1969.

46. Prominent attendees included: Berkeley Burrell (president, National Business League), Senator Edward Brooke, John Clay (Business Development Corporation), Joe Gomez (United Steel Workers of America), Dorothy Height (president, National Council of Negro Women), John Johnson (*Jet-Ebony* publisher), Napoleon Johnson (National Urban League), Myrtle Ollison (National Association of Colored Women's Clubs), and John Wooten (executive director, Black Economic Industrial Union).

47. Richard Nixon, "Prescribing Arrangements for Developing and Coordination a National Program for Minority Business Enterprise," 5 March 1969, in *The American Presidency Project*, University of California, Santa Barbara; "Nixon Sets Up Agency to Help Blacks Own, Manage Businesses," *Jet*, 20 March 1969; "Nixon Creates New Office

to Help Minority Business, *Baltimore Afro-American*, 15 March 1969; "Taking Care of Business," *Ebony*, September 1978.

48. In 1961, 13 percent of African Americans made more than $10,000 per year. Roughly ten years later, 30 percent earned this amount, while 12 percent received more than $15,000 ("America's Rising Black Middle Class," *Time*, 17 June 1974).

49. "Nixon Offers Solution to Urban Problem," *Chicago Tribune*, 26 April 1968; Edward W. Brooke, phone interview by the author, 21 August 2008.

50. Edward W. Brooke, phone interview by the author, 21 August 2008.

51. It is important to note that Brooke was not belittling the rationale *behind* the Great Society initiatives. In fact, he firmly agreed that such programs were needed in the battle against inequality. However, as Brooke noted, he could not accept certain problematic and discriminatory aspects of Democratic liberalism.

52. Brooke speech to NIA July 1967, CLT Papers.

53. The scholarship on self-help ideology is vast, focusing on the black bourgeoisie, working-class communities in the South, black clubwomen, classical black nationalists, black-power advocates, and many other categories that demonstrate the diversity of African Americans. In assessing the impact of self-help philosophies, criticisms tend to focus on intraracial class and status discrimination; scholars suggest that the ideology represented a capitulation to racism or segregation and exacerbated class differences and tensions. In contrast, those who argue in favor of self-help claim that it served a protective function—African Americans refused to rely on the external white world and determined their own success, creating their own socioeconomic systems. Finally, it is important to point out that Richard Nixon viewed black capitalism as a means of wooing black militants. He gained the support of a few; Robert Weems and Dean Kotlowski document this in their respective books and chapters on Nixon. For more information, please see Kevin Gaines, *Uplifting the Race: Black Leadership, Politics, and Culture in the Twentieth Century* (Chapel Hill: University of North Carolina Press, 1996); Charles T. Banner-Haley, *The Fruits of Integration: Black Middle-Class Ideology and Culture, 1960–1990* (Oxford: University Press of Mississippi, 1994); Stephanie J. Shaw, *What a Woman Ought to Be and to Do: Black Professional Women Workers during the Jim Crow Era* (Chicago: University of Chicago Press, 1996); Willard B. Gatewood, *Aristocrats of Color: The Black Elite, 1880–1920* (Bloomington: Indiana University Press, 1990); Joseph, *The Black Power Movement*; Hanes Walton, *African American Power*; and *Politics*; Weems, *Business in Black in White*, 110–26.

54. Richard Nixon had a number of reasons for advancing black capitalism, as historian Dean Kotlowski has analyzed at length in *Nixon's Civil Rights: Politics, Principle, and Policy* (Cambridge: Harvard University Press, 2001), 97–157. See also Weems, *Business in Black and White*, 110–56.

55. In terms of middle-class "black backlash politics," many African Americans were reacting to the violence that exploded across the nation in the wake of Martin Luther King Jr.'s assassination. In the days following King's death, for example, 202 race riots broke out in 172 cities. Approximately 43 people were killed, 3,500 were injured,

and 27,000 were arrested. This one month of rioting was comparable to all that oc-curred in 1967, during which 233 riots broke out in 168 cities, causing 82 deaths, 3,400 injuries, and 18,800 arrests ("Scorecard for the Cities," *Time*, 13 September 1968).

56. Quoted in Graham, *Collision Course*, 70.

57. Boneparth interviewed sixty black businessmen in the New York metropolitan area over a period of six months from September 1970 to March 1971. Her sample also included interviews with representatives from nine civic and civil rights organizations including NUL, Council of Concerned Black Executives, National Business League (formerly the National Negro Business League), and New York Urban Coalition. Many of the respondents also indicated they had worked with the NAACP, Operation Bread-basket of the SCLC, CORE, and the Black Panther Party (Ellen Boneparth, "Black Businessmen and Community Responsibility," *Phylon* 37, no. 1 (First Quarter, 1976).

58. Black Republicans Jackie Robinson and Samuel R. Pierce Jr. were among the founders of the Freedom National Bank of Harlem (FNB). Established in 1964, the bank was created as a black-owned and -operated alternative to mainstream institu-tions, which often rejected or denied African American customers. Furthermore, as Robinson explained, financial institutions could serve as civil rights vehicles if poten-tial African American entrepreneurs and leaders pooled their resources and "put their capital to work locally, in their own neighborhoods." Indeed, many embraced this idea; for example, Martin Luther King Jr. deposited his Nobel Peace Prize winnings in the bank, while the NAACP in October 1968 deposited $75,000. For more information, see Mary Kay Linge, *Jackie Robinson: A Biography* (Santa Barbara: Greenwood, 2007), 138; "Negroes Not Seeking Handouts Only Want to Help Themselves," *Call and Post*, 12 October 1968.

59. As assistant secretary of labor, Fletcher was responsible for wage and labor standards, manpower development projects, and local government and community outreach (Nixon Names Negro to Post in Labor Department," *Chicago Tribune*, 15 March 1969; "Fletcher Gets Key Labor Job," *Baltimore Afro-American*, 22 March 1969; "Nixon Appoints Negro Asst. Labor Secretary," *Cleveland Call and Post*, 22 March 1969; Virginia Olds, "Fletcher Spells Plan," *Ellensburg Daily Record*, 27 March 1969).

60. "New Office for Poor Businesses," *Afro-American*, 31 May 1969; Ethel L. Payne, "So This Is Washington," *Chicago Daily Defender*, 10 May 1969.

61. Michael Flynn, "Negro Running for Lt. Governor," *Washington Post, Times Herald*, 26 September 1968; Nicholas Lemann, *The Big Test: The Secret History of the American Meritocracy* (New York: Farrar, Straus, Giroux, 1999), 200.

62. "Negro Wins Primary in Wash. State," *Washington Post, Times Herald*, 19 Sep-tember 1968; Michael Flynn, "Negro Running for Lt. Governor," *Washington Post, Times Herald*, 26 September 1968; "Choice of GOP Incumbent Gov. Carries State," *New Pittsburgh Courier*, 5 October 1968. See also "GOP Black Runs Strong for Wash-ington State's No. 2 Office," *Christian Science Monitor*, 16 September 1968; "Gov. Evans Renominated," *New York Times*, 18 September 1968; "Black Man Wins GOP Slot for Lt. Governor," *Chicago Defender*, 19 September 1968; "Nominated for Lt. Governor; Re-publicans Pick Negro in State of Washington," *New Journal and Guide*, 28 September

1968; Daryl E. Lembke, "Negro Pressing Hard in Washington Contest," *Los Angeles Times*, 9 October 1968; and Daryl E. Lembke, "Negro Loses Election but Hails Big Vote," *Los Angeles Times*, 8 November 1968. See also Sam Reed, "Two Mainstream Republican Leaders Who Made History," *Washington Mainstream* 15, no. 2 (September 2005).

63. *Chicago Tribune*, 15 March 1969; *Afro-American*, 22 March 1969; *Cleveland Call and Post*, 22 March 1969.

64. As a condition of his appointment, Fletcher was allowed to select the head of the Office of Federal Contract Compliance (OFCC). He selected John Wilks, a black Republican, as the deputy head of the OFCC (see Robert C. Smith, *We Have No Leaders: African Americans in the Post-Civil Rights Era*, 145).

65. "Fletcher: Time to Put Up," *Sacramento Observer*, 30 April 1970; Virna M. Cason to Arthur Fletcher, 25 May 1970, Box 88, Folder "Arthur Fletcher," Garment Files.

66. Ernest C. Cooper to Arthur A. Fletcher, with attachments, 10 February 1970; "End to Job Discrimination by '80 Urged as Goal by Fletcher," *St. Louis Globe-Democrat*, 28 May 1970; Irving A. Williamson, "Secretary Fletcher Goes to the White House," unidentified newspaper article [St. Louis, Mo.], 4 June 1970, all in Box 88, Folder "Arthur Fletcher," Garment Files.

67. Arguably, Lyndon Johnson's June 1965 commencement address at Howard University illustrated a significant shift in the battle for civil rights, laying the groundwork for September's presidential executive order. The 1964 Civil Rights Act guaranteed freedom; however, as Johnson declared in his speech, "Freedom is not enough. . . . You do not take a person who, for years, as been hobbled by chains and liberate him, bring him up to the starting line of a race and then say 'you are free to compete with others' and still justly believe you have been completely fair. . . . It is not enough just to open the gates of opportunity. All our citizens must have the ability to walk through those gates" (see Lyndon B. Johnson, commencement address at Howard University, "To Fulfill These Rights," 4 June 1964, Presidential Speeches and Messages, Lyndon Baines Johnson Library, National Archives and Records Administration, Austin, Tex. [hereafter Johnson Library]).

68. It should be noted that American organized labor is far more intricate than blanket charges of nepotism or racism would imply. Nationwide, there *were* some unions that were integrating (in *Collision Course*, Hugh Davis Graham goes so far as to argue that organized labor was "nearly there"). Likewise, as *Time* detailed in September 1969 and *Jet* documented in March 1971, organized labor not only discriminated against minorities, it blocked "almost everyone" in an attempt to keep the labor pool lower than the number of available jobs, thus creating a demand for services that far exceeded the supply and "forcing top dollar wages." Nevertheless, those unions that continued to engage in "flagrant racial discrimination" by denying minorities "equal access to skilled, well-paid jobs" complicated these explanations (see "What Unions Are and Are Not Doing for Blacks," *Time*, 26 September 1969; and Theophilus Green, "The Man Behind Pittsburgh Labor Plan That Becomes Model for Nation," *Jet*, 11 March 1971.

69. Thomas J. Sugrue, "Affirmative Action from Below: Civil Rights, the Building Trades, and the Politics of Racial Equality in the Urban North, 1945–1969," *Journal of American History* 91 no. 1 (June 2004): 145–73; Thomas J. Sugrue, *Sweet Land of Liberty: The Forgotten Struggle for Civil Rights in the North* (New York: Random House, 2008), 363–64; Robert C. Smith, *We Have No Leaders*, 145–60.

70. In 1969, 106,000 (8.4 percent) of the nation's 1.3 million construction workers were African American. Among this small black group, 81,000 (76 percent) were laborers—the lowest-paid in the industry. In Philadelphia, the figures were abysmal among the most lucrative unions: black workers comprised 1.6 percent of carpenters, 0.6 percent of electricians, and 0.2 percent of plumbers. Consequently, the Philadelphia Plan only applied to the "worst offenders" in the construction industry in an attempt to provide minorities with "their fair share" of high-paying jobs. In truth, civil rights legislation did offer protection against discrimination, but the process was reactive—claims were filed only *after* discrimination occurred. Activists demanded preventive justice and objected to the slow legal process (claims could take weeks, months, or even years to resolve). Explaining organized labor's hostile reaction to the Philadelphia Plan, AFL-CIO president George Meany angrily remarked: "There is no question that [African Americans] have come a long way. . . . [But] the militants want instant solutions for all problems. Of course, they are not going to get them" (see "What Unions Are—and Are Not Doing for Blacks," *Time*, 26 September 1969; "A Narrow Victory for Blacks," *Time*, 5 January 1970; "The Philadelphia Problem," *Time*, 17 August 1970; and Graham, *Collision Course*, 65–70.

71. Richard Nixon's reasons for endorsing the Philadelphia Plan are complicated and myriad. Nixon scholars have provided diverse analysis that explores these motivations. The president used the policy as a wedge to create chaos among Democratic politicians by pitting their disparate coalitions in opposition (like organized labor and the civil rights establishment). Many of the scholars also indicate that Nixon agreed to the Philadelphia Plan out of a genuine interest in issues of race, employment and wealth; however, above all else—he was a politician, thus all rationales were justifiable as long as they somehow worked to his political advantage and contributed to his re-election efforts for 1972 (Graham, *Collision Course*, 67–68; Sugrue, *Sweet Land of Liberty*, 364–65; Joan Hoff, *Nixon Reconsidered* (New York: Basic Books, 1994, 92–93). See also "PR Man Named to Lead Labor's Compliance," *Jet*, 21 August 1969.

72. It is worth noting that Fletcher actually wrote the revised Philadelphia Plan and was involved deeply with its implementation, working closely with George Schultz and John Wilks (a black Republican and deputy director of the OFCC, brought in by Fletcher). There are thousands of primary-source articles from periodicals and records from the Nixon and Ford Presidential Libraries that provide evidence for this argument; Harry Dent also discusses Fletcher's role in his 1978 autobiography. Unfortunately, there is somewhat of a tendency to dismiss or overlook Fletcher's influence on the labor policy. Indeed, after the session in which Fletcher described his history with the Philadelphia Plan, his interviewer dismissed his claims as "overstated," and concluded that George Schultz was the real mastermind behind the initiative. For more

information, please see Harry S. Dent, *The Prodigal South Returns to Power* (New York: Wiley, 1978), 182; Arthur Fletcher, interview by Robert C. Smith, in Robert C. Smith, *We Have No Leaders*, 145.

73. As defined by the labor department in 1969, the established standard was 4–5 percent minority representation for the first year with a goal of reaching 25–26 percent within five years. Fletcher warned that contractors and unions would be monitored frequently to ensure that the stated goals were being honored. And while the first phase affected only Philadelphia and its surrounding counties, officials indicated that similar policies would be implemented in cities across the nation.

74. Arthur Fletcher, "Remarks on the Philadelphia Plan," n.d. [26 June 1969], from *The Civil Rights Movement*, ed. Peter B. Levy (Santa Barbara: Greenwood, 1998); "US to Order Minority Quotas for Contractors," *Los Angeles Times*, 28 June 1969.

75. The paradox, of course, was that the Philadelphia Plan rejected colorblind philosophy. In doing so, it advanced a theory of equality premised upon the same ideology that policy fundamentally denied. Proponents of the plan, and later, affirmative action, suggested that as a theory, color-blind philosophy was appropriate. In truth, however, the nation's history of racial discrimination rendered color-blind policies nearly ineffective; to achieve color-blind equality for the future, the government needed to employ color-conscious solutions in the immediate. Both Johnson and Fletcher articulate this in their equal opportunity speeches. Moreover, Fletcher's interest in the plan is a concrete example of the progressive conservatism espoused by many black Republicans; the Nixon official embraced a mixture of liberal and conservative principles so as to advance an alternative and viable solution for uplift.

76. In all, five people were sent to the hospital, and nine were arrested—including six of the black witnesses ("Whites Battle Blacks, Police," *Bryan Times,* 26 September 1969; Seth S. King, "Whites in Chicago Disrupt Hearing; 5 Hurt and 9 Arrested in Dispute," *New York Times*, 26 September 1969; Seth S. King, "Whites in Chicago Continue Protest; Plan to Take More Blacks into Building Union Scored," *New York Times*, 27 September 1969).

77. The rider was a reaction to a public split between critics and opponents of the Philadelphia Plan. Specifically, the comptroller general ruled the policy unconstitutional under the Civil Rights Act of 1964; in contrast, U.S. Attorney General John Mitchell declared that the plan was legal since "goals" were not "racial quotas." The Byrd rider took advantage of this schism by banning funding for any policy deemed illegal by the comptroller general.

78. It is important to note that the legal and political battles prompted by the Philadelphia Plan, as well as the motivations and maneuverings of the White House, are much more complicated than this essay allows. Countless scholars offer interesting and detailed analysis on this subject; for more information, please see "Philadelphia Plan: How White House Engineered Major Victory," *New York Times*, 26 December 1969; "A Narrow Victory for Blacks," *Time*, 5 January 1970; Richard Nixon, "Statement about Congressional Action on the Philadelphia Plan," 23 December 1969, *The American Presidency Project*; Skrentny, *Ironies of Affirmative Action*, 177–221; Graham,

*Collision Course*, 65–77; Graham, *The Civil Rights Era: Origins and Development of National Policy, 1960–1972*, 326–43.

79. While rarely discussed, Order No. 4 represented a critical shift in affirmative action policies. The 3 February 1970 announcement required *all* contractors across *all* industries receiving federal funds of more than $50,000 and employing more than fifty workers to submit detailed affirmative action plans with goals, timetables, and proposed remedies for "underutilization" of minorities. This dramatically expanded the scope and regulatory reach of compensatory treatment in employment ("Watchdog for U.S. Labor," *Ebony*, April 1971; George Schultz to Richard Nixon, White House Memo on Progress in Civil Rights, 18 May 1971, Box 3, Folder "Black Caucus Demands and Responses," WHCF SMOF Robert Finch, Nixon Library (hereafter Finch Files). See also Skrentny, *Ironies of Affirmative Action*, 286; and Graham, *Collision Course*, 74.

80. "Black Americans," *CSM*, April 1970.

81. At the end of his speech, Fletcher received a five-minute standing ovation from the 1,300 delegates ("End to Job Discrimination by '80 Urged as Goal by Fletcher," *St. Louis Globe-Democrat*, 28 May 1970; Irving A. Williamson, "Secretary Fletcher Goes to the White House," unidentified newspaper article [St. Louis, Missouri], 4 June 1970, Box 88, Folder "Arthur Fletcher," Garment Files).

82. Notably, the Philadelphia Plan spawned internal policies that also had an impact on black economic uplift. With the announcement of the plan, Bob Brown began prodding officials to implement fair hiring mandates across the federal government. The result was Executive Order 11478, launched on 8 August 1969. Although it encouraged affirmative action practices, however, it did not require goals or timetables. Unsurprisingly, the initiative produced uneven results as some departments blatantly ignored the policy. Still, the order appears to have had a significant impact on overall minority hiring. For example, between 1969 and 1971, black employment at the midrange level rose by 33.6 percent between 1969 and 1971, and by 55.7 percent at the supergrade (highest level). And, while overall hiring decreased by 12 percent during this period, minority employment increased by nearly 20 percent (Richard Nixon, "Statement on Executive Order 11478," 8 August 1969, *AMP*; Robert P. Turner, *Up to the Front of the Line: Blacks in the Political System* [Port Washington: Kennikat Press, 1975], 127–29; Linda Faye Williams, *The Constraint of Race*, 177).

83. Victor Riesel, "High Pay Jobs Open for Blacks," *Rome News-Tribune*, 13 February 1970.

84. OMBE also held training seminars and information sessions, including a spring 1970 conference on minority federal procurement, during which the five hundred participants learned how to supply their products to the government for purchase ("Minority Firms Hope for U.S. Contracts," *Jet*, 9 April 1970).

85. Boneparth, "Black Businessmen," *Phylon*.

86. Ibid.

87. In the spring of 1969, OMBE launched Operation Enterprise, a partnership with eighteen private companies that financed the entrepreneurial ambitions of minority businessmen. Maurice Stans ambitiously declared that by June 1970, the program

would include one hundred private sponsors and provide $500 million in loans. Unfortunately, OMBE was overambitious in its predictions; after one year, only nine companies had kept their promise. Officials blamed this on the economy, complaining "It's hard to imbue businessmen with social consciousness when business is bad." Other OMBE initiatives, however, did move rapidly in this period, including public-private partnerships with the automotive industry and OEO community development programs (see Paul Delaney, "Black Capitalism Program Falling Far Short of Goals," *New York Times*, 29 June 1970).

88. The median family income for a nonwhite family in 1970 was $6,520—50 percent higher than in 1960. On average, black families earned approximately 64 percent of what white families earned, a 53 percent increase from 1963. Likewise, by 1970, black households earning over $10,000 hit 21 percent (up from 8 percent in 1960). During this same period, total nonwhite employment increased by 22 percent, whereas black male unemployment fell to 4 percent. One of the most dramatic shifts occurred in black households—by 1970, employed black couples (under the age of thirty-five and living in the North and the West) earned approximately the same amount as their demographically similar white counterparts ("Nixon and Black Americans—Two Views," *Christian Science Monitor*, 23 April 1970; Arthur Fletcher, U.S. Delegation to the General Assembly, Press Release and Report, October 26, 1971, Box 14, Miscellaneous 1971, SSS Papers). Historians Robert Weems and Jonathan Bean both demonstrate that black capitalism ultimately failed. This essay acknowledges and recognizes the deep problems of black capitalism, especially as a policy of the Nixon administration; however, this essay also seeks to examine how the Black Cabinet members instituted policy changes and shifts, couched in their understanding of racial equality, within the Nixon administration (please see Jonathan Bean, *Big Government and Affirmative Action: The Scandalous History of the Small Business Administration* [Lexington: University Press of Kentucky, 2001]; and Weems, *Business in Black and White*, esp. chaps. 5–7).

89. Brown's appeal was triggered after a meeting with the National Association for Equal Opportunity in Higher Education (NAEOHE), a group representing 124 predominantly black colleges. Of note, between 1960 and 1970, the number of black students enrolled in college increased from 10 percent to 18 percent (approximately 7 percent of the nation's total). For comparison, during this same period, white students enrolled in school at a constant rate of 22 percent (please see Robert Brown, "The Nixon Administration," *American Visions* [February–March 1995]; "Black College Presidents Tell Nixon of Repression Fears" and Theophilus E. Green, "Name-Calling and Racial Hatred Cited Possible Reasons," *Jet*, 4 June 1970; Bob Brown to Len Garment, memo on black college presidents, 11 December 1970, Box 137, Folder "Minority Activities," Garment Files; "The Presidency and the Press," *Bulletin of the American Academy of Arts and Sciences* 24, no. 8 [May 1971]: 12–14; Arthur Fletcher, U.S. Delegation to the General Assembly, Press Release and Report, October 26, 1971, Box 14, Miscellaneous 1971, SSS Papers; "Good News, Bad News," *Time*, 31 July 1972; "America's Rising Black Middle Class," *Time*, 17 June 1974).

90. The presidents represented schools including Howard University, Morehouse College, Tuskegee Institute, Meharry Medical College, Lincoln University, North Carolina Central University, and Jackson State University. During the meeting, the administrators requested funding to cover additional student scholarships, increased faculty salaries, and improvements to libraries, laboratories, and dormitories. Interestingly, the presidents stated that as racial liberalism began to take root in academia, white northern universities had started to "raid" black colleges, taking the best faculty members. The black institutions—unable to compete with the resources and salaries of the northern schools—thereby found themselves in a struggle to remain competitive (Brown to Garment, Memo on Black College Presidents, December 1970, Garment Files).

91. During their meeting, the presidents told Nixon that the "prevailing mood" on their campuses was "one of fear and repression . . . and frustration over the low premium set on [black] lives." The educators were referring to a devastating incident that occurred on 15 May 1970 at Jackson State University. The Mississippi National Guard fired more than four hundred rounds into a women's dormitory, killing two unarmed men and injuring a dozen students (less than two weeks earlier, Ohio National Guardsmen had killed four students at Kent State University). African Americans placed blame squarely on the Nixon administration for fostering a culture of violent repression. "It is as wrong for top officials in our government to call people bums and rotten apples," Whitney Young criticized. Likewise, a barrage of civil rights leaders called for national justice; among them was Edward Brooke, who traveled to Jackson State and held a private session for students. "Political power," he encouraged, "is the key to your problem." For more information, see "Black College Presidents Tell Nixon of Repression Fears"; and Theophilus E. Green, "Name-Calling and Racial Hatred Cited Possible Reasons," *Jet*, 4 June 1970.

92. Dr. James Cheek of Morehouse was appointed the White House's special advisor on black colleges.

93. During the press conference, Finch and Brown indicated that the preliminary FICE findings (issued in February 1970) deeply concerned Nixon, as did the subsequent meeting with the black presidents and a separate report filed by Dr. James Cheek, head of Howard University (appointed as a temporary White House advisor on black colleges). As a result, HEW was authorized to provide the additional sources. Likewise, the government also provided work-study payments and subsidized loans for students whose family incomes were $10,000 or less in 1970–71. A few months later, in a 10 August 1970 letter to NAEOHE, Nixon declared his "vigorous support of equal education opportunity," writing: "The present financial plight of many of our small and the overwhelming majority of our black colleges clearly demonstrates to me that the federal government must strengthen its role in support of these institutions." For their part, the college presidents issued a press release, publicly applauding the administration for taking groundbreaking steps to fight discrimination. Although the solution was "not sufficient" for the long-term, the NAEOHE members firmly expressed con-

fidence that additional support would be forthcoming, and that the administration would create a viable solution to ensure longevity.

94. Brown was successful—Nixon met with the black college presidents regularly through 1974. As an interesting aside, the administration's initial actions received barely any mention in the press until a September 1970 *New York Times* article claiming that NAEOHE had denounced the administration for refusing aid to black colleges. Outraged, the members of the consortium demanded a retraction. Their request was ignored. The president of Clark College sharply rebuked the *Times*, characterizing the article as a "gross error of misrepresentation of what actually went on." The editors of the *Bulletin of the American Academy of Arts and Sciences* agreed, writing, "[Anyone] who read this account . . . would assume that the administration's attitude toward black colleges was virtually the opposite of what it, in fact, was" ("The Presidency and the Press," *Bulletin of the American Academy of Arts and Sciences* 24, no. 8 [May 1971]: 12–14; "Letters to the Editor," *New York Times*, n.d., September 1970).

95. In a 1995 interview, Brown claimed the administration provided $600 million to black colleges in 1974 (see Brown, "Nixon," 1995).

96. Farmer's plan required that 50 percent of HEW management interns be members of underrepresented minority groups (African Americans, Latinos, Asians, and Native Americans) (Farmer, *Lay Bare the Heart*, 318–21).

97. Overall, 25 percent of the slots in the GSA trainee pool were designated for minority recruits ("George Schultz to Richard Nixon, Memo on Progress in Civil Rights, May 18, 1971, Box 3, Folder "Black Caucus Demands and Responses," Finch Files; Len Garment, letter, 15 April 1971, Box 133, Folder "Minority Business Enterprise and Other Minority Programs," Garment Files. By 1972, there were more than 342,000 black managers, proprietors, and business owners—nearly double the total in 1960. Likewise, African American professionals—lawyers, engineers, doctors, writers, teachers, and entertainers—totaled more than 800,000, for an increase of 128 percent. Certainly, black capitalism was not the sole engine that developed the black middle class, nor was it even the most powerful engine. However, it undoubtedly complemented the extensive civil rights legislative gains of the 1960s, aiding in the development of a culture of minority enterprise and growth.

98. As mentioned, between 1960 and 1972, white college students enrolled in school at a constant rate of 22 percent. During this same period, total employment across all races rose by 23 percent; likewise, total job growth increased by 49 percent. According to the U.S. Census, African Americans were overrepresented (proportionally) in the federal government. That is, they comprised 15 percent of the federal workforce, despite making up only 11 percent of the U.S. population. However, it is important to note that among that 15 percent, most were employed in low-level positions. Once the number was adjusted for midlevel and high-ranking positions, it appears that African Americans were grossly underrepresented in 1971 ("America's Rising Black Middle Class," *Time*, 17 June 1974).

99. In the six-page spread, *Ebony* offered an in-depth analysis of Fletcher's woes

and successes in the Labor Department. It was difficult to measure the effectiveness of the policy after its first year because a number of contractors would deceive the government by hiring temporary black workers to meet the compliance rules. But *Ebony* concluded that "Hometown Plans" (voluntarily enacted in 102 cities) had facilitated the success of affirmative action policy. As African Americans moved into the 1970s, the writers argued, the federal and local policies would help the black community to obtain "its fair share" of 15 million new construction jobs. However, it should be noted that some scholars indicate that hometown plans were an attempt by the Nixon administration to "water down" affirmative action policy as a means of appealing to organized labor. For more information, see "Watchdog of U.S. Labor," *Ebony*, April 1971.

100. For comparison, in 1968, SBA provided $28 million in minority loans. The government provided eight black firms with $10.4 million in federal contracts, and purchased $12.6 million under the federal procurement program in 1969. Minority employment and training opportunities also experienced a surge: In 1972, the government created 1.25 million minority-training opportunities in the public sector, along with 700,000 jobs for enterprising black youth. Between 1969 and 1971, the number of black banks jumped from twenty-three to thirty-eight. The government initially deposited between $100 and 142 million during the first year of the program, and deposited more than $300 million by 1973 (of note: one source quotes Commerce Secretary Charles Walker as saying that deposits would hit $1 billion by the end of 1972). "The Minority Bank Deposit Program," wrote political scientist Robert Turner in 1975, "represents the largest single transfer of economic power into black-controlled economic institutions in the history of the country" ("The Beginnings of Black Capitalism," *Time*, 6 April 1970; Turner, *Front of the Line*, 128–29; "Statement on Civil Rights," memo, n.d. [1970–71], Box 49, Folder "Black Congressmen," Garment Files; George Schultz to Richard Nixon, memo on progress in civil rights, May 18, 1971, Box 3, Folder "Black Caucus Demands and Responses," Finch Files; Len Garment, letter, April 15, 1971, Box 133, Folder "Minority Business Enterprise and Other Minority Programs," Garment Files; "With Loss of $704,530, Harlem Bank Tops Others," *Jet*, 31 August 1972).

101. "U.S. Aid: Blacks, $119 Million; Whites, Billions," *Jet*, 6 August 1970; "Robert Brown Puts Black Consciousness in the White House," *Jet*, 4 March 1971.

102. To find more on class struggle and problems with black capitalism, please see Weems, *Business in Black and White*; Dean J. Kotlowski, *Nixon's Civil Rights: Politics, Principle, and Policy* (Cambridge: Harvard University Press, 2002); Manning Marable, *How Capitalism Underdeveloped Black America* (Boston: South End Press, 1999), 151–73, 190–243.

103. Draft White House Statement on Civil Rights, n.d. [1971], Box 49, Folder "Black Congressmen," Garment Files.

104. While black athlete-entrepreneurs were afforded the luxury of reputation, college education, and finances, it is important to recognize their "personal wealth" was not, in most cases, extraordinary (although it was higher than the majority of the

black population). Many of the grant recipients opened restaurants, gas stations, and automobile dealerships (and publicly declared loyalty to the Republican Party). Chamberlain and Keys, however, received their first SBA grants in 1967 under the Johnson administration. In that same year, Jim Brown, along with John Wooten of the Washington Redskins, received a $520,000 grant from the Ford Foundation and $251,000 in loans from the Commerce Department to start the BEU (formerly Negro Industrial and Economic Union). And yet, all were outspoken black Republicans and continued to receive financial support from the SBA (under the umbrella of OMBE) throughout the Nixon and Ford years. While most of the athlete-entrepreneurs campaigned for Richard Nixon in 1968 and 1972, Chamberlain also had a personal relationship with the Republican official; for example, the basketball player escorted Nixon to Martin Luther King Jr.'s funeral in April 1968 ("Birth Pangs," *Time*, October 1968; "A Disappointing Start," *Time*, 15 August 1969; see also "Into the Big Leagues," *Time*, 25 July 1969; and "Is Black Capitalism a Mistake?" *Time*, 12 January 1970.

105. Along similar lines, Nixon met with former Chicago Bear Gale Sayers on multiple occasions between 1972 and 1973. In one October 1972 meeting, Nixon expressed an interest in starting a program for retired black athletes, where they would "work with young people as a means of discouraging drug use and crime." Finally, it should be noted that during the first stages of the Watergate investigation, a link was discovered between CREEP and BEU (Robert J. Brown, White House Memo on Jim Brown, August 10, 1972; Robert J. Brown to Richard Nixon, Memo on Gale E. Sayers' Meeting [10/17/72], 5 December 1972, both in Box 18, Folder "Presidential Meetings 1972–1973," SSS Papers.

106. Bob Brown to Richard Nixon, memo, October 1970; Len Garment to Nixon, memo, November 1970; John Ehrlichman to Len Garment, memo, December 1970, all in Box 137, Folder "Minority Oriented Activities," Garment Files.

107. Most of these figures made the list multiple times. Others black Republicans included: Stan S. Scott (presidential aide to Nixon after Bob Brown's retirement in 1972), Samuel J. Simmons, Berkeley Burrell, Samuel R. Pierce Jr. (chief counsel, U.S. Treasury), Jewel S. Rogers LaFontant (deputy solicitor general), James E. Johnson, Leon Sullivan, Joseph H. Jackson (National Baptist Convention. Please note—Whitney Young was not included on the list after 1971 as he drowned in Nigeria in March 1971) ("The 100 Most Influential Black Americans," *Ebony*, April 1971). See also "The 100 Most Influential Black Americans," *Ebony*, May 1972, May 1973, and May 1974.

108. "The 100 Most Influential Black Americans," *Ebony*, May 1972.

109. Both Bob Brown and Stan Scott (who was hired in early 1971) pushed aggressively for a communications campaign geared toward the black media. Accordingly, after joining the administration, Brown documented weekly trends and statistics on the black press's positive and negative reaction to Nixon initiatives of concern to African Americans. In 1972, the black Republican was appointed a special assistant to Nixon, and successfully convinced the president to launch an aggressive paid advertising campaign targeted at black constituents. Still, Brown's tenure in the White

House was a constant "irreconcilable" battle, as he often acknowledged in his private handwritten notes (Stanley Scott, Memo on Minority Media, November 3, 1971, Box 1, Folder "Administration Initiative Minority Publishers 11/3/1971," SSS Papers).

110. During the NAACP's July 1970 convention, Bishop Steven Spottswood described the Nixon White House as the "most anti-Negro" administration since Woodrow Wilson. However, by July 1971, as Stan Scott recorded, NAACP leader Roy Wilkins admitted that the administration had made significant strides in civil rights, most notably in economic advancement. "The situation is better than it was a year ago," Wilkins grudgingly told Scott. "But it's often not fast or far enough for me as head of the NAACP." But, as Wilkins noted, NAACP leaders believed that it was "pure folly" for a racial group to "sit back and just criticize rather than try to develop a dialogue and working relationship" with the White House. In his notes, Stan recorded that the civil rights leader offered "private praise" for the president's "high moral character," but bemoaned his "political strategy." Nixon could "double or triple his vote in the black community . . . and would not lose votes in middle America," Wilkins wearily pointed out, "because he would gain some of the so-called white liberal votes" ("NAACP Judges Nixon More Fairly," unknown source, n.d. [July 1971]; Stan Scott to Herbert Klein, confidential memo on NAACP, 9 July 1971, all in Box 14, Folder "NAACP," SSS Papers. See also "Education, Jobs" *Jet*, July 1971.

111. Young told his audience that he was convinced that the administration would stop exemptions for the South's "private 'hate academies,'" desegregate southern schools, and move aggressively against job discrimination (see Cordell S. Thompson, "Young Hits Nixon Administration," *Jet* 38 (6 August 1970): 6–12.

112. Tom Buckley, "Whitney Young: Black Leader or 'Oreo Cookie,'?" *New York Times*, 20 September 1970.

113. Len Garment and John Ehrlichman attended the meeting, as did the secretaries of Labor, HUD, HEW, commerce, and transportation. Delegates for the U.S. Attorney General, the head of the Office of Economic Opportunity (OEO), and the secretary of defense also participated.

114. Nixon quotation from 22 December 1970 meeting with Whitney Young and cabinet members as discussed by George P. Schultz, Address to the National Urban League Conference, July 26, 1971, Patterson, Box 70, Urban League; see also George Schultz to Richard Nixon, Memo on Progress in Civil Rights, 18 May 1971, Box 3, Folder "Black Caucus Demands and Responses," Finch Files.

115. Dickerson, *Whitney Young*, 316.

116. Leonard Garment, Memo on Urban League and Attachments, 22 December 1970; Leonard Garment to Richard Nixon, memo, 25 January 1971, WHCF SMOF Patterson, Box 70, Urban League.

117. Garment to Nixon, memo, 25 January 1971, WHCF SMOF Patterson, Box 70, Urban League; Les Payne, "Vernon E. Jordan: In the Footsteps of Whitney Young," *Ebony*, July 1972.

118. Robert Brown to James D. Hodgson, memo, 2 June 1971; Robert Brown to John

D. Ehrlichman, memo, 25 June 1971; Robert Brown to Richard Nixon, memo, 25 June 1971, Box 70, Folder "Urban League," all in Patterson Files.

119. Young drowned while swimming at Lighthouse Beach in Lagos, Nigeria, on 11 March 1971. At the request of Richard Nixon, Young's body was transported back to the United States. The president also delivered the civil rights leader's eulogy at Young's Kentucky funeral service. For more information, see Dennis C. Dickerson, *Militant Mediator: Whitney M. Young, Jr.* (Lexington: University Press of Kentucky, 2004), 315–17; Richard Nixon, Statement on the Death of Whitney M. Young, Jr., March 11, 1971, *The American Presidency Project*, University of California, Santa Barbara.

120. NUL's claims were true, in part. While the program was proceeding smoothly, for the most part, some agencies were lagging or being uncooperative. Given the lax attitude toward intragovernment enforcement, the federal divisions could easily get away with misbehavior. After several months of misbehavior, though, Nixon officials finally clamped down (under pressure from Bob Brown and other black appointees). Overall, the NUL maintained a strained but relatively productive relationship with the GOP well into the late 1970s. Vernon Jordan regularly met with the president and corresponded with him in private. In public, however, Jordan often adopted an adversarial role antagonistic of the actions of the White House (a position he would also take with the Democratic Party, as well). Like most of these relationships, the one between the White House and the NUL was deeply nuanced and complicated.

Review of National Urban League Proposals, 17 September 1971, Box 88, Urban League, Garment Papers.

121. Robert Brown to John D. Ehrlichman, memo, 25 June 1971; Robert Brown to Richard Nixon, memo, 25 June 1971, Box 88, Urban League, Garment Files.

122. Les Payne, "Vernon E. Jordan: In the Footsteps of Whitney Young," *Ebony*, July 1972; George P. Schultz, Address to the National Urban League Conference, 26 July 1971, Box 70, Folder "Urban League," Patterson Files.

123. Weems, *Business in Black and White*, 127.

124. Most of the companies were concentrated in the major metropolitan areas of New York, Los Angeles, Chicago, Washington, D.C., and Detroit. Spanning an "imaginative and broad" range, the businesses included light manufacturers, auto dealerships, general contractors, food processors and distributors, beer and liquor wholesalers, entertainment businesses, publishing companies, and financial institutions. The 1974 list again highlighted top earners Motown and Johnson Publishing, but also included Fedco with $26 million and Johnson Products with $25 million. The largest black bank in the country, Independence Bank, reported assets of $55.6 million, while the biggest black-owned savings-and-loan company reported $61 million. North Carolina Mutual, the largest black life-insurance company, earned assets of $135.7 million ("Rise of Entrepreneurs," *Time*, 25 June 1973; "100 Black Businesses," *Jet*, June 1973; "JPC Ranks No. 2. among Top 100 Black Businesses," *Jet*, 20 June 1974). See also Alex Poinsett, "1973: Year of Watergate," *Ebony*, January 1974.

125. "Entrepreneurs," *Time*, June 1973.

126. In 1974, *Commentary* analysts Ben Wattenberg and Richard Scammon argued that the black middle-class annual base was $8,000 in the North and $6,000 in the South; *Time* noted that under these parameters, more than 50 percent of black people would be middle class. Black scholars scoffed at these "perilously low" figures, and instead suggested a base of $11,500; here, 25 percent of African Americans would be considered middle class (as compared to nearly 50 percent of whites).

127. It is important to point out that for all of the gains of the black middle class, approximately 30 percent of African Americans remained below the poverty line in the mid-1970s (as compared with 10 percent of whites). While the *Time* issue barely mentioned this issue, it did point out that the widening gulf between the black middle class and the black underclass posed a glaring dilemma for the black community; moreover, black middle-class citizens were well aware and deeply affected by the "sounds and sights of poverty, of deprivation and oppression" ("Black Middle Class," *Time*, June 1974; "Good News, Bad News," *Time*, 31 July 1972).

128. "America's Rising Black Middle Class," *Time*, 17 June 1974.

129. Arthur Fletcher, press release and statement, U.S. Delegation to the General Assembly, 26 October 1971, Box 14, Folder "Misc. 1971," SSS Papers.

130. In his article, West argues that one of the realities of the black freedom movement was the "ambiguous attitude of Democratic Party liberals to the movement." Given that members of the black middle class achieved their status against the "backdrop of undeniable political struggle, a struggle in which many of them participated," it is not unusual that some members of the black middle class would reject the Democratic Party, seeking alternative solutions. To those ends, as West also notes, the context of the civil rights movement made the black middle class more than likely to "refuse to opt for political complacency" as their identities were built around their continuing political participation, resistance to racism, and advocating for equal opportunities (Cornel West, "The Paradox of the Afro-American Rebellion, *Social Text*, no. 9/10 [Spring–Summer 1984]). See also Michael C. Dawson, *Black Visions: The Roots of Contemporary African-American Political Ideologies* (Chicago: University of Chicago Press, 2001), 39.

131. Milton Viorst, "The Blacks Who Work for Nixon," *New York Times*, 29 November 1970.

132. For example, Nixon's decision in January 1970 to nominate Florida federal judge G. Harrold Carswell infuriated African Americans, who accused him of playing to segregationist sensibilities by attempting to appoint a "white supremacist" to the court of national justice. For further analysis of Carswell's "politics of white resistance," please see Kevin Kruse, *White Flight: Atlanta and the Making of Modern Conservatism* (Princeton: Princeton University Press, 2005), 256; and Kotlowski, *Nixon's Civil Rights*, 88–90. For further discussion of Nixon's "Southern Strategy" and tumultuous relationship with African Americans, please see Dan T. Carter, *The Politics of Rage: The Origins of the New Conservatism, and the Transformations of American Politics* (Baton Rouge: Louisiana State University Press, 2000), 396–99; and Merle Black, *The Rise of Southern Republicans*, 120–22, 209–10.

133. Robert J. Brown, White House Questionnaire on Minority Affairs, n.d. [1972–73], Box 7, Folder "Robert J. Brown 1970–1972," SSS Papers. See also Clarence L. Townes Jr. to Yvonne Price, 31 March 1970, Box I: 115, Black Elected Republicans 1970, Folder "Leadership Conference on Civil Rights," Part I: Subject File, 1951–80, Manuscript Division, Library of Congress (hereafter BERO 1970—LOC).

134. For the Nixon administration's black outreach strategy, please see RNC, *Campaign Plan: A Strategy for the Development of the Black Vote in 1972*, n.d. [February 1971]; Jeb S. Magruder to Attorney General, Memo on the 1972 Black Vote, 3 December 1971; Bill Marumoto to Bob Brown, Memo on Black Capitalism in Election 1972, 1 September 1971; Fred Malek to Paul Jones, Memo on Campaign Plan for Black Vote, 22 February 1972; Robert Brown, Proposal for the Organization of a Network of "Young Black Friends for the Re-Election of the President," April 1972, all in Box 5, Folder "Black Vote 1972," SSS Papers.

135. For instance, Fletcher talked directly to 40,000 people through conferences and meetings. In Atlanta, Chicago, St. Louis, Topeka, San Diego, and Houston, he reached audiences ranging from 250,000 to 1 million through radio and television programs. Targeted groups (and attendance) included the Urban League of Cleveland and St. Louis (3,500), Operation Breadbasket in Chicago (3,500), Alabama A&M College (1,500), and the Washington Area Ministers' Retreat (700). See also RNC Research Division, Report on Black Political Participation 1971–72; RNC Research Division, Report on the Polls—Blacks 1971–1972, all in Box 5, Folder "Black Vote 1972," SSS Papers.

See, for example, Dent, *Prodigal South Returns*, 15–16, 176–180; Arthur Fletcher, White House Report on Black Outreach, 9 June 1970; Arthur Fletcher, 1970 Speech List, January 6, 1970–June 7, 1970, Box 88, Folder "Arthur Fletcher," Garment Files.

136. During the November 1969 elections, Virginia governor Linwood Holton tallied 55 percent of the black vote (in Richmond alone, 71 percent of the black electorate cast their ballots for the official). In Philadelphia, Arlen Specter was reelected as district attorney with the help of 31 percent of the black electorate, while in New Jersey, Governor William Cahill garnered 26 percent. These numbers and others compelled the *Chicago Defender* to wonder if this signaled the beginning of a "re-entry of black voters into the GOP fold" ("Impact of Black Vote," *Chicago Daily Defender*, 25 November 1969).

137. In an administration memo to Nixon, Ehrlichman, Rumsfeld, Garment, and Brown, Daniel Patrick Moynihan enthusiastically declared, "Without question, the Negro community as a whole is much more politically conservative than are the Negroes whom whites identify as 'spokesmen'" (Daniel P. Moynihan to Richard Nixon et al., memo on position of the Negro, 27 February 1970, Box 49, Folder "Black Congressmen," Garment Files). See also RNC, *Campaign Plan Black Vote 1972*, Box 5, Folder "1972 Black Vote," SSS Papers; and Dent, *Prodigal South*, 180–81.

138. Tom Tiede, "Black Silent Majority Speaks for Democracy," *Rome News-Tribune*, 29 October 1970; "Guest Editorials: Black Silent Majority," *Chicago Tribune*, 22 July 1970; Paul Delaney, "Blacks for Nixon Form G.O.P. Group; Panel Will Concern Itself with Policy and Jobs," *New York Times*, 20 January 1973; Vernon Jarrett, "Blacks

for Nixon Stress Equality," *Chicago Tribune*, 23 August 1972; Ronald Sarro, "Blacks See New Political Era," *Sunday Star*, 16 May 1971, Box 14, Folder "Black Elected Officials," Patterson Files; Wagner to Brad Patterson, Memo, October 15, 1971; Membership List, National Black Silent Majority Committee, n.d. [October 1971]; Philip Shandler, "Black Silent Majority Plans Crusade," *Evening Star*, 13 May 1971; Black Silent Majority Statement of Beliefs, n.d. [1971]; National Black Silent Majority Newsletter, n.d. [1971], all in Box 9, Folder "National Black Silent Majority Committee," Finch Files; List of Republican Black Elected Officials, 15 March 970, and List of Black Elected Republican Officials' Proposals, n.d. [March 1970], Box I: 115, Black Elected Republicans 1970, Folder "Leadership Conference on Civil Rights," Part I: Subject File, 1951–80, Manuscript Division, Library of Congress (hereafter BERO 1970—LOC); BERO Conference Agenda, 19–20 March 1970, all in Box 14, Folder "Black Elected Officials," Patterson Files; "How Blacks Got to President Nixon," *Jet*, 9 April 1970; Black GOP Leaders," *Chicago Defender*, 26 March 1970.

139. Booker, "Washington Notebook," *Ebony*, January 1977.

140. Booker specifically referred to Sam Jackson, Bob Brown, Arthur Fletcher, Ed Brooke, James Cummings of the NBRC, and U.S. Solicitor Jewel LaFontant (ibid.).

# 12

## M. E. Bradford, the Reagan Right, and the Resurgence of Confederate Nationalism

### FRED ARTHUR BAILEY

"In a Southern context the fight over the past is (and always has been) primarily a dispute concerning choices for the past and the future," proclaimed the Texas literary figure and political philosopher Melvin E. Bradford in 1987. Personally resistant to the profound social changes that swept over the American South after World War II, he emerged as an influential scholar whose interpretations of American history would at century's end help inspire a neo-Confederate resurgence. The author of scores of popular and professional articles, Bradford was also an accomplished orator who spoke with eloquence to crowds gathered in support of presidential candidate George Wallace or college and university assemblages throughout the world.[1]

Bold and consistent in his views, Bradford condemned faith in human equality while articulating the case for an ordered society premised upon the supposed innate inequality of mankind. He grounded his belief system in a grand historical paradigm which melded his comfortable conviction of white superiority with a distinctive interpretation of the ideological dynamics of both the American Revolution and the Confederate crusade.[2]

A professor of English at the Jesuit University of Dallas from 1967 to 1993, Bradford's forthright expression of his principles earned the respect of a certain cadre of southern intellectuals as well as those politicians fearful of a national government that might undermine the social customs they had long cherished. Although he proudly styled himself a conservative, in his candid moments he admitted to more radical and, to him, more virtuous inclinations. "'Reaction' is a necessary term in the intellectual context we inhabit late in the twentieth century," he reflected in 1990. "Merely to conserve is sometimes to perpetuate what is outrageous."[3]

The wholesale dismantling of the South's racist institutions seemed to Bradford a cultural catastrophe loosed upon the region by misguided reformers moved by dangerous egalitarian ideas. Influenced by conscience-driven

northern liberals and long-restive southern blacks, a powerful national government had nullified laws that mandated racial segregation, denied blacks
and large numbers of whites the elective franchise, and gerrymandered legislative districts that ensured patrician-driven rural counties' dominance over
southern cities with significant minority populations. Bradford considered
these alterations a crime against the natural order of mankind; he saw in civil
rights and related democratic reforms the fundamental destruction of a southern civilization whose genius derived from a select, white, talented few. "The
cult of equality," he wrote, "is the 'opiate of the masses' . . . part of the larger
and older passion for uniformity or freedom from distinction. It flatters in us
all that is worst."[4]

Although Bradford's admirers praised him as an original thinker, in reality
he merely perpetuated a long tradition among southern white intellectuals
that justified a cultural system in which race, class, and ethnic distinctions
took precedence over leveling democracy. While a graduate student at Tennessee's Vanderbilt University during the height of the civil rights crusades,
he partook of an academic environment that had long nurtured the South's
distinctive race and class customs. During the 1930s, it had been the special
domain of the "Nashville Agrarians," a loose association of twelve intellectuals
including the historian Frank W. Owsley, the poets Donald Davidson, Alan
Tate, and Andrew Lytle, and the emerging literary giant Robert Penn Warren. Overwhelmingly elitist and racist in their social philosophy, they detested
northern industrialism, criticized its impact upon the South, and condemned
those southern reformers who, they maintained, gave aid and comfort to the
Yankee colossus. Their works imagined an antebellum agricultural order in
which aristocratic planters, white yeomen, and black slaves resided together in
felicity with nature and in harmony with one another. In 1930, they produced
the controversial anthology *I'll Take My Stand*. Dedicated to "a Southern way
of life against . . . the American . . . way," it declared war on northern scholars
and southern progressives alike.[5]

A sixth-generation Texan, Bradford grew up in a South where many whites,
still bridling at the defeat of 1865, strove to preserve the essential trappings
of the Old South. He moved in a carefully structured society that valued a
southern version of Anglo-Saxon civilization as superior to all others and in
which the relegation of Negroes and Hispanics to a separate and inferior status
was made normative. Born in Fort Worth on May 8, 1934, Bradford matured
in a family proud of its Confederate heritage and moderate comfort from the
income of ranch lands in Texas and Oklahoma. His progenitors had migrated
from Tennessee and Alabama prior to the Civil War. "We were a storytelling

people," Bradford explained in 1992. "I had three great-grandfathers who fought for the Confederacy." One lost a leg at Chickamauga "and suffered the rest of his life." Reconstructing the past, he reflected, "helped my family define who we were."[6]

Bradford excelled in a school system whose curriculum, long shaped by the Confederate patriotic societies, reinforced his perception of what it meant to be southern. As late as 1976, the historian of Fort Worth's Julia Jackson chapter of the United Daughters of the Confederacy praised its campaigns to "pressure . . . textbook publishers to give accurate accounts of the War Between the States" and to disapprove of "Northern teachers in the local schools who presented a view slanted." Looking back as an adult upon his youth, Bradford yearned for "that remembered Texas, which I like very much better than the one I now inherit."[7]

Reared in a closed intellectual environment, Bradford never broke free from the culture that so narrowed his ideological horizons. He viewed the Civil War as an unmitigated tragedy, one that destroyed a just southern civilization and whose cause could be traced to the malignant ambitions of a single individual—Abraham Lincoln. Bradford considered the sixteenth president an unprincipled scoundrel who, rather than allow the southern states a peaceful exit from the Union in 1861, launched a war that slaughtered six hundred thousand men, all for the benefit of his personal ambition and the prosperity of his northern industrial allies. He admitted a hatred for Lincoln so corrosive that whenever he spied his memorial in Washington, D.C., "a visceral wave of loathing rack[ed] his entire body." Pressed to explain Bradford's anti-Lincoln bitterness, Harry Jaffa, who maintained with the Dallas professor a friendly debate over Lincoln's legacy, chuckled before responding: the Great Emancipator "stole Mel Bradford's great-grandfather's slaves."[8]

Graduating high school in 1952, Bradford entered college with a love for the southern culture of his upbringing and with an acute awareness of the gathering pressures for civil rights reforms and other challenges to the traditional entitlements of the South's white elites. In the two decades from his freshman year at the University of Oklahoma until his doctorate in literature at Vanderbilt in 1968, Bradford witnessed profound, and for him troubling, alterations in the southern way of life. From *Brown*'s seminal call to end public school segregation to the Civil Rights Act of 1964 and the Voting Rights Act of 1965, he imagined an aggressive national government forcing upon a righteously reluctant South a despised social leveling. This quest for equality was nothing more than "Old Liberalism hidden under a Union battle flag."[9] A Naval ROTC scholarship financed Bradford's bachelor's and master's degrees and plunged him into an intense period of military service critical to his intellectual development. Following brief deployment aboard a navy destroyer, he joined the teaching staff at Annapolis. There he enjoyed the fellowship of senior colleagues whose conservatism "of various kinds" helped him sort through his own ideological proclivities and apply them to his identity as a white southerner.[10]

Bradford's Annapolis friends also introduced him to the conservative quarterly *Modern Age* edited by Russell Kirk. Years later, he recalled that he eagerly awaited each of the publication's new issues, anticipating that its articles would serve as the basis of stimulating conversations with his fellow faculty. "In *Modern Age*," he reminisced, "I began to read . . . of a stream both broad and deep, coming down to us from antiquity in the multifaceted variety of European civilization. That there was a need to defend the West and that American intellectuals who understood the heritage would be in forefront of that defense was beyond dispute." Impressed that Donald Davidson, the last of the Nashville Agrarians at Vanderbilt, served as an editorial advisor of the journal, Bradford entered the university's English Department eager to earn his doctorate in a community famed as "a veritable nursery of intellectual conservatism."[11] A close friend and fellow graduate student remembered the school's English faculty as "utterly homogeneous . . . filled with Southern conservatives." Angered by assaults on Jim Crow, faculty defended the South in private and sometimes in public. "With such teachers, [Bradford] didn't have to waste time defending his convictions against the assaults of ideological adversaries."[12]

Bradford especially cherished his bonding with Donald Davidson. As an undergraduate troubled by attacks on his native region's racial polity, he had devoured the Agrarians' anthology *I'll Take My Stand* and later reflected: "I said to myself [here] is a voice for the deepest sentiments of the people I have known best . . . [the] wisdom of the world 'where I was born and raised.'" While at Vanderbilt, he sat at Davidson's feet, ingested his view on literary criticism, and absorbed his distaste for interpretations of American history contrary to those he believed. A powerful voice opposed to civil rights reforms, Davidson taught that the founding fathers never intended the phrase "all men are created equal" to apply to nonwhites, and encouraged his students to see both the Declaration of Independence and the Constitution as conservative scriptures designed to shield society from the anarchy of democracy. "I have not changed my mind since I was a graduate student at Vanderbilt," Bradford reflected in 1986. "Not my mind, or my method."[13] He considered himself the intellectual heir to the Nashville Agrarians. Bradford admired their concept of southern community as "an informally hierarchical social organism in which all Southerners (including the Negro, insofar as the survival of that community permitted) had a sense of investment and participation." The South was a land where unequal men—white and black, privileged and impoverished— lived in harmony. The white and privileged Agrarians appreciated that reality and gloried in the critical "role of the gentleman . . . in cementing the bonds between unequal men." They feared an aggressive national government committed to wrongheaded egalitarianism. A corrupt national government almost destroyed southern order during the Civil War and Reconstruction, and in the 1930s it stood poised again as a threat to the rational order of men. Little wonder, Bradford mused, that the Agrarians entitled *I'll Take My Stand* as an affirmation "from the spirited anthem of their warlike forefathers."[14]

Although Bradford groomed himself for a quiet academic career, his love for politics would thrust him into the dynamic company of those who contested for control of the fundamental institutions of American intellectual life. He, and those of similar persuasion, wished to define the cultural creed by which all other Americans must manage their society. While in the end Bradford failed to achieve victory on a hoped-for scale, his legacy held a certain import. Across the South, a coterie of white academicians would hail Bradford's interpretations of America's past and present, dedicating themselves to the reversal of nearly fifty years of civil rights progress. Bradford taught briefly at Hardin-Simmons University in Abilene, Texas, and at Northwestern State in Natchitoches, Louisiana, before settling into his permanent post at the University of Dallas. A prolific writer, he produced engaging essays on southern literary themes. Emboldened by his faith in his own abilities as a rhetorical critic and driven by his intense distaste for central government intent upon dismantling southern institutions of inequality, in 1971 Bradford moved beyond the limited confines of literature to launch an attack on Abraham Lincoln. The brash assault upon this icon of American civil religion proved pivotal. It projected him into ideological circles beyond narrow academia and established him as an intellectual leader among those white southerners set on reversing the tide of civil rights reforms.[15]

Published in the magazine *Triumph*, Bradford's article "Lincoln's New Frontier: A Rhetoric for Continuing Revolution" branded the Great Emancipator a cultural heretic who misconstrued the phrase "all men are created equal," gave it a meaning never intended by the founding fathers, and then employed that faulty interpretation to make of the Union cause a holy crusade. In Bradford's paradigm, Lincoln's Gettysburg Address conjoined with Julia Ward Howe's "The Battle Hymn of the Republic" to whip the North into a religious fervor against the South. "To state my argument briefly," Bradford wrote, "what the Emancipator accomplished by confirming the nation in (or 'institutionalizing') an erroneous understanding of the Declaration of Independence made possible the ultimate elevation of that same error in Mrs. Howe's 'war song' and set us forever to 'trampling out the grapes of wrath.'"[16]

Bradford instead interpreted the Declaration of Independence as "a lawyer's answer to lawyers, a counterplea to the English government." The Declaration, he argued, defined the proper relationship between a prince and his subjects. Lincoln's rhetoric and Howe's anthem violated the intent of the Declaration, converted a single statement ("all men are created equal") into a sacred dictum, and loosed a religious crusade for "equality" that threatened to undermine fundamental institutions of social order more than a century beyond the Civil War. "With 'equality,'" Bradford proclaimed, we enter "the French Jacobin satrapy, where men are dignified by abstract 'proposition' and loud musketry."[17]

Bradford considered himself at war with a society moving rapidly toward anarchy worse than that of the French Revolution. The urban riots of the 1960s reinforced that conviction, stirring in him the urge to seek a strong leader capable of reversing what he saw as a trend toward social disintegration, and leading to his championing of George Wallace's 1972 presidential bid. Crusading throughout the Dallas area, Bradford organized Wallace followers, ushered them into the local presidential caucuses, and then led a solid pro-Wallace delegation to the Democratic state convention in San Antonio.[18]

The Wallace faithful elected Bradford to the Democratic state committee, where from 1972 to 1974 he proved an embarrassment to party centrists. Anxious to separate their movement from its segregationist past and to include Texas's ethnically diverse population, they held little brief for Bradford's open boast that he received his orders directly from Montgomery, Alabama—Wallace's home and once the Confederacy's capital. By 1975, Bradford moved into the Republican Party and in 1980 supported California governor Ronald Reagan over Texan George H. W. Bush in the presidential primary. When Reagan entered the White House, he nominated Bradford to head the National Endowment for the Humanities (NEH).[19] Although Bradford had served on Reagan's NEH transition team, his nomination surprised Washington pundits. On September 20, 1981, the *New York Times* leaked news of Bradford's impending appointment by quoting a "high-ranking Washington" official that the administration was pressed to this action "as a concession to conservative supporters" angered by Reagan's choice of Sandra Day O'Connor for the Supreme Court. Reactionary southern Republican senators John Tower of

Texas and Jesse Helms and Bob East of North Carolina endorsed Bradford enthusiastically.[20]

Senator Helms had for months resisted several recommended candidates on the grounds that they lacked sufficient ideological commitment to the cause. He bristled at the policies of current NEH director Joseph D. Duffey, the former president of the Americans for Democratic Action. Believing Duffey had unfairly favored the funding of "leftist" scholars from "effete" northeastern universities and associations dedicated to left-wing social agendas, Helms and like-thinking senators condemned such recent NEH grants as that to heighten the heritage awareness of female employees. Helms demanded that the new director reverse the trend and reward "scholarship from the conservative end of the spectrum as well as from the liberal."[21]

Sharing Helms's concerns, Bradford boldly articulated his vision of a reformed NEH. At Michigan's radically rightist Hillsdale College, he condemned the current NEH director's "talk of 'human values' and 'deep needs'" as little more than a cloak for "cultural populism" designed to serve "the political issues of the day." Under a Bradford administration, the NEH would focus on preserving the best of American society. "Americans of all backgrounds and levels of education know that something is wrong," he told his audience, "if we neglect in the cultural fields our role as leaders and preservers of Western civilization; wrong if we fail to preserve and promote the finest products of human reason and imagination and the best discussion of these books and artifacts . . . [and] such old fashioned activities." He would "avoid with all possible rigor" special programs "which reflect 'pop' sociology, social-scientific approaches to problem solving, and literary or historical themes which suggest a position on questions of public policy"; and eliminate entirely all such efforts as "the 'Fellowship for College Teachers,'" a program he contemptuously termed "grants for second-rate scholars" because they amounted "to a hidden quota for minorities who have shown no academic promise but who have the right politics."[22]

Academicians, social activists, and newspaper publishers condemned Bradford's nomination, citing the professor's support for George Wallace, his published condemnations of Lincoln, and his alleged racism. One of his strongest foes, the neoconservative godfather Irving Kristol, circulated among White House staffers a document sarcastically entitled "Quotations from Chairman Mel." It revealed that Bradford had labeled Lincoln "a dangerous man" with a "very dark" and "indeed sinister" image. Bradford further held that slavery "was as good or as bad as the people who administered the regimen," and that it "seemed . . . both defensible . . . and civilized in its human results." As for the concept of equality of rights, Bradford dismissively commented that the subject belonged "to the post-Renaissance world of ideology—or political magic and the alchemical 'science' of politics. Envy is the basis for its broad appeal."[23]

Feeling himself unfairly maligned, Bradford called an impromptu press conference in the hallway of the Sam Rayburn Senate Office Building. His blunt way of talking, folksy style, and boisterous Texas humor served him well in private conversations with fellow ideologues and in public appearances before audiences predisposed to his views, but it failed to impress veteran journalists adept at unmasking the careful sophistry of government functionaries.[24]

Bradford's lack of political savvy lent to his comments an air of pettiness, vindictiveness, and insensitivity. How would Bradford change the National Endowment for the Humanities? "I'd stop washing money through the damn thing like Joseph Duffey has," he told the eager reporters. "I wouldn't give money to raise consciousness—for instance, that grant to the Ladies Garment Workers Union." Corrected, he repeated himself to properly reference the National Council of Working Women. Bradford then charged that the NEH had become far too partisan. "I wouldn't politicize it," he said. "I'd see that conservatives get a better shake than they did in Duffey's regime, not every thing would go to Harvard, Yale, Princeton and Chicago." Even as the Dallas professor promised to shepherd more grants toward Texas and Oklahoma, he also pledged to restrict the NEH chair's personal prerogative to fund small projects. "I think chairman's grants ought to be stopped," he chuckled, but only "after I give out two or three. Don't quote me on that. But there really are two or three deserving conservatives." Several reporters pressed Bradford on his published critiques of Abraham Lincoln, leading one to ask the obvious: would Bradford have been a Confederate in 1861?[25]

Two days after the interview, an unnamed White House source revealed that Reagan was considering William Bennett to be NEH chair. His nomination easily passed Senate scrutiny, and Bennett was inaugurated to the prestigious post in the week before Christmas 1981. Although Reagan would later appoint Bradford to the Board of Foreign Scholarships, which administers the Fulbright Program, the Dallas professor largely faded from the national scene, but not from the consciousness of his conservative admirers, most of whom were white southern academicians. They saw in him a martyr sacrificed in their war against the forces of liberalism and cultural anarchy. "In the long run," reflected one of his staunchest supporters, "the political assassination of this immensely learned man may well have been the proverbial blessing in disguise for Bradford and a Pyrrhic victory for his tormentors; for the period between 1983 and 1993 proved to be the most productive of his career, highlighted by an outpouring of important books and essays that would not have been possible had he been tied down with administrative chores."[26]

A prolific scholar, Bradford employed the essay as his preferred mode of expression; throughout his career, he authored scores of tightly focused but abstrusely written papers whose themes had large cultural and intellectual applications. Although he never systematized his works, he customarily re-published his more salient articles in book form, producing seven thick volumes.[27] He boldly asserted himself as an alternative voice to what he called the mandarins who teach in Northern universities. Among those enamored of Bradford's insights was the conservative Dartmouth College scholar Jeffery Hart, who proclaimed Bradford an "American Plutarch" whose thoughts were "profoundly rooted in the tradition of Western civilization, Roman and biblical and regional. . . . [H]is work is both historical and deeply philosophical."[28]

Insofar as Bradford's sense of history and philosophy led him to articulate concepts "biblical and regional," his ideas were actually rooted in a cosmology influenced less from the New Testament and more from a sectarian belief encapsulated in the term "Reconstruction Theology." This dogma sprang largely from the thinking of the late-nineteenth-century southern Presbyterian theologian Robert L. Dabney and was carried forward by Richard M. Weaver, in common with Bradford a disciple of Donald Davidson and the Nashville Agrarians.[29]

Both Dabney and Weaver assumed that a decline of biblical morality in America began with New England Unitarianism and its rejection of Jesus' divinity and gained momentum with northern intellectual enthusiasm for both the English Enlightenment's rational humanism and the French Revolution's egalitarian fervor. Dabney postulated that the antebellum South's defense of slavery and a stratified social order (which he grounded in his carefully selective interpretation of the Bible) enabled the region to retain its larger fidelity to the sanctity of Holy Scripture. Writing in the 1940s, Weaver espoused Dabney's essential themes, recasting them in light of the Agrarians' assertion that the antebellum South was a premodern society untainted by scientific rationalism. "The Southern people," he reflected, "reached the . . . Civil War one of the few religious peoples left in the Western World," and when the South went down in defeat in 1865, "the last barrier to the secular spirit of science, materialism, and pragmatism was swept away."[30]

Drawing his belief system from Dabney, Weaver, and like-minded southern chauvinists, Bradford presented the Civil War as a religious conflict, an American Armageddon that pitted the pious South against the secular North. He crafted a spiritual paradigm that contrasted a virtuous Bible-based South of aristocracy and slavery with the less worthy, humanistic North of democracy and social leveling. Abraham Lincoln's Union, he proclaimed, personified "modern man" whose prototype was "the figure of Dr. Faustus, the omnicompetent master of all the sciences, the alchemist who somehow summarizes the restless spirit of Western civilization." Bradford's imagined South, by contrast, had been largely unaffected by the scientific revolution, remained faithful to its traditions—especially its religious roots—and stood immune to secularism's soul-killing self-righteousness. The "Antebellum Southerner was not modern even though his adversary was," he lectured. "The Southerner could not believe that engineering, medicine, and the popular ballot could cure all the ills the flesh is heir to."[31]

Bradford worshiped reverent, gray-clad soldiers and the pious officers who led them. Referencing the Georgia historian E. Merton Coulter, he assured his audiences that "the Confederate Army was extraordinary among modern forces for its size—in this with no rival but Cromwell's host—in being free from vice." Just as the fervent Puritans of the English Civil War marched under the command of godly generals, so men of abiding faith similarly guided Johnny Reb. Bradford deemed Generals Thomas "Stonewall" Jackson and John Breckenridge and Admiral Raphael Semmes Christ-like exemplars whose saintliness stimulated the faith-professions of Generals Braxton Bragg, Joseph E. Johnston, William Hardee, Dick Ewell, and John B. Hood; and he saved his strongest accolades for the southern clergy.[32] "Almost to a man," he sermonized, "the religious leaders of the Antebellum Southern society called for secession and led the way in reconciling the people of the South to all the hardships secession would cost them." These zealot divines proclaimed that "separation from the North was a 'holy enterprise'" for they perceived something profoundly "wrong with Northern religion."[33]

The essential flaw with northern faith specifically and Yankee society in general was its failure to acknowledge the inerrant Word of God. Embracing the apostasy of science, northern intellectuals and clerics alike succumbed to the egalitarian heresies of the French Revolution, best illustrated in their antibiblical crusade against slavery. Clothing the institution of human bondage with the garb of divine sanction, Bradford declared that in "exalting their own religious sense above the historic witness of the Church, the abolitionist blasphemed." From this he argued that "if they behaved that way on one issue, using hieratic language to explore their own endless fresh revelations, they might well be expected to do the same in another context."[34]

Bradford preached that his own generation manifested that other context. For him the celebration of a spiritual South juxtaposed to a secular North meant far more than a mere exercise in antiquarian piety. If the infidel Yankee stood as the enemy in 1861, his spiritual descendants remained a threat more than a century later. "For all of the great issues fought out in the 1860s are with us still," he warned his listeners, "sometimes disguised, but in their fundamental character never changing." He sermonized that the post–World War II civil rights movement and the late-twentieth-century quest for multiculturalism emanated from the North's selfsame lack of biblical understanding and thus persisted as a threat to his native region's fundamental values. "The consequences of their admonitions are among us still, setting most Southerners aside from the primary delusions of our place and time," he averred. "Historians who wish to understand Southern persistence in character would do well to consider this . . . and be less concerned with explanations of Southern particularity which derive from slavery alone."[35]

Bradford's sense of religious and social righteousness rested upon his historical interpretations and underscored his essential faith in the virtues of human inequality. Widely read but never formally trained in the historian's craft, he approached the past as a dedicated ideologue rather than as a dispassionate observer of the human chronicle.[36] While a historian would, by his profession's canons, feel compelled to present documentary or other evidence to support his views of slavery's supposed efficacy or a biologist deem it essential to cite scientific research to substantiate any assertion of racial inferiority, no such compulsions moved the Texan. He issued his dictums grounded upon his personal proclivities and prejudices, feeling unobligated to justify his positions beyond this frame of reference. Bradford pleasured in his role as "a professor of literature" who was "free to range throughout the humanities and to combine insights from several disciplines with his particular skills as rhetor."[37] From his training as a student of language and its persuasive powers he assumed an intrinsic right to judge intuitively the worth of any document—poem, essay, political treatise, sermon, or history—and to determine which had the virtue of truth and which should be dismissed as polemic.

Bradford, of course, scaled the words of others with the measure of his predetermined sense of the past. Although the Dallas professor—in common with the Agrarians—disdained scientific analysis, he eagerly lent his imprimatur to Robert Fogel and Stanley Engerman's 1975 statistical study *Time on the Cross*, which concluded that enslaved antebellum blacks and independent subsistence farmers enjoyed almost equal levels of material comfort. "For those raised altogether inside" the "framework of Southern memory," Bradford declared, "there is no surprise at all." In his view, Fogel and Engerman validated the southern white tradition of benevolent slavery, a fact that should make it difficult—if not impossible—for liberal intellectuals to retain faith with their less-than-honest image of a malevolent slave system popularized in the "cult of Union, Father Abraham and the significance . . . of that great Gnostic fit that was our Civil War." Emboldened by *Time on the Cross*, he pledged his participation in future debates over the peculiar institution's merits—an effort he looked "forward to with warm anticipation."[38]

Given Bradford's sense of "Southern memory," he casually dismissed almost all of slavery's post-1950 historiography. "For reasons that have more to do with contemporary politics and the intellectual fashions of our times," he essayed in 1989, "we have experienced . . . a veritable explosion of commentary on the phenomenon of American Negro slavery." Those books were "so numerous and predictable" that they negated any "serious consideration of their subjects." Their only purpose, he complained, was "to give those who write . . . an opportunity to demonstrate their own moral refinement—as 'ethical proof' of their right to instruct those benighted conservatives" who do not "hate slavery to the point of distraction."[39]

To Bradford's disappointment, he felt that his would-be hero Robert Fogel succumbed to the liberals' blandishments. In a second edition of *Time on the Cross*, the author acknowledged that however good the material comforts provided slaves by the South's master class, they failed to make up for the Negro's lack of human liberty. "Fogel has . . . to prevent neo-abolitionist hostility," surrendered to "the vituperative political context of contemporary American historiography." Unrepentant himself, Bradford assured his audience that the original publication, minus any apology, had "given the American intellectual community not only all it would wish to know about slavery, but . . . a good deal more than it was and is ready to digest."[40]

However flawed Bradford's historical methodology, the value of his work lies in its consistent interpretation of American history as a fundamental struggle between order and anarchy, and in its influence upon other scholars who employ his views of the past to define their vision of the future. Bradford especially admired the American South and championed it as a society guided by a sagacious elite and dedicated to the preservation of fundamental white cultural values. A firm believer in virtuous aristocracy, he condemned all those he deemed social levelers, including French Jacobeans, Abraham Lincoln, and modern advocates of the civil rights movement. Bradford especially despised contemporary historians enamored with the concept of human equality. He airily dismissed these "gentlemen [as] greatly confused . . . about our early history" who "threaten what remains intact from an originally wholesome political inheritance."[41]

Bradford portrayed the past as a grandiose experience peopled with high-principled champions and their foils. He imagined the seventeenth-century settlers who first constructed plantations upon southern soil as men "from landed families" dedicated to a culture premised upon patriarchy, "a social system more like old Scotland" or Anglo-Saxon Britain. Committed to the improvement of life for themselves and for their progeny, they dreamed of the "acquisition and cultivation of land, 'real property.' . . . Theirs was a mind-set which presumed a culture of families, not atomistic individualism in the modern sense." Bradford held that long before Negro slavery came to symbolize the South, these men's commitment to place and kindred defined the region as they developed a sense of noblesse oblige, a dedication to the preservation of the communal weal. "The gentleman," Bradford claimed, "was no mere decorative creature; instead, he was an honored figure whose lofty status was matched by his function and large responsibility, encouraging the kind of deference which gives excellence to social unity." Born to privilege, the gentleman had a "heroic mission," the safeguarding "of civil life which gives meaning to the acts of the statesman, the warrior, the poet, and the priest." Aristocracy ensured social order and became the cement which shored up its "battlements within which all others found shelter."[42]

Bradford scoffed at the scholarship of those historians who would define the colonial South as a "debate over the merits and demerits of slavery as a social and economic system for half-wild Blacks and seventeenth-century Anglo-Saxons living uneasily together," or who would impose upon the region concepts of a white class struggle. Prior to the American Revolution, social stratification (class and slavery) was assumed to be normal and appropriate. "Egalitarianism got no foothold in the original South," he lectured, nor were there protests against an articulated society. "Bacon's Rebellion was . . . no outburst of democracy. Neither were the 'Regulators' of North Carolina. . . . These explosions were . . . 'against a governing class derelict in its duty,' not reductions of the idea of class."[43] For in the South, Bradford defined the struggle for independence from England as a conservative revolution, one designed "to preserve a familiar way of life." The region's oligarchy resented an all-powerful London government that threatened their local autonomy and prevented their "acting together against levellers, Indians, and the champions" of economic disorder. Thus to argue that the Declaration of Independence, written by a Virginia slave owner, was intended to affirm the equality of mankind sorely failed the test of logic. "This particular Declaration," Bradford reasoned, "makes it plain that Englishmen were in dispute with Englishmen . . . on English grounds." To Bradford, no modern-day "liberal, new or old, can make of that framework" a plea for universal equality.[44]

Bradford insisted that heresies associated with the Declaration threatened the destruction of American civilization. In the preface to his anthology *A Better Guide Than Reason*, he explained that "presupposed in every chapter is the necessity to correct conventional misreadings of the Declaration of

Independence: that is to say, the imperative to discourage compulsive filtering of our national beginnings through the first sentence of paragraph two in that instrument of separation." Jefferson, of course, was no egalitarian. Believing in the innate inferiority of the Negro race, he never intended that any non-Anglo-Saxon be included as citizens in the new American nation. "Jefferson," Bradford wrote, was "consistent with the ancients in maintaining that a republic should be racially homogeneous—in our case, Anglo-Saxon."[45]

Bradford believed that a later generation, one represented by Abraham Lincoln, would out of misguided humanitarianism forget the importance of homogeneity. "It is probable that Lincoln disliked slavery," Bradford reasoned, "just as it is obvious that most Southerners recognized slaves as human beings in that they hoped to see them accept Christianity." But while most white southerners never perceived the Negro as a potential citizen able to function on the same level with whites, Lincoln stretched the phrase "all men are created equal" beyond all reasonable interpretation and applied it to black men. This distortion of the Declaration of Independence became Lincoln's "lasting and terrible impact on the nation's destiny." His insistence that "the Negro was included in the promise" of the Declaration and that the "Declaration bound his countrymen to fulfill a pledge hidden in that document" moved the nation "toward a radical transformation of American society." While this application was to the issue of race, its larger implications involved the profound undermining of a properly articulated social structure. It was "the base and wheels of . . . the Trojan horse of our home-grown Jacobinism."[46]

Bradford emphasized that "the founders of the Southern Confederacy" saw themselves as emulating their ancestors who had earlier rebelled against George III. Southern statesmen considered secession "as an attempt to preserve a precious heritage, a known and agreed upon social, cultural, and political arrangement developed in an unbroken continuum from reverenced antecedents." For too long, white southerners had endured the North's disparagement of their social order. They could no longer tolerate the "closing of territories to Southern settlers," the North's glorification of John Brown, and the threats implied in Lincoln's "House Divided" speech. "The dangers and the indignities of 1860–61," he reasoned, "were worse than those of 1774–1776." In the end, the Confederate fathers "felt no hesitation in pleading the example of that past to resist what they perceived as obnoxious alterations of its nature: unsanctioned changes, however high-sounding might be the terms employed to rationalize this introduction."[47]

The North, of course, won the Civil War and with that validated Lincoln's interpretation of the Declaration. To Bradford, the ultimate and tragic result was the formation of a polyglot society bent on the establishment of a "classless, raceless, sexless, and cultureless melting pot." America had lost sight of its vital essence, the fundamental heritage of Anglo-Saxon civilization. School children mistakenly celebrated the "pietistic arrogance" enshrined "in the iconography of the Lincoln myth," praised the "civil disobedience" of Martin Luther King, and accepted as natural the invasion of their land by immigrants from south of the Rio Grande. "When our most refined moralists insist that . . . borders be ignored and distinctions of citizenship be set aside," Bradford warned, our "own institutions and identities" would be imperiled.[48]

As the twentieth century entered its last quarter, Bradford argued that the prospects of halting the American march toward cultural nihilism grew ever-dimmer. In spite of the partial successes of George Wallace and the consequent faithfulness of many southern Republicans to the values of a racist South, the hope of achieving a national conservative majority seemed remote. "There is, however . . . an example which might be employed in achieving the end of a durable conservative majority," he postulated in 1974, "the example . . . of the Old South. And the clearest proof was in the organization of the armies by means of which that society almost achieved its independence." Certainly the Nashville Agrarians had yearned for white southern cultural autonomy, and Bradford reflected that "there are others—clergymen, lawyers, journalists, and politicians who hear the same music." Such a circle formed around Bradford, sharing with him a worship of the Old South and the Confederacy it spawned, and despising what they together perceived as an overbearing, malignant North.[49] To Bradford and his closest confidants, the late Confederacy represented far more than a nostalgic might-have-been; to them it stood as a political and social model, an ordered alternative to the anarchy they associated with the late twentieth century. This informal cadre assembled on numerous occasions—sometimes as friends, sometimes as academics celebrating the Agrarians' philosophical legacy, and sometimes as political ideologues questing for a white southern version of the conservative ideal.[50]

Bradford's circle embraced the Lost Cause's iconography and the Texan often led them in its adoration. In 1974, he and his friends convened with the North Carolina Conservative Society, where for entertainment they screened *Birth of a Nation*, the silent-film classic that glorified a high-principled Old South, a courageous Confederate cause, and a heroic Ku Klux Klan. "There in the darkened hall," reminisced one participant, sat Mel Bradford "with scores of college students at his feet." He read "aloud each caption as it flashed upon the screen, and [did so] with no small gusto."[51] Bradford, the students, and the Tar Heel conservatives become one with the North Carolina native Thomas Dixon, his negrophobic novels, and the movie that animated his themes.

Enveloped by the intellectual culture of the racist South, such men resented all criticism of their region, which by extension was also criticism of them. Believing that there were "almost no public voices raised in defense of the South and its traditions," in 1979 Thomas Fleming and Clyde Wilson, two of Bradford's compatriots, published the inaugural issue of the *Southern Partisan*, a conservative magazine dedicated to reminding its readers "of all that was and is distinctively good about the South." Its editors promised to counteract the "barrage of [anti-South] propaganda from university lectures, magazines, movies and television programs" and to expose as well the traitorous "horde of intellectual Southerners—happily expatriate—who make their living ridiculing their homeland." Men of considerable academic clout themselves, Fleming, who possessed a doctorate in the classics from Chapel Hill, and Wilson, a historian at the University of South Carolina, envisioned their new periodical as a means of bridging the gap between their vision of a South restored to the value system of the Nashville Agrarians and those "affluent and educated Southerners who are in danger of losing their birthright."[52]

From the *Southern Partisan*'s first issue, Bradford played a major role in its development. Clyde Wilson encouraged him, praising him in its opening pages as a spokesman for the South in the "tradition . . . of Patrick Henry and Jefferson, John Taylor and John Randolph, Calhoun and [Jefferson] Davis, [and] the . . . 20th century agrarians." Bradford donated an article to its initial publication and contributed regularly thereafter, served on its editorial board, and, "after years of persuasion," became its principal editor in 1990. A magazine spokesman expressed delight to "have Mel Bradford officially installed at the helm of [the] journal" for, he reflected, Bradford had "always been our guardian of the tablets."[53]

These "tablets" projected an idealized image of the Confederacy and offered it, along with the Old South it protected, as a viable alternative to the Yankee-dominated South of their own era. With such regular features as the "CSA Today," the "Scalawag Award," and "Whistling Dixie," the *Southern Partisan*'s writers consistently ridiculed the political correctness they identified with civil rights, an economic culture homogenized by northern chain stores, and a wrongheaded, government-imposed spirit of egalitarianism. Contributors and readers alike saw themselves as champions of an unbroken thought process that stretched from John C. Calhoun and the antebellum fire-eaters to the regional chauvinism of the Nashville Agrarians. And, as true believers, they were hypersensitive to any and all who critiqued their beliefs.

When in 1992 an iconoclastic journalist for the Austin-based *Texas Monthly* disparaged Bradford, an editorialist for the *Southern Partisan* jumped to his defense. "What is one to make of an intellectual who despises Abraham Lincoln, believes that equality is a humbug, and compares the Klan . . . to the

French resistance of World War II?" asked the perplexed journalist. The answer, responded the *Southern Partisan*'s writer, was that Bradford represented a legitimate trend in contemporary southern thought. "A good many people agree with" the Dallas professor, who "operates in a well-defined historical tradition . . . that is coming back into prominence after several decades of eclipse." Had the *Texas Monthly* journalist "driven a few miles west" he "might have spoken to Grady McWhiney at [Texas Christian University], whose views on eighteenth- and nineteenth-century America often coincided with Bradford's, as do those of Clyde Wilson (South Carolina), Forrest MacDonald (University of Alabama), Marion Montgomery (University of Georgia), and many others." These men were but a small portion of Bradford's intellectual circle and they, along with many others, mourned his death in 1993.[54]

Inspired in large measure by Bradford's teachings, some prominent members of the Department of History at the University of Alabama—along with such cohorts as Fleming, Wilson, and McWhiney—met in Tuscaloosa in 1994 to organize the "League of the South" as a movement of southern thought-leaders dedicated to "secession [as] the best way to restore good government in the South" and to preserve its "Christian, Anglo-Celtic" civilization. They acknowledged Bradford as their prophet, for his writings warned of the dangers to their view of society, of the challenges to it from without by a powerful national government dedicated to multiculturalism, and from within by liberal college professors and special-interest groups promoting minority rights. The League's membership grew to include professors of history, religion, political science, literature, journalism, and philosophy at such respected schools as Clemson, Emory, Baylor, and Virginia Commonwealth University and the universities of Virginia, South Carolina, Georgia, and Houston as well as smaller institutions across the South.[55]

To counteract what the League designated as the "anti-South" textbooks used in public schools and university classrooms, it sponsored summer institutes and weekend seminars, staffed them with scholars from among their membership, and indoctrinated high school teachers and homeschooling parents with a canted version of the past. The League recognized that in order to shape the next generation of white southerners, it had to deal with the sensitive issue of race, but it pledged to do so "free of hatred and malice." This "does not mean," explained its president, that "we must subscribe to the flawed Jacobin notion of egalitarianism, nor does it mean that white Southerners should give control over their civilization and its institutions to another race, whether it be native blacks or Hispanic immigrants. Nowhere, outside of liberal dogma, is any nation called upon to commit cultural and ethnic suicide."[56] Bradford would have applauded the League of the South's goals, for he, too, longed for a South freed from oppressive forms of northern egalitarianism and bound once again by a glorious Anglo-Saxon order to the exclusion of all other races. Perhaps a clue to that desire exists in his presentation of his academic self. Like any good scholar, he carefully listed those organizations that defined his persona: the Modern Language Association, the American Political Science Association, the Southwestern American Literature Association, and, of course, the Sons of Confederate Veterans.[57]

## Notes

1. Melvin Eustace Bradford," *Contemporary Authors*, (Detroit: Gale Research, 1984), 13:69–70.

2. M. E. Bradford, "All to Do Over: The Revolutionary Precedent and the Secession of 1861," in *A Better Guide Than Reason: Studies in the American Revolution*, by Bradford (Peru, Ill.: Sugden. 1979), 153–68; Tomas H. Landess, "Partisan Conversation with M. E. Bradford," *Southern Partisan* 5 (Spring 1985): 37–42.

3. "Melvin Eustace Bradford," *Contemporary Authors*, (Detroit: Gale Research, 1984), 13:69–70; Bradford, *The Reactionary Imperative: Essays Literary and Political* (Chicago: Open Court, 1999), viii (quotation).

4. M. E. Bradford, "On Remembering Who We Are: A Political Credo," in *Remembering Who We Are: Observations of a Southern Conservative*, by Bradford (Athens: University of Georgia Press, 1985), 11 (quotations); Landess, "Partisan Conversation," 37–42.

5. Twelve Southerners, *I'll Take My Stand: The South and the Agrarian Tradition* (New York: Harper and Brothers, 1930).

6. "Melvin Eustace Bradford," *Contemporary Authors*, 69–70; Gary Cartwright, "Mr. Right," *Texas Monthly* 20 (March 1992): 60, 65 (quotations).

7. Dora Davenport Jones, *History of the Julia Jackson Chapter #141, United Daughters of the Confederacy, Fort Worth Texas, 1897–1976* (Fort Worth: "6333" Kwik-Kopy Printing Center, 1976), 34 (first quotation); M. E. Bradford quoted in Lee Cullum, "The Controversial Career of Professor Melvin E. Bradford," *Dallas Times-Herald*, 2 September 2, 1990 (second quotation).

8. Cartwright, "Mr. Right," 65 (first quotation), 66 (second quotation). Although Jaffa and Bradford shared many common values, for years they carried on a friendly disputation over the role Lincoln played in American history (see M. E. Bradford, Harry V. Jaffa, Jeffrey Hart, "Time on the Cross: Debate," *National Review* 27 [28 March 1974]: 340–42, 359; Harry V. Jaffa, "In Abraham's Bosom: A Lifelong Dispute about Abraham Lincoln Has Been Remanded to a Higher Court," *National Review* 45 [12 April 1993]: 50–51).

9. M. E. Bradford, "The Heresy of Equality: A Reply to Harry Jaffa," in *A Better Guide Than Reason*, by Bradford, 31 (quotation).

10. Cartwright, "Mr. Right," 65; M. E. Bradford, "Memories," *Modern Age* 26 (Summer/Fall 1982): 242 (quotations).

11. M. E. Bradford, "Memories," *Modern Age* 26 (Summer/Fall 1982): 242 (quotations).

12. "Melvin Eustace Bradford," *Contemporary Authors*, 69–70; Thomas H. Landess, "The Education of Mel Bradford: The Vanderbilt Years," in *A Defender of Southern Conservatism: M. E. Bradford and His Achievements*, ed. Clyde N. Wilson (Columbia: University of Missouri Press, 1999), 15–16 (quotations).

13. Landess, "The Education of Mel Bradford," 10–11; M. E. Bradford, "The Agrarian Tradition: An Affirmation," in *Remembering Who We Are*, by Bradford, 83 (first quotation); M. E. Bradford, "Rhetoric and Respectability: Conservatives and the Problem of Language," in *Reactionary Imperative*, by Bradford, 98 (second quotation). As early as 1939, Donald Davidson condemned the emerging young historian C. Vann Woodward for suggesting that "class conflict" played a role in the Populist movement. The problem with Woodward, he wrote, is that "the class approach" means, as it generally seems to mean nowadays, the obliteration of the color line in the South. . . . This alone is a solid and sufficient reason for the traditional Southern insistence that the Negro be put in a separate category and that his problems be treated separately. . . . In retrospect, it seems that it would have been a wise course, at the time of Negro emancipation, to remove the race question from politics by giving the Negro a status at least as special as that of the American Indian" (Donald Davidson, "The Class Approach to Southern Problems," *Southern Review* 5 [1939]: 272). Almost two decades later, Davidson wrote in a Canadian magazine that the "racial differences are simply too real for the South to accept an amalgamation of the Negro society with the white. The South's determined preference is to maintain white society as white. That preference cannot be removed by the decree of any court" (Donald Davidson, "Integration Means a Cold Civil War," *Toronto Star Weekly Magazine*, 9 November 1957, 36).

14. M. E. Bradford, "The Agrarian Tradition: An Affirmation," in *Remembering Who We Are*, by Bradford, 85 (third quotation), 86 (first quotation), 87 (second quotation).

15. "Melvin Eustace Bradford," *Contemporary Authors*, 69–70. One of Bradford's biographers incorrectly lists him as teaching at Abilene Christian College instead of Hardin-Simmons University; both institutions are in Abilene, Texas (Landess, "The Education of Mel Bradford," 16). The bulk of Bradford's early works were divided between essays that argued that liberal scholars largely misread and misinterpreted the Mississippi novelist and Nobel laureate William Faulkner and that touted the contributions to southern culture made by his mentor Donald Davidson and by Davidson's compatriots among the Nashville Agrarians. A bibliography of Bradford's works appears in Alan Cornett, "An M. E. Bradford Checklist," in *A Defender of Southern Conservatism*, ed. Wilson, 152–85.

16. M. E. Bradford, "Lincoln's New Frontier: A Rhetoric for Continuing Revolution," *Triumph* 6 (1971), reprinted as M. E. Bradford, "Lincoln, The Declaration, and Secular Puritanism: A Rhetoric for Continuing Revolution," in *A Better Guide Than Reason*, by Bradford, 187.

17. M. E. Bradford, "Lincoln, The Declaration, and Secular Puritanism," 187 (first quotation), 191 (second quotation), 192, 196–99.

18. Lee Cullum, "The Controversial Career of Professor Melvin E. Bradford," *Dallas Times-Herald*, 2 September 1990; untitled newspaper clipping, 23 September 1984, in Melvin E. Bradford file, Texas/Dallas History and Archives Division, Dallas Public Library (DPL), Dallas, Tex.

19. "Melvin Eustace Bradford," *Contemporary Authors*, 69–70; Lee Cullum, "The Controversial Career of Professor Melvin E. Bradford," *Dallas Times-Herald*, 2 September 1990; untitled newspaper clipping, 23 September 1984, in Melvin E. Bradford file, Texas/Dallas History and Archives Division, DPL; Cartwright, "Mr. Right," 64.

20. *New York Times*, 20 September 1981 (quotation); N. Cider, "Report from the Capitols: Bradford for the Humanities," *Southern Partisan* 2 (Fall 1981): 4–6. One of Bradford's former students and a participant in various administrative functions in both the Reagan and George H. W. Bush administrations argued that "Bradford from the outset was President Reagan's favorite for the NEH post not so much for his learning, as for his charm as a conversationalist and storyteller" (Benjamin B. Alexander, "The Man of Letters and the Faithful Heart," in *A Defender of Southern Conservatism*, ed. Wilson, 31.

21. *New York Times*, 20 September 1981 (first quotation), 27 December 1981 (second quotation); *Dallas Morning News*, 21 September 1981; *Washington Post*, 3 September 1980, 11 and 21 September 1981.

22. M. E. Bradford, "Culture and Anarchy: Federal Support for the Arts and Humanities," in *Remembering Who We Are*, by Bradford, 95 (first quotation), 97 (second quotation), 99–100 (third, fourth, fifth quotations). For later examples of Bradford's critiques of the National Endowment for the Humanities, see M. E. Bradford, "Subsidizing the Muses," in *Remembering Who We Are*, by Bradford, 102–9; M. E. Bradford, "The Form and Pressure of Our Time: The Social Role of Modern Drama," in *Reactionary Imperative*, by Bradford, 15–26.

23. *New York Times*, 24 September 1981; *Washington Post*, 14, 15, 20, 22 October 1981 (quotations); M. E. Bradford, "A Southern Candidate Recalls His Struggle," *Humanities in the South* 56 (Fall 1982): 1, 12–13; Marshall L. DeRosa, "M. E. Bradford's Constitutional Theory: A Southern Reactionary's Affirmation of the Rule of Law," in *A Defender of Southern Conservatism*, ed. Wilson, 123.

24. *New York Times*, 27 October 1981; *Washington Post*, 28 October 1981.

25. "Well," he responded, "who's to know what one would have done?" (*New York Times*, 27 October 1981; *Washington Post*, 28 October 1981 [quotations]).

26. *Washington Post*, 31 October 1981; *New York Times*, 14 November, 27 December 1981; James McClellan, "Walking the Levee with Mel Bradford," in *A Defender of Southern Conservatism*, ed. Wilson, 41 (quotation).

27. Bradford, *A Better Guide Than Reason*; M. E. Bradford, *A Worthy Company: Brief Lives of the Framers of the United States Constitution* (Marlborough, N.H.: Plymouth Rock Foundation, 1982); M. E. Bradford, *Generations of the Faithful Heart: On the Literature of the South* (La Salle, Ill.: Sugden, 1983); Bradford, *Remembering Who We Are*; Bradford, *Reactionary Imperative*; M. E. Bradford, *Against the Barbarians, and Other Reflections on Familiar Themes* (Columbia: University of Missouri Press, 1992);

M. E. Bradford, *Original Intentions: On the Making and Ratification of the United States Constitution* (Athens: University of Georgia Press, 1993).

28. M. E. Bradford, "Artists at Home: Froster and Faulkner," in *Reactionary Imperative*, by Bradford, 1 (first quotation); Jeffery Hart, "Introduction," in *A Better Guide Than Reason*, by Bradford, xiii (second quotation).

29. Edward H. Sebesta and Euan Hague, "The US Civil War as a Theological War: Confederate Christian Nationalism and the League of the South," *Canadian Review of American Studies* 32 (2002): 257–64. For a lengthy exposition on Dabney's theological ideas, see his *A Defense of Virginia and the South (And Through Her, Of the South) in Recent and Pending Contests against the Sectional Party* (1867; repr., Harrisonburg, Va: Sprinkle, 1999).

30. Sebesta and Hague, "The US Civil War as a Theological War," 258–59; Richard M. Weaver, "The Older Religiousness of the South," *Sewanee Review* 51 (Spring 1943); 248 (quotation). Weaver's article is reprinted in George M. Curtis III and James J. Thompson Jr., eds., *The Southern Essays of Richard M. Weaver* (Indianapolis: Liberty Press, 1987), 134–46.

31. M. E. Bradford, "The Theology of Secession," *Southern Partisan* 11 (Fourth Quarter 1991): 21.

32. Bradford, "Theology of Secession," 20, 22 (first quotation). Although Coulter and Bradford shared similar views about the righteousness of the Confederate cause and the spiritual virtues of the army that fought for it, Bradford broadened the historian's observation beyond its original context. Writing about the camp-meeting revivals that broke out among the Rebel armies during the winter of 1863–64, Coulter reflected that for "a time vice among the soldiers was routed, and the Confederate army took on the nature of Cromwell's Ironsides" (E. Merton Coulter, *The Confederate States of America, 1861–1865* [Baton Rouge: Louisiana State University Press, 1950], 526–27).

33. Bradford, "Theology of Secession," 23 (quotations), 25.

34. Ibid., 21.

35. Ibid., 24 (first quotation), 25 (second quotation).

36. "Piety, or better pietas, runs through M. E. Bradford's work," wrote Elizabeth Fox-Genovese and Eugene D. Genovese in their analysis of his historical vision. "Bradford considered himself, and faithfully assumed the responsibilities of, a steward—a custodian of the collective memory of the South and, beyond the South, of the essence of what it means to be an American" (Elizabeth Fox-Genovese and Eugene Genovese, "M. E. Bradford's Historical Vision," in *A Defender of Southern Conservatism*, ed. Wilson, 78).

37. M. E. Bradford, "Memories," 243.

38. M. E. Bradford, "Just as We Were Told," *National Review* 27 (28 March 1974), 340 (first quotation), 341 (second, third, fourth quotations).

39. M. E. Bradford, "The Ambiguous Muse," *National Review* 41 (24 February 1989): 50.

40. M. E. Bradford, "All We Would Want to Know," *National Review* 41 (31 December 1989): 39 (second quotation), 40 (first quotation).

41. M. E. Bradford, "And God Defend the Right: The American Revolution and the Limits of Christian Obedience," in *Remembering Who We Are*, by Bradford, 39.

42. M. E. Bradford, "First Fathers: The Colonial Origins of the Southern Tradition," in *A Better Guide Than Reason*, by Bradford, 177 (fourth and fifth quotations), 179 (first quotation); M. E. Bradford, "Where We Were Born and Raised: The Southern Conservative Tradition," in *Reactionary Imperative*, by Bradford, 118, 120 (second quotation); M. E. Bradford, "Is the American Experience Conservative?" in *Reactionary Imperative*, by Bradford, 136 (third quotation).

43. Bradford, "First Fathers," 174 (first quotation), 178 (second, third quotations); M. E. Bradford, "Word from the Forks of the Creek: The Revolution and the Populist Heritage," in *A Better Guide Than Reason*, by Bradford, 61; Bradford, "Where We Were Born and Raised," 118.

44. Bradford, "Where We Were Born and Raised," 121 (first quotation); Bradford, "The Heresy of Equality," 36, 37 (second quotation), 39 (third quotation).

45. M. E. Bradford, "Preface," in *A Better Guide Than Reason*, by Bradford, xi (first quotation); M. E. Bradford, "Franklin and Jefferson: The Making and Binding of Self," ibid., 143 (second quotation).

46. M. E. Bradford, "Against Lincoln: A Speech at Gettysburg," in *Reactionary Imperative*, by Bradford, 223 (first quotation); Bradford, "The Heresy of Equality," 32 (second quotation); M. E. Bradford, "The Lincoln Legacy: A Long View," in *Remembering Who We Are*, by Bradford, 144 (third quotation); M. E. Bradford, "A Fire Bell in the Night," ibid., 48 (fourth quotation).

47. M. E. Bradford, "All to Do Over: The Revolutionary Precedent and the Secession of 1861," in *A Better Guide Than Reason*, by. Bradford, 154 (first, second, fourth quotations), 159 (third quotation).

48. Bradford, "A Fire Bell in the Night," 52 (first quotation); Bradford, "The Heresy of Equality," 46 (second quotation); Bradford, "The Lincoln Legacy," 155 (third quotation); M. E. Bradford, "Rhetoric and Respectability: Conservatives and the Problem of Language," in *Reactionary Imperative*, by Bradford, 97–98 (fourth quotation); M. E. Bradford, "Sentiment or Survival: The Case Against Amnesty," in *Remembering Who We Are*, by Bradford, 114 (fifth quotation).

49. Bradford, "Lasting Lessons of Southern Politics," 56 (first quotation); Bradford, "The Agrarian Tradition," 89 (quotation).

50. Marion Montgomery, "Remembering Who M. E. Bradford Is," *Modern Age* 41 (Spring 1999): 115–16. In the preface to Bradford's discussion of the "Theology of Secession," the *Southern Partisan's* editor noted that paper had originally been presented before the "annual assembly of Southerners at Willie Pie's Store in Crozier, Virginia (Bradford, "Theology of Secession," 20).

51. T. Kenneth Cribb Jr., "M. E. Bradford: An Appreciation," *Southern Partisan* 12 (Fourth Quarter 1992 [1993]): 8 (quotation); Norman Stewart, "'Galloping Tintypes,' The Birth of the Movies: The Legacy of D. W. Griffith," *Southern Partisan* 13 (Fourth Quarter, 1993 [1994]): 45. Note that volumes 12 and 13 of the *Southern Partisan* were dated incorrectly. The actual years of publication are in brackets.

52. "Forward," *Southern Partisan* 1 (1979): n.p.

53. Clyde N. Wilson, Review of *A Better Guide Than Reason* by M. E. Bradford, *Southern Partisan*, 1 (1979), 35 (first quotation); "At the Helm," *Southern Partisan* 10 (Fourth Quarter, 1990), 10 (second, third, fourth quotations). For Bradford's contributions to the periodical, see M. E. Bradford, "William Henry Drayton, a Neglected Founding Father," *Southern Partisan* 1 (1979): 7–17; M. E. Bradford, "The Beast in Todd County," *Southern Partisan* 2 (Fall 1982): 20–24; M. E. Bradford, "Window on the West," *Southern Partisan* 3 (Fall 1983): 22–23; M. E. Bradford, "The Dark Side of Abraham Lincoln," *Southern Partisan* 5 (Fall 1985): 18–22; M. E. Bradford, "Samuel Chase," *Southern Partisan* 6 (Summer 1986), 40–44; M. E. Bradford, "The 'Gamecock' of South Carolina," *Southern Partisan* 6/7 (Fall 1986/Winter 1987): 41–43, 46; M. E. Bradford, "With No Love of Innovation: The Prophetic Politics of Rawlins Lowndes," *Southern Partisan* 7 (Spring 1987): 33, 35–37; M. E. Bradford, "The Nabob as Anti-Federalist: Benjamin Harrison of Virginia," *Southern Partisan* 7 (Summer 1987): 38–39; M. E. Bradford, "The Trumpet Voice of Freedom: Patrick Henry and the Southern Political Tradition," *Southern Partisan* 8 (Summer 1988): 16–19, 22; M. E. Bradford, "Steady Hand at the Wheel: Thomas Johnson of Maryland," *Southern Partisan* 10 (Second Quarter 1990): 37–39; Bradford, "Theology of Secession," 20–25.

54. Cartwright, "Mr. Right," 60 (first quotation); Matthew Sandel, "Triium," *Southern Partisan* 12 (First Quarter 1992): 7 (second, third, fourth, fifth quotations).

55. *Rome (Ga.) News-Tribune*, 7 January 1996, quoted in "The League of the South in the News, 1996," www.dixienet.org/_vti_bin/shtml.exc/press_quotes/1996news.html/mrpl; "The Right of Secession: A League of the South Position Paper," www.dixienet.org/positions/secede.htm (quotation).

56. "League of the South Institute for the Study of Southern Culture and History," www.dixienet.org/ls-institute/los-institute.htm; Michael J. Hill, "The Issue of Race in the Southern Independence Debate: A Call for Proportionality, Honesty, Integrity, Morality, and an End to Demagoguery," www.dixienet.org/positions/race.htm (quotations).

57. "Melvin Eustace Bradford," *Contemporary Authors*, 70.

# Conclusion

## America's Appointment with Destiny—A Cautionary Tale

GLENN FELDMAN

> I see in the future a crisis approaching that causes me to tremble for the safety of my country. . . . Corporations have been enthroned, an era of corruption in high places will follow, and the money-power of the country will endeavor to prolong its reign by working upon the prejudices of the people until the wealth is aggregated in a few hands and the Republic is destroyed.
>
> Abraham Lincoln

In November 2006, half of this country let out a huge sigh of relief; the other a loud cry of anguish.[1] Both could be heard all the way across the Atlantic, indeed the world. For in November 2006, what had seemed impossible actually happened: Democrats won a majority, not only in one house of Congress, but in *two*; and the Republican lock on all three branches of U.S. government was broken—suddenly, decisively, and potentially with epic repercussions. In November 2008, the apparently impossible happened again: a black man was elected president of the United States.

Actually, things had deteriorated rather quickly after the election of 2006 for Republicans and, more specifically, for the presidential administration of George W. Bush. The one thing Karl Rove and company publicly wagered would never happen, happened. Administration officials and their surrogates, so quick to repeat the mantra that "elections have consequences" when Democrats were in the minority, took on the look of deer in headlights as they tried to absorb the results of an election that was a tremendous shock to them.[2] As Congress changed hands, and as Democrats assumed control over committees and subpoena power—and the nation got its first female Speaker of the House—bodies that likely would have remained hidden until the historians eventually got around to them decades later (if ever) began to bob inconveniently to the surface.

In the wake of the 2006 midterm elections, a virtual cascade of scandals fell—bad news upon bad news for the GOP. Some were the foci of investigation; others involved misdeeds. But fall they did, pell-mell, one on top of the other: Scooter Libby; Walter Reed; Alberto Gonzalez; Pat Tillman; Paul

Wolfowitz and the World Bank; Dick Cheney, his obsession with secrecy, and the creative declaration that his office was not part of the executive branch after all; a prostitution ring in Washington involving the president's leading advocate for sexual abstinence; the forced silence of professional scientists on climate change; of professional prosecutors on official misconduct; of professional soldiers on colossal military blunders; of professional auditors on billions of dollars in tax money and military appropriations lost and unaccounted for. And always, always, floating above it all, seemed to be the name and visage of chief political adviser Karl Rove—the Rasputin of our age. Compounding previous public-relations disasters (Jack Abramoff, Duke Cunningham, Mark Foley, Larry Craig, "Pastor Ted" Haggard, Abu Ghraib, Guantanamo, Donald Rumsfeld, Tom DeLay) and the painful, national peeling back of the realization that our preemptive 2003 attack on another sovereign nation had nothing to do with finding weapons of mass destruction—or Saddam Hussein's nonexistent role in 9/11—it is clear now that the historical verdict on the Bush II administration will not be kind. With almost two years remaining in office and approval ratings slipping lower than previous records, a few Republican leaders actually mouthed the "*I* word" out loud (impeachment), and several distinguished historians dispensed with protocol to contemplate George W. Bush's likely occupancy of the deepest cellar in over two hundred years of American presidents.[3]

With all of this happening at a rapid—no, a blurring—pace, it was no doubt tempting for that half of the American population that had always resisted the Bush regime and the Republican lock on all three branches to get carried away. Denied a place at the table for so long, it was tempting for them to survey the smorgasbord of public scandal before them, the outrage and scandal and plummeting poll numbers of the Bush administration, and to become giddy—to stuff themselves with reckless abandon. Sudden feasting like that is dangerous for a starving man. That portion of the American electorate would do well to resist the temptation to binge. For this is a nation, it may be argued (even now after Barack Obama's election), that has only recently emerged from what will one day likely be recalled by historians as perhaps our worst and most ineffable crisis: the unsteady teetering on the edge of a precipice above a long drop into the abyss of an actual kind of American pseudo-fascism—replete with the possible mutation of our great democratic experiment into something utterly unrecognizable.

While the Bush II administration left with approval ratings at a record low, and a Democrat became the first African American president, Americans would still do well to remember that this has always been about far more than one president—even a figure as simultaneously simple and polarizing as

George W. Bush. The vehicle that brought so average a man to power—and us as a nation so close to possible ruin on a variety of fronts—is still largely intact. It is still out there. In many ways Bush's ascension was merely the culmination of a perfect storm that is not likely to happen in exactly the same way again; that much may be said with some small degree of certainty. It was a perfect storm of unchecked (even undefined) fundamentalist fervor, civic sloth, communications and technological revolution, a perverse epidemic of media cowardice, decades of extreme rightist vision, money, work, and a not inconsequential amount of Democratic complacency and (in the face of challenge) paralyzing dissension and timidity.

Yet this has also been about something more—something far darker and more frightening than the list of factors that made the storm so fantastic— something that, it may be said now, irrefutably wells up periodically from deep within the American nation and psyche, something with which we have never fully wrestled, much less defeated: the darkly reoccurring angels of our national conscience that feast so joyously on a self-destructive diet of hyper-patriotism, jingoistic nationalism, moral chauvinism, hatred of "the other" (even among our fellow citizens), and the most unattractive combination of certitude that God is on our side with the most ungodly indifference to the weakest and most vulnerable among us—or the collateral damage of our imperial overreach.[4] The most recent (and perhaps most horrible) installment in this experience, and the disastrous repercussions that exist, are still too fresh to warrant a glib "back to normal" response. If nothing else, the southern experience should teach us that. And if the southern example is not enough, the Great Recession should make it impossible to forget.

What seems clear—even if this nation is eventually to emerge (apparently) unscathed, even if most Americans remain blissfully and perpetually unaware that the country ever came close to an actual type of ruin—is that, in many respects, America is a nation in decline. Thirty-seven years ago our mainstream media and the leaders of both parties informed Richard Nixon that, due to his apoplectic excesses, his presidency was over. Some Democrats and a few Republicans called publicly for George W. Bush's impeachment. But it is not difficult to imagine our Nixon-era media leading the call for George W. Bush's impeachment instead of facilitating the parade of deceptions that led to a national carnival of bloodlust in Iraq, antiseptically termed "shock and awe." Increasingly deficient in healthy skepticism and elementary intellectual curiosity, America's embedded and so-called "liberal media" has disgraced itself again and again—and in the process failed the citizenry miserably. Thirty years ago Rush Limbaugh, Sean Hannity, and Bill O'Reilly would have been laughed off the public airwaves, recognized for the demagogic blowhards they are. Glenn Beck and Ann Coulter would have been hospitalized. They are no doubt highly paid entertainers, but today these figures are also lionized and feted by a disturbingly large segment of "mainstream" America—especially in the South. To the extremists who today call themselves "conservatives," these figures are rock stars. Although many of the essays in this volume document the ascension of reactionaries, demagogues, racists, and extremists, what we are experiencing today in terms of media support for, propagation of, and cultural acceptance of extreme voices is unparalleled. Perhaps more troubling, they are treated as legitimate journalists by people and news outlets that should (and often *do*) know better. They appear in *Time* magazine and on cable news instead of white power Aryan Web sites or *Thunderbolt* magazine.[5] Confronted by emerging evidence of climate change, forty years ago the country would have likely mobilized to meet this threat to continued human existence on the planet. Today a large part of the ink spilled on global warming is corporate-sponsored hack "science" designed to muddy the waters and create confusion and paralysis. Such an approach safeguards revenues from oil and conventional automobile production, and discourages innovation in the fields of alternative energy and transportation.[6] Fifty years ago, were this truly a nation at war, its people would have likely done more in the way of collective sacrifice to "support the boys" in Iraq than slap a yellow ribbon on the new, oversized SUV as they refilled its gas tank. Peddlers of hate in collars like Pat Robertson, James Dobson, and the late Jerry Falwell would have been ignored—if not ridiculed—by most rather than have their faux, commercial, and bloody brand of piety accepted with any degree of seriousness—and their coffers lined with contributions.[7] Yes, it can be argued seriously that this country is clearly in decline. What is not yet apparent is if the decline will be permanent or if the nation can recover, and what role the American South— always the most critical of regions—will play in the drama.

In large part, this question will turn on whether the United States will choose to preserve the New Deal or jettison it for an earlier, simpler, more starkly divided time. In all of this, the South will be critical, for it was the American South more than any other place that first led the revolt against the New Deal (after profiting from it more than any other region—a situation not unlike today's tax revolts). It was southern Democrats who met in Macon, Georgia, in 1936 to plot against the Roosevelt presidency. It was southern Democrats who led the way in organizing and issuing the 1938, ten-point "Conservative Manifesto" against the New Deal. It was southern Democrats who rebelled openly in the 1948 "Dixiecrat Revolt." And it was southern Democrats who took their rejection of the New Deal to the point of leaving their party in droves to become Republicans. Surveying the situation today, one is likely to have the sinking realization that much of today's status quo (and certainly the "conservative" agenda) looks more like the Gilded Age (or at least the 1920s) than it does the New Deal. This has been true in virtually every imaginable sector: free-market fundamentalism as the answer to every one of society's problems; worship of unrestricted free trade; deep-seated animus toward governmental regulation; neoimperialism; yellow journalism; Social Darwinism with its fixation on "personal responsibility" and blindness to systemic causes and solutions; the robber barons and their modern parallels in CEO pay and a shocking roster of corporate scandal; yawning income and wealth disparities; downward pressure on the middle class; assaults on labor rights, environmental protections, and Social Security; and a willingness to do or say anything to "win"—in politics or in business. It is impossible not to recall the public comparisons made between George W. Bush and William McKinley, or Karl Rove and Marc Hanna (made by Rove himself), or Grover Norquist's public pining for the 1880s. It is difficult to forget that one of the only things the Bush administration did quickly or decisively in the wake of Hurricane Katrina was to propose that the 1938 Davis-Bacon protection of prevailing wage rates in the construction industry be annulled so the Gulf Coast could be rebuilt with cut-rate, nonunion wages. It is impossible not to notice that the targets of many Republican domestic policies (Social Security, "card-check" union organization) are children of the New Deal. It *has* been, unfortunately, possible for most Americans to miss it when the venerated octogenarian conservative and radio icon Paul Harvey reminisces about the good old days, when America wasn't "made of sugar candy," when it realized that chattel slavery and distributing smallpox-infected blankets to Native Americans was merely the price one paid to "grease the skids" so we could "elbow our way . . . across this continent," fulfill our destiny to become a "great nation-state" and "grow prosperous."[8]

Actually a good case can be made that the New Deal was, indeed, "un-American." Not in the sense that its critics meant—then or now—but in the sense that the New Deal represented an aberration in the reality of much of American history as it has unfolded over two-and-a-half centuries. Most fundamentally, the New Deal and its values called the nation to put community on par with self, and to try, at least, to approach this nation's perhaps unreachable ideals of equality, inclusiveness, and opportunity for all. The South's pattern of resistance to New Deal ideals (after reaping the first and greatest portion of its windfall) may, in fact, put the region more squarely within the dominant narrative of American history than it is comfortable to think about.[9] As with all things historic, only time will tell.

I

The results of 2006 and 2008, as momentous as they are, do not erase the results—or the meaning—of the American presidential elections in 2000 and 2004. In some ways, those contests seem a lifetime away, an ancient relic of a bygone era of blustering preachers, unrepressed homophobia, Supreme Court justices turning themselves into pretzels to annul a lifetime of states'-rights decisions, and sabers, flags, and Bibles rattled at any who would dare question the course of a wartime administration—even Georgia senators with only one limb remaining from their real (not imagined) war service in the jungles of Vietnam.[10] Yet if and *until* the national policy results of 2000 and 2004 are reversed, it is this cautionary tale, as much as the surprising verdicts of 2006 and 2008, that should remain in the forefront of our consciousness.

In the wake of the 2004 election, there emerged a great deal of focus on 1968 or even 1964 as "the moment" when the South became Republican—when Barry Goldwater's debacle signaled the emergence of a Republican majority in the United States—and many liberals took some solace in the thought that their party, too, could rise dramatically after such a disaster.[11] If the Republicans could rise from the ashes of defeat phoenix-like, then surely Democrats could as well.

This line of thinking misses at least a few points.

First, for all of the talk and scholarship about a "New South," a more compelling argument can be made that the South has never changed fundamentally in a *political* sense or even a cultural one. Yes, it has changed party affiliations—really quite often in national races. But through its various partisan incarnations, the South has generally maintained an unswerving devotion to cultural predilections born out of the Reconstruction trauma—racial, supremely emotional, plutocratic, anti-federal, anti-"foreigner," anti-tax, anti-social service, romantically martial, blindly patriotic, and illiberal. This has been especially true of the Deep South. Conservative Democrats, Dixiecrats, many of their regular party adversaries, George Wallace's independent Democrats, and now many Republicans largely share these fundamental and bedrock characteristics. While the names of the parties have changed, the aims have remained essentially the same.

What *has* happened since the 1960s is that "the southern way" of politics has increasingly become the national way. For the "Republican South," there was no great awakening or pull to the GOP. There was, rather, an almost wholesale substitution of the GOP for the Democratic Party that lurched to the left on civil rights, Vietnam, and moral/social issues. People like former labor secretary Robert Reich are fond of saying that pocketbook issues dictate how Americans vote.[12] Maybe. But not in the South, never in the South. In the South, this refusal, this stubborn, shortsighted, self-destructive, "cut off your nose to spite your face" kind of obstinacy is, in many quarters, a source of great pride. And, it may be said, it is this which is distinctly *southern*. The capacity of the South's "better sorts" to repeatedly manipulate plain folk into supporting a conservative economic program by putting emotional issues to work—race, religion, morality, hyperpatriotism—is *the* ultimate basis for the region's persistent distinctiveness. Before 1965 and the Voting Rights Act, overt racism worked its magic, but increasingly that has been replaced by an effective "politics of emotion" characterized by more subtle, coded references to race that could be termed the "new racism." The "new racism," while employing careful wording and muted rhetoric, is also characterized by religious bigotry, authoritarianism, overt moral chauvinism, and an almost gleeful kind of public narrow-mindedness and intolerance in the guise of a rejection of "elitist" political correctness, scientific knowledge, rationality, and, of course, liberalism in all its various guises.[13]

In actuality, the white South has never really changed politically or fundamentally. Despite the volumes written about a New South, a Sunbelt South, a modern South, a suburban South, the region, as measured by perhaps its most defining element, has moved very little, if at all. The parties that have been willing to cater to the white South's ingrained, seemingly endemic, and largely immutable conservatism have, turn by turn, "won" the South. But the South, especially the Deep South, has never really been conquered by a political party. It has simply chosen the party that, at the time, most closely mirrors the region's essential and enduring conservative self. The South's *partisan* allegiances are transitory; its fundamental *political* allegiance is unchanging.

Nor has this conservatism been purely a race-based phenomenon. To be sure, race has been at the heart, soul, and center of it—even in its more muted and coded forms. But recent southern history makes clear that the old "politics of emotion" that could preclude the poor and middle class from voting their economic interests includes other, powerful, issues that constitute a "new racism" (war, taxes, terror, abortion, guns, gays, prayer in schools) and "new negroes" (liberals, gays, feminists, the pro-choice, religiously pluralistic, or antiwar). The menu is much broader and deeper than what has been pigeonholed by "suburban school" historians as merely a "white backlash." And the prospects for white southerners to vote their material interests over these hot buttons is just as slim as ever—perhaps the very essence of southern exceptionalism. Hence the allegedly sectional nature of the partisan realignment of the South has been nothing of the sort. The South didn't move so much as the nation did. It was the *national* Democratic Party's move toward racial and economic liberalism that doomed continued southern devotion. It has been the explosion of the *national* appetite for a "tabloid politics" and the allied transformation of news into round-the-clock entertainment that has allowed the rise of extremists masquerading as conservatives to ascend in the GOP and especially the Republican South. It has been national changes combined with the refinement and popularization of southern continuities.

The American Heartland learned these lessons from the South (thanks to Fox News and Rupert Murdoch's ceaseless adumbrations), and it has become more "southern" and thus more susceptible to the Far Right's noise-machine messages of conservative excess and distraction on issues of abortion, gay marriage, tax fury, school prayer, and whatever else comes down the pike.[14] After November 2, 2004, and its now-famous exit polls, liberals and pundits spent their time wringing their hands over which was more important—moral issues or things like war and terrorism.[15] A greater percentage of the up-for-grabs vote probably went for Iraq and terrorism (which the vice president and president worked overtime to conflate into one and the same thing, as the mainstream media largely complied). But in the larger scheme it doesn't really matter because in 2004, regardless of how the exit poll questions were framed, *both* issues were presented as two sides of the same coin—not separate and competing categories. Karl Rove and company used both morality and Iraq/terrorism quite successfully in 2004 as emotional issues to deflect the attention of middle-class and working-class people (especially whites) away from the shoals of economic reason and rationality—that is, away from the reality of a lawless quagmire in Iraq; away from a "growing" economy and economic policies mercilessly shrinking and pressuring the middle class, the environment, and worker protections; and away from the aggrandizement of the nation's privileged to an extent and extreme unseen in this country since the 1920s or perhaps the Gilded Age.[16]

In the 2010 midterm elections, voters were largely distracted from economic malaise and obscene levels of corporate profit by kindred emotional methods of scapegoating immigrants and making a fetish of taxes. It must also be admitted that two towering ironies doomed Democratic fortunes: the Obama administration's lack of audacity to act on a scale sufficient to stem the national hemorrhaging it inherited on joblessness, and perhaps the ineffectiveness of the finest political communicator of the age in communicating what his administration had done right on the economy. Both factors contributed to a national deficit of hope and a bonanza for Republicans.

But, as much criticism as Karl Rove has received from a variety of sources, it is important to recognize that he did not invent the wheel. A Texan, Rove simply rode—perhaps more ruthlessly and brazenly than ever before—the same southern horse that South Carolinians Lee Atwater, Harry Dent, and Strom Thurmond did before him; the one Alabama's George Wallace and the Dixiecrats did before *them*; and one that looks an awful lot like the one southern Bourbons used to suppress class-consciousness during Reconstruction and the turn-of-the-century disfranchisement movement.[17]

There is quite another sort of problem with pinpointing the birth of modern-day national Republicanism to the 1964/1968 parallel and the Goldwater experience. What we witnessed in 2004—growth of 3 percent for George Bush among black voters over his 2000 totals, a 15 percent increase in the Catholic Republican vote from 1996 to 2004, even the rises in Republican votes among Jews and Hispanics, not to mention virtual ownership of evangelical whites—is the fruit of a movement that is now nearly four decades old. While it is true that a lingering and questionable war in Iraq and a moribund economy damaged Republican prospects in 2008, it is equally true that Democrats still have nothing remotely like the GOP's deeply funded media/think-tank/policy-center machine that runs with something akin to military discipline and a repetitive message drive that would make any PR firm envious.

There were undeniable and significant problems with John Kerry's campaign in 2004 (voting for war authority in Iraq, war appropriations, acquiescing to the "war on terror" narrative with George Bush as national father-figure, a refusal to integrate minimum-wage initiatives in battleground states, allowing Mary Beth Cahill to confront Karl Rove's brass knuckles with school-marmish civility, and Kerry's own exasperating propensity to give convoluted ten-minute responses to one-sentence questions). But the most daunting challenges to Kerry's campaign were structural: hate/talk radio, the Internet, Religious Right money and organization, and the $300 million-a-year think-tank and policy-center industry dominated by what reasonable people once recognized as the *Far* Right.[18] While some of this has been blunted by Howard Dean's and Barack Obama's revolutionary use of the Internet for fund-raising and communications, Clear Channel alone still reaches 100 million Americans daily. What did Air America do?[19]

Another type of structural problem that should give pause to liberals poised to assume a new Democratic future is electoral. Although numerous conspiracy theories swirling around Florida in 2000 and Ohio in 2004 have never been proven conclusively, it is nothing less than a scandal that the "world's greatest democracy" still has in place a system whereby Diebold, ES & S, and other companies with close ties to the GOP actually program the voting machines that much of the American public uses in presidential elections; that secretaries of state in Florida, Ohio, and other battleground states counted and certified votes while simultaneously directing the Bush campaign in-state; and this country still does not have the paper trail for voting that any self-respecting ATM or gas pump might have. This—along with amply documented minority and youth vote suppression by GOP operatives cycle in and cycle out—is so because somebody wants it so.[20] It benefits someone and is not likely to go away.

Finally, there does not yet appear to be a very close connection between an emerging global and interdependent economy that might not reward "geographic areas that do not embrace cultural diversity and do not make tolerance a premier virtue," as one esteemed historian recently speculated.[21] Would that our trade system did so. On the contrary, the way free trade was designed under Bill Clinton and the Democratic Leadership Council—not to mention Clinton's successor in the White House—had very little to do with environmental protection and worker rights. Instead, the sacred cow of "free trade" as practiced by the United States exists primarily as a collection of political euphemisms and economic presumptions masquerading as "natural laws." Yet this system remains foreign to anything Adam Smith or even Edmund Burke might have sanctioned. Rather than anything "natural," it may be fairly said that current rules of free trade more closely resemble a free-market economy on steroids: a neoliberal dream that has accompanied the neoconservative fantasy in Iraq—one in which trade unions are outlawed; water, natural resources, and oil revenues are privatized; and every meaningful obstacle to uncontrolled material exploitation—even that which would jeopardize areas as large as the Gulf of Mexico—is removed.[22]

## II

For those who persist, in the wake of all this, in doubting whether the American South still exists as a distinct and distinguishable reality,[23] they need go no further than the Catholic vote in 2000 and 2004—long the single-most accurate index of American presidential preference. In 2000, George W. Bush (a Southern Methodist) lost the Catholic vote narrowly (49–47 percent) to Al Gore, a Southern Baptist. Four years later—after a ceaseless drumbeat about gays, abortion, Hollywood, and a "culture of life" that curiously included death for an estimated six hundred thousand Iraqis—Bush won the Catholic vote 53–47 percent over an actual Catholic, John Kerry. In fact, Bush dramatically increased his Catholic vote between the two elections by some 3.3 million votes. Now, class and the South: Bush's take of the Catholic vote among upper-income Catholics rose in 2004 to a 59–41 percent margin over Kerry. Among *southern* Catholics of all incomes, Bush registered a whopping 67–33 percent margin of victory over Kerry.[24]

It is impossible not to notice that, in conjunction with these electoral realities, American entertainment patterns have also taken a decided turn toward the new "reality" show: *Big Brother, Fear Factor, Survivor, Dog the Bounty Hunter, American Idol, America's Next Top Model,* and all the rest. Much of this, no doubt, has to do with the fact that our country was founded on, at best, a paradox—at worst, a troubling falsity. All men were indeed not created equal. And this claim did not begin to pretend inclusion for that half of the population that was women, or any male who was not free, white, and the owner of significant property. Yet the persistence of the paradox, and its repetition for centuries in civics schoolrooms throughout the country, has invariably contributed to a nation bred on a love of myth, fairy tale, folklore, legend—in a word, "unreality." It has also made many Americans allergic to actual reality when it comes in doses too large to handle (body bags from Iraq, for example). Thus our susceptibility to a media-synthesized "reality" that has come to include not simply reality shows—that are, after all, staged entertainment—but also a heightened susceptibility after the trauma of 9/11 to undertaking wars based on dissembling and cooked intelligence, and a simultaneous detachment from the consequences of those wars: civilian deaths that are "collateral damage" and an aversion to seeing injured troops or the coffins in which the unlucky of our young people return home. In all of this, the South has demonstrated that it is the section of America most at ease with this duality, and it has exported the appetite for it to the rest of the country— unfortunately to our collective national detriment. Southerners have shown themselves repeatedly to be the most enthusiastic consumers of Hollywood-produced "reality," and those most stubbornly resistant to the actual realities that can be found in Iraq or Afghanistan, with a minimum of effort, on the BBC, public radio, or the Internet.[25]

The deliberate compromise of a reality-based world has insidious possibilities far beyond the decline of quality entertainment. Journalist Chris Mooney actually traced this strategy to methods perfected by the tobacco industry and anti-environmental interests during the Reagan years. More recently, the Christian Right and corporate conservatives have applied them to a whole gamut of issues including climate change, stem-cell research, evolution, abortion and breast cancer, contraception, the protection of endangered species, reliance on petroleum products, and more—wherever profits are to be found. "*Doubt is our product,*" a notorious 1969 Brown & Williamson internal memo about tobacco (uncovered in the 1980s) boasted, "since it is the best means of competing with the 'body of fact' that exists in the mind of the general public. It is also the best means of establishing a controversy." As Harvard physicist Lewis Branscomb reminds us, "Policymaking by ideology requires that reality be set aside, [and] it can be maintained only by moving towards ever more authoritarian forms of government." Longtime *New York Times* bureau chief Chris Hedges concurred: The recent "war on truth" creates "a world where facts become interchangeable with opinions, where lies become true—the very essence of the totalitarian state. And it . . . empowers a rapacious oligarchy whose god is maximum profit at the expense of citizens."[26]

The racism that drove southern electoral politics for at least a hundred years is a bird of a feather with "the new racism" that afflicts our national electoral politics today. More than anything else, racist politics in the South were white-supremacist politics, and taught white southerners, most elementally, how to *feel* better than other people; how to feel superior to others no matter the reality of their hardscrabble existence. This lesson—even more than the race issue, per se—is what endures about the southern political experience, and what forms the basis for the modern Republican appeal in the South currently based on (fill in the blank) religion, patriotism, nationalism, militarism, masculine toughness, morality, and tax revolt. The specific topic actually matters very little because, like race or, more correctly, white supremacy, these topics are in large part only means to an end. The end is the feeling of psychological superiority vis-à-vis "the other" that lets the class-challenged white southerner suspend disbelief and transcend the reality of his or her economic existence to vote Republican and, thus, feel special, superior, and part of an elite—in spirit if not in flesh . . . or wallet.[27]

In fact, it has been argued that very modest gains in income may actually act as a *depressor* of resentment among poor and working-class people—if they are properly framed. Because wealth attainment is cast in popular American and capitalist mythology as the sole product of personal merit and effort (rather than the result of a more complex combination of factors including state aid, education, opportunity, inheritance, and others), people are programmed to believe their economic achievements, however modest, are the sole result of personal merit—and thus to take pride in those accomplishments however meek. So it is the Walmart associate making just over minimum wage with a wretched benefits package that taxes the public for adequate health-insurance coverage—rather than resenting the scandals of executive pay and Wall Street bonuses, the economic accoutrements of the super-rich, and the unlevel playing field and gamed markets that keep things that way— who applauds his own initiative in getting ahead, even if he moves two inches back for every one forward.[28] On a macro level, this phenomenon depresses the capacity for resentment, as do the Calvinistic notions of piety that still flourish so strongly in the white South. If persons are directly responsible for whatever economic gains they make, the poor are also personally responsible for their poverty. If wealth is a sign of God's favor, so poverty is a sign of disfavor, of personal depravity. This accounts in large part for the retarded capacity of many of those wedded to such a "prosperity gospel" to empathize—much less sympathize—with the poor, or to connect state aid, a level playing field, or the robustness of collective action through the efforts of labor unions or government agencies to the question at hand.[29]

If anything, the biggest surprise of postwar American politics is not that the South stopped being distinctively southern, but that the South exported its southern-ness (and often the most unfortunate aspects of it) to a nation that used it to build a Republican majority. Perhaps the greatest surprise in all this is the assumption of many that the South's worst traits (a kind of anti-intellectual religious and free-market fundamentalism, bigotry, intolerance, anti-unionism, and others) would gradually be ameliorated by southern integration into the American mainstream. Obviously, this has not turned out to be the case. In fact, instead of the southern way on race, economics, taxation, social policy, federalism, and the rest being softened, the worst molecules of southern society have not been dispersed—they have been infused into the bloodstream of much of the rest of the nation. The actual reverse of what many progressives hoped for—and fully expected after the civil rights movement—has taken place. Eighty years after the Scopes Trial in Tennessee, and we have evolution once again on the defensive (furnishing, ironically, some of the best evidence we have to date *against* the theory that human beings advance); neo-liberal economics everywhere; supernationalism and warmongering as the order of the day; and quasi-fascist repression of dissent. We have Sarah Palin and a Tea Party revolt with a racist and xenophobic agenda burbling and frothing just inches below its surface. A "neo-Kluxism," not unlike the 1920s' and 1940s' brands of actual Ku Kluxism, is again in vogue. Relying on a warped amalgam of hyperpatriotism and fundamentalist religion, it targets women out of "their place," the godless, the morally unfit, and anything that smacks of liberalism, modernism, or critical thought.[30]

Nor has religion helped things much (although there are some recent encouraging signs of moderation). Religion in these formative years—at least folk theology (or the predominant religious beliefs of nonelites)—curried two main themes that would have appreciable significance for the future course of conservative politics in the South—and, to a growing extent—outside of it. Both themes are best stated in the negative, ironically as aversions to two of the most basic and fundamental tenets of American government (as understood by most scholars and most Americans): separation of church and state, and the principle of majority rule with respect for minority rights. Deep South folk theology (with some few exceptions) does not accept either. This folk religion is profoundly uncomfortable with separation between church and state because acceptance of the Jeffersonian premise logically removes government or "the state" from the same realm as "church" or religion. Placing the two in separate realms makes it logically impossible for religion to dominate the state in temporal matters; makes it impossible for God's law to exercise sovereignty over all laws—including man's law—precisely because the two occupy different realms. Hence the profound discomfort of the Religious Right in witnessing the state (executive, legislative, and especially judicial) pass down "liberal" rulings on race and civil rights during the 1950s and 1960s—and later on abortion, gay rights, prayer in school, and public displays of religion—that clearly, in their view, violate divine law. Figures like Tim LaHaye and the late Jerry Falwell personified these developments as they segued seamlessly from enthusiastic opposition to Martin Luther King and the "civil wrongs movement" to, later, rights and respect for women, gays, and religious and cultural minorities.[31] In the southern fundamentalist view, if the wall between church and state could, in fact, be torn down, then society would be free to witness a cosmic clash between the two, and God's law would inevitably supersede man's. Such thought is a hallmark (perhaps only partially conscious) of today's Tea Party movement.

Nor does white, southern, Christian conservatism believe in the second bedrock principle of American government: majority rule with respect for minority rights. Perhaps the *leadership* of mainline southern Protestant and Catholic churches accepts both tenets—as do most black folk religionists—but not the bulk of white southerners and their folk understanding of theology.[32] They believe wholeheartedly in the first half of the proposition (majority rule) but not the second. During the civil rights movement, and more recently, theirs is more closely an adherence to the principle of majority rule . . . period. As with their rejection of church-state separation, this deep antipathy toward the notion of minority rights applied to African Americans during the 1940s and 1950s—leading directly to a contempt for the concept of judicial review by federal courts—and later to women, gays, war protesters, and non-Christian Americans in the "culture wars" and recently even largely imaginary threats such as the "War on Christmas." Those Americans (if indeed they could be called real Americans) who were not white, Anglo-Saxon, Protestant Christian, and native-born were expected to know their place and take a backseat to the true Americans who were. This extended to keeping one's mouth shut in a public classroom or courtroom during the recital of the Lord's Prayer and not making a peep when tax monies were used to install Christian monuments and statues in public buildings. As a Birmingham man explained at the height of the Dixiecrat Revolt in 1948: "We are . . . a WHITE Nation, 90% are still white. If there are ten men in a comfortable room and one wants to let in soot, dust, dirt . . . the other nine are within their rights to prevent such minority-rule. . . . Theoretically all [people] are equal; but I can't picture . . . my daughter sitting alongside greasy, smelly and uncivilized Japs, Hunkies, Negroes, etc. in either café or school. Can you?!!!!!!! . . . [T]he North and West . . . [nor] the South . . . desire . . . [the] ruling of the 90% by the 10%." Or as a circuit prosecutor charged with enforcing the law in several Alabama hill counties put it: The "law of segregation is a natural law. . . . All . . . black people . . . are . . . inferior and servile. . . . Only Hitler, Mussolini, Tojo, and Joe Stalin and their kind suffer with such insanity that man can repeal either a natural or Divine law. . . . [So] it is pitiful . . . to see our Supreme Court of the U.S. sending out its edicts contrary to this Mandate, as though they had the power and authority to overrule it."[33]

Actually, this folk religious creed was so pervasive that it extended to many business and political elites. Chauncey Sparks—Alabama governor and Democratic loyalist in 1948, described by some as a racial "moderate"—reacted to civil rights rulings by comparing the Supreme Court to the "Polit Bureau." Northern allies referred to it as the "JewDeal Supreme Court" with its "mongrel decisions." Business leaders combined denouncements of communists "boring-in" to undermine American and southern life by assaults on segregation and fair-employment agitation with praise for the "incontrovertible Americanism" that resulted in "a howl" going up anytime a "small, though vociferous minority . . . attempts to over-rule the vast majority's vote or customs" on racial, religious, or economic matters. Sam M. Johnston, a prominent Mobile attorney and Dixiecrat leader, also couched much of his lament against civil rights in what he termed a dictatorship of minority rights.[34]

Yet it must be realized that very little of this happened by accident or in some natural course of events. Instead, it has all, more or less, followed a carefully choreographed elite script. Beginning in the late 1930s, an increasingly important goal for the economic conservatives who opposed the New Deal was to fashion what can be termed a "Great Melding" with social conservatives. Above all its other sins, perhaps, the New Deal's most egregious offense was its implicit challenge to the presumed omniscience and omnipotence attributed to business interests in America for decades—"a near spiritual belief," as one analyst put it, that business "simply by pursuing profit, had the power to redeem society." During World War II, organized business interests increasingly realized that their cold war with social conservatives was becoming a drag on their success and their profits. In response, they launched a concerted propaganda campaign that presented business as the military and economic savior of America—and labor as selfish, unpatriotic, and even subversive. More important, the campaign set out to preserve the traditional American suspicion of concentrated power but to recast that suspicion in a monumental way.[35]

The numbers themselves were staggering. In 1934, for example, the National Association of Manufacturers (NAM) had an annual public-relations budget of $360,000 (equivalent to $5.5 million today). Throughout the New Deal years, that budget grew exponentially as the group bankrolled pamphlets, speaker bureaus, newspaper ads, press releases, and radio shows—all in what they termed an "everlasting battle for the minds of men . . . to check the steady, insidious, and current drift toward socialism." In 1941, the NAM proposed joining the National Education Association to sponsor a series of conferences to inculcate young students with pro-business values, disparage the "blight" of federal aid to education, and portray the belief that government had anything to do with economic prosperity as "childlike." By 1950, the NAM had distributed 4.5 million pamphlets and comic books to the nation's schoolchildren, 8 million "information packets" to newspapers, recruited right-wing priests to combat what they called the churches' "'inherent sympathies' for the weak," and provided free pro-business, antiunion, "right-to-work" material to 265 dailies and almost 1,900 small-town newspapers across the country. Of course, the NAM was especially active in the American South, where its pro-business seed fell on fertile soil. The group also sponsored its own $1.4 million radio show and provided the leadership of several past presidents to the founding of the John Birch Society—the same one that smeared President Dwight Eisenhower and his brother, Milton, as communist agents. By 1954, school authorities estimated that they had received $50 million in free NAM materials, roughly half what the public schools spent yearly on their regular textbooks.[36]

The campaign achieved success beyond its architects' wildest dreams. In the most basic way, it substituted a "Big Gov'mint Devil" for the old big-business "fat cat" stereotype, and changed the New Deal–American view of "government" fundamentally—as something that *gives* to something that *takes away*. This extraordinary change paved the way for antifederal animus to become the critical glue of a new economically rightist and racially conservative alliance that had its nerve center in the American South. Yet this stroke of genius had other, national implications—fully intended or not. Because antifederalism became the focal point of the new alliance among social and economic conservatives, it locked together those sections of the country that already had the longest and deepest traditions of antipathy to taxes and the central government: the South and West. In effect, it was the old Populist alliance in reverse—this time with nosey Yankees and a federal leviathan playing the villainous part of the elite "interests."[37]

The South, the section most familiar with contentious relations with the central government (even to the point of armed conflict), became a proving ground in all of this. Rapprochement took the form first of a fusion between economic conservatism and racial conservatism that, of course, served Whiggish business interests by winning plain-white votes for conservative political platforms and parties. After the "failed" Dixiecrat Revolt of 1948, this fusionism did the same for the GOP and its economically conservative policies, underwritten by white supremacy and hostility to civil rights and employment discrimination laws.[38]

In the South, fusion had long produced considerable dividends for bigbusiness interests, not the least of which was a popular and powerful argument against labor unionism steeped in folk religion. During the Great Depression, the North Carolina Piedmont found itself roiling in textile strikes, put down brutally by a white populace aroused by religious charges that the union was actually a "hellish serpent . . . creeping into the Garden of Eden" to bring only bloodshed and death. A Gastonia, North Carolina, newspaper encouraged community hysteria that led to massive violence against the striking textile workers and their organizers by charging that the strike meant "world revolution, irreligion, racial mixing, and free love" and the "overthrowing of this government."[39] Such emotional language and imagery was a notable part of the community backlash among thousands of ordinary whites during the 1965 march from Selma to Montgomery and other events of the civil rights period.[40] Late in the twentieth century, religious radio and TV evangelists could still motivate many in the South by damning union challenges to the authority of secular bosses as a surefire way to get oneself to hell. Nor were such sermons reserved for the unsophisticated, the poor, or the fundamentalists in the New South. The "better sorts" heard the same thing. In 2002, privileged white Catholics in an affluent "over-the-mountain" section of Birmingham could hear their priest instruct them from the pulpit that God's plan for eternal happiness was simple. It consisted merely of unquestioning obedience to the earthly representatives of His authority: priests, teachers, *and employers*. Deviation from the plan invited unhappiness and actually jeopardized the soul's chances for salvation. "Labor unions should study and read the Bible instead of asking for more money," the Moral Majority's Jerry Falwell proselytized. "When people get right with God, they are better workers." "I think we should take the shackles off business and get rid of outfits like OSHA," he offered on another occasion. The political training manual of the Christian Coalition, founded by the 700 Club's Pat Robertson, phrased it this way: "Christians have a responsibility to submit to the authority of their employers since they are designated as part of God's plan for the exercise of authority on the earth by man." Tim LaHaye, best-selling coauthor of the *Left Behind* series, former John Birch Society lecturer, and Reagan booster, put it simply: "Unions are one of the organizations leading the world to wickedness."[41] After 9/11, prominent southern conservatives like House majority whip Tom DeLay upped the ante by adding terrorism to the equation—despite the heroic role played that day by union-organized police officers, firefighters, emergency personnel, and ironworkers. DeLay declared that labor unions present a "clear and present danger to the security of the United States."[42]

The southern alliance between economic rightists and social conservatives actually long predated its manifestation at the national level. Tension between the coalition partners had as well. The 1928 presidential election—in which a racially moderate, New York Catholic held the Democratic standard—posed a particularly difficult challenge to elite business conservatives and their more common social counterparts. Yet it also hinted at the possibilities of a successful resolution that, if it could ever be accomplished, promised to transform the partisan beneficiary of its reconciliation into an insurmountable entity in the majority white South. Much had to be overcome if this were ever to take place, though, not least considerable elite disdain for the "priest-ridden ignorance to which our people now seem utterly lost," as the business-booster and Alabama newspaper mogul Victor Hanson put it. Other representatives of the southern business class exhibited similar unease with the moral and religious attitudes of the plain folk: their tendency to be moved by "intolerance, hatred, [and] . . . religious bigotry . . . [their] lust for witch-burning . . . [and their] Christian appetite for hatred," as one Bourbon editor characterized it.[43]

The Republican genius in the modern South has been the amicable resolution of this tension by putting emotionalism to work in uniting conservatives instead of allowing it to divide them. First using race, then a more muted racism combined with moralism, the modern GOP accomplished no mean feat below the Mason-Dixon Line, thanks mostly to the ministrations of Strom Thurmond, Harry Dent, Lee Atwater, and, most recently, Atwater's protégé, Karl Rove. "Country-club Republicans have been forced to accept it [cultural populism]," wrote Fred Barnes, the arch-conservative editor of the *Weekly Standard*. "Country-club Democrats can't." "This must be the most blindingly honest admission by any Republican pundit this year," a stunned former *New York Times* editor Howell Raines wrote about Barnes's comment, "for it exposes the contract at the heart of the new Republican pandering. As long as affluent, educated Republicans are allowed to control wealth in this country, they're willing for the rednecks to pray in the public schools that rich Republicans don't attend, to buy guns at Wal-Marts they don't patronize, to ban safe abortions that are always available to the affluent, and to oppose marriage for gays who don't vote Republican anyway."[44]

Today, in the post–Voting Rights Act South, individuals like Ralph Reed, Richard Land, Trent Lott, and (previously) Jerry Falwell profess to be great racial progressives and admirers of Martin Luther King. But among these Religious Rightists, there remains fusionism's core commitment to economically conservative values. Pat Robertson, James Dobson, and "Pastor Ted" Haggard portray themselves as civil rights champions, as do kindred Catholic Rightists such as George Weigel, Robert P. George, and the late Richard John Neuhaus.[45] How did this happen? Did it simply occur in the natural order of things?

In large part, the answer lies in the civil rights acts that liberals wrote into law during the 1960s: the 1964 Civil Rights Act, John Kennedy's executive order banning employment discrimination in the federal workforce, and the 1965 Voting Rights Act. The 1965 law, in particular, rendered the traditional racial and economic melding, in its unvarnished mode, untenable. Court decisions like *Engel v. Vitale* and *Row v. Wade* hinted at morality and religion as the new American flashpoint.[46] Gradually the old racism was replaced with the new. While racial appeals in conservative politics were recalibrated away from George Wallace's bluster about segregation now and forever and schoolhouse doors to more muted and implicit Nixonian code about busing, quotas, and affirmative action, right-wing notions of religion and morality largely replaced conservative racism as the public face of "The Great Melding." Lee Atwater, the master GOP strategist from South Carolina, actually announced the sea change: "By 1968, you can't say 'nigger'—that hurts you. Backfires. So you say stuff like forced busing, states' rights, and all that stuff." Allegiance to extreme rightist economic conservatism, heroically personified by newly popular libertarians who had long been considered fringe figures (Milton Friedman, F. A. Hayek, Ayn Rand) remained a constant in the alliance. The new racism combined muted white supremacy, Religious Right moral chauvinism, and even a morality-based hatred, with neoliberal rightist economic extremism. People like James Dobson, Jerry Falwell, Pat Robertson, Murray Rothbard, Ted Haggard, and Tim LaHaye personified the alliance, even as some country-club types held their noses.[47]

More recently, moralism and militaristic nationalism increasingly play the public role that white supremacy used to play for the southern conservative meld. Reliance on focus group–tested topics such as gay marriage, abortion, school prayer, the Ten Commandments, war, and terrorism bring in the votes and the checks of southern white folks who have little idea of the neoliberal agenda behind the emotional appeals.[48] Average Christians continue to buy into the morality-based rhetoric and thus find themselves supporting an economic agenda of tax cuts, free trade, anti-unionism, and privatization that is not only hostile to their own interests but also embarrassingly difficult to reconcile with the New Testament message of Jesus Christ. Hence the reliance by Religious Right figures in their public pronouncements on Old Testament staples like Exodus and Leviticus rather than the Beatitudes in the Sermon on the Mount, Mary's Magnificat, Luke, or the overtly socialistic Acts of the Apostles.[49]

Like the old racism, the new kind also uses the primacy of emotion-based politics over the rational to further an economically conservative agenda. It is the old marriage of neo-Kluxism and neo-Bourbonism that originally birthed the GOP into power in the modern South. While a growing number of evangelicals struggle to make sense of economic, trade, and environmental policies that seem at odds with Christ's message in the Gospels, there remains the flawed assumption that the apparently oxymoronic alliance between religion and right-wing economics just kind of "happened."[50] Yet nothing just happens—especially in the world of politics. This melding—like the one in the infamous 1901 Alabama constitution, like the 1948 Dixiecrats, like the 1964 Goldwater win in the South—happened because elite economic conservatives *wanted* it to happen and worked very hard and effectively to tap into powerful emotional issues (race, white supremacy, law and order, evangelical religion and moralism, abortion, gay marriage, and tax revolt) to encourage ordinary Americans to forget their own economic interests. While pundits like resident *New York Times* conservative David Brooks continue to write editorials celebrating the fact that financially challenged Americans put social and emotional issues ahead of economics, others—notably former Republican national chairmen Ken Mehlman and Michael Steele, at least one *Wall Street Journal* editor, and Christian Right pioneer Ralph Reed—have publicly lamented that conservatives and the GOP were on the wrong side of civil rights.[51]

Nor is the phenomenon of using emotion-laden strategy reliant on themes such as patriotism and religion isolated or accidental. "This alliance between religion and politics didn't just happen," evangelical titan Paul Weyrich explained with evident satisfaction. "I've been dreaming and working on this for years."[52] Indeed, a moment of indisputable import was Barry Goldwater's 1964 campaign, when the conservative wing of the Republican Party seized power from Old Guard liberal Republicans of the stripe of Nelson Rockefeller, George Romney, and Everett Dirksen, and waged a presidential campaign that netted just six states. In addition to Goldwater's home state of Arizona, they were the former-Dixiecrat states plus Georgia, Alabama, Mississippi, Louisiana, and South Carolina. George Wallace would win the exact same states in 1968 (minus Arizona). In the wake of the Goldwater defeat, Republican operative Richard Viguerie volunteered to raise funds for Wallace's presidential campaign with the condition that he get to keep the Alabamian's contributors list of urban ethnics, blue-collar workers, and southern Democrats alienated by their national party's leftward drift on race. Thus was born the vaunted direct-mail operation of Viguerie and the new Republican Party. After an ill-fated attempt to take over Wallace's American Independent Party, the Religious Right set its sights on the capture of one of the two major political parties. They chose the GOP and sealed the decision with a formal 1979 summit that merged Viguerie's organization with the other forces of the Religious Right represented by Jerry Falwell, Tim LaHaye, Howard Phillips, and Paul Weyrich.[53]

The mid- to late 1970s were of vital importance in changing the rules of American politics in the most fundamental ways. As another essay in this book points out, 1979 was the same year theological and political conservatives routed moderates in the Southern Baptist Convention (SBC). In 1976, *Buckley v. Valeo* radically altered the amount of money private interests could contribute to political campaigns and advertisements. Labor union membership began to slide precipitously as subcontracting, outsourcing, foreign imports, and global relocating slashed membership rolls. Ronald Reagan's forceful interference in the Professional Air Traffic Controllers (PATCO) strike of 1981 and his antiworker appointments to the National Labor Relations Board (NLRB) delivered devastating blows to labor. The demise of the "Fairness Doctrine" a few years later (in 1986) ushered in the new age of hate/talk radio and the phenomenon of political/entertainment figures using the public airwaves to rant nonstop, without a legally mandated proportionate response or even elementary fact-checking or an impartial ombudsman to moderate the discourse and "news" imparted. The confluence of these forces and developments—the entry of the Religious Right into Republican politics, the conservative takeover of the SBC, the revolution in cable, Internet, and AM radio media, changes in campaign finance laws, the decline of the modern labor movement, the birth of a billion-dollar right-wing think-tank/policy-institute web, and more—resulted in the construction of a new set of rules for America's political and social arena. The new rules made virtually no topic or tactic off-limits in a scorched-earth, winner-take-all, take-no-prisoners politics that increasingly took on millennial and apocalyptic language and the accompanying characteristics of good versus evil, right and wrong, and total victory and eradication of the opposition.[54]

For decades, race was the most reliable fuel for a politics that ran on emotion. In the Jim Crow South through the mid-1960s, it was perfectly acceptable, even advantageous, for the region's political figures to race-bait opponents openly and directly. With federal intervention in the area of voting rights, a growing black electorate, and the maturation of a post-*Brown* generation of white southerners who reject segregation—at least in public and in principle—it is no longer acceptable to do this. More subtle race appeals still exist, of course: clever and thinly disguised references to "law and order," welfare, quotas, taxes for social programs, food stamps, states' rights and local government, urban decay, "big government," crime, and "personal responsibility." But, to a large extent, conventional race-baiting has been supplanted by the new racism, and its muted racism combined with religious-moral baiting of political opponents on the basis of "character," "values," and the like. It is no longer socially acceptable in the South to call a political opponent a "nigger lover." It is acceptable—even commonplace and shrewd—to paint political opponents as moral reprobates of flawed character, inferior values, suspect religious orientation, and questionable integrity—basically, of being morally and religiously inferior human beings.

The result is essentially the same as the old racism. That is, in a South once compelled by notions of racial orthodoxy and now equally compelled by conceptions of moral and religious orthodoxy, political figures gain ground by questioning an opponent's moral fiber—his "character"—in much the same way they once did by impugning their commitment to white supremacy. Elite politicians can tap into mass white support for a neoliberal economic agenda of low taxation, corporate welfare, anti-unionism, gutted social services, fiscal retrenchment, inadequate funding of public education, decreased worker safety, lower environmental standards, and the like by using morality in the same way that conservatives once used race alone: by morality-baiting in the same way they once race-baited. And in the inner councils of conservative religious strategists, there is a barely restrained euphoria about this ability. "We can elect Mickey Mouse to the Senate," the late Terry Dolan, head of the National Conservative Political Action Committee, rejoiced in 1982. "People will vote against the liberal candidate and not [even] remember why." The key to raising funds from Christian conservatives, this pioneering Catholic rightist lectured, was to "make them angry and stir up hostilities. The shriller you are, the easier it is to raise funds. That's the nature of the beast." Paul Weyrich agreed: "In the past we conservatives paraded all those Chamber of Commerce candidates with Mobil Oil strapped to their backs. It doesn't work," said Weyrich, who served as one of George W. Bush's top advisers on religious and political matters. There are "rural people in West Virginia who don't understand Reaganomics and who are being hurt by Reaganomics and who wouldn't like it if they did understand it." The way to reach that mass of people is through emotional issues like "the issue of prayer in the schools."[55] James Dobson and Focus on the Family is their logical successor.

When religious moralism outlives its usefulness as white supremacy eventually did—or it becomes too stale or transparently hypocritical to be of further use (as might be happening now)—economic conservatives can and will substitute hypermilitaristic patriotism and the raw, corrosive, unrelenting fear that is its corollary to curry the support they need from average Americans.[56] Regardless if the blunt instrument used is race, moralism, militarism, or anti-tax mania—or some mixture thereof—we end with an alliance harboring profound and disturbing contradictions: economic rightism and the preservation of wealth fortified by religious people who are avowed white supremacists and opponents of civil rights (who eventually end up apologizing for that); or religious people who call themselves pro-civil rights yet celebrate hostility toward gays and other moral nonconformists as zealously as any race-baiter ever did; or religious people who are enthusiastic, even callous, Social Darwinists in their treatment of Austrian economics as a fetish, privatizing Social Security, cutting Medicare and programs for the poor, and ravaging the environment in pursuit of profit; or, in yet another variant, religious people who are rabidly prowar in places like Iraq even though the Papal See opposed invasion, and the war itself failed every possible test of Just War theory.[57] Logical consistency does not seem to be prerequisite as long as the emotion is powerful and the ultimate end served is the perpetuation of economic privilege.

## III

The results of November 2006 and 2008 were so shattering and unexpected that subsequent interpretations have proved stunningly divergent. Yet time and again, the South has been the focus for much of the post-election fallout and analysis. One contributing writer for the *Nation* was so happy about the 2006 election that he argued it was proof positive that the South could not be written off by Democrats and progressives, and actually provided the most fertile ground for future Democratic development. Bob Moser was so elated by the results that he channeled "the South" itself to publicly answer the "Democratic wizards" who had recommended bypassing Dixie to concentrate precious party resources in winnable states and districts—all outside the South. His trenchant reply: "No, fuck you." The essay was a not-so-subtle rejoinder to, among others, Maryland political scientist Tom Schaller, whose pre-election book *Whistling Past Dixie* garnered great attention by calling for Democrats to devise a winning electoral blueprint by cobbling together a plan that relied on a coalition of states distinctly outside the South.[58]

Moser's was an interesting article with some interesting insights. But it was obvious from the start that his "new Southern strategy" could be taken too far (as could, to a lesser extent, the "Whistling Past Dixie" stratagem). Yes, Democrats, even in the South and rural areas all over the country, needed desperately to return to their old, blue-collar, working-class, New Deal roots after 2004. The Clinton/Kerry/DLC retreat on this point was nothing less than a disaster—and allowed Republicans to easily play the game of pseudopopulist appeal to working-class whites everywhere. Genuine New Deal and populist-type progressivism could only help everywhere, would resonate everywhere, and constitutes an honest and noble approach for Democrats to pursue.

But "the South" isn't just "the South." Tennessee isn't Virginia, and it darn sure isn't Missouri. Substitute Georgia or Alabama or Mississippi for Tennessee, and the contrast is even more dramatic. Yes, Jim Webb and Claire McCaskill are to be congratulated for having had the guts and foresight to campaign in rural, previously Republican sections of Virginia and Missouri. But can anyone doubt the significance of George W. Bush's unpopularity and the "reverse coattail effect" created by Cheney, Rumsfeld, Iraq, Foley, and Pastor Ted? Can anyone question the urban importance of the D.C. suburbs, northern Virginia, Kansas City, and St. Louis? Can anyone doubt the significance of the shrinking of the "God Gap" among Protestants and the reversal of the all-important Catholic vote from 2004? Between 2004 and 2006, Democrats learned how to talk to religious Americans (read: most Americans) in a language they could understand; a language in which Democratic economic values could be translated into terms of salve and cover that would allow religious folks to cast a vote for a Democrat and not feel guilty about it. Democrats cut the 2004 Republican advantage among weekly churchgoers from 22 to 12 percentage points in 2006, and won the Catholic vote over Republicans in what was largely a referendum on the Bush administration in more-than-reverse proportion to 2004: 55–45 percent. Those trends only continued in 2008.[59]

The message of 2006 and 2008 is that, to win, Democrats need to campaign their honest beliefs and values—economically progressive to be sure—but adapt to the particular "section" of the South where they are. If Harold Ford is pro-gun and somewhat more socially conservative than some other Democrats, and is campaigning closer to the Deep South, so what? Does that reduce him to a simple panderer? Is the Democratic Party no longer a big tent?

Ford did not win—but his combination of social conservatism and economic progressivism (while not everyone's cup of tea) allowed him to do better than anyone ever imagined a black man could do in Tennessee. And, in the end, the GOP had to resort to the old racist/sexist stereotypes to seal Bob Corker's win and a U.S. Senate seat. A more nuanced, and perhaps more accurate, way to look at those election results is to factor in that "the South"—still the most conservative, evangelical, hierarchical, pro-military, pro-gun, homophobic, antilabor section of the country—is the only section that, overall, *still* voted for Republicans, even in the historic 2006 "thumpin'" that the Democrats gave the Republicans: East 64–36 (Dem); Midwest 53–47 (Dem); West 56–44 (Dem); South 54–46 (Rep). This realization—that 2006 reveals the GOP has "become a nasty rump of Dixie"—is essentially shared by scholars, journalists, and pundits as varied on the political spectrum as Paul Krugman, Dick Armey, Rick Perlstein, Andrew Sullivan, and Sidney Blumenthal. The Obama election of 2008 merely underscored this conclusion—leading to rounds of soul-searching and circular firing squads within the GOP.[60]

## IV

While the rise of the modern GOP in the South is obviously about more than just race, just as clearly it is about race more than anything else. Several recent studies—especially those of Matthew Lassiter, Joseph Crespino, and Byron Shafer and Richard Johnston—have emphasized the nonracial in this massive partisan shift. It would be unfortunate if other recent scholarship were also lumped into this rather myopic approach.[61] It is essential to go back to the basics. The South did not become Republican so much as the Republican Party became *southern*. White supremacy was the first and most powerful wedge the modern GOP learned to use in Dixie, often to retard mass white class-consciousness. But the party's skillful—even masterful—manipulation of other emotional issues ingrained in its post-Reconstruction culture (religious, moral, hyperpatriotic, martial) has allowed Republicans to profit from recent southern changes like civil rights while at the same time capitalizing on powerful constants in the white southern cultural experience. These constraints have been there since at least Reconstruction (antifederalism, illiberalism, fear and dislike of the racial, religious, or sexual "other") and include race at a center spot, but are not limited to just racism. The southern experience is one that has repeatedly privileged white wealth over both black and white work and poverty. Once the GOP melded economic conservatism to the racial (and then social) kind, southern soil became an exceptionally hospitable garden in which Republican politics could take root. This, perhaps above anything, is the most important white southern response to civil rights.

It is tempting to ask if meaningful civil rights change would ever have come to a South left to its own devices—without the direct action of blacks and Yankee agitators, or the unwanted interference of the federal government. While the question is hypothetical (and thus technically unanswerable), the practical answer is obvious: No. Over a century's worth of proof backs that conclusion. And, in the end, celebration of the "wide" diversity of white southern responses to civil rights must be tempered with that most sobering of realities.

Like the careful historian he is, Sheldon Hackney has considered a number of qualifiers to his solution of what he has termed "Fermat's Last Theorem of Southern History"—the problem of whether the U.S. South is still a distinctive region. Hackney is right about a lot of things—first and foremost the reality and persistence of southern distinctiveness—but also the idea that the South has long been both the "land of super-patriotism and the locus of dissent"; the "molting South" that disappears only to reemerge in a different yet still distinctive way; and evidence of the survival of the centrality of race in the southern experience in its embodiment as the most Republican region in the country in national elections. It is race that most accounts for modern Republican ascendance, Hackney asserts: "It is certainly not because the South contains a disproportionate share of the economic elite that benefit from Republican policies."[62]

But it can be argued that, in some ways, Hackney does not go far enough. He is right that there is a molting quality to the South, but through all of these periods—conservative Democratic to newly Republican—the white southerners who dominated the region—both elite and mass—have been moved by emotional considerations bound up in prevailing notions of cultural regularity; indeed, they are notions that have long been in conflict with much of the rest of the country. After 1865, this dominant cultural ethos took the form of white supremacy and Reconstruction enmity to the federal leviathan and found its purest expression in the Solid Democratic South. Later it took the form of a "politics of emotion" that distracted plain folks from their class interests. After the Second Reconstruction, it emerged in a "new racism" predicated on more muted racial themes but also on a cultural orthodoxy resting on moral and patriotic chauvinism, and narrow forms of judgmental proscription that have found enunciation primarily through the modern Republican South. Hackney is correct that white supremacy and the rise of the Religious Right have been prime factors in the ascendant GOP in the recent South, but he has not yet discussed two others that are equally important: the technology revolution in cable TV, talk radio, and Internet media that has, paradoxically, led to mass suspicion of modern media unless it reinforces extant prejudices and stereotypes—and the rise of massive, coordinated, and well-heeled conservative think tanks like the Heritage Foundation and the American Enterprise Institute, whose work has led to a conservative dominance in agenda setting for southern *and* American politics—the spiritual fruition of the economic Right's World War II–era investment blitz in propaganda. The rest of America may indeed be becoming more southern as James Cobb suggested in a 1999 address,[63] but it is doing so in a manner—thanks to Fox News, Rush Limbaugh, and WorldNet Daily—that is popularizing and perpetuating the less tolerant, less humane, and frankly less attractive side of the South's essentially dual personality

Southern politics is not now—nor has it ever been—predominantly about politics. It's about culture. This is, perhaps, the great irony of southern politics (and increasingly, if the rest of the country is not careful, about American politics as well): that most people in the South are fueled by cultural dictates, not political ones.

Over the decades, this thesis has found expression in various ways: the power of the "Reconstruction Syndrome," the salience of a politics of emotion, the resonance of "God and country" issues, the portability of the new racism, the continued strength of a race-based and morality-based political and social conformity, the relevance of "fast-food politics" (based on quick consumption, immediate gratification, and superficial satisfaction from being on the "right"-values side of one issue without critical analysis or deeper, actual knowledge or digestion of issues), and the perpetual power of perception over reality.[64] At root, despite their differences in emphasis and in time period, all of these things are about culture: what is the predominant culture in the South, and what is presented by its elite as the dominant culture. Race has long served as the vital core for this cultural orthodoxy, but the outer layers are cultural in their essence as well—prevailing regional orthodoxies on class, gender and sex, war, religion, patriotism, jingoism, morality, nativism and xenophobia, taxes, and the federal government.

In such a polity, cultural IQ matters much more than knowledge about actual policies or matters of governance. For the bulk of the citizenry, knowledge of what constituted the "southern way of life" was enough to know how to stand on civil rights. Cognizance of what comprises regional mores on religion, not constitutional requisites or science, is sufficient for many voters to form a position on school prayer or display of the Ten Commandments, on climate change or evolution—and to demand that their elected officials do the same. For the Lee Atwaters and Karl Roves of the world, it is enough to know how people *perceive* candidates and character rather than any correlation with actual reality or the electorate's knowledge about a real issue. Now, with the apparent decline of a reality-based world, that approach has been taken national. In the white, male, rural and small-town, working-class culture of the "NASCAR Dads," it is enough to perceive that voting for Democrats is "for wusses" and that the Democrats are somehow "out of control" or "socialists."[65] No actual knowledge about a specific policy or how what was once Goldwater-era extremism has been converted into present-day mainstream "conservatism" need be necessary—especially new knowledge that might complicate or contradict long-standing beliefs and prejudices. It is what Thomas Aquinas called, in long-ago Rome, a "'cultivated ignorance' . . . [one] so useful that one protects it, keeps it from the light, in order to continue using it."[66]

At root, this state of affairs reveals an ugly but important truth about much of our democracy in the early twenty-first century. It makes plain that once the two major political parties stopped being Tweedledee and Tweedledum on race, once one of the major parties actually tried to make the country live up to part of its founding creed of "equal rights for all," it doomed itself to electoral defeat and, according to some, increasing irrelevance. The ascendance of "The Social Issue," as Scammon and Wattenberg famously dubbed it, did not bespeak the essential wisdom of much of the electorate.[67] On the contrary, it betrayed a fundamental and difficult truth about much of white America—certainly a majority in the South, and perhaps a majority overall. Both white ethnic northerners and white southerners were a lot more comfortable with a racially, ethnically, and sexually exclusive polity, society, and economy—even those who did not share in a significant way in the economic rewards associated with this status quo—than in striving toward a genuinely inclusive America. Far from comprising a wise and moderating influence in politics, "the people" have too often been—especially once mass media and modern religion caught up to the elite rhetoric—ever-susceptible to a demagogy that preys on their most primal and irrational fears, jealousies, prejudices, and emotions. As a country and as a people, we have not been the better for it.

Like a spurned and sometimes-scorned lover, the South has consistently been the most vulnerable region in this regard. Rejected by the whole like no other section—militarily and decisively—the American South and its people have been the most eager to prove their love (and their worthiness) through self-conscious and grandiloquent exhibitions: acts of patriotism, piety, and martial willingness—no matter the individual merits of the case. Like a jilted lover desperate for a second chance, southerners have combined sectional defensiveness with something near desperation to be loved again. Thus—despite its several and significant exceptions—it has ever been the region most ready to substitute emotion for reason, conformity for caution, fantasy for reality, insecurity for rationality, and unquestioning "patriotic" and martial obedience for critical thought. In all of this, its contribution to the aggrandizement of interests dedicated to private power and individual wealth has been serious; its neglect of progressive, shared, and community values considerable. The ineluctable inequalities and imbalances that result from such a value system have proliferated nowhere more than in the American South. Sadly, the greatest lesson the South can offer the rest of the country is a cautionary tale—a tragic example the country should watch closely, learn well, and then, by all means, avoid.

## Notes

1. This essay was originally written in the summer of 2007, six months after the 2006 midterm elections and a year and a half before Barack Obama was elected president. Some of it appeared in Glenn Feldman, "Our Appointment with Destiny," 244–54, in *American Crisis, Southern Solutions: From Where We Stand, Promise and Peril*, ed. Anthony Dunbar (Montgomery: NewSouth Books, 2008). Quotation from Abraham Lincoln to Col. William F. Elkins, 21 November 1864, in *The Lincoln Encyclopedia*, ed. Archer H. Shaw (New York: Macmillan, 1950).

2. "How many presidential and senatorial elections must Republicans win before the Democratic Party accepts the fact that elections have consequences?" a typical *Washington Times* editorial asked on 19 May 2005. An early sign that things had changed in Washington occurred when Senate Environment and Public Works Committee chair Barbara Boxer (D-CAL) dealt with Senator James Inhofe's (R-OK) repeated interruptions of the testimony on climate change by former vice president Al Gore by reminding Inhofe, in public, that "You're not making the rules . . . anymore. Elections have consequences" ("Inhofe Finds Out 'Elections Have Consequences,'" www.cnn.com, 22 March 2007).

3. "White House Backs Cheney's Disregard for Executive Order," *Washington Post* and San *Francisco Chronicle*, www.sfgate.com, 23 June 2007; Steve Benen, "Cheney Rejects His Own Argument," *CBS News*, www.cbsnews.com, 28 June 2007; "Bush Impeachment on the Table, Hagel Says," *Los Angeles Times*, 26 March 2007, www.latimes. com, concerned Senator Chuck Hagel (R-NEB). Sean Wilentz, "The Worst President in U.S. History?" *Rolling Stone*, 21 April 2006. Jay Tolson, "Ten Worst Presidents: Introduction," *U.S. News & World Report*, 16 February 2007, www.usnews.com; Catherine Dodge, "Bush Iraq Plan May Be Last Chance to Avoid History's 'Dustbin,'" Bloomberg News, www.Bloomberg.com, "Politics," 22 January 2007; Eric Foner, "He's the Worst Ever," *Washington Post*, 3 December 2006; Rick Shenkman, "George Bush's Misplaced Hope That Historians Will Rank Him Higher Than His Contemporaries," *History News Network*, http://hnn.us, 1 January 2007. Strangely, President Bush repeatedly

expressed optimism that history would judge him more kindly than the present. There are signs that this type of thinking has its basis in Bush's and Dick Cheney's close ties to Andrew Roberts, a self-described "extremely right wing" and "reactionary," but little-known British historian. Indeed, Roberts's work itself has been described as linked to, and inspired by, white supremacy, the most unrepressed glorification of imperialism, massive violence, and an "ahistorical catalogue of apologies and justifications for mass murder that even blames the victims of concentration camps for their own deaths." The Harvard historian Caroline Elkins called Roberts's work "incredibly dangerous and frightening." Bush's confidence that history will judge him kindly seems rooted in his own explanation that "When it's all said and done, when Laura and I head back home . . . I will . . . look in the mirror, and I will say, 'I came with a set of principles and I didn't try to change my principles to make me popular'"—words that take on more significance when one considers the advice Roberts has given Bush and Cheney: "adopt a supreme imperial indifference to public opinion . . . there can be no greater test of statesmanship than sticking to unpopular but correct policies"; and in another passage, "The greatest danger . . . come[s] not from declared enemies without, but rather from vociferous enemies within their own society" (Jim Ruttenberg, "Bush, on Friendly Turf, Suggests History Will Be Kind to Him," New York Times, 20 April 2007 [Bush quotation]; Johann Hari, "White Man for the Job: Bush's Imperial Historian," New Republic, www.tnr.com, 13 April 2007 [all other quotations in note]).

4. These tendencies have been amply documented by some of America's finest scholars. See, e.g., Richard Hofstadter, The Paranoid Style in American Politics and Other Essays (New York: Knopf, 1965); Seymour Martin Lipset and Earl K. Raab, The Politics of Unreason: Right-Wing Extremism in America, 1790–1970 (New York: Harper and Row, 1970); and David Brion Davis, The Fear of Conspiracy: Images of Un-American Subversion from the Revolution to the Present (Ithaca: Cornell University Press, 1971).

5. On the "rock star" reception given to extreme-right incendiaries, see Ben Adler, "Why Liberals Should Keep Complaining about Ann Coulter," New Republic, www.tnr.com, 16 March 2007; and Sherie Gossett, "Ann Coulter 'Raghead' Comments Spark Blogger Backlash," Cybercast News Service, www.cnsnews.com, 13 February 2006. One important reason extremist right comment has enjoyed entrée into mainstream venues is that modern radical Right media has been highly successful at pretending that there are two co-equal sides to every question, and that they are simply taking one legitimate, if differing, viewpoint that deserves to be heard and treated with seriousness in an open society. Yet every now and then a member of the extreme-right chattering class lets the open secret slip. Matt Labash, a young writer for Rupert Murdoch's Weekly Standard and, formerly, the American Spectator, admitted that the modern right-wing media simultaneously rejects the conventional "standards of fairness, accuracy, and unbiased coverage that they [simultaneously] demand from the 'liberal media.'" As Labash himself put it: "We've created this cottage industry in which it pays to be un-objective. . . . It's a great way to have your cake and eat it too. Criticize other

people for not being objective. Be as subjective as you want. It's a great little racket" (David Brock, "The Mighty Windbags," www.salon.com, 11 May 2004 [quotations]). The aggregate effect of this, of course, has led to extreme timidity on the part of the mainstream media (the so-called MSM or "liberal media") who do not want rightist charges of bias to stick.

A corollary is widespread confusion over what the word "conservative" really means. Since modern rightists have termed extreme positions "conservative"—and been allowed to do so by a mainstream media more enamored with "balance" and ratings than actual reality—there are signs that the word "conservatism" is headed toward "becoming totally meaningless altogether" (Bill Zide, "The 'C' Word," www. truthout.org, 13 June 2006 [quotation]). A priceless Orwellian example is former Bush speechwriter Michael Gerson's op-ed piece arguing that President Bush's tenure has represented pro-poverty, Catholic concern for the "common good" and centrist politics (see "Two Parties Fleeing the Center," *Washington Post*, 13 June 2007). Another by-product, as Andrew O'Hehir put it in his comments on "the mainstream media's fetish for journalistic 'balance,' regardless of its relevance to reality" is that it takes months or even years for the mainstream media or regulatory agencies to sort out competing "scientific" claims made by organized business interests—which is exactly the point of paying for the generation of competing scientific claims on matters such as climate change and the environment ("The Know-Nothings," www.salon.com, 14 September 2005 [quotation]). Nor is this unintentional. As Donald Devine, a lecturer at a "conservative boot camp" in Santa Barbara that schools its college-age recruits on F. A. Hayek, Milton Friedman, Frank Meyer, and William F. Buckley, explained: Four decades ago "we had to make the term 'conservative' respectable. Now 'conservatism' has become such a popular word it doesn't mean anything" (Jason DeParle, "Passing Down the Legacy of Conservatism," *New York Times*, 31 July 2006 [quotation]). The rub is that now even progressive scholars and sources casually, perhaps unconsciously, refer to extreme rightist thought and policy proposals as "conservative" (see, e.g., George Lakoff, Marc Ettlinger, and Sam Ferguson, "Bush is Not Incompetent!" Rockridge Institute, www.truthout.org, 26 June 2006). And, among the luminaries that are canonical at the "boot camp" for college students in Santa Barbara above, a number (F. A. Hayek and Milton Friedman) spent decades being considered extremists. Others (William F. Buckley Jr.) trace their rightism to a strange fusion of Catholicism and capitalism that has definite antidemocratic roots. Or, as Buckley put it in 2004, "Democracy just doesn't work, much of the time" (Sam Tanenhaus, "Athwart History," *New Republic*, 19 March 2007, 31–33; Buckley quotation on 32). This is a kindred kind of extreme right Catholicism that now passes for "conservatism," such as that which animated a 1996 *First Things* symposium titled "The End of Democracy: The Judicial Usurpation of Politics" featuring Hadley Arkes, Robert P. George, Richard John Neuhaus, George Weigel—at which there was open questioning of the legitimacy of democracy and the advocacy of mass civil disobedience to court decisions on abortion and gay rights (Max Blumenthal, "Rick Santorum's Beastly Politics," *Nation*, 13 November 2006).

In point of fact, this antidemocratic strain is strongly represented in the writings of neoliberal or Austrian economic thinkers such as Milton Friedman and F. A. Hayek, who are heroes to many on this Catholic right (see Glenn Feldman, "Putting Uncle Milton to Bed: Reexamining Milton Friedman's Essay on the Social Responsibility of Business," *Labor Studies Journal* 32 [June 2007]: 125–41). A distinct irony is supplied by Russell Kirk. Often called the "father of conservatism," Kirk is venerated at conservative "boot camp" as well. His extremist tendencies are evident perhaps in reverse. Not unlike Hayek, Friedman, and Ludwig von Mises, he tarred New Deal liberalism as the herald of collectivist tyranny—and engaged in the transitive game of equating liberalism with collectivism, collectivism with communist tyranny, and, then consequently, liberalism with communism and tyranny. What is interesting about Kirk, though, is that he, like Buckley and the early *National Review* staff, was also possessed of a "Catholic sacramental vision." Only his vision was decidedly of the less popular premelding or prefusionist type ("Russell Kirk [1918–1994]," *Religion & Liberty* 4 [May and June 1994], Acton Institute, www.acton.org, [quotation]). Because ownership of property was, for Kirk, the foundation of human separation from animals, "the rights of property are more important than the right to life" (Joanne Ricca, "The American Right," unpublished report presented at the annual meeting of the United Association of College and Labor Educators, Los Angeles, Calif., April 2002, p. 4 [quoted]). This is a stunningly obsolete argument that would today give public lie to the fusionist fiction that moral values really do matter as much as economic ones.

Good recent pieces on the state of the "mainstream media" in the United States that deal with the changing concept of "reality" are Paul Craig Roberts, "Economic Unreality Revealed," http://vdare.com/roberts, 15 February 2006; Frank Rich, "All the President's Press," *New York Times*, 29 April 2007; and Gene Lyons, "Rhetoric over Reality," *Arkansas Democrat-Gazette*, 28 June 2006. Rick Perlstein explores why it is the modern mainstream media has handicapped its own ability to accurately describe reality in "Southern Discomfort," *New Republic*, www.tnr.com, 29 November 2006. On political extremism being repackaged as "conservatism," see "Revenge of the Irate Moderates," *New York Times*, 9 August 2006; Paul Krugman, "Nonsense and Sensibility," *New York Times*, 11 August 2006; Joe Conason, "War Critics Are Mainstream, Not Fringe," www.Truthdig.com, 10 August 2006; Stephen Lendman, "A Short History of the Christian Right," www.counterpunch.org, 23 April 2007; and O'Hehir, "The Know-Nothings."

6. O'Hehir, "The Know-Nothings"; Chris Mooney, *The Republican War on Science* (New York: Basic Books, 2005). Mooney traces this strategy to methods perfected by the tobacco industry and anti-environmental interests during the Reagan years. Recently they have been applied by the Christian Right and corporate conservatives to a whole gamut of issues including climate change, stem-cell research, evolution, abortion, breast cancer, contraception, the protection of endangered species, and more. "Doubt is our product," a notorious Brown and Williamson tobacco internal memo declared in 1969, "since it is the best means of competing with the 'body of fact' that exists in the mind of the general public. It is also the best means of establishing a

controversy." There are obvious dangers involved. "Policymaking by ideology," Harvard physicist Lewis Branscomb reminds us, "requires that reality be set aside, [and] it can be maintained only by moving towards ever more authoritarian forms of government" (O'Hehir, "The Know-Nothings" [quotations]).

7. As political scientist Alan Wolfe wrote upon Falwell's recent death, "Instead of pondering Jerry Falwell's legacy, we would be better off asking how this man ever became a public figure in the first place" ("The Stone Is Cast," www.salon.com, 15 May 2007 [quoted]). Christopher Hitchens made, essentially, the same point in a much more acerbic piece, "Faith-Based Fraud" (www.slate.com, 16 May 2007).

8. Harvey also argued against the media referring to women and children killed in Afghanistan as "civilians" and compared them to the hijackers who perpetrated 9/11 ("ABC's Paul Harvey Compares 'Women and Children' Killed in Afghanistan to 9/11 Hijackers," http://thinkprogress.org, 2 May 2007 [quotations]). Interview with Grover Norquist in Pablo Pardo, "In Twenty Years, the American Welfare State Will No Longer Be Needed," *El Mundo*, 12 September 2004, reprinted in *E Messenger: The Electronic Newsletter of the Florida AFL-CIO*, www.flaaflcio.org, 8 October 2004. Yoshi Tsurumi, Bush's Harvard Business School MBA professor for economics, remembers that the future president made the statement, "The government doesn't have to help poor people"—including people on fixed incomes who needed heat—"because they are lazy." He sneered at Tsurumi for showing the film *The Grapes of Wrath*, based on the John Steinbeck novel of the Great Depression. He also called FDR's New Deal policies "socialism," and "denounced labor unions, the Securities and Exchange Commission, Medicare, Social Security, you name it. He denounced the civil rights movement as socialism. To him, socialism and communism were the same thing" (see Mary Jacoby, "The Dunce," www.salon.com, 16 September 2004 [quotations]). Paul Krugman, "Gilded Once More," *New York Times*, 27 April 2007.

9. Likewise it is unsettling to consider that our present-day revival of fundamentalist religious intolerance in this country may, in fact, mark more of a return to form than an aberration in our historical development. For that disturbing development, see, for example, Nancy Lusignan, ed., *Fear Itself: Enemies Real or Imagined in American Culture* (West Lafayette, Ind.: Purdue University Press, 1999); David Harry Bennett, *The Party of Fear: From Nativist Movements to the New Right in American History* (Chapel Hill: University of North Carolina Press, 1988); and note 4 above.

10. This refers of course to Republican attack ads that linked incumbent U.S. senator Max Cleland with Osama bin-Laden and Saddam Hussein, which helped a candidate hand-picked by Karl Rove (Saxby Chambliss, who did not serve in Vietnam due to a knee injury) to unseat the Georgia senator who lost three limbs in Vietnam. While Chambliss never claimed to have served, the GOP and its supporters clearly appropriated the "patriotism" and "support for the military" issues away from the Democrats. ("Ad Uses Saddam, bin Laden to Question Cleland's Record," Associated Press, 11 October 2002; Mary McGrory, "Dirty Bomb Politics," *Washington Post*, 20 June 2002; Eric Boehlert, "The President Ought to Be Ashamed," www.salon.com, 21 November 2003;

"Commander-in-Chief Lands on USS *Lincoln*," www.cnn.com, 2 May 2003; "'Mission Accomplished' Whodunit," www.cbsnews.com, 29 October 2003).

11. Joshua Kurlantztick, "Democrat Lessons," *Prospect*, www.prospect-magazine. co.uk, December 2004; Josh Marshall, "It's Tough to Have a Goldwater Moment When You're So Close," www.thehill.com, 4 November 2004; George F. Will, "A Goldwater Revival," *Washington Post*, 2 September 2004. For a variation on this theme, see John Fund, "Internet Rules," *Wall Street Journal*, www.wsj.com, 31 October 2005; and "What Now for Democrats?" *Washington Post*, 9 November 2002.

12. Robert B. Reich, "Who Really Picks the Next President," 26 August 2004; "The Real Battle in the Battle Ground," 22 September 2004, Public Radio's Marketplace Commentaries, www.robertreich.org; D. Stephen Voss, "Strength in the Center," www. digitas.harvard.edu, ca. 2004.

13. I have discussed concepts such as the "Reconstruction Syndrome," a "politics of emotion," "neo-Kluxism," and "The New Racism," in various places. See, for example, Glenn Feldman, "The Status Quo Society, The Rope of Religion, and The New Racism," in *Politics and Religion in the White South*, ed. Glenn Feldman, 287–352 (Lexington: University Press of Kentucky, 2005); and Glenn Feldman, "Ugly Roots: Race, Emotion, and the Rise of the Modern Republican Party in Alabama and the South," in *Before Brown: Civil Rights and White Backlash in the Modern South*, ed. Feldman, 268–309 (Tuscaloosa: University of Alabama Press, 2004).

14. Michael Lind, *Made in Texas: George W. Bush and the Southern Takeover of American Politics* (New York: Basic Books, 2003); Peter Applebome, *Dixie Rising: How the South Is Shaping American Values, Politics, and Culture* (New York: Harvest Books, 1997); David Herbert Donald, "The Southernization of America," *New York Times*, 30 August 1976; John Egerton, *The Americanization of Dixie, the Southernization of America* (New York: HarperCollins, 1974).

15. Maggie Gallagher, "The Rise of the Values Voters," *National Review*, www. nationalreview.com, 23 November 2004; "Media Overplayed 'Moral Values' as 'Decisive' Election Issue," www.mediamatters.org, 10 November 2004, supplied commentary by Dan Rather, *CBS Evening News*, 3 November 2004; Anderson Cooper, 3 November 2004, *Anderson Cooper 360*, 3 November 2004; Paula Zahn, CNN, *Paula Zahn Now*, 3 November 2004; Pat Buchanan, MSNBC, *Scarborough Country*, 3 November 2004; and Bill Plante, CBS, *The Early Show*, 4 November 2004 as evidence of an overemphasis on "moral values" as the decisive issue. Other pundits soon argued that the Iraq War and the War on Terror had been downplayed incorrectly (see, for example, "Moral Values Malarkey," www.cbsnews.com, 5 November 2004).

16. For an example of the pressure being applied to the middle classes in today's economy, see David Wessel, "As Rich-Poor Gap Widens in the U.S., Class Mobility Stalls," *Wall Street Journal*, 13 May 2005.

17. On this final topic, see Glenn Feldman, *The Disfranchisement Myth: Poor Whites and Suffrage Restriction in Alabama* (Athens: University of Georgia Press, 2004). Another exhibit in the evidence supporting the reality of political distraction is that, in

poll after poll, most Americans demonstrate liberal or progressive beliefs on economic and social issues and even foreign policy (see Ted Rall, "The Right Stuff . . . Long Live Fictional Conservatism!" *Boise Weekly*, www.boiseweekly,com, 28 March 2007; Paul Krugman, "Emerging Republican Minority," *New York Times*, 26 March 2007; and for CBS and Gallup polls, Katrina vanden Heuvel, "The Progressive Gap," *Nation*, www.TheNation.com blog, 19 April 2007).

18. Laurie Goodstein and David D. Kirkpatrick, "Conservative Group Amplifies Voice of Protestant Orthodoxy," *New York Times*, 22 May 2004; Nicholas Confessore, "Welcome to the Machine: How the GOP Disciplined K Street and Made Bush Supreme," *Washington Monthly*, www.washingtonmonthly.com, July/August 2003; Don Hazen, "The Right-Wing Express," www.alternet.org, 7 February 2005; Michael Dolny, "What's in a Label?" *Fairness & Accuracy in Reporting*, www.fair.org, May/June 1998; Paul Krugman, "Supply-Side Virus Strikes Again: Why There Is No Cure for this Virulent Infection," *Slate*, http://web.mit.edu, 15 August 1996; Eric Alterman, "How We Got Here," Center for American Progress, *Think Again*, www.cfap.org, 28 August 2005; David Callahan, "$1 Billion for Conservative Ideas," *Nation*, www.thenation.com, 26 April 1999. David Brock, "The Mighty Windbags," www.salon.com, 11 May 2004; David Brock, *The Republican Noise Machine: Right-Wing Media and How it Corrupts Democracy* (New York: Crown, 2004); Jessica Clarke and Tracy Van Slyke, "Making Connections," *In These Times*, www.alternet.org, 27 April 2005; Kim Campbell, "A Call to the Right," *Christian Science Monitor*, 25 July 2002. In fact, among right-wing media managers, the inability of liberals to reduce complex issues down to the level of black-and-white sound bites, in misleading and moralistic terms, is actually lampooned as a "weakness" that, they are confident, should ensure conservative dominance in talk radio for years to come. See comments by various right-wing media figures about Al Franken's liberal talk show on "Air America," in Leonard Pitts Jr., "Just What We Need: More On-Air Yahoos," *Miami Herald*, 24 February 2003 (quotation).

19. The answer is: not much, relatively speaking. A report released in June 2007 documented the overwhelming advantage right-wing radio programming has over progressive programming on America's public radio airwaves. Among other notable findings, the study revealed that of the 257 news/talk radio stations controlled by the nation's top five commercial owners, weekday conservative programming held a 91 to 9 percent edge over progressive news/talk. Cut other ways, the data revealed the same basic trend. Each weekday more than ten times as much conservative programming as progressive is aired on these 257 stations: 2,570 hours to 254 hours. In four of the nation's top-ten radio markets (Atlanta, Dallas, Houston, and Philadelphia), conservative radio programming holds an even higher edge over progressive: between 96 and 100 percent (*The Structural Imbalance of Political Talk Radio*, a joint report by the Center for American Progress and Free Press, www.thinkprogress.org, 21 June 2007). Air America actually declared bankruptcy and went off the air.

20. Gregory Korte, "Blackwell Revels in the Hot Seat: Promoting Bush—and Himself," *Cincinnati Enquirer*, 25 October 2004; Jo Becker, "Behind the Scenes, Officials Wrestle over Voting Rules," *Washington Post*, 10 October 2004; Robert F. Kennedy Jr.,

"Was the 2004 Election Stolen?" *Rolling Stone*, 1 June 2006; Bob Fitrakis and Harvey Wasserman, "Why Is the Man Who Stole Ohio Campaigning with a White Suprema-cist?" www.freepress.org, 9 October 2006; Harold Meyerson, "The GOP's Shameful Vote Strategy," *Washington Post*, 27 October 2004; Art Levine, "Salon's Shameful Six," www.salon.com, 15 August 2006; Richard Byrne Reilly, "Election Day Has Its (Dirty) Tricks, Too," *Pittsburgh Tribune-Review*, 28 October 2004. The historian Dan T. Carter has also made the important point in a number of places that our current "rotten borough" system of gerrymandered congressional districts disproportionately favors Republican candidates. For example, Carter reports that from 2000 to 2006, Repub-lican candidates actually won less than 47 percent of the total vote but occupied 55 of the chamber's 100 seats (Carter, "Is There Still a Dixie?: The Southern Question and the Triumph of American Conservatism," paper presented at the University of Sussex, October 2006, p. 3; I am grateful to Professor Carter for making a copy of this paper available to me). See also Dan T. Carter to author, e-mail, 9 November 2004 (in pos-session of the author). "I don't want everybody to vote," the religious right activist Paul Weyrich bluntly informed 15,000 conservative preachers at a 1980 political training session in Dallas. "Elections are not won by a majority of the people. They never have been from the beginning of our country and they are not now. As a matter of fact, our leverage in the elections quite candidly goes up as the voting populace goes down" (*The Long Shadow of Jim Crow: Voter Suppression in America, 2004,* A Report by the People for the American Way and the National Association for the Advancement of Colored People [NAACP], www.pfaw.org, 2004, p. 1 [quotation]). See also Greg Gor-don, "Justice Official Accused of Blocking Suits into Alleged Violations," McClatchy Newspapers, 19 June 2007; Greg Gordon, "Complaints Abound over Enforcement of Voter Registration Law," McClatchy Newspapers, 6 June 2007; "Disenfranchisement Strategy at Heart of Modern Right Wing," www.rightwingwatch.org, 8 June 2007; and Zachary A. Goldfarb, "Hearing on FEC Pick Could Add Fuel to Debate over Justice Dept," *Washington Post*, 8 June 2007.

21. Sheldon Hackney to author, e-mail, 3 December 2004 (e-mail in possession of the author).

22. See Glenn Feldman, "Putting Uncle Milton to Bed." On the critical, post-1960s Democratic abandonment of the American working classes and working-class union issues, see Michael Lind, "Red State Sneer," *Prospect*, 16 December 2004; Chris Hedges, "The Rise of Christian Fascism and Its Threat to American Democracy," www.alternet. org, 8 February 2007; and, of course, Thomas Byrne Edsall and Mary D. Edsall, *Chain Reaction: The Impact of Race, Rights, and Taxes on American Politics* (New York: Nor-ton, 1992). Alison Fitzgerald, "BP Ready for Spill 10 Times Gulf Disaster, Plan Says (Update 1), *Bloomberg/Business Week*, 31 May 2010, www.businessweek.com

23. The two most notable recent books to do this are Matthew D. Lassiter, *The Silent Majority: Suburban Politics in the Sunbelt South* (Princeton: Princeton Univer-sity Press, 2005); and Byron E. Shafer and Richard Johnston, *The End of Southern Exceptionalism: Class, Race, and Partisan Change in the Postwar Period* (Cambridge: Harvard University Press, 2006). For an insightful and penetrating critical look at this

question, see Dan T. Carter, "Is There Still a South?: And Does It Matter?" *Dissent* 53 (Summer 2007): 92–96.

24. Glenn Feldman, "Unholy Alliance: Suppressing Catholic Teachings in Subservience to Republican Ascendance in America," *Political Theology* 7 (April 2006): 137–79, see esp. 138–39.

25. Richard Goldstein, "Red Sluts, Blue Sluts," *Nation*, www.thenation.com, 16 December 2004; Jeffrey Friedman, "Not What They Do," *New Republic*, www.tnr.com, 29 November 2004; Pam Belluck, "To Avoid Divorce, Move to Massachusetts," *New York Times*, 14 November 2004; Lee Seigel, "Reality in America," *New Republic*, www.tnr. com, 16 June 2003; Dan Carlin (Washington University, St. Louis), "Chasing Images of the Dead: The Unreality of the Iraq War in American Media," The Elie Wiesel Prize in Ethics, Third Prize, 2004.

26. O'Hehir, "The Know-Nothings" (first and second quotations). See also Mooney, *The Republican War on Science*. Hedges reminds us that before the 2006 elections, 45 U.S. senators and 186 members of the House had approval ratings of between 80 and 100 percent from the Christian Coalition, the Eagle Forum, and the Family Resource Council, "the three most influential Christian right advocacy groups" (Hedges, "The Rise of Christian Fascism and Its Threat to American Democracy" [second Hedges quotations in text and quotation in note]). The award-winning journalist Bill Moyers has concurred that "for the first time in our history, ideology and theology hold a monopoly of power in Washington" (Lendman, "A Short History of the Christian Right" [first Hedges quotation in text, Moyers quotation in note]). Perhaps the best-known essay on this subject is Maureen Dowd's now-legendary 25 April 2004 piece in the *New York Times*, "The Orwellian Olsens," which provided the basis for her book *Bushworld* (New York: Putnam, 2004).

27. "Their problem is they think they're Republicans," is a common refrain heard from frustrated southern labor leaders in talking about the propensity of much of their rank-and-file to vote on the basis of social conservatism (author's notes). "America is utterly enthralled with what is perhaps the most ironically misnamed product ever unleashed on the opiated American public: 'reality' TV. . . . I worry because we hear virtually nothing about it, and because the change [in media] is so felicitous to our moral and economic masters. . . . This neutralization of class consciousness . . . an unprecedented dissociation of preferences from realistic self-interest . . . has been the religious right's greatest achievement," one alternative columnist wrote perceptively. "Convincing ordinary folks that gay marriage, activist judges and the like are greater threats than their own economic distress is a virtually unprecedented feat. It allowed the constellation of Christian churches to create a civil religion full of bombast and devoid of charity—a God-blessed dystopia where the meek inherit nothing but debt and the actual rich reap the manna that flows from the rich-any-day-now's myopia. . . . The shrapnel from lower-class America's identification with the upper class is the angry renunciation of the social contract by those who need it most. And so poor people and middle-class Americans support tax cuts for the wealthy, because deep down they just know . . . any day now they are going to be rich" (John Steinberg, "Unreality

TV: The New Opiate of the Masses," The Raw Story, www.rawstory.com, 26 May 2006 [quoted]). See also Michelle Cottle, "That's Life: Unreality," *New Republic*, www.tnr. com, 21 March 2003 (references "Shocknawe" and "embedded" as catchphrases).

28. On this point, I have profited from an ongoing discussion and numerous conversations with Birmingham attorney James M. "Jimmy" Wooten and colleague Edwin L. Brown ("Executive Pay," *Business Week*, www.businessweek.com, 19 April 2004 and 16 April 2001).

29. See, for example, "Lutheran Leader Condemns Prosperity Gospel," Associated Press, 30 March 2007; and Jeff Sharlet, "Soldiers for Christ: Inside America's Most Powerful Megachurch," *Harper's*, May 2005, 41–54. Such notions were prominent during the late nineteenth century, no doubt correlated with the pervasive mentality of Social Darwinism (see, for example, Robert Bartels, ed., *Ethics in Business* [Columbus: Bureau of Business Research, Ohio State University, 1963], 35).

30. One of the few studies that has recognized the irony of the nationalizing of southern thought and culture, especially the worst aspects of it, is George Lewis, *The White South and the Red Menace: Segregationists, Anticommunism, and Massive Resistance, 1945–1965* (Gainesville: University Press of Florida, 2004). Lindman, "A Short History of the Christian Right," notes the tie between patriotism and religion in right-wing thought. On the evolution controversy, a *Los Angeles Times* editorial stipulated that "This would be risible if anti-evolution forces were confined to a lunatic fringe, but they are not" ("Yabba-Dabba Science," 24 May 2007 [quotation]). George W. Bush contributed to public perception that there was an ongoing, legitimate scientific controversy by proclaiming that "the jury is still out" on evolution (Timothy Noah, "George W. Bush, The Last Relativist," *Slate*, 31 October 2000 [quotation]; Peter Slevin, "Battle on Teaching Evolution Sharpens," *Washington Post*, 14 March 2005). By 2007, a Gallup Poll concluded that almost seven in ten Republicans did not believe in evolution ("Poll: Most Republicans Doubt Evolution," *Christian Post*, 21 June 2007). See also Arian Campo-Flores, "Are Tea Partiers Racist?" *Newsweek*, 26 April 2010, www.newsweek.com; Linda Feldmann, "Rand Paul: Civil Rights Brouhaha Clouds Senate Campaign," *Christian Science Monitor*, 20 May 2010; and David Espo, "GOP Senate Hopes Ride with Tea Party Activists," Associated Press, 29 May 2010.

31. Ralph Reed, *After the Revolution: How the Christian Coalition Is Impacting America* (Dallas: Word Publishing, 1996), 236; John Nichols, "The Old Time Hypocrisy Hour," www.thenation.com, 16 May 2007 (quotation); Timothy Noah, "Jerry Falwell's Greatest Hits," www.slate.com, 16 May 2007. See also the conservative, former editor of the right-leaning religious journal *First Things*, Damon Linker, "Jerry Falwell's Nasty Contributions to American Political Life," www.tnr.com, 17 May 2007. See also Sean Alfano, "Christine O'Donnell, Tea Party Hopeful, Doesn't Believe in Separation of Church and State," *New York Daily News*, 19 October 2010; Brian Montopoli, "Delaware GOP Candidate: Ask Liberals Why They're Nazis" *CBS News*, www.cbsnews.com, 17 September 2010 (regarding Tea Party candidate Glen Urquhart's denial of "separation of church and state"); and "Ken Buck: 'I Disagree Strongly with Concept of Separation of Church and State," 26 October 2010, http://blogs.abcnews.com, original from

George Zornick, "GOP Candidate Ken Buck: 'I Disagree Strongly with Concept of Separation of Church and State," 26 October 2010, www.thinkprogress.org.

32. This has been the subject of some considerable historiographical controversy. David L. Chappell's provocative work is probably the best example of the school of thought that casts "religion" as something that was not an obstacle to the modern civil rights movement (see *A Stone of Hope: Prophetic Religion and the Death of Jim Crow* [Chapel Hill: University of North Carolina Press, 2003]). Professor Paul Harvey's work does not. See *Freedom's Coming: Religious Culture and the Shaping of the South from the Civil War through the Civil Rights Era* (Chapel Hill: University of North Carolina Press, 2005). Ironically, Religious Right luminary Ralph Reed sides here against the Chappell thesis (see Reed, *After the Revolution*, 235–48). For commentary on the Chappell thesis, see Feldman, ed., *Politics and Religion in the White South*, 8–9, 28 n. 1, 105, 122 n. 6.

33. Frank Cheney to Charles Ross, 12 December 1948 (first quotation), Box 1510, Folder 596-A, Official Files, Harry S. Truman Papers, Harry S. Truman Library (HST), Independence, Mo.; J. J. Cockrell to James E. Folsom, 30 January 1948, with enclosure (second quotation), Box SG 13441, Folder 5, Alabama Governors Papers, James E. Folsom Papers, Alabama Department of Archives and History (ADAH), Montgomery; William Fisher commented on what he called modern conservative intolerance for "the other," and its southern heritage, by pointing to Virginia Republican congressman Virgil Goode's prediction that cultural ruin and an avalanche of Muslim in-migration would occur if Minnesota's newly elected congressman, Keith Ellison, was allowed to take his oath of office on the Koran. "The former bastion of the Confederacy lingers with those like Goode who have no respect or tolerance for anyone different from them" (Fisher, "Here Are the Christians!" www.truthout.org, 29 December 2006 [quoted]).

34. *Montgomery Advertiser*, 4 February 1948 (first quotation). Paul Bernard Williamson to Mr. Editor, 22 November 1946 (fourth quotation), Box 376, Folder 5, J. Lister Hill Papers, W. Stanley Hoole Special Collections Library, University of Alabama (UA), Tuscaloosa; Sam M. Johnston to John Sparkman, 3 July 1948, Box 2, Folder 2, Frank M. Dixon Personal Papers, Alabama Department of Archives and History (ADAH), Montgomery; An American Northerner to Honored Sirs, 17 February 1948 (second quotation), and W. E. Bush, Chicago, "A Letter to Southern Leaders. . . . ," 25 February 1948 (third quotation), both in Box SG 13427, Folder 11, Folsom Papers, ADAH.

35. On traditional deference toward business and the New Deal challenge to that, see George A. Steiner and John F. Steiner, *Business, Government, and Society: A Managerial Perspective*, 9th ed (Boston: Irwin, McGraw-Hill, 2000), 88–89, 124 (quotation), 373; and Robert L. Heilbroner, *The Worldly Philosophers: The Lives, Times, and Ideas of the Great Economic Thinkers*, rev. ed., 7th ed. (New York: Touchstone Books, Simon and Schuster, 1999), 277.

36. Rick Perlstein, "Rigging the Marketplace of Ideas," www.tompaine.com, 30 May 2007 (quotations). Perlstein's piece is partially a review of Elizabeth A. Fones-Wolf's,

*Selling Free Enterprise: The Business Assault on Labor and Liberalism, 1945–1960* (Urbana: University of Illinois Press, 1995). For the NAM's National Industrial Information Committee's activity in the South, see Stetson Kennedy, *Southern Exposure* (1946; repr., Boca Raton: Florida Atlantic University Press, 1991], 194–97).

37. After the legal victories of the modern civil rights movement made it necessary to tone down explicit appeals to white supremacy, "personal responsibility" became common coin for a *New Racism*, a kindred coalition of economic and social/religious conservatives. "Personal responsibility" augmented and, to some degree eclipsed, the antifederalism coin of the old racism, as the melding alliance of economic and social conservatives adjusted to new racial and voting realities.

38. Various scholars and journalists have discussed the importance of "fusionism" but have not recognized its important southern, and much earlier roots, which go back to at least Reconstruction and the turn of the twentieth century disfranchising movement. A former protégé of conservative icon William F. Buckley, Michael Lind dates the origins of national fusionism at the mid-1950s and attributes it to conservative theorist Frank S. Meyer (see *Up from Conservatism: Why the Right Is Wrong for America* [New York: Free Press, 1996]: 53–54). Lind, more than others, understands the more general importance of southern history and politics for the American pattern (see, for example, *Made in Texas*. Libertarians Brink Lindsey, Ryan Sager, and John Tierney also date conservative fusionism to the mid-1950s (see Lindsey, "Liberaltarians," *New Republic*, www.tnr.com, 4 December 2006; Shawn Macomber, "Save the Elephant," *American Spectator*, www.spectator.org, 15 September 2006; an interview with Ryan Sager on his book, *The Elephant in the Room: Evangelicals, Libertarians,, and the Battle to Control the Republican Party* [New York: John Wiley, 2006]; and Tierney, "Can This Party Be Saved?" *New York Times*, 2 September 2006. The liberal Princeton economist Paul Krugman puts the origins of this "movement conservatism" even later, in the 1960s and 1970s. See "The Great Revulsion," *New York Times*, 10 November 2006. Jean Hardisty, leftist political scientist and founder of Political Research Associates, traces it to the early 1970s in *Mobilizing Resentment: Conservative Resurgence from the John Birch Society to the Promise Keepers* (Boston: Beacon Press, 2000). *Salon.com* writer Andrew O'Hehir described it as a post-1980 coalition in the "The Know-Nothings." Yet fusionism's actual roots date to the late-nineteenth-century South.

39. George Brown Tindall, *The Emergence of the New South, 1913–1945* (Baton Rouge: Louisiana State University Press, 1967), *Gastonia (N.C.) Gazette* quoted on p. 345 (second quotation) and also see p. 347 (first quotation).

40. William L. Dickinson, a Republican congressman from Alabama, took a leading role on the national scene in trying to discredit the whole voting-rights movement as immoral based on the allegation that incidents of interracial sex took place around the march activities at Selma (see William L. Dickinson, ed., *South: The News Magazine of Dixie*, March 1967, 4, and November 1969, 4).

41. Ricca, "The American Right," 18 (Falwell quotation), 19 (LaHaye quotation), 20 (Robertson quotation). On LaHaye, see also Steve Weismann's five-part series, including pt. 4, "Pie in the Sky," www.truthout.org, 28 April 2005; and Robert Dreyfuss,

"Reverend Doomsday," *Rolling Stone*, www.rollingstone.com, 28 January 2004. See also notes from the sermon of Father Michael J. Deering, n.d., September 2002, Our Lady of Sorrows Catholic Church, Homewood, Ala. (notes in possession of author). It is also worth noting that the new priest who gave this sermon became a member of the cloth only after a twenty-plus-year sales/management career with the Eastman-Kodak Company. After only two years in the priesthood, Deering had so ingratiated himself with the conservative Catholic hierarchy in Alabama that he was elevated to the position of chancellor of the Birmingham Diocese, a lofty office just below that of bishop.

42. Christopher Brauchli, "A Short Primer on DeLay Tactics," *Boulder Daily Camera*, 15 March 2003 (quotation).

43. Yet Hanson also recognized the long-term importance of the project. "The treatment must be a sparing administration gradually applied. . . . [W]e must not excite too many of their prejudices at once," he cautioned one of his more gifted Bourbon editors, "but must work at it very slowly and tactfully, violating as little as possible their sacred taboos" (Victor Hanson to Grover C. Hall, 12 August 1927 [first quotation], box 67, folder 1, Grover C. Hall Papers, ADAH; Charles Fell editorials in the *Birmingham Age-Herald*, 14–15 August 1928 [second quotation]).

44. "In their heart of hearts," Raines agreed, Republican leadership "in Washington and the conservative think tanks disdain the social rigidity and common tastes of the party's NASCAR wing. They worry a bit that George W. Bush seems to have a genuine liking for the slumming required of a self-created cultural populist. But GOP strategists and think tankers are able to stifle these concerns, because there's been no one since Ronald Reagan so good at getting votes from Southern Baptists trying to raise families on 40 grand a year." This is "the shell game by which the GOP uses 'cultural populism' to get millions of Middle Americans to vote against their financial, medical and educational interests" (Howell Raines, "Winning the Populism PR War," *Washington Post*, 2 July 2004 [Barnes and Raines quotations]).

45. Garry Wills, "Fringe Government," *New York Review of Books* 52 (6 October 2005): 46–50. See the formal ECT statement with a list of original signatories, "Evangelicals & Catholics Together: The Christian Mission in the Third Millennium," *First Things* 43 (May 1994): 15–22; Tom Strode, "Land: Religious Right Has Won Fight with Secular Fundamentalists," *Baptist Press*, 26 January 2005; Reed, *After the Revolution*, 235–48. For the Orwellian use of abortion by the far right as the new civil rights, see, for example, Greg Pierce, "Inside Politics: Civil Rights Award," *Washington Times*, www.washingtontimes.com, 5 December 2006; John-Henry Westen, "Pastor Warren, Would You Permit a White Supremacist to Speak at Your Church?" *Christian Post*, www.christianpost.com, 6 December 2006; Strode, "Land"; and Dimitri Cavalli, "A Liberal Mix of Religion and Politics," *Wall Street Journal*, 8 June 2007; and comments of Richard Land at the conference "Role of Religion in Public Life," James Madison Institute, Princeton University, Robert P. George, presiding, C-SPAN, www.c-span.org, 24 December 2005. Of course, Lott's newfound and professed racial tolerance ignores a long personal history of intolerance, beginning with his apprenticeship to Mississippi Democratic (Dixiecrat) congressman William Colmer and continuing at

the University of Mississippi and in the U.S. Congress (see Nicholas Lemann, "What Is the South?" *New Republic*, 29 January 2007, 24–28).

46. *Engel v. Vitale*, 370 U.S. 421 (1962) dealt of course with public school prayer. *Row v. Wade*, 410 U.S. 113 (1973).

47. Others, like the conservative journalist Robert Novak, moved far to the right over time to become an apologist for more extreme views. His book *The Agony of the GOP, 1964* (New York: Macmillan, 1965) reads as almost as a primer in moderation and centrism next to his columns of the past decade and a half. The mutation of race prejudice was not complete, even in this transition viz the career of Rand acolyte Murray Rothbard, who supported Dixiecrat candidate Strom Thurmond for president in 1948 (see David Leonhardt, "Free For All: A History of Libertarianism from the Austrians to Ayn Rand and Beyond," *New York Times Book Review*, 1 April 2007, 16; Bob Herbert, "The Howls of a Fading Species," *New York Times*, 1 June 2009 [Atwater quote]).

48. On the focus group–tested nature of the gay rights issue as a dynamite fundraiser for the religious right, see conservative Andrew Sullivan's report of the Rev. Jim Wallis's discussions with Focus on the Family in "Wallis: Focus Admits Gays Not the Problem with American Families—Just a Fundraising Canard," www.rightwingwatch.org, 5 June 2007.

49. Of course, George Wallace was too shrewd to be taken in by any of this: "I talked about the Supreme Court usurpation of power . . . about the big central government. Isn't that what everybody talks about now? Isn't that what Reagan got elected on? . . . Reagan got elected by one of the biggest votes . . . ever . . . by saying those very same things I said way back yonder" (Jason Sokol, *There Goes My Everything: White Southerners in the Age of Civil Rights* [New York: Knopf, 2006], 252 [Wallace quotation]). On another occasion, Wallace mused: "You know, I should have copyrighted all of my speeches. If I had, the Republicans in Alabama, throughout the South, and all over the nation would be paying me hundreds of thousands of dollars. They owe everything they have to my kind of Democratic thinking" (Glenn Feldman, "Ugly Roots," 286 [Wallace quotation]). Right-wing economics, religion, and militarism are deeply linked in fusionism or *The Great Melding*. Stephen Lendman argues that plain people observe religious-right notables flaunting wealth as they identify with them and soak up a "prosperity gospel" that, they think, may make them rich too. All the while "unrestrained free-market capitalism divinely sanctioned . . . create[s] a global marketplace of (non-Christian, non-believing) serfs . . . left to the mercy of . . . corporate predators." Thus military, economic, and religious allegiance is demanded for a neo-liberal "Christian America where freedom means the freedom of the powerful to dominate the weak," as Chris Hedges writes (Lendman, "A Short History of the Christian Right" [quotations in note]). These arguments are reminiscent of liberal philosopher Isaiah Berlin's famous remark about unrestricted laissez-faire: "Freedom for wolves is death to the lambs." For a sample blogger who understands the chasm between the religious right and the New Testament, see Tom Degan, "Christ vs. Conservatism: A Serious Conflict," http://tomdegan.blogspot.com, 21 July 2006.

50. For an example of a young evangelical with progressive inclinations struggling to understand how religion and libertarian economics ever became linked, see Stacia Brown, "Growing Up Evangelical: How Does Childhood Faith Influence Political Engagement?" *Sojourners*, www.sojo.net, 2 June 2005, 20–25.

51. David Brooks, "Dollars & Sense," *New York Times*, 26 January 2006; Jason L. Riley, "President Bush Needs to Lead His Party on Race," *Wall Street Journal*, 16 January 2003; Richard Benedatto, "GOP: 'We Were Wrong' to Play Racial Politics," *USA Today*, www.usatoday.com, 14 July 2005, regarding RNC chair Ken Mehlman. In 2006, an Emory University study actually demonstrated a correlation between racial prejudice and Republican voter identification (see Shankar Vendatam, "Study Ties Political Leanings to Hidden Biases," *Washington Post*, 30 January 2006). The former Christian Coalition director and Republican political strategist Ralph Reed recognized and publicly apologized for the "past complicity of the white church in the mistreatment of African-Americans and Jews . . . too large a blot on our history to deny. . . . George Wallace may have stood in the schoolhouse door, but evangelical clergy provided the framework for his actions." Of course, Reed's remarks must be tempered with the realization that he was simultaneously proposing a cross-color alliance between white and black religious conservatives that would also supersede class, a precursor to the Bush–Rove "faith-based initiative" (Reed, *After the Revolution*, 236 and 237 [quotations]). See also Abdon W. Pallasch, "GOP Chairman: African Americans Not Given Good Reason to Vote for Party," *Chicago Sun-Times*, 20 April 2010.

52. Ricca, "The American Right," 15 (Weyrich quoted).

53. Ibid., 8–9. As one California Republican ally predicted about Goldwater near the time of the 1964 "purge" of the progressive wing of the GOP, "the nigger issue will put him in the White House" (Rick Perlstein, *Before the Storm: Barry Goldwater and the Unmaking of the American Consensus* [New York: Hill and Wang, 2001], 374 [quoted]). See note 49 above on George Wallace.

54. *Buckley v. Valeo*, 424 U.S. 1 (1976).

55. Ricca, "The American Right," 11 (Dolan's first quotation) and 15 (Weyrich quotation). One of the tragic ironies of Dolan's life and his right-wing, homophobic brand of Christianity was that he died in 1984, of AIDS, as a closeted homosexual (see David B. Smith, "You're Talking About Them, Not Me, Right God," *Voice of Prophecy*, www.vop.com, 27 July 2004 [second Dolan quotation]). John Gallagher and Chris Bull, "Perfect Enemies: The Religious Right, the Gay Movement, and the Politics of the 1990s," *Washington Post*, ca. 1996 (second Dolan quotation repeated). See also Gallagher and Bull, *Perfect Enemies: The Religious Right, the Gay Movement, and the Politics of the 1990s* (New York: Crown, 1996).

56. Nobel laureate and Nigerian playwright Wole Soyinka spoke of religious intolerance replacing racism worldwide, while the moral scandals surrounding Republican congressman Mark Foley, Pastor Ted Haggard, former Speaker of the House Newt Gingrich, abstinence advocate and deputy to Condoleezza Rice, Randall Tobias, among others, have plagued the GOP (see K. Connie Kang, "Nobel Winner Assails Religious Intolerance in L. A. Visit," *Los Angeles Times*, 27 January 2007; Steven Thomma,

"GOP Grapples with Marriage Revelations," *Houston Chronicle*, 28 March 2007; Anne Gearan, "Bush Official Resigns over Escort Scandal," *Yahoo News*, http://news.yahoo. com, 28 April 2007; Ari Berman, "Another GOP Sex Scandal," www.thenation.com, 3 November 2006; Marcus Mabry, "A Political Limbo: How Low Can the Republicans Go?" www.msnbc.msn.com, 7 October 2006, in conjunction with the *Newsweek* poll "GOP in Meltdown"; and Dick Polman, "How the GOP Presidential Candidates Apply Their Christian Moral Ethics," *Philadelphia Inquirer*, 12 June 2007). An April 2007 Harris Poll put George W. Bush's approval rating at 28 percent ("Bush Approval Rating Falls to 28%, Lowest Level So Far, in Harris Poll," *Wall Street Journal*, 26 April 2007). A sidelight of the Republican free fall has been watching some conservative columnists contort themselves into pretzels to effect damage control. One pundit weighed the spate of moral scandals involving Newt Gingrich, Pastor Ted Haggard, and Congressman Mark Foley—and the pro-life positions and marital affairs, divorces, and other ethical baggage of leading 2008 candidates John McCain, Rudy Giuliani, and Mitt Romney—and actually argued that the ability of conservative evangelicals to look past Republican moral failings in a way they did not look past those of Bill Clinton in the 1990s was—not hypocrisy at all—but instead an encouraging sign of "maturity" (Cal Thomas, "The Maturing Christian Right Voter," nationally syndicated column appearing in the *Florence [Ala.] Times*, www.TimesDaily.com, 13 March 2007).

57. The parade of Vatican prelates who made their opposition public to the United States' 2003 preemptive war on Iraq include Pope John Paul II, Cardinal Josef Ratzinger (later Pope Benedict XVI), Cardinal Pio Laghi, papal envoy to President Bush, Archbishop Jean-Louis Tauran, Vatican secretary for relations with states, and Archbishops Renato Martino and Celestino Migliore, permanent observers of the Holy See to the United Nations. See also Garry Wills, "What Is a Just War?" *New York Review of Books* 51 (18 November 2004); and Jean Bethke Elshtain, "Arguing about War," *New York Review of Books* 51 (16 December 2004).

58. Bob Moser, "The New Southern Strategy," www.thenation.com, 9 November 2006 (quotations). Thomas F. Schaller, *Whistling Past Dixie: How Democrats Can Win Without the South* (New York: Simon and Schuster, 2006). Paul Waldman concurred with Schaller by stressing the possible fertility of the Southwest vs. the barrenness of the South, for progressive chances in *Being Right Is Not Enough: What Progressives Must Learn from Conservative Success* (New York: Wiley, 2006).

59. The 49 percent spread Republicans enjoyed over Democrats in 2004 among white evangelicals dropped 7 points to 42 percent as the 2004 Republican margin of victory (74–25) was cut to 70–28 in House races. For this and the percentages mentioned in the main text, see Alan Cooperman, "Democrats Win Bigger Share of Religious Vote," *Washington Post*, 11 November 2006; and Joe Feuerherd, "God Gap Narrows as Democrats Take a Majority of Catholic Vote," *National Catholic Reporter*, 17 November 2006.

60. The Dixie rump quotation is conservative scholar and blogger Andrew Sullivan's from "A Political Katrina?" http://andrewsullivan.theatlantic.com, 7 March 2007. The MIT-trained economist Paul Krugman wrote, "we're seeing an emerging

Republican minority" and a "great regional realignment, in which a solid Northeast has replaced a solid South" (see Paul Krugman, "Emerging Republican Minority," *New York Times,* 26 March 2007 [first Krugman quotation]; and "The Great Revulsion," *New York Times*, 10 November 2006 [second Krugman quotation]). In this second column, Krugman also intimated that "we may be seeing the downfall of "movement conservatism" (what I have referred to in this essay as "fusionism" or "The Great Melding"). Dick Armey's sentiments appear in Ryan Sager's, *The Elephant in the Room*. For some of Armey's quotes, see Paul Krugman, "Things Fall Apart," *New York Times*, 2 October 2006. In this column, Krugman also suggested that the GOP's seemingly "permanent winning strategy" of using value issues to keep white working-class Americans distracted enough to keep them from realizing, or voting, their economic interests, "may be cracking up." He was addressing his remarks specifically about the Thomas Frank book, *What's the Matter With Kansas?: How Conservatives Won the Heart of America* (New York: Metropolitan Books, 2004). If I may be so bold, I might note that I explored the same issue of the power of emotion-based politics to distract the class interests of plain whites, and originated the term "politics of emotion" to describe the strength and durability of this kind of politics in a book that was published the same month as Frank's, in a scholarly monograph on an earlier time period that made connections to contemporary politics: Glenn Feldman, *The Disfranchisement Myth*. On the Thomas Frank thesis, Michael Lind makes the interesting argument that there never was a romantic time when "working-class Americans voted for liberals whose values they rejected." Lind points out that debates on divisive social issues (abortion, gay rights, censorship) were, prior to the 1960s, fought out in state and local arenas, which facilitated working-class Americans voting liberal and Democratic on national and economic issues, but another way on divisive social issues at the state and local levels. Thus Roosevelt, Truman, Kennedy, and Johnson, as he points out, never had to take stands on abortion or gay rights (Lind, "The Red State Sneer"). The GOP has "become a regional party of the South," Sidney Blumenthal wrote in dubbing the 2006 election another "American Revolution,"—and there are "the makings of a further realignment" in 2008 "and beyond" (Blumenthal, "The American Revolution of 2006 and Beyond," *Guardian*, www.guardian.co.uk, 9 November 2006 [quoted]). Another, probably sanguine assumption that underlay the post-election optimism in 2006, was that conservative values voters are "starting to get it." That is, they realize that if they can't "get meaningful action" on abortion and gay marriage with Republican control of all three branches of government, "it's not going to happen" (Rall, "The Right Stuff. . . . Long Live Fictional Conservatism!" [first quotation]; and Rod Dreher, "Last Hurrah for Conservative Culture Warriors," *Dallas Morning News*, 4 March 2007 [second and third quotations]). Libertarian Ryan Sager recognized frustration among the Religious Right about its lack of tangible accomplishment, but was less certain than Rall and Dreher that they are "starting to get it." He pointed to the increase in home-schooling as a coping mechanism of retreat and self-seclusion (see Macomber, "Save the Elephant"). Election Day 2006, Rick Perlstein wrote, "may well go down in history as the day the modern Republican Party became a mere Southern faction" ("Southern

Discomfort," *New Republic*, www.tnr.com, 29 November 2006 [quoted]). Perlstein also noted that former congressman and political science Ph.D. Glen Browder of Alabama, like Bob Moser, dubbed Thomas Schaller's "whistling past Dixie" theory to be "foolishness." The sectional percentages are from the *New York Times*, 9 November 2006. It is impossible not to note the religious difference between these regions. Catholics, the largest, single, denomination in the United States, comprise 21 percent of America's religious people, but that is highly concentrated: 35 percent of the East and only 12 percent of the South. Evangelicals make up only 13 percent of the East but more than half of the U.S. South (see "What Is a Christian?: New Moral Values. . . . ," *Anderson Cooper 360 Degrees,* Cable News Network [CNN], http://transcripts.cnn.com, 14 December 2006). "Thumpin,'" of course, is how President Bush described the 2006 loss in his post-election press conference (see, for example, "Bush: Several Factors Determined Vote," United Press International, www.upi.org, 8 November 2006 [first quotation]).

61. Lassiter, *The Silent Majority*; Shafer and Johnston, *The End of Southern Exceptionalism*; Joseph A. Crespino, *In Search of Another Country: Mississippi and the Conservative Counterrevolution* (Princeton: Princeton University Press, 2007); Matthew D. Lassiter and Joseph A. Crespino, eds., *The Myth of Southern Exceptionalism* (New York: Oxford University Press, 2010). Two recent works have not followed this lead (see Sokol, *There Goes My Everything*; and Kevin M. Kruse, *White Flight: Atlanta and the Making of Modern Conservatism* [Princeton: Princeton University Press, 2005]).

62. Sheldon Hackney, "The Ambivalent South," in *Warm Ashes: Issues in Southern History at the Dawn of the Twenty-First Century*, ed. Winfred B. Moore Jr., Kyle S. Sinisi, and David H. Whyte Jr., 385–95 (Columbia: University of South Carolina Press, 2003), esp. 387, 390, 392 (quotations).

63. James C. Cobb, "An Epitaph for the North: Reflections on the Politics of Regional and National Identity at the Millennium," *Journal of Southern History* 66 (February 2000): 3–24.

64. I have discussed these concepts in a number of places. See note 13 above.

65. The "reality-based" quotation is taken from a piece that has now passed into legend: Ron Suskind, "Without a Doubt," *New York Times Magazine*, 17 October 2004. A Democratic aide to North Carolina senator John Edwards and Virginia governor Mark Warner in Mara Liason, "Democrats Seek to Fire up 'NASCAR Dad' Vote," *Morning Edition*, on National Public Radio, www.npr.org, 19 September 2003 (first and second quotations). Scott Shepard, "GOP Owns the Votes of 'NASCAR Dads,'" *Atlanta Journal-Constitution*, 31 August 2003 (second quotation). For a sample of how far the bar of what constitutes mainstream conservatism has moved rightward over the past few decades, see Nixonian conservatism described as "liberal" by recent standards in Matthew Miller, "Something to Talk About," *New York Times*, 4 September 2003. See also Christopher Weber, "Newt Gingrich Defends Comparing 'Socialist' Agenda of Democrats to Nazis, Stalinist Russia," *Politics Daily*, 18 May 2010, www.politicsdaily.com.

66. One final illustration on the morphing of Goldwater-era "extremism" into what

passes today for mainstream "conservatism." During the 1960s, moderate Republicans ridiculed Barry Goldwater's contempt for what he called the "pinhead intellectuals" of the eastern elite and George Wallace's disdain for the liberal media, worrying that these tendencies might "doom their party to know-nothing irrelevance." "Little did they know," Andrew O'Hehir wrote, "how dominant [this critique] would become" ("The Know-Nothings" [quotations in note]). Garry Wills, *Papal Sin: Structures of Deceit* (New York: Doubleday, 2000), 9 (Aquinas quotation).

67. Richard M. Scammon and Ben J. Wattenberg, *The Real Majority: An Extraordinary Examination of the American Electorate* (1970; New York: Primus, 1992).

# Contributors

Fred Arthur Bailey is professor and head of the Department of History at Abilene Christian University. He is the author of *William Edward Dodd: The South's Yeoman Scholar* (1997) and *Class and Tennessee's Confederate Generation* (1987).

Michael Bowen is visiting lecturer in the Department of History and assistant director of the Bob Graham Center for Public Service, both at the University of Florida.

Tim Boyd is a history teacher at Nashville's Montgomery Bell Academy. His forthcoming book examines the impact of the civil rights movement on Democrats in Georgia between 1946 and 1976.

Glenn Feldman is a historian and professor in the College of Arts and Sciences at the University of Alabama at Birmingham. He is the author or editor of seven other books on politics, economics, religion, and race relations in the U.S. South.

Katherine Rye Jewell is assistant professor in the Economics, History, and Political Science Department at Fitchburg State College.

Barclay Key is assistant professor of history at Western Illinois University. He is the recipient of a Fulbright Lecturing Award.

John A. Kirk is chair and Donaghey Professor of History in the Department of History at the University of Arkansas at Little Rock. He is the author of *Redefining the Color Line: Black Activism in Little Rock, Arkansas, 1940–1970* (2002), *Martin Luther King Jr.* (2005), and *Beyond Little Rock: The Origins and Legacies of the Central High Crisis* (2007), as well as the editor of two other books.

George Lewis is a reader in American history and director of the Centre for American Studies at the University of Leicester. He is the author of *Massive Resistance: The White Response to the Civil Rights Movement* (2006) and *The White South and the Red Menace: Segregationists, Anticommunism, and Massive Resistance, 1945–1965* (2004).

J. Eric Pardue is a law student at the University of Virginia.

Frederick V. Slocum is associate professor in the Department of Political Science/Law Enforcement at Minnesota State University, Mankato. He has published numerous articles.

John W. White is an archivist of special collections at the College of Charleston Library. He has contributed essays to a number of collections.

Daniel K. Williams is assistant professor of history at the University of West Georgia. He is the author of *God's Own Party: The Making of the Christian Right* (2010).

Leah M. Wright is assistant professor of history and African American studies at Wesleyan University.

# Index

Abe, Kojire, 209

Abolition, 14

Abortion, 4, 9, 11, 17n6, 29, 30, 31, 32, 59–63, 186, 320, 321, 323, 324, 327, 332–33, 343n5, 345n6; as an election issue, 323, 332–33; civil disobedience and, 343n5; compared to civil rights, 354n45; death penalty for providers of, 9, 73n16; debated at state and local level, 357n60; judicial rulings on, 327

Abramoff, Jack, 315

Abu Ghraib, 315

Acts of the Apostles, 333

Aderholt, Robert, 73n11

Affirmative Action, 255–58, 277n67, 332, 335; Philadelphia Plan and, 255, 263, 280n79, 280n82

Afghanistan War, 324; deaths of civilian women and children, 346n8

Africa, 44

African Methodist-Episcopal Zion Church, 248, 274n38

*Against the Grain*, 50

Agnew, Spiro, 42; disliked by blacks, 241–42, 269n9

*The Agony of the GOP, 1964*, 355n47

AIDS, 356n55

Air America, 322, 348n19

Alabama, 1, 2, 5, 9, 21, 22, 44, 45, 64, 74n20, 106, 114, 223–24, 292, 322, 328, 331, 337, 353n40, 357n60; as a GOP stronghold, 1, 71, 355n49; as contested terrain, 16n1; Birmingham, 2, 100, 111, 113, 328, 351n28, 353n41; Black Belt of, 2; Christian Coalition and, 32; Constitution of 1901 and, 333; DeKalb County, 56; Etowah County, 57–58; evolution and, 75n37; gay and lesbian rights and, 58–59; Goldwater and, 234–35; Mobile, 105, 328; Montgomery,

330; Pike County, 56, 65, 72n7; prayer in schools and, 56, 57, 65–66, 72n7; Selma, 44, 100, 113, 330, 353n40; Southside of Birmingham, 2; strength of McCain-Palin ticket in, 32; tax reform and, 10; Ten Commandments and, 57–58, 73n11; unpledged electors in 1960 and, 153

Alabama Mills, 211

Alaska, 32

Alberti, Dino, 122

Almond, J. Lindsay, Jr., 98, 105

Alsop, Joseph, 228, 229

Alsop, Stewart, 228

American Civil Liberties Union, 58, 65, 109

American Enterprise Institute, 340

American exceptionalism, 316. *See also* "Americanism"; Militarism; Patriotism

American Independent Party, 175, 334

"Americanism," 4, 7, 13, 23, 104, 327, 328; dissent and, 4

American Legion, 104

American Revolution. *See* Declaration of Independence

Americans for Democratic Action, 297

*American Spectator*, 343n5

"American way of life," 40, 41, 204, 292

Anglo-Saxon (Western) civilization, 291–313

Annapolis, 294

Anti-civil rights thought, 39–41

Anti-Defamation League, 38

Antidemocratic impulses, 7–8, 12, 226, 291–313, 343n5, 348n20. *See also* Apportionment; Gerrymandering; Republic; Vote suppression

Anti-intellectualism. *See* Liberalism; Media; Reality; Science

Antilynching acts, 207

Antioch College, 105

Appalachia, 72, 82, 85, 95n9, 98

Applebome, Peter, 62
Apportionment. *See Baker v. Carr*; County-
unit system; Gerrymandering
Aquinas, St. Thomas, 341
Arizona, 81, 105
Arkansas, 6, 8, 10, 38–54, 74n20, 81, 105, 154,
172–97; Fayetteville, 174; gay marriage
and, 59; Hot Springs, 105; importance of
black vote in, 187, 196n68; Little Rock,
41–42, 174; Petit Jean Mountain, 176, 185,
188; Searcy, 38. *See also* Harding College;
Little Rock
Arkansas Delta, 174, 181, 192
Arkansas Industrial Development Commis-
sion, 177, 185, 192
Arkes, Hadley, 343n5
Armey, Dick, 71, 338, 357n60
Arnall, Ellis G., 87
Atheism, 24, 40, 65, 91, 124, 179; God-
lessness and, 13, 124, 326. *See also*
Communism
*Atlanta Constitution*, 91, 208
Atwater, Lee, 11, 322, 331, 332, 340–41
Austrian School. *See* Economic
fundamentalism
Avondale Mills, 201–6

Bailey, Fred Arthur, 4, 9, 14
*Baker v. Carr*, 110, 120n53
Bales, James, 13, 39–40, 45–46; book attack-
ing Martin Luther King and, 45–46
Baptists, 23; moderates and, 62; race and,
145–46. *See also* Southern Baptist Con-
vention; Southern Baptists
Barkley, Alben, 209
Barnes, Fred, 331
Barnett, Ross, 100, 101, 105
Barr, Bob, 71
Barr, John U., 208. *See also* Dixiecrats
Barrow, John, 74n20
Barth, Jay, 181
Bartley, Numan V., 116n8, 117n12
Bass, Jack, 174
"Battle Hymn of the Republic," 295–96
Baylor University, 307
Bean, Jonathan, 281n88
Beatitudes, 333
Beck, Glenn, 317
Bell, Joann, 56, 65

Bell, L. Nelson, 25
Bennett, William, 298
Benson, George, 6, 8; Harding College and,
38–54; pro-segregation sermons and, 42,
43; support for anti-Martin Luther King
book and, 46
Bentley, James L. "Jimmy," 88, 91–92
Berlin, Isaiah, 355n49
Bible. *See* Religion
bin-Laden, Osama, 346n10
Birmingham. *See* Alabama
Birth control. *See* Sex
*Birth of a Nation*, 305
*Bison*, 40, 42–46, 48
Black, Earl, 55, 70, 98, 186; "conservative
advantage" and, 70
Black, Merle, 55, 70, 98; "conservative
advantage" and, 70
"Black and Tans," 230–32, 234; versus "Lily
Whites" in Mississippi, 230–34
Black Americans for Nixon-Agnew, 248
Black Belt, 2, 85, 87, 88, 139–41, 143–45,
147–48, 152, 156
Blackburn, Ben, 88
Black Republicans, 137n94, 240–90; in
Atlanta and, 79, 82, 83, 86
Black vote. *See* Apportionment; Bloc voting;
Democratic Party; Race; Selma-to-Mont-
gomery march; Vote suppression; Voting
Rights Act
Blackwell, Ken (referred to), 323
Blair, Diane D., 181
Bloc voting, 125, 132, 137n93, 162. *See also*
Apportionment; Civil rights; Race
Bloom, George I., 107
Blumenthal, Sidney, 338, 357n60
Bob Jones University, 23, 24
Boineau, Charles E., Jr., 155–56, 160, 166
Boles, John B., 116n1
Bonaparth, Ellen, 252–53, 258, 276n57
Bond, Julian, 92–93
Boozman, John, 189
Bork, Judge Robert, 31
Bourbons, 322, 331, 354n43. *See also* Neo-
Bourbonism; Redeemers
Bowen, Michael, 10, 14, 16
Boxer, Barbara, 342n2
Boyd, Tim, 16, 17n3
Bradford, Melvin E., 4–5, 7, 8, 9, 12, 14,

291–313; approach to history and, 301–2; attack on Lincoln and, 293, 295–98, 301–2, 304–5, 308n8; blame of those seeking equality as envious, 297–98; concern for the commonweal, 303; defense of aristocracy and, 303; defense of patriarchy, 303; defense of slavery and, 297, 299–302; defense of slavery on religious grounds, 300; justification of Civil War on religious grounds and, 300; ties to Reagan and, 296–99, 310n20; ties to Wallace and, 291, 296, 297

Bradley, Graham, and Hamby. *See* Hamby, Dorothy

Branscomb, Lewis, 325, 345n6

Breckenridge, Gen. John, 300

Briggs, W. C. "Colley," 225, 228–29

*Briggs v. Elliott*, 139, 145

Britain, 64, 342n3

British Broadcasting Corporation (BBC), 324

Brooke, Edward, 241, 243, 247–49, 251–52, 254, 263, 269n8, 271nn18–19, 275n51, 282n91

Brooks, David, 333

Brooks, Overton, 122, 133

Browder, Glen, 357n60

Brown, Edwin L., 351n28

Brown, James, 248, 273n36

Brown, Jim, 262, 284n104

Brown, Judge Janice Rogers, 13, 50

Brown, Robert J. "Bob," 244–45, 249, 251, 261–62, 265, 267–68, 273n78, 280n82, 281n89, 282n91, 283nn94–95, 285n109, 287n199, 289n135; black education and, 259–60

Brown & Williamson, 324, 345n6

Brownell, Herbert, 220–32, 234, 235; ideological adversaries reap rewards of his work and, 234–35

*Brown II*, 174

*Brown v. Baskin*, 139, 140

*Brown v. Board of Education*, 84, 85, 99–103, 114, 141, 145–49, 173–74, 185, 212, 293, 335

Bryan, William Jennings, 73n8

Bryant, Anita, 6, 28

Buckley, William F., 4, 12, 38, 343n5, 353n38

*Buckley v. Valeo*, 334

Bumpers, Dale, 188, 189

Bunning, Jim, 71

Burke, Edmund, 323

Burns, Leon, 42

Busbee, George, 92–93

Bush, Alvin C., 98, 106–8

Bush, George H. W., 190, 296, 310n20

Bush, George W., 9, 70–71, 314, 315–16, 318, 336, 356n51; approval rating and, 356n56; attitude toward liberalism, 346n8; attitude toward the poor, 346n8; Catholics and, 323–24, 357n57; election of 2000 and, 55; election of 2004 and, 55, 63, 71, 321, 322, 323–24; election of 2006 and, 357n60; foreign policy of, 9; free trade and, 323; hostility to, 9–10, 315, 337, 356n56; impeachment spoken of, 315, 316; Israel and, 67; on evolution, 351n30; pseudo-populism and, 354n44; rating by historians and, 342n3; reality and, 343n5; religion and, 336; Terri Schiavo controversy and, 69; as a southern president, 11; terror of 9/11 and, 67; view of the New Deal, 346n8; war in Iraq and, 69

Bush, Laura, 342n3

*Bush v. Gore* (referred to), 319

*Bushworld*, 350n26

Business, 328; as heroic and omniscient, 13, 40, 41, 328–29, 330–31; culture of, 318; government aid to, 3–4. *See also* Labor; Propaganda; Ruthlessness

Busing, 91, 161, 163–65, 266, 332

"Buy American," 215–16

Byrd, Harry Flood, Sr., 98–100, 102, 110, 113, 114, 147; "golden silence" of, 99; trade and, 204, 206, 209, 214

Byrd, Robert, 257, 279n77

Byrnes, James F. "Jimmy," 140, 141, 143, 144, 145, 147, 152, 158, 182; support for Republicans in 1952 and, 141, 143; support for Goldwater and, 182; support for Nixon and, 152; support for Albert Watson as a Republican candidate and, 158

*Caddo Republican*, 127, 133

Cahill, Mary Beth, 322

Cahill, William, 289n136

Calhoun, John C., 103, 205, 306

Calhoun, John H., 86

California, 5, 29, 42, 59, 356n53

California State University, 260

Callaway, Howard "Bo," 86–88, 91, 187

Calvinism, 326

Cambodia, 27

Campaign finance, 334, 335–36, 355n48

Cancer, 324, 345n6

Cao, Joseph, 74n20

Capitalism. *See* "Americanism"; Business; CEO pay; Corporate welfare; Economic fundamentalism; Entrepreneurship; Free trade; Imperialism; Industry; Labor; Oil; Patriotism; Tariffs; Taxes; Textiles; Tobacco; Wall Street

Capitalist mythology, 325

Capital punishment. *See* Death penalty

"Card-check," 318

Carlton, David L., 203

Carswell, G. Harrold, 288n132

Carter, Dan T., 221, 288n132, 348n20, 349n23; racism in the suburbs and, 121n76

Carter, Jimmy, 28–29, 30–31, 188, 190, 268; Georgia and, 92, 94n2; leaves SBC, 62; referred to, 1; relationship with Religious Right, 28–29, 30–31, 62, 63; submission of wives and, 62

Castro, Fidel, 131

Catholics, 55; alliance with evangelicals and, 22, 29; conservatism of, 29, 38, 42, 323–24, 330, 332, 335, 343n5, 353n41, 354n45; fear of, 6, 24–25, 27, 31; exposure to antilabor thought, 330; extremism and, 343n5; gay rights and, 58–59, 73n12; leadership of, 327; liberalism of, 336; presidential candidate, 224, 331; southern, 324, 330, 353n41; upper-class, 323–24, 330; vote of, 322, 323–24, 337, 357n60; war and, 336, 357n57. *See also* Abortion; "Culture of life"; Death penalty; Economic fundamentalism; Poverty; War

Cattle, 224–25

Central government. *See* Federal government

Central High School. *See* Little Rock (confrontation)

CEO Pay, 318, 325

Chamberlain, Wilt, 284n104

Chamber of Commerce, 214, 215, 335. *See*

*also* National Association of Manufacturers; Propaganda; Southern States Industrial Council

Chambliss, Saxby, 68, 346n10

Chandler, Chan, 63, 72

*Chandler v. James,* 56

Chappell, David L., 17n6, 352n32

Character. *See* Moral chauvinism; Morality

Charleston Naval Base and Shipyard, 139–40

Chase National Bank, 175

Cheek, Dr. James, 282nn92–93

Chemicals, 205–6

Cheney, Dick, 315; election of 2004 and, 63, 321; election of 2006 and, 337; ties to right-wing historians, 342n3

Chicago, 9, 44

*Chicago Defender,* 289n136

Chicago School. *See* Economic fundamentalism

China, 39, 124, 132

Christ, Jesus, 21, 22, 333; second coming of, 9, 67

Christian Coalition, 31–32, 56, 62, 331, 350n26, 356n51

Christian College Coalition, 49

*Christianity Today,* 26

Christian Reconstructionism, 9

Churches of Christ, 38, 39, 42. *See also* Harding College

Citizens' Councils. *See* White Citizens' Councils

Civil rights, 3, 5, 7, 8, 14, 21, 25–26, 40, 41, 186–88, 203, 207, 212, 215, 326, 327, 328, 330, 331, 332, 333, 336, 338, 339, 340, 341, 346n8, 353n40; abortion compared to, 354n45; black capitalism and, 240–90; judicial rulings on, 327; rejected as wrong-headed, 291–313; religion and, 21, 25–26, 352n32; Republican Party and, 7, 13, 79–97, 333, 346n8, 356n51; socialism and, 40, 41; "suburban strategy" and, 79–97; tax exemptions and, 28–29; token desegregation of religious schools, 28–29. *See also* Civil Rights Act; Race; Token desegregation; Voting Rights Act; "White backlash" thesis

Civil Rights Act (of 1866), 103

Civil Rights Act (of 1964), 17n6, 26, 113,

121n68, 176–77, 293, 332; only one Deep South congressman votes for, 86; Southern Baptist Convention endorses before takeover, 26

Civil War, 41, 65–66, 70, 140, 206, 222, 292–93, 295; attack on Lincoln's character and, 293, 295–96; conflict justified religiously, 300, 311n36; cultural import for conservatism and, 299–302, 304–5; tied to the New Deal, 295; tied to Reconstruction, 295; referred to, 341. *See also* Confederacy; Neo-Confederacy

Clark, Sheriff Jim, 100, 104, 115

Clark College, 260

Class, 13, 14, 23, 149, 292, 302–4, 309n13, 318, 320–22, 323–24, 334, 340; black middle class, 240–90; class hatred, 23; rejected as an adequate explanation, 303, 309n13; Republicans and the middle class, 22, 29, 84, 140, 142, 149, 151–53, 161, 164–65, 223; suburban middle class, 173; working class, 147, 154, 156, 161, 184, 221, 337. *See also* Class consciousness; Labor; Middle class; "New racism"; "Politics of emotion"; Pseudo-populism; "Suburban school"

Class consciousness, 3–4, 23, 318, 320–22, 325–26, 331–32, 333, 336, 337–41, 350n27, 355n49, 356n51, 357n60; of Catholic voters, 323–24. *See also* Class; "New racism"; "Politics of emotion"; Pseudo-populism

Clear Channel, 322

Cleland, Max, 346n10; referred to, 319

Clemson College (and University), 155, 307

Climate change, 315, 317, 324, 340, 342n2, 343n5, 345n6

Clinton, Bill, 11, 94n2, 337, 356n56; Arkansas and, 188–90; free trade and, 323; investigation by Ken Starr, 45

Clinton, Hillary Rodham, 38, 190

Coal, 205–6

Cobb, James C., 340

Coble, Howard, 67

Coburn, Tom, 9, 71; death penalty for abortion providers and, 73n16; gay and lesbian rights and, 59

Coclanis, Peter, 203

Coded appeals (to race), 7, 76n50, 123, 320, 332, 339; on civil rights and, 263. *See also*

Atwater, Lee; Civil rights; Race (and racism); "Southern strategy"

Cohen, Dov, 64, 66

Cold War, 6, 7, 22, 23, 24, 31, 124, 143; trade and, 201, 203, 215, 216. *See also* McCarthyism

"Collateral damage," 324

Colmer, William, 354n45

Color-blind issues. *See* "Suburban school"

Comer, Donald, 201–3, 205, 208–15. *See also* Dixiecrats

Common good, 343n5

Communications. *See* Media

Communism, 4, 7, 9, 13, 38, 39, 40, 42, 64, 67, 81, 123–24, 202, 208, 210, 211, 328, 329, 343n5, 345, 346n8; anticommunism and, 22–23, 25, 38, 39, 40, 42, 45, 46; Democrats and, 104, 122–24, 126–27; religion and anticommunism, 22–25, 29, 38, 40, 42, 46. *See also* McCarthyism; Socialism; "Transitive law of politics"

*The Communist Blueprint for the American Negro*, 49

Concentrated power (American suspicion of), 329–30

Confederacy, 1, 6, 14, 40, 352n33; glorified, 41, 291–313; troops of compared to Puritans, 300, 311n32

Confederate flag, 6, 40

Conformity, 13, 336, 340, 341–42; business and, 13–14, 42–43, 47

*Congressional Record*, 113

Congress of Industrial Organizations, 205, 213

Congress of Racial Equality, 273n30. *See also* Farmer, James; Freedom Rides

Connor, "Bull," 100, 104, 115

Connors, Marty, 58–59, 73n12

Conservatism, 3, 5, 7, 8–9, 12, 14, 291–313, 320, 335, 338; character assassination and, 8–9; complexity of issues and, 348nn18–19; neo-Confederacy and, 291–313; religion and, 21–37, 55–76; varied meanings of, 343n5. *See also* Civil rights; Class consciousness; Continuity; Cultural continuity; Economic fundamentalism; Extremism; Media; Moral chauvinism; Morality; Nashville Agrarians; "New racism"; "Politics of emotion"; Race;

Conservatism—*continued*
Religion; Religious Right; Southern Baptist Convention; "Status quo society"
"Conservative Manifesto," 317
Constitutionalism, 13, 15, 39, 40, 98–121, 123, 124, 129, 131, 133, 143, 147, 155, 184, 204, 224, 295–96, 340. *See also* Freedom
Continuity (of southern history), 3, 13, 55, 319–21, 325, 338–42, 351n30; example of, 216; race and, 161; versus change, 55–56
Contraception, 324, 345n6
Conyers, John, 259
Cook, Rodney Mims, 86, 93
Cooksey, John, 67
Cooperative Baptist Fellowship, 62
Coral Ridge Ministries, 58, 63
Corker, Bob, 338
Corporal punishment, 64
Corporate welfare, 3–4, 335
Cosman, Bernard, 234
Coulter, Ann, 13, 50, 317
Coulter, E. Merton, 300, 311n32
County-unit system, 83–86, 95n15
Craig, Larry, 315
Creager, Col. Rentfro B., 225, 226, 228
Crespino, Joseph, 221, 338
Crime. *See* "Law and order"; Riots
Criswell, W. A., 6, 25
Cromwell, Oliver, 300, 311n32
Cuba, 67, 124, 131, 132
Cullen, H. R., 225
"Cultivated ignorance," 341
Cultural continuity, 3, 13, 319, 325, 338–42, 351n30
"Cultural defense," 11, 63–68, 69–72
Cultural IQ, 340–41
Cultural populism. *See* Fusionism; "Great melding"; Pseudo-populism
"Culture of honor," 64, 67, 69–72
"Culture of life," 323
"Culture wars," 14, 30, 31, 32, 327
Cunningham, Duke, 315

Dabney, Robert L., 9, 299
*Danger on the Right*, 38
Dartmouth College, 299
Daschle, Tom, 11
Davidson, Donald, 12, 292, 294, 299, 309n15; criticism of C. Vann Woodward

and, 309n13; defense of white supremacy and, 309n13
Davis, James C., 79, 83–84, 86
Davis, Jefferson, 306
Davis-Bacon Act, 318
Dean, Howard, 322
Death penalty, 9, 58–59, 67, 188
Declaration of Independence (as misunderstood), 295–96, 303–5
Deep South, 2, 86, 99, 319
Deering, Fr. Michael J., 353n41
Defense industries, 139–40, 147
DeLay, Tom, 8, 69, 70, 71, 315; terrorism and hostility to unions and, 331
Demagoguery, 316–17, 341
Deming, Jim, 59
DeMint, Jim, 71
Democratic Leadership Council, 323, 337
Democratic Party: abandonment of working-class and, 349n22; conservative Democrats, 41, 319, 328, 337–38; dissatisfaction with by southern industrialists, 201–19; importance of black vote and, 157, 159, 161–63, 187, 196n68, 270n10; liberalism of national party, 319–20, 321; "New South Democrats," 85, 86, 92; religious voters and, 31; timidity and ineptitude of, 11, 316, 321; as un-American, 40. *See also* Democratic Leadership Council; Dixiecrats; Fair Deal; New Deal; Reconstruction; "Reconstruction Syndrome"
Dent, Harry S., 160–64, 245, 268, 273n27, 278n72, 322, 331. *See also* "Southern strategy"
Devine, Donald, 343n5
DeVries, Walter, 174
Dewey, Thomas A., 10, 82–83, 95n11, 220–39
Dickerson, Dennis, 264
Dickinson, William L., 353n40
Diebold, 322
Dirksen, Everett, 333
Discrimination. *See* Race
Disfranchisement, 322; roots of fusionism and, 353n38
Distinctiveness (of the South), 2, 3, 5, 16, 320–21, 323–24, 325, 326, 338–42; argument against and, 207; based on conservatism, hierarchy, and religious-based justification for slavery and, 301. *See also*

"Southern strategy"; "Suburban school"; "White backlash" thesis

Diversity, 323

"Dixie" (the song), 48, 92

Dixiecrat revolt, 317, 328

Dixiecrats, 3, 8, 25, 70–71, 110, 139–41, 145–47, 151–52, 174, 202, 221, 227, 317, 319, 322, 328, 333, 334, 354n45, 355n47; alleged failure of, 330; leaving for GOP, 317, 334. *See also* States' Rights Party

Dixon, Rev. Thomas, 305

Dobbs, John Wesley, 86

Dobson, James, 317, 332, 336. *See also* Focus on the Family

*Doe, et al. v. Rhea County Board of Education*, 56–57

*Doe v. Santa Fe Independent School District*, 57

Dolan, Terry, 335, 356n55

Dominionism, 9

Dorsey, Jack, 86

Dowd, Maureen, 350n26

Drugs, 45

Dual Sovereignty Committee, 109–14

DuBois, W.E.B., 10; "Talented Tenth," 10

Duffey, Joseph D., 297, 298

DuPont Chemical, 39

Eagle Forum, 350n26

Earth Day, 91

East, Bob, 5, 296–97

Eastland, James O., 103, 118n21, 209, 214

East Pasco Cooperative Association, 253–54

East Waynesville Baptist Church, 63

*Ebony*, 249, 261, 263, 264, 268

Economic fundamentalism, 8, 10–11, 13, 15, 318, 323, 326, 332–36, 343n5, 355n47, 355n49, 356n50; antipathy to New Deal, 328–29; evangelicalism and, 356n50; South Carolina and, 168n39. *See also* Friedman, Milton; Hayek, F. A.; New Deal; Rand, Ayn; Rothbard,Murray; Taxes; Thatcher, Margaret

Economic populism, 7, 23, 32, 156, 161

Economics, 4, 16, 201–19, 322, 324, 326, 341; black capitalism and, 240–90. *See also* Capitalism; Communism; Economic fundamentalism; Economic populism; Fair Deal; Industry; "Great melding";

Great Recession; New Deal; Privatization; "Prosperity Gospel"; Socialism; Tariffs; Taxes

Edsall, Mary Byrne, 221

Edsall, Thomas, 221

Education, 38–54, 99–102, 107, 116n7, 124, 307, 329, 332, 335; blacks and, 259–61, 263, 281n89, 282nn90–93, 283nn94–95, 283n98. *See also* Home-schooling; Prayer in schools

Edwards, James B., 164–66; coded racism and, 164; opposition to collective bargaining for public employees, 165

Edwards, John, 359n65

Egalitarianism, 8, 14, 291–313, 324, 341; desire for a function of envy, 297–98. *See also* Antidemocratic impulses; Civil rights; Inequality; Superiority; "Superiority gene"

Ehrlichman, John D., 286n113

Eisenhower, Dwight D., 10, 23–24, 99, 107, 130, 139, 141–48, 151, 153, 157–58, 220–39; Little Rock and, 173, 177–78, 182; smeared as a communist agent, 329; suburbs and, 83, 84, 85, 88, 95n14; trade issues and, 202–3, 207–12, 215

Eisenhower, Edgar, 38

Eisenhower (family), 10

Eisenhower, Milton, 10; smeared as a communist agent, 329

Eleventh Circuit Court of Appeals, 58

Elkins, Caroline, 342n3

Elliott, Chris, 6, 40–41

Ellison, Keith, 68, 352n33

Emory University, 31, 307, 356n51

Emotion (in politics), 44, 319, 321, 330–36, 338, 339, 341–42, 357n60. *See also* "Politics of emotion"

Employment discrimination, 41, 124, 328, 330, 332. *See also* Fair Employment Practices Committee; Kennedy, John F.; Truman, Harry

*The End of Southern Exceptionalism*, 16

*Engel v. Vitale*, 6, 17n6, 26–27, 332, 355n46. *See also* Prayer in schools; "Separation of church and state"

Engerman, Stanley, 301–2

England, 64, 303; English Enlightenment and, 299

Enlightenment. *See* Science

Entrepreneurship, 10; black capitalism and, 240–90

Environment, 91, 318, 324, 333, 335, 336, 343n5, 345n6. *See also* Climate change

Episcopalians, 32, 110–11

Equality. *See* Egalitarianism; Inequality

Equal Rights Amendment, 27–28, 165

ES & S, 322

Eskew, Tucker, 11

Establishment Clause, 58, 75n36. *See also* "Separation of church and state"

*Eternity*, 27

Ethnicity, 5, 13, 292, 334, 341; immigration and, 327, 328

Evangelicals, 21–37, 322, 333, 338, 356n50, 356n56, 357nn59–60; education and, 38–54; militarism and, 69–72; movement away from Democratic Party, 21–54; ties to Republican Party, 21–37. *See also* Protestants; Religion

Evangelicals & Catholics Together, 354n45

Evolution, 55, 75n37, 324, 326, 340, 345n6, 351n30

Exeptionalism (of the South). *See* Distinctiveness

Exodus, 333

Extremism (of modern Republican Party), 4, 9, 10, 11, 12–13, 15, 291–313, 317, 321, 322, 326, 341, 343n5, 351nn30–31, 355n47, 359nn65–66. *See also* "Status quo society"

Fair Deal, 13, 211–12

Fair Employment Practices Committee, 41, 202, 204, 207, 224, 225, 229, 236n10

Fairness Doctrine, 334

"Faith-based initiative," 356n51

False consciousness. *See* Class consciousness

Falwell, Jerry, 6, 63, 317, 327, 330, 332; birth of the Religious Right and, 22, 26, 29, 30, 31, 334; denounced as an "agent of intolerance," 32; hostility to the federal government, 29, 30; legacy of, 346n7; on Muslims, 67. *See also* Liberty Baptist University; Moral Majority

Family, 27–28, 29; "Family values" and, 28. *See also* Religious Right; Sex, feminism

Family Research Council, 350n26

Farm Bureau, 124

Farmer, Andrew S., 14–15

Farmer, James, 140, 246–47, 260, 267, 273n30, 283n96

Fascism, 9, 39. *See also* Pseudo-fascism

"Fast-food politics," 340

Faubus, Orval, 13, 25, 42, 101, 105, 173, 177–83, 186, 187

Fear, 44, 45, 101–2, 336, 338, 341, 343n4, 346n9. *See also* McCarthyism; Terrorism

Federal government: black employment in, 283n98; hostility to, 3, 13, 28–30, 44, 45, 106–14, 123–24, 291–313, 319, 326, 329–30, 335, 338, 339, 340, 353n37, 355n49. *See also* "Reconstruction Syndrome"

Feminism. *See* Sex

"Fermat's Last Theorem of Southern History," 339

Fifth Circuit Court of Appeals, 232

Fifties, 82–85; race and, 223–25, 231–32, 234, 235

Finch, Robert N., 245

"First Southern strategy," 220–39

*First Things*, 343n5, 351n31

Fisher, William, 352n33

Fleming, Thomas, 14, 306

Fletcher, Arthur, 241–43, 249–50, 253–57, 263, 266–68, 276n59, 277n64, 282n91, 283nn94–95, 285n109, 287n119, 289n135; Philadelphia Plan and, 255–61, 278n72, 279n73, 279n75, 280n81, 283n99

Florida, 2, 15, 28, 71, 72, 74n20, 105, 172, 193n1, 211, 223, 227, 230, 231, 322; Atlantic Coast of, 2; Barack Obama and, 72; Brian Darling and, 76n45; carried by Eisenhower in 1952 and, 231; conservative propaganda groups and, 105; constitutionalism and, 105; Coral Ridge Ministries and, 58, 63; delegates contested at 1952 convention, 230; election controversy and, 71; election of Claude Kirk and, 172; election of 2000 and, 71, 322, 323; election of 2010 and, 74n20; gay and lesbian rights and, 59; I-4 Corridor and, 2; Mel Martinez and, 76n45; Miami, 18n11; nomination of G. Harrold Carswell to the Supreme Court and, 288n132; Orlando, 2; Panhandle of, 2; praised, 227; Republican

Party and, 211, 227; segregation and, 105; Tampa, 2, 3, 231; Tampa Bay, 231; Ten Commandments and, 58; Terri Schiavo controversy and, 69, 76n45; William Cramer elected to Congress and, 231

Florida (delegates contested), 230

Florida Citizens for Eisenhower-Nixon, 230

Floyd, Bill, 42–43

Focus Groups. *See* Marketing

Focus on the Family, 56, 63, 336, 355n48

Fogel, Robert, 301–2

Foley, Mark, 315, 337, 356n56

"Folk Theology," 326–28, 336, 352n32; anti-unionism and, 330–31; race and, 145–46

Fones-Wolf, Elizabeth A., 352n36

Food Stamps, 335

Ford, Gerald, 268

Ford, Harold, 337–38

Fordice, Kirk, 71, 73n9

Foreign Policy, 124, 229. *See also* Cold War; Communism; China; Cuba; USSR; War

Forum Club, 102, 106

Fourteenth Amendment, 103

Fowler, Donald, 148

Fox News, 190, 321

Frank, Thomas, 357n60

Franken, Al, 348n18

Frederick, Carolyn E., 160, 166

Frederickson, Kari, 202

Freedom, 3–4, 41, 42, 44, 59, 123–24, 173; cooptation of term by the Right, 13, 15, 355n49; economic power and, 242, 239, 254, 256, 277n67; rightist religion and, 24–25, 38. *See also* Constitutionalism

"Freedom Forums," 12–13, 40, 41, 50

Freedom National Bank of Harlem, 276n58

"Freedom of choice," 15, 91, 100, 160–62. *See also* Civil rights; Race

Freedom Rides, 101, 124, 132, 154, 246, 273n30

Free Trade, 8, 201–19, 318, 323, 333, 334

French (language), 76n50

French Revolution, 50; disparaged for misguided notions about equality and civil rights and, 296, 299–300, 302, 304

Friedman, Milton, 4, 12, 332, 343n5; antipathy to democracy, 8, 343n5. *See also* Economic fundamentalism

Frist, Bill, 69

Fulbright, William, 189, 191

Fulton Republican Planning Commission, 81

Fundamentalism (and fundamentalists), 4, 9, 10–11, 13, 14, 23–37, 55–76, 316, 326–27, 334–36, 346n9

Fusionism, 330–33, 343n5, 353n38, 354n44, 355n49, 357n60; employment discrimination and, 41; religion and tax exemptions, 29, 31. *See also* "Great melding"

Gabrielson, Guy, 227

Gallup Poll, 29, 351n30

Ganus, Clifton L., 47, 48–49

Garment, Len, 245–46, 267, 273n28, 286n113

Gaty, John, 38

Gay and Lesbian rights, 4, 11, 28, 29, 31, 55, 58–60, 62, 73n8, 320, 321, 327, 336, 355n48, 356n55; as an election issue, 323; civil disobedience and, 343n5; death penalty for homosexuals, 9, 58–59; debated at state and local level, 357n60; fund-raising and, 355n48; gay marriage, 76n50, 321, 332–33, 350n27; homophobia and, 319, 336, 338, 356n55; sodomy laws and, 59

Gender, 13, 27, 149, 340. *See also* Sex

General Agreement on Trade and Tariffs, 207–8, 214, 216

George, Robert P., 6, 332, 343n5

George, Walter, 209

Georgia, 1, 2, 28, 31, 67, 71, 74n20, 79–97, 317, 319, 337, 346n10; Atlanta and suburbs, 2, 58, 79, 83, 88, 91, 92, 93–94, 348n19; Augusta, 85; Christian Coalition and, 32; Cobb County, 62, 92, 97n57; Columbus, 85; DeKalb County, 83, 88, 92, 97n57; Douglasville, 56; evolution and, 75n37; Fulton County, 79, 81–82, 86, 92, 94; gay marriage and, 59; Goldwater and, 234–35; Gwinnett County, 97n57; Macon, 92, 317; prayer in schools, 56; Rockdale County, 83; Savannah, 85; Ten Commandments and, 58

Gerrymandering, 8, 15, 161, 292, 348n20

Gerson, Michael, 343n5

GI Bill, 39

Gilded Age, 318, 321

Gingrich, Newt, 22, 71, 93, 356n56
Giuliani, Rudy, 356n56
Global warming. *See* Climate change
"God and country" issues, 7, 340; religion and patriotism and, 332–36
"God gap." *See* Religion
Goldfield, David, 62, 69–70, 75n37; prayer in schools and, 65–66
Goldwater, Barry, 12, 18n11, 38, 112, 115, 121n64, 159–60, 215, 241–42, 249, 270n10, 319, 322, 333, 334, 341, 359n66; Georgia and, 81–82, 85–87, 93; not a precursor to GOP in Louisiana, 123, 133, 134; race issue and, 356n53; South Carolina and, 157–60; versus Johnson, 174–75, 180, 184, 195n34; Virginia and, 112, 115, 121n64
*Gone With the Wind*, 6, 40
Gonzalez, Alberto, 314
Goode, Virgil, 68, 352n33
Gore, Al, 323, 342n2
Gore, Albert Sr . 209
Gospels, 333
Gowan, Kay, 48
Graham, Billy, 7, 22, 24, 25, 26, 27, 67
Graham, Franklin, 67; on Islam, 67
Graham, Hugh Davis, 277n68
*Grapes of Wrath*, 346n8
Grassroots Republicanism, 138–71
Gray Commission, 100; Garland "Peck" Gray and, 100
Great Depression. *See* New Deal
"Great melding," 13, 328–31, 332, 333–36, 338, 343n5, 353nn37–38, 355n49, 357n60; examples of, 155–56, 203, 205. *See also* Fusionism
Great Recession, 316
Great Society, 87, 164–66, 244, 251, 275n51
Green, John, 62, 69
Griffith, Parker, 74n20
Groove Phi, 47–48, 49
Guantanamo, 315
Gulf Coast, 318, 323
Gulf of Mexico, 323
Gun control, 91, 320, 332, 337, 338

Hacker, Jacob, 70
Hackney, Sheldon, 339–40, 349n21; referred to, 323
Haggard, "Pastor Ted," 315, 332, 337, 356n56

Haldeman, H. R., 27
Ham (curse of), 6, 42
Hamby, Dorothy, 142–43, 145, 151–52, 155–57; and not using "southern strategy," 157, 163–64
Hammerschmidt, John Paul, 179, 183, 189
Hampton Institute, 176
Hanna, Marc, 318
Hannity, Sean, 13, 15, 50, 316
Hanson, Victor, 331, 354n43
Harding College, 6, 8, 12–13, 15, 38–54; "Freedom Forums" of, 12–13, 15
Harding University, 50
Hardin-Simmons College, 295, 309n15
Hardisty, Jean, 353n38
Hargis, Billy James, 6, 23, 25
Harris, Katherine (referred to), 323
Harrison, Albertis S., Jr., 98–99
Harris Poll, 268, 356n56
Hart, Jeffrey, 299
Harvard University, 298, 325, 342n3, 345n6, 346n8
Harvey, Paul (historian), 17n6, 352n32
Harvey, Paul (radio personality), 318, 346n8
Hatred, 332–36. *See also* Civil rights; "Great melding"; "New racism"; Race; Radio
Hayek, F. A., 4, 12, 332, 343n5; antipathy to democracy, 8, 343n5. *See also* Economic fundamentalism
Health insurance, 325. *See also* Medicare
Hedges, Chris, 325, 350n26, 355n49
Helm, W. Stuart, 98, 108–12, 119n44
Helms, Jesse, 5, 28, 71, 296–97
Henry, Patrick, 108, 306
*Herdahl v. Pontotoc County School District*, 56, 65, 75n34
Herding, 64
Heritage Foundation, 28, 67, 340
Hierarchy, 338, 353n41
Hill, Lister, 234
Hillsdale College, 297
Hispanics, 49, 72, 322; danger of immigration of, 292, 305, 307
Hitchens, Christopher, 346n7
Hitler, Adolf, 5, 8–9, 328
Hodges, Luther, 105
Hollings, Fritz, 59, 105, 157, 159
Hollywood, 323, 324
Holocaust (Nazi), 68, 342n3

Holton, Linwood, 289n136
Home-schooling, 307, 357n60
Homophobia. See Gay rights
Homosexuality. See Gay rights
Honor, 11, 64
Hoover, J. Edgar, 50n2
House Un-American Activities Committee, 23
Howard, Perry, 230, 233–34
Howard University, 277n67
Howe, Julia Ward, 295–96
Huckabee, Mike, 190–91
Hudson, Jimmy, 176
Humphrey, Hubert H., 161, 240, 269n1, 269n5, 273n36
Hunt, H. L., 225
Hussein, Saddam, 315, 346n10
Hutchinson, Asa, 189–90
Hutchinson, Tim, 189–90

Idaho, 114
Ignorance. See "Cultivated ignorance"; Media; Reality
Illinois, 24
I'll Take My Stand, 292, 294–95
Immigrants. See Ethnicity
Impeachment, 315, 316
Imperialism, 316, 342n3
Independents: Democrats, 319
Indiana University, 105
Indians. See Native Americans
Individualism. See "Personal responsibility"; Self-help; Social Darwinism
Industry, 8, 201–19. See also National Association of Manufacturers; Southern States Industrial Council; Tariffs
Inequality, 318, 321, 341–42; as a virtue, 291–313
Ingrebretsen (case), 66
Inheritance, 325
Inhofe, James, 342n2
Institutional racism, 256
Intelligence (cooked), 324
Internal Revenue Service, 29
International Women's Year Conference, 28
Internet. See Media; Technology
Interposition, 105, 109
Intolerance. See Hatred; Ku Klux Klan;

McCain, John; Moral chauvinism; Neo-Kluxism; Religious Right
Iran, 9, 67
Iraq War, 9, 62, 66–67, 315, 316, 317, 321, 324, 336; deaths and, 323, 324; issue in 2004 election, 322, 347n15; issue in 2006 election, 337
Irion, Val, 129, 131
Islam. See Muslims
Israel, 9, 67

Jackson, Gen. Thomas "Stonewall," 300
Jackson, Sam C., 263
Jackson Clarion-Ledger, 72
Jackson State University, 282n91
Jaffa, Harry, 293, 308n8
James, Fob, 66
Japan, 67, 201–2, 206–9, 213, 214, 328
Jefferson, Thomas, 108, 143, 303–4, 306, 327. See also "Separation of church and state"
Jenkins, Micah, 151, 153; White Citizens' Councils and GOP, 151, 153
Jet, 240, 241, 258
Jewell, Katherine Rye, 8, 10
Jews, 5, 9, 38, 55, 56, 65, 68, 75n34, 322, 356n51; conservatism and, 5; forcible conversion of, 9; New Deal Supreme Court and, 328. See also Israel
Jim Crow, 26, 82, 85, 125, 335. See also Race, segregation
John Birch Society, 10, 104, 111, 329, 331; seen as "a bunch of nuts" by Virginia conservatives, 104
Johnson, Albert W., 98
Johnson, James D. "Justice Jim," 177–78, 182–87, 191; Moral Majority and, 191; support for Reagan and, 191
Johnson, Lyndon B., 11, 87, 121n64, 150, 242, 244, 256, 271n15, 273n27, 279n75, 357n60; Great Society criticized and, 251, 254, 275n51; Philadelphia Plan and, 255, 277n67; versus Goldwater, 174–75, 180, 184, 195n34. See also Great Society
Johnston, Olin, 139–40, 152–54, 155–57, 210
Johnston, Richard, 16, 338, 349n23
Johnston, Sam M., 328
Jones, Bob, Jr., 6, 23. See also Bob Jones University

Jordan, Vernon, 265–66, 287n120. *See also*
    Urban League
Judicial review, 327–28, 350n27. *See also*
    Supreme Court
Just War theory, 336, 357n57

Kalk, Bruce H., 143, 148
Kansas, 38, 111, 357n60; Wichita, 38
Kasper, John, 195n34
Katrina (Hurricane), 7, 318
Kefauver, Estes, 209
Kendrick, Judge I. B., 149
Kennedy, Earl, 272n21
Kennedy, John F., 6, 11, 24–26, 86, 94n2,
    107–8, 109, 122–37, 150–53, 214, 234,
    273n27, 357n60; and 1960 election,
    150–53; black vote and, 270n10; civil
    rights and, 332; employment discrimi-
    nation and, 332; Protestant hostility to
    candidacy of, 24–26
Kennedy, Kathleen, 107
Kennedy, Rev. D. James, 58
Kennedy, Robert F., 127, 244
Kennedyphobia, 122–37; in South Caro-
    lina, 155
Kentucky, 5; gay marriage and, 59; Ten
    Commandments and, 57
Kerry, John, 63, 71, 72, 76n50, 322, 323–24,
    337
Key, Barclay, 6, 8, 9, 13
Key, V. O., 55, 174, 221–22
Keys, Brady, 262, 284n104
Kilpatrick, James Jackson, 98, 102, 104, 111
King, Coretta Scott, 150
King, Martin Luther, 26, 45–47, 86, 150,
    177, 244, 247, 269n9, 273n30, 275n55,
    305, 327, 332; book attacking him,
    45–46; reaction to death of, 46; recent
    uses of, 46
Kinstler, Guy A., 107–8
Kirk, John A., 10
Kirk, Russell, 12, 294, 343n5
Koran, 352n33
Kristol, Irving, 5, 297–98
Krugman, Paul, 10, 338, 353n38, 357n60
Kruse, Kevin, 221
Ku Klux Klan, 55, 148–49, 187, 326. *See
    also* Neo-Kluxism

Labash, Matt, 343n5
Labor, 4, 216, 224, 278n70, 326, 328–29,
    334, 335, 338, 346n8; anti-union senti-
    ment and religion, 330–31, 338; decline
    of unions, 334; Democratic Party and,
    349n22; divisions between leadership
    and rank-and-file, 350n27; opposition to
    collective bargaining for public employ-
    ees, 165; portrayed as selfish and unpa-
    triotic, 329; portrayed as undesirables,
    45; protections and rights of, 318, 323,
    335; race and, 255–57, 277n68, 278n70;
    safety standards and, 335; strikes, 45, 70,
    330, 334; violence and, 256–57. *See also*
    Business; Class; Class consciousness;
    Free trade; National Labor Relations
    Act; National Labor Relations Board;
    "Operation Dixie"; Philadelphia Plan;
    Taft-HartleyAct
Lafferty, Ed, 108
Laghi, Cardinal Pio, 357n57
LaHaye, Tim, 28, 327, 331, 332, 334
Laissez faire. *See* Economic fundamentalism
Land, Richard, 332
Lassiter, Matthew D., 16, 80, 172–73, 221,
    338, 349n23
Latinos. *See* Hispanics
Lausche, Frank, 38
"Law and order," 7, 22, 26, 27, 101–2, 222,
    241, 244, 269nn8–9, 335; understood as
    not racial, 154. *See also* Riots
*Lawrence v. Texas*, 59
Lawton, Brayton, 213
League of the South, 307–8
*Left Behind* (series), 331
Lendman, Stephen, 355n49
Lenin, V. I., 91
*Let Freedom Ring*, 15
Leviticus, 333
Lewis, George, 10, 14, 15, 16
Libby, "Scooter," 314
Liberalism, 2, 14; communitarian values
    and, 342; complexity of issues and,
    348n18; debasement of term, 12; equation
    to communism, 23, 25, 31; equation to
    socialism, 23, 25, 31, 122–24, 129–31; hos-
    tility to, 122–37, 291–313, 319, 326, 343n5;
    judicial rulings seen as, 327; of New Deal,

8–9; popular polls and, 347n17; progressive values and, 342, 347n17; southern bastions of, 2. *See also* "Status quo society"; "Transitive law of politics"
Libertarianism. *See* Economic fundamentalism
Liberty Baptist University, 30
*Life*, 211
"Lily Whites." *See* "Black and Tans"
Limbaugh, Rush, 316, 340
Lincoln, Abraham, 5, 99; character and reputation attacked and, 293, 295–98, 301–2, 304–5, 308n8
Lincoln, Blanche, 189
Lind, Michael, 63–64, 66, 67, 353n38, 357n60
Lindsey, Brink, 353n38
Link, William A., 221
Linker, Damon, 351n31
Little Rock (confrontation), 41–42, 99, 101, 107, 131, 173, 177–78, 182
Lodge, Henry Cabot, 151, 153
Long, Alecia P., 18n7, 18n14
Lost Cause. *See* Romanticization of the Old South
Lott, Trent, 14, 18n15, 70–71, 76n50, 332; racial tolerance and, 354n45
Louisiana, 7, 8, 14, 15, 67, 74n20, 81, 105, 106, 122–37; Bossier Parrish, 123; Caddo Parrish, 127, 129, 130, 132; Christian Coalition and, 32; evolution and, 75n37; gay marriage and, 59; Goldwater and, 234–35; New Orleans, 7, 14, 74n20, 124, 233; Shreveport, 122, 125, 130, 132, 233. *See also* Katrina (Hurricane)
Louisiana State University, 125–26
Lublin, David, 8, 15
Lucy, Arthurine, 146, 148
Luke (Gospel of), 333
Lumber, 205–6
Lynching. *See* Antilynching acts
Lyons, Charlton, 122–37
Lytle, Andrew, 292

MacArthur, Gen. Douglas, 201, 209, 229
MacDonald, Forrest, 14, 307
Maddox, Lester, 87–88, 162, 187
Magnificat, 333

Majority rule (with Minority rights), 327–28
Malapportionment. *See* Apportionment
Malcolm X, 45
Manion, Clarence, 38, 42
March. *See* Selma-to-Montgomery march
Marketing, 332–33. *See also* Propaganda
Marriage, 31
Marshall, Thurgood, 154, 248
Martinez, Mel, 76n45
*The Martin Luther King Story*, 45–46
Martino, Archbishop Renato, 357n57
Marx, Karl, 4, 132
Mary, 333
Maryland, 2, 337
Massachusetts, 76n50
"Massive resistance," 15, 81, 84, 85, 92, 101, 108–9, 113–16, 116n8, 117n12, 121n76, 147–48, 154–55. *See also* Civil rights; Race
Matthews, J. B., 23
Mattingly, Mack, 93
Mays, David J., 100–106, 108, 110–16, 121n64
McCain, John, 21, 32, 79, 190, 356n56; denouncing Jerry Falwell and Pat Robertson as "agents of intolerance," 32
McCarthy, Joseph, 23; attacks on Democrats and, 23. *See also* McCarthyism
McCarthyism, 7, 23. *See also* "Americanism"; Communism; Fear
McCaskill, Claire, 337
McClanahan, Fred, 133
McClellan, John, 42
McConnell, Mitch, 71
McCord, Lucille, 56
*McCreary v. ACLU of Kentucky*, 57
McDowell, Hobart, 225, 228–29
McGill, Ralph, 208
McKinley, William, 318
McKissick, Floyd, 242, 259
McLean, Marrs, 225
McWhiney, Grady, 14, 307
Meaney, George, 278n70
Media, 8, 12–13, 16–17, 316–17, 321, 322, 324, 329, 334–35, 339–40, 341, 343n5, 348nn18–19; attacked as liberal, 359n66; cowardice of, 316; reality and, 324–25, 350n27. *See also* Propaganda
Medicare, 336, 346n8

Mehlman, Ken, 333, 356n51
Methodists, 323; race and, 146
Meyer, Frank S., 343n5, 353n38
Miami (national convention), 18n11
Michelet, Jules, 50
Middle class, 22–23, 173, 318, 320, 321,
    347n16, 349n22, 350n27, 354n44; blacks
    and, 240–90. *See also* Class; Class con-
    sciousness; "New racism"; "Politics of
    emotion"; "Suburban strategy"
Middle East, 9. *See also* Afghanistan War;
    Iran; Iraq War; Muslims
Midterm elections: 2006, 314, 319, 336–38,
    342n1, 348n20, 350n26, 357n60; 2010,
    74n20, 321
Migliore, Archbishop Celestino, 357n57
Militarism, 4, 9, 11, 39, 41, 66, 69–72, 319,
    325, 326, 332–33, 336, 338, 341–42,
    355n49; exceptions from tax fury for
    military and defense and, 165; ties to
    business and, 329; use of as issue, 346n10.
    *See also* "Americanism"; Honor; Patrio-
    tism; Xenophobia
Minimum wage, 154, 156, 188, 322, 325
Minnesota, 67, 352n33
Mises, Ludwig von, 343n5
Mississippi, 14, 21, 42, 71, 74n20, 105, 223,
    230–35, 337, 354n45; "Black and Tans"
    versus "Lily Whites" in, 230–34; gay and
    lesbian rights and, 59; gay marriage,
    59; Goldwater and, 234–35; integra-
    tion of the University of Mississippi, 42;
    Neshoba County, 76n50; Oxford, 42, 154;
    prayer in schools, 56, 57, 65; Ten Com-
    mandments and, 66; unpledged electors
    in 1963 and, 153
Mississippi River, 41
Mississippi State University, 72
Missouri, 2; Kansas City, 337; St. Louis, 337
Mitchell, John, 279n77
Mobil Oil, 336
*Modern Age*, 12, 294
Modernism. *See* Science
Mohammed, 67
Money in campaigns. *See* Campaign finance
*Monroe World*, 172, 173, 175
Monsanto Chemical, 206
Montgomery, Marion, 307

Mooney, Chris, 324, 345n6
Moore, Alice, 28
Moore, Judge Roy, 9, 57–58, 66, 73n11,
    75n36; gay and lesbian rights and, 58–59.
    *See also* Ten Commandments
Moral chauvinism, 316, 320, 332–36, 339,
    340
Morality (and moralism), 30, 31, 40, 45,
    55–76, 129, 179–80, 191, 320, 321, 325, 326,
    332–36, 340, 347n15, 348n18
Moral Majority, 30, 191, 330
Morehouse College, 282nn92–93
Moser, Bob, 336–37, 357n60
Mountain Republicanism, 221–22. *See also*
    Appalachia
Movement conservatism. *See* Fusionism;
    "Great melding"
Moye, Charlie, 83–85
Moyers, Bill, 350n26
Moynihan, Daniel Patrick, 289n137
Murdoch, Rupert, 321, 343n5
Muse, William T., 111
Muslims, 9–10, 352n33; Islamic extremism
    and, 67. *See also* Terrorism
Mussolini, Benito, 328
Myrick, Sue, 67

Nagin, Ray, 14
"NASCAR dads," 341
NASCAR wing, 354n44
Nashville Agrarians, 8, 12, 292, 294–95, 299,
    306, 309n15
*Nation*, 336
National Association for the Advance-
    ment of Colored People (NAACP), 263,
    270n12, 273n30, 286n110
National Association of Manufacturers, 13,
    123, 214; propaganda blitz of, 329, 352n36
National Conservative Political Action
    Committee, 335
National Education Association (NEA), 329
National Education Program, 38–39, 40
National Endowment for the Humanities
    (NEH), 5, 296–99, 310n22
National Industrial Information Commit-
    tee, 352n36
Nationalism. *See* Militarism; Patriotism
National Labor Relations Act, 203–4

National Labor Relations Board (NLRB), 334
National Religious Affairs Briefing, 30
*National Review*, 158, 343n5
National Urban League. *See* Urban League
Native Americans, 303, 309n13, 318
Natural laws. *See* Economic fundamentalism
Neo-Bourbonism, 333
Neo-Confederacy, 14, 291–313. *See also* Confederacy
Neoconservatism, 323
Neo-Kluxism, 326, 333, 347n13
Neoliberalism. *See* Economic fundamentalism
Neo-Nazism, 317
Neuhaus, Fr. Richard John, 6, 332, 343n5
New conservatism, 99, 115, 116
New Deal, 39, 40–41, 85, 86, 139, 142, 211–12, 337; anti-New Deal sentiment, 6, 7, 8–9, 13, 39–41, 317–18, 328–30, 343n5, 346n8; as an aberration, 318; critical nature of, 317–18; fundamental change in view of, 329–30; popularity of, 22; the South and, 22, 23, 317, 318, 329. *See also* Economic fundamentalism
New England, 9
New Frontier, 86, 127
"New Negroes," 320
"New racism," 320, 325, 332, 333–36, 339, 340, 347n13, 353n37. *See* Emotion; "Politics of emotion"
New Rules. *See* Seventies
New South, 319, 320, 330
New South Democrats, 188–89. *See also* Carter, Jimmy; West, John
*Newsweek*, 29
New Testament, 299, 333, 355n49
New York, 175, 176, 331
*New Yorker*, 38
*New York Times*, 41, 263, 264, 269n8, 296, 325, 331, 333; criticized for coverage and, 283n94; criticism of Nixon's "Black Cabinet" and, 267
Nicaragua, 67
Nickles, Don, 71
Nigeria, 356n56
Nisbett, Richard, 64, 66

Nixon, Richard, 7, 101–2, 115, 132, 138, 151, 152, 160–64, 175, 215, 222, 240–90, 332; black cabinet and, 242–90; black capitalism and, 240–90; black middle class and, 240–90; black vote and, 270n10; blacks in administration compared, 271n15, 273n27; looming impeachment of, 316; and 1960 election, 150–53; as a relative liberal today, 10, 359n65; religious voters and, 22, 24, 25, 26, 27; "Silent Majority" and, 222; "Southern strategy" and, 101–2, 115, 245, 250, 267, 288n132, 332; southern voters and, 47, 101–2, 115; "Suburban strategy," and, 85, 88; support from white evangelicals, 47. *See also* "Law and order"; Philadelphia Plan; "Silent Majority"; Southern strategy"; "Suburban strategy"
Nobel Prize, 10, 356n56
Nock, Albert Jay, 18n12
Nolte, Mike, 226
Noonjin, Lonnie, 223–24
Norquist, Grover, 318
North Carolina, 2, 5, 21, 24, 25, 63, 67, 72, 74n20, 359n65; Apex, 22; Chapel Hill, 2; Charlotte, 3, 70; Christian Coalition and, 32; evolution and, 75n37; Gastonia, 330; Piedmont, 330; textile strikes and, 330; Waynesville, 72
Northern Republicans, 7, 98, 106–14, 213, 214; move to Democratic Party, 32, 33
Notre Dame. *See* University of Notre Dame
Novak, Robert, 355n47
Nunn, Sam, 92

Obama, Barack, 6, 11, 21, 55, 71, 72, 190, 315, 322, 338, 342n1; midterm elections of 2010 and, 71, 321
O'Callaghan, James O., 79
Occupational Safety and Health Administration (OSHA), 330–31
O'Connor, Sandra Day, 296
O'Daniel, "Pappy," 8
Office of Minority Business Enterprise, 250–52, 257–58, 261, 280n84, 280n87
O'Hehir, Andrew, 343n5, 353n38
Ohio, 322; election of 2004 and, 322, 323

Oil, 122, 123, 224–25, 228, 229, 323, 324. *See also* Gulf of Mexico; Iraq War

Oklahoma, 2, 9, 23, 27; gay and lesbian rights and, 59; gay marriage, 59; Little Axe, 56; prayer in schools, 56, 65; Tulsa, 23

Old, Judge William "Wild Billy," 104–5

Old Guard (Republicans), 86, 140, 178, 189, 191, 222, 224, 226–30, 231, 233, 333

Old racism. *See* "New racism"

Old rules. *See* Seventies

Old South. *See* Romanticization of the Old South

Old Testament, 333

Ole Miss. *See* University of Mississippi

*Operation Breakthrough*, 79–80, 81, 86

"Operation Dixie," 205, 213

O'Reilly, Bill, 316

Organized labor. *See* Labor

Orwell, George (and Orwellian). *See* Reality

Outer South, 2, 99

Outsourcing. *See* Privatization

Ownby, Ted, 75n31

Owsley, Frank W., 292

Pacifism, 39, 41, 320

Palin, Sarah, 21, 32, 326

Pardue, J. Eric, 8, 15

Patriotism (hyper), 4, 13, 39, 40, 316, 319, 320, 325, 326, 332–33, 336, 338, 339, 340, 341–42, 351n30; business and, 329; use of as issue, 346n10. *See also* "Americanism"; Honor; Militarism; Xenophobia

Patterson, John M., 105

Paul, Rand, 5

Pelosi, Nancy (referred to), 314

Pennsylvania, 98; Republican connections to southern Democrats, 98, 106–14

People for the American Way, 58, 65

Perception (over reality), 340, 341

Perlstein, Rick, 338, 343n5, 352n36, 357n60

Perot, Ross, 216

"Personal responsibility," 318, 326, 335, 353n37. *See also* Social Darwinism

Philadelphia, 107, 110, 111, 348n19

Philadelphia Plan, 255–61, 263, 277n67, 278nn71–72, 279n73, 279n75, 275nn77–78, 280n79, 280nn81–82, 283n99

Phillips, Howard, 334

Phillips, Kevin, 9–10; coined term "Southern strategy," 193n3

Phillips-Fein, Kim, 203

Pierce, Samuel R., Jr., 276n58

Pierson, Paul, 70

Pine Belt, 2

Pittsburgh, 110

"Pocketbook issues," 320

Poles, 328

"Politics of emotion," 3–4, 17n3, 320, 339, 340, 347n13, 357n60. *See also* Emotion (in politics); "New racism"

Poll tax, 136, 181

Pope. *See* Catholics

Pope Benedict XVI, 357n57. *See also* Ratzinger, Cardinal Josef

Pope John Paul II, 357n57

Populism, 329–30, 337, 341; southern economic, 7

Populist alliance (in reverse), 329–30

Pornography, 31, 63

Porter, H. Jack, 225, 228–29; race and the GOP and, 235, 238n29

Post Office Republicans, 221–223, 231

*Pottsville Republican*, 110

Poverty, 10, 288n127, 326, 336, 346n8, 350n27. *See also* Taxes; Welfare

Powell, Adam Clayton, 45

Prayer in schools, 4, 6, 55–57, 62, 320, 321, 327, 332–33, 340, 355n46; "cultural defense" and, 65

Prentice, George R., 111

Presbyterians, 25, 32. *See also* Southern Presbyterianism

Presidential elections: of 1928, 22, 331; of 1948, 355n47; of 1948 as overrated, 139; of 1952, 23–24, 40; of 1964, 319, 322, 333–34, 356n53; of 1964 as overrated, 139; of 1968, 26, 319, 322, 334; of 1968 as overrated, 139; of 1976, 1, 28–31; of 1988, 31; of 1996, 322; of 2000, 319, 322, 348n20; of 2000, 319, 321, 322, 337, 346n10, 347n15, 357n59; of 2008, 21, 32, 314, 319, 322, 336–37, 338

Princeton University, 298

Privatization, 333, 334, 342

Professional air traffic controllers, 334

Progressivism. *See* Liberalism

Prohibition, 22

Propaganda, 15, 100–121, 322, 340, 343n5;
Nixon and outreach to black middle
class and, 285n109; pro-business, 12–13,
328–29, 330, 340, 352n36; religious col-
leges and, 38–54
Property rights, 80, 343n5
"Prosperity Gospel," 326, 351n29, 355n49
Protestants, 6, 7, 11, 21–37, 322, 337
Pryor, Bill, 73nn11–12
Pryor, David, 189, 190
Pryor, Mark, 190, 193
Pseudo-fascism, 315, 326
Pseudo-populism, 337, 341, 354n44
Public aid, 325, 326
Public radio, 324
Public relations. *See* Propaganda
Public schools. *See* Education; Prayer in
schools
Puritans, 300, 311n32
Putnam, Carleton, 104

Quotas. *See* Affirmative Action

Race (and racism), 1–2, 3, 4, 5–6, 12, 13,
16, 21, 25–26, 41–42, 44–45, 203, 207,
212, 215, 320, 325, 326, 328, 333–36, 339,
340, 341, 356n53; alternative to "massive
resistance," 98–121; as not vital to development of South Carolina GOP, 158–59;
black entrepreneurship, 10, 240–90; black
middle class and professionals, 240–90;
blacks in the GOP, 86, 240–90; bloc voting and, 132, 137n93; election of a black
president, 314, 315; employment discrimination and, 328; "freedom of choice" and,
15, 91, 100; history and, 342n3, 356n51;
in the Fifties, 223–25, 231–32, 234, 235;
judicial rulings on, 327; labor and, 330;
miscegenation, 328, 330; move to GOP
in South and, 1–2, 3, 4, 5–6, 7, 48–50,
320–21, 338–39, 355n47; religion and,
21, 25–26, 48, 327; segregation, 6, 10, 15,
28–29, 39–42, 62, 81, 98–137, 328, 335;
segregation and federal funds, 43–44, 45,
47; segregation as Christian, 42; slavery,
9, 14; states' rights and, 15, 332; student
dissension on segregation, 42–43; systemic causes and consequences of, 46;
taxes and, 335; token desegregation of

religious schools, 28–29, 43–45, 47; white
supremacy as a virtue, 291–313. *See also*
Bloc voting; Civil rights; Dixiecrats; Fed-
eral government; "Great melding"; Ham
(curse of); Institutional racism; "Massive
resistance"; "New racism"; "Politics of
emotion"; Token desegregation; Voting
rights
*Race and Reason,* 104
Radicalism, 4. *See also* Communism;
McCarthyism
Radio, 8, 322, 324, 334, 340, 348nn18–19;
evangelists and, 23, 25. *See also* Media
Rainach, William, 123, 125
Raines, Howell, 331–32, 354n44
Rand, Ayn, 4, 332, 355n47. *See also* Economic fundamentalism
Randolph, John, 306
Rasputin, 315
Ratzinger, Cardinal Josef, 357n57
Ravenel, Arthur, 163–64
Reagan, Ronald, 5, 7, 22, 93, 241, 291–313,
324, 331, 345n6; air-traffic controllers
strike and, 334; economics and, 336;
election of 1980 and, 38; hostility to
federal government, 29–30; ideas similar
to George Wallace's and, 355n49; labor
and, 334; nomination of M. E. Bradford
and, 296–99, 310n20; pseudo-populism
and, 354n44; Religious Right and, 29–30,
31, 38, 42; supported by "Justice Jim"
Johnson, 191
Reaganomics, 336
Reagan Right, 291–313
Reality (and unreality), 324–25, 334–35,
340–42, 343n5, 345n6, 348nn18–19,
350nn26–27, 359nn65–66. *See also* Extremism; Media; Propaganda; Science
Reciprocal Trade Agreements Act, 202–8,
210, 212, 214, 216
Reconstruction, 8, 14, 319, 322, 338, 339;
irony of GOP using as issue and, 129, 131;
roots of fusionism and, 353n38. *See also*
"Reconstruction Syndrome"
"Reconstruction Syndrome," 340, 347n13
Reconstruction theology, 299
Redeemers, 8, 129
Redmond, Paul, 211
Reece, B. Carroll, 231

Reed, Ralph, 6, 22, 31–32, 332, 333, 352n32, 356n51. *See also* Christian Coalition

Reed, Walter (hospital), 314

Reich, Robert, 320

Religion, 9, 14, 21–37, 40, 45, 46, 179–80, 184, 186, 320, 322, 325, 326, 332–34, 336, 340, 341; American exceptionalism and, 316; apocalyptic, 334–35; blacks at religious colleges, 47–48; class and, 326, 336; colleges and, 38–54; conservatism and, 4, 6–7, 21–37, 320, 327, 336, 337, 341–42; conservatism at religious colleges as suffocating, 47; division of evangelicals and fundamentalists over civil rights, 26; divisions between leadership and rank-and-file, 26, 327; education and, 38–54, 357n60; extremism and, 9; liberalism and, 333; move to GOP and, 38–76; patriotism and, 7, 39, 40; poverty and, 326; race and, 6–7, 13, 336, 352n32; religious colleges, 13–14; scandal and, 356n56; tax exemptions and civil rights, 28–29. *See also* African Methodist-Episcopal Zion Church; Calvinism; Catholics; Christian Reconstructionism; Civil War; Churches of Christ; Dominionism; Episcopalians; Evangelicals; "Folk theology"; Fundamentalism; "God and country" issues; "Great melding"; Ham (curse of); Jews; Methodists; "Moral chauvinism"; Morality; Muslims; "New racism"; "Politics of emotion"; Prayer in schools; Presbyterians; "Prosperity Gospel"; Protestants; Reconstruction Theology; Religious Right; "Separation of church and state"; Slavery; Southern Baptist Convention; Southern Baptists; Southern Methodists; Southern Presbyterianism; "Status quo society"; Ten Commandments; Theology of secession; Unitarians

Religious Right, 6–7, 9, 21–37, 55–76, 322, 324, 327, 332, 333, 334–36, 341, 345n6, 355n49; colleges and, 38–54; fund-raising and, 355n48; home-schooling and, 357n60; voting and, 21–37, 348n20, 350nn26–27. *See also* Catholics; Fundamentalism; Evangelicals; Religion; "Separation of church and state"

Republic, 7–8, 122

Reuther, Walter, 213, 215

Reverse discrimination. *See* Affirmative Action

Reynolds, Grant, 273n28

Rhode Island, 94n2

Rice, Condoleeza, 356n56

Rice, John R., 23

*Richmond News Leader*, 98, 102

Riggs, Robert R., 111

Right-to-work laws, 203–4

Riley, Bob, 10, 73n12

Riots, 252, 275n55, 296. *See also* "Law and order"; Urban issues

Rivers, Mendel, L., 25, 141–46, 152, 153, 157; support for Eisenhower, 143–46. *See also* Dixiecrats

Robber barons, 318

Roberts, Andrew, 342n3

Robertson, Pat, 6, 29, 31, 32, 317, 331, 332; denounced as an "agent of intolerance," 32; on Muslims, 67; presidential candidacy of, 31, 63; takeover of the GOP and, 29; the 700 Club and, 331. *See also* Christian Coalition

Robinson, Jackie, 241–42, 276n58

Rockefeller, Jay, 191

Rockefeller, John D., Jr., 175

Rockefeller, John D., Sr., 175

Rockefeller, Nelson, 180, 241, 242, 333

Rockefeller, Winthrop, 10, 172–97

Rockefeller, Winthrop Paul, 191

*Roe v. Wade*, 63, 332. *See also* Abortion

Rogers, Adrian, 62

Romanticization of the Old South, 291–313

Rome, 341

Romney, George, 333

Romney, Mitt, 356n56

Roosevelt, Franklin Delano, 6, 8–9, 40, 140, 317, 346n8, 357n60; hostility to, 40; internment of Japanese and, 67; popularity with religious voters, 22; popularity with southerners, 22. *See also* New Deal

"Rope of religion," 13

Rothbard, Murray, 332, 355n47

Rove, Karl, 11, 314, 315, 318, 331, 340–41, 356n51; election of 2004 and, 321, 322, 346n10

Rumsfeld, Donald, 315, 337

Rural values, 341

Rural voters, 80, 87, 88, 93, 174. *See also* Apportionment; Black Belt; County-unit system; "Suburban strategy"

Russia. *See* USSR

Ruthlessness, 69–70. *See also* Democratic Party, timidity of

Safety. *See* Labor

Sager, Ryan, 353n38, 357n60

Sanders, Carl E., 87

Sanders, Claudia, 148–49

Santa Barbara, 343n5

*Santa Fe ISD* (case), 66

Sayers, Gale, 285n105

Scammon, Richard M., 288n126, 341

Scandals, 314–15, 337, 356n56

Schafly, Phyllis, 28

Schaller, Thomas F., 15, 337, 357n58, 357n60

Schiavo, Terri, 69, 76n45

School of American Studies, 41

School prayer. *See* Prayer in schools

Schools. *See* Education; Prayer in schools

Schultz, George P., 253, 255–57, 265–66, 278n72

Schwarz, Fred, 42

Science: assault on rationality and Enlightenment values, 9, 14, 299–301, 317, 320, 326, 340–42, 343n5, 345n6, 359nn65–66. *See also* Climate change; Evolution; Fundamentalism

Scopes Trial, 56–57, 73n8, 326

Scotland, 64

Scott, Hugh, 227

Scott, Stan, 263, 285n109, 286n110

Scranton, William W., 107, 109, 112, 119n44

Sears, Barbara, 176

Second Reconstruction, 8, 339

Secularism (and "Secular humanism"), 26–27, 28, 39, 57. *See also* Supreme Court

Securities and Exchange Commission, 346n8

Segregation. *See* Race

Self-help, 252–54, 275n53. *See also* Personal responsibility

Selma-to-Montgomery march, 44, 100, 330, 353n40

Semmes, Admiral Raphael, 300

Sensing, Thurman, 207, 211, 212

"Separation of church and state," 6, 17n6, 73n9, 327, 332, 351n31. *See also* Establishment Clause

Sermon on the Mount, 333

Seventies (and the assault on the old rules), 9, 11, 334–35; evangelical power and, 29; tax exemption for religious schools and, 29 Sex, 11, 338, 341; abstinence, 315, 356n56; contraception, 324; feminism, 11, 23, 27–28, 29, 30, 31, 62, 320, 327; gender, 13, 340; interracial, 331, 353n40; machismo politics, 325, 341; patriarchy defended and, 303; religious scandals and, 356n56; rights of women, 324; women's Republican clubs, 232. *See also* Abortion; Gay rights; Religion; Scandal

Shafer, Byron E., 16, 338, 349n23

Shartzer, Bill, 85

*Shelley v. Kraemer*, 103

Shivers, Allan, 151; support for Nixon and, 151

"Shock and awe," 316

Shook, P. G., 212–13

*Shreveport Journal*, 125, 128, 129–30, 131, 132

*Shreveport Times*, 123, 125, 127, 129, 130

"Silent amendments," 109–12

"Silent Majority," 222

*The Silent Majority*, 16

Simkins, Modjeska, 159

Sit-ins, 103

Slavery, 9, 14, 55, 62, 318; defended and, 297, 299–302; defended on religious grounds, 300

Slavic peoples, 328

Slocum, Frederick V., 8, 9, 11, 15

Small Business Administration, 261, 284n100

Smallpox, 318

Smith, Adam, 323

Smith, Al, 22, 224; referred to, 331

Smith, Bailey, 69

Smith, "Cotton Ed," 140

Smith, J. Craig, 206, 212, 213

Smith, Margaret Chase, 214

Smith, Oran P., 57

*Smith v. Allwright*, 103

Smoot-Hawley, 202

Social Darwinism, 5, 318, 336, 351n29

Socialism, 6, 7, 13, 23, 38, 40–41, 84, 122–24, 129–31, 142–43, 210, 211, 341, 343n5, 346n8; the Bible and, 333; coded speech and race, 142, 143; label applied to the Fair Deal, 23; label applied to the New Deal, 23, 38, 40–41. See also Communism; "Transitive law of politics"

"Social issue," 341

Social justice. See Economic fundamentalism; Liberalism

Social responsibility. See Economic fundamentalism; Liberalism

Social Security, 84, 318, 336, 346n8

Sons of Confederate Veterans, 308

South. See Civil rights; Class; Continuity; Cultural continuity; Deep South; Distinctiveness; Federal government; "Great melding"; New Deal; "New racism"; Outer South; "Politics of emotion"; Race; "Reconstruction Syndrome"; Religion; Sex

South Carolina, 2, 23, 25, 59, 71, 74n20, 138–71, 322, 332; Charleston Naval Base, 139–40; Christian Coalition and, 32; Columbia, 147, 160; evolution and, 75n37; Gaffney, 148–49; Goldwater and, 234–35; liberalism and, 148; race and, 138–71; Richland County, 160

South Carolina State College, 146–47

South Carolinians for Eisenhower, 140–47, 151

Southern Baptist Convention, 6, 7, 11, 17n6, 23, 26, 55, 57, 334; conservative takeover of, 62- 63; endorsement of Civil Rights Act before takeover of, 26; endorsement of "separation of church and state," 27, 31; Engel v. Vitale and, 27, 31; hostility to Catholics and, 27, 31; resolution against a Catholic president, 24–25; reversal of position on abortion, 30; ties to GOP and, 11, 55, 57, 62

Southern Baptists, 22, 23, 26, 55–76, 354n44. See also Southern Baptist Convention

Southern Governors' Conference, 105

Southern Methodists, 22, 323

Southern Partisan, 14, 306–7

Southern Presbyterianism, 9, 299

Southern States Industrial Council, 203–8, 210–12, 214, 215

"Southern strategy," 16, 101–2, 115, 245, 250, 267, 288n132, 332; described as "so-called," 138, 250; not applicable to Winthrop Rockefeller, 172–73; not used in South Carolina, 157, 163–64; versus a "Suburban strategy," 79–97. See also "First Southern strategy"

"Southern way of life," 125, 204, 205, 292, 293, 319, 326, 340

Southwest, 357n58

Soviet Union. See USSR

Soyinka, Wole, 356n56

Sparkman, John, 212–13, 218n29

Sparks, Chauncey, 328

Specter, Arlen, 289n136

Spence, Floyd, 156, 166; segregation and GOP and, 156–57

Spottswood, Bishop Steven, 263, 286n110

Stalin, Joseph, 328

Standard Oil, 175

Stanley, Charles, 67

Stanley, Thomas "Bahnse," 100, 102

Stans, Maurice, 258, 280n87

Starr, Ken, 13, 45; attitude toward cities, 45; attitude toward drug addicts, 45; attitude toward unions, 45; investigation of Bill Clinton, 45

States' rights, 15, 101–2, 115, 123–24, 147, 319, 332. See also Dixiecrats; Race

States' Rights Party, 123. See also Dixiecrats

"Status quo society," 9–10, 12, 13, 18n9

Stauffer, Bill, 108, 119n49

"Stealth strategy," 32

Steele, Michael, 333

Steinbeck, John, 346n8

Stem-cell research, 324, 345n6

Stevenson, Adlai, 24, 83

Stock market. See Wall Street

Stone v. Graham, 57

Strikes. See Labor

Student Congress of Young Americans for Freedom, 105

Student Non-Violent Coordinating Committee (SNCC), 45, 181

Students for a Democratic Society (SDS), 45

Sturm, Phil, 44

Subcontracting. *See* Privatization
"Suburban school," 16, 320, 338; Georgia
    example of, 79–97; South Carolina
    example of, 138–71. *See also* Class; Class
    consciousness; Middle class; Rural voters;
    "Suburban strategy"; Suburbs; "White
    backlash" thesis
"Suburban strategy," 16, 79–97; color-blind
    issues and, 81, 84, 173; education and
    prosperity of voters, 82–93, 94; "massive
    resistance" not part of, 83–86; Nixon
    considered representative of instead of a
    "Southern strategy," 85, 88; not appli-
    cable to Winthrop Rockefeller, 172–73;
    "progressive conservatism" of, 81; racial
    moderation and, 80, 81; socialism charge
    as part of, 84; stress on merit over race,
    84; urban areas becoming Democratic
    and, 97n57. *See also* "White backlash"
    thesis
Suburbs, 14, 16, 79–97, 320, 337
Suit, Hal, 82, 91–92
Sullivan, Andrew, 338, 355n48, 357n60
Sullivan, Rev. Leon, 272n23
Sunbelt, 3, 320
Sun Oil, 107, 112
Superiority (and supremacy), 4–5, 7–8, 12,
    291–313, 325, 335. *See also* Antidemo-
    cratic impulses; Civil rights; Egalitarian-
    ism; Moral chauvinism; Race
"Superiority gene," 5
Supply-side economics. *See* Reaganomics
Supreme Court, 26–27, 28, 30, 31, 55–76,
    99–104, 138–71, 319, 328, 343n5, 355n49.
    *See also* Civil rights; Judicial review;
    Secularism
Suskind, Ron, 359n65
*Sword of the Lord*, 23

"Tabloid politics," 321
Taft, Robert A., 10, 40, 220–39
Taft-Hartley Act, 203–4
Talk-radio. *See* Radio
Talmadge, Herman, 83, 87, 93, 154, 209
Tammany Hall, 45
Tariffs, 8, 10, 201–19. *See also* Free trade
Tate, Alan, 292
Tauran, Archbishop Jean-Louis, 357n57

Taxes, 28–29, 80, 164–66, 229, 319, 320, 325,
    326, 333, 340; exceptions for military and
    defense and, 165; race and, 28–29, 335;
    religious exemption and, 28–29; social
    programs and, 335; tax fury and, 3, 4, 10,
    13, 16, 317, 321, 325, 326, 329–30, 333, 336,
    340, 350n27. *See also* Economic funda-
    mentalism; Tea Party
Tea Party, 5, 12, 326, 327, 351n31
Technology (revolution in), 316, 334,
    339–40, 341
Television, 330, 350n27; cable, 334, 340
Ten Commandments, 55, 57–58, 73n11,
    332–33, 340
Tennessee, 2, 41, 42, 69, 71–72, 74n20, 211,
    231, 326, 337, 338; Columbia, 42; Dayton,
    73n8; gay marriage and, 59; Nashville, 8,
    12; prayer in schools, 56–57, 73n8; Rhea
    County, 56–57, 73n8. *See also* Nashville
    Agrarians
Tenth Amendment, 103
Terrorism, 4, 320, 321, 322, 332–33, 336,
    347n15; attack of 9/11 and, 66–67, 315,
    331, 346n10. *See also* Militarism; Patrio-
    tism; War on Terror
Texas, 2, 5, 7, 8, 14, 15, 27, 69, 71–72, 73n9,
    74n20, 114, 220, 223–26, 228–30, 231, 292,
    321; Austin, 2, 57; Bexar County, 226;
    Christian Coalition and, 32; Dallas, 14,
    25, 30, 296, 348nn19–20; death penalty
    and, 67; evolution and, 75n37; Fort
    Worth, 292, 293; gay and lesbian rights
    and, 59; Houston, 3, 14, 27–28, 348n19;
    prayer in schools and, 57; Ten Com-
    mandments and, 57
"Texas Steal," 230
Textiles, 8, 201–19; strikes and, 70, 330
Thatcher, Margaret, 12
Theology of secession, 299–301
Think tanks (and policy institutes), 12–13,
    38, 316, 322, 329, 334–35, 340. *See also*
    Media; Propaganda
Thomas, Cal, 356n56
Thompson, Fletcher, 88, 92
Thompson, Judge Myron, 58
Thompson, Ronnie, 92–93
Thrower, Randolph, 84–85
*Thunderbolt*, 317

Thurmond, Strom, 14, 18n15, 25, 70–71, 112, 139, 142, 147, 151–52, 157–58, 174, 182, 214, 322, 331, 355n47; as a GOP candidate, 159–60; not part of the "Suburban strategy" and, 83, 93, 95n14; ties to Nixon and, 241–42, 245

Tidelands oil (issue), 228–29. *See also* Dixiecrats

Tierney, John, 353n38

Tillman, Pat (cover-up about death of), 314

*Time*, 240, 259, 317

*Time on the Cross*, 301–2

Timmerman, George Bell, Jr., 145–47

Timmerman, George Bell, Sr., 145–46

Tobacco, 324–25, 345n6

Tobias, Randall, 356n56

Tojo, 328

Token desegregation, 148, 150, 160, 177, 187; of religious schools, 28–29, 43–45, 47. *See also* Civil rights; Race

Torture, 4, 67

Tower, John, 38, 296–97

Townes, Clarence, 244, 249, 272n21

Trade. *See* Free trade

Trade unions. *See* Labor

Traditional Values Coalition, 63

"Transitive law of politics," 7, 343n5; examples of, 210, 211; rightist religion and, 23, 25, 31. *See also* Communism; Democrats; Liberalism; Socialism

Transportation, 317

Tribble, Joe, 86

"Trickle-down economics." *See* Reaganomics

*Triumph*, 295–96

Truman, Harry, 6, 11, 23, 24, 40, 98–99, 140, 142, 174, 357n60. *See also* Fair Deal

Trumbull, Lyman, 103

Tsurumi, Yoshi, 346n8

Tucker, Bishop Charles Ewbank, 248, 274n38

Tuttle, Elbert, 231, 235

Twenties (inequality of), 321

Unions. *See* Labor

Unitarians, 24

United Daughters of the Confederacy, 293

United Fruit Company, 233

United Nations, 84, 124

University of Alabama, 146, 148

University of Arkansas, 174; law school and, 174; medical school and, 174

University of Chicago, 298. *See also* Economic fundamentalism

University of Dallas, 291, 295, 296

University of Georgia, 31, 105, 307

University of Houston, 307

University of Mississippi, 354n45

University of North Carolina, 306

University of Notre Dame, 38, 42; law school and, 38, 42

University of Oklahoma, 293, 298

University of South Carolina, 306, 307

University of Texas, 125, 298

University of Virginia, 307

Upper South. *See* Outer South

Urban issues, 45, 335; versus rural, 97n57, 341. *See also* "Law and order"; Riots

Urban League, 264–66, 270n12, 273n30, 287n120

Urquhart, Glen, 351n31

USSR, 23, 132. *See also* Cold war; Communism; McCarthyism; Socialism

Values. *See* Moral chauvinism; Morality

Vanderbilt University, 292–94, 309n15. *See also* Nashville Agrarians

Vandiver, Ernest, 87

*Van Orden v. Perry*, 57

Vardaman, Claude, 223–24

"Vast right-wing conspiracy," 38

Vatican, 357n57

Vietnam, 7, 45, 67, 319, 346n10; evangelical support for war in, 47, 67; Southern Baptist support for war in, 27, 67

Viguerie, Richard, 334

Violence, 64, 330, 342n3. *See also* War

Viorst, Milton, 267

Virginia, 2, 10, 13, 14, 15, 21, 67, 72, 74n20, 98–121, 211, 231, 337, 352n33; Charlottesville, 100; Christian Coalition and, 32; Front Royal, 100; gay and lesbian rights and, 59; Lynchburg, 26, 30; Norfolk, 100; northern Virginia, 337; Richmond, 98, 106; suburbs, 337; Williamsburg, 98, 99, 101, 106, 108

Virginia Commission of Constitutional Government, 15, 101–21

Virginia Commonwealth University, 307
Vote suppression, 7–8, 44, 45, 322–23, 348n20; and voter registration, 124
Voting Rights Act (of 1965), 8, 113, 159, 162–63, 293, 320, 332, 335; movement toward, 44, 45, 353n40

Waggoner, Joe, 123–37
Wagner Act. *See* National Labor Relations Act
Waldman, Paul, 357n58
Wallace, George C., 5, 14, 26, 100–101, 112–13, 115, 121n76, 154, 160–64, 175, 186–87, 269n1, 319, 322, 334; anti-intellectualism of, 359n66; attacks on liberal media, 359n66; debt owed by GOP and, 355n49; Georgia and, 88, 93, 94n2; ideas similar to Reagan's, 355n49; segregation and, 47, 332, 356n51; support from white evangelicals, 47; ties to M. E. Bradford, 291, 296, 297; white vote and, 332
*Wallace v. Jaffree*, 56
Wallenstein, Peter, 120n53
Wallis, Rev. Jim, 355n48
Wall Street, 325
*Wall Street Journal*, 333
Wal-Mart, 325, 332
War, 62, 320, 321, 324, 327, 332–33, 336, 340, 341. *See also* Civil War; Confederacy; Iraq; Just War theory; Militarism; Pacifism; Patriotism; Reconstruction; Vietnam; World War II
Ward, John, 59
Ward, Mary, 59
Warner, Mark, 359n65
"War on Christmas," 327
War on Terror, 322
Warren, Earl, 99, 109, 131, 145. *See also* Supreme Court
Warren, Robert Penn, 292
Washington, Booker T., 10
Washington, Walter, 274n39
Washington, D.C., 2, 29, 129, 315, 337. *See also* Federal government
*Washington Times*, 342n2
Water, 323
Watson, Albert, 153, 160–64, 166; as a GOP candidate, 158–60; as not subtle enough on busing, 163; segregation and GOP

and, 156–58; support for Nixon and Lodge, 151, 153; ties with Thurmond and, 151–52
Wattenberg, Ben J., 288n126, 341
"Weapons of mass destruction," 315
Weaver, Richard M., 9, 299
Webb, Jim, 337
*Weekly Standard*, 331, 343n5
Weems, Robert, 266, 281n88
Weigel, George, 6, 332, 343n5
Welfare, 45, 335. *See also* Corporate welfare; Poverty
Welfare state, 129, 346n8
Weltner, Charles, 86; only Deep-South vote against the Civil Rights Act and, 86
West, 329–30
West, Cornel, 267, 288n130
West, John, 159–64; busing issue versus Watson, 163
Weyrich, Paul, 28, 333, 334, 335–36, 348n20. *See also* Heritage Foundation
*What's the Matter with Kansas?*, 357n60
Whigs, 330
*Whistling Past Dixie*, 337
Whitaker, Mary Ann, 41
White, Hugh V., 111
White, John W., 16
"White backlash" thesis, 3–4, 16, 17n3, 221, 320; slowing movement to GOP, 80–81; Arkansas and, 172–73; importance of 1970 gubernatorial elections and, 81, 82; mentioned, 269nn8–9; question about why it took so long, 80, 94n4; waged too aggressively, 80–81; *See also* "Southern strategy"; "Suburban school"; "Suburban strategy"
White Citizens' Councils, 105, 111, 123, 177, 178, 186–87, 208; Republicans and, 146, 147, 151, 152, 153, 159, 208
White supremacy. *See* Race
Wilkins, Roy, 263, 270n12, 273n30, 286n110. *See also* National Association for the Advancement of Colored People (NAACP)
Wilks, John, 277n64, 278n72
Williams, Daniel K., 6, 7, 11, 13, 16
Wills, Garry, 269n9
Wilson, Charles Reagan, 70
Wilson, Clyde, 14, 306–7
Winrock Farms, 176, 178, 179, 191

Wisdom, John Minor, 231, 232–33, 235
Wiseman, Marty, 72
Wolfe, Alan, 346n7
Wolfowitz, Paul, 314–15
Women. *See* Gender; Sex
Woodward, C. Vann, 3; work attacked by Donald Davidson and, 309n13
Wooten, James L. "Jimmy," 351n28
Workers. *See* Labor
Working class. *See* Class; Class consciousness; Labor
Workman, William D., 155–57; segregation and GOP and, 156–57; versus Olin Johnston, 155–57
WorldNet Daily, 340
World Outlook Conference, 23
World War II, 22, 39, 79, 82, 123, 139, 328–29, 340

Wright, Leah M., 10, 16
Wyatt-Brown, Bertram, 75n32

Xenophobia, 143, 152, 316, 319, 338, 340

Yale University, 175, 298
Yankees, 3, 9, 14, 41, 104, 172, 175, 292, 300, 306, 339
Yeager, Wirt, 234; race and GOP in Mississippi and, 234–35
Young, Whitney, 245–46, 249, 263–65, 270n12, 273nn28–30, 286n111, 287n119
Young America's Foundation, 50
Youth, 126–27, 284n100; vote, 323

Zweifel, Henry, 220, 228, 229

NEW PERSPECTIVES ON THE HISTORY OF THE SOUTH
Edited by John David Smith, Charles H. Stone Distinguished Professor of American History
University of North Carolina at Charlotte

*"In the Country of the Enemy": The Civil War Reports of a Massachusetts Corporal*, edited by William C. Harris (1999)

*The Wild East: A Biography of the Great Smoky Mountains*, by Margaret L. Brown (2000)

*Crime, Sexual Violence, and Clemency: Florida's Pardon Board and Penal System in the Progressive Era*, by Vivien M. L. Miller (2000)

*The New South's New Frontier: A Social History of Economic Development in Southwestern North Carolina*, by Stephen Wallace Taylor (2001)

*Redefining the Color Line: Black Activism in Little Rock, Arkansas, 1940–1970*, by John A. Kirk (2002)

*The Southern Dream of a Caribbean Empire, 1854–1861*, by Robert E. May (2002)

*Forging a Common Bond: Labor and Environmental Activism during the BASF Lockout*, by Timothy J. Minchin (2003)

*Dixie's Daughters: The United Daughters of the Confederacy and the Preservation of Confederate Culture*, by Karen L. Cox (2003)

*The Other War of 1812: The Patriot War and the American Invasion of Spanish East Florida*, by James G. Cusick (2003)

*"Lives Full of Struggle and Triumph": Southern Women, Their Institutions and Their Communities*, edited by Bruce L. Clayton and John A. Salmond (2003)

*German-Speaking Officers in the United States Colored Troops, 1863–1867*, by Martin W. Öfele (2004)

*Southern Struggles: The Southern Labor Movement and the Civil Rights Struggle*, by John A. Salmond (2004)

*Radio and the Struggle for Civil Rights in the South*, by Brian Ward (2004, first paperback edition, 2006)

*Luther P. Jackson and a Life for Civil Rights*, by Michael Dennis (2004)

*Southern Ladies, New Women: Race, Region, and Clubwomen in South Carolina, 1890–1930*, by Joan Marie Johnson (2004)

*Fighting Against the Odds: A History of Southern Labor since World War II*, by Timothy J. Minchin (2005, first paperback edition, 2006)

*"Don't Sleep With Stevens!": The J. P. Stevens Campaign and the Struggle to Organize the South, 1963–1980*, by Timothy J. Minchin (2005)

*"The Ticket to Freedom:" The NAACP and the Struggle for Black Political Integration*, by Manfred Berg (2005)

*"War Governor of the South": North Carolina's Zeb Vance in the Confederacy*, by Joe A. Mobley (2005)

*Planters' Progress: Modernizing Confederate Georgia*, by Chad Morgan (2005)

*The Officers of the CSS Shenandoah*, by Angus Curry (2006)

*The Rosenwald Schools of the American South*, by Mary S. Hoffschwelle (2006)

*Honor in Command: The Civil War Memoir of Lt. Freeman Sparks Bowley, 30th United States Colored Infantry*, edited by Keith P. Wilson (2006)

*A Black Congressman in the Age of Jim Crow: South Carolina's George Washington Murray*, by John F. Marszalek (2006)

*The Spirit and the Shotgun: Armed Resistance and the Struggle for Civil Rights*, by Simon Wendt (2007)

*Making a New South: Race, Leadership, and Community after the Civil War*, edited by Paul A. Cimbala and Barton C. Shaw (2007)

*From Rights to Economics: The Ongoing Struggle for Black Equality in the U.S. South*, by Timothy J. Minchin (2008)

*Slavery on Trial: Race, Class, and Criminal Justice in Antebellum Richmond, Virginia*, by James M. Campbell (2008)

*Welfare and Charity in the Antebellum South*, by Timothy James Lockley (2008)

*T. Thomas Fortune the Afro-American Agitator: A Collection of Writings, 1880–1928*, by Shawn Leigh Alexander (2008)

*Francis Butler Simkins: A Life*, by James S. Humphreys (2008)

*Black Manhood and Community Building in North Carolina, 1900–1930*, by Angela Hornsby-Gutting (2009)

*Counterfeit Gentlemen: Manhood and Humor in the Old South*, by John Mayfield (2009)

*The Southern Mind under Union Rule: The Diary of James Rumley, Beaufort, North Carolina, 1862–1865*, edited by Judkin Browning (2009)

*The Quarters and the Fields: Slave Families in the Non-Cotton South*, by Damian Alan Pargas (2010)

*The Door of Hope: Republican Presidents and the First Southern Strategy, 1877–1933*, by Edward O. Frantz (2011)

*Painting Dixie Red: When, Where, Why, and How the South Became Republican*, edited by Glenn Feldman (2011)